PENGUIN CLASSICS

THE DIVINE COMEDY 1: INFERNO

DANTE ALIGHIERI was born in Florence in 1265 into a family from the lower ranks of the nobility. He may have studied at the university of Bologna. When he was about twenty, he married Gemma Donati, by whom he had four children. He first met Bice Portinari, whom he called Beatrice, in 1274, and when she died in 1290 he sought consolation by writing *La Vita nuova* and by studying philosophy and theology. During this time he became involved in the conflict between the Guelf and Ghibelline factions in Florence; he became a prominent White Guelf and, when the Black Guelfs came to power in 1302, Dante was, during his absence from the city, condemned to exile. He took refuge initially in Verona but eventually, having wandered from place to place, he settled in Ravenna. While there he completed the *Commedia* which he began in about 1307. Dante died in Ravenna in 1321.

ROBIN KIRKPATRICK graduated from Merton College, Oxford. He has taught courses on Dante's *Commedia* in Hong Kong, Dublin and – for more than twenty-five years – at the university of Cambridge, where he is Fellow of Robinson College and Professor of Italian and English Literatures. His books include *Dante's Paradiso and the Limitations of Modern Criticism* (1978), *Dante's Inferno: Difficulty and Dead Poetry* (1987) and, in the Cambridge Landmarks of World Literature series, *Dante: The Divine Comedy* (2004). His own published poetry includes *Prologue and Palinodes* (1997); he is currently working on a long poem (in five acts) entitled 'Paradise Rag'.

DANTE ALIGHIERI

The
Divine Comedy 1:
Inferno

Translated and edited by
ROBIN KIRKPATRICK

PENGUIN BOOKS

PENGUIN CLASSICS

Published by the Penguin Group
Penguin Books Ltd, 80 Strand, London WC2R ORL, England
Penguin Group (USA) Inc., 375 Hudson Street, New York, New York 10014, USA
Penguin Group (Canada), 90 Eglinton Avenue East, Suite 700, Toronto, Ontario, Canada M4P 2Y3
(a division of Pearson Penguin Canada Inc.)
Penguin Ireland, 25 St Stephen's Green, Dublin 2, Ireland
(a division of Penguin Books Ltd)
Penguin Group (Australia), 250 Camberwell Road, Camberwell, Victoria 3124, Australia
(a division of Pearson Australia Group Pty Ltd)
Penguin Books India Pvt Ltd, 11 Community Centre, Panchsheel Park, New Delhi – 110 017, India
Penguin Group (NZ), cnr Airborne and Rosedale Roads, Albany, Auckland 1310, New Zealand
(a division of Pearson New Zealand Ltd)
Penguin Books (South Africa) (Pty) Ltd, 24 Sturdee Avenue, Rosebank, Johannesburg 2196, South Africa

Penguin Books Ltd, Registered Offices: 80 Strand, London WC2R ORL, England

www.penguin.com

This translation first published in Penguin Classics 2006
3

Translation copyright © Robin Kirkpatrick, 2006
The text of the *Commedia* is reprinted from *La Commedia secondo l'antica vulgata*,
edited by Giorgio Petrocchi, Edizione Nazionale delle Opere di Dante Alighieri a cura della Società
Dantesca, copyright © 1994 by Casa Editrice Le Lettere – Firenze
Lines from *The Unnameable* by Samuel Beckett are quoted by permission of
the estate of Samuel Beckett.
Every effort has been made to contact copyright holders. The publishers will make good
in future printings any errors or omissions brought to their attention.
All rights reserved

The moral right of the editor has been asserted

Set in 10.25/12.25 pt PostScript Adobe Sabon
Typeset by Rowland Phototypesetting Ltd, Bury St Edmunds, Suffolk
Printed in Great Britain by Clays Ltd, St Ives plc

Except in the United States of America, this book is sold subject
to the condition that it shall not, by way of trade or otherwise, be lent,
re-sold, hired out, or otherwise circulated without the publisher's
prior consent in any form of binding or cover other than that in
which it is published and without a similar condition including this
condition being imposed on the subsequent purchaser

ISBN 13: 978-0-140-44895-5
ISBN 10: 0-140-44895-0

Contents

Acknowledgements   vii
Chronology   viii
Editor's Note   x
Introduction   xi
Further Reading   cv
A Note on the Manuscript
     Tradition   cviii
Map of Italy *c.*1300   cx
Plan of Hell   cxii

Commedia Cantica 1: *Inferno*

Commentaries and Notes   315

Acknowledgements

Thanks of many kinds are due. To those, especially Vittorio Montemaggi and Matthew Treherne, who endured with great good humour the many hours of obsessive discussion concerning words and rhythms that I have willed upon them. To those who have given, in their great authority, both encouragement and criticism: Pat Boyde, Zyg Baranski, David Wallace and the early readers of the original proposal. To Hilary Laurie for painstaking and perceptive attention to the details of the text as it was prepared for press. Also to Sally Holloway, as copy-editor, for her meticulous and flexible work. To Anna and Laura for taking a far more lively interest in this text than filial duty required and for providing, at need, advice on demotic usage. The dedication of this volume recalls a debt incurred over decades to the Cambridge undergraduates with whom I have been lucky enough to be associated. Some of my happiest hours have been spent discussing the deficiencies of extant translations. I offer this translation, knowing that it will provide much food for similar discussion in the future.

This translation is dedicated to all those in the English faculty at Cambridge University, now represented by Amelia, Cheema, Frances and Tom, with whom reading even the *Inferno* has been a pleasure since 1978.

Chronology

1224 Saint Francis receives the stigmata

1250 Death of Emperor Frederick II

1260 Defeat of the Guelfs at the battle of Montaperti, leading to seven years of Ghibelline domination in Florence

1265 Dante born, probably 25 May

1266 Defeat of imperial army by the Guelfs and the French under Charles d'Anjou at the battle of Benevento

1267 Birth of Giotto; restoration of Guelf rule in Florence under the protection of Charles d'Anjou

1274 Death of Thomas Aquinas and Bonaventura

1282 The influence of the guilds starts to grow in Florence

1283 Dante begins his association with the poet Guido Cavalcanti

1289 Dante fights at the battle of Campaldino; Florence, having defeated Arezzo and Ghibelline factions at Campaldino, begins to extend its supremacy over Tuscany

1290 Death of Bice (Beatrice) Portinari

1292 Dante compiles the *Vita nuova*

1293 *Ordinamenti di Giustizia* promulgated in Florence

1294 Election and abdication of Pope Celestine V; election of Pope Boniface VIII

1295 Dante enrols in a guild

1296 For five years, Dante is actively involved in the political life of the Florence commune; *Rime Petrose* probably composed

1300 Dante elected to the office of prior; fictional date of the *Commedia*

1301 Crisis and *coup d'état* in Florence; Charles de Valois enters the city; return of Corso Donati; defeat of the White Guelfs by the Black Guelfs

1302 In his absence, Dante formally exiled and sentenced to death by the Blacks

1303 Dante seeks refuge for the first time in Verona; death of Pope Boniface VIII

1304 Dante probably engaged until 1307 on the *Convivio* and the *De Vulgari Eloquentia*; birth of Petrarch

1305 Pope Clement V detained in Avignon

1307 Possible date for when Dante started the *Commedia*; accession of Edward II to English throne

1308 Henry VII of Luxembourg elected Holy Roman Emperor in Rome

1310 Dante writes his epistle to Henry: '*Ecce nunc tempus acceptabile*'; Henry enters Italy

1312 Possible (though much debated) date for when Dante started *De Monarchia*; Henry crowned Holy Roman Emperor

1313 Emperor Henry VII dies; Boccaccio born

1314 Dante begins living for six years in Verona, under the protection of Can Grande della Scala

1318 Dante in Ravenna: in close contact with Guido Novello da Polenta

1320 Dante in Latin verse correspondence with the humanist Giovanni del Virgilio; lectures at university of Verona: *Questio de Aqua et Terra*

1321 Dante dies in Ravenna, 13 September

Editor's Note

Dante called his poem a 'comedy', or *commedia*. Only in the sixteenth century was the now-familiar adjective 'divine' attached to Dante's original title, by readers impressed with the ambition of the work and eager to enhance its reputation. This adjective has been kept on the title page of the present translation. However, there are good reasons, which will be discussed at a later stage, for retaining Dante's less showy designation and, beyond the title page, his original one-word title has been preserved.

The *Commedia* is a single poem of one hundred cantos, subdivided into three parts – the *Inferno*, the *Purgatorio* and the *Paradiso*, each part constituting a *cantica*. The present translation will appear in three separate volumes: the *Inferno* first, then the *Purgatorio* and *Paradiso*, both of which are in active preparation.

In each volume there is an introduction specific to the *cantica* within it. The current volume also contains a general introduction to the *Commedia* as a whole.

The introductions, commentaries and notes have been edited according to standard practice. However, the text of the translation – in an attempt to respond to the density and variety of Dante's poetic practice – frequently employs non-standard forms of punctuation and capitalization.

Introduction

Dante: Life and Times

In January 1302, at the age of thirty-six, Dante Alighieri was exiled from his native Florence. In the five or six years before that date he had played an increasingly important role in the political life of the Florentine commune and in 1300 was elected to the governing authority of the city, the Council of Priors. It is this period of Dante's life that is celebrated in a fresco painted by his contemporary, Giotto di Bondone (1267–1337), which depicts the poet – keen, gaunt, defiant yet capable (almost) of smiling – among the most prominent citizens of his day. (The fresco is to be found on the walls of the chapel of the Bargello, the medieval palace of the Florentine police, now the Museo Nazionale.) But thirteenth-century Florence was wracked with internal dissension and susceptible to pressures from the world beyond its civic boundaries. In 1301, Dante's party was ousted from power by a *coup d'état*, and the poet, 'midway on [his] path in life' (*Inferno* canto 1, line 1), was condemned to exile. He never returned to Florence. Accused – falsely, one presumes – of the corrupt exercise of his public office, Dante refused to admit to the charges or accept any ignominious offer of amnesty, preferring, until his death in 1321, to remain as a voice in the wilderness, travelling from place to place in the northern part of the Italian peninsula. He was accompanied for some of this time by two of his three sons – these two being among the first people to write commentaries on their father's work – and by a daughter who became a nun and took 'Beatrice' as her name in religion. Dante's wife appears to have remained in Florence.

Little more than this is known about Dante's life, save for
what Dante himself relates – often obliquely – in the *Commedia*.
It is possible that he travelled as far as Paris and visited the
great schools of philosophy at the Sorbonne. He must certainly
at some time, possibly before his exile, have reached Bologna,
about sixty miles from Florence, and been able to develop at
its civic university the interests in philosophy that he had pur-
sued as an amateur in Florence. Subsequently, his reputation as
a politician, philosopher and poet seems to have secured him a
livelihood at some of the great courts of north-east Italy, not-
ably those of Can Grande della Scala (1291–1329), ruler of
Verona, and Guido Novello da Polenta (fl. mid-thirteenth cen-
tury), in Ravenna. Indeed, within fifty years of Dante's death,
Florence itself came to recognize the merits of the erstwhile
outlaw – whose writings by now existed in a great many copies,
though no autograph script has ever been found. By 1373
Giovanni Boccaccio (1313–75) had organized a series of public
lectures in Florence on the *Commedia*. But Dante died in exile
on 13 September 1321, having perhaps contracted malaria
while on a diplomatic mission to Venice. He was buried in
Ravenna with great honour at the church of San Pier Maggiore.

For Dante himself, his early involvement in Florentine politics
and the long experience of exile persisted as irremovable factors
in his intellectual and emotional complexion. For instance, in
his many political letters, which react with almost paranoid
animus to the divided state of Florence and Italy at large, Dante
repeatedly signs himself 'a Florentine by birth but not in moral
character'. His philosophical writings betray a similarly fraught
ambiguity of sentiment: the *Convivio* (c. 1304) invites his fellow
citizens to a 'banquet' of knowledge and ethical inquiry, as if
this might reveal to them the true foundations of civic life and
lead them to recognize (as after his death they did) how much
they had lost in driving Dante out. *De Monarchia* (c. 1312)
seeks, as a work of political theory, to rise above factional
politics and demonstrate the necessity of a world empire cap-
able of replacing the crude aggressions and divisive appetites
that thrived in the soil of local politics. Nor is the *Commedia*
itself by any means free of factional sentiment. Anger, along

with bitterness in the face of exile, is a recurrent feature of Dante's authorial voice. The poem was begun (probably) in 1307 and concluded only a few months before the poet's death. Dante, however, chooses significantly to set the journey that his narrative depicts in the year 1300, at the point in his career when his own political success as prior must also have given him an acute understanding of how fragile the state of Florentine politics would shortly prove to be. The *Inferno* – the first volume, or *cantica*, of Dante's three-part poem – is punctuated by agonizing evidence of all that Florence, for good or ill, meant to Dante. Yet even in the heights of its final *cantica*, the *Paradiso* – where politics, one might suppose, would at last have been left behind as Dante embarks upon his final journey towards God – the poet inveighs against the corruptions of city life; and nowhere does he more painfully record the misery of exile – 'climbing another man's stair', 'eating another man's bread and salt' (*Paradiso* 17: 55–60) – than in the central cantos of this *cantica*.

For all that, Dante's politics were not the politics of disappointed nostalgia. On the contrary, friction and frustration generated in the poet an extreme intensity of historical analysis and an inventiveness – even, indeed, a hopefulness – in the search for remedies. The *Commedia* is the expression of such energies and, in the course of this relatively short but long-meditated poem, it slowly becomes apparent that political disasters and political solutions can never be isolated, in Dante's view, from the whole spectrum of human possibilities. For him, politics cannot be divorced from intellectual and ethical ambition, or from emotional sensitivity and religious enlightenment. Likewise, a true city is one in which philosophy and the observation of natural phenomena, as well as the exercise of literary talent, all make a recognized contribution to the riches of civic life.

The dark wood of *Inferno* 1 must in large part be taken to represent Dante's own entanglement in the world of Florentine politics, a place of sterile barbarity, remote from all true civilization. Yet few aspects of Dante's poem are more surprising, or ultimately more problematic, than his decision to represent

Virgil as his guide through Hell, and even as his mentor in Purgatory. Virgil is the poet who spoke of how the Roman empire grew triumphantly out of the ruins of Troy to become, in Dante's view, a model of what civilization might properly be. His function in the *Commedia* is, partly at least, to reveal a perspective in which the political disaster that Dante suffered in 1301 and his subsequent exile can be viewed as a matter of hope, as the beginning of a journey comparable to that undertaken by the Trojans on their way to Rome, which will end with the establishment of justice. As, in Virgil's vision, the Trojans are aided by the gods, so too providence works in the depths of Dante's despair.

Dante enters his dark wood on Good Friday, when Christ suffered at the hands of history and, by doing so, redeemed it. Dante, in assimilating his own sufferings to those of Christ, begins an exploration of Christian possibilities which grows ever richer as the poem proceeds. This process of discovery compels him to engage with the most sophisticated thinkers of the late Middle Ages, such as Saint Thomas Aquinas (1224– 74). But it also leads him to explore the implications of the Christian understanding that came to him originally in Florence through his love for Beatrice – the girl whom he saw first at the age of nine and to whom he devotes the only work he completed before his exile, the *Vita nuova* (1292). Contemplating the beauty of Beatrice and her early death (in 1290), Dante comes to believe in a providence that creates and sustains human beings in all aspects of their existence. In the end, it is charity that underlies Dante's political vision – a love which seeks not to possess or to violate, but rather to promote the good of others and nurture one's own self in relationship with others. The *Commedia* is truly a comedy, not merely in the happy ending that providence is seen to have reserved for Dante but, above all, in the unlikely confidence and exhilaration which Dante, as poet, progressively displays on his way to that conclusion.

Despair, then, is no part of Dante's vision – except as a prevailing element in the minds of the damned souls of the *Inferno*. But the generosity and scope of his thinking is by no means easily won. On the contrary, the narrative of the

Commedia is largely the narrative of an intellectual and spiritual struggle, fought out before us on the pages of the poem. With painstaking intensity of detail, Dante analyses the impediments to happiness that he encounters in the events and personalities of his own time; and with equal intensity he depicts the many contributions that other persons have made to his own thought in the legitimate advancement of human happiness. In the course of this progressive investigation, exile itself begins to alter its meaning. The awful pain of exile informs Dante's representation of Hell, which is a state of absolute alienation from human or divine companionship. But exile in Purgatory is transformed into the condition of pilgrimage, of a quest for distant truth; and in Paradise it finally becomes clear that exile, in spiritual terms, is a metaphor expressing the true nature of charity: '*caritas*' demands nothing less than exile; it is that absolute and willing dispossession of self which allows that God is the source of all things, and, in recognizing that, participates in the plenitude of divine creation.

Exile, too, had a powerful effect on Dante's imagination and intellect, nurturing a habit of mind that – almost uniquely among philosophers – encouraged the poet's vision to move constantly between the perception of detail and the construction of universal ideas. The *Commedia* is punctuated by references to landscapes and to historical episodes that must originally have presented themselves to Dante in the course of his many journeys. There are mafioso killings in the marshes near Oriaco (*Purgatorio* 5); there are hermits in *Paradiso* 21 from regions in the Apennines so high that thunderstorms break out beneath their level; there are stunning waterfalls in *Inferno* 16. Such details are caught by the hypersensitive eye of a man who has no home of his own to go to – of one who observes all alien things as sharply as if they were splinters of glass. But in seeking to rediscover and reconstruct a home for himself, the poet simultaneously brings to bear upon these brilliant fragments the perspectives of theology and philosophy which he always carried in his mind. The large view illuminates the detail; the detail – depriving the poet of any complacent point of rest – continually demands that he should make all new.

Far afield as Dante's travels took him, however, it is Florence that remains the epicentre of the shocks and opening vistas that he records in the course of the *Commedia*. And it is in the Florence of 1300 that the reader of the *Commedia* must begin. For it is here that Dante's history is most closely linked to our own. Thirteen hundred is not perhaps a date that we now see as a watershed in European history. Yet on Dante's analysis it ought to be. The forces that were unleashed against Dante in the year of his exile were forces that had been gathering momentum over the later centuries of the Middle Ages. But as they reformulated themselves in the course of the thirteenth and fourteenth centuries, the institutions – social, governmental and economic – which began to develop are recognizably the institutions of the modern world. So, too, are many of the problems and possibilities that these new formulations introduced. Dante is a modern poet in that he reveals, in his response to the events of 1301, the nature of the changes – for good as well as ill – that were taking place at this particular moment in European history. He remains an indispensable voice in any response we may now need make to the reverberation of those changes.

Florence 1300: The Historical and Intellectual Context of Dante's *Commedia*

Throughout the thirteenth century, the political and economic life of the Italian peninsula was driven by the interaction of three forces. Two of these – the Holy Roman Empire and the Roman Catholic Church – laid claim to universal jurisdiction. The third force, generated by the emerging economies of the mercantile Italian city states, did not initially make any such claim – though, in effect, the hegemony of the global market place that has developed over the last seven hundred years owes much to its origins in late medieval Italy.

From the time of Charlemagne (742–814), who was crowned Holy Roman Emperor in AD 800 by Pope Leo III (d. 816), Europe had at least a notional principle of unity in feudal allegiance to the imperial throne. There was, of course, little hard reality to support this principle; and by Dante's time dynastic aspirations began to display themselves in the territories of present-day France and Italy, which, over the coming centuries, were progressively to displace imperial authority in favour of the ambitions of the several nation states. To Italian eyes – and particularly to Dante's – there were a few decades at the beginning of the twelfth century when imperial power seemed to have gained ascendancy in the peninsula. By various accidents of lineage, the Emperor Frederick II (1272–1337) came to rule his Germanic domain from his Sicilian power base in the southern regions of Italy. A flourishing imperial culture developed – drawing some of its motifs from classical Rome – in which notions of the emperor as the embodiment of universal justice were consciously cultivated. At the same time, the first stirrings of vernacular poetry were found at his court and there was even some development of science: Frederick himself not only wrote verse but also composed a volume on hunting birds, which speculated, no less than Leonardo da Vinci eventually would, on the aerodynamic principles of flight. By 1265, the claims of Frederick's Hohenstauffen dynasty to political control in Italy had been extinguished by a lack of legitimate descendants and through the armed opposition of Church and city state. Imperial ambitions were shortly to be replaced by the growing claims of national dynasties such as the House of Anjou. However, as late as 1313 Dante maintained the passionate, if ill-founded, hope that the Empire would return to Italy in the person of Henry VII of Luxembourg (c. 1269–1313) and restore the unity and peace once enjoyed under the rule of ancient Rome.

Throughout the twelfth and thirteenth centuries, the Empire was in conflict, on both ideological and territorial grounds, with a Church that displayed increasing efficiency and appetite as a political institution. Organizational reforms in the twelfth century had helped to centralize the power and authority of the Church. The advance of the Papal Curia as an extremely well-regulated civil service encouraged the development of bureaucratic technologies that strengthened central control and allowed the Church to respond rapidly and rapaciously to the decline of imperial power in Italy. A manifestation of what this might produce is the papacy of Boniface VIII, in office from 1294 to 1303. An aristocrat of the ancient Caetani clan, and a lawyer experienced in the wheelings and dealings of the Curia, Boniface (c. 1235–1303) claimed the right as Pope to intervene directly (if not always successfully) in the local politics of Italy, and was an important protagonist in the *coup* that led to Dante's exile. Dante himself speaks of Boniface with often brilliant sarcasm (see especially *Inferno* 19). Nor was he alone in the odium he expressed. A posthumous trial of Boniface conducted in France accused the Pope of heresy, witchcraft, embezzlement, nepotism and sodomy.

The third feature of the Italian scene was the emergence in the course of the thirteenth century of a considerable number of city states. As they gathered momentum, these urban centres increasingly asserted their independence and were inclined to forge self-interested alliances. These were established, sometimes, with the Empire against neighbouring city states. But cities also formed alliances with the Church against the Empire which – though in decline – could still claim suzerainty over lands that were now increasingly subject to the influence of mercantile and banking interests. The huge energies of the city state were to find expression not only in trade but also in intellectual ambition and artistic achievement. Dante's own work draws upon, and critically modifies, these achievements. It was in this complex and highly charged arena that the poet most directly encountered the intersecting currents that impelled and wracked the social order into which he was born.

Florence, although it had been a city of some standing since Roman times, made a comparatively late entry into the commercial world of late medieval Italy. Pisa, for instance – which stood at that time on the coast – had been developing its maritime trade since the late eleventh century, and at an early date had begun to devise political constitutions that encouraged the participation of new mercantile interests. By the end of the twelfth century, however, Florence, too, was expanding rapidly as a workshop for luxury goods and, increasingly, as a centre of financial expertise. Migrant workers from the surrounding countryside flooded in – bringing the population of the city from approximately 30,000 in 1200 to something like 100,000 in 1300, and leading to a corresponding expansion of the city limits. The feudal nobility also began to set up working establishments in the city, which allowed them to share in its economic success. The cityscape which characteristically developed at this time must have resembled present-day San Gimigniano, where a brutal profile of towers expresses the determination of each incoming clan to defend itself from, or outdo, the next. Energies and tensions ran high. Rivalries – often between aristocratic factions or between noblemen and *nouveaux riches* – were rife. Clan opposed clan. And, where marriage alliances failed, murder was likely to prove the alternative. (William Shakespeare's Montagues and Capulets are mentioned in *Purgatorio* 6 with acute disgust for their political – and historical – divisiveness.)

In the course of the thirteenth century two partisan groupings, along with lesser and more shifting factions, developed aggressively visible identities. One of these, the Ghibelline party, proclaimed allegiance to the increasingly beleaguered Empire. The Guelfs, on the other hand, even though they themselves were often nobles of feudal origin, tended to look pragmatically to the future, associating with the new power of the papacy while also supporting the dynastic claims of northern dynasties such as the Angevin. These conflicting allegiances did not, however, erase the common investment in commercial success. The middle classes of merchants, notaries and bankers were able to establish forms of broadly popular government to voice and promote the economic interests of the city. Here, as in San Gimigniano, towers may have been built. But in Florence these towers were also systematically knocked down as ascendancy in the turf wars of the period switched from Ghibelline to Guelf and back again. In all of which, civic and ecclesiastical planning prospered. Florence became remarkable in the eyes of visitors for the vigour and beauty of its building programme. Just as importantly, accounting methods of considerable sophistication began to develop. Most significant of all, the golden florin was minted in 1252 (under the regime of the middle-class party, the Primo Popolo). This coin rapidly became an international currency, greatly advancing the banking activity of the city.

The 1260s, the decade in which Dante was born, saw a number of crucial developments. In 1260s, the Ghibellines, riding on a final surge of imperial influence, won a military victory over the Guelfs, which was apparently so decisive that they could easily have chosen to raze the city of Florence to the ground (see *Inferno* 10). Yet by 1266, the influence of the Empire in Italy had been extinguished and the Guelf cause came to prevail, producing a period of stability which was to endure for at least thirty-five years. Dante's own family was a minor scion of an aristocratic Guelf clan. But political involvement had, by mid-century, come to depend upon membership of the great trade guilds that oversaw the interests of the commercial commune. Dante's father, Alighiero Alighieri (born ?1266), who died in or before the poet's eighteenth year (his mother had died much earlier), seems to have worked on the shadier margins of the banking industry, possibly as a moneylender. He did not qualify to belong to any guild. Alighiero Alighieri, though known to contemporary texts, is never mentioned by Dante himself. But Dante (unlike his father) became a nominal member of the Guild of Physicians and Pharmacists. Thus, while he came to detest many aspects of Guelf polity, he was formally qualified to take an active part in the political life of the city. Among the notable achievements of the city in this period were the *Ordinamenti di Giustizia* in January 1293, which sought to establish the trade guilds rather than the élite magnate families at the centre of power. These ordinances included invidious clauses against the aristocratic magnates, but still pointed to a greater appetite for inclusive and associational politics than most other European countries could boast of at this time.

The resilience of the Florentine state was tested to the full in 1300. In the late 1290s the endemic divisiveness of the magnate classes had begun once again to display itself. Even the Guelf party had now divided into two factions, the Blacks and the Whites. The Blacks (who by 1301 were temporarily in exile)

were led by Corso Donati (d. 1308), who is described by the
contemporary White historian Dino Compagni as 'noble of
lineage, handsome in bodily form and charming in his public
speaking but arrogant, with a mind always intent on evil, who
ordered many acts of arson and rapine'. Dante in his turn (at
Purgatorio 24: 82–7) describes Corso as 'the most blame-
worthy of all, being dragged towards Hell at the tail of a horse'.
It is an indication of how finely drawn were the lines of internal
division (and also perhaps of Dante's open-mindedness and
delicacy in discrimination) that Corso's brother, Forese Donati
(d. 1296), was one of Dante's closest friends – and appears as
a redeemed sinner in *Purgatorio* 23 – while Corso's sister,
Piccarda Donati (?1266–?1298), is found among the blessed in
Paradiso 3 delivering one of the most important accounts of
love and order in the whole *Commedia*.

Corso, however, had a clearer eye for political advantage
than Dante himself. The Church at this time, under Pope
Boniface VIII, was looking for dominion over Tuscany, and
Angevin armies, encouraged by the Pope, were marching close
to Florence. Corso forged alliances with both. The city, under a
supposedly non-partisan government, sought to rally the guilds,
who failed, however, to muster any unified defiance to the
military threat. In early November 1301, while Dante was out
of the city on a last-ditch diplomatic mission to Rome, the
French armies under Charles de Valois (1270–1325) came
within striking distance of Florence and installed the Blacks in
power.

In many respects, Florence itself came through this crisis just
as, forty years later, it was to weather the impact of the Black
Death. As early as 1265, an inscription on the gates of the
Bargello defiantly proclaimed the right of Florence to pursue
its own imperial destiny and spread justice throughout the
whole of the world. In the coming centuries this destiny was to
be fulfilled, at least in terms of artistic and economic hegemony.
Among the many early migrants to Florence was the peasant
Medici family. Surreptitiously, the Medici advanced their inter-
est as economic success began to fuel the Renaissance phase of
Florentine culture. They became bankers to the Pope, and by

the sixteenth century were able to supply from their own ranks not only incumbents of the papal office (such as Clement VII and Leo X), but also consorts for the kings of France, notably Catherine, queen of Henry II.

To the eyes of the exiled Dante, however, such social, economic and political developments seemed symptomatic of a radical dislocation in understanding; a perversion indeed of all that human beings at their best could hope to achieve. (He was not likely to have been mollified by the thought that these developments led directly to the Florentine Renaissance.) And his feelings were all the more painful in that human beings, on the philosophical understanding that Dante came to develop, could only truly realize their human possibilities when they lived and worked together – as they might in a small and peaceful city – in the common pursuit of intellectual and ethical interests. Civic living is the most natural form of human existence; and in the *Convivio*, written in the first shock of exile, Dante speaks movingly – and with a strongly literal emphasis – of how a man 'uprooted' from his native city is comparable to a water plant torn out of its natural habitat and set down in the desert.

Throughout the *Commedia* Dante looks back with anguished contempt at a Florence that has forgotten how to flourish – in the way that its very name (the 'flowering' place) suggested that it might. In *Inferno* 26, for instance, he consciously parodies the words on the gates of the Bargello, sarcastically professing amazement that Florentine ambitions should have borne its citizens even to the depths of Hell. The newly minted florin is, for Dante, the '*maladetto fiore*' – the accursed flower; and usury is an unnatural vice, punished in Hell alongside sodomy. The Church is the target of no less agonized venom. There can be no question, of course, as to the depth of Dante's Christian sensibility. In *Paradiso* 23, he speaks of himself as one who, day and night, invokes the name of the Blessed Virgin. Likewise, the place in Florence to which his thoughts invariably tend is the great octagonal Baptistery – 'my own beloved Saint John's' (*Inferno* 19: 17) – which, since Charlemagne's time, had been the civic and liturgical focus of Florentine life. Indeed, in

Dante's view, Florence was at its best when it was at its smallest, when every citizen could hear the chime of bells from the church of the Badia. For all that, Dante is never more Christian than when he vibrates in horror at the corruption disseminated by the institutional politics of the contemporary Church, the Whore of Babylon. As for France, the Capetian dynasty (of which the Angevin invaders were a cadet branch) is pictured in *Purgatorio* 20, in words given penitentially to its founder Hugo Capet (*c.* 938–96), as the very anti-type of everything that a social order ought to be, impelled in all its decisions by avarice and violence.

Faced with the decadence of the modern world, it is a part of Dante's response, as he travels the paths of exile, to look ever wider to the ways in which philosophy and the true traditions of Christian thinking might help him to construct in his mind an intellectual and spiritual homeland that could remain immune to the corruptions of local politics. Casting his eyes beyond the confines of his own Florentine Guelfism, he is prepared to re-assess his political allegiances and to recognize that the imperial cause which his Ghibelline opponents have fostered has much to recommend it. This is to say that, up to a point, he recognizes the intellectual merit of the culture promoted by Frederick II. But Frederick himself is consigned to Hell as a heretic (though his illegitimate son Manfred, thrice-excommunicated, is redeemed and found in Purgatory, while Frederick's mother, Constance, appears in Paradise). More importantly, Dante begins to recall the ancient merits of imperial Rome. Florence, Dante reminds himself (in *Inferno* 1 and 15 and *Paradiso* 15–18), was a Roman foundation; and when he meets the figure of Virgil in the dark wood, this, among many things, represents a return to long-forgotten roots and a rediscovery of the values that the modern descendants of Rome have so disgracefully deserted.

At the same time, corrupt as the institutional Church might be, there are still resources in the Christian life that could nurture the exile in his attempt to rebuild his shattered city. In the spirit of Saint Francis of Assisi (1182–1226), Dante realizes the value of willing and consensual poverty. The teachings

of Saint Francis represent, of course, a counterblast to the
corruptions of church and mercantile life. More than that,
however, Dante – on the evidence of *Paradiso* 11 – also saw
Franciscan poverty as an intellectual and spiritual virtue, as a
form of total dispossession through which the mind of the finite
creature could become aware of its relationship with an infinite
Creator. All things are dependent upon that relationship and,
through their acceptance of poverty, sustain the condition of
that dependency. (It has recently been suggested that Dante at
one point intended to become a Franciscan friar.)

Equally, there was the tremendous example of intellectual
community offered by figures such as Saint Thomas Aquinas at
the schools of Paris. Here, in the fifty years before Dante's birth,
the rediscovery of Aristotle's logic had led to the development
of a Christian rationalism which, as well as displaying an
enthusiastic appetite for intellectual debate, encouraged the
confident and scientifically systematic study of God, of human
relationships with God, of ethics and natural phenomena.
Aristotle – as read in scholastic translations (Dante did not read
Greek) – came to be one of the central influences on Dante's
thought.

The *Commedia* ranges wide in its survey of the European
scene. Yet Dante never lost sight of the city as the best form of
organization for the ethical and intellectual life of the human
being. Indeed, in *Paradiso* 25, the poet imagines how his poem
will return to Florence and win for its author renewed recog-
nition of his literary and intellectual achievements – which will
be bestowed upon him in the church of the Baptistery where he
first received his baptismal name. And at every point in his exile
he carries with him a legacy drawn directly from Florence,
where developments in the sphere of philosophy, art and culture
kept pace with, and at times were encouraged by, developments
in the sphere of economics and politics.

Three figures, all of whom were known to Dante and were
of personal importance to him, may here indicate the richness
of Florentine culture in three particular fields – those of moral
philosophy, vernacular poetry and the visual imagination –
to which Dante in the *Commedia* makes his own complex

contribution. The first is Brunetto Latini (c. 1220–94), a notary and rhetorician who served in the popular government of the 1250s, was exiled to France and, on his return to Florence, became, effectively, first minister of the Guelf Republic. Brunetto exerted considerable intellectual influence over the circles that Dante seems to have moved in. The second is the poet Guido Cavalcanti (c. 1250–1301), – described by Dante in his earliest writings as his 'closest friend' – a Guelf aristocrat whom historians of Florence praise as 'a philosopher of considerable ability in the natural sciences'. The third is Giotto di Bondone, who, among his many other artistic achievements, designed the belltower of the Duomo in Florence to stand as monument to civic pride. Early commentaries on the *Commedia* suggest Dante and Giotto may have been in communication during Dante's exile, and may even have discussed ways in which Giotto might represent the Last Judgement on the walls of the Arena chapel in Padua.

The most significant of Brunetto's writings are *La Rettorica* (1260) (an annotated translation of Cicero's *De Inventione*) and the *Livres dou Trésor* (1262–6), which is one of the earliest encyclopaedias of learning and curious information to be found in the western tradition. Both works display a profound concern with a proper development of the civic life. Thus, in the *Rettorica* Brunetto writes: 'A city is a coming-together of persons as one, so as to live according to reason. Citizens are not simply those who live in the same community, surrounded by the same city walls, but those who are brought together to live according to rational principle.' A true city, therefore, is not merely a market place or a stock exchange. On the contrary, its unity depends directly upon a sharing of ethical and intellectual interests, upon a devotion – common to all its citizens – to rational principles and justice. It is the task of the rhetorician to reveal by his eloquence these principles to his fellow citizens and to persuade them that they are worthy of attention. In the same spirit, the 'treasures' that the author of the *Trésor* has to offer are the riches of wisdom and science: 'jewels' are here Brunetto's discourses on the vices and virtues; and 'gold' – far from being the stuff of monetary exchange – is the educated sagacity that an honest politician requires if he is truly to serve the city in his charge.

As the economies of the city states developed, so too did an ideology which sought to re-interpret – or, occasionally, to justify – the materialism on which these cities depended. Brunetto is not alone in voicing such an ideology. For instance, Guittone d'Arezzo (c. 1230–94), whose writings dominated the intellectual life of Tuscany in the 1260s, provided the new city bourgeoisie with a strong anti-imperial and anti-aristocratic programme when he insisted that true nobility can never be defined by social class but rather derives from the exercise of reason in the context of city life. Nor can there be any doubt that Dante was much impressed by this ideal. In the early years of his exile, he himself wrote the prose work the *Convivio*, which mirrors (and modifies) Brunetto's encyclopaedia and also Brunetto's understanding of rhetoric, language and eloquence.

Yet Brunetto Latini is, on Dante's view, damned to Hell, and the imagined encounter between the living Florentine and his now-dead mentor is the painful subject of *Inferno* 15. This encounter takes place in the region of the underworld where ostensibly those who have sinned against nature, in particular the sodomites, are punished. It is true that Dante does not explicitly accuse Brunetto of sodomy. Indeed, the words he attributes to himself in this canto speak of Brunetto movingly as 'a dear, good father' who 'taught me how a man becomes eternal'. There is, none the less, an unmistakable sense that Brunetto in some way delivered a traumatic shock to Dante's sensibility, and that he failed to live up to the civic ideal or to fulfil the promise of his own best sentiments. If unity of ethical purpose is the defining characteristic of true fellow citizens, it is clear that Brunetto, and the Guelf Florence which he represents, have, in Dante's view, deserted the ideals that once made it flourish. It is Virgil, not Brunetto, that Dante turns to in the dark wood, and Virgil is a silent but significant participant in Dante's meeting with Brunetto: the Florentine master has been replaced by a Roman who knows better than Brunetto how cities may be destroyed and yet, it seems, be rebuilt by the heroic efforts of their citizens.

The central cantos of the *Inferno* are peopled by a great many figures drawn, like Brunetto, from the generation preceding Dante's own, who are shown to have left a valuable yet contaminated legacy. In canto 10, Dante engages with one of the most prominent representatives of his own generation, his close associate Guido Cavalcanti. In this canto, Dante travels through an infernal graveyard where the tombs contain the souls of those who have denied the Christian doctrine of human immortality. Here he encounters Cavalcanti's father, who demands in anguish to know why his son is not travelling with Dante on his epic journey: 'If you . . . pass on by height of intellect, my son, where is he? And why not here with you?' This is one of only two explicit references to Guido in the *Commedia*. But it expresses much of the dramatic relationship that came to develop between Dante and Cavalcanti, from the time when, as the opening chapters of the *Vita nuova* record, Dante sent an early example of his love poetry to Guido for his opinion. Flattered by the subtlety, or 'height of intellect', that Cavalcanti showed in his response to this poem, Dante proudly acknowledges him as his '*primo amico*' – at least in the early chapters of that volume.

Guido was some ten years older than Dante, and, by the time that Dante came to know him, had brought Florentine poetry to a peak of sophistication. He revealed to Dante the ways in which the Florentine avant-garde might develop and extend the traditions established by earlier Italian poets. Vernacular verse had been written in Italy for little more than a century before the Florentines inherited it. Its origins, on the account that Dante himself offers in his study of linguistics and poetics, *De Vulgari Eloquentia* (1304), can be traced to a Sicilian school of poets, many of them associated with the court of Frederick II, active in the first three decades of the thirteenth century. These poets (including Pier della Vigna, who appears as a suicide in *Inferno* 13) had introduced into Italian verse some of the techniques and motifs characteristic of the troubadour poetry of the *langue d'oc*, or Occitan language of southern France. In some cases, they had given a peculiarly scientific twist to these motifs, interesting themselves in the psychology of love and the peculiar optics of the imagination, which render the lady so powerful an object in the lover's mind. By the middle of the thirteenth century, Tuscan poets had developed their own version of the Sicilian originals. In particular, Guittone d'Arezzo added a powerful concern over civic politics to the prevailing interest in love, producing verse with an especially rich rhetorical texture.

However, neither Cavalcanti nor Dante was greatly impressed by Guittone. Both wrote poems that derided Guittone's lack of intellectual and emotional sophistication, and both affected to despise the clumsiness of his rhetoric. Cavalcanti, as the leader of a Florentine coterie, laid claim to a style which combined something of the scientific interests that had characterized the Sicilian schools with an appetite for philosophical speculation and an extreme finesse in the handling of remote and often melancholic emotional registers. Above all, along with the poet and jurist Guido Guinizzelli of Bologna (c. 1225–76), he pioneered the way of writing which Dante was to call 'the sweet new style' (*Purgatorio* 24: 52). 'Sweetness' here does not mean mellifluous sentiment. Rather, it refers to a rarefied elevation of mind in contemplation of the effects of love, which brings its own intellectual satisfaction. Brunetto or Guittone had defined nobility in terms of rational exercise; the élite poets of the new style claimed a similar nobility on the grounds of intelligence and sensibility. Nobility and the capacity for love were now perceived as identical. At the same time, the capacities of Italian vernacular – still in its infancy as a literary language – were greatly advanced by Cavalcanti's example. Simplicity of diction, a tensile elegance of rhythm, unforced cadences and rhyming schemes are all properties of Cavalcanti's verse, and all made an impression on Dante that endured from the poetry of the *Vita nuova* to the last cantos of the *Paradiso*.

When Cavalcanti writes, '*Chi è questa che vien ch' ogn'uom la mira . . .*' ('Who is she who comes that every man gazes at . . .'), the lightness of metrical stress, the indefinite reference to the woman – signified only by the feminine ending of '*questa*' – the mysteriously unresolved interrogative, as if the woman could never be known, all reflect an elegance and delicacy of touch that Dante himself in his lyric poetry can hardly match. Similarly, Cavalcanti's immensely arduous poem '*Donna mi priega*' establishes a standard of philosophical ambition that Dante seems to have been peculiarly eager to emulate. But the philosophy that Dante wished to pursue was very different from that which characterized Cavalcanti's writing. Moreover, the growing distance between the two poets can only have been accentuated when, during his term of office as city prior, Dante was obliged to exile Cavalcanti from Florence in the interests of balancing the partisan rivalries that had broken out in the city. The tight-lipped reference to Cavalcanti in *Inferno* 10 suggests how deep the divisions were to become. Here Cavalcanti is accused, by association, of the same sin that brought his father to Hell: a philosophical form of materialism that denies any eternal existence to the human being. Cavalcanti's father is one among the many who held that the soul dies with the body (see *Inferno* 10: 15). This corresponds to some of the most characteristic features of Cavalcanti's own poetry. Though the poet frequently displays a flamboyance, and even an arrogance, in his authorial demeanour, there lies beneath that a profoundly melancholic message. For Cavalcanti, the finest responses of the human psyche are motivated by purely physical agencies and will not endure. He is deeply aware of the fragility of human identity and cultivates an unremitting sense that love, so far from enlivening the mind and promising some ultimate harmony, is a conflictual power descended from the influence of the war god Mars. In the last line of the *Commedia* Dante claims that his being is moved by an eternal power, 'by the love that moves the sun and the other stars'. He could not have written this if he had followed obediently in Cavalcanti's fatalistic footsteps.

It says a great deal for the intellectual vivacity of the Florentine élite that it could entertain ideas as daring and heterodox as Cavalcanti's. Dante, too, is vehemently original in the development of his own philosophical position, and is not himself immune to charges of heresy. Yet the thrust of almost all of Dante's thinking is to reject the melancholia and fatalism implicit in Cavalcanti's poetry. Thus, the opening chapters of the *Vita nuova* do indeed follow Cavalcanti in their introspective response to the shattering power of love. But two moments of revelation lead Dante in a wholly different direction from his '*primo amico*'.

The first is the realization that, in loving Beatrice, he should not seek in any way to possess or even to understand her, but rather rejoice that she should exist at all. His task as a poet is not to assert his own claims or to draw attention to his own exquisite sufferings, but rather to praise Beatrice. For Dante, love is no more comprehensible than it is for Cavalcanti. However, where Cavalcanti saw love as a destructive, embattled experience, for Dante love is henceforth a source (in his own repeated phrase) of 'miracles' – taxing to the mind, yet also an illumination, redemptive in its impact. This understanding goes on to support and inspire every move that Dante subsequently makes in his intellectual exploration of Christian belief. The same understanding lies at the core of Dante's authorial practice and, in pursuing it, he liberates a poetic voice quite distinct from Cavalcanti's. His own theme will be disinterested love (or charity). He will not speak any longer to the empty interiority of his own suffering. He will instead turn outwards in unself-conscious confidence to celebrate the virtue and value displayed in the life of Beatrice.

But then, as the second test of such confidence, Beatrice died at the early age of twenty-four. This could easily have confirmed in Dante a Cavalcantian pessimism. Yet it is precisely at this point that Dante finds corroboration for his belief in providential design. Beatrice is now distant from human eyes, but only because she is in the presence of the God who first created her and will ensure her resurrection on the Day of Judgement. Far from the soul dying with the body, as the heretics of canto 10 believe, the body itself will not die. Dante's thinking always returns to these fundamental truths. They lead directly to the vision of the afterlife contained in the *Commedia*, and speak of a commitment simultaneously to divine values and to a value in human nature which, in Dante's view, the materialist is bound to deny.

   The distance between Cavalcanti and Dante is, in part, the distance between an intellect absorbed in the analysis of its own nature and one which, no less acutely, investigates the grounds of faith and love and locates them in the manifestations of order, in beauty and in the delicacy of human sentiment. It is a part of Dante's search that it should lead him to a new valuation of the human body, as the finest expression of the material world. Considering the rampant materialism that was unleashed in the mercantile ethos of the city state, the physical body could easily have been regarded by the moralist as an unregenerate and contemptible agent of base appetites. Cavalcanti himself, in his aristocratic intellectualism, sometimes suggests as much. But Dante, with due qualification, is closer in his representation of physical realities to Giotto – the third representative here of Florentine culture – than he is to Cavalcanti.

   Giotto had painted a fresco portrait of the young Alighieri. In *Purgatorio* 11: 94–6, Dante dedicates an important allusion to the painter, declaring that, in the shifting world of artistic fashion, Giotto has now replaced Cimabue as the *dernier cri*. Historians of Renaissance art have always been quick to appropriate this comment, and to regard it as an indication that a new spirit of realism was alive in the visual arts of thirteenth-century Florence. There are reasons to accept this judgement. Compare Cimabue's great panel depicting the Virgin and Child (1285–6) with Giotto's equally massive version (*c.* 1305–10) (both to be found now in the first room of the Uffizi Gallery in Florence). The former proves to be a magnificent devotional fantasy in which the Virgin floats upwards on a stylized throne, and where her robes – folds and swirls of fabric, edged calligraphically in gold – are seen essentially in two dimensions. Gold dominates the panel, performing a symbolic function as the token of eternal permanence and value. Giotto, however, painting his version only a decade after Cimabue, depicts the Virgin in a massively settled and unmistakably maternal pose, her feet firmly planted, her dress gathering around her knees to indicate their sculpted roundness. These are both religious works. But while Cimabue's painting invites attention to the spiritual and symbolic attributes of the Virgin, Giotto's emphasizes the interpenetration of divine and human purpose.

The mercantile world of weights and measures, fabrics and barrels, generates a peculiar sensitivity to the material structure of the human environment. Giotto shares this sensitivity and puts it to a revolutionary use which, in at least two respects, runs parallel to Dante's own: firstly, in regard to the human body viewed in its natural environment; secondly, in the development of an extremely subtle narrative art.

In depicting Christ's first miracle at the Marriage at Cana (1304–6), Giotto opens up a theatrical space, recognizably a banqueting hall. The bride sits in the centre of the picture but is rather blank and isolated, so that the viewer's attention is likely to drift to the right, where Giotto has painted the wonderful roundness of a paunchy innkeeper and posed him – as if in visual rhyme – against three equally rotund wine jars. Only perhaps at third glance does one notice Christ at the extreme left of the painting, modestly, even tentatively, raising a hand to transform the water into wine. The composition is dominated by a skilful placing of natural bodies, all commanding their own volumetric space, in convincing relationship one to the other. There is a religious meaning here. It is not, however, to be sought by adopting – as though in viewing an icon – any specifically devotional or contemplative attitude. We need rather to be streetwise, agile and alert in our reading of nuance and gesture, responsive even to an element of comedy. The undemonstrative miracle – performed by an incarnate God to enhance an everyday celebration – requires of the viewer a comparably natural act of observation.

There is scarcely a canto in the *Commedia* where Dante's highly visual narrative does not display a sensitivity comparable with Giotto's to space, volume, heft and gesture. Leaden-cloaked hypocrites (in *Inferno* 23) observe the wobbling of Dante's Adam's apple. Belacqua in *Purgatorio* 4 is so slow and bulky that he cannot raise his chin from its resting place on his own thigh. The souls of *Paradiso* 14 dance forwards and back like the ripples of water in a round vessel ('*un ritondo vaso*')

when its rim is gently tapped. Such observations can all intro-
duce a comic inflection. Even in his tragic meeting with Caval-
canti's father in *Inferno* 10, Dante insinuates a certain
Giotto-esque humour by inviting a silent comparison between
the elder Cavalcante – who only manages to peek a feeble nose
over the rim of his infernal tomb – and an earlier figure, the
Ghibelline warrior Farinata, who is seen from the waist up,
puffing out his heroic chest and raising an eyebrow in contempt
of both Dante and his own damnation. This is the circle of
those heretics who denied that any integral relationship of soul
and body would endure beyond death. But for Dante, it seems,
even in Hell the expressive significance of the human body
cannot be erased.

There was much, then, that nurtured Dante in the Florentine
culture of his day and, as he went into exile, there were many
intellectual goods that he carried with him from his native
city. Yet these goods were liable to wither or reveal inner
contradictions. And Dante now needed, in his enforced iso-
lation, to develop remedies of his own against the destructive
effect of such tensions. Above all, committed as he would
always remain to the service of the secular world, he needed to
discover how best he could save that world from the cruel
delusions that the secular mind can so easily propagate.

Dante's Intellectual Itinerary: The Minor Works

Travelling in exile through Italy, Dante began a series of broadly
philosophical writings which display remarkable independence
and ambition of mind and would be worth attending to, even
if he had not written the *Commedia*, as a contribution to the
developing intellectual life of Florence and Italy. A striking
feature of these works, which are often unfinished, is a restless
experimentalism. To arrive at the *Commedia*, however, Dante
needed to make the extraordinary leap in experimental under-
standing which occurred around 1307, when he seems to have
begun his poetic narrative. All the same, the minor works re-
flect the pressures and sometimes the frustrations that the
Commedia was eventually to tackle so decisively.

The most original and most authoritative of these works is *De Monarchia* (or, as it is sometimes translated, *Concerning World Government*) written, probably, around 1315, when Dante was composing the early cantos of the *Paradiso*. Here the one-time prior of the Guelf Republic argues the case for a world empire. For some time, Dante's factional sympathies had been swinging towards an interest in the fading claims of the Holy Roman Empire. The treatise, however, goes far beyond the pragmatic devotion to the imperial cause that was displayed by the Ghibelline party. Writing in Latin, expert in the professional techniques of argumentation, drawing on both biblical and classical sources, in *De Monarchia* Dante develops a comprehensive vision of political history, in which the ideal emperor is seen as a divinely appointed philosopher-king whose God-given function is to ensure justice and peace throughout the world. The great enemy of justice in the world – as Dante had reason to know from his own experience of Florentine mercantilism – is *cupiditā* or *cupidigia* (avarice, greed or 'cupidity'), which leads each individual to seek a disproportionate share of the finite supply of worldly goods. For Dante, the good things of the world truly are good, but only if distributed equitably from the hand of the emperor. The emperor himself, as a matter of logic, simply cannot be subject to greed, since, by providential sanction, he already possesses everything that there is in the world. This means in part that the emperor can exercise power disinterestedly in defence of a just distribution of scarce resources. However, the function of the emperor is not simply to control or police the world community but also, as a perfect embodiment of perfect justice, to illuminate and inspire the ethical ambitions of all human individuals. In this sense, the emperor is not a territorial potentate but the pattern and model of the highest virtues, moral and intellectual, that the human being at its best might display. For Dante, justice is not simply a utilitarian or managerial instrument. It is a virtue, a defining characteristic of humankind in its truest nature. In response to the emperor's example, justice will be exercised purely for its own sake. Even if all cupidity disappeared from the world, human beings, in the light of the emperor's example, would still enjoy being honest and just.

There are recognizable similarities between the emperor of *De Monarchia* and the Virgil of the *Commedia*, that firm but illuminating presence who directs Dante's journey. Indeed, just as Virgil appears as a divinely appointed guide for the Dante of *Inferno* 1, saving him from the rapacious greed of the wolf (lines 88–90), so too the emperor will save the world from cupidity. When Dante looks for historical evidence that a perfect empire is possible, it is to the ancient Roman empire that he looks, with scant attention to the realities of Roman politics. Thus, the sign that this worldly empire was providentially ordained is (as Dante continues to argue in *Paradiso* 6 and 7) that Christ should have chosen to enter the world and be crucified, justly, under the perfect justice of Roman law. These claims are in many ways as astonishing as Dante's choice of the pagan Virgil to be his guide on a Christian journey. But beneath the surface of Dante's sometimes capricious logic, there are considerations that flow from the deepest and most persistent currents of his thinking. Above all, Dante in the *Monarchia* defines his belief – unshaken even by exile or by his penetrating perception of human depravity – that the temporal world is inherently good and that its goodness can be realized anew by the unimpeded exercise of rational justice. We are redeemed by the sacrifices of Christ and may, through the sacramental offices of the Church, expect to arrive at perfect happiness in the world to come. For Dante, however, if only human beings could exercise their God-given reason to the full, they could then expect to be happy in their earthly lives also. On Dante's view, there are two forms of beatitude promised to humanity and, correspondingly, two authorities established by providence to ensure that we arrive at these modes of beatitude. The Church is required to lead us to fulfilment in the life to come. But the emperor is designated by God, independent of the Church, to lead us in our rational lives and bring about, in effect, a paradise on earth. Needless to say, when the Church chooses, as it did in Dante's day, to meddle in matters of politics and territorial possession, it deserts its eternal destiny and distorts, by its avarice, the proper workings of imperial justice. (Not surprisingly, the late medieval Church took violent exception to Dante's views and, as soon as it had instituted an *Index* of prohibited books, placed *De Monarchia* – though not the *Commedia* – on it.)

It has been said that a prevailing characteristic of Dante's philosophical thinking is a tendency to reduce to a minimum the dependence of the human mind upon the actions of divine grace. It is even suggested at times that Dante veers towards a version of the Pelagian heresy in which the powers we possess as creatures of God are themselves thought to be sufficient to ensure our redemption. The *Monarchia* may seem to give credence to that view. On the other hand, Christianity in its truest form is never simply a mystery religion, but also a history religion. Its concern is with a God who chose to enter history and to suffer in doing so. The promise that it holds out points to no simple escape from the world, but rather to a passion within the world, which offers redemption and a bodily resurrection that restores the physical reality of the human person to full perfection. Some such understanding, which underlies the *Commedia* from first to last, was present (though not fully formed) in Dante's mind from the *Vita nuova* onwards, in his contemplation of a Beatrice whose beauty, as a 'miracle', revealed God's purposes in the streets of Florence itself and who, through her death, inspired in Dante the certain hope of resurrection. Nor is this understanding absent from the *Monarchia*. There are 'miracles' here as well: when Roman citizens submit themselves to torture and death for the good of their countrymen, these acts are themselves, miraculously, instances of secular martyrdom, displaying the providential election of the Roman people (*De Monarchia* 2: 4–5).

The line of thought that Dante was attempting to tread was precarious and difficult to sustain. Much of the drama and subtlety of the *Commedia* resides in the delicacy of Dante's footwork. And something of this is already evident in Dante's earliest and most ambitious work of philosophy, the *Convivio*. This work, which is an extended prose commentary on certain of Dante's lyric *canzoni*, was written in the early years of the poet's exile (with enthusiasm prevailing at times over discretion), and intended to demonstrate how the virtues of the rational life may themselves instil true ethical sustenance into the secular living. So by the fourth book – which is the last that he wrote, though he had originally intended to compose fourteen – Dante had already begun to outline the arguments for empire that were to be developed in *De Monarchia*.

From first to last the *Convivio* is intended to be read and digested by a Florentine audience, in particular by those public men who are too distracted by the claims of office to give due time to the pursuit of learning. For that reason (among others), the *Convivio* is written in the vernacular. Dante is aware that to employ the vernacular rather than scholarly Latin in pursuit of a philosophical aim is a daring departure; the whole of the first book is a defence of his decision to do so. Little space, however, is given to the apparently obvious argument that the vernacular will ensure easy, widespread access. On the other hand, a great deal is said about Dante's own love for his mother tongue and for the ways in which the vernacular may establish a relationship of love between those who speak it. These are arguments that Dante goes on to develop in his great defence of the vernacular, *De Vulgari Eloquentia*, which he was writing almost simultaneously with the *Convivio* – though, paradoxically, in Latin. But in the *Convivio* – meaning 'The Banquet' – language is the palpable food that will restore those bonds of community that factionalism and exile have sundered, drawing both author and audience together in a passionate love of learning and wisdom. Latin might serve to clarify or provide professional argument; the vernacular will inspire.

Dante's 'banquet' is dependent upon, yet differs radically from, the recipes and resources that Florentine culture had hitherto provided. Brunetto's *Livres dou Trésor* had been an encyclopaedia. It was written, however, in French – perversely so, if its intention was to contribute to the intellectual well-being of Florence. Moreover, it had offered 'treasure' not nutriment, a scattering of nuggets of information rather than a digest of vital understanding through which the mind might live and work the better. Where Brunetto expounds, Dante argues and seeks to convince. Then, too, there is the ever-present but silent Cavalcanti. Guido's 'height of intellect' displayed itself in the philosophical *canzone* '*Donna mi priega*'. But just as his morbid intelligence had refused to attend to the redemptive 'miracles' of love, so also it denied itself the wonder and generosity of knowledge in favour of an élitist and often abrasively technical rigour. Philosophy, Dante now argues, is literally *philo-sophia* or 'love of wisdom', and he finds no shame in confessing himself an 'amateur'. The mind, as well the heart, can experience love, and does so whenever it delights in a book, an argument or an elegant calculation. And for Dante (as for Aristotle), wonder is the stimulus to philosophical appetite. Philosophy is born whenever we are surprised by some everyday object or apparently ordinary phenomenon, and begin to ask why this star or that flower, or any particular muscle or act of love is as it is and displays itself precisely as it does.

In defining the distance between himself and his Florentine antecedents, Dante draws increasingly upon a fund of international learning that began to interest him even before his exile. He offers some account of this philosophical education in the *Vita nuova* as well as in the *Convivio*. Stricken, as he says, by the first disaster in his life, the death of Beatrice, he began to distract and console himself by immersing his mind in the study of books, to a point at which he nearly destroyed his eyesight (see *Convivio* 3). His early reading clearly included the *Consolation of Philosophy* (523) by Anicius Boethius, the sixth-century Roman Christian whose response to political disgrace must have resonated in Dante's mind when the second disaster, his exile from Florence, afflicted him. At the same time, it seems likely that the libraries in which Dante pursued his philosophically ambitious studies would have been located in study rooms administered by Franciscan and Dominican friars. The influence, both spiritual and intellectual, exerted by these mendicant orders over the life of urban Italy cannot be overestimated. In Dante's time, the Dominican church of Santa Maria Novella had begun construction, in 1246, and, at the other end of the city, the great Franciscan basilica of Santa

Croce (started in 1296) was being built, close to Dante's home. Preachers of great power, such as Remigio de' Girolami, made regular visits to the city. Lay spirituality flourished in societies such as the *laudesi* companies, which originally met for the purposes of choral performance but came to act as mutual assurance agencies. News of reforming tendencies, and of recent advances and controversies in the faculties of the Sorbonne, would have spread almost as rapidly as news of Jacques Derrida or Michel Foucault did in the 1970s.

Dante would thus have had access to the whole spectrum of Christian debate and religious observance – which had run a very varied and sometimes controversial course since the eleventh century. In its earliest stages, this debate had a Platonic or Neoplatonic character. Dante certainly makes this part of his formation. His final guide in the *Paradiso* is the contemplative Saint Bernard de Clairvaux (1090–1153), who had enriched and re-invigorated the Neoplatonic tradition with his sermons on the Song of Songs. However, by the middle of the thirteenth century, the Christian schools of Paris had produced, in Thomas Aquinas, a revolutionary development of philosophical procedure derived from a renewed engagement with Aristotelian philosophy.

The incisiveness and argumentative rigour of Saint Thomas's writings clearly made a great impression on Dante. This is reflected in the circle of Paradise (*Paradiso* 10–15) devoted to Christian philosophy. It should be said that Dante is not as single-mindedly devoted to Aquinas as was once supposed. His purpose in the *Paradiso* episode is to celebrate the intersection of the many different strands of thinking which contributed harmoniously to his own intellectual formation. Nor does the *Convivio* pursue in terms of technical argumentation the model offered in Aquinas's teaching, but rather displays the eclectic delight of the gifted amateur in intellectual pyrotechnics. There is, however, one figure above all (eventually consigned to the Limbo regions of Hell) who seems to have left an indelible mark on Dante's thinking and taught him how to advance beyond both Brunetto and Cavalcanti in philosophical skill. This figure is Aristotle, or rather the scholastic version of Aristotle that he would have read in Aquinas's annotated translations. For Aquinas, Aristotle's works (initially transmitted to the west by Arab translators) had provided, in range and methodological rigour, an example of the thinking that would be required of any Christian thinker who wished to give a rational account of the workings of divine creation. Aristotle is above all interested in 'causes', in those movements in the cosmos that communicate life downwards from the 'Unmoved First Mover' to the vacillating sphere of human endeavour. He is also interested in the observation of both physical phenomena and human behaviour. It is Aristotle who has bequeathed to the scholastic mind the dictum – with which Dante wholeheartedly agrees – that 'there is nothing in the mind that is not first in the senses'. Likewise, in his syllogistic logic Aristotle develops the intellectual instruments (metaphorically speaking, the scalpel, theodolite and telescope) which permit the construction of logically valid models of the universe. These instruments, properly employed, may lead us, as both Dante and Aquinas believed, to an accurate understanding of God's working in the universe.

'All human beings by nature desire to know': the *Convivio* opens with this quotation from Aristotle. Just as strikingly, in the opening pages of *Convivio* 2, Dante declares that he will now – temporarily, at least – forbear to speak further of Beatrice. Nor will he address those ultimate questions concerning immortality, resurrection and providence which are always aroused by his meditation on her existence. He has, he says, discovered the attractions of another lady. This lady is philosophy; and – as if to outdo not only Brunetto and Guido but also his own earlier self – he proceeds to interpret a series of his own love poems as allegorical investigations of the cosmic order. Geography, astronomy and philosophical speculation are the menu of his banquet; and, in offering these, he seeks to lay before his fellow citizens an intellectual vision, properly supported by argument, of the greater order that rational understanding can deliver. The exile will come home when others are able to feed with him on that vision:

O ineffable wisdom that made these dispositions [in the geographical and astronomical order], how poor our mind is in comprehending you. And you, for his whose benefit and delight I compose these words, how deep is the darkness and blindness in which you live, failing to raise your eyes to things such as these, keeping them fixed in the mire of your own stupidity.

Convivio 3: 5: 22

With hindsight, one can see that there is much that Dante will later regret (or at least revise) in this indulgence of intellectual enthusiasm. Certainly, in the final cantos of the *Purgatorio*, Beatrice berates him for having dallied after her death with attractions 'other' than hers, which lead him away from the consideration of the religious truths delivered by revelation. Moreover, canto 26 of the *Inferno* unambiguously consigns to Hell a figure whose only fault seems to have been a burning desire for knowledge. Indeed, even by the end of the *Convivio* (which Dante never completed), Aristotle seems gradually to have been displaced in Dante's intellectual affections by a growing interest in and possible rereading of Virgil, who is no professional philosopher but a poet who speaks of disasters, journeys and hard-won victories.

Yet the *Commedia* would be inconceivable if Dante had not first written the *Convivio*. For one thing, the very language of the work produces a tautness of argumentative syntax which remains a central feature of Dante's writing in the *Commedia*. Similarities have frequently been observed between the three-line verse that Dante devises for his poem and the syllogistic progress of an Aristotelian argument, which runs thesis/antithesis/synthesis. Indeed, one of the differences between Brunetto's prose and Dante's is the evident delight that Dante takes in those moments when thought is productively connected to thought by a triumphant 'therefore'. Such moments punctuate the *Commedia*, enhanced very often through the balance introduced by a caesura or the bite of some conclusive rhyme.

Like Aristotle, Dante is a passionate observer of things, persons and gestures, and, also like Aristotle, he can move with perfect coherence from the microscopic to the macroscopic vision. The *Convivio*, in common with the *Commedia*, fixes the reader's attention, for example, upon the behaviour of travellers in a field of snow, and draws from this observation ethical conclusions about our duties to tradition. But Dante can also produce the geometry necessary for a diagrammatic description of the motions of the heavenly bodies. Thus, in *Convivio* 3, Dante constructs an experimental model of the earth to show the distances and relationships between the northern and southern hemispheres. (Dante knew the earth was round.) Yet, in doing so he anticipates the imaginative leap – amounting almost to a piece of science fiction – that allows him to imagine Purgatory as an island in the southern hemisphere. Above all, the Aristotelian idea that our ethical lives are intrinsically related to our intellectual lives is always a central strand in Dante's thinking. Human knowledge, when assessed against the realities of eternal life, may threaten to imprison us in perspectives merely of our own construction. But the *Convivio*, like the *Monarchia* and the *Commedia*, asserts that knowledge is the primary and most essential food of human existence, its sustenance and its greatest pleasure. The sharing of knowledge is, comparably, a pure manifestation of justice and good will.

The *Commedia*

To many of its readers, the *Commedia* is remarkable above all as a great intellectual synthesis, a *summa* sustained by the confidence that all things in the universe can be fully understood and all things explained. On this reading, Dante's poem has frequently been compared to a great Gothic cathedral. And those who favour such an analogy are likely to argue that the work is a characteristic product of the late Middle Ages, of a period in which Christian faith joined hands with Christian reason and confidently developed (as did the writings of Saint Thomas Aquinas) a comprehensive account of God and of the cosmos that God had created.

With a similar eye for structural coherence, there are others who insist that the Dantean synthesis extends beyond the intellectual sphere to include the emotions and even the imagination.

The sharper Dante's thinking, the more acute is his awareness of the shades of emotion and human drama. Dante offers a concentrated analysis of the human psyche, which he maps out in the geographical plan of the other world. Hell is a pit perfectly planned to contain confusion. Purgatory is a mountain designed to make possible steady, if difficult, ascent. Paradise is a universe of planetary spheres in perfect motion. Each sin or virtue or mode of happiness is assigned a carefully graded position on an ethical scale. And this scale progressively reveals a comprehensive spectrum of human intentions, passions and potentialities, ranging from the violence and horror of Hell, through the courage, charm and generosity displayed in Purgatory, to the solemnity and *joie de vivre* of Paradise. In a similar way, the poem may be thought to cohere around its images. This is a poem that begins in the lonely isolation of a dark wood, and ends in a vision of the white rose – which is the communal shape assumed in Heaven by all the ranks of human beings as they contemplate the order of divine creation. Dante's imagination here speaks of sterility, growth and flowering (as it does throughout of light and dark, water and rock, motion and stasis). It thus delivers a pattern of archetypal suggestions in which subliminal coherence is as tightly drawn as any philosophical or theological system.

No one can ignore the architectonic design of Dante's poem or doubt that Dante in the *Commedia* (no less than in the encyclopaedic *Convivio*) numbers the appetite for scientific information among the most characteristic compulsions of the human psyche. We do not know exactly how Dante composed his poem. It is clear, however, that he wrote with an acute eye for structural development, significant cross-reference and imaginative pattern. A narrative that begins at a point midway in the journey of our life shows a marked interest in beginnings, processes and ends. It is hardly conceivable that Dante should not have known how the poem would conclude.

For all that, too strong an emphasis upon the coherence and architectural characteristics of Dante's poem can sometimes prove misleading and distort the character of his thinking and achievement. It is in the first place doubtful whether a continued insistence upon the 'unity' of the intellectual world to which Dante belonged is appropriate. That understanding of the late Middle Ages was cultivated in the early twentieth century, often by writers who, in the wasteland of that century, were nostalgic for a long-lost harmony of systematic understanding. It is now apparent that the medieval period was a time of extreme intellectual ferment, impelled by diverse intellectual experiments, riven by controversy and often by heresy. Dante himself – always controversial, always polemical, sometimes inclined to heretical emphases – offers evidence of this. The *Commedia* is a poem that dramatizes conflict on the intellectual as well as the political level, providing its reader, even in the *Paradiso*, with a multiplicity of competing or finely differentiated considerations. The desire for order and the celebration of order as displayed in divine creation is without question a dominant feature of Dante's thinking. But so, in the *Inferno*, is the vision of disorder and (in the *Purgatorio* and *Paradiso*) the awareness that order is mere tyranny unless it acknowledges the claims of difference and variety. (See *Paradiso* 8: 97–135.)

In the second place, the emphasis upon Dante's intellectual orderliness should never be allowed to obscure the dynamism of his narrative. As most first-time readers will testify, the *Commedia* is, supremely, a narrative poem, shaped and orchestrated at every point by an incomparable skill in the handling of episode, surprise, cliffhanger, fades-to-black, unexpected changes of tempo. Such effects are an intrinsic part of a text in which the narrative unit (or, so to speak, the cinematic frame) is never more than 160 lines in length, thus encouraging a constant attention to critical moments, to beginnings, transitions and unexpected conclusions. (For examples, the reader may turn to *Inferno* 8–9 and 16–17; also to *Purgatorio* 9 and 20–21 and *Paradiso* 1, 10 and 21–2.) Nor should it be supposed that features such as these are incidental to Dante's poetic intention or intellectual purpose. In setting himself to write a narrative, even an epic, poem, Dante at a stroke abandons the lyric genres which were cultivated by all the poets of his day, and which, hitherto, had been central to his own poetic practice.

He likewise leaves unfinished the *Convivio*, the prose encyclo-
paedia in which he had attempted to embody his earlier philo-
sophical speculations. From this point on, Dante's concerns –
whether political or philosophical, emotional or spiritual – are
expressed almost exclusively in narrative form, in the depic-
tion of a journey in the form of a fiction rather than as an
argument.

In the light of so radical a departure, the *Commedia* demands
to be considered less as an encyclopaedia than as the record of
a quest, or even as a work-in-progress. At every point in the
poem, Dante finds ways to dramatize the issues that most con-
cern him, presenting them in terms of specific confrontations
and conversations which resist the easy application of any
pre-established formula. Frequently, he shows as much interest
in the impact of a question as in the statement of an answer. In
some cases, too, as Dante's spiritual story progresses from
stage to stage, he corrects or adjusts positions that he adopted
at earlier points in his career. (For examples of such re-
adjustments, see *Inferno* 27 and *Paradiso* 2 and 28.) Engaged
upon the composition of the poem for well over a decade,
Dante created a narrative that was to prove flexible enough to
reflect a living mind, constantly responsive to new develop-
ments and the implications of thoughts newly pondered.

Doubt, for Dante, is a productive state of mind. This is true
even in the *Paradiso*, where, were one to suppose that Christian
faith was simply a matter of comforting certitude, one might
imagine that Dante would have been content to rely upon the
reaffirmation of established doctrine. Yet in the fourth canto of
the *Paradiso*, at lines 124–32, the poet declares that doubt
springs like a growing shoot from the base of truth and drives
the mind onwards to ever greater understanding. The same
impetus is evident throughout the poem, and it is unlikely that
anyone will read Dante's narrative aright who is not prepared
at many moments in its progress to accept perplexity as the
fertile precursor of comprehension. The *Inferno*, indeed, begins
with a notable example, which both draws attention to the
originality and daring of Dante's decision to write a narrative

poem and introduces a series of ethical and political questions
that resonate throughout the rest of the *Commedia*.

For the first great surprise of the *Commedia* – Dante's first
coup de théâtre – is that he should have chosen as his guide for
the journey ahead the epic poet Virgil. Why Virgil? A Christian
sinner might have expected a Christian guide; and – given
Dante's philosophical and religious interests – Saint Thomas
Aquinas or Saint Francis of Assisi would appear the obvious
candidates. Why choose a pagan? Or if, for some reason, Dante
felt compelled to choose a pagan, then why not a philosopher
such as Aristotle, for whom he held the utmost admiration?
These questions point to the core of Dante's ethical vision. Yet
from the first they are inextricably linked to questions that
concern Dante's ambitions and intentions as an author. What
kind of response might he be thought to have made, in terms
of form and language, to the example offered by Virgil's
Aeneid? At *Inferno* 1: 85–7, Dante writes:

> You are my teacher. You, my lord and law.
> From you alone I took the fine-tuned style
> that has, already, brought me so much honour.

What does he mean by this claim, as resounding on his own
account as it is on Virgil's?

If there are answers to all these questions, they are not
developed fully until the very end of the *Paradiso*. (And even
in the *Paradiso*, at canto 19, line 69, Dante speaks of the
doubts that are always stirred in his mind when questions arise
concerning the value of pagan culture.) This much, however, is
clear: that Dante considers his own distinction, as a poet and
equally as a political thinker, to depend upon his attention to
and constant consideration of Virgil's example. Taking Virgil
as his guide, he decisively marks himself off from those in the
vernacular tradition, such as his friend the love poet Cavalcanti,
who disregarded the importance of the classical model. From
the first, Dante claims the right to offer his own very distinctive
understanding of Virgil's significance. Throughout the Middle
Ages, Virgil had been regarded principally as a seer, even as a

magician. He was thought to have journeyed to the depths of Hell at the behest of a witch. He was also thought, more sympathetically, to have prophesied the coming of Christ when, in his fourth *Eclogue*, he spoke of how the return of a golden age would be heralded by the birth of a baby boy. Dante knew of these traditions and alludes to them in *Inferno* 20 and *Purgatorio* 21. However, his first move in *Inferno* 1 is to re-establish Virgil as the poet of the Roman empire. This departure, as we have already seen, corresponds to Dante's growing belief that the political factionalism of Florence could only be solved by a return to the ethical standards of Rome, of justice and public duty, as exemplified above all by Virgil's Aeneas. It also identifies Virgil as the poet of history, with the right to speak, as he does in *Inferno* 1, of the long story enacted in time which will only conclude with the Second Coming. This itself may be considered a problematical emphasis, if one regards Dante as a Christian poet who concerns himself only with the eternal world. But, by following Virgil, Dante is in some measure claiming for his own poetry a public role on the stage of political history.

Dante's first meeting with Virgil is an account of both a spiritual and a literary re-awakening. And the adoption of Virgil as a guide has profound implications for an understanding of the central principles of thought on which Dante's philosophical vision is constructed. But the ambition which Dante displays by leaping so daringly into the epic genre expresses an appetite for literary experimentation which immediately gathers strength and quickly leads him to call into question or qualify his initial devotion to Virgil and the classical tradition. Thus, in canto 4 of the *Inferno*, Dante refers to himself (some might say hubristically) as the latest graduate in that 'lovely college' of classical poets which was founded by Homer, Horace, Lucan and Ovid. But as the *De Vulgari Eloquentia* and *Convivio* make plain, Dante is always unwilling to admit the superiority of Latin over the vernacular. By cantos 25 and 26 of the *Inferno* he is triumphantly able to silence the poets Ovid and Lucan, demanding that they recognize the greater artistry of his own vernacular verses. The superiority that Dante claims here is also connected to a belief that Christian culture, though dependent on classical culture, must also outdo and transcend its progenitor.

Dante never deals so brashly with Virgil. Indeed, his main tribute to the poet is his account of a fictional journey – sustained over sixty-four cantos of the *Commedia* – which depicts his relationship with the Latin poet in terms as subtle as, say, those that Miguel de Cervantes employs in his portrayal of Don Quixote and Sancho Panza. None the less, there is no question of any slavish or inert imitation of the Virgilian model. The early cantos of the *Inferno* draw much of their imagery and *dramatis personae* from the sixth book of the *Aeneid*. But when, in canto 5 of the *Inferno*, Dante introduces the Virgilian figure of Minos – who for Virgil himself is the unanswerable judge of the underworld – Dante immediately endows the figure with an absurdly coiling tail, introducing an element of grotesque comedy into the otherwise awe-inspiring scene. Incongruity and narrative surprise replace the sombre tonalities of Virgil's original. In keeping with this, Dante abandons from the first the narrative continuum and dignified solemnity that are characteristic of Virgil's style in favour of a contrastive and episodic procedure. His cantos are far shorter than the epic books in which Virgil writes and, correspondingly, more capable of sudden changes of pace and tone. By introducing modifications of this sort, Dante – as if suddenly alive to a whole spectrum of narrative possibilities – draws into the experiment features that derive from classical writings other than Virgil's own, combining these with techniques from those few models of narrative art that were available to him in the medieval tradition.

In terms purely of technique, a greater influence on the *Commedia* than Virgil is, in some ways, Ovid. Ovid's *Metamorphoses* are deliberately anti-Virgilian in their spectacular and often amoral portrayal of a shifting and unstable world of physical transformations. The appeal of Ovid's narrative lies in its cultivation of sensuous effect, shock, horror and fictional extravagance. Yet even in the *Paradiso* – as Dante imagines his own unimaginable transformation on entering a world of pure intelligence – the text he draws upon is Ovid's account of how Glaucus became a sea god (see *Paradiso* 1: 67–72). In the same canto, at lines 18–20, when the poet invokes the Muses, he also recalls the Ovidian story of Marsyas, the satyr who challenged Apollo to a flute-playing contest and, on losing, was flayed alive.

Similarly, in regard to medieval narrative, it becomes clear as early as canto 2 of the *Inferno* – where Beatrice appears as the inspiration of Dante's journey – that the *Commedia* is to be not only an epic account of spiritual warfare but also a romance, a quest for lost love, an ordeal displaying the virtues and prowess of the lover in the eyes of the lady. Indeed, in *Inferno* 1, Virgil's enigmatic appearance carries with it something of the aura of a fable and far-off legend, as – refusing to name himself – he lays before Dante a series of cryptic hints as to who he is. Most important of all, however, in terms of contemporary cultural reference, Dante's has constant recourse to the narratives of the Judaic and Christian traditions as embodied in the Bible. Dante's knowledge of the Bible is attested in quotations (far outnumbering his references to classical literature) from the Psalms and prophetic books to the Gospels and Revelation. In places, Dante will produce, in support of his main narrative, rapid and elliptical vignettes on biblical subjects (as in the illustrative examples of vice and virtue that run through the central cantos of the *Purgatorio*).

Dante can also build up very complex polyphonies of classical and scriptural narrative, where the one strand casts a notable influence or cross-light over the other. In *Purgatorio* 21, Dante describes an encounter with the one soul in Purgatory who completes his due penance during Dante's visit. Strikingly, the author chooses to take as his example the Roman poet Publius Papinius Statius, the author of the epic *Thebaid* (c. AD 80–92). There is no record of Statius ever having been a Christian. But he had lived a few years within the Christian era, and Dante, in a daring invention, builds on this flimsy evidence to credit Statius with a covert conversion to Christianity. Statius greets Virgil – who had died before Christ's incarnation – with the utmost deference. So, up to a point, Dante here demonstrates a

continuing interest in the traditions that underlay the develop-
ment of Latin poetry. But that is not all. For the whole scene is
compared almost scandalously to the meeting of Christ with
two of his disciples on the way to Emmaus. The narrative
invention here, which is deliberately problematic, demands that
we should think simultaneously of the classical tradition and
the scriptural tradition – and indeed witness how Dante's own
narrative claims to go beyond both of them.

In the notes and commentaries to the present translation, par-
ticular attention has been paid to the narrative and linguistic
features of each canto of the *Commedia*, in the belief that the
originality of Dante's thought can only be appreciated through
a close attention to the details of the forms that he develops.
However, on a number of issues which are central to his philos-
ophy, Dante's commitment to narrative poetry produces many
very challenging angles of interpretation. Foremost among
these are questions that concern the representation and charac-
ter of the human individual. The most distinctive feature of
Dante's narrative is its concern with the psychology, actions
and fate of the human individual. It is this concern that has
led readers to place the *Commedia* alongside the plays of the
Elizabethan period and the great novels of the nineteenth cen-
tury. Shakespeare is unlikely to have read Dante's work, but he
shares with him an interest in representing people at points of
crisis. Honoré de Balzac in his *Comédie humaine* (1842–53)
consciously attempts to emulate the detail and variety that
Dante brings to his observation of human beings. The sculptor
Auguste Rodin – whose representation of 'The Thinker' (1904)
surmounts his own portrayal of the gates of Hell – was well
aware of the connection between Balzac and Dante. There are,
none the less, significant differences in philosophical emphasis
between Dante's conception of the individual and conceptions
which have developed since his time and may sometimes colour
our reading of his work. Most importantly, attention needs
to be paid to the particular meaning that Dante gives to the
concept of reason and the crucial role of the body in his rep-
resentation of the individual.

In some sense, Dante may be regarded as a great rationalist, and Virgil – as depicted in the *Commedia* – is frequently taken to be an allegorical representation of how reason acts within us. Yet Dante's view of what reason is must be distinguished from the understanding that has become familiar since the European Enlightenment (and still dominates the popular view). Taking science as our model, we may now suppose that hypothesis, experiment and the dispassionate assessment of evidence are the essential characteristics of rational procedure. Dante would not wholly dissent. To this understanding, however, with its emphasis upon neutrality of view and dispassionate assessment, he would add the realization that reason is the central factor in our ethical lives and is deeply engaged in our pursuit of happiness. On the account offered in the central cantos of the *Purgatorio* (cantos 16 and 17), the core of human personality is freedom of the will. For Dante, will is not some blind compulsion; on the contrary, it is the intellectual appetite that impels us constantly to pursue those objects and purposes that properly bring to fruition the complex possibilities of human living. We exercise our wills, moreover, not only for ourselves but also for those in collaboration with whom our lives are carried through. As the *Inferno* demonstrates, Hell is the condition of those who refused in the course of their lives to free themselves from destructively self-imprisoning appetites. The *Purgatorio* and *Paradiso* proceed to investigate how wide the field of human possibilities might be if human beings set their minds upon the pursuit of rational freedom. Dantean reason, therefore, is concerned less with the production of valid assertions than with the search for what is truly good. It is also the common bond between all human beings engaged upon this search. In this respect the possession of reason carries with it a commitment to discourse: to argument, but also to conversation and persuasion; to logic, but also to rhetoric. This is evident in Dante's portrayal of Virgil. Virgil, as Dante's guide in the other world, exercises his powers of discourse on behalf of his pupil. Equally, as author of the *Aeneid*, he inspires in the author of the *Commedia* a confidence that cultures and texts can connect across the centuries, and thus be enlisted to explore and expand the possibilities of human relationship across time as well as in time. Measured against that standard, irrationality is a refusal to enter upon that communal endeavour in which discourse must always involve us.

For Dante, then, our possession of reason commits us to a quest in which we must as much participate actively in the processes of truth-telling as assess or control the world around us. A journey narrative is an exact model for such a quest. So, the situations that Dante's poem describes almost invariably reflect the intense pressures on the rational will that the poet observed in the political and intellectual world of his day. Correspondingly, the characters whom Dante condemns or celebrates represent the many historical figures from whom he sought to disassociate himself or towards whom, as members of the intellectual community, he owed some particular debt of gratitude. Throughout, the strains of the journey articulate a view of the choices and challenges to which the moral will must always respond, especially in the disoriented state of political or spiritual exile.

Where the mind is engaged in the pursuit of rational good, what part does the body have to play in such a journey? As we have already seen, Dante shares with Giotto a profound interest in the bodily presence of the human being. There is scarcely an episode in the *Commedia* that does not in some way focus upon the human body, its gestures and dynamics. Sodomites dance like greased gymnasts under a rain of fire (see *Inferno* 16); blind penitents tilt back their heads – as the visually impaired observably do (*Purgatorio* 13); Dante's mind rushes to God like a baby seeking milk at its mother's breast (*Paradiso* 33). Behind such details lies a philosophical perspective, infused by Christian belief, that marks Dante off from any school of thought that disparages or recoils from the physicality of the human condition.

Nothing would seem more natural than to insist upon a division between body and spirit, and to locate the core of human identity in its spiritual characteristics. Modern readers, swayed by Cartesian or faded Neoplatonic prejudices, are particularly inclined to this position, all too ready to suppose this must also be Dante's view. But Dante is no dualist. His very conception of a human soul denies that he could be. For Dante – as for Aristotle – the soul, or (in Italian) *anima*, is neither more nor less than the *animating* form of the body. All forms of life that are capable even of minimal self-motivation are endowed with a soul, whether vegetable, animal or rational, which impels them to seek what is good for their existence, be it food, procreation or pleasure. Human beings differ from other life forms only in having more complex goods to pursue if they are to survive and flourish: books, music, friendship and social cohesion are just some of these. But none of them are attainable without physical effort and thus include and subsume animal motivations. Reading requires a healthy and attentive eye; friendship requires a handclasp. We are rational beings. But we live our lives in and through the specific stories that our physical existence in space and time demands that we should enter. This is what being human means and, for Dante, it is good that this should be so.

Such an insistence is entirely at one with the Christian demand that human beings should rejoice in their own particular mode of existence, uniquely constituted from both physical and intellectual components. Dante believed in angels. He did not, however, believe that human beings could themselves become angels, or that they should even want to. Any such aspiration, if *per impossibile* it were fulfilled, would leave a gap in the hierarchy of created order, a lacuna between the angels and the beasts. Thus, in *Purgatorio* 25, Dante considers how the union of soul and foetus, once formed, can no more be put asunder than the union of grape juice and solar heat that constitutes the substance of wine. Similarly, in *Paradiso* 14, the philosophers who appear in Heaven as sempiternal flames are not contented with this apparently magnificent transformation but long for the Day of Resurrection when their '*carne*' – their 'flesh' or 'meat' – will be restored to them in recognizably human form (lines 61–6). Expressions of this doctrine penetrate the *Commedia* from beginning to end, and are associated throughout with both Aristotle and the Christian implications of Beatrice's death and resurrection.

Human beings can themselves, however, traduce and distort the value of the body. Gluttons, for instance, are guilty of this, and in *Inferno* 6 are shown to have reduced the world around them to a morass of undifferentiated matter. Gluttony is an unending and unchanging appetite for one type of object – the edible – and so distracts attention from the many other objects of intelligent attention to which human beings must freely choose to turn if they are to satisfy the requirements of their complex and subtle nature. So, too, Hell, in some illustrations of Dante's poem, is portrayed as a gigantic and unregenerate body, consuming, possessing and digesting, but in no way celebrating, the value of the human person. (See in particular the artist Tom Phillips's portrayal in *The Inferno* (1985).) This, of course, is what any dualist would expect. One would also expect that a wholly different view of human dignity would emerge from the *Paradiso*. And so it does. The difference, however, arises not through some vision of an impossible spiritual purity, but rather through a new appreciation of the extent to which human beings exist and speak through their bodily forms. The great mystery with which the third *cantica* concludes is that God and the truth that has been sought so long throughout the *Commedia* has in fact a human form – '*nostra effigie*': 'our image' – which fixes its intelligent attention firmly on our own.

The human individual is, for Dante, best seen as neither purely rational nor fixedly material, but rather as psychosomatic in essential character. The body displays its value when it moves, when it shifts, when it suffers or when it poises itself (as Beatrice does) in the pursuit of some freely chosen purpose. The body is also the register of our dependency and fragility, and calls upon others to acknowledge this. Thus Dante constantly invites the reader to attend to a kinetic (and often cinematic) interplay of physical actions, whether in the phantasmagoric mingling of human and reptilian flesh that occurs in canto 25 of the *Inferno* or in the ever-varied choreography of patterned lights and illuminated faces that appears throughout the *Paradiso*. Indeed, the meaning of Dante's text is frequently best appreciated through a close attention to the shifting detail

of the visual scene. For instance, in *Inferno* 12, Dante encoun-
ters the Minotaur. A scutter of stones dislodged by Dante's feet
runs down the slope, leading the reader's eye to discover, at the
base, the demented figure of a half-bull half-man. But the visual
accent provided by this physical detail also alerts us to the fact
that the scene includes not one but *two* hybrid creatures: Dante
is no mere spirit in Hell. He is, rather, a bodily presence whose
foot can act on the stones that lie beneath it. The Minotaur, as
the first of these two hybrids, acts with the self-affirmative
violence of a brute beast. The second – assured though he is
of salvation – is as tentative and vulnerable as only a human
can be.

Another case – that of Buonconte da Montefeltro (d. 1289),
in *Purgatorio* 5 – illustrates the extent to which the self may
realize its Christian destiny through loss and physical suffering.
Here, a great political leader and warrior, who fought against
the young Dante at the battle of Campaldino in 1289, drags
himself away from the battlefield. He is mortally wounded in
the throat. Yet he staggers something like two miles, leaving
behind him a trail of blood across the countryside. So far, it
seems that Buonconte's last action is an attempt to escape and
save himself from further harm. Yet this is not the end. With
his last free act, Buonconte places his arms across his body to
signify his emulation of Christ. He falls into a river, but, even
after the departure of the spirit, his body, with unrelenting grip,
maintains the pose that gave significance to his dying gesture.
There is a heroism here, and an affirmation of selfhood, but
not self-glorification. The dignity that Buonconte achieves lies
in an act of abnegation, in which he assimilates his bodily
passion to a passion beyond his own.

Whether viewed in its rational or its physical aspect, individu-
ality is not, for Dante, a steady or self-sufficient state. Rather,
it is a capacity for relationship. As beings that exist in historical
time, we live by virtue of our rational discourse with others. As
physical beings, we are dependent upon – and can give our aid
to – all others who share our bodily nature. As created beings,
we are ultimately dependent on our Creator. These are all
considerations that both Aristotelianism and Christianity

would have driven deep into Dante's thinking. While Aristotle insists that we are only truly ourselves when we live as social beings, in community with others, Christian belief correspondingly insists that we are only truly human when, in humility and charity, we acknowledge our dependence on the divine.

Yet these are all hard sayings, and largely at odds with conceptions of the individual that have come into prominence since Dante's time. We are accustomed now to think of the human individual in terms of identifiable personality traits or psychological structures. Many novels, in particular, encourage us to look for those 'rounded' and consistent characters whom we can discuss, understand and possess – as though they were statuettes on some connoisseur's collecting shelf. Yet the *Commedia* calls into question any such conception. And the question is the more searching insofar as Dante instinctively anticipates a good deal of the individualism that has, since his day, come to seem natural and, equally, many of the interests that we are now encouraged to pursue in our reading of fiction.

On the one hand, Dante is undoubtedly sensitive to the appeal exerted by the voices of particular and recognizable people. He is supremely skilful at creating such voices on the page, and is plainly sensitive to the deep pathos that arises in contemplating the loss or destruction of these particular beings. The most familiar example occurs in *Inferno* 5, where Dante represents the delicate figure of the adulterous Francesca trapped in the filigree of her own fine sentiments. Here he imagines a figure who may well be seen as a direct antecedent of Gustave Flaubert's Madame Bovary. There are almost as many such characters as there are cantos in the *Commedia*. And many readers of the poem – especially if they are influenced by nineteenth-century styles of interpretation – are not unreasonably content to focus their attentions on such dominant personalities as the Florentine patriot Farinata (*Inferno* 10), the intellectual adventurer Ulysses (*Inferno* 26) or Count Ugolino, the agonized but cannibalistic father of *Inferno* 33. Yet, in the perspective of the whole *Commedia*, the deeper pathos of all these apparent heroes is that they are imprisoned in their own obsessive and narcissistic selves, and tragically destroy a potentiality which would flourish in the cultivation of a discourse with others.

Dante's Hell is a region – immensely attractive to many later generations – in which we become the victims of our own best ambitions, paralysed by the image we see in our self-regarding mirrors. However, in the *Purgatorio*, another view of the individual is brought into focus. In the second *cantica*, as throughout the *Commedia*, Dante's literary experimentalism runs in parallel with his thought experiments and ethical investigations. Suddenly, the tragic posturings of the characters in Hell are replaced by conversation, by inquiry and by subtle reciprocations of response which draw attention rather to the workings of a group than the presumptions of any single figure. In an evident sense, the realm of Purgatory demands the penitential abandonment of selfhood. Yet it would be wholly out of keeping with Dante's high estimation of humanity to suppose that penance involved any diminution of human dignity. Nor is the purpose of penance simply to comply with the demands of a tyrannical God. On the contrary, its aim is the liberation of the very capacity for change and creative interaction which Dante locates at the core of the human psyche. Purgation is a condition of quest and, time and again in the second *cantica*, Dante dramatizes the ways in which the narrative of a penitential life contributes to, or collaborates with, the narrative of his own spiritual explorations. (See, for instance, *Purgatorio* 3, 14 and 23.) Nor is this quest suspended in the *Paradiso*. The third *cantica* emphatically does not represent a realm of unrelievedly monotonous beatitude – though those who have not read it often suppose it does. It imagines, rather, the infinite variety of ways of living that is possible when our capacity for self-alteration is fully realized. Heaven for Dante is a '*primavera sempiterna*' (*Paradiso* 28: 116), perpetual spring, a constant refreshment, a purposeful new beginning. The final *cantica* of the *Commedia* emerges from the delusions of grandeur that Dante himself, with all his poetic ambitions, had clearly been attracted by in the earlier parts of his work. He now envisages a condition of willing change and reciprocal enlargement, in harmony both with other persons and the person of God.

Of all the individuals who appear Dante's *Commedia*, none is more significant than Dante himself. The opinion we form of this individual will have a considerable bearing upon the way in which we read the Dantean epic. From the opening canto of the *Inferno*, the reader's eye is trained upon a tremulous and sometimes comic figure who bears all the distinguishing marks of the historical Dante, an unfortunate Florentine traversed by the antipathies and sympathies that exile has stirred within him. Or would it be better to say that our attention has been drawn to *two* Dantes: one who appears as an authorial presence in his own text, and another who is a highly developed character in the narrative? For instance, in *Paradiso* 25, Dante speaks of how, in writing a poem to which 'both Heaven and Earth have set their hands', he hopes – albeit faintly – to overcome the enmity of his fellow citizens and return in poetic triumph to his native place. This, one may safely say, is the voice of the historical Dante, an exile keenly aware of his own talents, yet painfully dependent upon the response and regard that others might afford him. On that evidence, we might be inclined to read the *Commedia* as Dante's sustained defence of his sullied reputation. (Movingly Dante equates literary recognition with the sacrament of baptism when he longs, at lines 8 and 9 of *Paradiso* 25, to receive the laurel crown in the Baptistery of Florence where he was first given his civic and baptismal name.) Yet the same Dante, on the one occasion when he allows his name to be spoken in the *Commedia*, chooses to represent himself in a condition of utter confusion and childlike weakness (see *Purgatorio* 30). The scene is set on the summit of Mount Purgatory and, since Dante has now completed two-thirds of his arduous journey, one might have predicted that his arrival at that summit would be marked by celebration and triumph. It is not. On the contrary, the poet brings into play the utmost of his narrative art, devising a recognition scene in which all expectations are reversed. Here, for the first time since her death, Dante meets Beatrice, and the first word that Beatrice speaks is Dante's name. Yet, far from this being a moment of gentle acknowledgement, Beatrice proceeds to attack Dante vehemently for his past sins and his present unworthiness. The great poet is reduced to inarticulate sighs and tears, unable even to make audible the 'yes' he wishes to speak in assent to Beatrice's strictures. In the *Paradiso* passage, we are called to admire an artist. In the earthly Paradise, we are asked to sympathize with (or, arguably, to condemn) a feeble fellow human being.

It has become a commonplace of Dante criticism to draw a clear distinction between the two aspects of Dante's presence in the poem, speaking of 'Dante pilgrim', or protagonist, and 'Dante author' (sometimes adding a third Dante, if we assume that behind the implied author there is the silent activity of its true begetter). The present commentary does not insist on that distinction, preferring to speak often indiscriminately of 'Dante' as both poet and protagonist. None the less, there is something to be said for the standard view. It can, for instance, allow the reader to see in the representation of Dante pilgrim a peculiarly subtle piece of fictional art whereby Dante spins from his own experience an everyman figure whose responses at each turn illuminate the weaknesses and strengths of anyone engaged in a spiritual pilgrimage.[1] Conversely, readers are sometimes encouraged to see in the dichotomy between author and character a vertiginous piece of legerdemain where, in place of receiving a realistic portrayal of Everyman's spiritual education, we are offered a peculiarly sophisticated pleasure: to the critical eye the very claims that Dante makes to speak the truth can be revealed as artful illusions.[2]

There is, however, an alternative to positions such as these. Could we not agree that the story of the *Commedia* is a story of self-discovery – for its author no less than for its protagonist? Could we not take Dante's view of the human individual seriously and refuse to allow that Dante, as either author or protagonist, could ever claim for himself total self-sufficiency or control over his own destiny – or even over his own text?

On such a view, the poem displays an awareness of the ways in which any human being (or Everyman) can betray himself, distancing himself from truth and allying himself with fiction. But, given Dante's view of the human individual, it is also a work in which the author has come to recognize that the self must always be a fiction until it recognizes a dependency on truths beyond itself. In modern literary theory, we have become accustomed to the view that the self is not an essential identity. We have also come to appreciate that, as language animals, human beings are constantly constructing themselves: selves truly are fictions, engaged in their own unrolling narratives. Yet such an understanding is entirely consistent with Dante's thinking. For him, as we have seen, individuals do not exist autonomously, but rather as points of activity within a communal order and, ultimately, within the created order that God – who is, by definition, the supreme point of activity – has willed into existence. Whether in anxiety or desire, a human is a being constantly in search of itself, constituted out of dependency, need and unrealized possibilities. There is also another story to tell. We are always the stories that we tell to others and others tell about us. Dante acknowledges as much when he ascribes the one utterance of his own name to the lips of Beatrice.

Throughout the *Commedia*, Dante presents himself in a double part – as a being, within this unremittingly experimental text, always himself, always other than himself. And this is an indication that we should read the poem as, in the fullest sense, a confessional work, a conscious engagement with his own divided and, as yet, unrealized nature. The '*personaggio*' identifies issues and propensities that the author, as he lives and writes, has still to face – as, for example, when the Dante character is almost swept away by his admiration for Ulysses or sympathy for Francesca. But instead of supposing that the author is able to stand apart from these questions, in some all-controlling posture, we can see him better as one who, in the course of his narrative, constantly re-opens those questions that must always arise in the course of any intellectual and spiritual quest. This is strikingly exemplified at both the beginning and the end of the *Commedia*. Thus the first emotion that is registered in the dark wood of *Inferno* 1: 7 is, notably, not the fear experienced by the protagonist, but the acute apprehension which fills the author's own mind as he contemplates the task ahead. This thought is so bitter that 'death is hardly worse'. Writing may be the way in which – to adopt the modern idiom – we 'construct ourselves'. It is also the way in which we abandon ourselves to all those possibilities of discourse that lie dormant until the tongue moves or the paper is marked. So, at the end of the poem, Dante refuses to claim any authorial triumph. On the contrary, his words cannot, he declares, encompass the remotest degree of divine reality. All tongues when speaking of the Divine Being will fall as short as the tongue of an infant still suckling at its mother's breast. But this humility is itself the ground of Dante's participation in divine creation. We cannot, by logic, possess God entirely. But our acceptance that we cannot is the source of infinitely new activity, in the moral as also in the authorial life. For Dante (see *Paradiso* 19: 46–8), Satan fell not through an act of rebellion but rather through stupid impatience. God, as infinity of being, can and will answer the desire that finite creatures have for illumination. But Lucifer, the summit of all light-bearing beings, simply would not wait for light, progressively, to reveal itself: '*per non aspettar lume cadde acerbo*': 'through not waiting for light, he fell unripe'.

When Dante speaks at *Purgatorio* 32: 103 of his purposes in writing the *Commedia*, he declares that he writes 'for the benefit of the world that lives amiss'. This dictum immediately points a finger at the reader – particularly, perhaps, at the modern reader who is unused to literature that directs itself so unambiguously at the conscience. What does it mean to read a work that is driven by such an intention? What 'benefit' is likely to accrue from our doing so? Supposing there were a benefit for Dante's original readers, is it likely to be the same for the many subsequent generations that have valued Dante's poem so highly?

One familiar answer leads us to assume that Dante is writing an allegorical poem in which, beyond the complications of narrative surface, there are other meanings that reflect some clear and comprehensive vision of an ultimate truth. It may be that we cannot share that vision now. But it is worth knowing – at the very least, for historical reasons – what a vision of that sort once appeared to be.

Over the centuries, the allegorical reading of Dante's poem has produced significant results. For instance, we should hardly be able to make the useful distinctions between Virgil as a figure for unaided reason and Beatrice as a figure for revelation if a long tradition of allegorical exegesis had not sanctioned such a reading. Dante was clearly interested in that tradition. In the *Convivio* he offers an allegorical reading of three of his own *canzoni*, and allegory is a feature of the few vernacular narratives that preceded Dante's own. *Il Fiore* (1285–?95), an Italian version of the French *Romance de la Rose*, may have been the work of Dante himself. Brunetto Latini's verse allegory *Tesoretto* (1260–67) also displays strong allegorical tendencies. As for the famous *Epistle to Kan Grande*, which offers an allegorical reading of the opening lines of the *Paradiso*, this work (of uncertain date) may not after all have been written by Dante. (The debate continues.) Yet if it is not by Dante himself, it must still represent the interpretation of one of Dante's near contemporaries. Certainly, allegorical readings of the *Commedia* are dominant in most early commentaries.

It is, for all that, doubtful whether we can describe the *Commedia* as a 'medieval allegory' without considerable qualification. For one thing, even in his explicitly allegorical *Convivio*, Dante noticeably tires of seeking a multiplicity of levels of meaning in his own text. Increasingly his attention falls not upon the *other* meanings that might lie beneath the text (*allegoria* means to speak 'otherwise', strangely or differently) but upon the interest of the *literal* meaning. A planet, for instance, may be viewed allegorically as one of the liberal arts, which, like the heavenly bodies, exert their influence over the human mind. So Venus in the *Convivio* is designated as a figure for rhetoric, while Mars may stand for music. (There is some residual sense of this in the plan of the *Paradiso*.) But a planet is also a planet, inviting the 'mind in love' (as Kenelm Foster terms it) to discourse, in scientific attention to the facts, about its intricate movements – its orbit and epicycles – in the planetary system. Such a reading, far from directing us to any hidden meaning, asks us to contemplate directly the design that God has wrought within His universal creation. In a similar vein, it is doubtful whether, for Dante, the cryptic or enigmatic utterances of allegory have any greater interest than the records of historical fact or the analysis of political situations. It is arguably part of Dante's experimentation in narrative form that *Inferno* 1 should start in a simple allegorical fashion – with three dreamlike beasts, representing three forms of vice, who impede Dante's advance towards salvation. Yet the same experimental spirit demands, with the appearance of the Roman Virgil, that the poem should immediately translate itself into an epic of political engagement. Henceforth, Dante, either as pilgrim or as author, is less concerned with conceptual abstractions than with the brute realities of political corruption or with the ethical example offered in the lives of many historical individuals. This is not to deny that there are many moments in the *Commedia* which are formally constructed – often with staggering inventiveness – in the allegorical mode. The great pageant of the Church in *Purgatorio* 29–33 – which so excited Sandro Botticelli and William Blake with its visual exuberance – is one such example. Yet the fact that such passages are so easy to isolate suggests that allegory is not consistently present in Dante's text but is conspicuously displayed at certain moments as an act of virtuosity, adding yet further to the wide spectrum of genres that Dante claims to command.

Dante's allegory has been the subject of vigorous discussion over recent decades; and the best thinking on the subject has always taken full account of the primacy that Dante accords to the literal sense. On one understanding – which contributes greatly to an appreciation of Dante's enormous literary ambition – the literal text should be treated in the way that the text of the Bible would have been treated by its Christian commentators. In God's own book, historical fact itself becomes significant insofar as we can perceive there the workings of an eternal providence. Thus, at every point the events recorded in the Old Testament can be read as prefigurations of truths revealed by the coming of Christ. For instance, when

Jonah is swallowed by a whale he is physically swallowed by a whale. Yet this event also leads us to think of the descent of Christ into Hell on the day before His resurrection – and therefore of the history of providential redemption. Or consider (as Dante does in *Purgatorio* 2) the escape of the Israelites from servitude in Egypt. The exodus did occur at a certain point in history. But in God's book this event is also a certain promise of the deliverance of the soul from the servitude of sin. If, to follow the same prescription, Dante suffers exile or escapes to Purgatory from the captive condition of Hell, then the literal fact (or its fictional correlative) may be rewritten in terms similar to Jonah's fate or the wanderings of the Israelites in the desert.

There is much in all of this to encourage yet another possibility, which is that Dante regarded himself as a latter-day prophet or scribe of God. The vehemence of the poet and his polemical drive, as well as his frequent references to prophetic literature, go some way towards substantiating that contention. Of course, claims of this order would now seem extravagant to the point of megalomania. Yet in one respect – in which the *Commedia* may still have much to contribute – Dante's prophetic pretensions express a realization that undoubtedly lies close to the heart of his poetic purpose. This is the realization that the world, in its natural and human manifestations, is full of signs and overflowing with significance. Yet these signs are likely to grow obscure or fall into confusion. The voice of the prophetic imagination will always be called upon to ensure that they do not.

In Dante's own day, as the new wilderness of mercantile capitalism began to establish itself, there appeared an irrigating surge of prophetic voices, declaring that too great a concentration on the here-and-now – on simple or utilitarian conceptions of significance – could only diminish the scope of human possibilities. Some of these prophets are promoted in the *Commedia* to Heaven, as, for instance, is Joachim da Fiore (*c.* 1130–1202) (see *Paradiso* 10). Others, such as the communistical Fra Dolcino (d. 1307) (see *Inferno* 28), are consigned as schismatics to Hell. But biblical prophets – like, for instance, Jeremiah, to whom Dante paid much attention – would have been constantly in the ears of anyone who attended to the Church liturgy. Moreover, the liturgy itself, with its constant reconciliation of Old and New Testament citations, would have provided then (as it may still do) a way of reading the world which revealed perspectives unknown in the market place. In its true, though not its corrupted form, the Church encouraged in its liturgy a form of communal attention that transcended the material purposes of any single individual. As a daily exercise, the liturgy continually concerns itself with prophecy and its fulfilment, and continually brings the prophetic past into union with the ethical present. It is an exact reflection of this that in Dante's Purgatory – which is deliberately set in a temporal landscape – the lives of the penitents are punctuated by the observance of the canonical hours and ritual offices. This is more than merely a pious piece of dramatic colouration. Rather, the poet here points to the ways in which the liturgical mentality constantly sees the signs of the created cosmos anew, as pointing always to the actions of the transcendent Providence that sustains them.

The mind of the Middle Ages – along with all its philosophy and all its allegory – needs to be seen against the constant background of liturgical practice in which signs and texts could be converted from their immediate meaning and thus contribute to the enactment of the story of divine creation. Liturgical practice undoubtedly was the background for the most extended allegorical writings of the period, that is to say in Saint Bernard's sermons on the Song of Songs, originally written for the monks of Clairvaux, where the erotic love described in the Old Testament text is evoked in often highly sensuous language as the legitimate vessel for the truths of divine charity. Significantly, Saint Bernard is Dante's final guide in his spiritual journey, succeeding both Virgil and Beatrice. And it is a constant feature of Dante's thinking that he should see human love as a proper and acceptable sign of the love of God. Nor is Dante ever more vehemently prophetic than when he sees love abandon its conversional and regenerative role to fix itself, single-mindedly, on those defective and fading objects of trade that the citizens of Florence had begun to traffic in. Such single-mindedness is cupidity, the sin which Dante in the *Commedia* never ceases to denounce. Few poets have a greater sense of the value and dignity of the material world than Dante has. None speaks more violently against a mentality which seeks to measure objects in this world against the yardstick of other objects in this world – a florin for a bolt of silk; a painting comprising the finest lapis lazuli for fifteen florins. So, at every point, Dante's prophetic imagination strives to re-assert the order of conversion over the order of exchange. For him, intelligence will simply waste itself – and sully the beauty of material objects – if it contents itself with shuffling coins across the counter or with rolling the rocks of financial information (see *Inferno* 7 and 17). Love, however – which can so tragically shrivel to an obsessive desire for possession – expresses itself most fully in an unending desire to interpret the words and utterances of others, in ever-wider circles of understanding. All things, in that view, should be seen as signs, an expanding universe of brilliant particulars, all acting as mirrors – to use Dante's repeated metaphor – to the intentions of the Supreme Intelligence.

What, finally, can this all mean for our reading of the poem now? How in the end are we best to read the *Commedia*?

It is tempting to emphasize that cupidity and rampant egoism are possibly more in need of criticism in the present age than they were even in Dante's own. Yet if this polemical emphasis suggested that there was one single way, and one way only, in which to read Dante's poem, it would foolishly distort the character of a work which, in its narrative fashion, presents all discourse as potentially fruitful. Like any poem – like any narrative – the *Commedia* is an open book, a tissue of suggestions and implications that the reader is entitled to approach with a free and interpretive eye. At first sight, of course, Dante's voice is more authoritative, and sometimes more aggressive, than other poetic voices ever have been. Even so, it is doubtful whether Dante would have thought it reasonable to insist upon the absolute authority of his own utterances. In the more detailed discussion of *Paradiso* in volume three of this translation, it is argued that Dante sees the abandonment of any such claim as a precondition of approaching truth at all. Correspondingly, it can be seen in the *Paradiso* and, indeed, throughout his career, that Dante is constantly aware of his audience. Which is to say that he is aware of the need for his reader to collaborate with him in the construction of a meaning to which both author and reader can consent. The *Commedia* is a quest as much for its reader as for its author. Dante stands in a similar relation to his own readers, past and present, as Virgil does to Dante himself.

The conclusion to which these suggestions lead can be summarized in a single word – a word that points to both the profit and the pleasure of reading the *Commedia*. 'Why?' Why is it that a great teacher such as Brunetto may still become or be considered a corrupting influence? Why is the Roman suicide Cato promoted to the guardianship of the Christian realm of Purgatory (see *Purgatorio* 1)? Why is Piccarda Donati, a failed nun and the sister of Dante's most vicious enemy, triumphantly entrusted (in *Paradiso* 3) with one of the poet's most important discussions of freedom and divine harmony? We ask 'why' in these cases (and in all the other cases which these three exemplify), and immediately we begin to participate in the ethical endeavours of the poet himself – in the exercise of intelligence, in the attempt to see things afresh and free from confusion.

The *Commedia*, then, through its constant interrogatives avoids any arrogant affirmation of certitude and acknowledges the essential relativity and interdependence of all human activity. (In this respect, it has much in common with other great comedies.) To ask 'why?' is, of course, an act of dispossession and humility, an abdication of single-mindedness. But it is also a source of pleasure. And this is where the benefit of reading the *Commedia* may still reside. For Dante, ethical benefit is not, in the end, the product of constraint, rule, duty or devotion to infallible principles. It is a matter, rather, of the flourishing that occurs when the possibilities latent in human nature are most fully exercised. It is a condition of pleasure. The last words that Virgil – hitherto the voice of common-sense restraint – speaks to Dante (in *Purgatorio* 27) are: 'Take pleasure as your guide.'

The implication must be that the time for teaching is over, and for the games to begin. Against the popular view that the *Paradiso* is all sermons and sanctimony, the notes to this translation continually emphasize that the final *cantica* is a game. But – in common with the *Commedia* at large – it is an intelligent game, where 'why' is the necessary dice. It is the game of the 'mind in love'. Dante saw more acutely than any modern thinker how the institutions and practices of the modern world – its cupidity, as he would say – might come to threaten the essential humanity that leads us to welcome the utterance of our 'why?' But he also devised a narrative that freshens and trains intelligence on every facet and feature of the literal or historical world. Nothing is more important in the *Commedia* than that we, through our questions, should achieve an ever more precise and ever more varied appreciation of the excellence that all things in creation can display, and especially of the excellence of which human beings themselves are capable.

The Future of Dante's *Commedia*

Dante's position in the canon of European literature is a peculiar one. Since the beginning of the nineteenth century the poet has been recognized, with increasing confidence, as (to quote Ruskin) 'the most central man in all the world'. Henry Cary, Percy Bysshe Shelley, Dante Gabriel Rossetti, and even Alfred, Lord Tennyson and Henry Wadsworth Longfellow give colour to this view. The twentieth century, in its own more analytical and hard-headed way, added to this claim. Dante over the last eighty years has become an awe-inspiring but none the less practical model for writers as different as T. S. Eliot and James Joyce, Osip Mandelstam and Samuel Beckett, Jorge Luis Borges, Seamus Heaney, Primo Levi and Derek Walcott. More recently still, the artist Tom Phillips and the film-maker Peter Greenaway in a *TV Dante* (1989) seem to have discovered in the *Commedia* a stimulus to visual experimentation in the modern medium.

This is not to say that Dante's importance went unrecognized in earlier centuries. In his native Florence, especially, during the fourteenth and fifteenth centuries the *Commedia* became an icon of the cultural and, sometimes, political prestige to which his native city increasingly laid claim. Commentaries were written on Dante's work by Florentines and others throughout the fourteenth century. Boccaccio, in the last years of his life, contributed to the cult with lectures on the *Commedia* and a *Treatise in Praise of Dante* (*c.* 1351–5). Botticelli executed a long sequence of supremely intelligent drawings illustrating the *Commedia*. Michelangelo not only drew motifs from the *Inferno* in painting his *Last Judgement* (1535–41) in the Sistine Chapel, but longed, in his sonnets, to emulate the supposedly melancholic genius of his Florentine master. Beyond Florence, Dante's reputation as a poet affected Geoffrey Chaucer very deeply – and no one has written more intelligent parodies of Dante's work than Chaucer in *The Wife of Bath's Prologue* (1387–92?) and *The House of Fame* (1374–85). Marguerite de Navarre, the brilliant sister of the French king, François I, provides a very searching treatment of the *Commedia* in her evangelical poem *Les Prisons* (1548). Others were impressed by Dante's political and religious thinking which – especially in its anti-ecclesiastical aspect – provided ammunition to the Protestant movement. His *De Monarchia* was cited by members of the court of the English King Henry VIII.

For all that, the continuity of Dante's influence was noticeably interrupted, and even eclipsed, for a span of nearly five hundred years, during the centuries that are now conventionally designated as the Renaissance and the Enlightenment. But the poet who might be thought most significantly to have anticipated the Renaissance is Francesco Petrarch (1304–74) who by descent, if not by domicile, was himself a Florentine. Petrarch's reaction to Dante indicates in large part the nature of the prejudices against Dante's poem which were to prevail for so long, and would eventually lead the French Enlightenment (until Charles Sainte-Beuve and Honoré de Balzac brought other views into prominence) to regard Dante as a 'disgusting' example of Gothic extravagance.

The influence of Dante's writing on Petrarch's is indisputable. There would have been no Laura if there had not first been a

Beatrice. Yet in an early manifestation of the 'anxiety of influ-
ence' (as the critic Harold Bloom conceives it), Petrarch refused
to allow a copy of Dante's *Commedia* on to his bookshelf.
Plainly, Petrarch wished to escape from Dante's long shadow,
and, in doing so, he set European poetry on a course that for
several centuries would largely distract it from the merits of
Dante's way of writing. In choosing, for instance, lyric verse as
the principal medium of his art, he turned his back on Dante's
narrative poetry. Likewise, in favouring the sonnet, Petrarch
gave kudos to a genre that, in Dante's eyes, was trivial compared
with the great lyric form of the *canzone* and far too unsophisti-
cated in its metrical schemes to be adopted in the treatment of
grand philosophical themes. Above all, Petrarch developed a
form of highly refined poetic diction that sought to avoid all
the controversial frictions and spurts of aggression that charac-
terize Dante's essentially public voice. Dante never hesitated to
use a vulgarism, if that is what was needed, and generally
developed a vocabulary of the widest possible range (see *Inferno*
21 and 22). Petrarch deliberately restricted the spectrum of his
vocabulary, and cultivated a melodic elegance which, for much
of the Renaissance, was taken as the standard of what poetic
diction should be.

A full account of how Dante's poetry came eventually to
dominate the modern imagination would require a longer
examination of shifting tastes and cultural expectations than
is appropriate here. But this dominance is consistent with a
realization that dawned first upon the Romantics – with their
appetite for the medieval world – and spread more widely in
recent decades, that revealed the serious deficiencies inherent
in the Enlightenment project, as also in the Renaissance as a
precursor of that project. New conceptions of what rationality
might be and a profound interest in the place that language
holds in all human dealings have consequently come to be
developed. And these all find a sympathetic footing in the modes
of thought that Dante supremely exemplifies. Any new transla-
tion of the *Commedia* must in some way be driven by a mission-
ary desire to promote the rediscovery of long-forgotten
resources (as in the dark wood Dante rediscovered Virgil). It

consequently needs to establish its own orientation within the sometimes conflicting tides of Dantean adulation which have flowed unabated now for at least two hundred years.

Something of what is at stake is illustrated by the popular phrase 'It was just like Dante's *Inferno*', to denote some scene of mayhem or conflagration. This saying ignores the fact that Dante's Hell is characterized more by ice than fire and is a highly organized juridical construction. It also betrays a common tendency to think of the *Commedia* in terms only of that fraction of it – a mere third of the whole – that Dante devotes to damnation. Still, this phrase resonates with the shock, horror and imaginative sublimity that nineteenth-century readers or illustrators such as Gustave Doré and Eugène Delacroix initially prized in the poem. The minds of both author and reader are tested to the full by the scope of the poem and stretched beyond their normal competence. An energy beyond the control of urbanity or good taste was unleashed by the ambitions of Dante's imagination. And to some, such as Shelley and Blake, this could be put to political use in their offensive against the constrictions of eighteenth-century culture.

In its vision of the 'heart of darkness', to borrow Joseph Conrad's phrase, the *Inferno* continued in the twentieth century to excite the general reader. The *Commedia* as a whole could also offer a remarkable resource to many who, in their own lives, were compelled to confront those hellish consequences of supposedly enlightened thinking that were revealed in the progressivism of the early communist regimes and the industrial horrors of the concentration camps. Osip Mandelstam, persecuted by the Soviet state, not only felt a kinship with the exiled Dante (as Fyodor Dostoevsky had also) but also embraced Dante's political vision of Rome as a just and universal authority. So, too, Primo Levi took Dante's understanding of knowledge as the truest human requirement to be an indispensable source of hope amidst the unremitting horrors of Auschwitz. It is not merely the vision that Dante offers, but also his precision of thought and language that appealed to the minds of Mandelstam and Levi. As an example of how disaster may be encountered and transformed, Dante offers to both of these writers a poem which succeeds because it attends with scientific honesty to the details of the world and, equally, recognizes that exactitude of observation and phrase is the preconditions of any honest communication between human beings.

Others, too, in the twentieth century, from Ezra Pound to Seamus Heaney, have in their different ways realized a similar truth: that when faced with the collapse of a civilized order or the day-to-day evidence of malice in a divided community, the tongue and eye must refresh and reinvigorate the very roots of perception and language. In *The Cantos* (1917–69) Pound attempts to weld an alliance between Chinese thinking and medieval thought (drawing on Cavalcanti as well as upon Dante), which could conceivably re-animate the language of the lost tribes of Europe. Heaney – particularly in his collection from 1991, *Seeing Things* – repeatedly turns to Dante (as Joyce did also) in his attempt to record those epiphanies, or moments of revelation, that can arise from the sudden perception of value in, for instance, a dust-veined beam of light.

It is notable that in the twentieth century attention shifted away from the excitements of the *Inferno* to a subtler understanding of process and the modest but constantly renewed attention to detail that Dante pursues in the *Purgatorio*. The only remote analogy for Dante's highly original conception of Purgatory, as an island located in the southern hemisphere, is Station Island in Lough Derg, County Donegal – still a site of penitential practice. Seamus Heaney recognized this in his 1984 collection entitled *Station Island*. It was, however, T. S. Eliot and Samuel Beckett – the one a founding father of modernism, the other the acknowledged patron of post-modernism – who between them made the most sustained claims for the *Purgatorio*, as will be seen in subsequent volumes of this translation. Here it is enough to emphasize that these great experimentalists each discovered in Dante ways of writing and thinking that offered a release from the encumbrances of more recent cultural baggage.

At the conclusion of *The Waste Land* (1922) Eliot alludes to the episode in canto 26 of the *Purgatorio* where Dante depicts the soul of the troubadour poet Arnaut Daniel 'hiding himself in the fire that refines'. The way to redemption – and to linguistic vitality – lies through a constant and often-agonizing return to our origins and the roots of our tradition. This becomes Eliot's Christian theme in *Four Quartets* (1943): 'We shall not cease from exploration/ and the end of all our exploring will be to arrive where we started/ And know the place for the first time.' Dante in exile discovered a similar truth and translated it into the questing experience of the second *cantica*.

Beckett died with a copy of the *Commedia* at his bedside. Throughout his writing career he had taken, as his own *alter ego*, the character of the indolent Belacqua who appears in *Purgatorio* 4. Above all, Beckett's concern with 'waiting' as a condition of human existence exactly mirrors a dominant theme of the early *Purgatorio*. Resisting the dualistic claims of Cartesian thought, Beckett looks, as Dante always does, at the incalculable shifts of word and physical movement that, in the experience of waiting, so vividly animate even the most indolent mind. Here, like Dante, he reclaims the body as a comic determinant of human identity.

What, then, of the *Paradiso*? Italians even now tend to warn readers away from this *cantica* on the grounds that the passions and excitements of the *Inferno* have dwindled here to an endless sequence of doctrinal debates. No unprejudiced reader is likely to arrive at the same conclusion. It is here that Dante's linguistic and narrative art is at its most highly developed, and indeed its most experimental. This translation attempts to reveal something of how exhilarating the *cantica* can be if one abandons the presumption that the only proper subject for literature is darkness and disaster. Dante is a supremely intelligent poet and he would not have written the *Inferno* and *Purgatorio* if he had not known from the first the extent to which intelligence is fulfilled in the perception and propagation of the good. Goodness, for Dante, is not some Platonic abstraction, nor even some Aristotelian 'cause'. It is a particular property of any mode of existence. The psychometrics of the market place may in the modern era attempt to concentrate the human personality on a limited number of desirable goods. In resisting this, one needs to acknowledge without anxiety – as Dante does

– that, by virtue of its freedom of will, the human person is always undetermined. It is the nature of human beings always to be in exile, but always to be alert to the perception of unexpected goods, always responsible for specific acts of creativity. The *Paradiso* strengthens this understanding. The vision it offers is one in which person speaks to person in the continuing liberation of human possibilities.

The *Inferno*

One of the many surprises that the *Inferno* holds for the modern reader is that the climax of the *cantica*, with its final vision of Satan, proves in effect to be an *anti*-climax. Satan is spectacularly ugly, a three-faced abomination whose gigantic limbs are covered with clumps of shaggy hair. In spite of this, he is far from being a threatening presence. He is, after all, capable only of two endlessly repeated actions: his bat-like wings flapping perpetually to refrigerate the frozen depths of Hell; his three mouths endlessly gnawing away at the three sinners who are located between his jaws. But these sinners induce surprises of their own. They are supreme examples of treachery. Why is treachery – rather than, say, cupidity or lust – the worst of sins in Dante's estimation? And why – alongside the obvious exemplar of treachery, Judas Iscariot – does Dante condemn such Roman patriarchs as the canny Cassius and the noble Brutus?

We have become accustomed to the idea that evil is interesting. John Milton contributes to this familiar supposition with a depiction of Lucifer which seems, if only for a while, to suggest that Milton himself was, according to Blake, 'of the devil's party without knowing it'. Since Blake first ventured this suggestion, it has become a wearisome cliché that spectacular displays of wickedness which in real life would be abominable are somehow more engaging in a literary work than a concern with goodness. To Dante this would have been an utter nonsense. The great achievement of the *Paradiso* and, to some degree, the *Purgatorio* is to show that goodness, properly understood, is the very source of variety and refreshment in human existence. The *Inferno* makes its contribution by displaying, in the final encounter with Satan, the sheer banality and tedium of evil. Satan is nothing but a cold, mechanical and ultimately absurd bulk over whom Dante scrambles on his way out of Hell – as if the traveller were a child negotiating some theme-park bogey. This is theologically accurate. Evil is not a self-existent principle. It exists only as a silhouette of goodness. Dante himself suggests this when he endows Satan with his three faces, which are nothing except a parodic copy of God's existence in the Trinity. If evil possesses any power at all, it is, at most, the power of a vortex or wastepipe, drawing water into a void. Having in the course of the *Inferno* demystified evil, Dante – in common with other medieval thinkers and the authors of the English mystery plays – can finally represent evil in a mode of comic bathos.

The conception of sin that the *Inferno* offers is, largely, compatible with Dante's conception of evil. Sin is the way in which human beings, with varying degrees of consciousness, abandon themselves to the emptiness of evil. A profound expression of this is to be found in the theological invention that leads Dante unexpectedly to represent, as the first group of sinners in Hell, the 'apathetic' of canto 3. These are 'wretched souls [who] were never truly live' (line 64), in the sense that they could never bring themselves to exercise their freedom of will in choosing either the good or ill, and have consequently allowed the central principle of their human existences to degenerate. Such sinners, it seems, are particularly offensive to a mind as zealous and as driven as Dante's. From this point on, it is clear that all the sinners in Dante's Hell, however impressive they might at first appear, have all in some way denied themselves a full realization of their human potentiality and fallen into an alliance with dullness and death. T. S. Eliot shares this understanding, and translates directly from canto 3 of the *Inferno* when, writing in *The Waste Land* of the crowds that flow over London Bridge, he declares that he 'had not thought death had undone so many'. What Eliot does not, however, fully represent is Dante's understanding of how various and violent the tentacles of apathy can be. Nor are the solutions he seeks the same as – or as unrelentingly vigorous as – those that Dante pursues in the *Inferno*.

Immediately preceding the comic conclusion of the first *cantica*, Dante provides the most tragic account of human self-destructiveness that the *Commedia* contains. This is the historical story of Count Ugolino della Gherardesca, who was starved to death, along with his sons and grandsons, by his political enemies in a tower at Pisa in 1289. When the tower was at last opened, it became evident that Ugolino, in his death throes, had committed acts of cannibalism on the corpses of his relatives. The pathos of this episode has led it to be treated more frequently than any other in the *Commedia* by English authors, from Chaucer to Blake to Heaney. Dante, however, is less concerned with pathos than with an awful vision of how the human will to live and to sustain life in others may come to be extinguished. In canto 33, Ugolino is himself condemned to Hell as a traitor whose punishment is to be frozen into an ice field, where he gnaws unrelentingly at the skull of the man – the Archbishop Ruggieri – who on earth had contrived his imprisonment and death. Ugolino's action anticipates the action of Satan as he gnaws away at Judas, Cassius and Brutus. But worse, even, than this action is the way in which he tells the story of his dreadful end. Moving as the story is – shot through by a stark understanding of human fragility, penetrated by a perception of our dependency upon the love and care of others – Ugolino wholly distorts the sympathy that the narrative, if taken from context, would undoubtedly elicit. As he himself declares, the point of his story is to turn all of its pathetic power to the purposes of hatred. When fully known, the facts of this tragedy will serve to defame all the more effectively the archbishop whom, in Hell, Ugolino is already seeking physically to consume. Murder is wrong, eating people is wrong. But the final condition of sin is a conscious perversion of those energies of love and generosity that any listener to the story must at first experience. These sentiments, if Ugolino has his way, will become the fuel of hatred. The bond of rational speech will itself become a source of contamination.

Ugolino is condemned to Hell not as a cannibal but as a traitor, and the fact that traitors lie at the bottom of Hell as the worst of sinners is highly significant in assessing Dante's view of sin. It is a signal that, for Dante, the most heinous offences that a human being can commit are those which threaten to destroy the unity and cohesion of the social order. For T. S. Eliot, the city is a place of utter disaffection and alienation. The proto-capitalist Florence of Dante's day anticipated this alienation. None the less, for Dante the city remains the true habitat of the human being. For that reason, in his attempts to remedy the betrayals he suffered at the hands of his own city, Dante's first task is to call into play the bonds of Roman loyalty that Virgil celebrated in the *Aeneid*, and which Brutus and Cassius, in rebelling against the empire, so violently sought to disrupt.

It is a notable extension of this principle that leads Dante, in mapping and categorizing the circles of Hell, to develop a scheme drawn largely from Aristotle and Cicero (see notes to *Inferno* 11). A common misapprehension supposes that in the *Inferno* Dante is concerned with the seven capital vices. Yet consideration of that scheme is reserved for *Purgatorio*. In the *Inferno*, Dante makes common cause with those moralists who have analysed sin from a rational point of view, unaided or unimpeded by specifically Christian categories of thought. One might indeed say (as does Father Kenelm Foster, the most celebrated of modern English Dante scholars) that the sins Dante depicts in the *Inferno* would be sins 'by any standard that was human at all'. Sin is thus an offence against humanity rather than against God. For Dante, the effects of sin and the remedies to be sought for sin are (in large part) both discernible to the rational mind.

The first remedy for sin is to summon up the best understanding that rational discrimination can produce. And this Dante does in planning the highly organized underworld of the *Inferno*. But since Dante is a poet as well as a philosopher, the ethical distinctions that he draws stimulate in his imagination finely tuned distinctions of landscape and style. At all points, Dante's categorization of sin is accompanied by and embodied in narrative images that reflect the nature of any particular sin and represent the consequences in dramatic form.

The ethical plan of Hell (see p. cxii) confirms the view that the worst of sins are those that arise from the perversion of intellectual purpose. Thus the first seven cantos are devoted to the (relatively) insignificant sins that arise from a surrender to urges and appetites of disruptive sexual passions or greed, avarice, anger and sluggishness of mind. The scenery in these cantos tends to be correspondingly dominated by effects of unruly weather – buffeting winds and drearily fruitless rain. Worse than any such sins are those in which the mind, in pursuit of its supposed advantage, consciously contradicts some self-evident or fundamental principle of its own existence. For instance, the will to sustain oneself in existence turns on itself in the act of suicide (see *Inferno* 13). Thus in the central cantos, dealing with other comparably self-destructive acts of violence, the infernal landscape correspondingly pictures the wasteland that sin has created, peopled very often by emblems of divided nature – the Minotaur, Harpies, centaurs. Worse still are the sins of lying and cheating and, worst of all, the sin of treachery. For in all of these cases, intelligent stratagems are spun out to the disadvantage of other human lives. Fraud and falsehood are punished in a region where the dominant features, far from alluding to a natural or perverted landscape, are those of a cityscape, with sewer-like channels and alleys cut into solid rock. If a city, properly understood, is a realm of thriving relationships, fraud and falsehood are parasites upon the social body, turning the city into a place of malicious opportunities. Last of all is the frozen lake of the traitors. All life is extinguished here. For, in treachery, all responsiveness is silenced or, worse still, hidden beneath a mask of betrayal, deluding guests and friends no less than fellow citizens. On such a scheme, no sin is simply a private matter, or an offence against some inner principle of conscience. All sins, even those of greed and lust, are shown to have public consequences, corroding our faith in, and love of, our fellow human beings. By the same token, sins arising in the intellect, and, therefore, consciously willed, are more serious than sins of the flesh. (Or better say – since to the non-dualist Dante the body cannot sin at all except by mental motivation – sins of the fleshly *mind*.) Thus the sins committed by politicians, such as the eminent and highly sophisticated Guido da Montefeltro of *Inferno* 27, are worse (and more stupid) than any committed by adulterers, thugs or thieves.

To a certain degree, the *Inferno* (like the *Convivio* and also *De Monarchia*) represents an experiment in agnosticism, an attempt to see what the human mind can achieve when, accompanied only by 'Virgil', it anatomizes its own psyche and adjusts its own ethical apparatus to achieve a better performance. Such agnosticism is not necessarily irreligious. Whenever the institutional Church dangles before the eye some supposedly authoritative conception of God, there is reason to suspect that it is verging on idolatry, and consequently to turn once again to a rational analysis of human needs and interests. The scathingly absurd portrayal of corrupted popes in *Inferno* 19 is an illustration of this. And the fact that Dante allows Virgil to accompany him into Purgatory, acting, at times, as a sort of secular priest, adds further to this suggestion. But the second half of the *Inferno* is somewhat different in tenor from the first. Here, human beings largely lose the heroic and pseudo-heroic dimensions that had led in cantos such as 10, 13 and 15 to a series of searching and even tragic encounters with fellow citizens, and Dante's vision now descends to a realm where comic triviality is the key note. In this sequence Dante is prepared to represent himself – and even Virgil, at times – in a ridiculous light (see cantos 21, 22 and 24). An understanding begins to dawn that if human beings are ever to be truly human, they are bound to seek for a transcendent 'other' beyond their own self-destructive inclinations. This understanding is explored in a positive light throughout the *Purgatorio* and *Paradiso*. In the *Inferno*, it is expressed in a repeated demand that human justice be illuminated by the coming of the Day of Judgement. To say this, however, is not simply to hand the responsibility for action to some *deus ex machina*. It is rather to say that human discourse – and, indeed, all our physical realities of body and hunger – depends upon a relationship to 'otherness'. We are required to acknowledge the reality beyond us of a Being (or beings) distinct from ourselves and therefore capable of eliciting from us speech and response. Ugolino makes no such acknowledgement. His frozen, imprisoned existence is a picture of human self-enclosure – of denial, silence and the terminal diminution of possibility.

But how, finally, do such considerations square with a Dante who, in the popular imagination, thinks nothing of consigning friend and enemy alike to Hell? What bearing do they have upon the works of a poet who was undoubtedly led by the massive ambitions of his literary project to presume that he can (apparently) record the judgements that God has passed, or will pass, at Judgement Day? Such questions inevitably arise in considering a feature of the *Inferno* that is sometimes assumed to be as central to its moral system as it is to its moral geography: the so-called '*contrapasso*'. The *contrapasso* – a term drawn perhaps from Saint Thomas Aquinas and used once (though only once) by Dante, in *Inferno* 28: 142 – means very simply that a punishment should fit the crime it punishes. This is an extremely primitive moral principle, and Dante, in terms of moral sophistication, eventually moves far beyond it. Yet there can be no doubt that, in developing the imaginative implications of this principle (and sometimes in resisting its moral crudity), Dante produces a series of tremendously exhilarating literary effects.

In devising appropriate punishments, Dante far outdoes the standard iconography of his time. There are very few horny or pitchfork-wielding devils in Dante's Hell (except, to special effect, in cantos 18, 21 and 22). Nor are gluttons stuffed to bursting point like infernal Strasbourg geese or adulterers suspended for ever (as they are in Giotto's Paduan *Last Judgement* (1304–6)) from strings and hooks around their genitals. Against such barbarism, Dante, especially in the early cantos of the *Inferno*, tends to recall the elegantly heroic punishments that Virgil devised in book 6 of the *Aeneid* for Sisyphus or Ixion. But his searching mind is always likely to imagine as well a punishment that reflects the psychological or social damage that a sin may precipitate. In effect, sinners are not punished by God, but rather by the consequences of their own deficient or malicious actions. The lustful, therefore, swirl in the typhoons of passion that, on earth, might have brought all productive life to a halt or, if extended to eternity, would have proved to be an eternal irritation or distraction. The 'unnatural' sinners – who, for Dante, include blasphemers, sodomites and bankers alike – restlessly inhabit a terrain where nothing natural can flourish, and where even the rain and snow that descend on their naked forms are sticky splodges of burning chemicals. Flatterers and seducers plod unrelievedly through excrement, a loathsome reminder of the fundamental realities that they sought to conceal (canto 18). As for the venal popes, these are stacked head-down in wells, and the feet of the uppermost are oiled and set alight with flames that flicker from toe to heel (canto 19). The exquisite correspondence that Dante has excogitated in this particular case produces a parodic inversion of Christian understanding in three specific ways. In this instance, the *contrapasso* alludes firstly to the apostolic succession (here passed ridiculously down the pillar of upturned clerics). Secondly, the burning oil is a corrupt version of the chrismatic ointment that a priest receives at ordination. Thirdly, the tongues of flickering flames are analogous to the fires that came down at Pentecost on the heads of the true Apostles. And if one asks why *feet* are so prominent in this canto, the answer must be that any feet that fail to follow in Christ's footsteps, as Christ demanded they should, deserve no other punishment.

The opportunities, in all of this, for psychopathology and sociopsychopathology are endlessly variable. Yet it is very doubtful whether, in the perspective of the whole *Commedia*, the *contrapasso* should be taken as a key to Dante's ethical thinking. This is in part to say that Dante is less concerned with absolute certainties or final judgements than many have supposed he is. It is also to say that anyone who is concerned with absolute certainties is hardly likely to be satisfied with a tit-for-tat conception of ethical tariffs. That mentality belongs to a vendetta world, or a merely mercantile assessment of exchange values. Its literary critical equivalent is the *tricoteuse* calculus to which modern editions of the *Inferno* have been especially inclined, constantly repeating the reductive formula:

'As in life X did Y, so X in the afterlife will suffer Y to the power of infinity.'

This is not a Dantean conception of justice. By the time he is writing the *Paradiso* (or even the *De Monarchia*), it is clear that Dante thinks of justice not merely as a useful distributive instrument, but as a vital component – '*viva giustizia*': 'living justice' – in the human personality, a love of order and relationship as a condition of all existence (see *Paradiso* 6 and 19). In the *Inferno*, one of the many struggles that Dante has to engage in, not only against the sinners of the world but also against himself as one of those sinners, is the temptation to yield to a merely vindictive conception of justice. In *Inferno* 29: 25–36, this struggle becomes explicit when Dante ignores the demand of a murdered kinsman that he should avenge him in pursuance of a family feud. On a theological level, however, the issue has been alive since Dante wrote at the opening of *Inferno* 3:

> Justice inspired my exalted Creator.
> I am a Creature of the Holiest Power,
> of Wisdom in the Highest and of Primal Love.

Here we seem to know, absolutely, where we stand. Horrible as it might be to contemplate, Hell is a logical consequence of divine existence. Ignore God and we likewise ignore the love that created us. We ignore the justice that rules our dealings both with God and all the other beings that God has willed into existence. We ignore the wisdom that inspires our delight in the order of creation. Damnation is the consequence. But is it? After all, Dante passes beyond Hell Gate and therefore beyond the very words that announce this consequence. In doing so, he has to believe that the words do not apply to him. He has to show, absurdly, faith that he is an exception. He has to hope that he can escape from an entirely just and rational sentence. He has to demonstrate love in response to a love – whether Beatrice's or God's – that sustains him in his apparently ridiculous journey (see *Inferno* 2). Damnation results not from the contradiction of a judicial rule but rather from a failure of belief in the ways that rules can be broken.

The damned damn themselves throughout the *Inferno* by insisting upon an utterly definitive conception of their own human possibilities. Thus, a patriotic hero such as Farinata in *Inferno* 10 unchangingly insists on being that alone, and not (say) a father or a lover. A father, such as Cavalcante in the same canto, insists upon being a father alone and not (say) a patriot or a philosopher. A court official is a court official and not a human being (*Inferno* 13). A human being such as Ulysses in *Inferno* 26 may be moved by an understanding of our intellectual dignity, yet refuse to be either son, husband or father. Above all, in *Inferno* 5, a lover who is represented with the utmost sympathy fails utterly to realize that love, so far from being a matter of obsession, is a source of liberation. This is Francesca, who declares that she has been brought to Hell because 'Love' (as if this were some impersonal fatality) has swept her away, along with her consort, into unresisting oblivion. Love can and does sweep people away. In *Purgatorio* 32, Dante's love for Beatrice and God is shown to do precisely that. But in this latter case, love, so far from being obsessive, is represented as an opening of attention to the offerings of the 'other'.

The *Commedia* is one poem, not three. And beyond the *Inferno*, in the narrative unfolding of the whole work, there are *cantiche* in which justice is seen as the way to human flourishing, and not a restraint upon it. That is why in the *Purgatorio* the penitents actively seek to submit to justice (in an impulse that anyone will understand who has ever asked for an essay to be properly marked or a performance fairly adjudicated). The *Commedia* is a narrative poem and its ethics are the ethics of a narrative. Frequently enough, the rebellious readers will ask why it is that Francesca or Brunetto or Pier della Vigna or Ulysses should be condemned to Hell. It is right that this question should be asked. After all, Dante's own text has put the question in the reader's mind, and sometimes the text (or its commentators) has also provided the answers. But the question itself is more important than any confident explanation. As finite beings, we enjoy the absolute only through a continual unfolding of its implications. We enjoy the *Inferno* best through an appreciation of the many ambiguities that are brought into play by the temporary assumption, on Dante's part, of absolute authority.

Dante's Language and the Question of Translation

In the *Convivio* 1: 7 Dante declares that 'nothing which is bound together in harmonious form by musical ligatures can possibly be translated from one language into another without losing entirely its sweetness and harmony'. In other words, it is impossible to translate poetry because it is impossible to find exact phonetic equivalents for the original. For this reason, says Dante, 'Homer has not been translated into Latin'. For this reason, too, the Psalms do not sound harmonious. They did so in their original Hebrew, but lost their melodic structure on being translated first into Greek and then into Latin.

These are all hard sayings for a translator of the *Commedia*. Yet they indicate the extent to which Dante – impelled, he would have said, by an ardent love of his native language – concerned himself with the finest detail of his art. The *Convivio* and the *De Vulgari Eloquentia* provide an extended discussion of both linguistic theory and poetic technique. The focus of attention in these early texts is the lyric *canzoni* of the early Italian and Occitan canons, including Dante's own. The *Commedia* goes far beyond any of these writings in its restless experimentalism. There are, none the less, considerations here that remain central to Dante's poetic practice and which need to be borne in mind, by both translators and their readers.

Dante's emphasis upon physical sound as a distinguishing property of poetry is of far-reaching significance. In the *De Vulgari Eloquentia*, he reminds us that words are sensuous as well as rational signs – as, on reflection, they evidently are, whether they be received as vibrations in the air or as marks inscribed on a printed page. Other poets, of course, share something of this understanding. Stéphane Mallarmé, for instance, insists that poetry is made with words, not ideas; and Ezra Pound, who was much influenced by the *De Vulgari Eloquentia*, develops a profound understanding of 'melopoeia', the melodic aspect of the poetic line. Yet Dante's particular emphasis remains remarkable, especially in a poet who is frequently regarded as a philosopher, or even as a visionary – and so, conceivably, concerned above all with the transcendent or ideal. There can be no doubt that in the *Commedia* Dante attempts, more than any modern poet ever has, to make poetry serve a philosophical purpose. Indeed, in emphasizing Dante's interest in the physical properties of words, one must not overlook an equally original aspect of his style, which is the concern he shares with all philosophers to be as clear as he can in his arguments and propositions. From the *Vita nuova* onwards, Dante demands that a poet should make himself responsible for the meaning of his verses and offer paraphrases and commentaries when the meaning fails to be apparent. In the *De Vulgari Eloquentia* he declares that 'it is more human to *be* understood than to understand'. This is to demand a high degree of precision and conceptual lucidity in poetic utterance, and immediately sets Dante apart from any writer of a modernist or twentieth-century persuasion who thinks of poetry as a matter of oblique suggestion or exquisite feeling. But precision of thought is, for Dante, entirely consistent with precision of form. As any translator of the *Commedia* knows, the harder one concentrates on the cadence, shape and rhythm of Dante's verses, the clearer the meaning of his sentences becomes. To read a poem by Dante is, in a real sense, to enter into responsible and responsive connection with another 'person', body as well as mind. For bodily form occupies a central position in Dante's philosophical thinking; and words, in belonging as much to the sensuous as to the conceptual sphere, offer an exact analogy to those psychosomatic interrelations of body and rational spirit that constitute human identity. (There are, indeed, cases in the early *canzoni* – see, for instance, the envoi of '*Tre Donne intorno al cor . . .*' (*c.* 1303–4) – where Dante formally addresses the poem he has written as if it were in fact a human person, capable of independent life or even of suffering the wandering existence of the exile himself.)

It follows from Dante's high valuation of the material nature of language that the act of composition should be viewed, not as the product of ecstatic or imaginative rapture, but rather as a matter of craft, of technical artistry, of painstaking labour. Dante, indeed, is inclined to describe words in terms drawn from the wool-making industry that dominated the Florentine economy: some words are silky, some are combed out and some are 'hairy', as if they shared their characteristics with velvet or Harris tweed (*De Vulgari Eloquentia* 2: 20). These are striking and even polemical metaphors. The Florence that Dante hated depended on trade in cloth; the fabric of Dante's poetry offers a philosophical and linguistic alternative. In a similar vein, Dante speaks throughout the *Commedia* of the poet as a '*fabbro*', or smith, using a 'file' to shape and smooth his utterances (see *Purgatorio* 26), or else as a scribe, carefully taking dictation from a superior mind (*Purgatorio* 24). The poet for Dante is a maker, but not a Platonic maker of golden ideas, nor a God-like creator of vast designs, but rather a labourer in the workshop of rhetoric (see *Convivio* 3:3). To be sure, there are a number of occasions on which Dante does invoke the Muses (as in *Inferno* 2, *Purgatorio* 1 and *Paradiso* 1). And certainly, he can produce subtle tissues of pure feeling, worthy of the modern lyricist (as in the incomparable opening of *Purgatorio* 8 to which Thomas Gray refers in the first lines of his *Elegy Written in a Country Churchyard* (1751)). Yet even in the furthest flights of the *Paradiso*, Dante recognizes that the purpose of inspiration is to allow him to perform the labour of composition: 'Make me a vessel to do what I can and need to do in human words to win the laurel crown' (paraphrase of *Paradiso* 1: 13–15).

Neither translator nor reader can safely ignore the 'texture' of Dante's text. In the following example even such concepts as central to Dante's thinking as '*E 'n la sua volontade è nostra pace . . .*' ('In [*God's*] will is our peace . . .') are contained, or, better, embodied in a play of alliterations and rhetorical variations on the words '*voglia*' and '*volontade*': 'will' and 'freedom of will':

Anzi è formale ad esto beato esse
tenersi dentro a la divina voglia,
per ch'una fansi nostre voglie stesse;
  sì che, come noi sem di soglia in soglia
per questo regno, a tutto il regno piace
com'a lo re che 'n suo voler ne 'nvoglia.
  E 'n la sua volontade è nostra pace:
ell' è quel mare al qual tutto si move
ciò ch'ella cria o che natura face.

(In formal terms, our being in beatitude
entails in-holding to the will of God,
our own wills thus made one with the divine.
  In us, therefore, there is, throughout this realm,
a placing, rung to rung, delighting all
– our King as well in-willing us in will.
  In his volition there's peace we have.
That is the sea to which all being moves,
be it what that creates or nature blends.)

Paradiso 3: 79–87

The concept of free will is fundamental to Dante's moral philosophy, but this is no mere piece of versified prose. From the first word, the poet is concerned to expound his meaning with the utmost lucidity. The technical terms '*formale*' and '*esse*' – difficult as they may be now – are as precise for Dante as 'neutrino' or 'quark' would be to a modern scientist. Syntax, here as everywhere in the *Commedia*, is of the utmost importance. It is syntax that carries the argument clearly from one point to the next, as in the '*sì che*' of line 82 – which is here translated as 'therefore' to emphasize that logical consequence is one of Dante's most central concerns. But syntax is intimately related to verse structure in Dante's poetry. Line endings and caesurae mark off the subordinate clauses and subdivisions of the sentence (as in lines 85–7), and rhyme clinches the conclusion of each phase of thought. Yet this is also the utterance of a 'mind in love' with logic and precision, a mind that delights (as the reader may also come to delight) in the exact placing of

a technical term or a well-timed 'therefore'. Nor is logic the
only feature of the passage. Craftsmanship and aural sensitivity
are no less important in contributing directly to the pleasure it
offers. '*Voglia*' varies to the plural '*voglie*' then to '*voler*' (an
infinitive used as a noun) and on to the neologistic construc-
tion ''*nvoglia*' ('in-wills'). Then finally there is the phonetic
variation which sees the two-syllable '*voglia*', with its relatively
closed vowels, open up into the four-syllable '*volontade*', which
is distinguished also by its open third syllable and sharply
articulated consonants. The weave of these verses is no less
significant than their lucidity in demonstrating what it means
for a mind thoroughly to absorb a philosophical truth.

If translation is impossible, then the version offered here will
plainly indicate why. An attempt has been made to register
some of the patternings and variations of the original. Indeed,
such an attempt has to be made, otherwise these lines will
descend into a mere exposition of doctrine and lose much of
the meaning that arises in and through the pleasure of seeing –
or, better, experiencing – thought so beautifully orchestrated.
Prose translations of the *Commedia* are almost invariably far
muddier and more confused than the original, precisely because
they cannot replicate the articulation of thought that Dante
achieves in establishing a close correspondence between metri-
cal and syntactical division. In the translation above (as in
response to every other nano-inflection that Dante's text pro-
duces) no account is given of the repetition of '*regno*' at line
83, of the alliterations (but contrast of vowel sounds) that occur
in line 86 with '*mare*' and '*move*'. Nor does the translation
replicate the effect of the rhyme *pace/face* in line 85 which
associates 'peace' ('*pace*') with active 'doing' ('*fare*') and pre-
vents any suggestion that peace for Dante could ever be a matter
of tranquil complacency.

The identity of a poetic text is established, in Dante's view,
by the interplay of a number of formal features. Two of these
– the effects of rhythm and rhyme – correspond to the 'body'
of the text. The other two reflect its 'mind', or conscious intent
– these being grammatical structure and rhetoric, as displayed

in the poet's choice of word or figurative ornamentation. Thus, in the *De Vulgari Eloquentia*, Dante had spoken of poetry as the product of musical expertise in the treatment of organized sound, of grammatical understanding in the proper ordering of sentences and rhetorical learning in the effective use of words and figures of speech. The poet is one who has worked 'with strenuous intelligence' on all four aspects of the art (*De Vulgari Eloquentia* 2: 4: 10). Any translator will be well advised to do likewise.

Before turning to each of these specific demands, there is a fifth, peculiar to the *Commedia*, which serves to modify the prescriptions of the *De Vulgari Eloquentia*. While in technical detail the *Commedia* clearly benefits from both the theory and the practice of Dante's earlier work, its overall conception is wholly distinctive. The *De Vulgari Eloquentia* is in essence a theoretical account of Dante's practice in his lyric poetry, and particularly in the *canzoni* that he wrote in the early years of his exile. These *canzoni* are, in Dante's understanding of the term, 'tragic' works. By which he signifies, not dramatic form or melancholy subjects, but an extreme elevation of style appropriate to the treatment of equally elevated subjects, such as love, justice and wisdom. The *canzoni* and the theory that accompanies them are 'courtly' in that they speak to an élite audience of aristocratic intellects. Yet, now, attempting a work that from the first he clearly regarded as the summation of his thought and experience, Dante surprisingly chooses to write a 'comedy'. This term did not for Dante (or for medieval rhetoric in general) refer either to a theatrical genre or even, necessarily, to an interest in happy endings. It does, however, imply a new realization on Dante's part of the virtues of a moderate or median level of writing. The comic style occupies a position from which it is possible to rise (as Dante often does) to the heights of rhetorical display but also, as needed, to descend to the lower registers of diction and construction, either to plumb the depths of human degradation or else to demonstrate (as again Dante often does, at least in the *Inferno*) a perverse genius in the treatment of vulgar, scatological or obscene locutions. Such flexibility of style directly serves the purposes of both narrative and ethical aim. Where the lyric *canzoni* are univocal, and seek always to defend or affirm the dignity of the poet's moral *persona*, the *Commedia* dares to unleash from the echo chamber of Dante's political and intellectual memory a multiplicity of voices and tones. Many of these are vicious and contentious, as in the Babel of Hell. Many, as in the *Purgatorio*, are capable of conversational nuance. Many, too, in the *Paradiso* are able to generate the unity and variety of a polyphonic chorus. Such diversity contributes to the dramatic impact of the *Commedia*. At the same time, the resources of common speech that Dante now claims to employ also add urgency and directness to the exposition of his philosophical understanding. With characteristic, even comic bluntness, Dante is prepared to assert, even in the *Paradiso*, that he will speak the truth boldly and openly; and as for those who resist the truth, well, 'Let them scratch wherever they itch' (*Paradiso* 17: 127).

There is, then, a fundamental tendency in the *Commedia* – consistent with its narrative and 'prophetic' character – towards a certain plainness of style. Many modern translators of the poem have recognized this, and have rightly sought enough to avoid archaism and artificiality. Not all, however, have realized that plainness is different from flatness, and that directness of address cannot always be best achieved by the adoption of merely colloquial registers. Too often those who speak most loudly of plainness have produced versions that are lexically inert and intellectually flaccid. But Dante is never loose in his choice of word, or anything less than 'strenuous' in his pursuit of meaning and effect. Just as a brilliant musical performance can frequently be accounted for by years of practice at scales and arpeggios, so the tension and intelligence of even the drabbest lines in the *Commedia* can (usually) be traced to some exercise which is consistent with the attention given in the *De Vulgari Eloquentia* to metre, rhythm and rhyme (the phonetic properties of the text) and to grammar and rhetoric (its structural and conceptual components). The translator needs to have at least some sense of what these preparatory exercises were like.

The standard unit of metre – throughout the *Commedia*, as

in most of Dante's lyric poems – is an eleven-syllable line, which concludes (almost) invariably with a stressed followed by an unstressed syllable. It is our expectation of this final cadence that governs the musical pattern of the line, and though Dante's versification acknowledges the importance of stress, it does not rely as heavily upon it in the first nine syllables of a line as does the English iambic pentameter. Dante's regular eleven syllables can, in most cases, only be numbered as eleven if account is taken of elisions between adjacent vowels. 'Puckerings and pleatings' (to quote Eric Griffiths) occur, as vowel flows into vowel; and these elisions can be reduced to eleven in a line that may include as many as fourteen otherwise separate syllables. It is usual (but again not invariable) for any single line to subdivide, according to the demands of clause or phrase structure, around some midpoint, either at the fourth or sixth syllable, bringing an accent on to one or the other of these syllables. The result is a line which is very responsive to the voice as it shapes its meaning and pursues the melodic current towards the last two, rhyming syllables.

Rhyme – as any translator is acutely aware – is the second and more prominent feature of the textual body. The 'musical' structure of Dante's early lyrics is the product of extremely complex rhyme schemes. The sonnet, complex as this itself might seem to modern eyes, is for Dante far less 'noble' a form than the *canzone*, which allows a highly variable concatenation of interlocking units. Behind Dante's *canzoni* (and in particular his so-called *Rime Petrose*) lies the example of extreme virtuosity that was developed in the Occitan language by troubadour poets such as Arnaut Daniel (who appears in canto 26 of the *Purgatorio*). By contrast with his own earlier work and the Occitan example, Dante devises for the *Commedia* a three-line verse form, the *terzina*, for which no precursor has convincingly been found. The *terzina* aims at and makes possible a simplicity or fluidity of structure evidently desirable in a narrative poem. Yet the inherent elegance and lightness of this form is also a result of rhyme. The scheme here runs: ABA BCB CDC, and so on. That is to say, the sequence knits itself together by taking the central line ending of one *terzina* and employing it as the initial and concluding rhyme of the following verse. The meaning of a *terzina* can sometimes be clinched as rhythm and rhyme produce an emphatic closure at the final line. It is, however, equally possible for Dante to build up larger units or verse paragraphs, all held together by the bond between the middle line and the opening line of the subsequent verse. Paragraphing of this sort displays its importance when Dante sets himself to produce a sustained piece of argumentation, with logical consequences and conclusions all being grouped by the rhyming pattern (as in the example quoted above from *Paradiso* 3). Simultaneously, such paragraphs serve the demands of narrative form, allowing for a continual variation of tempo between sustained sequences and sudden interruptions.

No translation is likely even to approach the voice print of Dante's verse unless it pays attention to effects such as these. But there is no real reason (save a lack of Dantean talent) why the rhythms of Dante's 11-syllable lines should not broadly be adopted in English. The translator needs to abandon too strong a commitment to the iamb as an organizing principle of a line. But free verse (along with Shakespeare) has taught us a great deal about how this might be achieved. The speaking voice never produces regular beats or equal stresses, but rather a constantly varied melody of half tones and quarter tones. English poets have much to learn from Dante as to how such melodies can be produced and brought to the reader's attention.

All in all, Dante's text – though it builds distinctly into an authoritative philosophical tome – is also a speaking volume, requiring a visceral as well as an intellectual response (Dante takes seriously the notion of knowledge as nutriment). One test of the validity of a translation is that, while keeping a pace comparable to Dante's own, it can be read aloud with some conviction. Which is not to say that its rhythms should conform any more compliantly than Dante's to the rhythms of everyday speech. Strangeness and inventiveness are as much a quality of poetic rhythm as they are of poetic word. We should, however, feel compelled, by a translation as by Dante's original, to remain physically in the presence of the poem.

Rhyme is altogether a more contentious matter. Some translators have abandoned all attempts at rhyme, tending to justify the departure by maintaining that Italian has an unfair advantage over English. Italian verse is dominated by end vowel words, not least because all Italian words end in vowels. In any case, Italian rhymes on a stressed–unstressed pair of syllables and therefore produces a far less obtrusive effect than the monosyllabic rhymes of English. (The most common rhymes in the *Commedia* are generated by the syllables *–ore*, *–ia*, *–ate*, *–ente* and *–etto*.) Others, however, have bravely contended that, granted the use of half rhyme, translators need only gird up their rhyming loins and get on with the task ahead. There may be some virtue in this approach, and perhaps a successful version in these terms awaits us somewhere in the future. But past examples are not encouraging. All too often rhyme becomes the dominant point of interest in a line, drawing undue attention to itself and often distorting the subtleties of cadence or inflection and thrust of Dante's narrative. At worst – and the worst often happens – an obsession with regular rhyme can distract translator and reader alike from the precise implications of Dante's meaning, which is itself almost invariably precise. Conscious of such possible distortions, the translation offered here does not usually rely upon end rhyme, though at times – when a particularly conclusive effect is called for – it will produce such a rhyme. This translation does, however, make consistent use of internal rhyme, assonance and alliterative patterning, seeking in this respect to create a discernible phonetic design and simultaneously to replicate those effects of paragraphing and narrative orchestration which are central to Dante's enterprise.

In this respect, the grammatical intelligence of the text has a structural significance as great as that of rhythm or rhyme. In English we are not accustomed to poets who are thrilled by the sequences of cause, effect, concession and logical linkage that syntax is designed to indicate. Milton may have enjoyed the sonorities that Latinate syntax can produce but, in syntactical terms, he is the polar opposite of Dante. Syntax for Dante is, as has already been seen, the very voice of the mind in love,

seeking not sonority for its own sake but precision of under-
standing, psychological consequence and philosophical affir-
mation. This is a poet who relishes the word 'therefore'. The
structure of any *terzina* is determined by the interplay of
rhythm, rhyme and the syntactic articulation of the sentence. It
is often easier, once the non-Italian reader has got the gist of
Dante's meaning, to follow this meaning in the original text
than in the English translation; and one reason for this is the
clarity with which Dante's metrical effects combine with his
syntax to clarify and highlight the progress of a thought from
point to point.

It is impossible to overstate the importance of syntax to
Dante's style, or the damage that translators can do to his text
by disregarding it. Indeed, in the moments of intellectual drama
that punctuate the *Commedia*, syntactical motifs themselves
can become active protagonists. When, in line 8 of *Inferno* 1,
Dante writes: '*ma per trattar del ben ch'i' vi trovai . . .*' his
conjunction '*ma*' ('but') marks a determination to seek a new
direction, which is immediately confirmed by the purpose
expressed in the preposition *per* ('in order to . . .'). To ignore
this is to miss the energy of new intellectual engagement. Yet
some translators do ignore it. '[Y]et there was good there . . .'
substitutes for 'but' the logically and phonetically weaker 'yet',
and further dissipates any sense of intellectual purpose with a
perverse mistranslation (of very simple Italian) which denies to
Dante all active involvement in the search for goodness. It is no
better to write: '[B]ut if I would show the good that came of
it . . .' 'But' is immediately fluffed by 'if'; 'would' is very confus-
ing as a piece of English grammar; and the enfeebled rhythm,
touching on the baleful idiom 'no good will come of it', allows
no attention to the 'good' that henceforth will be the object of
Dante's exploration. The sinewy drive of Dante's syntax is here
transformed into the bleat of a tentative curate on encounter-
ing some infernal egg. (How the present translator's attempt
measures up can be decided from the lines below.)

There can scarcely be a single *terzina* in the *Commedia* that
does not revolve around some similar instance of finely muscled
syntax. And whether any one translator can match this effect

faultlessly, English, on the whole, possesses the resources to register many of these effects. Here it is enough to alert the reader to certain aspects of syntax that will prove particularly significant.

Take the example of prepositions. The poem opens with a preposition 'Nel *mezzo* . . .' (literally, '*In* the middle . . .') and proceeds in the second line to speak of Dante finding himself '*per*' (which in this case means 'through') a dark wood. English translations almost always repeat 'in' as their translation of '*per*', and by doing so obscure the transition from the stasis of line 1 to the forward movement (albeit minimal) that is registered in the second line. Such a beginning bodes ill for the accurate treatment of a work which, through Dante's own meticulous use of prepositions, always ensures that we know exactly where he stands in any scene, what is above him, what is below, where his foot is placed, or where his gaze is angled. The solution offered in the present translation is:

> At one point midway on our path in life,
> I came around and found myself now searching
> through a dark wood, the right way blurred and lost.

The rationale for this (to speak only of prepositions) is to enhance the stasis of the first line with 'at' and 'in' and likewise (admittedly with more emphasis than Dante himself) to draw attention to the movement and purpose implied by '*per*' to stretch the purposes of 'searching' and the direction expressed by 'through' across the momentary suspense created by an enjambed second line.

Consider, similarly, the effect of the verb in Dante's text. Statistically, Dante registers an exceptionally high proportion of verbs when compared with most writers of his time. On particular occasions, Dante can choose very recondite verbal contructions, or even invent his own (see notes to *Paradiso* 8). For the most part, however, the verbs that Dante relies upon are the fundamental verbs of being, seeing, thinking, doing, walking, answering. These are the verbs that indicate the essential modalities of human existence, and Dante's use of them directly reflects his interest, as a philosopher, in those actions that human beings can (or should) perform in pursuit of ethical or spiritual good. Thus Dante shows an almost obsessive interest – which the translator should not politely overlook – in the repetition of the verbs to ask, to reply, to answer. The force of Dante's narrative as well as the power and torsion of his plain style depends upon such emphases. His verbs are the sinews of narrative, focusing upon the actions, physical and intellectual, that Dante wishes to dramatize. And because he invests these actions with the utmost ethical meaning (as the motivations of a quest), the plainest reference to a movement can take on exceptional significance: '*Allor si mosse*' at the end of the first canto might tempt one to the idiomatic 'And then he put his best foot forward'. But the cheery emotion registered in any such phrase would obscure the interest that Dante takes in this movement – as the first in a sequence that is eventually reconciled with the love that *moved* the sun and other stars (*Paradiso* 33, concluding line). Sometimes, too (in a way that can prove especially taxing to English grammar), the form of the verb takes on heightened significance. For instance, in *Purgatorio* 16, where Dante gives his fullest account of the relationship of delight that exists between the Creator and the human creature, he speaks of how God loves the soul '*prima che sia*' – before it actually exists – where *sia* is the subjunctive form of the verb *essere*: to be. The Italian subjunctive is the grammatical mood for a virtual or unrealized reality, existing purely in the mind or in our hopes. English cannot match this deft syntactical turn. But somehow it must seek to register the profound theology that is contained in Dante's *sia*: before we enter the world of physical reality, we already exist as the object of divine intelligence and desire.

Similar problems arise with the gerund or participle – the expression of a continuing or infinite action – which English denotes with the suffix '-ing'. The Italian equivalent are the suffixes '-*ando*' and '-*endo*'. The Italian suffixes, in phonetic terms, possess a sonority which the rather pinched pronunciation required for '-ing' can hardly equal. Yet something needs to be done, for when Dante wishes to speak of those in Purgatory who are involved in their continuing search for moral liberty, it is the gerund he turns to: Dante in Purgatory is one who '*libertà va cercando*' ('goes seeking liberty') (*Purgatorio* I: 71). Correspondingly, when Dante speaks of the Holy Trinity he writes: '*Guardando suo Figlio con l'Amore ...*' ('Looking upon his Son with the Love ...') (*Paradiso* 10: 1). Here the activity of God the Father in his relationship with Son and Holy Ghost is directly represented in the opening gerund: this action is 'infinite' action.

Finally, there is the matter of rhetoric – where Dante's mind is visible in his choice of diction and in the rhetorical figures that his text employs. In both respects, modern English may prove not so much lacking as superabundant. The range of synonyms available to an English translator and the possibilities of semantic shading that are offered by a language as diverse in its origins as English, are far greater than Italian, in its essentially Romance formation, can ever command. So, too, the rhetorical flexibility of all European languages since Dante's day has greatly expanded, especially under the influence of Renaissance humanism. Shakespeare, for instance, on the strength of a humanist education at Stratford, is capable of (and brilliantly indulges in) displays of linguistic pyrotechnics that are wholly beyond the scope of Dante's Italian. This is not to imply the poetic superiority of English over Italian, or Shakespeare over Dante. It is to suggest, rather, that Dante's Italian – in its deliberate plainness and ethical gravity – may be distorted if its translator is swayed too strongly by an appetite for words (as perhaps Henry Cary was in his proto-Romantic translation of 1814). The fundamental austerity of Dante's lines may easily be overvarnished when unnecessary concessions are made to later taste.

The Dante of the *Commedia* is a writer who has broken free in his comic narrative from the strict observances that he imposed upon himself in the *De Vulgari Eloquentia*, yet still can maintain – often with ethical implications – an evenness of tenor, even a humility, in the exercise of his newfound freedoms. The aristocratic *De Vulgari Eloquentia* would not allow such words as 'mummy' and 'daddy' in a 'tragic' poem. Yet in

Purgatorio 21: 97–8, the Latin poet Statius refers to his mentor, Virgil, as his 'mummy': '*mamma fummi, e fummi nutrice poetando*': 'you were my mummy and my nurse in poetic writing'. Likewise, in *Paradiso* 10, the ranks of Christian philosophers respond to an extraordinarily elevated hymn, celebrating the doctrine of the Resurrection, with the shout of '*Amme*' – which is vernacular Florentine for 'Amen' – rhyming with the '*mamme*' (or 'mummies') that they hope to see again on the Day of Judgement. So, too, in *Inferno* 32, Dante will burst forth with a string of hard, exotic rhymes and locutions – '*plebe*', '*zebe*', '*converebbe*' – displaying a virtuoso delight in this extravagant sequence while also registering how dangerously far such extravagance might take him from the 'sweetness' of the poetry he wrote for Beatrice. The spectrum of Dante's linguistic choices is a reflection of his power to dramatize an extreme multiplicity of voices and an indication of his irrepressible virtuosity. The translator must reconcile the full range of Dante's choice of words with an orientation towards simplicity and even silence. The contemplatives of *Paradiso* 21: 81 can be described, in unexpectedly colloquial terms, as 'rapid mill wheels' whirling in their circles of light. But in the following canto, at line 49, Dante relies on the simplest components – the verb to be, the use of proper names, a central caesura – to denote the austerity and harmony that two of these contemplatives have arrived at in their monastic lives: '*Qui è Maccario. Qui è Romoaldo*': 'Maccario is here; Romoaldo here.'

Last, but in some ways most importantly, there is the matter of figurative speech. We have come to suppose that metaphor is the supreme, even defining figure in poetic utterance, a crucible in which the imagination transforms reality as we know it to reality on some deeper level: 'Light thickens,' says Shakespeare's Macbeth thus invoking impossible corruptions, profound pollutions and limitless evil. Dante rarely attempts such imaginative flights. His metaphors are more likely to be scarcely perceptible resurrections of long-dead tropes: a hill – in *Inferno* 1: 16–17 – has 'shoulders'. Not a striking image, yet relevant in context: Dante needs security and guidance; the hill momentarily provides it but, in the barely noticed metaphor, a space is opened that can only be filled by a guide with real shoulders, a human being rather than a physical object, whose discourse can lead Dante, as Virgil shortly does, towards his goal.

It is, however, in simile – which to the post-Romantic reader may seem a plain and uninteresting rhetorical figure – that the Dante of the *Commedia* finds his imaginative centre. Thus, the most evident way in which Dante may be said to derive his 'fine style', to use his own words, from Virgil lies in the use he makes of Virgilian simile. As early as canto 2 of the *Inferno* he employs the simile of a flower sinking down on its stalk which in book 9 of the *Aeneid* was used to picture the death of the young warrior Euryalus. Even more directly, in *Inferno* 3 Dante describes the souls of the dead assembling before the Virgilian figure of Charon as autumn leaves lying scattered on the ground (see *Aeneid* 6). Yet no sooner does Dante use these figures than he departs from the original, and introduces effects and implications entirely of his own. In Virgil's poem, similes are used pictorially and emotively. They impose a pause upon some moment of action, to intensify our perception of its dynamics and to suggest the emotional key – whether of pity, terror or melancholy – in which the episode is to be read.

Dantean similes likewise display a pictorial dimension. Indeed, if Dante is so often and so accurately described as 'a visual poet', it is because T. S. Eliot, in his 1929 essay on Dante, drew attention to the visual impact of the simile in *Inferno* 15 which describes Brunetto Latini, squinting through the darkness of Hell, as being like an old tailor peering into the eye of a needle. Yet in all of these cases the Dantean simile works in a way wholly different from the Virgilian model. For one thing, Virgil would never descend to the 'comic' register that provides Dante with his reference to tailors and needles. And Dante's simile, in risking that descent, abandons the dignity – or sublimity – that Virgil looks for, in favour of a much more ambiguous engagement with the strains, stresses and mixed emotions that are evoked by the picture of an old man in this scene. Or else, when Dante compares himself with a flower bent down by frost (at *Inferno* 2: 127–32), he shows more interest than Virgil ever does in the scientific observation of phenomena,

tracing in very measured phrases the processes by which frost
causes a flower to droop while the heat of the sun helps it to
rise again:

> As little flowers bend low on freezing nights,
> closed tight, but then, as sunlight whitens them,
> grow upright on their stems and fully open,
>   now so did I. My wearied powers reviving,
> there ran such wealth of boldness to my heart
> that openly – all new and free – I now began . . .

Most important of all, Dante is inclined, exactly and know-
ingly, to reverse the implications of the Virgilian trope. Where
Virgil's flower simile expresses its author's characteristically
elevated fatalism in the face of human frailty, Dante's verse,
just as characteristically, speaks of the new life and re-
invigoration of energies that may unexpectedly be born in the
human being. The simile carries with it the Christian perception
that we are sustained providentially by the forces of the natural
world, just as we are also sustained – as Dante is in canto 2
– by the miraculous intervention of Beatrice into his story.
Conversely, when Dante makes a comparison between sinners
and fallen leaves, his point is that the sinners are precisely *not*
leaves, nor can they participate any longer in any natural cycle;
natural leaves are renewed (as in the simile that concludes
Purgatorio 33: 143). The sinners, however, are 'evil seed', in
that they have consciously chosen to set themselves apart from
the regenerative process. Here, as very frequently, the purpose
of a Dantean simile is to stimulate a critical recognition of
difference rather than similitude.

To Osip Mandelstam, Dante is 'the Descartes of simile: I
compare therefore I am'. These words pithily suggest the extent
to which simile, far from being a gratuitous ornament, reflects
many of the essential features of Dante's vision and processes
of thought. As we have seen, the created world for Dante is not
(as it might be for certain Platonists) a world of illusions that
we need to transform and transcend in pursuit of a higher truth.
Rather, we must look clearly at the world around us, and

employ the resources of sense perception and even emotional sympathy in a way that reveals the significant relationships and differences between its various phenomena. To exist, on this understanding, is not to retreat into some Cartesian cell of intellect, but to encounter this world anew in all its ordered variety. The true value of objects in the world is that they provide significant opportunities for the sharpening of our minds and perceptions. Thus, in *Paradiso* 15: 109–17, the souls of Christian warriors – scintillating as sparks of fire in the twin beams of a celestial cross – can be compared to motes of dust dancing in a beam of sunlight that falls through a hole in a hovel roof. We see the scene, of course, more clearly because of this homely comparison. There is also comedy here, in the incongruity of the comparison and in the generous suggestion that even motes of dust are allowed, by association, the status of heroic beings: once perceived in relation to the Christian crusaders, the contribution of dust particles to the created order takes on wholly unexpected significance. Comparison reveals their *raison d'être*.

A Dantean simile is an invitation to participate in a process of perception and interpretation (which could easily involve in every instance an hour or more of interpretative conversation). The task of the translator must be to allow each simile space for attention, so that the implications of the reference can unroll in parallel with the main narrative of the canto. It is usually not enough simply to introduce a simile with the sort of apparatus – 'As when . . .', 'Like as to . . .' – that, since Dante, has been developed (as in Miltonic usage) to signal the onset of a standard epic simile. For that reason, the formula frequently adopted in the following pages is 'Compare: . . .' The hope is that here, as in other respects, the reader is invited into a critical and collaborative venture, seeing what Dante sees and constructing along with him (as he himself asks his reader to do, for instance, in *Paradiso* 13: 1–18) the relationships that define us humans in our own participation in existence.

The notes accompanying each canto in this translation are designed to indicate those aspects of linguistic texture – and often of linguistic drama – that are generated in Dante's text by the play of register, the thrust of grammatical construction and the processes of simile construction. The translation attempts its own response, point by point, to these searching considerations.

Here, finally, to return to Dante's own forbidding strictures: is translation really possible? The answer must be 'no'. Yet such an answer need not invalidate the attempt. Nothing can replace the authentic melody – varying from extremes of 'sweetness' to harsh and acrid danger – that Dante's Italian unfailingly produces. (Compare, for instance, *Inferno* 5:100 and so on with *Inferno* 18: 103–8). Nor can any translation ever at all points encourage that critical attention to subtext, implication and subliminal word play that is a permissible part of our reading of the original text. What can a translator do, for example, in a sequence such as *Inferno* 13: 59, when we note the recurrent use of the word *fede* (faith) and the ironic mention of a faithless emperor whose name is *Fede*rigo (*Frede*rick)? Or what can be done with Dante's teasing play upon truth and illusion, suggested in *Paradiso* 28: 7–8 by the proximity in Italian of the word *vero* (truth) to the word *vetro* (looking-glass)?

There is still no reason for despair. In the first place, even bad translations (or *especially* bad translations) can be very instructive. The truly bad translation at least allows one to recognize, even in a cursory reading of the original, details and dimensions which might easily have been taken account of until they were crudely hidden from view by the translator's clumsy rendering.

More positively, however, one may regard a translation as a sustained critical performance. Compare: a violinist opens the score of the *Kreutzer Sonata*, picks up her instrument and begins – through a series of infinitesimal adjustments to finger-placing and bow speed – to engage with Ludwig van Beethoven's musical intentions; every note counts and, though the movements of mind and hand are too rapid to be defined by explanation, the process involves the constant exercise of critical discrimination. We do not in the end hear Beethoven's own rendition; and another violinist may play with wholly different emphases. But we do hear a valid interpretation. So, too, with a translation. Behind the choice of any one word or rhythm there may be many hours of critical analysis. And often that analysis could have been expressed in many pages of prose interpretation. A translation, in common with all forms of communication, is an act of interpretation. It is, above all, a performance.

But translation can also be an education. It was regularly so in the seventeenth and eighteenth centuries (as, for instance, in John Dryden's translation of Boccaccio or Alexander Pope's translation of Homer). In attempting to translate, translators can enrich their own linguistic repertoire and even encourage in their native language tendencies and qualities that would otherwise remain undiscovered. Pound, for instance, seeks to refresh the tired tongues of modern Europe by introducing to them the implications of the Chinese ideogram. This can mean imparting elements of linguistic strangeness into the English text. And that consideration leads one to ask whether a translator should, in principle, seek to deliver a wholly naturalized version of the original, which reads as it would if it had been written in a native and contemporary idiom. Or should the translated version in some way preserve the density, oddness and resistive characteristics of the original? This is a particularly pertinent question in the case of the *Commedia*. There is a great deal in Dante – above all in his plain style and syntax – which has yet to be absorbed into the repertoire of English poetry. Paradoxically, in this case strangeness derives from a simplicity, directness and particularity of address. We should lose much that Dante has to offer if this strangeness were reduced merely to some approachable but commonplace measure of modern English. Dante's language is, on the one hand, anything but archaic and, on the other, rarely – except for special effect – neologistic in character. Its own form of ever-renewable modernity derives, firstly, from its moral urgency to engage the reader, and to make the reader answer its author's questions from the reader's own point in history. Secondly, the text thrives on a profound inventiveness that drives author and reader alike to search the whole thesaurus of linguistic potentialities. A translation of this text – like any reading of it – needs to be impelled by a linguistic curiosity akin to Dante's own, and by all the anxieties and *joie de vivre* that arise in talking with an interlocutor as sharp-witted as Dante invariably is.

NOTES

1 An excellent reading along these lines is offered by Patrick Boyde in *Dante, Philomythes and Philosopher* (Cambridge, 1981).
2 An excellent reading along *these* lines can be found in Teodolinda Barolini's *The Undivine Comedy: Detheologizing Dante* (Princeton, 1992).

Further Reading

Auerbach, E. *Mimesis: The Representation of Reality in Western Literature* (Princeton, 1953).

—, *Literary Latin and Its Public in Late Latin Antiquity* (New York, 1965). These two seminal studies, written with great critical sensitivity, identify crucial issues in regard to Dante's allegory and his relation to classical tradition.

Barolini, T. *Dante's Poets: Textuality and Truth in the Comedy* (Princeton, 1984).

—, *The Undivine Comedy: Detheologizing Dante* (Princeton, 1992). Interesting attempts to detach Dante's poem from an over-insistence on moral issues which reveal the virtuosity of Dante's fiction in creating a 'hall of mirrors'.

Boitani, P., *The Tragic and the Sublime in Medieval Literature* (Cambridge, 1989).

—, *The Shadow of Ulysses* (Oxford, 1994). Highly original studies of issues such as 'recognition' and the search for knowledge as central issues in Dante's poem.

Boyde, P., *Dante, Philomythes and Philosopher: Man in the Cosmos* (Cambridge, 1981).

—, *Perception and Passion in Dante's Comedy* (Cambridge, 1993).

—, *Human Vices and Human Worth in Dante's Comedy* (Cambridge, 2000). A magisterial trilogy expounding all the central principles of Dante's philosophical system.

Curtius, E. R., *European Literature and the Latin Middle Ages*, trans. Willard R. Trask (New York, 1953). Dante seen as the culminating figure in the tradition of medieval Latinity.

Davis, C. T., *Dante and the Idea of Rome* (Oxford, 1957). An important study of Dante's political thinking.

Dronke, P., *Dante and Medieval Latin Traditions* (Cambridge, 1986). Detailed essays on Dante's use of classical and medieval motifs.

Eliot, T. S., *Dante* (London, 1929). Not in itself a particularly illuminating essay, but crucial in pointing to issues that concerned Eliot as a poet throughout his long apprenticeship to Dante.

Fergusson, F., *Dante* (New York, 1966). A stimulating introduction by a passionate Dantist.

Foster, K., *The Two Dantes* (London, 1977). The most penetrating study available of Dante's conception of free will and love.

Fowlie, W., *A Reading of Dante's Inferno* (Chicago and London, 1981). A valuable point-by-point study of the first *cantica* of the *Commedia*.

Freccero, J. (ed.), *Dante: A Collection of Critical Essays* (Englewood Cliffs, 1965).

—, *The Poetics of Conversion* (Cambridge MA, 1986). Freccero's edited volume includes extremely important essays on Dante's philosophy of love and learning and also on his poetic experimentalism.

Gilson, E., *Dante and Philosophy* (London, 1948). An indispensable study of Dante's political theory, by the most influential medievalist of the twentieth century.

Griffiths, E. and Reynolds, M., *Dante in English* (London, 2005). An exhilarating account of English versions of Dante's work beginning with Chaucer and including William Ewart Gladstone.

Hawkins, P., *Dante's Testaments* (Stanford CA, 1999). A study of Dante's indebtedness to the Scriptures, notable for many critical insights.

Holmes, G., *Dante* (Oxford, 1980). A concise introduction to the history of Dante's time and also to his political theory.

Jacoff, R. (ed.), *The Cambridge Companion to Dante* (Cambridge, 1993). Good introductory essays on a range of essential subjects.

Kirkpatrick, R., *Dante's Inferno: Difficulty and Dead Poetry* (Cambridge, 1987). A canto-by-canto study of the first *cantica*.

Lansing, R. (ed.), *The Dante Encyclopedia* (New York and London, 2000). A comprehensive study of Dantean issues, drawing on the best of modern scholarship.

Mandelstam, O., 'Conversation about Dante', in *Collected Critical Prose and Letters*, trans. J. G. Grey (London, 1991). A poet's account – sometimes extravagant but always interesting.

Phillips, T., *The Inferno* (London, 1985). A highly imaginative and penetrating critique of the first *cantica*, in the form of canto-by-canto illustrations and notes, from the hand of a major modern artist.

Quinones, R., *Dante Alighieri* (Boston, 1979). A good account, especially of historical themes in the *Commedia*.

Williams, C., *Religion and Love in Dante: The Theology of Romantic Love* (London, 1941). A subtle but accessible introduction to Dante's theological imagination.

A Note on the Manuscript Tradition

Dante appears to have published parts of the *Commedia* in manuscript form before the work as a whole was completed. The *Inferno* appeared around 1315 and the *Purgatorio* around 1320, a year before the author's death, by which time groups of cantos from the *Paradiso* may also have been available to patrons. No manuscript in Dante's own hand has ever been identified. But the immediate popularity of the work ensured that, from the earliest times, there were a great many copies available. The oldest manuscript of the work complete in all three of its parts appears to have been produced in Florence between 1330 and 1331. The success of this publication is attested by an anecdote in which a Florentine copyist active in the 1330s is said to have made provision for the dowries of his daughters by producing no less than 100 redactions of the *Commedia*. A further wave – of largely de luxe editions, produced in Tuscany, beyond the walls of Florence – began to emerge in the 1350s. This second tradition seems to have been stimulated by the interest that Boccaccio took in Dante's poem. Boccaccio himself seems to have copied out the *Commedia* at least three times, and had one of these delivered to Petrarch in Avignon in 1351. In all, something approaching 900 manuscripts were available before printed editions began to appear in 1472. These editions, too, of which there were many, were quickly sold. They included an octave edition in 1502 from the prestigious house of Aldine – important enough to be pirated in the same year at Lyons. No less than 100 of the early manuscripts were scrupulously illustrated, establishing a collaboration between poet and painter which reached its height in

Botticelli's extraordinarily subtle treatment of all of the cantos of the *Commedia* produced in Florence during the 1480s, and which continued unabated in the works of William Blake, Gustave Doré and Tom Phillips.

The text reproduced in the present volume (with, on a few occasions, silent emendation) is that established by Giorgio Petrocchi in *La commedia secondo l'antica vulgata* (Milan, 1966–7). Petrocchi's text is based on some thirty of the earliest Florentine manuscripts. Debate continues over the detail of some of Petrocchi's readings. However, it is a testimony to the clarity of Dante's thought and style that his copyists seem only rarely to have lapsed in concentration. In very few cases do variant readings lead to significantly different interpretations. This is the more remarkable in that punctuation was negligible in early copies. Dante's use of rhyme and caesurae fulfils most of the functions that are now ascribed to punctuation. The scholarly reader, therefore, of both Petrocchi's text and the present translation may reasonably complain at the very high level of editorial punctuation that these both display. Their justification lies in an attempt to articulate and clarify the subtlety, nuance and polyphonic variety of the author's original voice.

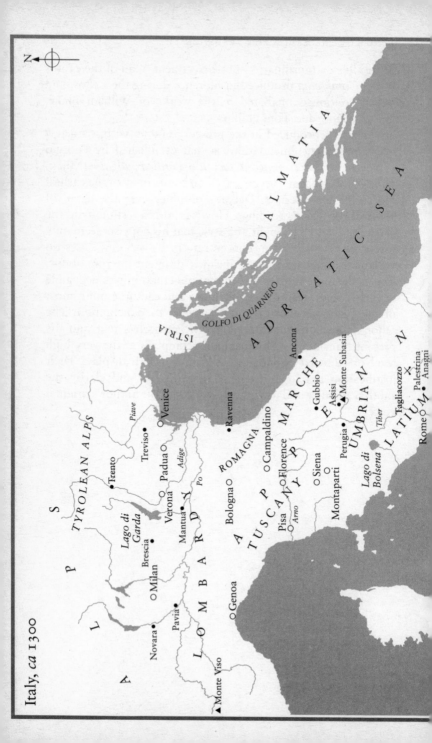

Italy, *ca* 1300

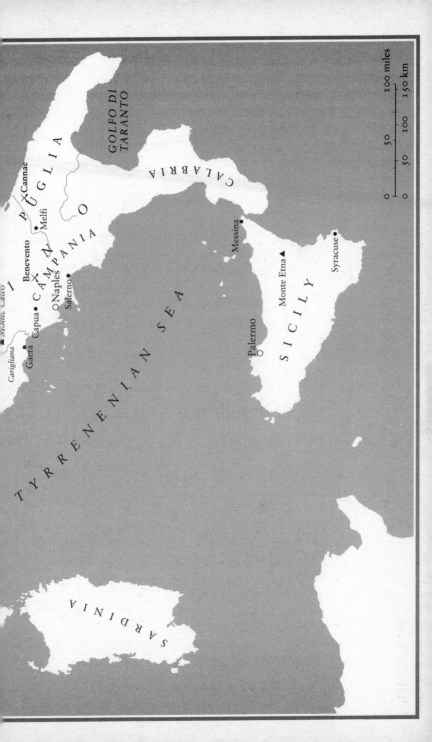

GOLFO DI
TARANTO

CALABRIA

Cannae

PUGLIA

Melfi

Benevento

CAMPANIA

Naples
Capua
Salerno

Gaeta

Carigliana

TYRRENENIAN SEA

Messina

Monte Etna

Palermo

SICILY

Syracuse

SARDINIA

0   50   100 miles
0   50   100   150 km

Plan of Hell

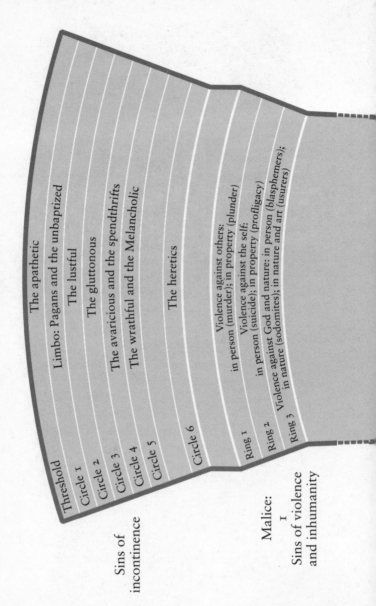

The apathetic
Limbo: Pagans and the unbaptized
The lustful
The gluttonous
The avaricious and the spendthrifts
The wrathful and the Melancholic

The heretics

Violence against others:
in person (murder); in property (plunder)
Violence against the self:
in person (suicide); in property (profligacy)
Violence against God and nature: in person (blasphemers);
in nature (sodomites); in nature and art (usurers)

Threshold
Circle 1
Circle 2
Circle 3
Circle 4
Circle 5

Circle 6

Ring 1

Ring 2

Ring 3

Sins of
incontinence

Malice:
1
Sins of violence
and inhumanity

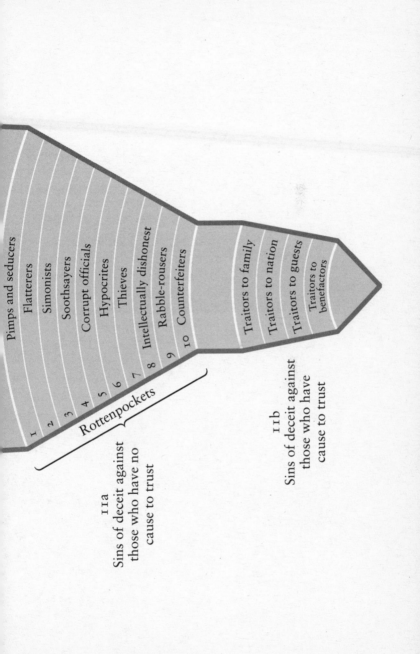

Pimps and seducers
Flatterers
Simonists
Soothsayers
Corrupt officials
Hypocrites
Thieves
Intellectually dishonest
Rabble-rousers
Counterfeiters

1
2
3
4
5
6
7
8
9
10

Rottenpockets

11a
Sins of deceit against those who have no cause to trust

Traitors to family
Traitors to nation
Traitors to guests
Traitors to benefactors

11b
Sins of deceit against those who have cause to trust

Commedia Cantica 1: *Inferno*

CANTO 1

1   Nel mezzo del cammin di nostra vita.
mi ritrovai per una selva oscura,
ché la diritta via era smarrita.

4   Ahi quanto a dir qual era è cosa dura
esta selva selvaggia e aspra e forte
che nel pensier rinova la paura!

7   Tant' è amara che poco è più morte;
ma per trattar del ben ch'i' vi trovai,
dirò de l'altre cose ch'i' v'ho scorte.

10   Io non so ben ridir com'i' v'intrai,
tant' era pien di sonno a quel punto
che la verace via abbandonai.

13   Ma poi ch'i' fui al piè d'un colle giunto,
là dove terminava quella valle
che m'avea di paura il cor compunto,

16   guardai in alto, e vidi le sue spalle
vestite già de' raggi del pianeta
che mena dritto altrui per ogne calle.

19   Allor fu la paura un poco queta
che nel lago del cor m'era durata
la notte ch'i' passai con tanta pieta.

22   E come quei che con lena affannata,
uscito fuor del pelago a la riva,
si volge a l'acqua perigliosa e guata:

25   così l'animo mio, ch'ancor fuggiva,
si volse a retro a rimirar lo passo
che non lasciò già mai persona viva.

CANTO 1

At one point midway on our path in life,   1*
I came around and found myself now searching
through a dark wood, the right way blurred and lost.

How hard it is to say what that wood was,   4
a wilderness, savage, brute, harsh and wild.
Only to think of it renews my fear!

So bitter, that thought, that death is hardly worse.   7*
But since my theme will be the good I found there,
I mean to speak of other things I saw.

I do not know, I cannot rightly say,   10
how first I came to be here – so full of sleep,
that moment, abandoning the true way on.

But then, on reaching the foot of a hill   13*
which marked the limit of the dark ravine
that had before so pierced my heart with panic,

I looked to that height and saw its shoulders   16
already clothed in rays from the planet
that leads all others, on any road, aright.

My fears, at this, were somewhat quieted,   19
though terror, awash in the lake of my heart,
had lasted all the night I'd passed in anguish.

And then, like someone labouring for breath   22
who, safely reaching shore from open sea,
still turns and stares across those perilous waves,

so in my mind – my thoughts all fleeing still –   25
I turned around to marvel at that strait
that let no living soul pass through till now.

28   Poi ch'èi posato un poco il corpo lasso,
ripresi via per la piaggia diserta
sì che 'l piè fermo sempre era 'l più basso.

31   Ed ecco, quasi al cominciar de l'erta,
una lonza leggera e presta molto,
che di pel macolato era coverta;

34   e non mi si partia dinanzi al volto,
anzi 'mpediva tanto il mio cammino
ch'i' fui per ritornar più volte voltò.

37   Temp' era del principio del mattino,
e 'l sol montava 'n sù con quelle stelle
ch' eran con lui quando l'amor divino

40   mosse di prima quelle cose belle;
sì ch' a bene sperar m'era cagione
di quella fiera a la gaetta pelle

43   l'ora del tempo e la dolce stagione.
Ma non sì che paura non mi desse
la vista che m'apparve d'un leone.

46   Questi parea che contra me venisse
con la test' alta e con rabbiosa fame,
sì che parea che l'aere ne tremesse.

49   Ed una lupa, che di tutte brame
sembiava carca ne la sua magrezza,
e molte genti fé già viver grame,

52   questa mi porse tanto di gravezza
con la paura ch' uscia di sua vista,
ch' io perdei la speranza de l'altezza.

55   E qual è quei che volontieri acquista,
e giugne 'l tempo che perder lo face,
che 'n tutti suoi pensier piange e s'attrista:

58   tal mi fece la bestia sanza pace,
che, venendomi 'ncontro, a poco a poco
mi ripigneva là dove 'l sol tace.

61   Mentre ch'i' rovinava in basso loco,
dinanzi a li occhi mi si fu offerto
chi per lungo silenzio parea fioco.

And then – my weary limbs a little rested –   28*
I started up the lonely scree once more,
the foot that drives me always set the lower.

But look now! Almost as the scarp begins,   31*
a leopard, light and lively, svelte and quick,
its coat displaying a dappled marking.

This never ceased to dance before my face.   34
No. On it came, so bothering my tread
I'd half a mind at every turn to turn.

The time, however, was the hour of dawn.   37
The sun was mounting, and those springtime stars
that rose along with it when Holy Love

first moved to being all these lovely things.   40
So these – the morning hour, the gentle season –
led me to find good reason for my hopes,

seeing that creature with its sparkling hide.   43
Yet not so far that no fear pressed on me,
to see, appearing now, a lion face.

This, as it seemed, came on and on towards me   46
hungrily, its ravening head held high,
so that, in dread, the air around it trembled.

And then a wolf. And she who, seemingly,   49
was gaunt yet gorged on every kind of craving –
and had already blighted many a life –

so heavily oppressed my thought with fears,   52
which spurted even at the sight of her,
I lost all hope of reaching to those heights.

We all so willingly record our gains,   55
until the hour that leads us into loss.
Then every single thought is tears and sadness.

So, now, with me. That brute which knows no peace   58
came ever nearer me and, step by step,
drove me back down to where the sun is mute.

As I went, ruined, rushing to that low,   61
there had, before my eyes, been offered one
who seemed – long silent – to be faint and dry.

64   Quando vidi costui nel gran diserto,
       'Miserere di me,' gridai a lui,
       'qual che tu sii, od ombra od omo certo!'

67   Rispuosemi: 'Non omo, omo già fui,
       e li parenti miei furon lombardi,
       mantoani per patria ambedui.

70   Nacqui sub Iulio, ancor che fosse tardi,
       e vissi a Roma sotto 'l buono Augusto
       nel tempo de li dèi falsi e bugiardi.

73   Poeta fui, e cantai di quel giusto
       figliuol d'Anchise che venne di Troia
       poi che 'l superbo Ilión fu combusto.

76   Ma tu perché ritorni a tanta noia?
       Perché non sali il dilettoso monte
       ch' è principio e cagion di tutta gioia?'

79   'Or se' tu quel Virgilio e quella fonte
       che spandi di parlar sì largo fiume?'
       rispuos' io lui con vergognosa fronte.

82   'O de li altri poeti onore e lume,
       vagliami 'l lungo studio e 'l grande amore
       che m'ha fatto cercar lo tuo volume.

85   Tu se' lo mio maestro e 'l mio autore,
       tu se' solo colui da cu' io tolsi
       lo bello stilo che m'ha fatto onore.

88   Vedi la bestia per cu' io mi volsi:
       aiutami da lei, famoso saggio,
       ch' ella mi fa tremar le vene e i polsi.'

91   'A te convien tenere altro viaggio,'
       rispuose, poi che lagrimar mi vide,
       'se vuo' campar d'esto loco selvaggio;

94   ché questa bestia, per la qual tu gride,
       non lascia altrui passar per la sua via,
       ma tanto lo 'mpedisce che l'uccide;

97   e ha natura sì malvagia e ria,
       che mai non empie la bramosa voglia,
       e dopo 'l pasto ha più fame che pria.

Seeing him near in that great wilderness,   64*
to him I screamed my '*Miserere*': 'Save me,
whatever – shadow or truly man – you be.'

His answer came to me: 'No man; a man   67*
I was in times long gone. Of Lombard stock,
my parents both by *patria* were Mantuan.

And I was born, though late, *sub Iulio*.   70
I lived at Rome in good Augustus' day,
in times when all the gods were lying cheats.

I was a poet then. I sang in praise   73
of all the virtues of Anchises' son. From Troy
he came – proud Ilion razed in flame.

But you turn back. Why seek such grief and harm?   76
Why climb no higher up that lovely hill?
The cause and origin of joy shines there.'

'So, could it be,' I answered him (my brow,   79
in shy respect, bent low), 'you are that Virgil,
whose words flow wide, a river running full?

You are the light and glory of all poets.   82
May this serve me: my ceaseless care, the love
so great, that's made me search your writings through!

You are my teacher. You, my lord and law.   85
From you alone I took the fine-tuned style
that has, already, brought me so much honour.

See there? That beast! I turned because of that.   88
Help me – your wisdom's known – escape from her.
To every pulsing vein, she brings a tremor.'

Seeing my tears, he answered me: 'There is   91
another road. And that, if you intend
to quit this wilderness, you're bound to take.

That beast – you cry out at the very sight –   94*
lets no one through who passes on her way.
She blocks their progress; and there they all die.

She by her nature is cruel, so vicious   97
she never can sate her voracious will,
but, feasting well, is hungrier than before.

100   Molti son li animali a cui s'ammoglia,
        e più saranno ancora, infin che 'l veltro
        verrà, che la farà morir con doglia.

103   Questi non ciberà terra né peltro,
        ma sapienza, amore e virtute,
        e sua nazion sarà tra feltro e feltro.

106   Di quella umile Italia fia salute
        per cui morì la vergine Cammilla,
        Eurialo e Turno e Niso di ferute.

109   Questi la caccerà per ogne villa,
        fin che l'avrà rimessa ne lo 'nferno,
        là onde 'nvidia prima dipartilla.

112   Ond' io per lo tuo me' penso e discerno
        che tu mi segui, e io sarò tua guida,
        e trarrotti di qui per loco etterno,

115   ove udirai le disperate strida,
        vedrai li antichi spiriti dolenti,
        ch'a la seconda morte ciascun grida;

118   e vederai color che son contenti
        nel foco, perché speran di venire,
        quando che sia, a le beati genti.

121   A le quai poi se tu vorrai salire,
        anima fia a ciò più di me degna:
        con lei ti lascerò nel mio partire;

124   ché quello Imperador che là sù regna,
        perch' i' fu' ribellante a la sua legge,
        non vuol che 'n sua città per me si vegna.

127   In tutte parti impera e quivi regge;
        quivi è la sua città e l'alto seggio:
        oh felice colui cu' ivi elegge!'

130   E io a lui: 'Poeta, io ti richeggio
        per quello Dio che tu non conoscesti,
        acciò ch'io fugga questo male e peggio,

133   che tu mi meni là dov' or dicesti,
        sì ch'io veggia la porta di san Pietro
        e color cui tu fai cotanto mesti.'

136   Allor si mosse, e io li tenni dietro.

She couples, a mate to many a creature,   100
and will so with more, till at last there comes
the hunting hound that deals her death and pain.

He will not feed on dross or cash or gelt,   103
but thrive in wisdom, virtue and pure love.
Born he shall be between the felt and felt.

To all the shores where Italy bows down   106
(here chaste Camilla died of wounds, Turnus,
Euryalus and Nisus, too), he'll bring true health.

Hunting that animal from every town,   109
at last he'll chase her back once more to Hell,
from which invidia has set her loose.

Therefore, considering what's best for you,   112
I judge that you should follow, I should guide,
and hence through an eternal space lead on.

There you shall hear shrill cries of desperation,   115
and see those spirits, mourning ancient pain,
who all cry out for death to come once more.

And then you'll see those souls who live in fire,   118
content to hope – whenever that time comes –
they too will be among the blessed choirs.

To which if you shall ever wish to rise,   121
a soul will come far worthier than me.
I must, at parting, leave you in her care.

Reigning on high, there is an Emperor   124
who, since I was a rebel to His law,
will not allow His city as my goal.

He rules there, sovereign over every part.   127
There stands His capital, His lofty throne.
Happy the one He chooses for His own.'

'Poet,' I answered, 'by that God whose name   130
you do not know, I beg – so I may flee
this ill, or worse – lead me to where you say,

to find the gates where now Saint Peter stands –   133
and all those souls that you say are so sad.'
He made to move; and I came close behind.

CANTO 2

1   Lo giorno se n'andava, e l'aere bruno
toglieva li animai che sono in terra
da le fatiche loro; e io sol uno

4   m'apparecchiava a sostener la guerra
sì del cammino e sì de la pietate,
che ritrarrà la mente che non erra.

7   O muse, o alto ingegno, or m'aiutate;
o mente che scrivesti ciò ch'io vidi,
qui si parrà la tua nobilitate.

10   Io cominciai: 'Poeta che mi guidi,
guarda la mia virtù s'ell' è possente,
prima ch'a l'alto passo tu mi fidi.

13   Tu dici che di Silvio il parente,
corruttibile ancora, ad immortale
secolo andò, e fu sensibilmente.

16   Però, se l'avversario d'ogne male
cortese i fu, pensando l'alto effetto
ch'uscir dovea di lui, e 'l chi e 'l quale,

19   non pare indegno ad omo d'intelletto;
ch' e' fu de l'alma Roma e di suo impero
ne l'empireo ciel per padre eletto:

22   la quale e 'l quale, a voler dir lo vero,
fu stabilita per lo loco santo
u' siede il successor del maggior Piero.

25   Per quest' andata onde li dai tu vanto,
intense cose che furon cagione
di sua vittoria e del papale ammanto.

CANTO 2

Daylight was leaving us, and darkened air   1*
drawing those creatures that there are on earth
from all their labours. I alone, I was
    the only one preparing, as in war,   4
to onward-march and bear the agony
that thought will now unfailingly relate.
    I call the Muses. You great Heights of Mind   7
bring help to me. Memory, you wrote down all I saw.
Now shall be seen the greatness of your power.
    'You,' I began, 'my poet and my guide,   10
look at me hard. Am I in spirit strong enough
for you to trust me on this arduous road?
    As you once told, the sire of Silvius   13*
travelled, though still in fragile flesh, to realms
immortal, and his senses all alive.
    Nor will it seem (to those of intellect)   16
unfitting if the enemy of ill
should thus so greatly favour him, recalling
    what would flow from him, his name and who he was.   19
He was ordained, in empyrean skies,
father of Rome – its noble heart and empire.
    To speak the truth: that city – and the sphere   22
it ruled – was founded as the sacred seat
for all inheritors of great Saint Peter.
    You have proclaimed the glory of that march.   25
He on his way heard prophecies that led
to all his triumphs and the papal stole.

28   Andovvi poi lo Vas d'elezione,
      per recarne conforto a quella fede
      ch'è principio a la via di salvazione.

31   Ma io, perché venirvi? o chi 'l concede?
      Io non Enea, io non Paulo sono;
      me degno a ciò né io né altri 'l crede.

34   Per che, se del venire io m'abbandono,
      temo che la venuta non sia folle.
      Se' savio; intendi me' ch'i' non ragiono.'

37   E qual è quei che disvuol ciò che volle
      e per novi pensier cangia proposta,
      sì che dal cominciar tutto si tolle:

40   tal mi fec' io 'n quella oscura costa,
      perché, pensando, consumai la 'mpresa
      che fu nel cominciar cotanto tosta.

43   'S'i' ho ben la parola tua intesa,'
      rispuose del magnanimo quell' ombra,
      'l'anima tua è da viltade offesa,

46   la qual molte fiate l'omo ingombra
      si che d'onrata impresa lo rivolve,
      come falso veder bestia quand' ombra.

49   Da questa tema acciò che tu ti solve,
      dirotti perch' io venni e quel ch' io 'ntesi
      nel primo punto di te mi dolve.

52   Io era tra color che son sospesi,
      e donna mi chiamò beata e bella,
      tal che di comandare io la richiesi.

55   Lucevan li occhi suoi più che la stella;
      e cominciommi a dir soave e piana,
      con angelica voce, in sua favella:

58   "O anima cortese mantoana,
      di cui la fama ancor nel mondo dura,
      e durerà quanto 'l mondo lontana,

61   l'amico mio, e non de la ventura,
      ne la diserta piaggia è impedito
      sì nel cammin, che volt' è per paura;

And then Saint Paul, the chosen Vessel, came –   28*
to carry back a strengthening of that faith
from which salvation always must begin.

But me? Why me? Who says I can? I'm not   31
your own Aeneas. I am not Saint Paul.
No one – not me! – could think I'm fit for this.

Surrendering, I'll say I'll come. I fear   34
this may be lunacy. You, though, are wise.
You know me better than my own words say.'

And so – as though unwanting every want,   37
so altering all at every altering thought,
now drawing back from everything begun –

I stood there on the darkened slope, fretting   40
away from thought to thought the bold intent
that seemed so very urgent at the outset.

'Supposing I have heard your words aright,'   43
the shadow of that noble mind replied,
'your heart is struck with ignominious dread.

This, very often, is the stumbling block   46
that turns a noble enterprise off-course –
as beasts will balk at shadows falsely seen.

I mean that you should free yourself from fear,   49
and therefore I will say why first I came,
and what – when first I grieved for you – I heard.

With those I was whose lives are held in poise.   52*
And then I heard a lady call – so blessed,
so beautiful – I begged her tell me all she wished.

Her eyes were shining brighter than the stars.   55
Then gently, softly, calmly, she began,
speaking, as angels might, in her own tongue:

"You, Mantuan, so courteous in spirit,   58
your fame endures undimmed throughout the world,
and shall endure as still that world moves onwards.

A man most dear to me – though not to fate –   61
is so entrammelled on the lonely hill
that now he turns, all terror, from the way.

64   e temo che non sia già sì smarrito
      ch'io mi sia tardi al soccorso levata,
      per quel ch'i' ho di lui nel cielo udito.

67   Or movi, e con la tua parola ornata
      e con ciò c'ha mestieri al suo campare,
      l'aiuta sì ch'i' ne sia consolata.

70   I' son Beatrice che ti faccio andare;
      vegno del loco ove tornar disio;
      amor mi mosse, che mi fa parlare.

73   Quando sarò dinanzi al segnor mio,
      di te mi loderò sovente a lui."
      Tacette allora, e poi cominciai' io:

76   "O donna di virtù, sola per cui
      l'umana spezie eccede ogne contento
      di quel ciel c'ha minor li cerchi sui,

79   tanto m'aggrada il tuo comandamento
      che l'ubidir, se già fosse, m'è tardi;
      più non t'è uo' ch'aprirmi il tuo talento.

82   Ma dimmi la cagion che non ti guardi
      de lo scender qua giuso in questo centro
      de l'ampio loco ove tornar tu ardi."

85   "Da che tu vuo' saver cotanto a dentro,
      dirotti brievemente," mi rispuose,
      "perch' i' non temo di venir qua entro.

88   Temer si dee di sole quelle cose
      c'hanno potenza di fare altrui male;
      de l'altre no, ché non son paurose.

91   I' son fatta da Dio, sua mercé, tale
      che la vostra miseria non mi tange,
      né fiamma d'esto 'ncendio non m'assale.

94   Donna è gentil nel ciel che si compiange
      di questo 'mpedimento ov' io ti mando,
      sì che duro giudicio là sù frange.

97   Questa chiese Lucia in suo dimando
      e disse: 'Or ha bisogno il tuo fedele
      di te, e io a te lo raccomando.'

My fear must be he's so bewildered there   64
that – hearing all I've heard of him in Heaven –
I rise too late to bring him any aid.

Now make your way. With all your eloquence,   67
and all that his deliverance demands,
lend him your help so I shall be consoled.

For me you'll go, since I am Beatrice.   70
And I have come from where I long to be.
Love is my mover, source of all I say.

When I again appear before my Lord,   73
then I shall often speak your praise to Him."
She now fell silent. I began to speak:

"Lady of worth and truth, through you alone   76
the human race goes far beyond that bourne set
by the lunar sphere, smallest of all the skies.

To me, so welcome is your least command,   79
I'd be too slow had I obeyed by now.
You need no more declare to me your will.

But tell me why you take so little care   82
and, down to this dead middle point, you leave
the spacious circle where you burn to go."

"Since you desire to know so inwardly,   85
then briefly," she replied, "I'll tell you why
I feel no dread at entering down here.

We dread an object when (but only when)   88
that object has the power to do some harm.
Nothing can otherwise occasion fear.

I was created by the grace of God –   91
and so untouched by all your wretchedness.
Nor can the flames of this great fire assail me.

In Heaven, a Lady, gracious, good and kind,   94*
grieves at the impasse that I send you to,
and, weeping, rives the high, unbending rule.

She called Lucia, seeking her reply.   97
'Your faithful one,' she said to her, 'has now
great need of you. I give him to your care.'

100 Lucia, nimica di ciascun crudele,
si mosse, e venne al loco dov' i' era,
che mi sedea con l'antica Rachele.

103 Disse: 'Beatrice, loda di Dio vera,
ché non soccorri quei che t'amò tanto
ch'uscì per te de la volgare schiera?

106 Non odi tu la pieta del suo pianto,
non vedi tu la morte che 'l combatte
su la fiumana ove 'l mar non ha vanto?'

109 Al mondo non fur mai persone ratte
a far lor pro o a fuggir lor danno,
com' io, dopo cotai parole fatte,

112 venni qua giù del mio beato scanno,
fidandomi del tuo parlare onesto,
ch'onora te e quei ch'udito l'hanno."

115 Poscia che m'ebbe ragionato questo,
li occhi lucenti lagrimando volse,
per che mi fece del venir più presto.

118 E venni a te così com' ella volse:
d'inanzi a quella fiera ti levai
che del bel monte il corto andar ti tolse.

121 Dunque che è? perché, perché restai,
perché tanta viltà nel core allette,
perché ardire e franchezza non hai,

124 poscia che tai tre donne benedette
curan di te ne la corte del cielo,
e 'l mio parlar tanto ben ti promette?'

127 Quali fioretti dal notturno gelo
chinati e chiusi, poi che 'l sol li 'mbianca,
si drizzan tutti aperti in loro stelo:

130 tal mi fec' io di mia virtude stanca,
e tanto buono ardire al cor mi corse,
ch'i' cominciai come persona franca:

133 'Oh pietosa colei che mi soccorse!
e te cortese ch'ubidisti tosto
a le vere parole che ti porse!

Lucia is the enemy of harm.   100
Leaving her place, she came at once to where
I sat – Rachel, long-famed, beside me.

'You, Beatrice, are, in truth, God's praise.   103
Why not,' she said, 'make haste to him? He loves you,
and, loving you, he left the common herd.

Can you not hear the pity of his tears?   106
Do you not see the death that beats him down,
swirling in torrents that no sea could boast?'

No one on earth has ever run more rapidly   109
to seek advantage or to flee from harm,
than I in coming – when her words were done –

down from that throne of happiness, to trust   112
in your great words, their dignity and truth.
These honour you and those who hear you speak."

When she had said her say, in tears, she turned   115
her eyes away – which shone as she was weeping.
And this made me far quicker still for you.

So now, as she had willed, I made my way,   118
to raise you from the face of that brute beast
that stole your pathway up that lovely hill.

What is it, then? What's wrong? Why still delay?   121
Why fondle in your heart such feebleness?
Why wait? Be forthright, brave and resolute.

Three ladies of the court of Paradise,   124
in utmost happiness watch over you.
My own words promise you the utmost good.'

As little flowers bend low on freezing nights,   127
closed tight, but then, as sunlight whitens them,
grow upright on their stems and fully open,

now so did I. My wearied powers reviving,   130
there ran such wealth of boldness to my heart
that openly – all new and free – I now began:

'How quick in compassion her aid to me!   133
And you – so courteous, prompt to accede
to all the words of truth that she has offered!

136   Tu m'hai con disiderio il cor disposto
sì al venir con le parole tue,
ch'i' son tornato nel primo proposto.

139   Or va, ch'un sol volere è d'ambedue:
tu duca, tu segnore e tu maestro.'
Così li dissí; e poi che mosso fue,

142   intrai per lo cammino alto e silvestro.

You, as you speak, have so disposed my heart   136
in keen desire to journey on the way
that I return to find my first good purpose.

Set off! A single will inspires us both.   139
You are my lord, my leader and true guide.'
All this I said to him as he moved on.

I entered on that deep and wooded road.   142

CANTO 3

1   'Per me si va ne la citta' dolente.
Per me si va ne l'etterno dolore.
Per me si va tra la perduta gente.

4   Giustizia mosse il mio alto fattore;
fecemi la divina podestate,
la somma sapienza e'l primo amore.

7   Dinanzi a me non fuor cose create
se non etterne, e io etterno duro.
Lasciate ogne speranza, voi ch'intrate.'

10   Queste parole di colore oscuro
vid' io scritte al sommo d'una porta,
per ch'io: 'Maestro, il senso lor m'è duro.'

13   Ed elli a me, come persona accorta:
'Qui si convien lasciare ogne sospetto,
ogne viltà convien che qui sia morta.

16   Noi siam venuti al loco ov' i' t'ho detto
che tu vedrai le genti dolorose
c'hanno perduto il ben de l'intelletto.'

19   E poi che la sua mano a la mia puose
con lieto volto, ond' io mi confortai,
mi mise dentro a le segrete cose.

22   Quivi sospiri, pianti e alti guai
risonavan per l'aere sanza stelle,
per ch'io al cominciar ne lagrimai.

25   Diverse lingue, orribili favelle,
parole di dolore, accenti d'ira,
voci alte e fioche, e suon di man con elle

CANTO 3

'Through me you go to the grief-wracked city.   1*
Through me to everlasting pain you go.
Through me you go and pass among lost souls.

    Justice inspired my exalted Creator.   4
I am a creature of the Holiest Power,
of Wisdom in the Highest and of Primal Love.

    Nothing till I was made was made, only   7
eternal beings. And I endure eternally.
Surrender as you enter every hope you have.'

    These were the words that – written in dark tones –   10
I saw there, on the summit of a door.
I turned: 'Their meaning, sir, for me is hard.'

    And he in answering (as though he understood):   13
'You needs must here surrender all your doubts.
All taint of cowardice must here be dead.

    We now have come where, as I have said, you'll see   16*
in suffering the souls of those who've lost
the good that intellect desires to win.'

    And then he placed his hand around my own,   19
he smiled, to give me some encouragement,
and set me on to enter secret things.

    Sighing, sobbing, moans and plaintive wailing   22
all echoed here through air where no star shone,
and I, as this began, began to weep.

    Discordant tongues, harsh accents of horror,   25
tormented words, the twang of rage, strident
voices, the sound, as well, of smacking hands,

28   facevano un tumulto, il qual s'aggira
sempre in quell'aura sanza tempo tinta,
come la rena quando turbo spira.

31   E io ch'avea d'orror la testa cinta,
dissi: 'Maestro, che è quel ch' i' odo?
e che gent' è che par nel duol sì vinta?'

34   Ed elli a me: 'Questo misero modo
tegnon l'anime triste di coloro
che visser sanza 'nfamia e sanza lode.

37   Mischiate sono a quel cattivo coro
de li angeli che non furon ribelli
né fur fedeli a Dio, ma per sé fuoro.

40   Caccianli i ciel per non esser men belli,
né lo profondo inferno li riceve,
ch'alcuna gloria i rei avrebber d'elli.'

43   E io: 'Maestro, che è tanto greve
a lor che lamentar li fa sì forte?'
Rispuose: 'Dicerolti molto breve.

46   Questi non hanno speranza di morte,
e la lor cieca vita è tanto bassa
che 'nvidiosi son d'ogne altra sorte.

49   Fama di loro il mondo esser non lassa;
misericordia e giustizia li sdegna:
non ragioniam di lor, ma guarda e passa.'

52   E io, che riguardai, vidi una 'nsegna
che girando correva tanto ratta
che d'ogne posa mi parea indegna;

55   e dietro le venìa sì lunga tratta
di gente, ch'i' non averei creduto
che morte tanta n'avesse disfatta.

58   Poscia ch'io v'ebbi alcuno riconosciuto,
vidi e conobbi l'ombra di colui
che fece per viltade il gran rifiuto.

61   Incontanente intesi e certo fui
che questa era la setta d'i cattivi,
a Dio spiacenti e a' nemici sui.

together these all stirred a storm that swirled   28
for ever in the darkened air where no time was,
as sand swept up in breathing spires of wind.

I turned, my head tight-bound in confusion,   31
to say to my master: 'What is it that I hear?
Who can these be, so overwhelmed by pain?'

'This baleful condition,' he said, 'is one   34*
that grips those souls whose lives, contemptibly,
were void alike of honour and ill fame.

These all co-mingle with a noisome choir   37
of angels who – not rebels, yet not true
to God – existed for themselves alone.

To keep their beauty whole, the Heavens spurned them.   40
Nor would the depths of Hell receive them in,
lest truly wicked souls boast over them.'

And I: 'What can it be, so harsh, so heavy,   43
that draws such loud lamentings from these crowds?'
And he replied: 'My answer can be brief:

These have no hope that death will ever come.   46
And so degraded is the life they lead
all look with envy on all other fates.

The world allows no glory to their name.   49
Mercy and Justice alike despise them.
Let us not speak of them. Look, then pass on.'

I did look, intently. I saw a banner   52
running so rapidly, whirling forwards,
that nothing, it seemed, would ever grant a pause.

Drawn by that banner was so long a trail   55*
of men and women I should not have thought
that death could ever have unmade so many.

A few I recognized. And then I saw –   58*
and knew beyond all doubt – the shadow of the one
who made, from cowardice, the great denial.

So I, at that instant, was wholly sure   61
this congregation was that worthless mob
loathsome alike to God and their own enemies.

64   Questi sciaurati, che mai non fur vivi,
      erano ignudi e stimolati molto
      da mosconi e da vespe ch'eran ivi.

67   Elle rigavan lor di sangue il volto,
      che, mischiato di lagrime, a' lor piedi
      da fastidiosi vermi era ricolto.

70   E poi ch'a riguardar oltre mi diedi,
      vidi genti a la riva d'un gran fiume,
      per ch'io dissi: 'Maestro, or mi concedi

73   ch'i' sappia quali sono, e qual costume
      le fa di trapassar parer sì pronte,
      com' i' discerno per lo fioco lume.'

76   Ed elli a me: 'Le cose ti fier conte
      quando noi fermerem li nostri passi
      su la trista riviera d'Acheronte.'

79   Allor con li occhi vergognosi e bassi,
      temendo no 'l mio dir li fosse grave,
      infino al fiume del parlar mi trassi.

82   Ed ecco verso noi venir per nave
      un vecchio, bianco per antico pelo,
      gridando: 'Guai a voi, anime prave!

85   Non isperate mai veder lo cielo:
      i' vegno per menarvi a l'altra riva
      ne le tenebre etterne, in caldo e 'n gelo.

88   E tu che se' costì, anima viva,
      pàrtiti da cotesti che son morti.'
      Ma poi che vide ch'io non mi partiva,

91   disse: 'Per altra via, per altri porti
      verrai a piaggia, non qui, per passare:
      più lieve legno convien che ti porti.'

94   E 'l duca lui: 'Caron, non ti crucciare:
      vuolsi così colà dove si puote
      ciò che si vuole, e più non dimandare.'

97   Quinci fuor quete le lanose gote
      al nocchier de la livida palude,
      che 'ntorno a li occhi avea di fiamme rote.

These wretched souls were never truly live.   64
They now went naked and were sharply spurred
by wasps and hornets, thriving all around.

The insects streaked the face of each with blood.   67
Mixing with tears, the lines ran down; and then
were garnered at their feet by filthy worms.

And when I'd got myself to look beyond,   70
others, I saw, were ranged along the bank
of some great stream. 'Allow me, sir,' I said,

'to know who these might be. What drives them on,   73
and makes them all (as far, in this weak light,
as I discern) so eager for the crossing?'

'That will, of course, be clear to you,' he said,   76
'when once our footsteps are set firm upon
the melancholic shores of Acheron.'

At this – ashamed, my eyes cast humbly down,   79
fearing my words had weighed on him too hard –
I held my tongue until we reached the stream.

Look now! Towards us in a boat there came   82*
an old man, yelling, hair all white and aged,
'Degenerates! Your fate is sealed! Cry woe!

Don't hope you'll ever see the skies again!   85
I'm here to lead you to the farther shore,
into eternal shadow, heat and chill.

And you there! You! Yes, you, the living soul!   88
Get right away from this gang! These are dead.'
But then, on seeing that I did not move:

'You will arrive by other paths and ports.   91
You'll start your journey from a different beach.
A lighter hull must carry you across.'

'Charon,' my leader, 'don't torment yourself.   94
For this is willed where all is possible
that is willed there. And so demand no more.'

The fleecy wattles of the ferry man –   97
who plied across the liverish swamp, eyeballs
encircled by two wheels of flame – fell mute.

100   Ma quell' anime, ch'eran lasse e nude,
cangiar colore e dibattero i denti,
ratto che 'nteser le parole crude.

103   Bestemmiavano Dio e lor parenti,
l'umana spezie e 'l loco e 'l tempo e 'l seme
di lor semenza e di lor nascimenti.

106   Poi si ritrasser tutte quante insieme,
forte piangendo, a la riva malvagia
ch'attende ciascun uom che Dio non teme.

109   Caron dimonio, con occhi di bragia,
loro accennando tutte le raccoglie;
batte col remo qualunque s'adagia.

112   Come d'autunno si levan le foglie
l'una appresso de l'altra, fin che 'l ramo
vede a la terra tutte le sue spoglie:

115   similemente il mal seme d'Adamo
gittansi di quel lito ad una ad una
per cenni, come augel per suo richiamo.

118   Così sen vanno su per l'onda bruna,
e avanti che sien di là discese,
anche di qua nuova schiera s'auna.

121   'Figliuol mio,' disse 'l maestro cortese,
'quelli che muoion ne l'ira di Dio
tutti convegnon qui d'ogne paese;

124   e pronti sono a trapassar lo rio,
ché la divina giustizia li sprona
sì che la tema si volve in disio.

127   Quinci non passa mai anima buona;
e però, se Caron di te si lagna,
ben puoi sapere omai che 'l suo dir suona.'

130   Finito questo, la buia campagna
tremò sì forte che de lo spavento
la mente di sudore ancor mi bagna.

133   La terra lagrimosa diede vento
che balenò una luce vermiglia
la qual mi vinse ciascun sentimento,

136   e caddi come l'uom cui sonno piglia.

But not the other souls. Naked and drained,   100
their complexions changed. Their teeth began
(hearing his raw command) to gnash and grind.

They raged, blaspheming God and their own kin,   103
the human race, the place and time, the seed
from which they'd sprung, the day that they'd been born.

And then they came together all as one,   106
wailing aloud along the evil margin
that waits for all who have no fear of God.

Charon the demon, with his hot-coal eyes,   109
glared what he meant to do. He swept all in.
He struck at any dawdler with his oar.

In autumn, leaves are lifted, one by one,   112*
away until the branch looks down and sees
its tatters all arrayed upon the ground.

In that same way did Adam's evil seed   115
hurtle, in sequence, from the river rim,
as birds that answer to their handler's call.

Then off they went, to cross the darkened flood.   118
And, long before they'd landed over there,
another flock assembled in their stead.

Attentively, my master said: 'All those,   121
dear son, who perish in the wrath of God,
meet on this shore, wherever they were born.

And they are eager to be shipped across.   124
Justice of God so spurs them all ahead
that fear in them becomes that sharp desire.

But no good soul will ever leave from here.   127
And so when Charon thus complains of you,
you may well grasp the sense that sounds within.'

His words now done, the desolate terrain   130
trembled with such great violence that the thought
soaks me once more in a terrified sweat.

The tear-drenched earth gave out a gust of wind,   133
erupting in a flash of bright vermilion,
that overwhelmed all conscious sentiment.

I fell like someone gripped by sudden sleep.   136

CANTO 4

1   Ruppemi l'alto sonno ne la testa
un greve truono, sì ch'io mi riscossi
come persona ch'è per forza desta;

4   e l'occhio riposato intorno mossi,
dritto levato, e fiso riguardai
per conoscer lo loco dov' io fossi.

7   Vero è che 'n su la proda mi trovai
de la valle d'abisso dolorosa
che 'ntrono accoglie d'infiniti guai.

10   Oscura e profonda era e nebulosa
tanto che, per ficcar lo viso a fondo,
io non vi discernea alcuna cosa.

13   'Or discendiam qua giù nel cieco mondo,'
cominciò il poeta tutto smorto.
'Io sarò primo, e tu sarai secondo.'

16   E io, che del color mi fui accorto,
dissi: 'Come verrò, se tu paventi
che suoli al mio dubbiare esser conforto?'

19   Ed elli a me: 'L'angoscia de le genti
che son qua giù, nel viso mi dipigne
quella pietà che tu per tema senti.

22   Andiam, ché la via lunga ne sospigne.'
Così si mise e così mi fé intrare
nel primo cerchio che l'abisso cigne.

25   Quivi, secondo che per ascoltare,
non avea pianto mai che di sospiri
che l'aura etterna facevan tremare;

CANTO 4

    Thunder rolling heavily in my head   1
shattered my deep sleep. Startled, I awoke –
as though just shaken in some violent grip.

    And then once more my sight grew firm and fixed.   4
Now upright and again afoot, I scanned,
intently, all around to view where I might be.

    I found I'd reached – and this is true – the edge   7
of the abyss, that cavern of grief and pain
that rings a peal of endless miseries.

    The pit, so dark, so wreathed in cloud, went down   10
so far that – peering to its deepest floor –
I still could not discern a single thing.

    'Let us descend,' the poet now began,   13
'and enter this blind world.' His face was pale.
'I shall go first. Then you come close behind.'

    I was aware of his altered colour.   16
'How can I come, when you,' I said, 'my strength
in every time of doubt, are terrified?'

    'It is the agony,' he answered me,   19
'of those below that paints my features thus –
not fear, as you suppose it is, but pity.

    Let us go on. The long road spurs our pace.'   22
So now he set himself – and me as well –
to enter Circle One, which skirts the emptiness.

    Here in the dark (where only hearing told)   25
there were no tears, no weeping, only sighs
that caused a trembling in the eternal air –

28   ciò avvenia di duol sanza martìri
      ch'avean le turbe, ch'eran molte e grandi,
      d'infanti e di femmine e di viri.

31   Lo buon maestro a me: 'Tu non dimandi
      che spiriti son questi che tu vedi?
      Or vo' che sappi, innanzi che più andi,

34   ch'ei non peccaro; e s'elli hanno mercedi
      non basta, perché non ebber battesmo,
      ch'è porta de la fede che tu credi;

37   e s'e' furon dinanzi al cristianesmo,
      non adorar debitamente a Dio:
      e di questi cotai son io medesmo.

40   Per tai difetti, non per altro rio,
      semo perduti, e sol di tanto offesi
      che sanza speme vivemo in disio.'

43   Gran duol mi prese al cor quando lo 'ntesi,
      però che gente di molto valore
      conobbi che 'n quel limbo eran sospesi.

46   'Dimmi, maestro mio, dimmi, segnore,'
      comincia' io per volere esser certo
      di quella fede che vince ogne errore:

49   'uscicci mai alcuno, o per suo merto,
      o per altrui, che poi fosse beato?'
      E quei, che 'ntese il mio parlar coverto,

52   rispuose: 'Io era nuovo in questo stato,
      quando ci vidi venire un possente
      con segno di vittoria coronato.

55   Trasseci l'ombra del primo parente,
      d'Abèl suo figlio e quella di Noè,
      di Moisè legista e ubidente,

58   Abraàm patriarca e Davìd re,
      Israèl con lo padre e co' suoi nati
      e con Rachele, per cui tanto fè,

61   e altri molti, e feceli beati.
      E vo' che sappi che, dinanzi ad essi,
      spiriti umani non eran salvati.'

sighs drawn from sorrowing, although no pain.   28
This weighs on all of them, those multitudes
of speechless children, women and full-grown men.

'You do not ask,' my teacher in his goodness said,   31
'who all these spirits are that you see here?
Do not, I mean, go further till you know:

these never sinned. And some attained to merit.   34
But merit falls far short. None was baptized.
None passed the gate, in your belief, to faith.

They lived before the Christian age began.   37
They paid no reverence, as was due to God.
And in this number I myself am one.

For such deficiencies, no other crime,   40
we all are lost yet only suffer harm
through living in desire, but hopelessly.'

At hearing this, great sorrow gripped my heart.   43
For many persons of the greatest worth
were held, I knew, suspended on this strip.

'Tell me, sir, tell me, my dearest teacher,'   46*
so I began, determined – on a point
of faith, which routs all error – to be sure,

'has anyone, by merit of his own   49
or else another's, left here then been blessed?'
And he, who read the sense my words had hid,

answered: 'I still was new to this strange state   52
when, now advancing, I beheld a power
whose head was crowned with signs of victory.

He led away the shadow of our primal sire,   55
shades of his offspring, Abel and Noah,
Moses, who uttered (and observed) the law,

of Abraham the patriarch, David the king,   58
Israel, his father and his own twelve sons,
with Rachel, too, for whom he laboured long,

and many more besides. All these He blessed.   61
This too I mean you'll know: until these were,
no human soul had ever been redeemed.'

64   Non lasciavam l'andar perch' ei dicessi,
        ma passavam la selva tuttavia,
        la selva, dico, di spiriti spessi.

67   Non era lunga ancor la nostra via
        di qua dal sonno, quand' io vidi un foco
        ch'emisperio di tenebre vincia.

70   Di lungi n'eravamo ancora un poco,
        ma non sì ch'io non discernessi in parte
        ch'orrevol gente possedea quel loco.

73   'O tu ch'onori scienzia e arte,
        questi chi son c'hanno cotanta onranza,
        che del modo de li altri li diparte?'

76   E quelli a me: 'L'onrata norminanza
        che di lor suona sù ne la tua vita,
        grazia acquista in ciel che sì li avanza.'

79   Intanto voce fu per me udita:
        'Onorate l'altissimo poeta:
        l'ombra sua torna, ch'era dipartita.'

82   Poi che la voce fu restata e queta,
        vidi quattro grand'ombre a noi venire:
        sembianz' avevan né trista né lieta.

85   Lo buon maestro cominciò a dire:
        'Mira colui con quella spada in mano,
        che vien dinanzi ai tre sì come sire:

88   quelli è Omero, poeta sovrano;
        l'altro è Orazio satiro che vene;
        Ovidio è 'l terzo, e l'ultimo Lucano.

91   Però che ciascun meco si convene
        nel nome che sonò la voce sola,
        fannomi onore, e di ciò fanno bene.'

94   Così vid' i' adunar la bella scola
        di quel segnor de l'altissimo canto
        che sovra li altri com' aquila vola.

97   Da ch'ebber ragionato insieme alquanto,
        volsersi a me con salutévol cenno,
        e 'l mio maestro sorrise di tanto;

Speak as he might, our journey did not pause,   64
but on we went, and onward, through the wood –
the wood, I mean, of spirits thronging round.

Our steps were still not far from where, in sleep,   67
I fell, when now, ahead, I saw a fire
that overcame a hemisphere of shade.

From this we were, as yet, some paces off,   70
but not so far that I should fail to see
that men of honour made this place their own.

'Honour you bring, my lord, to art and learning.   73
Inform me who these are – their honour great –
who stand apart in some way from the rest.'

He answered me: 'The honour of their name   76
rings clear for those, like you, who live above,
and here gains favour out of Heaven's grace.'

And then there came upon my ear a voice: 79
'Honour be his, the poet in the heights.
His shadow now returns which had departed.'

The voice was still and silent once again.   82
And now, I saw, there came four noble shades,
no sorrow in their countenance, nor joy.

My teacher – that good man – began to speak: 85
'Look on. Behold the one who, sword in hand,
precedes, as their true lord, the other three.

This is that sovereign Homer, poet.   88*
Horace the satirist is next to come,
Ovid is third. Then (see!) there is Lucan.

All these, by right, must duly share with me   91
the name that sounded in that single voice.
They do me honour thus, and thus do well.'

And so I saw, assembling there as one,   94
the lovely college of that lord of song
whose verses soar like eagles over all.

Some little time they talked among themselves,   97
then turned to me and offered signs of greeting.
On seeing all of this, my teacher smiled.

100   e più d'onore ancora assai mi fenno,
       ch'e' sì mi fecer de la loro schiera,
       sì ch'io fui sesto tra cotanto senno.

103   Così andammo infino a la lumera,
       parlando cose che 'l tacere è bello,
       sì com' era 'l parlar colà dov' era.

106   Venimmo al piè d'un nobile castello,
       sette volte cerchiato d'alte mura,
       difeso intorno d'un bel fiumicello.

109   Questo passammo come terra dura;
       per sette porte intrai con questi savi;
       giugnemmo in prato di fresca verdura.

112   Genti v'eran con occhi tardi e gravi,
       di grande autorità ne' loro sembianti:
       parlavan rado, con voci soavi.

115   Traemmoci così da l'un de' canti
       in loco aperto, luminoso e alto,
       sì che veder si potien tutti quanti.

118   Colà diritto, sovra 'l verde smalto,
       mi fuor mostrati li spiriti magni,
       che del vedere in me stesso m'essalto.

121   I' vidi Eletra con molti compagni,
       tra 'quai conobbi Ettòr ed Enea,
       Cesare armato con li occhi grifagni.

124   Vidi Cammilla e la Pantasilea;
       da l'altra parte vidi 'l re Latino,
       che con Lavina sua figlia sedea.

127   Vidi quel Bruto che cacciò Tarquino,
       Lucrezia, Iulia, Marzia e Corniglia;
       e solo, in parte, vidi 'l Saladino.

130   Poi ch'innalzai un poco più le ciglia,
       vidi 'l maestro di color che sanno
       seder tra filosofica famiglia.

133   Tutti lo miran, tutti onor li fanno:
       quivi vid' io Socrate e Platone,
       che 'nnanzi a li altri più presso li stanno,

And greater honour still they paid me now: 100
they summoned me to join them in their ranks.
I came and walked as sixth among such wisdom.

So on we went to reach the dome of light   103
and spoke of things which, proper where I was,
are relegated, rightly, here to silence.

We reached the footings of a noble fort,   106
circled around by seven curtain walls
and also, as its moat, a lovely stream.

We passed this brook as though it were dry land.   109
Through seven gates I went with these five sages.
We then came out upon a verdant lawn.

Here there were some whose eyes were firm and grave –   112
all, in demeanour, of authority –
who seldom spoke; their tones were calm and gentle.

And so we drew aside and found a space,   115
illuminated, open, high and airy,
where all of these were able to be seen.

And there, across that bright enamelled green,   118
these ancient heroes were displayed to me.
And I within myself am still raised high

at what I saw: Electra, many round her.   121*
Hector I recognized, Aeneas, too,
and Caesar in arms, with his hawk-like eyes.

Camilla I saw and Penthesilea,   124
and King Latinus on the other side –
his daughter seated with him, his Lavinia.

Brutus (he drove proud Tarquin out), Lucrece   127
and Julia, Marcia, Cornelia – all these I saw,
and there alone, apart, the sultan Saladin.

And then – my brow raised higher still – I saw,   130*
among his family of philosophers,
the master of all those who think and know.

To him all look in wonder, all in honour.   133
And, closer to his side than all the rest,
I now saw Socrates, I saw now Plato,

136   Democrito che 'l mondo a caso pone,
         Diogenès, Anassagora e Tale,
         Empedoclès, Eraclito e Zenone;

139   e vidi il buono accoglitor del quale,
         Diascoride dico; e vidi Orfeo,
         Tulio e Lino e Seneca morale,

142   Euclide geomètra e Tolomeo,
         Ipocràte, Avicenna e Galieno,
         Averoìs che 'l gran comento feo.

145   Io non posso ritrar di tutti a pieno,
         però che sì mi caccia il lungo tema
         che molte volte al fatto il dir vien meno.

148   La sesta compagnia in due si scema:
         per altra via mi mena il savio duca
         fuor de la queta, ne l'aura che trema.

151   E vegno in parte ove non è che luca.

and one, Democritus, who claims the world is chance,   136
Diogenes and Tales, Anaxagoras,
Empedocles, Heraclitus and Zeno.

Then one I saw who gathered healing herbs –   139
I mean good Dioscorides. Orpheus I saw,
and Seneca the moralist, Linus, Tully,

Euclid (geometer) and Ptolemy,   142
Hippocrates, Avicenna and Galen,
Averroes, too, who made the *Commentary*.

I cannot here draw portraits of them all;   145
my lengthy subject presses me ahead,
and saying often falls far short of fact.

That company of six declines to two.   148
My lord in wisdom leads a different way,
out of that quiet into trembling air.

And nothing, where I now arrive, is shining.   151

CANTO 5

1   Così discesi del cerchio primaio
giù nel secondo, che men loco cinghia
e tanto più dolor che punge a guaio.

4   Stavvi Minòs orribilmente, e ringhia;
essamina le colpe ne l'intrata;
giudica e manda secondo ch'avvinghia.

7   Dico che quando l'anima mal nata
li vien dinanzi, tutta si confessa;
e quel conoscitor de le peccata

10   vede qual loco d'inferno è da essa;
cignesi con la coda tante volte
quantunque gradi vuol che giù sia messa.

13   Sempre dinanzi a lui ne stanno molte;
vanno a vicenda ciascuna al giudizio,
dicono e odono e poi son giù volte.

16   'O tu che vieni al doloroso ospizio,'
disse Minòs a me quando mi vide,
lasciando l'atto di cotanto offizio,

19   'guarda com' entri e di cui tu ti fide:
non t'inganni l'ampiezza de l'intrare!'
E 'l duca mio a lui: 'Perché pur gride?

22   Non impedir lo suo fatale andare:
vuolsi così colà dove si puote
ciò che si vuole, e più non dimandare.'

25   Or incomincian le dolenti note
a farmisi sentire; or son venuto
là dove molto pianto mi percuote.

CANTO 5

And so from Circle One I now went down   1
deeper, to Circle Two, which bounds a lesser space
and therefore greater suffering. Its sting is misery.

Minos stands there – horribly there – and barking.   4*
He, on the threshold, checks degrees of guilt,
then judges and dispatches with his twirling tail.

I mean that every ill-begotten creature,   7
when summoned here, confesses everything.
And he (his sense of sin is very fine)

perceives what place in Hell best suits each one,   10
and coils his tail around himself to tell
the numbered ring to which he'll send them down.

Before him, always, stands a crowd of souls.   13
By turns they go, each one, for sentencing.
Each pleads, attends – and then is tipped below.

'You there, arriving at this house of woe,'   16
so, when he saw me there, the judge spoke forth,
(to interrupt a while his formal role),

'watch as you enter – and in whom you trust.   19
Don't let yourself be fooled by this wide threshold.'
My leader's thrust: 'This yelling! Why persist?

Do not impede him on his destined way.   22
For this is willed where all is possible
that is willed there. And so demand no more.'

But now the tones of pain, continuing,   25
demand I hear them out. And now I've come
where grief and weeping pierce me at the heart.

28   Io venni in loco d'ogne luce muto,
   che mugghia come fa mar per tempesta,
   se da contrari venti è combattuto.

31   La bufera infernal, che mai non resta,
   mena li spirti con la sua rapina;
   voltando e percotendo li molesta.

34   Quando giungon davanti a la ruina,
   quivi le strida, il compianto, il lamento;
   bestemmian quivi la virtù divina.

37   Intesi ch'a così fatto tormento
   enno dannati i peccator carnali,
   che la ragion sommettono al talento.

40   E come li stornei ne portan l'ali
   nel freddo tempo, a schiera larga e piena,
   così quel fiato li spiriti mali

43   di qua, di là, di giù, di sù li mena;
   nulla speranza li conforta mai,
   non che di posa, ma di minor pena.

46   E come i gru van cantando lor lai,
   faccendo in aere di sé lunga riga,
   così vid' io venir, traendo guai,

49   ombre portate da la detta briga;
   per ch'i' dissi: 'Maestro, chi son quelle
   genti che l'aura nera sì gastiga?'

52   'La prima di color di cui novelle
   tu vuo' saper,' mi disse quelli allotta,
   'fu imperadrice di molte favelle.

55   A vizio di lussuria fu sì rotta
   che libito fé licito in sua legge,
   per tòrre il biasmo in che era condotta.

58   Ell' è Semiramìs, di cui si legge
   che succedette a Nino e fu sua sposa:
   tenne la terra che 'l Soldan corregge.

61   L'altra è colei che s'ancise amorosa,
   e ruppe fede al cener di Sicheo;
   poi è Cleopatràs lussuriosa.

And so I came where light is mute, a place   28
that moans as oceans do impelled by storms,
surging, embattled in conflicting squalls.

The swirling wind of Hell will never rest.   31
It drags these spirits onwards in its force.
It chafes them – rolling, clashing – grievously.

Then, once they reach the point from which they fell . . . 34
screams, keening cries, the agony of all,
and all blaspheming at the Holy Power.

Caught in this torment, as I understood,   37
were those who – here condemned for carnal sin –
made reason bow to their instinctual bent.

As starlings on the wing in winter chills   40*
are borne along in wide and teeming flocks,
so on these breathing gusts the evil souls.

This way and that and up and down they're borne.   43
Here is no hope of any comfort ever,
neither of respite nor of lesser pain.

And now, as cranes go singing lamentations   46
and form themselves through air in long-drawn lines,
coming towards me, trailing all their sorrows,

I saw new shadows lifted by this force.   49
'Who are these people, sir?' I said. 'Tell me
why black air scourges them so viciously.'

'The first of those whose tale you wish to hear,'   52*
he answered me without a moment's pause,
'governed as empress over diverse tongues.

She was so wracked by lust and luxury,   55
licentiousness was legal under laws she made –
to lift the blame that she herself incurred.

This is Semiramis. Of her one reads   58
that she, though heir to Ninus, was his bride.
Her lands were those where now the Sultan reigns.

The other, lovelorn, slew herself and broke   61
her vow of faith to Sichaeus's ashes.
And next, so lascivious, Cleopatra.

64   Elena vedi, per cui tanto reo
      tempo si volse, e vedi 'l grande Achille,
      che con Amore al fine combatteo.

67   Vedi Parìs, Tristano'; e più di mille
      ombre mostrommi e nominommi a dito,
      ch'Amor di nostra vita dipartille.

70   Poscia ch'io ebbi 'l mio dottore udito
      nomar le donne antiche e' cavalieri,
      pietà mi giunse, e fui quasi smarrito.

73   I' cominciai: 'Poeta, volontieri
      parlerei a quei due che 'nsieme vanno
      e paion sì al vento esser leggeri.'

76   Ed elli a me: 'Vedrai quando saranno
      più presso a noi; e tu allor li priega
      per quello amor che i mena, ed ei verranno.'

79   Sì tosto come il vento a noi li piega,
      mossi la voce: 'O anime affannate,
      venite a noi parlar, s'altri nol niega!'

82   Quali colombe dal disio chiamate
      con l'ali alzate e ferme al dolce nido
      vegnon per l'aere, dal voler portate,

85   cotali uscir de la schiera ov' è Dido,
      a noi venendo per l'aere maligno,
      sì forte fu l'affettuoso grido.

88   'O animal grazïoso e benigno
      che visitando vai per l'aere perso
      noi che tignemmo il mondo di sanguigno,

91   se fosse amico il re de l'universo,
      noi pregheremmo lui de la tua pace,
      poi c'hai pietà del nostro mal perverso.

94   Di quel che udire e che parlar vi piace,
      noi udiremo e parleremo a voi,
      mentre che 'l vento, come fa, ci tace.

97   Siede la terra dove nata fui
      su la marina dove 'l Po discende
      per aver pace co' seguaci sui.

Helen. You see? Because of her, a wretched   64
waste of years went by. See! Great Achilles.
He fought with love until his final day.

Paris you see, and Tristan there.' And more   67
than a thousand shadows he numbered, naming
them all, whom Love had led to leave our life.

Hearing that man of learning herald thus   70
these chevaliers of old, and noble ladies,
pity oppressed me and I was all but lost.

'How willingly,' I turned towards the poet,   73
'I'd speak to those two there who go conjoined
and look to be so light upon the wind.'

And he to me: 'You'll see them clearer soon.   76
When they are closer, call to them. Invoke
the love that draws them on, and they will come.'

The wind had swept them nearer to us now.   79
I moved to them in words: 'Soul-wearied creatures!
Come, if none forbids, to us and, breathless, speak.'

As doves, when called by their desires, will come –   82
wings spreading high – to settle on their nest,
borne through the air by their own steady will,

so these two left the flock where Dido is.   85
They came, approaching through malignant air,
so strong for them had been my feeling cry.

'Our fellow being, gracious, kind and good!   88
You, on your journeying through this bruised air,
here visit two who tinged the world with blood.

Suppose the Sovereign of the Universe   91
were still our friend, we'd pray He grant you peace.
You pity so the ill perverting us.

Whatever you may please to hear or say,   94
we, as we hear, we, as we speak, assent,
so long – as now they do – these winds stay silent.

My native place is set along those shores   97
through which the river Po comes down, to be
at last at peace with all its tributaries.

100   Amor, ch'al cor gentil ratto s'apprende,
       prese costui de la bella persona
       che mi fu tolta, e 'l modo ancor m'offende.

103   Amor, ch'a nullo amato amar perdona,
       mi prese del costui piacer sì forte
       che, come vedi, ancor non m'abbandona.

106   Amor condusse noi ad una morte.
       Caina attende chi a vita ci spense.'
       Queste parole da lor ci fuor porte.

109   Quand' io intesi quell' anime offense,
       china' il viso, e tanto il tenni basso
       fin che 'l poeta mi disse: 'Che pense?'

112   Quando rispuosi, cominciai: 'Oh lasso,
       quanti dolci pensier, quanto disio
       menò costoro al doloroso passo!'

115   Poi mi rivolsi a loro e parla' io,
       e cominciai: 'Francesca, i tuoi martìri
       a lagrimar mi fanno tristo e pio.

118   Ma dimmi: al tempo d'i dolci sospiri,
       a che e come concedette Amore
       che conosceste i dubbiosi disiri?'

121   E quella a me: 'Nessun maggior dolore
       che ricordarsi del tempo felice
       ne la miseria; e ciò sa 'l tuo dottore.

124   Ma s'a conoscer la prima radice
       del nostro amor tu hai cotanto affetto,
       dirò come colui che piange e dice.

127   Noi leggiavamo un giorno per diletto
       di Lancialotto come amor lo strinse;
       soli eravamo e sanza alcun sospetto.

130   Per più fiate li occhi ci sospinse
       quella lettura, e scolorocci il viso;
       ma solo un punto fu quel che ci vinse.

133   Quando leggemmo il disiato riso
       esser basciato da cotanto amante,
       questi, che mai da me non fia diviso,

Love, who so fast brings flame to generous hearts,   100
seized him with feeling for the lovely form,
now torn from me. The harm of how still rankles.

Love, who no loved one pardons love's requite,   103
seized me for him so strongly in delight
that, as you see, he does not leave me yet.

Love drew us onwards to consuming death.   106*
Cain's ice awaits the one who quenched our lives.'
These words, borne on to us from them, were theirs.

And when I heard these spirits in distress,   109
I bowed my eyes and held them low, until,
at length, the poet said: 'What thoughts are these?'

I, answering in the end, began: 'Alas,   112
how many yearning thoughts, what great desire,
have led them through such sorrow to their fate?'

And turning to them now I came to say: 115
'Francesca, how your suffering saddens me!
Sheer pity brings me to the point of tears.

But tell me this: the how of it – and why –   118
that Love, in sweetness of such sighing hours,
permitted you to know these doubtful pangs.'

To me she said: 'There is no sorrow greater   121*
than, in times of misery, to hold at heart
the memory of happiness. (Your teacher knows.)

And yet, if you so deeply yearn to trace   124
the root from which the love we share first sprang,
then I shall say – and speak as though in tears.

One day we read together, for pure joy   127
how Lancelot was taken in Love's palm.
We were alone. We knew no suspicion.

Time after time, the words we read would lift   130
our eyes and drain all colour from our faces.
A single point, however, vanquished us.

For when at last we read the longed-for smile   133
of Guinevere – at last her lover kissed –
he, who from me will never now depart,

136   la bocca mi basciò tutto tremante.
       Galeotto fu 'l libro e chi lo scrisse:
       quel giorno più non vi leggemmo avante.'
139   Mentre che l'uno spirto questo disse,
       l'altro piangea sì che di pietade
       io venni men così com' io morisse,
142   e caddi come corpo morto cade.

touched his kiss, trembling to my open mouth.   136
This book was *Galehault* – pander-penned, the pimp!
That day we read no further down those lines.'

And all the while, as one of them spoke on,   139
the other wept, and I, in such great pity,
fainted away as though I were to die.

And now I fell as bodies fall, for dead.   142

CANTO 6

1   Al tornar de la mente, che si chiuse
dinanzi a la pietà d'i due cognati,
che di trestizia tutto mi confuse,

4   novi tormenti e novi tormentati
mi veggio intorno come ch'io mi mova
ch'io mi volga, e come che io guati.

7   Io sono al terzo cerchio, de la piova
etterna, maladetta, fredda e greve;
regola e qualità mai non l'è nova.

10   Grandine grossa, acqua tinta e neve
per l'aere tenebroso si riversa;
pute la terra che questo riceve.

13   Cerbero, fiera crudele e diversa,
con tre gole caninamente latra
sovra la gente che quivi è sommersa.

16   Li occhi ha vermigli, la barba unta e atra
e 'l ventre largo, e unghiate le mani;
graffia li spirti ed iscoia ed isquatra.

19   Urlar li fa la pioggia come cani;
de l'un de' lati fanno a l'altro schermo;
volgonsi spesso i miseri profani.

22   Quando ci scorse Cerbero, il gran vermo,
le bocche aperse e mostrocci le sanne;
non avea membro che tenesse fermo.

25   E 'l duca mio distese le sue spanne,
prese la terra, e con piene le pugna
la gittò dentro a le bramose canne.

CANTO 6

As now I came once more to conscious mind –   1
closed in those feelings for the kindred souls
that had, in sudden sadness, overcome me –

wherever I might turn I saw – wherever   4
I might more look around or send my gaze –
new forms of torment, new tormented souls.

I am in Circle Three. And rain falls there,   7
endlessly, chill, accursed and heavy,
its rate and composition never new.

Snow, massive hailstones, black, tainted water   10
pour down in sheets through tenebrae of air.
The earth absorbs it all and stinks, revoltingly.

Cerberus, weird and monstrously cruel,   13*
barks from his triple throats in cur-like yowls
over the heads of those who lie there, drowned.

His eyes vermilion, beard a greasy black,   16
his belly broad, his fingers all sharp-nailed,
he mauls and skins, then hacks in four, these souls.

From all of them, rain wrings a wet-dog howl.   19
They squirm, as flank screens flank. They twist, they turn,
and then – these vile profanities – they turn again.

That reptile Cerberus now glimpsed us there.   22
He stretched his jaws; he showed us all his fangs.
And me? No member in my frame stayed still!

My leader, bending with his palms wide-spanned,   25
scooped dirt in each, and then – his fists both full –
hurled these as sops down all three ravening throats.

28   Qual è quel cane ch'abbaiando agogna
e si racqueta poi che 'l pasto morde,
ché solo a divorarlo intende e pugna,

31   cotai si fecer quelle facce lorde
de lo demonio Cerbero, che 'ntrona
l'anime sì ch'esser vorrebber sorde.

34   Noi passavam su per l'ombre che adona
la greve pioggia, e ponavam le piante
sovra lor vanità che par persona.

37   Elle giacean per terra tutte quante,
fuor d'una ch'a seder si levò, ratto
ch'ella ci vide passarsi davante.

40   'O tu che se' per questo 'nferno tratto,'
mi disse, 'riconoscimi, se sai:
tu fosti, prima ch'io disfatto, fatto.'

43   E io a lui: 'L'angoscia che tu hai
forse ti tira fuor de la mia mente,
sì che non par ch'i'ti vedessi mai.

46   Ma dimmi chi tu se' che 'n sì dolente
loco se' messo e hai sì fatta pena
che, s'altra è maggio, nulla è sì spiacente.'

49   Ed elli a me: 'La tua città, ch'è piena
d'invidia sì che già trabocca il sacco,
seco mi tenne in la vita serena.

52   Voi cittadini mi chiamaste Ciacco;
per la dannosa colpa de la gola,
come tu vedi, a la pioggia mi fiacco.

55   E io anima trista non son sola,
ché tutte queste a simil pena stanno
per simil colpa.' E più non fé parola.

58   Io li rispuosi: 'Ciacco, il tuo affanno
mi pesa sì ch'a lagrimar mi 'nvita;
ma dimmi, se tu sai, a che verranno

61   li cittadin de la città partita;
s'alcun v'è giusto; e dimmi la cagione
per che l'ha tanta discordia assalita.'

A hungry mongrel – yapping, thrusting out,   28
intent on nothing but the meal to come –
is silent only when its teeth sink in.

In that same way, with three repulsive muzzles,   31
the demon Cerberus. His thunderous growlings
stunned these souls. They wished themselves stone deaf.

Over such shadows, flat in that hard rain,   34
we travelled onwards still. Our tread now fell
on voided nothings only seeming men.

Across the whole terrain these shades were spread,   37
except that one, at seeing us pass by,
sat, on the sudden, upright and then cried:

'You there! Drawn onwards through this stretch of Hell,   40
tell me you know me. Say so, if so you can.
You! Made as man before myself unmade.'

And I replied: 'The awful pain you feel   43
perhaps has cancelled you from memory.
Till now, it seems, I've never even seen you.

Then tell me who you are, and why you dwell   46
in such a place? And why a pain like this?
Others may well be worse, none so disgusting.'

And he: 'That burgh of yours – that sack of bile   49
that brims by now to overflow – I lived
as hers throughout my own fine-weather years.

You knew me, like your city friends, as Hoggo.   52
So here I am, condemned for gullet sins,
lying, you see, squashed flat by battering rain.

I'm not alone in misery of soul.   55
These all lie subject to the self-same pain.
Their guilt is mine.' He spoke no further word.

'Hoggo, your heavy labours,' I replied,   58*
'weigh on me hard and prompt my heavy tears.
But tell me, if you can, where they'll all end,

the citizens of that divided town?   61
Is there among them any honest man?
Why is that place assailed by so much strife?'

64   E quelli a me: 'Dopo lunga tencione
verranno al sangue, e la parte selvaggia
caccerè l'altra con molta offensione.

67   Poi appresso convien che questa caggia
infra tre soli, e che l'altra sormonti
con la forza di tal che testè piaggia.

70   Alte terrà lungo tempo le fronti,
tenendo l'altra sotto gravi pesi,
come che di ciò pianga o che n'aonti.

73   Giusti son due, e non vi sono intesi;
superbia, invidia e avarizia sono
le tre faville c'hanno i cuori accesi.'

76   Qui puose fine al lagrimabil suono.
E io a lui: 'Ancor vo' che mi 'nsegni
e che di più parlar mi facci dono.

79   Farinata e 'l Tegghiaio, che fuor sì degni,
Iacopo Rusticucci, Arrigo e 'l Mosca,
e li altri ch'a ben far puoser li 'ngegni,

82   dimmi ove sono e fa ch'io li conosca;
ché gran disio mi stringe di savere
se 'l ciel li addolcia o lo 'nferno li attosca.'

85   E quelli: 'Ei son tra l'anime più nere;
diverse colpe giù li grava al fondo:
se tanto scendi, là i potrai vedere.

88   Ma quando tu sarai nel dolce mondo,
priegoti ch'a la mente altrui mi rechi:
più non ti dico e più non ti rispondo.'

91   Li diritti occhi torse allora in biechi;
guardommi un poco e poi chinò la testa:
cadde con essa a par de li altri ciechi.

94   E 'l duca disse a me: 'Più non si desta
di qua dal suon de l'angelica tromba,
quando verrà la nimica podesta:

97   ciascun rivederà la trista tomba,
ripiglierà sua carne e sua figura,
udirà quel ch'in etterno rimbomba.'

His answer was: 'From each side, long harangues.   64
And then to blood. The Wildwood boys
will drive the others out. They'll do great harm.

But then, within the span of three brief suns,   67
that side will fall and others rise and thrive,
spurred on by one who now just coasts between.

For quite some time they'll hold their heads up high   70
and grind the others under heavy weights,
however much, for shame, these weep and writhe.

Of this lot, two are honest yet not heard.   73
For pride and avarice and envy are
the three fierce sparks that set all hearts ablaze.'

With this, his tear-drenched song now reached an end.   76
But I to him: 'I still want more instruction.
This gift I ask of you: please do say more.

Tegghiaio, Farinata – men of rank –   79*
Mosca, Arrigo, Rusticucci, too,
and others with their minds on noble deeds,

tell me, so I may know them, where they are.   82
For I am gripped by great desire, to tell
if Heaven holds them sweet – or poisonous Hell.'

And he: 'These dwell among the blackest souls,   85
loaded down deep by sins of differing types.
If you sink far enough, you'll see them all.

But when you walk once more where life is sweet,   88
bring me, I beg, to others in remembrance.
No more I'll say, nor answer any more.'

His forward gaze now twisted to a squint.   91
He stared at me a little, bent his head,
then fell face down and joined his fellow blind.

My leader now addressed me: 'He'll not stir   94
until the trumpets of the angels sound,
at which his enemy, True Power, will come.

Then each will see once more his own sad tomb,   97
and each, once more, assume its flesh and figure,
each hear the rumbling thunder roll for ever.'

100   Sì trapassammo per sozza mistura
de l'ombre e de la pioggia, a passi lenti,
toccando un poco la vita futura;

103   per ch'io dissi: 'Maestro, esti tormenti
crescerann' ei dopo la gran sentenza,
o fier minori, o saran sì cocenti?'

106   Ed elli a me: 'Ritorna a tua scienza,
che vuol, quanto la cosa è più perfetta,
più senta il bene, e così la doglienza.

109   Tutto che questa gente maladetta
in vera perfezion già mai non vada,
di là più che di qua essere aspetta.'

112   Noi aggirammo a tondo quella strada,
parlando più assai ch'i' non ridico;
venimmo al punto dove si digrada.

115   Quivi trovammo Pluto, il gran nemico.

So on we fared across that filthy blend   100
of rain and shadow spirit, slow in step,
touching a little on the life to come.

Concerning which, 'These torments, sir,' I said,   103
'when judgement has been finally proclaimed –
will these increase or simmer just the same?'

'Return,' he said, 'to your first principles: 106*
when anything (these state) becomes more perfect,
then all the more it feels both good and pain.

Albeit these accursed men will not   109
achieve perfection full and true, they still,
beyond that Day, will come to sharper life.'

So, circling on the curve around that path,   112
we talked of more than I shall here relate,
but reached the brow, from which the route descends,

and found there Plutus, the tremendous foe.   115*

CANTO 7

1   '*Pape Satàn, pape Satàn aleppe!*'
cominciò Pluto con la voce chioccia;
e quel savio gentil, che tutto seppe,

4   disse per confortarmi: 'Non ti noccia
la tua paura; ché poder ch'elli abbia
non ci torrà lo scender questa roccia.'

7   Poi si rivolse a quella 'nfiata labbia
e disse: 'Taci, maladetto lupo!
consuma dentro te con la tua rabbia.

10   Non è sanza cagion l'andare al cupo:
vuolsi ne l'alto, là dove Michele
fé la vendetta del superbo strupo.'

13   Quali dal vento le gonfiate vele
caggiono avvolte, poi che l'alber fiacca:
tal cadde a terra la fiera crudele.

16   Così scendemmo ne la quarta lacca,
pigliando più de la dolente ripa
che 'l mal de l'universo tutto insacca.

19   Ahi giustizia di Dio! tante chi stipa
nove travaglie e pene quant' io viddi?
e perché nostra colpa sì ne scipa?

22   Come fa l'onda là sovra Cariddi,
che si frange con quella in cui s'intoppa:
così convien che qui la gente riddi.

25   Qui vid' i' gente più ch'altrove troppa,
e d'una parte e d'altra, con grand' urli,
voltando pesi per forza di poppa.

CANTO 7

'*Popoi Satan, popoi Satan! Alezorul!*'   1
So Plutus – shrill voice clucking on – began.
But Virgil, wise and noble, knowing all,
    spoke out, to comfort me: 'Let not your fears   4
occasion you distress. Despite his powers,
he cannot steal your right to scale this rock face.'

    And then he turned to meet those rabid lips.   7*
'Silence, you execrable wolf!' he said.
'May fury gnaw you inwardly away.

    To these dark depths, with every right he treads.   10*
All this is willed where Michael, in the heights,
avenged the rapine wrought by prideful hordes.'

    As sails, inflated by a furious wind,   13
fall in a tangle when the main mast snaps,
so too he flopped, this predator, to ground.

    Then downwards to the seventh sink we went,   16
advancing further down the curving wall
that bags up all the evil of the universe.

    God in all justice! I saw there so many   19
new forms of travail, so tightly crammed. By whom?
How can our guilt so rend and ruin us?

    Over Charybdis, the sea surge swirls   22*
and shatters on the swell it clashes with.
So must these people dance their morisco.

    I saw, in numbers greater than elsewhere,   25
two factions, hollering, this one to that,
who rolled great boulders, thrust by rib and tit.

28   Percoteansi 'ncontro; e poscia pur lì
        si rivolgea ciascun, voltando a retro,
        gridando: 'Perché tieni?' e 'Perché burli?'

31   Così tornavan per lo cerchio tetro
        da ogne mano a l'opposito punto,
        gridandosi anche loro ontoso metro;

34   poi si volgea ciascun, quand' era giunto
        per lo suo mezzo cerchio a l'altra giostra.
        E io, ch'avea lo cor quasi compunto,

37   dissi: 'Maestro mio, or mi dimostra
        che gente è questa, e se tutti fuor cherci
        questi chercuti a la sinistra nostra.'

40   Ed elli a me: 'Tutti quanti fuor guerci
        sì de la mente in la vita primaia
        che con misura nullo spendio ferci.

43   Assai la voce lor chiaro l'abbaia,
        quando vegnono a' due punti del cerchio
        dove colpa contraria li dispaia.

46   Questi fuor cherci, che non han coperchio
        piloso al capo, e papi e cardinali,
        in cui usa avarizia il suo soperchio.'

49   E io: 'Maestro, tra questi cotali
        dovre' io ben riconoscere alcuni
        che furo immondi di cotesti mali.'

52   Ed elli a me: 'Vano pensiero aduni:
        la sconoscente vita che i fé sozzi
        ad ogne conoscenza or li fa bruni.

55   In etterno verranno a li due cozzi;
        questi resurgeranno del sepulcro
        col pugno chiuso, e questi coi crin mozzi.

58   Mal dare e mal tener lo mondo pulcro
        ha tolto loro, e posti a questa zuffa:
        qual ella sia, parole non ci appulcro.

61   Or puoi, figliuol, veder la corta buffa
        d'i ben che son commessi a la Fortuna,
        per che l'umana gente si rabuffa;

Their stones would clash. Then wheeling they'd retreat   28
and yell, across their shoulders, cry and counter-cry.
'You miser! Why?' 'Why fling it all away?'

So back along that dismal curve they went,   31
to reach, at either end, the diametric points,
still screaming shamefully insulting chants.

Arriving back, each by its own half-circle,   34
each whisked around to tilt against the other.
At this – my heart transfixed, or very nearly:

'Sir,' I spoke up, 'make clear to me what folk   37
these are, and whether – to our left – all those
with tonsured scalps could really have been clerics.'

'Without exception, all of these,' he said,   40
'when first they lived, had such strabismic minds
they'd bear no check or measure on expense.

And when they reach the two points in the round   43*
where converse crimes uncouple each from each,
they bark their meaning out and sound it clear.

Clerics they were – all those whose heads aren't dressed   46
with shaggy hair. All popes – or cardinals.
In that lot, avarice displays its worst.'

'Well, sir,' I said, 'in any group like this,   49
I surely ought to recognize some few
who bore in life the taint of this disease.'

'You seek,' he said, 'to form an idle thought.   52
The mindless lives that made them all so foul
darken them now against all acts of mind.

Both, to eternity, will buck and butt.   55
These from their tombs will rise with first tight shut,
the others with their curly manes cropped short.

Their frenzied sprees or febrile hoardings-up   58
have wrung from them the beauty of the world,
and brought them firmly to this ugly brawl.

You now can see, dear son, the short-lived pranks   61
that goods consigned to Fortune's hand will play,
causing such squabbles in the human ranks.

64   ché tutto l'oro ch'è sotto la luna
        e che già fu, di quest' anime stanche
        non poterebbe farne posare una.'

67   'Maestro mio,' diss' io, 'or mi dì anche:
        questa Fortuna di che tu mi tocche,
        che è, che i ben del mondo ha sì tra branche?'

70   E quelli a me: 'Oh creature sciocche,
        quanta ignoranza è quella che v'offende!
        Or vo' che tu mia sentenza ne 'mbocche.

73   Colui lo cui saver tutto trascende
        fece li cieli, e diè lor chi conduce
        sì ch'ogne parte ad ogne parte splende,

76   distribuendo igualmente la luce.
        Similemente a li splendor mondani
        ordinò general ministra e duce

79   che permutasse a tempo li ben vani
        di gente in gente e d'uno in altro sangue,
        oltre la difension d'i senni umani;

82   per ch'una gente impera e l'altra langue,
        seguendo lo giudicio di costei,
        che è occulto come in erba l'angue.

85   Vostro saver non ha contasto a lei;
        questa provede, giudica, e persegue
        suo regno come il loro li altri dèi.

88   Le sue permutazion non hanno triegue;
        necessità la fa esser veloce,
        sì spesso vien chi vicenda consegue.

91   Quest' è colei ch'è tanto posta in croce
        pur da color che le dovrien dar lode,
        dandole biasmo a torto e mala voce;

94   ma ella s'è beata e ciò non ode;
        con l'altre prime creature lieta
        volve sua spera e beata si gode.

97   Or discendiamo omai a maggior pieta:
        già ogne stella cade che saliva
        quand' io mi mossi, e 'l troppo star si vieta.'

For all the gold that lies beneath the moon –   64
or all that ever did lie there – would bring
no respite to these worn-out souls, not one.'

'Please tell me, sir,' I said, a little more,   67
'what can it be, this Fortune that you touch on,
that clasps all earthly goods between its claws?'

And he to me: 'You idiotic creatures,   70
so greatly hurt by your own ignorance!
Feed on my words. I'd have you grasp their sense.

He who transcends in wisdom all that is,   73*
wrought every sphere and gave to each a guide,
so every part shines out to every part

always in equal distribution of light.   76
So, too, above the splendours of the world,
He set a sovereign minister, ordained to move –

in permutations at the proper time –   79
vain goods from tribe to tribe, from blood to blood,
in ways from which no human wisdom hides.

And this is why, where one race rules supreme,   82
another faints and languishes: they all pursue
her judgements, secret as a snake in grass.

Your powers of mind cannot contend with her.   85
She, looking forwards, will pronounce her law,
advancing, as do other gods, her own domain.

Her permutations never come to rest.   88
It is necessity that makes her quick,
so thick they come by turns to meet their fate.

She is the one so often crossed and cursed   91
by those who, rightly, ought to sing her praise,
yet vilify her name and speak her ill.

But she, a holy being, pays no heed.   94
Happy, with all the other primal powers,
she turns her sphere, rejoicing in beatitude.

So let us now go down to greater pain.   97*
The stars that rose when I first stirred now fall.
We cannot stay too long. That is forbidden.'

100   Noi ricidemmo il cerchio a l'altra riva
sovr' una fonte che bolle e riversa
per un fossato che da lei deriva.

103   L'acqua era buia assai più che persa;
e noi, in compagnia de l'onde bige,
intrammo giù per una via diversa.

106   In la palude va c'ha nome Stige
questo tristo ruscel, quand'è disceso
al piè de le maligne piagge grige.

109   E io, che di mirare stava inteso,
vidi genti fangose in quel pantano,
ignude tutte, con sembiante offeso.

112   Queste si percotean, non pur con mano
ma con la testa e col petto e coi piedi,
troncandosi co' denti a brano a brano.

115   Lo buon maestro disse: 'Figlio, or vedi
l'anime di color cui vinse l'ira;
e anche vo' che tu per certo credi

118   che sotto l'acqua è gente che sospira,
e fanno pullular quest' acqua al summo,
come l'occhio ti dice, u' che s'aggira.

121   Fitti nel limo dicon: "Tristi fummo
ne l'aere dolce che dal sol s'allegra,
portando dentro accidïoso fummo:

124   or ci attristiam ne la belletta negra."
Quest' inno si gorgoglian ne la strozza,
ché dir nol posson con parola integra.'

127   Così girammo de la lorda pozza
grand' arco, tra la ripa secca e 'l mézzo,
con li occhi vòlti a chi del fango ingozza.

130   Venimmo al piè d'una torre al da sezzo.

   Cutting across the circle, we approached   100
the margins of a spring – which, seething, spilled
and ran from there along an outer sluice.

   The waters here were darker, far, than perse.   103
So, on – accompanied by murky waves –
downwards we travelled by a weirder route.

   Into a swamp (by name, the loathsome Styx)   106
this melancholy brook makes way, and finds
the foot of those malignant, grey-black slopes.

   As there I stood, intent and wondering,   109
I saw there, plunged within that stagnant fen,
a peevish people, naked, caked with mud.

   Each battered each – and not with fists alone,   112
also with head butts, kicks and charging chests.
Their teeth, too, tore them, bit by bit, to shreds.

   'You witness now,' my gentle teacher said,   115*
'the souls of those whom anger overthrew.
And this I'd also have you know: be sure,

   beneath the surface of this slick are some   118
whose sighs – as you can see at every turn –
now aerate that pullulating film.

   So, stuck there fast in slime, they hum: "Mournful   121
we were. Sunlight rejoices the balmy air.
We, though, within ourselves nursed sullen fumes,

   and come to misery in this black ooze."   124
That is the hymn each gurgles in his gorge,
unable to articulate a single phrase.'

   So, on around this sour, revolting pit,   127
between the sludge and arid rock, we swung
our arc, eyes bent on those who gulped that slop.

   We reached, in fine, the bottom of a tower.   130

CANTO 8

1   Io dico, seguitando, ch'assai prima
che noi fossimo al piè de l'alta torre,
li occhi nostri n'andar suso a la cima

4   per due fiammette che i vedemmo porre,
e un'altra da lungi render cenno
tanto ch'a pena il potea l'occhio tòrre.

7   E io mi volsi al mar di tutto 'l senno;
dissi: 'Questo che dice? e che risponde
quell'altro foco? e chi son quei che 'l fenno?'

10   Ed elli a me: 'Su per le sucide onde
già scorgere puoi quello che s'aspetta,
se 'l fummo del pantan nol ti nasconde.'

13   Corda non pinse mai da sé saetta
che sì corresse via per l'aere snella,
com' io vidi una nave piccioletta

16   venir per l'acqua verso noi in quella,
sotto 'l governo d'un sol galeoto,
che gridava: 'Or se' giunta, anima fella!'

19   'Flegiàs, Flegiàs, tu gridi a vòto,'
disse lo mio segnore, 'a questa volta:
più non ci avrai che sol passando il loto.'

22   Qual è colui che grande inganno ascolta
che li sia fatto e poi se ne rammarca,
fecesi Flegiàs ne l'ira accolta.

25   Lo duca mio discese ne la barca
e poi mi fece intrare appresso lui;
e sol quand' io fui dentro parve carca.

CANTO 8

And so I say (continuing) that, long before   1
we reached the bottom of that lofty tower,
our eyes had travelled upwards to its summit,

  drawn by a pair of tiny flames, set there –   4
as now we saw – to signal to a third,
so far away the eye could hardly grasp it.

  I turned towards the ocean of all wisdom: 7
'What do they mean?' I said to him. 'What answer
follows from the farther fire? Who makes these signs?'

  And he: 'Across these waves of foaming mire,   10
you may already glimpse what they've been waiting for,
unless it still goes hidden by these marshy fumes.'

  No bow string ever shot through air an arrow   13
rapider than now, at speed, I saw come on
towards us there, a mean little vessel,

  within it – as pilot plying these waters –   16
a single galley man who strained the oar,
squealing: 'You fiend! You've got it coming now!'

  'Phlegyas, Phlegyas!' my master said.   19*
'Your screams and shouts have, this time, little point.
We're yours – but only while we cross this marsh.'

  Like someone hearing that a massive hoax   22
has just, to his disgruntlement, been pulled on him,
so Phlegyas now stood, in pent-up rage.

  My lord stepped down, and, entering the boat,   25
he made me, in my turn, embark behind.
The hull seemed laden only when I did.

28 Tosto che 'l duca e io nel legno fui,
    segando se ne va l'antica prora
    de l'acqua più che non suol con altrui.

31 Mentre noi corravam la morta gora,
    dinanzi mi si fece un pien di fango,
    e disse: 'Chi se' tu che vieni anzi ora?'

34 E io a lui: 'S'i' vegno, non rimango;
    ma tu chi se', che sì se' fatto brutto?'
    Rispuose: 'Vedi che son un che piango.'

37 E io a lui: 'Con piangere e con lutto,
    spirito maladetto, ti rimani;
    ch'i' ti conosco, ancor sie lordo tutto.'

40 Allor distese al legno ambo le mani;
    per che 'l maestro accorto lo sospinse,
    dicendo: 'Via costà con li altri cani!'

43 Lo collo poi con le braccia mi cinse;
    basciommi 'l volto e disse: 'Alma sdegnosa,
    benedetta colei che 'n te s'incinse!

46 Quei fu al mondo persona orgogliosa;
    bontà non è che sua memoria fregi:
    così s'è l'ombra sua qui furiosa.

49 Quanti si tegnon or là sù gran regi
    che qui staranno come porci in brago,
    di sé lasciando orribili dispregi!'

52 E io: 'Maestro, molto sarei vago
    di vederlo attuffare in questa broda
    prima che noi uscissimo del lago.'

55 Ed elli a me: 'Avante che la proda
    ti si lasci veder, tu sarai sazio:
    di tal disio convien che tu goda.'

58 Dopo ciò poco vid' io quello strazio
    far di costui a le fangose genti,
    che Dio ancor ne lodo e ne ringrazio.

61 Tutti gridavano: 'A Filippo Argenti!'
    e 'l fiorentino spirito bizzarro
    in sé medesmo si volvea co' denti.

At once – my leader boarded, me as well –   28
the ancient prow put out. It sawed the waves
more deeply than it would with other crews.

So, rushing forwards on that lifeless slick,   31*
there jerked up, fronting me, one brimming slime
who spoke: 'So who – you come too soon! – are you?'

And my riposte: 'I come, perhaps; I'll not remain.   34
But who might you be, brutishly befouled?'
His answer was: 'Just look at me. I'm one

who weeps.' And I to him: 'Weep on. In grief,   37
may you remain, you spirit of damnation!
I know who *you* are, filth as you may be.'

And then he stretched both hands towards our gunwales.   40
My teacher, though – alert – soon drove him back,
saying: 'Get down! Be off with all that dog pack!'

And then he ringed both arms around my neck.   43*
He kissed my face, then said: 'You wrathful soul!
Blessed the one that held you in her womb.

That man, alive, flaunted his arrogance,   46
and nothing good adorns his memory.
So here his shadow is possessed with rage.

How many, in the world above, pose there   49
as kings but here will lie like pigs in muck,
leaving behind them horrible dispraise.'

'Sir,' I replied, 'this I should really like: 52
before we make our way beyond this lake,
to see him dabbled in the minestrone.'

He gave me my answer: 'Before that shore   55
has come to view, you'll surely have your fill.
And rightly you rejoice in this desire.'

Then, moments on, I saw that sinner ripped   58
to vicious tatters by that mud-caked lot.
I praise God still, and still give thanks for that.

'Get him,' they howled. 'Let's get him – Silver Phil!'   61
That crazy Florentine! He bucked, he baulked.
Turning, the Guelf turned teeth upon himself.

64   Quivi il lasciammo, che più non ne narro;
     ma ne l'orecchie mi percosse un duolo,
     perch'io avante l'occhio intento sbarro.

67   Lo buon maestro disse: 'Omai, figliuolo,
     s'appressa la città c'ha nome Dite,
     coi gravi cittadin, col grande stuolo.'

70   E io: 'Maestro, già le sue meschite
     là entro certe ne la valle cerno,
     vermiglie come se di foco uscite

73   fossero.' Ed ei mi disse: 'Il foco etterno
     ch'entro l'affoca le dimostra rosse,
     come tu vedi in questo basso inferno.'

76   Noi pur giugnemmo dentro a l'alte fosse
     che vallan quella terra sconsolata;
     le mura mi parean che ferro fosse.

79   Non sanza prima far grande aggirata,
     venimmo in parte dove il nocchier forte:
     'Usciteci,' gridò: 'qui è l'intrata.'

82   Io vidi più di mille in su le porte
     da ciel piovuti, che stizzosamente
     dicean: 'Chi è costui che sanza morte

85   va per lo regno de la morta gente?'
     E 'l savio mio maestro fece segno
     di voler parlar loro segretamente.

88   Allor chiusero un poco il gran disdegno
     e disser: 'Vien tu solo, e quei sen vada
     che sì ardito intrò per questo regno.

91   Sol si ritorni per la folle strada:
     pruovi, se sa; ché tu qui rimarrai,
     che li ha' iscorta sì buia contrada.'

94   Pensa, lettor, se io mi sconfortai
     nel suon de le parole maladette,
     ché non credetti ritornarci mai.

97   'O caro duca mio, che più di sette
     volte m'hai sicurtà renduta e tratto
     d'alto periglio che 'ncontra mi stette,

We left him there. Of him, my story tells no more.   64
And yet my ears were pierced with cries of pain.
At which, I barred my eyes intently forwards.

'Dear son,' my teacher in his goodness said,   67
'we now approach the city known as Dis,
its teeming crowds and weighty citizens.'

'Already, sir,' I said, 'I clearly can   70
make out the minarets beyond this moat,
as bright and red, it seems, as if they sprang

from fire.' 'Eternal fire,' he answered me,   73
'burning within, projects, as you can see,
these glowing profiles from the depths of Hell.'

We now arrived within the deep-dug ditch –   76
the channel round that place disconsolate,
whose walls, it seemed to me, were formed of iron.

Not without, first, encircling it about,   79
we came to where the ferry man broke forth:
'Out you all get!' he yelled. 'The entry's here.'

I saw there, on that threshold – framed – more than   82
a thousand who had rained from Heaven. Spitting
in wrath. 'Who's that,' they hissed, 'who, yet undead,

travels the kingdom of the truly dead?'   85
He gave a sign, my teacher in all wisdom,
saying he sought some secret word with them.

At which they somewhat hid their fierce disdain.   88
'You come, but on your own!' they said. 'Let him,
so brazen entering our realm, walk by.

He may retrace his foolish path alone –   91
or try it, if he can – while you'll stay here.
You've been his escort through this dark terrain.'

Reader, imagine! I grew faint at heart,   94
to hear these cursed phrases ringing out.
I truly thought I'd never make it back.

'My guide, my dearest master. Seven times –   97
or more by now – you've brought me safely through.
You've drawn me from the face of towering doom.

100   non mi lasciar,' diss' io, 'così disfatto;
        e se 'l passar più oltre ci è negato,
        ritroviam l'orme nostre insieme ratto.'

103   E quel segnor che lì m'avea menato
        mi disse: 'Non temer, ché 'l nostro passo
        non ci può tòrre alcun: da tal n'è dato.

106   Ma qui m'attendi, e lo spirito lasso
        conforta e ciba di speranza buona,
        ch'i' non ti lascerò nel mondo basso.'

109   Così sen va, e quivi m'abbandona
        lo dolce padre, e io rimagno in forse,
        ché sì e no nel capo mi terciona.

112   Udir non potti quello ch'a lor porse;
        ma ei non stette là con essi guari,
        che ciascun dentro a pruova si ricorse.

115   Chiuser la porta que' nostri avversari
        nel petto al mio segnor, che fuor rimase
        e rivolsesi a me con passi rari.

118   Li occhi a la terra e le ciglia avea rase
        d'ogne baldanza, e dicea ne' sospiri:
        'Chi m'ha negate le dolenti case?'

121   E a me disse: 'Tu, perch' io m'adiri,
        non sbigottir, ch'io vincerò la prova,
        qual ch'a la difension dentro s'aggiri.

124   Questa lor tracotanza non è nova,
        ché già l'usaro a men segreta porta,
        la qual sanza serrame ancor si trova:

127   sovr' essa vedestù la scritta morta.
        E già di qua da lei discende l'erta,
        passando per li cerchi sanza scorta,

130   tal che per lui ne fia la terra aperta.'

Do not, I beg you, leave me here undone.   100
If we are now denied a clear way on,
then let us quickly trace our footsteps back.'

My lord had led me onwards to that place –   103
and now he said: 'Do not be terrified.
No one can take from us our right to pass.

Wait here a while. Refresh your weary soul.   106
Take strength. Be comforted. Feed on good hope.
I'll not desert you in this nether world.'

So off he went. He there abandoned me,   109
my sweetest father. Plunged in 'perhapses',
I so remained, brain arguing 'yes' and 'no'.

What he then said to them I could not tell.   112
Yet hardly had he taken up his stand
when all ran, jostling, to return inside.

They barred the door, these enemies of ours,   115
to meet his thrust. My lord remained shut out.
With heavy tread, he now came back to me.

Eyes bent upon the ground, his forehead shaved   118
of all brave confidence, sighing, he said:
'Who dares deny me entrance to this house of grief?'

To me he said: 'You see. I'm angry now.   121
Don't be dismayed. They'll fuss around in there.
They'll seek to keep us out. But I'll win through.

This insolence of theirs is nothing new.   124*
At some less secret gate they tried it once.
But that still stands without its lock, ajar.

You've seen the door, dead words scribed on its beam.   127
And now already there descends the slope –
passing these circles, and without a guide –
someone through whom the city will lie open.'   130

CANTO 9

1   Quel color che viltà di fuor mi pinse,
veggendo il duca mio tornare in volta,
più tosto dentro il suo novo ristrinse.

4   Attento si fermò com' uom ch'ascolta;
ché l'occhio nol potea menare a lunga
per l'aere nero e per la nebbia folta.

7   'Pur a noi converrà vincer la punga,'
cominciò el, 'se non . . . Tal ne s'offerse.
Oh quanto tarda a me ch'altri qui giunga!'

10   I' vidi ben sì com' ei ricoperse
lo cominciar con l'altro che poi venne,
che fur parole a le prime diverse;

13   ma nondimen paura il suo dir dienne,
perch' io traeva la parola tronca
forse a peggior sentenzia che non tenne.

16   'In questo fondo de la trista conca
discende mai alcun del primo grado,
che sol per pena ha la speranza cionca?'

19   Questa question fec' io; e quei: 'Di rado
incontra,' mi rispuose, 'che di noi
faccia il cammino alcun per qual io vado.

22   Ver è ch'altra fiata qua giù fui,
congiurato da quella Eritón cruda
che richiamava l'ombre a' corpi sui.

25   Di poco era di me la carne nuda,
ch'ella mi fece intrar dentr' a quel muro
per trarne un spirto del cerchio di Giuda.

CANTO 9

The colour that failing courage brought out   1
so quickly in me, seeing my leader retreat,
made him, the sooner, check his own new pallor.
   Intently, as though listening hard, he stopped.   4
Eyesight unaided – in that blackened air,
through foggy, dense swirls – could not carry far.
   'This contest, even so, we're bound to win.   7*
If not . . .' he began. 'Yet granted such a one . . .
How long to me it seems till that one comes!'
   I saw quite clearly how he covered up   10
his opening thoughts with those that followed on –
words inconsistent with the first he spoke.
   Yet fear came over me at what he had said.   13
And so, from these truncated words, I drew
a meaning worse, perhaps, than he'd intended.
   'Into the hollow deep of this grim bowl   16
do any make their way from that first rung
where nothing, save for thwarted hope, brings pain?'
   I put this question to him. 'Seldom,' he said.   19
'It happens rarely that our people take
the path that I am venturing to tread.
   It's true, of course, I've been here once before,   22*
conjured to come by bitter Erichtho –
she who called shadows back into their limbs.
   A short while only was I bare of flesh   25
until, as she compelled, I breached these walls
to fetch a spirit from the Judas ring.

28   Quell' è 'l più basso loco e 'l più oscuro,
e 'l più lontan dal ciel che tutto gira:
ben so 'l cammin; però ti fa sicuro.

31   Questa palude che 'l gran puzzo spira
cigne dintorno la città dolente,
u' non potemo intrare omai sanz' ira.'

34   E altro disse, ma non l'ho a mente;
però che l'occhio m'avea tutto tratto
ver' l'alta torre a la cima rovente,

37   dove in un punto furon dritte ratto
tre furie infernal di sangue tinte,
che membra feminine avieno e atto,

40   e con idre verdissime eran cinte;
serpentelli e ceraste avien per crine,
onde le fiere tempie erano avvinte.

43   E quei, che ben conobbe le meschine
de la regina de l'etterno pianto,
'Guarda,' mi disse, 'le feroci Erine.

46   Quest' è Megera dal sinistro canto;
quella che piange dal destro è Aletto;
Tesifón è nel mezzo'; e tacque a tanto.

49   Con l'unghie si fendea ciascuna il petto;
battiensi a palme e gridavan sì alto
ch'i' mi strinsi al poeta per sospetto.

52   'Vegna Medusa: sì 'l farem di smalto,'
dicevan tutte riguardando in giuso;
'mal non vengiammo in Teseo l'assalto.'

55   'Volgiti 'n dietro e tien lo viso chiuso;
ché se 'l Gorgón si mostra e tu 'l vedessi,
nulla sarebbe di tornar mai suso.'

58   Così disse 'l maestro; ed elli stessi
mi volse, e non si tenne a le mie mani,
che con le sue ancor non mi chiudessi.

61   O voi ch'avete li 'ntelletti sani,
mirate la dottrina che s'asconde
sotto 'l velame de li versi strani.

That is the utmost deep, the darkest place,   28
the furthest from the sky's all-turning sphere.
I know the way. Be confident, be sure.

This marsh, exhaling such a nauseous stench,   31
forms in a belt around the mournful town
and not without due anger shall we enter in.'

He said much more. But what I can't recall.   34
My eyes in all attention now were drawn
towards the blazing summit of that gate,

where suddenly, at one point, there had sprung   37*
three blood-stained Furies from the depths of Hell.
In pose and body they were, all three, women,

wound round about with water snakes, bright green.   40
Fringing their vicious brows they bore, as hair,
entwining snakes. Their curls were sharp-horned vipers.

And he – who knew quite well that these were slaves   43
who served the empress of unending tears –
said to me: 'Look! The cruel Eumenides!

That one's Megaera, on the left-hand side.   46
Weeping there stands Alecto, on the right.
Tisiphone's between these two.' He paused.

Each rent her breast with her own fingernails.   49
With slapping palm, each beat herself and screamed –
so loud I strained, all doubt, against the poet.

'Come now, Medusa! Turn him – quick! – to stone!'   52*
Staring hard down they spoke in unison.
'The Theseus raid went unavenged! We're wrong!'

'Turn round! Your back to them! Your eyes tight shut!   55
For if the Gorgon shows and you catch sight,
there'll be no way of ever getting out.'

He spoke and then, himself, he made me turn   58
and, not relying on my hands alone,
to shield my eyes he closed his own on mine.

Look hard, all you whose minds are sound and sane,   61
and wonder at the meaning lying veiled
beyond the curtain of this alien verse.

64   E già venìa su per le torbide onde
un fracasso d'un suon pien di spavento,
per cui tremavano amendue le sponde,

67   non altrimenti fatto che d'un vento
impetuoso per li avversi ardori,
che fier la selva e sanz' alcun rattento

70   li rami schianta, abbatte e porta fori;
dinanzi polveroso va superbo,
e fa fuggir le fiere e li pastori.

73   Li occhi mi sciolse e disse: 'Or drizza il nerbo
del viso su per quella schiuma antica
per indi ove quel fummo è più acerbo.'

76   Come le rane innanzi a la nimica
biscia per l'acqua si dileguan tutte
fin ch'a la terra ciascuna s'abbica:

79   vid' io più di mille anime distrutte
fuggir così dinanzi ad un ch'al passo
passava Stige con le piante asciutte.

82   Dal volto rimovea quell' aere grasso,
menando la sinistra innanzi spesso,
e sol di quell' angoscia parea lasso.

85   Ben m'accorsi ch'elli era da ciel messo,
e volsimi al maestro; e quei fé segno
ch'i' stessi queto ed inchinassi ad esso.

88   Ahi quanto mi parea pien di disdegno!
Venne a la porta e con una verghetta
l'aperse, che non v'ebbe alcun ritegno.

91   'O cacciati del ciel, gente dispetta,'
cominciò elli in su l'orribil soglia,
'ond' esta oltracotanza in voi s'alletta?

94   Perché recalcitrate a quella voglia
a cui non puote il fin mai esser mozzo,
e che più volte v'ha cresciuta doglia?

97   Che giova ne le fata dar di cozzo?
Cerbero vostro, se ben vi ricorda,
ne porta ancor pelato il mento e 'l gozzo.'

Already across the turbid swell there came   64
a shattering resonance that, charged with panic,
evoked great tremors down each river bank.

In this way, too, a driving wind – impelled   67
by clashing currents through the burning air –
strikes at a grove and, meeting no resistance,

splinters the branches flat and bears them off.   70
So, proudly on it goes, in clouds of dust,
shepherds and beasts all fleeing in its path.

He loosed my eyes, 'And now,' he said, 'stretch straight   73
your strings of sight across this age-old scum
to where the fumes are thickest, stinging most.'

Like frogs that glimpse their enemy the snake,   76
and vanish rapidly across the pond –
diving till each sits huddling on its bed –

I saw a thousand ruined souls or more   79
scattering in flight, ahead of one whose pace
passed, yet kept dry, across the river Styx.

The greasy air he wafted from his face,   82
his left hand drawn before him, as a fan.
And this was all the strain, it seemed, that tired him.

I saw full well that he was sent from Heaven,   85
I turned towards my teacher, and he signed
that I should bend in silent deference.

How full he seemed to me of high disdain!   88
He reached the gates. And, simply with his rod,
he opened them. For nothing held them firm.

'Outcasts from Heaven, driven beyond contempt!'   91
Thus, in that dreadful doorway, he began:
'How is such truculence bred up in you?

Why so recalcitrant against that will   94
whose aim and purpose never can be maimed,
which has so often now increased your pain?

What is the point? Why kick against your fate?   97*
Your guard dog Cerberus is still (remember?)
hairless for doing so, at chin and neck.'

100   Poi si rivolse per la strada lorda,
e non fé motto a noi, ma fé sembiante
d'omo cui altra cura stringa e morda

103   che quella di colui che li è davante;
e noi movemmo i piedi inver' la terra,
sicuri appresso le parole sante.

106   Dentro li 'ntrammo sanz' alcuna guerra;
e io, ch'avea di riguardar disio
la condizion che tal fortezza serra,

109   com' io fui dentro, l'occhio intorno invio:
e veggio ad ogne man grande campagna,
piena di duolo e di tormento rio.

112   Sì come ad Arli, ove Rodano stagna,
sì com' a Pola, presso del Carnaro
ch'Italia chiude e suoi termini bagna,

115   fanno i sepulcri tutt' il loco varo,
così facevan quivi d'ogne parte,
salvo che 'l modo v'era più amaro:

118   ché tra li avelli fiamme erano sparte,
per le quali eran sì del tutto accesi
che ferro più non chiede verun' arte.

121   Tutti li lor coperchi eran sospesi,
e fuor n'uscivan sì duri lamenti
che ben parean di miseri e d'offesi.

124   E io: 'Maestro, quai son quelle genti
che, seppellite dentro da quell' arche,
si fan sentir coi sospiri dolenti?'

127   E quelli a me: 'Qui son li eresiarche
con lor seguaci, d'ogne setta, e molto
più che non credi son le tombe carche.

130   Simile qui con simile è sepolto,
e i monimenti son più e men caldi.'
E poi ch'a la man destra si fu vòlto,

133   passammo tra i martìri e li alti spaldi.

He then turned back along the filthy road.   100
He spoke no word to us. He had the look
of someone gnawed and gathered up by care –
    though not the cares that here confronted him.   103
And now we set our tread towards that land.
The holy words had made us confident.
    We entered. And no force was offered us.   106
So, eager to survey what such a fort
could lock within the confines of its wall,
    when once inside, I cast my eyes about.   109
I see a plain, extending all around.
And everywhere is grief and wracking pain.
    Compare: at Arles (the Rhône there forms a marsh),   112*
or else at Polj by the Kvarner gulf,
which shuts the door on Italy and bathes its bounds,
    are sepulchres that make the ground uneven.   115
And so, too, here, a tomb at every turn,
except that all was done more bitterly.
    For flames were scattered round among these tombs.   118
The pits were therefore so intensely fired,
no tradesman needs his brand iron half so hot.
    The covers of the tombs all stood half-raised;   121
and out of each there came such cruel lamenting
these must have been the cries from pain within.
    And I to my master: 'Who can they be,   124
these people buried in the sepulchres?
They make their presence felt in such pained sighs?'
    The answer: 'These are the master heretics,   127
with all their followers from every sect.
These tombs are filled with more than you suspect.
    Those of like mind are buried each with each.   130
The monuments are all at differing heats.'
He turned towards the right, then on we went,
    between the torments and high battlements.   133

CANTO 10

1   Ora sen va per un secreto calle
     tra 'l muro de la terra e li martìri
     lo mio maestro, e io dopo le spalle.

4   'O virtù somma, che per li empi giri
     mi volvi,' cominciai, 'com' a te piace,
     parlami, e sodisfammi a' miei disiri.

7   La gente che per li sepolcri giace
     potrebbesi veder? già son levati
     tutt' i coperchi, e nessun guardia face.'

10   E quelli a me: 'Tutti saran serrati
     quando di Iosafat qui torneranno
     coi corpi che là sù hanno lasciati.

13   Suo cimitero da questa parte hanno
     con Epicuro tutti suoi seguaci,
     che l'anima col corpo morta fanno.

16   Però a la dimanda che mi faci
     quinc' entro satisfatto sarà tosto,
     e al disio ancor che tu mi taci.'

19   E io: 'Buon duca, non tegno riposto
     a te mio cuor se non per dicer poco,
     e tu m'hai non pur mo a ciò disposto.'

22   'O Tosco che per la città del foco
     vivo ten vai così parlando onesto,
     piacciati di restare in questo loco.

25   La tua loquela ti fa manifesto
     di quella nobil patria natio
     a la qual forse fui troppo molesto.'

CANTO 10

Onward along a secret path – confined   1
between those ramparts and the shows of pain –
my teacher led and I was at his shoulder.

'You,' I began, 'true power and height of strength,   4
you bring me, turning, through these godless whirls.
Speak, if this pleases you. Feed my desires.

Those people lying in the sepulchres –   7
what chance is there of seeing them? The lids
are off already. No one stands on guard.'

'These tombs,' he said, 'will finally be shut   10*
when, from Jehoshaphat on Judgement Day,
sinners bring back their bodies left above.

This circle is the cemetery for all   13*
disciples of the Epicurus school,
who say the body dies, so too the soul.

The question, therefore, that you've put to me,   16
once you're within, will soon be satisfied,
so, too, the longing that you keep unsaid.'

'I never would – my lord, my trusted guide –   19
keep, save for brevity, my heart from you.
And brevity you've urged on me before.'

'O Tuscan! You go through the city of fire   22
alive and speaking as a man of worth.
Come, if you will, and rest in this domain.

Your accent manifests that you were born   25
a son of that great fatherland on which,
perhaps, I wreaked too harsh an injury.'

28   Subitamente questo suono uscìo
       d'una de l'arche; però m'accostai,
       temendo, un poco più al duca mio.

31   Ed el mi disse: 'Volgiti! Che fai?
       Vedi là Farinata che s'è dritto:
       da la cintola in sù tutto 'l vedrai.'

34   Io avea già il mio viso nel suo fitto;
       ed el s'ergea col petto e con la fronte
       com' avesse l'inferno a gran dispitto.

37   E l'animose man del duca e pronte
       mi pinser tra le sepulture a lui,
       dicendo: 'Le parole tue sien conte.'

40   Com' io al piè de la sua tomba fui,
       guardommi un poco, e poi, quasi sdegnoso,
       mi dimandò: 'Chi fuor li maggior tui?'

43   Io, ch'era d'ubidir disideroso,
       non gliel celai, ma tutto gliel' apersi;
       ond' ei levò le ciglia un poco in suso;

46   poi disse: 'Fieramente furo avversi
       a me e a miei primi e a mia parte,
       sì che per due fiate li dispersi.'

49   'S'ei fur cacciati, ei tornar d'ogne parte,'
       rispuos' io lui, 'l'una e l'altra fiata;
       ma i vostri non appreser ben quell'arte.'

52   Allor surse a la vista scoperchiata
       un'ombra, lungo questa, infino al mento:
       credo che s'era in ginocchie levata.

55   Dintorno mi guardò, come talento
       avesse di veder s'altri era meco;
       e poi che 'l sospecciar fu tutto spento,

58   piangendo disse: 'Se per questo cieco
       carcere vai per altezza d'ingegno,
       mio figlio ov' è? e perché non è teco?'

61   E io a lui: 'Da me stesso non vegno:
       colui ch'attende là per qui mi mena
       forse cui Guido vostro ebbe a disdegno.'

This sound, so suddenly, came ringing out   28
from one among the sepulchres. Fearful,
I shrank still closer to my leader's side.

'What's wrong?' he said to me. 'Just turn around!   31*
And see there, upright, risen, Farinata.
From cincture upwards you will see him whole.'

My gaze was trained already into his,   34
while he, brow raised, was thrusting out his chest,
as though he held all Hell in high disdain.

My leader (hands in animated aid)   37
drove me towards him down the line of vaults.
He counselled: 'Let your words be duly measured.'

So there, beneath his sepulchre, I stood.   40
He looked me up and down a while, and then
inquired, half-scornfully: 'Who were your forebears?'

I – eager, as always, and obedient –   43
concealing nothing, laid all plainly forth.
At which he arched his brows a little more.

And then: 'In fierce hostility, they stood   46
against myself, my ancestors, my cause.
And so, on two occasions, they were scattered wide.'

'Scattered,' I answered, 'so they may have been,   49
but all came back from all sides, then and now.
And your men truly never learned that art.'

Then there arose, revealed before my eyes,   52
a shadow near the first, seen from chin up,
which had, as I suppose, just risen to its knees.

It looked me all around, as though intent   55
on seeing whether, with me, was another.
But when its doubting glance was wholly spent,

weeping he called: 'If you, through this eyeless   58
prison, pass on through height of intellect,
my son, where is he? And why not here with you?'

'I come,' I said, 'though not through my own strength.   61
The man who waits there leads me through this place
to one, perhaps, whom once your Guido scorned.'

64   Le sue parole e 'l modo de la pena
m'avean di costui già letto il nome;
però fu la risposta così piena.

67   Di sùbito drizzato gridò: 'Come
dicesti? "elli ebbe"? non viv' elli ancora?
non fiere li occhi suoi il dolce lome?'

70   Quando s'accorse d'alcuna dimora
ch'io facea dinanzi a la risposta,
supin ricadde e più non parve fora.

73   Ma quell'altro magnanimo, a cui posta
restato m'era, non mutò aspetto,
né mosse collo, né piegò sua costa;

76   e sé continuando al primo detto,
'S'elli han quell'arte,' disse, 'male appresa,
ciò mi tormenta più che questo letto.

79   Ma non cinquanta volte fia raccesa
la faccia de la donna che qui regge,
che tu saprai quanto quell'arte pesa.

82   E se tu mai nel dolce mondo regge,
dimmi: perché quel popolo è sì empio
incontr' a' miei in ciascuna sua legge?'

85   Ond' io a lui: 'Lo strazio e 'l grande scempio
che fece l'Arbia colorata in rosso,
tal orazion fa far nel nostro tempio.'

88   Poi ch'ebbe sospirando il capo mosso,
'A ciò non fu' io sol,' disse, 'né certo
sanza cagion con li altri sarei mosso.

91   Ma fu' io solo, là dove sofferto
fu per ciascun di tòrre via Fiorenza,
colui che la difesi a viso aperto.'

94   'Deh, se riposi mai vostra semenza,'
prega' io lui, 'solvetemi quel nodo
che qui ha 'nviluppata mia sentenza.

97   El par che voi veggiate, se ben odo,
dinanzi quel che 'l tempo seco adduce,
e nel presente tenete altro modo.'

The way he spoke – and what he suffered, too –   64
had now already spelled for me his name.
And that was why my answer was so full.

Upright suddenly: 'What's that you say?'   67*
he wailed. '"He once . . ."? You mean, he's not alive?
And are his eyes not struck by bonny light?'

But then, in noticing that slight delay   70
which came before I offered my reply,
he fell back flat, and did not re-appear.

The other noble soul (at whose command   73
I'd come to rest) in no way changed expression.
He neither moved his neck nor bent his waist.

But still continuing in what he'd said: 76*
'If,' he went on, 'they learned that art so ill,
that is more torment than this bed of pain.

And yet no more than fifty times that face   79
(the moon's, who is our sovereign here) will shine
till you shall learn how heavy that art weighs.

If you once more would gain the lovely world,   82
tell me: how dare those burghers, in their laws,
oppose themselves so viciously to mine?'

My answer was: 'The massacre, the mindless waste   85
that stained the flowing Arbia with blood,
led, in our oratories, to these demands.'

Sighing, he did now move his head. 'In none   88
of that,' he said, 'was I alone. And I
would not, without good cause, have gone with them.

I was alone – where all the rest could bear   91
to think that Florence might be swept away –
and boldly stood to speak in her defence.'

'Well (may your seed find sometime true repose!)   94
untie the knot for me,' I now besought,
'so tightly twined around my searching thoughts.

You see, it seems (to judge from what I hear)   97*
far in advance what time will bring to pass,
but otherwise in terms of present things.'

100   'Noi veggiam, come quei c'ha mala luce,
       le cose,' disse, 'che ne son lontano:
       cotanto ancor ne splende il sommo duce.

103   Quando s'appressano o son, tutto è vano
       nostro intelletto, e s'altri non ci apporta
       nulla sapem di vostro stato umano.

106   Però comprender puoi che tutta morta
       fia nostra conoscenza da quel punto
       che del futuro fia chiusa la porta.'

109   Allor, come di mia colpa compunto,
       dissi: 'Or direte dunque a quel caduto
       che 'l suo nato è co' vivi ancor congiunto;

112   e s'i' fui, dianzi, a la risposta muto,
       fate i saper che 'l fei perché pensava
       già ne l'error che m'avete soluto.'

115   E già 'l maestro mio mi richiamava;
       per ch'i' pregai lo spirto più avaccio
       che mi dicesse chi con lu' istava.

118   Dissemi: 'Qui con più di mille giaccio:
       qua dentro è 'l secondo Federico
       e 'l Cardinale; e de li altri mi taccio.'

121   Indi s'ascose; e io inver' l'antico
       poeta volsi i passi, ripensando
       a quel parlar che mi parea nemico.

124   Elli si mosse; e poi, così andando
       mi disse: 'Perché se' tu sì smarrito?'
       E io li sodisfeci al suo dimando.

127   'La mente tua conservi quel ch'udito
       hai contra te,' mi comandò quel saggio;
       'e ora attendi qui,' e drizzò 'l dito:

130   'quando sarai dinanzi al dolce raggio
       di quella il cui bell' occhio tutto vede,
       da lei saprai di tua vita il viaggio.'

'We see like those who suffer from ill light.   100
We are,' he said, 'aware of distant things.
Thus far he shines in us, the Lord on high.

    But when a thing draws near to us, our minds   103
go blank. So if no other brings us news,
then nothing of your human state is known to us.

    You will from this be able to deduce   106
that all our knowledge will be wholly dead
when all the doors of future time are closed.'

    And then I said, as though my heart were pierced   109
with guilt, 'Go, say to him, that fallen soul,
his first-born son is still among the living.

    And if, before I answered, I fell mute,   112
I did so (make him understand) because
my thoughts – which you have solved – had strayed to
        doubt.'

    By now, my teacher had already called.   115
And so, with greater urgency I begged that soul
that he should tell me who was with him there.

    'I lie,' he answered, 'with a thousand, more.   118*
Enclosed beside me is the second Frederick.
Cardinal Octavian, too. Of others, I keep silent.'

    And then he hid: and I, towards that great   121
poet of the ancient world, turned my steps backwards,
musing on words that seemed my enemy.

    He went his way and, as he walked, he asked: 124
'Why is it you're so lost in thought, so blurred by doubt?'
And I responded fully to his words.

    'Keep well in mind,' my lord in wisdom said,   127
'the things that you have heard against yourself.
But now,' his finger raised, 'attend to this:

    when once again you stand within the rays   130*
that she, whose lovely eyes see all things, casts,
you'll learn from her what your life's course will be.'

133   Appresso mosse a man sinistra il piede;
       lasciammo il muro e gimmo inver' lo mezzo
       per un sentier ch'a una valle fiede
136   che 'nfin là sù facea spiacer suo lezzo.

And then he swung, to tread towards the left.   133
We quit the wall and headed for the middle.
The path we took cut straight into a gorge,
    and even from above the stench was foul.   136

CANTO 11

1　　In su l'estremità d'un'alta ripa
che facevan gran pietre rotte in cerchio,
venimmo sopra più crudele stipa;

4　　　e quivi, per l'orribile soperchio
del puzzo che 'l profondo abisso gitta,
ci raccostammo, in dietro, ad un coperchio

7　　　d'un grand' avello, ov' io vidi una scritta
che dicea: 'Anastasio papa guardo,
lo qual trasse Fotin de la via dritta.'

10　　'Lo nostro scender conviene esser tardo,
sì che s'ausi un poco in prima il senso
al tristo fiato; e poi no i fia riguardo.'

13　　　Così 'l maestro; e io: 'Alcun compenso,'
dissi lui, 'trova che 'l tempo non passi
perduto.' Ed elli: 'Vedi ch'a ciò penso.'

16　　'Figliuol mio, dentro da cotesti sassi,'
cominciò poi a dir, 'son tre cerchietti
di grado in grado, come que' che lassi.

19　　　Tutti son pien di spirti maladetti;
ma perché poi ti basti pur la vista,
intendi come e perché son costretti.

22　　　D'ogne malizia, ch'odio in cielo acquista,
ingiuria è 'l fine, ed ogne fin cotale
o con forza o con frode altrui contrista.

25　　　Ma perché frode è de l'uom proprio male,
più spiace a Dio; e però stan di sotto
li frodolenti, e più dolor li assale.

CANTO 11

Now near the brink of a sheer escarpment　　　　　1
formed in a circle from great, shattered stones,
we found, below, a crueller bunch of souls.

And there, against an awful overflow –　　　　　4
a stink arising from the utmost depths –
we huddled back together by the lid

of one vast sepulchre, inscribed, I saw,　　　　　7*
in words that said: 'I guard Pope Anastasius,
drawn by Photinus from the rightful road.'

'Best not descend too rapidly, but first　　　　　10
get more accustomed in our sense of smell
to this grim belch. We'll then not notice it.'

These were my teacher's words. To him I said,　　　　　13
'Find something that will compensate, to waste
no time.' 'I'm thinking, as you see,' he said,

and then began: 'Dear son, within this rock-rimmed pit　　　　　16
three lesser circuits lie. And these (like those
you leave behind) go down by due degrees.

Each rung is crammed with spirits of the damned.　　　　　19
But listen now – so sight may henceforth serve –
and hear the "what" and "why" of their constraints.

Malice is aimed in all its forms – and thus　　　　　22
incurs the hatred of Heaven – at gross injustice,
and, aiming so, harms others, by deceit or force.

Deceit, though, is specifically a human wrong,　　　　　25*
and hence displeases God the more. Liars
are therefore deeper down, and tortured worse.

28   D'i violenti il primo cerchio è tutto;
        ma perché si fa forza a tre persone,
        in tre gironi è distinto e costrutto.

31   A Dio, a sé, al prossimo si pòne
        far forza, dico in loro e in lor cose,
        come udirai con aperta ragione.

34   Morte per forza e ferute dogliose
        nel prossimo si danno, e nel suo avere
        ruine, incendi e tollette dannose;

37   onde omicide e ciascun che mal fiere,
        guastatori e predon, tutti tormenta
        lo giron primo per diverse schiere.

40   Puote omo avere in sé man violenta
        e ne' suoi beni; e però nel secondo
        giron convien che sanza pro si penta

43   qualunque priva sé del vostro mondo,
        biscazza e fonde la sua facultade,
        e piange là dov' esser de' giocondo.

46   Puossi far forza ne la deitade
        col cor negando e bestemmiando quella,
        e spregiando natura e sua bontade;

49   e però lo minor giron suggella
        del segno suo e Soddoma e Caorsa
        e chi, spregiando Dio col cor, favella.

52   La frode, ond' ogne coscienza è morsa,
        può l'omo usare in colui che 'n lui fida
        e in quel che fidanza non imborsa.

55   Questo modo di retro par ch'incida
        pur lo vinco d'amor che fa natura;
        onde nel cerchio secondo s'annida

58   ipocresia, lusinghe e chi affattura,
        falsità, ladroneccio e simonia,
        ruffian, baratti e simile lordura.

61   Per l'altro modo quell'amor s'oblia
        che fa natura e quel ch'è poi aggiunto,
        di che la fede spezial si cria;

Ring One throughout is meant for violent wills.   28
But violent acts may fall upon three persons.
And so this ring is shaped and formed in three.

To God, to self, to neighbours hurt is done   31
(to persons, of course, but also their possessions)
in ways that you will now hear argued out.

To those around us, death or grievous wounds   34
are wrought by violent hands, the things we own
ruined by outrage, extortion or fire.

So in the agonies of Sub-ring One,   37
in different squads, are homicides and thugs,
vandals and looters, bandits and brigands.

In violence, too, we turn against ourselves,   40
or else our own belongings. And thus
in Sub-ring Two are those (regret now vain)

who by their own free will stripped off your world   43
or gambled all their competence away,
and weep where, properly, they should rejoice.

Force, too, is offered to the Deity   46
by hearts, blaspheming, that deny His power,
or else scorn Nature and her great largesse.

And so the imprint of the smallest ring   49*
falls on Cahorsian bankers, as on Sodom,
and those who speak at heart in scorn of God.

As for deceit – which gnaws all rational minds –   52*
we practise this on those who trust in us,
or those whose pockets have no room for trust.

Fraud of the second kind will only gash   55
the ligature of love that Nature forms:
and therefore in great Circle Two there nests

smarm and hypocrisy, the casting-up of spells,   58
impersonation, thievery, crooked priests,
embezzlement and pimping, such-like scum.

Fraud of the other sort forgets no less   61
the love that Nature makes, but then, as well,
the love particular that trust creates.

64   onde nel cerchio minore, ov' è 'l punto
      de l'universo in su che Dite siede,
      qualunque trade in etterno è consunto.'

67   E io: 'Maestro, assai chiara procede
      la tua ragione, e assai ben distingue
      questo baràtro e 'l popol ch'e' possiede.

70   Ma dimmi: quei de la palude pingue,
      che mena il vento, e che batte la pioggia,
      e che s'incontran con sì aspre lingue,

73   perché non dentro da la città roggia
      sono ei puniti, se Dio li ha in ira?
      e se non li ha, perché sono a tal foggia?'

76   Ed elli a me: 'Perché tanto delira,'
      disse, 'lo 'ngegno tuo da quel che sòle?
      o ver la mente dove altrove mira?

79   Non ti rimembra di quelle parole
      con le quai la tua Etica pertratta
      le tre disposizion che 'l ciel non vole,

82   incontenenza, malizia e la matta
      bestialitade? e come incontenenza
      men Dio offende e men biasimo accatta?

85   Se tu riguardi ben questa sentenza
      e rechiti a la mente chi son quelli
      che sù di fuor sostegnon penitenza,

88   tu vedrai ben perché da questi felli
      sien dipartiti, e perché men crucciata
      la divina vendetta li martelli.'

91   'O sol che sani ogne vista turbata,
      tu mi contenti sì quando tu solvi,
      che, non men che saver, dubbiar m'aggrata.

94   Ancora in dietro un poco ti rivolvi,'
      diss' io, 'là dove di' ch'usura offende
      la divina bontade, e 'l groppo solvi.'

97   'Filosofia,' mi disse, 'a chi la 'ntende,
      nota, non pure in una sola parte,
      come natura lo suo corso prende

So in the smallest ring of all – that point   64
within the universe where Satan sits –
consumed eternally, are traitors, every one.

'Your explanation, sir,' I said, 'proceeds   67
with great lucidity. You clarify
the levels of this grim abyss and all within.

Yet tell me, too: those souls in that gross marsh,   70
those swept by winds, those creatures lashed by rain,
and those that clash with such abrasive tongues,

if they all, likewise, face the wrath of God,   73
then why not racked within these flame-red walls?
Or if they don't, why are they as they are?'

'Why,' he replied, 'do your frenetic wits   76
wander so wildly from their usual track?
Or where, if not fixed here, are your thoughts set?

Do you, at any rate, not call to mind   79
the terms in which your *Ethics* fully treats
those three dispositions that the Heavens repel:

intemperance, intentional harm and mad   82
brutality? Or that intemperance
offends God least, and least attracts His blame?

If you think carefully of what this means,   85
and summon into thought what those souls are
who serve their sentence in the upper ring,

you'll plainly see why these are set apart   88
from those condemned as felons, and, in pain,
less sharply hammered by divine revenge.'

'You are the sun who heals all clouded sight.   91
Solving my doubts, you bring me such content
that doubt, no less than knowing, is delight.

But still,' I said, 'turn backwards to the point   94
where you declared that usury offends
God's generosity. Untie that knot.'

'Philosophy, as those that read it know,   97*
takes note,' he said, 'on more than one occasion,
of how the course that Nature runs is drawn

100   dal divino 'ntelletto e da sua arte;
e se tu ben la tua Fisica note,
tu troverai, non dopo molte carte,

103   che l'arte vostra quella, quanto pote,
segue, come 'l maestro fa 'l discente;
sì che vostr' arte a Dio quasi è nepote.

106   Da queste due, se tu ti rechi a mente
lo Genesì dal principio, convene
prender sua vita e avanzar la gente;

109   e perché l'usuriere altra via tene,
per sé natura e per la sua seguace
dispregia, poi ch' in altro pon la spene.

112   Ma seguimi oramai, che 'l gir mi piace;
ché i Pesci guizzan su per l'orizzonta,
e 'l Carro tutto sovra 'l Coro giace,

115   e 'l balzo via là oltra si dismonta.'

directly from the mind and art of God.   100
And if you read your *Physics* with due care,
you'll see, before you're many pages through,

   that your art takes, as best it can, the lead   103
that Nature gives – as student does from master.
Your art is nearly grandchild, then, to God.

   From these two principles – if you recall   106
the opening lines of Genesis – we're bound to draw
our living strength and multiply our people.

   But usurers adopt a different course.   109
They place their hopes in other things, and thus
make mock of Nature's self and her close kin.

   But follow on. I'm ready now to go.   112*
The writhing Fish have swum to the horizon.
The Wain lies high above the Western Wind.

   The leap we now must make lies far beyond.'   115

CANTO 12

1   Era lo loco ov' a scender la riva
venimmo alpestro e, per quel che v'er' anco,
tal ch'ogne vista ne sarebbe schiva.

4   Qual è quella ruina che nel fianco
di qua da Trento l'Adice percosse,
o per tremoto o per sostegno manco,

7   che da cima del monte, onde si mosse,
al piano è sì la roccia discoscesa
ch'alcuna via darebbe a chi sù fosse:

10   cotal di quel burrato era la scesa;
e'n su la punta de la rotta lacca
l'infamïa di Creti era distesa

13   che fu concetta ne la falsa vacca;
e quando vide noi, sé stesso morse,
sì come quei cui l'ira dentro fiacca.

16   Lo savio mio duca inver' lui gridò: 'Forse
tu credi che qui sia 'l duca d'Atene,
che sù nel mondo la morte ti porse?

19   Pàrtiti, bestia, ché questi non vene
ammaestrato da la tua sorella,
ma vassi per veder le vostre pene.'

22   Qual è quel toro che si slaccia in quella
c'ha ricevuto già 'l colpo mortale,
che gir non sa; ma qua e là saltella:

25   vid' io lo Minotauro far cotale;
e quello accorto gridò: 'Corri al varco;
mentre ch'e' 'nfuria, è buon che tu ti cale.'

CANTO 12

The place we'd reached – to clamber down that bank –   1
was alpine crag. No eye, considering
what else was there, would not have flinched away.

Compare: an avalanche in Adige,   4*
southwards of Trent, once struck the mountain flank,
triggered perhaps by landslip or earthquake;

and boulders from the summit shifted down   7
in steps and stages to the valley floor,
to offer those up there a downward route.

Likewise the path we trod down this ravine.   10*
And on the angle where the incline broke,
there lay stretched out the infamy of Crete,

spawned in the womb of Pasiphae's fake heifer.   13
And when he saw us there he gnawed himself,
as though flailed flat within by utter rage.

My leader in his wisdom called towards him: 16
'You may suppose that he's the duke of Athens,
who dealt you, in the world above, your death.

You monster! Move aside! This one's not come   19
provided with instructions from your sister.
He comes to see what you are suffering here.'

A stunned bull, stricken by its mortal blow,   22
wrenches, that instant, free from noose and rope.
It cannot walk but skips and hops about.

The Minotaur, I saw, behaved like that.   25
'Run!' shouted Virgil, watching out. 'A gap!
Better get down while still his fury bites.'

28   Così prendemmo via giù per lo scarco
di quelle pietre, che spesso moviensi
sotto i miei piedi per lo novo carco.

31   Io gia pensando; e quei disse: 'Tu pensi
forse a questa ruina, ch'è guardata
da quell'ira bestial ch'i' ora spensi.

34   Or vo' che sappi che l'altra fiata
ch'i' discesi qua giù nel basso inferno,
questa roccia non era ancor cascata.

37   Ma certo poco pria, se ben discerno,
che venisse colui che la gran preda
levò a Dite del cerchio superno,

40   da tutte parti l'alta valle feda
tremò sì ch'i' pensai che l'universo
sentisse amor, per lo qual è chi creda

43   più volte il mondo in caòsso converso;
e in quel punto questa vecchia roccia,
qui e altrove, tal fece riverso.

46   Ma ficca li occhi a valle, chè s'approccia
la riviera del sangue in la qual bolle
qual che per violenza in altrui noccia.'

49   Oh cieca cupidigia e ira folle,
che sì ci sproni ne la vita corta,
e ne l'etterna poi sì mal c'immolle!

52   Io vidi un'ampia fossa in arco torta,
come quella che tutto 'l piano abbraccia,
secondo ch'avea detto la mia scorta;

55   e tra 'l piè de la ripa ed essa, in traccia
corrien centauri, armati di saette,
come solien nel mondo andare a caccia.

58   Veggendoci calar, ciascun ristette,
e de la schiera tre si dipartiro
con archi e asticciuole prima elette;

61   e l'un gridò da lungi: 'A qual martiro
venite voi che scendete la costa?
Ditel costinci; se non, l'arco tiro.'

So down across the scree we picked our way.   28
Beneath my feet, the stones would often move,
teetering beneath the strange new weight they bore.

I walked on, deep in thought. 'Perhaps,' he said,   31
'you're thinking of this landslide? Or else that guard
whose brutal anger I have just eclipsed?

When once before (I'd like you now to know)   34
I came down here and entered lower Hell,
these cliffs had yet to suffer any rock fall.

But certainly, if I have got this right,   37
there once came One who gathered up from Dis
the stolen treasure of its highest place.

Moments before, a tremor in every part   40
disturbed these fetid depths. The universe
must then, I think, have felt that love through which

it often turns (so some suppose) to chaos.   43
At that same point, these age-old crags were rent
and left both here and elsewhere as they are.

But fix your eyes upon the valley floor.   46
We now are nearing the river of blood.
There simmer all whose violence damaged others.'

What blind cupidity, what crazy rage   49
impels us onwards in our little lives –
then dunks us in this stew to all eternity!

I saw there (as my guide had said I would)   52
a ditch of great dimensions in an arc
that stretched its wide embrace around the plain.

And there, between the hill foot and those banks,   55*
were centaurs, running in a long-drawn line,
armed – as they'd been on earth to hunt – with arrows.

On seeing us descend, they all reined in.   58
Three of that company then sallied forth,
their barbs and bow strings already well picked.

And one, still distant, shouted out: 'What pain   61
have you to meet, now making down that butte?
Tell us from there. Or else I draw my bow.'

64   Lo mio maestro disse: 'La risposta
      farem noi a Chirón costà di presso:
      mal fu la voglia tua sempre sì tosta.'

67   Poi mi tentò, e disse: 'Quelli è Nesso,
      che morì per la bella Deianira
      e fé di sé la vendetta elli stesso.

70   E quel di mezzo, ch'al petto si mira,
      è il gran Chirón, il qual nodrì Achille;
      quell'altro è Folo, che fu sì pien d'ira.

73   Dintorno al fosso vanno a mille a mille,
      saettando qual anima si svelle
      del sangue più che sua colpa sortille.'

76   Noi ci appressammo a quelle fiere isnelle;
      Chirón prese uno strale, e con la cocca
      fece la barba in dietro a le mascelle.

79   Quando s'ebbe scoperta la gran bocca,
      disse a' compagni: 'Siete voi accorti
      che quel di retro move ciò ch'el tocca?

82   Così non soglion far li piè d'i morti.'
      E 'l mio buon duca, che già li er' al petto,
      dove le due nature son consorti,

85   rispuose: 'Ben è vivo, e sì soletto
      mostrar li mi convien la valle buia;
      necessità 'l ci 'nduce, e non diletto.

88   Tal si partì da cantare *alleluia*
      che mi commise quest'officio novo;
      non è ladron, né io anima fuia.

91   Ma per quella virtù per cu' io movo
      li passi miei per sì selvaggia strada,
      danne un de' tuoi a cui noi siamo a provo

94   e che ne mostri là dove si guada;
      e che porti costui in su la groppa,
      ché non è spirto che per l'aere vada.'

97   Chirón si volse in su la destra poppa,
      e disse a Nesso: 'Torna, e sì li guida,
      e fa cansar s'altra schiera v'intoppa.'

My teacher in response then said: 'To Chiron –   64
there, just next to you – we'll make reply.
You are too headstrong. And you always were.'

'That's Nessus there,' he said, alerting me.   67
'He died for love of lovely Deianira,
but then avenged himself with his own blood.

The middle one (eyes fixed upon his chest)   70
is Chiron the Great. He nurtured Achilles.
Pholus, who lived so full of wrath, is third.

Around this ditch, in thousands these all run,   73
and loose their arrows at those souls that strain
higher beyond the blood than guilt allows.'

We drew now closer to those swift-foot beasts.   76
Then Chiron plucked a shaft and, with its notch,
he combed his beard and tucked it from his jaw.

And, once he'd made his noble mouth thus free,   79
he said to his companions: 'Have you yet seen
the one behind, how all he touches moves?

A normal dead man's feet would not do that.'   82
My trusted leader was now standing where,
around the waist, the double nature weds.

He answered thus: 'He is indeed alive.   85
To me it falls to show him this dark vale.
Necessity, not pleasure, leads us on.

Someone whose hymn is the "Alleluia"   88*
paused in that song to hand me this new task.
He is no robber, I no thievish soul.

Now in the name of that True Power by which   91
I move each step along this tangled way,
allot a guide to us from your own band

to show us where the ford might be, and bear   94
this man beside me on his crupper.'
He is no spirit walking through the air.

Now Chiron turned, to pivot to his right.   97
'Go back!' he said to Nessus. 'Be their guide.
Make any troop you stumble on give way.'

100   Or ci movemmo con la scorta fida
       lungo la proda del bollor vermiglio,
       dove i bolliti facieno alte strida.

103   Io vidi gente sotto infino al ciglio;
       e 'l gran centauro disse: 'E' son tiranni
       che dier nel sangue e ne l'aver di piglio.

106   Quivi si piangon li spietati danni;
       quivi è Alessandro, e Dionisio fero,
       che fé Cicilia aver dolorosi anni.

109   E quella fronte c'ha 'l pel così nero
       è Azzolino; e quell'altro ch'è biondo
       è Opizzo da Esti, il qual per vero

112   fu spento dal figliastro sù nel mondo.'
       Allor mi volsi al poeta, e quei disse:
       'Questi ti sia or primo, e io secondo.'

115   Poco più oltre il centauro s'affisse
       sovr' una gente che 'nfino a la gola
       parea che di quel bulicame uscisse.

118   Mostrocci un'ombra da l'un canto sola,
       dicendo: 'Colui fesse in grembo a Dio
       lo cor che 'n su Tamisi ancor si cola.'

121   Poi vidi gente che di fuor del rio
       tenean la testa e ancor tutto 'l casso;
       e di costoro assai riconobb' io.

124   Così a più a più si facea basso
       quel sangue, sì che cocea pur li piedi;
       e quindi fu del fosso il nostro passo.

127   'Sì come tu da questa parte vedi
       lo bulicame che sempre si scema,'
       disse 'l centauro, 'voglio che tu credi

130   che da quest'altra a più a più giù prema
       lo fondo suo, infin ch'el si raggiunge
       ove la tirannia convien che gema.

133   La divina giustizia di qua punge
       quell'Attila che fu flagello in terra,
       e Pirro e Sesto; e in etterno munge

The escort by our side, we now moved on   100
along the shore of boiling vermilion
where souls, well boiled, gave vent to high-pitched yells.

Some, so I saw, were plunged there to the brow.   103
'And these,' the mighty centaur said, 'are tyrants.
They lent their hands to violent gain and blood.

So here, in tears for their unpitying sins,   106*
with Alexander there is vicious Dionysius,
who brought on Sicily such grieving years.

That forehead there – its quiff as black as jet –   109
is Azzolino. At his side the blond
Opizzo d'Este, who – and this is true –

was done to death by his own bastard son.'   112
I turned towards the poet, who now said:
'Let him go first and I'll be next to come.'

A little further on, the centaur stopped,   115
arched over people who emerged, it seemed,
throat high above the seething of that stream.

There, to one side, he pointed out a shade.   118
'He stabbed,' he said, 'in the bosom of God,
the one whose heart drips blood still on the Thames.'

I now saw some with heads above the flood,   121
then others further on, their torsos clear.
And these, in greater numbers, I could recognize.

Then, gradually, the blood race grew more shallow –   124
so that by now it only stewed their toes.
And there we found the crossing of the ditch.

'On this side – see? – the boiling stream grows less.   127
So, correspondingly,' the centaur said,
'I'd have you understand that, over there,

the bed is pressed, in process point by point,   130
still further down until it finds the place
at which in pain great despots wring out moans.

Justice divine on that side sharply stings   133
the hun Attila – scourge of all the earth –
Pyrrhus and Sextus. There it also milks

136   le lagrime che col bollor diserra
a Rinier da Corneto, a Rinier Pazzo,
che fecero a le strade tanta guerra.'
139   Poi si rivolse e ripassossi 'l guazzo.

the tears eternally that boiling wave unlocks   136
from Renier the Mad to Renier da Corneto,
who wrought such strife upon the open roads.'
    And then he turned and passed the ford once more.   139

CANTO 13

1   Non era ancor di là Nesso arrivato,
quando noi ci mettemmo per un bosco
che da neun sentiero era segnato.

4   Non fronda verde, ma di color fosco,
non rami schietti, ma nodosi e 'nvolti,
non pomi v'eran, ma stecchi con tòsco.

7   Non han sì aspri sterpi né sì folti
quelle fiere selvagge che 'n odio hanno
tra Cécina e Corneto i luoghi cólti.

10   Quivi le brutte Arpie lor nidi fanno,
che cacciar de le Strofade i Troiani
con tristo annunzio di futuro danno.

13   Ali hanno late, e colli e visi umani,
piè con artigli, e pennuto 'l gran ventre;
fanno lamenti in su li alberi strani.

16   E 'l buon maestro 'Prima che più entre,
sappi che se' nel secondo girone,'
mi cominciò a dire, 'e sarai mentre

19   che tu verrai ne l'orribil sabbione.
Però riguarda ben; sì vederai
cose che torrien fede al mio sermone.'

22   Io sentia d'ogne parte trarre guai
e non vedea persona che 'l facesse,
per ch'io tutto smarrito m'arrestai.

25   Cred'io ch'ei credette ch'io credesse
che tante voci uscisser, tra quei bronchi,
da gente che per noi si nascondesse.

CANTO 13

No, Nessus had not reached the other side   1
when we began to travel through a wood
that bore no sign of any path ahead.

No fresh green leaves but dismal in colour,   4
no boughs clean arced but knotty and entwined,
no apples were there but thorns, poison-pricked.

No scrubby wilderness so bitter and dense   7*
from Cécina as far as Corneto
offers a den to beasts that hate ploughed farmlands.

Their nest is there, those disgusting Harpies   10
who drove the Trojans from the Strophades,
with grim announcements of great harm to come.

Wings widespreading, human from neck to brow,   13
talons for feet, plumage around their paunches,
they sing from these uncanny trees their songs of woe.

Constant in kindness, my teacher now said: 16
'Before you venture further in, please know
that you now stand in Sub-ring Number Two,

and shall until you reach the Appalling Sands.   19
So look around. Take care. What you'll see here
would drain belief from any word I uttered.'

A wailing I heard, dragged out from every part,   22
and saw there no one who might make these sounds,
so that I stopped, bewildered, in my tracks.

Truly I think he truly thought that, truly,   25
I might just have believed these voices rose
from persons hidden from us in the thorn maze.

28   Però disse 'l maestro: 'Se tu tronchi
        qualche fraschetta d'una d'este piante,
        li pensier c'hai si faran tutti monchi.'

31   Allor porsi la mano un poco avante
        e colsi un ramicel da un gran pruno;
        e 'l tronco suo gridò: 'Perché mi schiante?'

34   Da che fatto fu poi di sangue bruno,
        ricominciò a dir: 'Perché mi scerpi?
        non hai tu spirto di pietade alcuno?

37   Uomini fummo, e or siam fatti sterpi:
        ben dovrebb' esser la tua man più pia
        se state fossimo anime di serpi.'

40   Come d'un stizzo verde ch'arso sia
        da l'un de' capi, che da l'altro geme
        e cigola per vento che va via:

43   sì de la scheggia rotta usciva insieme
        parole e sangue, ond'io lasciai la cima
        cadere, e stetti come l'uom che teme.

46   'S'elli avesse potuto creder prima,'
        rispuose 'l savio mio, 'anima lesa,
        ciò c'ha veduto pur con la mia rima,

49   non averebbe in te la man distesa;
        ma la cosa incredibile mi fece
        indurlo ad ovra ch'a me stesso pesa.

52   Ma dilli chi tu fosti, sì che 'n vece
        d'alcun' ammenda tua fama rinfreschi
        nel mondo sù, dove tornar li lece.'

55   E 'l tronco: 'Sì col dolce dir m'adeschi
        ch'i' non posso tacere; e voi non gravi
        perch' io un poco a ragionar m'inveschi.

58   Io son colui che tenni ambo le chiavi
        del cor di Federigo e che le volsi,
        serrando e diserrando, sì soavi

61   che dal secreto suo quasi ogn'uom tolsi;
        fede portai al glorioso offizio,
        tanto ch'i' ne perde' li sonni e 'polsi.

Therefore: 'If you,' my teacher said, 'will wrench   28*
away some sprig from any tree you choose,
that will lop short your feeling in such doubt.'

And so I reached my hand a little forwards.   31*
I plucked a shoot (no more) from one great hawthorn.
At which its trunk screamed out: 'Why splinter me?'

Now darkened by a flow of blood, the tree   34
spoke out a second time: 'Why gash me so?
Is there no living pity in your heart?

Once we were men. We've now become dry sticks.   37
Your hand might well have proved more merciful
if we had been the hissing souls of snakes.'

Compare: a green brand, kindled at one end –   40
the other oozing sap – whistles and spits
as air finds vent, then rushes out as wind.

So now there ran, out of this fractured spigot,   43
both words and blood. At which I let the tip
drop down and stood like someone terror-struck.

'You injured soul!' my teacher (sane as ever)   46
now replied. 'If he had only earlier
believed what my own writings could have shown,

he'd not have stretched his hand so far towards you.   49
This, though, is all beyond belief. So I was forced
to urge a deed that presses on my own mind still.

But tell him now who once you were. He may,   52
in turn, as remedy, refresh your fame,
returning to the world above by leave.'

The trunk: 'Your words, sir, prove so sweet a bait,   55*
I cannot here keep silence. Don't be irked
if I a while should settle on that lure and talk.

I am the one who held in hand both keys   58
to Federigo's heart. I turned them there,
locking so smoothly and unlocking it

that all men, almost, I stole from his secrets.   61
Faith I kept, so true in that proud office
I wasted sleep and lost my steady pulse.

64   La meretrice che mai da l'ospizio
di Cesare non torse li occhi putti,
morte comune e de le corti vizio,

67   infiammò contra me li animi tutti;
e li 'nfiammati infiammar sì Augusto
che 'lieti onor tornaro in tristi lutti.

70   L'animo mio, per disdegnoso gusto,
credendo col morir fuggir disdegno,
ingiusto fece me contra me giusto.

73   Per le nove radici d'esto legno
vi giuro che già mai non ruppi fede
al mio segnor, che fu d'onor sì degno.

76   E se di voi alcun nel mondo riede,
conforti la memoria mia, che giace
ancor del colpo che 'nvidia le diede.'

79   Un poco attese, e poi: 'Da ch'el si tace,'
disse 'l poeta a me, 'non perder l'ora;
ma parla, e chiedi a lui, se più ti piace.'

82   Ond' io a lui: 'Domandal tu ancora
di quel che credi ch'a me satisfaccia;
ch'i' non potrei, tanta pietà m'accora.'

85   Perciò ricominciò: 'Se l'om ti faccia
liberamente ciò che 'l tuo dir priega,
spirito incarcerato, ancor ti piaccia

88   di dirne come l'anima si lega
in questi nocchi; e dinne, se tu puoi,
s'alcuna mai di tai membra si spiega.'

91   Allor soffiò il tronco forte, e poi
si convertì quel vento in cotal voce:
'Brievemente sarà risposto a voi.

94   Quando si parte l'anima feroce
dal corpo ond' ella stessa s'è disvelta,
Minòs la manda a la settima foce.

97   Cade in la selva, e non l'è parte scelta,
ma là dove fortuna la balestra,
quivi germoglia come gran di spelta.

That harlot Scandal, then (her raddled eyes   64
she never drags from where the emperor dwells,
the vice of court life, mortal blight of all)

enflamed the minds of everyone against me.   67
And they in flames enflamed the great Augustus.
So, happy honours turned to hapless grief.

My mind – itself disdainful in its tastes –   70
believing it could flee disdain by dying,
made me unjust against myself so just.

By all these weird, new-wooded roots, I swear   73
on oath before you: I did not break faith,
nor failed a lord so worthy of regard.

Will you – should either head back to the world –   76
bring comfort to my memory, which lies
still lashed beneath the stroke of envious eyes?'

Pausing a while, he said (my chosen poet),   79
'He's silent now, so waste no opportunity.
If there is more you wish to know, then say.'

'You,' I replied, 'must speak once more and ask   82
what you believe will leave me satisfied.
I could not do it. Pity wrings my core.'

And so he did once more begin: 'Suppose   85
that freely, from a generous heart, someone
should do, imprisoned ghost, what your prayers seek,

tell us, if you should care to, this: how souls   88
are bound in these hard knots. And, if you can:
will anyone be ever loosed from limbs like these?'

At that (exhaling heavily) the trunk   91
converted wind to word and formed this speech:
'The answer you require is quick to give:

When any soul abandons savagely   94
its body, rending self by self away,
Minos consigns it to the seventh gulf.

Falling, it finds this copse. Yet no one place   97
is chosen as its plot. Where fortune slings it,
there (as spelt grains might) it germinates.

100 Surge in vermena e in pianta silvestra;
     l'Arpie, pascendo poi de le sue foglie,
     fanno dolore e al dolor fenestra.

103 Come l'altre verrem per nostre spoglie,
     ma non però ch'alcuna sen rivesta,
     ché non è giusto aver ciò ch'om si toglie.

106 Qui le strascineremo, e per la mesta
     selva saranno i nostri corpi appesi,
     ciascuno al prun de l'ombra sua molesta.'

109 Noi eravamo ancora al tronco attesi,
     credendo ch'altro ne volesse dire,
     quando noi fummo d'un romor sorpresi:

112 similemente a colui che venire
     sente 'l porco e la caccia a sua posta,
     ch'ode le bestie, e le frasche stormire.

115 Ed ecco due da la sinistra costa,
     nudi e graffiati, fuggendo sì forte
     che de la selva rompieno ogne rosta.

118 Quel dinanzi: 'Or accorri, accorri, morte!'

     E l'altro, cui pareva tardar troppo,
     gridava: 'Lano, sì non furo accorte

121 le gambe tue a le giostre dal Toppo!'
     E poi che forse li fallia la lena,
     di sé e d'un cespuglio fece un groppo.

124 Di rietro a loro era la selva piena
     di nere cagne, bramose e correnti
     come veltri ch'uscisser di catena.

127 In quel che s'appiattò miser li denti,
     e quel dilaceraro a brano a brano;
     poi sen portar quelle membra dolenti.

130 Presemi allor la mia scorta per mano,
     e menommi al cespuglio che piangea
     per le rotture sanguinenti in vano.

133 'O Iacopo,' dicea, 'da Santo Andrea,
     che t'è giovato di me fare schermo?
     che colpa ho io de la tua vita rea?'

A sapling sprouts, grows ligneous, and then   100
the Harpies, grazing on its foliage,
fashion sharp pain and windows for that pain.

We (as shall all), come Judgement Day, shall seek   103
our cast-off spoil, yet not put on this vestment.
Keeping what we tore off would not be fair.

Our bodies we shall drag back here; and all   106*
around this melancholy grove they'll swing,
each on the thorn of shades that wrought them harm.'

Attention trained entirely on that stock   109
(thinking, in truth, it might as yet say more),
we now were shocked by a sudden uproar,

as if (to make comparison) you'd heard some hog   112
and all the boar hunt baying round its stand –
a sound composed of beasts and thrashing twigs.

And look there, on the left-hand side, there came,   115*
at speed, two fleeing, naked, scratched to bits,
who broke down every hurdle in that scrub.

One was ahead: 'Quick, quick! Come, death! Come
        now!'   118
The other (seeming, to himself, too slow)
was yelling: 'Lano! Oh, your nimble heels

weren't half so sharp at the Toppo rumble!'   121
And then (it may be his breath was failing),
he sank to form a clump beside a shrub.

Behind these two, the wood was teeming, full   124
of black bitches, ravenous and rapid,
as greyhounds are when slipping from their leads.

These set their teeth on that sad, hunkered form.   127
They tore him all to pieces, chunk by chunk.
And then they carried off those suffering limbs.

My guide then took me gently by the hand,   130
and led me to the bush, which wept (in vain)
through all of its blood-stained lacerations,

saying: 'O Jacopo da Santo Andrea!   133
What use was it to take me as your shield?
Am I to blame for your wild, wicked ways?'

136   Quando 'l maestro fu sovr' esso fermo,
      disse: 'Chi fosti, che per tante punte
      soffi con sangue doloroso sermo?'

139   Ed elli a noi: 'O anime che giunte
      siete a veder lo strazio disonesto
      c'ha le mie fronde sì da me disgiunte,

142   raccoglietele al piè del tristo cesto.
      I' fui de la città che nel Batista
      mutò 'l primo padrone, ond' ei per questo

145   sempre con l'arte sua la farà trista.
      E se non fosse che 'n sul passo d'Arno
      rimane ancor di lui alcuna vista,

148   que' cittadin che poi la rifondarno
      sovra 'l cener che d'Attila rimase,
      avrebber fatto lavorare indarno.

151   Io fei gibetto a me de le mie case.'

My teacher came and stood above that bush.   136
'So who were you,' he said, 'who, pierced to bits,
breathes painful utterance in jets of blood?'

    'You souls,' he said, 'you come – but just in time –   139
to see the massacre, in all its shame,
that rends away from me my fresh green fronds.

    Place all these leaves beneath this grieving stump.   142*
I too was from that city, once, which chose
Saint John as patron over Mars – its first –

    whose arts, since spurned, have always brought us harm. 145
And were there not, beneath the Arno bridge,
some traces visible of what he was,

    those citizens who built it all anew   148
on ashes that Attila left behind
would then have laboured with no end in view.

    Myself, I made a gallows of my house.'   151

CANTO 14

Poi che la carità del natio loco
mi strinse, raunai le fronde sparte
e rende'le a colui, ch'era già fioco.

Indi venimmo al fine ove si parte
lo secondo giron dal terzo, e dove
si vede di giustizia orribil arte.

A ben manifestar le cose nove,
dico che arrivammo ad una landa
che dal suo letto ogne pianta rimove;

la dolorosa selva l'è ghirlanda
intorno, come 'l fosso tristo ad essa:
quivi fermammo i passi a randa a randa.

Lo spazzo era una rena arida e spessa,
non d'altra foggia fatta che colei
che fu da' piè di Caton già soppressa.

O vendetta di Dio, quanto tu dei
esser temuta da ciascun che legge
ciò che fu manifesto a li occhi miei!

D'anirne nude vidi molte gregge
che piangean tutte assai miseramente,
e parea posta lor diversa legge.

Supin giacea in terra alcuna gente,
alcuna si sedea tutta raccolta,
e altra andava continuamente.

Quella che giva 'ntorno era più molta,
e quella men che giacea al tormento,
ma più al duolo avea la lingua sciolta.

CANTO 14

Seized, in pure charity, by love of home,   1
I gathered up those scattered leaves, then bore them
to my countryman, his voice grown dim.

And then, from there, we reached the boundary   4
of circuits two and three and witnessed now,
in awe and horror, how skilful justice is.

To make more manifest what now was new,   7
we'd reached, I'd better say, an open plain
that dusts all vegetation from its floor.

Round this, the wood of pain creates a fringe   10
(as likewise, round that wood, the wretched ditch).
And here we halted at the very edge.

The ground beneath was brushed with coarse, dry sand,   13*
no different from those arid Libyan wastes
on which the feet of Cato marched to war.

Great God! Your vengeance must be rightly feared   16
by all who read the verses I compose
to say what there was straight before my eyes.

I saw ahead a flock of naked souls.   19
And all were weeping, very mournfully.
But each was subject to a different law.

Some of these folk lay supine on the ground,   22
and some sat huddling, tight about themselves.
Others again strode endlessly around.

The latter were, in number, far the more.   25
Those lying flat, though fewer, were in tongue
more free at voicing their sharp miseries.

28   Sovra tutto 'l sabbion, d'un cader lento,
      piovean di foco dilatate falde,
      come di neve in alpe sanza vento.

31   Quali Alessandro in quelle parti calde
      d'India vide sopra 'l suo stuolo
      fiamme cadere infino a terra salde,

34   per ch'ei provide a scalpitar lo suolo
      con le sue schiere, acciò che lo vapore
      mei si stingueva mentre ch'era solo:

37   tale scendeva l'etternale ardore,
      onde la rena s'accendea, com' esca
      sotto focile, a doppiar lo dolore.

40   Sanza riposo mai era la tresca
      de le misere mani, or qundi or quinci
      escotendo da sé l'arsura fresca.

43   I' cominciai: 'Maestro, tu che vinci
      tutte le cose, fuor che' demon duri
      ch'a l'intrar de la porta incontra uscinci,

46   chi è quel grande che non par che curi
      lo 'ncendio e giace dispettoso e torto,
      sì che la pioggia non par che 'l maturi?'

49   E quel medesmo, che si fu accorto
      chi'io domandava il mio duca di lui,
      gridò: 'Qual io fui vivo, tal son morto.

52   Se Giove stanchi 'l suo fabbro da cui
      crucciato prese la folgore aguta
      onde l'ultimo dì percosso fui –

55   o s'elli stanchi li altri a muta a muta
      in Mongibello a la focina negra,
      chiamando 'Buon Vulcano, aiuta, aiuta!'

58   sì com' el fece a la pugna di Flegra,
      e me saetti con tutta sua forza –
      non ne potrebbe aver vendetta allegra.'

61   Allora il duca mio parlò di forza
      tanto, ch'i' non l'avea sì forte udito:
      'O Capaneo, in ciò che non s'ammorza

And over all that barren sand there fell – 28
as slow as Alpine snow on windless days –
a shower of broad-winged fire flakes drifting down.

Recall how Alexander, on his march 31*
across the climes of scorching India,
saw clouds of fire that fell around his troops

and reached the earth still whole. He therefore made 34
his squadrons stamp the ground, since, broken down,
these vapours proved far easier to quell.

So, too, eternally, the flames fell here. 37
The sand caught fire, like tinder under flint,
and doubled – from beneath – the upper punishment.

Unrestingly, their wretched hands jived on – 40
now up, now down, now high, now low, slap, clap! –
to shake fresh drops of ardour from their skin.

So I began: 'You, sir, in everything 43
have conquered all, though not those demons, hard-faced
at the gate of Dis, who stopped us on that step.

That hero there, who's he? Heedless he seems 46
of these incendiaries. Scowling in scorn,
it seems he lies unripened by the rain.'

The man himself roared forth (for he had seen 49
that I, in questioning my lord, meant him):
'What I, once living, was, so dead I am.

Yes! Jupiter may tire the blacksmith out 52
from whom he tore in wrath the thunder spear
by which I stood, on my last day, drilled through;

and others, too, he may exhaust, in shifts 55*
that stoke that black forge under Mount Jabal,
bellowing: "Vulcan! Aid, more aid! Good man!"

just as he did when battle raged at Flegra, 58
and loose his bolts at me with all his force . . .
But no! No sweet revenge he'd have on me!'

My leader then spoke out with greater strength 61
than ever I, till then, had heard him use:
'Oh, Capaneus! Pride yet uninterred!

64   la tua superbia, se' tu più punito;
        nullo martirio, fuor che la tua rabbia,
        sarebbe al tuo furor dolor compito.'

67   Poi si rivolse a me con miglior labbia,
        dicendo: 'Quei fu l'un d'i sette regi
        ch'assiser Tebe; ed ebbe, e par ch'elli abbia,

70   Dio in disdegno, e poco par che 'l pregi;
        ma, com' io dissi lui, li suoi dispetti
        sono al suo petto assai debiti fregi.

73   Or mi vien dietro, e guarda che non metti
        ancor li piedi ne la rena arsiccia,
        ma sempre al bosco tien li piedi stretti.'

76   Tacendo divenimmo là 've spiccia
        fuor de la selva un picciol fiumicello,
        lo cui rossore ancor mi raccapriccia.

79   Quale del Bulicame esce ruscello
        che parton poi tra lor le peccatrici,
        tal per la rena giù sen giva quello.

82   Lo fondo suo e ambo le pendici
        fatt' era 'n pietra, e' margini dallato,
        per ch'io m'accorsi che 'l passo era lici.

85   'Tra tutto l'altro ch'i' t'ho dimostrato
        poscia che noi intrammo per la porta
        lo cui sogliare a nessuno è negato,

88   cosa non fu da li tuoi occhi scorta
        notabile com' è 'l presente rio,
        che sovra sé tutte fiammelle ammorta.'

91   Queste parole fuor del duca mio;
        per ch'io 'l pregai che mi largisse 'l pasto
        di cui largito m'avea il disio.

94   'In mezzo mar siede un paese guasto,'
        diss' elli allora, 'che s'appella Creta,
        sotto 'l cui rege fu già 'l mondo casto.

97   Una montagna v'è che già fu lieta
        d'acqua e di fronde, che si chiamò Ida;
        or è diserta come cosa vieta.

This punishment, in consequence, is yours.   64
No agony, except your own great rage,
would serve as proper answer to your ire.'

And then – a better look around his lips –   67
he turned to me. 'This man,' he said, 'a king,
was one of seven laying siege to Thebes.

God he disdained – he seems to, still – and seemed   70
to pay Him scant regard. So, as I said:
disdain alone must be his sole medallion.

And now keep close behind. Take every care.   73
Do not set foot upon these blistering sands.
Follow the wood's verge round at every step.'

In silence now, continuing, we came   76
to where a rill flows spurting from the grove.
Remembering its redness, I still squirm.

As in Viterbo there's the Bubble Brook –   79*
which scarlet women, bathing, share between them –
so this stream took its course across the sand.

That rivulet, in bed and bank, was formed   82
of stone, as also were the margins by its side.
This, I could tell, was where our best path lay.

'Among so many other things that I –   85
since entering the gate through which
no foot is ever disallowed an entry –

have shown to you, nothing your eyes have spied   88
has been more notable than this stream here,
above which all the sparks grow dim and die.'

These were the words my leader spoke to me.   91
And I besought him, through his great largesse,
to grant the food in granting me the hunger.

'Mid-sea,' he said, 'there lies a land now waste.   94*
To us, this land is known as Crete, where once,
when Saturn ruled as king, the world was chaste.

A mountain stands there, Idaeus its name.   97*
This, once, rejoiced in streams and leafy fronds.
But now it stands abandoned like forbidden ground.

100   Rea la scelse già per cuna fida
del suo figliuolo, e per celarlo meglio
quando piangea, vi facea far le grida.

103   Dentro dal monte sta dritto un gran veglio,
che tien volte le spalle inver' Dammiata
e Roma guarda come suo speglio.

106   La sua testa è di fin oro formata,
e puro argento son le braccia e 'l petto,
poi e' di rame infino a la forcata;

109   da indi in giuso è tutto ferro eletto,
salvo che 'l destro piede è terra cotta;
e sta 'n su quel, più che 'n su l'altro, eretto.

112   Ciascuna parte, fuor che l'oro, è rotta
d'una fessura che lagrime goccia,
le quali, accolte, fóran quella grotta.

115   Lor corso in questa valle si diroccia;
fanno Acheronte, Stige e Flegetonta;
poi sen van giù per questa stretta doccia

118   infin, là ove più non si dismonta,
fanno Cocito; e qual sia quello stagno
tu lo vedrai; però qui non si conta.'

121   E io a lui: 'Se 'l presente rigagno
si diriva così dal nostro mondo,
perché ci appar pur a questo vivagno?'

124   Ed elli a me: 'Tu sai che 'l loco è tondo;
e tutto che tu sie venuto molto,
pur a sinistra, giù calando al fondo,

127   non se' ancor per tutto 'l cerchio voltò;
per che, se cosa n'apparisce nova,
non de' addur maraviglia al tuo volto.'

130   E io ancor: 'Maestro, ove si trova
Flegetonta e Letè? ché de l'un taci,
e l'altro di' che si fa d'esta piova.'

133   'In tutte tue question certo mi piaci,'
rispuose, 'ma 'l bollor de l'acqua rossa
dovea ben solver l'una che tu faci.

Once, Rhea – when seeking a sanctuary –   100
chose here to lay her boy child, Jove. And then,
to hide his wailings, called for dance and din.

Within those caves an aged man stands tall.   103
His back is turned to Egypt and Damiatta.
Rome is the mirror into which he stares.

His head is modelled in the finest gold.   106
Of purest silver are his arms and breast.
Then downwards to the fork he's brightest brass,
    and all below is iron of choicest ore.   109
The right foot, though, is formed of terracotta.
On that he puts more weight than on the left.

And every part that is not gold is cracked.   112
Tears drizzle down through this single fissure,
then, mingling, penetrate the cavern wall.

Their rocky course cascades to this deep hollow.   115*
They form the Acheron, Styx and Phlegethon.
These then disgorge themselves through this tight race,
    until (since there is no way further on)   118
they all collect as Cocytus. But you yourself
will see that pool. So I'll not tell the tale.'

'If,' I now put to him, 'this gutter flows   121
from somewhere in our human world, then why
do we just see it at this selvage hem?'

'You know,' he said, 'this place is circular.   124
Yet, far as you have sunk in your descent,
your path has always tended to the left.

So you have still not spanned the circle round;   127
and if new things now show themselves to us,
it should not stir amazement on your brow.'

And I kept on at him: 'And so, sire, where   130
are Phlegethon and Lethe found? The one, you say,
rains down in tears. The other you are silent of.'

'By everything you ask,' he said, 'I'm pleased.   133
And yet, as one solution, you should note
the seething redness of the waters here.

136   Letè vedrai, ma fuor di questa fossa,
là dove vanno l'anime a lavarsi
quando la colpa pentuta è rimossa.'

139   Poi disse: 'Omai è tempo da scostarsi
dal bosco; fa che di retro a me vegne:
li margini fan via, che non son arsi,

142   e sopra loro ogne vapor si spegne.'

Lethe you'll see, but far beyond this ditch.   136*
Its waves are where the soul will go to wash,
when guilt, repented, is at last removed.'

    And then: 'It's time for you to leave this wood.   139
So come. Keep close behind me as you do.
The banks, which are not burned, provide a road.

    These vapours are extinguished over it.'   142

CANTO 15

1   Ora cen porta l'un de' duri margini,
e 'l fummo del ruscel di sopra aduggia,
sì che dal foco salva l'acqua e li argini.

4   Qual i Fiamminghi tra Guizzante e Bruggia,
temendo 'l fiotto che 'nver' lor s'avventa,
fanno lo schermo perché 'l mar si fuggia;

7   e quali Padoan lungo la Brenta,
per difender lor ville e lor castelli,
anzi che Carentana il caldo senta:

10   a tale imagine eran fatti quelli,
tutto che né sì alti né sì grossi,
qual che si fosse, lo maestro félli.

13   Già eravam da la selva rimossi
tanto ch'i' non avrei visto dov' era,
perch' io in dietro rivolto mi fossi,

16   quando incontrammo d'anime una schiera
che venian lungo l'argine, e ciascuna
ci riguardava come suol da sera

19   guardare uno altro sotto nuova luna;
e sì ver' noi aguzzavan le ciglia
come 'l vecchio sartor fa ne la cruna.

22   Così adocchiato da cotal famiglia,
fui conosciuto da un, che mi prese
per lo lembo e gridò: 'Qual maraviglia!'

25   E io, quando 'l suo braccio a me distese,
ficcai li occhi per lo cotto aspetto,
sì che 'l viso abbrusciato non difese

CANTO 15

We're carried down by one of those hard shores,   1
while vapours from the brook rise, arching up,
to save both stream and margins from the fire.

Flemings, enflamed – from Wissant on to Bruges –   4
in terror of the floods that blast towards them,
construct great screens to put the sea to flight.

So, too, the Paduans, along the Brent,   7
attempt to shield their castles and estates,
before its source (Carinthia) is touched by heat.

Modelled on some original like these   10
(whatever master hand contrived them so)
these breaks were formed, though not that high or broad.

By now, we'd left the grove so far behind   13
that, even had I turned around to look,
I'd not have glimpsed the tract where it was found.

But here we came across a band of souls   16
who milled around the ditch and met our tread.
And each one peered at us – as people will

on evenings when the moon is new – their brows   19
towards us, wrinkled into squinting blades,
like those of some old tailor at his needle.

Eyed up and down so closely by this clan,   22
I now was recognized, as known, by one
who plucked my hem and cried: 'How marvellous!'

And I – as he then stretched an arm towards me –   25
fixed eyes so keenly through his fire-baked look
that these singed features could not fend away

28   la conoscenza sua al mio 'ntelletto;
        e chinando la mano a la sua faccia,
        rispuosi: 'Siete voi qui, ser Brunetto?'

31   E quelli: 'O figliuol mio, non ti dispiaccia
        se Brunetto Latino un poco teco
        ritorna 'n dietro e lascia andar la traccia.'

34   I' dissi lui: 'Quanto posso, ven preco;
        e se volete che con voi m'asseggia,
        faròl, se piace a costui, che vo seco.'

37   'O figliuol,' disse, 'qual di questa greggia
        s'arresta punto, giace poi cent' anni
        sanz' arrostarsi quando 'l foco il feggia.

40   Però va oltre: i' ti verrò a' panni,
        e poi rigiugnerò la mia masnada,
        che va piangendo i suoi etterni danni.'

43   Io non osava scender de la strada
        per andar par di lui, ma 'l capo chino
        tenea com' uom che reverente vada.

46   El cominciò: 'Qual fortuna o destino
        anzi l'ultimo dì qua giù ti mena?
        e chi è questi che mostra 'l cammino?'

49   'Là sù di sopra, in la vita serena,'
        rispuos' io lui, 'mi smarri' in una valle,
        avanti che l'età mia fosse piena.

52   Pur ier mattina le volsi le spalle:
        questi m'apparve, tornand' io in quella,
        e reducemi a ca per questo calle.'

55   Ed elli a me: 'Se tu segui tua stella,
        non puoi fallire a glorioso porto,
        se ben m'accorsi ne la vita bella;

58   e s'io non fossi sì per tempo morto,
        veggendo il cielo a te così benigno
        dato t'avrei a l'opera conforto.

61   Ma quello ingrato popolo maligno
        che discese di Fiesole *ab* antico,
        e tiene ancor del monte e del macigno,

my mind from knowing, truly, who he was.   28
And, reaching down a hand towards his face,
I answered him: 'Brunetto, sir, are you here?'

'Do not, my dearest son,' he said, 'be vexed,   31
but let Brunetto Latino turn and walk
a while along with you. The troops can run!'

'I pray, sir, to the utmost, do. Or should   34
you wish,' I said, 'I'll sit with you, so long
as this man here agrees. I go with him.'

'Dear boy,' he said, 'if any in this herd   37
should ever pause, he lies a hundred years
powerless to fan these searing fires away.

And so move on. I'll follow at your coat-tails,   40
then catch up later with that entourage,
which, as it goes, bewails eternal loss.'

I did not dare climb down to quit the causeway   43
and walk with him on equal terms. But still,
as though in reverence, I kept my head bowed low.

'What chance or destiny,' he then began,   46
'leads you down here before your final day?
And who is this that shows the way to you?'

'There, up above,' I answered him, 'where life   49
is halcyon, I lost myself – my path all blurred –
in some great deep before my years were full.

Only as dawn rose, yesterday, I turned   52
aside. Then he – as yet again I turned –
appeared, and guides me on the road back home.'

'If,' so he answered, 'you pursue your star,   55
then doubtless you will reach a glorious goal,
supposing, in the happy life, I knew you well.

And I myself (had not I died too soon),   58
seeing how kind the Heavens looked on you,
would willingly have helped you in your work.

But that malignant and ungrateful race   61*
descending *ab antico* from Fiesole
(they still retain the taint of crag and hill)

64   ti si farà, per tuo ben far, nimico;
        ed è ragion, ché tra li lazzi sorbi
        si disconvien fruttare al dolce fico.

67   Vecchia fama nel mondo li chiama orbi;
        gent' è avara, invidiosa e superba:
        dai lor costumi fa che tu ti forbi.

70   La tua fortuna tanto onor ti serba
        che l'una parte e l'altra avranno fame
        di te; ma lungi fia dal becco l'erba.

73   Faccian le bestie fiesolane strame
        di lor medesme, e non tocchin la pianta,
        s'alcuna surge ancora in lor letame,

76   in cui riviva la sementa santa
        di que' Roman che vi rimaser quando
        fu fatto il nido di malizia tanta.'

79   'Se fosse tutto pieno il mio dimando,'
        rispuos' io lui, 'voi non sareste ancora
        de l'umana natura posto in bando;

82   ché 'n la mente m'è fitta, e or m'accora,
        la cara e buona imagine paterna
        di voi quando nel mondo ad ora ad ora

85   m'insegnavate come l'uom s'etterna;
        e quant' io l'abbia in grado mentr'io vivo
        convien che ne la mia lingua si scerna.

88   Ciò che narrate di mio corso scrivo,
        e serbolo a chiosar con altro testo
        a donna che saprà, s'a lei arrivo.

91   Tanto vogli' io che vi sia manifesto,
        pur che mia coscienza non mi garra,
        ch'a la Fortuna, come vuol, son presto.

94   Non è nuova a li orecchi miei tal arra:
        però giri Fortuna la sua rota
        come le piace, e 'l villan la sua marra.'

97   Lo mio maestro allora in su la gota
        destra si volse in dietro e riguardommi;
        poi disse: 'Bene ascolta chi la nota.'

will act, because you act so well, as bitter foes.   64
That much is logical: no luscious fig
can rightly thrive where small, sour sorbus grows.

The world, since ancient times, has known they're blind.   67
The tribe is grasping, envious and proud.
Keep yourself clean of habits of their kind.

Fortune for you reserves such great renown   70
that both these factions – Black and White – will seek
to set their teeth in you. Keep goats from grass!

Well may these cattle from Fiesole   73
make themselves straw but never touch the sprout
that springs (if any does within their dung)

to bring to life the sacred seed of Rome –   76
of those remaining when that ancient place
became the very home and nest of malice.'

'If all,' I said to him, 'that I might ask   79
were answered, and in full, then you would not
be exiled, as you are, from human nature.

Fixed in my thoughts, and working at my heart,   82
an image of you still endures – a dear, good father –
as, in the world, you were when hour by hour

you taught me how a man becomes eternal.   85
How great my gratitude must be, will show,
while I still live, in all my tongue will tell.

I write, as you recount it here, the story   88
of my future course, and keep your words with others.
A lady, if I come to her, will comment.

On this point only I would have you clear: 91
that I, so long as conscience does not chide,
am well prepared for all that Fortune wills.

In what you vouch, my ears hear nothing new.   94
Let Fortune, therefore, do as Fortune pleases –
whirl at her wheel like yokels at their hoe.'

My teacher, who had now turned right-about,   97
looked back at me and fixed me with his eye.
'Those listen well,' he said, 'who take good note.'

100   Né per tanto di men parlando vommi
con ser Brunetto, e dimando chi sono
li suoi compagni più noti e più sommi.

103   Ed elli a me: 'Saper d'alcuno è buono;
de li altri fia laudabile tacerci,
ché 'l tempo saria corto a tanto suono.

106   In somma sappi che tutti fur cherci
e litterati grandi e di gran fama,
d'un peccato medesmo al mondo lerci.

109   Priscian sen va con quella turba grama,
e Francesco d'Accorso anche; e vedervi,
s'avessi avuto di tal tigna brama,

112   colui potei che dal servo de' servi
fu trasmutato d'Arno in Bacchiglione,
dove lasciò li mal protesi nervi.

115   Di più direi, ma 'l venire e 'l sermone
più lungo esser non può, però ch'i' veggio
là surger nuovo fummo del sabbione.

118   Gente vien con la quale esser non deggio.
Sieti raccomandato il mio Tesoro,
nel qual io vivo ancora, e più non cheggio.'

121   Poi si rivolse, e parve di coloro
che corrono a Verona il drappo verde
per la campagna; e parve di costoro

124   quelli che vince, non colui che perde.

So on I go, speaking with lawyer Brunetto.   100
I ask who his companions are, the great
and good, the eminent, and men of note.

    'Of some,' he said, 'you're right to want to know.   103
More laudable of others not to speak.
Our time would be too short for all that din.

    But all of them, be sure, were men of learning,   106
authorities and dons of world renown,
besmirched, when living, with the self-same sin.

    And so, among this dismal crowd, runs Priscian.   109*
D'Accorso, too – the Prof. And if you yearn
to set your eyes on such-like mangy scabs,

    you could. That bishop there! The Slave of Slaves   112
transferred him to Vicenza from the Arno.
He left his muscles, ill-distended, there.

    I would say more. Yet further I may not   115
advance nor any longer talk with you.
I see new smoke there, rising from the sand.

    I can't consort with those who now draw near.   118*
My Treasury, may that commend itself.
In that, I still live on. I ask no more.'

    Around he swung. To me he seemed like one   121*
who, in the fields around Verona, runs
for that prize, a length of green festoon.

    He seemed to be the one that wins, not loses.   124

CANTO 16

1   Già era in loco onde s'udia 'l rimbombo
de l'acqua che cadea ne l'altro giro,
simile a quel che l'arnie fanno rombo,

4   quando tre ombre insieme si partiro,
correndo, d'una torma che passava
sotto la pioggia de l'aspro martiro.

7   Venian ver' noi, e ciascuna gridava:
'Sòstati tu ch'a l'abito ne sembri
essere alcun di nostra terra prava.'

10 Ahimè, che piaghe vidi ne' lor membri,
ricenti e vecchie, da le fiamme incese!
Ancor men duol pur ch'i' me ne rimembri.

13 A le lor grida il mio dottor s'attese;
volse 'l viso ver' me, e: 'Or aspetta,'
disse, 'a costor si vuole esser cortese.

16 E se non fosse il foco che saetta
la natura del loco, i' dicerei
che meglio stesse a te che a lor la fretta.'

19 Ricominciar, come noi restammo, ei
l'antico verso; e quando a noi fuor giunti,
fenno una rota di sé tutti e trei.

22 Qual sogliono i campion far nudi e unti,
avvisando lor presa e lor vantaggio
prima che sien tra lor battuti e punti:

25 così rotando, ciascuno il visaggio
drizzava a me, sì che 'n contraro il collo
faceva ai piè continuo viaggio.

CANTO 16

    I stood already where the roar and boom   1
of waters falling to the next great ring
could now be heard – a rumble like a beehive.

    But then appeared, together, at the run,   4
three shadows, swerving from a further squad
of those in rasping torment from the rain.

    Towards us, as they came, each cried aloud: 7
'Stop there! To us, it seems, you're dressed like one
who travels from our own degenerate homeland.'

    No! No! I saw how branded by the bite   10
of fire their limbs all were. New wounds! Old scars!
This, though mere memory, still brings me pain.

    My teacher paused, attending to their cries.   13
And then, his eyes on me, he said: 'Now wait.
We owe to these men here some courtesy.

    Indeed, were not the nature of this place   16
to shoot down barbs of fire, then haste (I'd say)
should properly be shown by you, not them.'

    And so again, as now we came to rest,   19
they all began the song they'd sung before
and, turning, formed among themselves a wheel.

    Compare: prize wrestlers, with their bare skin oiled, 22
circle – until they clash, then punch and gouge –
in search of some advantage, grip or hold.

    These likewise. As they wheeled around, each fixed 25
their glances hard on me. And so their necks
turned counter always to the track they trod.

28   E: 'Se miseria d'esto loco sollo
      rende in dispetto noi e nostri prieghi,'
      cominciò l'uno, 'e 'l tinto aspetto e brollo,

31   la fama nostra il tuo animo pieghi
      a dirne chi tu se', che i vivi piedi
      così sicuro per lo 'nferno freghi.

34   Questi, l'orme di cui pestar mi vedi,
      tutto che nudo e dipelato vada,
      fu di grado maggior che tu non credi:

37   nepote fu de la buona Gualdrada;
      Guido Guerra ebbe nome, e in sua vita
      fece col senno assai e con la spada.

40   L'altro, ch'appresso me la rena trita,
      è Tegghiaio Aldobrandi, la cui voce
      nel mondo sù dovria esser gradita.

43   E io, che posto son con loro in croce,
      Iacopo Rusticucci fui, e certo
      la fiera moglie più ch'altro mi nuoce.'

46   S'i' fossi stato dal foco coperto,
      gittato mi sarei tra lor di sotto,
      e credo che 'l dottor l'avria sofferto;

49   ma perch' io mi sarei brusciato e cotto,
      vinse paura la mia buona voglia
      che di loro abbracciar mi facea ghiotto.

52   Poi cominciai: 'Non dispetto, ma doglia
      la vostra condizion dentro mi fisse,
      tanta che tardi tutta si dispoglia,

55   tosto che questo mio segnor mi disse
      parole per le quali i' mi pensai
      che qual voi siete, tal gente venisse.

58   Di vostra terra sono, e sempre mai
      l'ovra di voi e li onorati nomi
      con affezion ritrassi e ascoltai.

61   Lascio lo fele e vo per dolci pomi
      promessi a me per lo verace duca;
      ma 'nfino al centro pria convien ch'i' tomi.'

'The misery,' thus one began, 'of these   28
vile sands may render us, and all our prayers,
contemptible, our faces, too, now black and burned.

But let our reputations bend your heart.   31
And who are you – now tell – whose living step,
in perfect safety, scours the paths of Hell?

This man, whose prints my own feet trample on,   34
although he now goes naked, shorn of hair,
was once of higher rank than you'd imagine.

Grandson by birth of our good Gualdrada,   37*
he was, by title, Conte Guido Guerra.
Much he achieved alive with mind and sword.

The other next to him who flails the sand   40
is Lord Tegghiaio of the Aldobrands.
He ought to have more pleased the world in word.

I, in excruciating pain with them,   43
was Iacopo Rusticucci. And, yes,
it was my wife who did me greatest harm.'

If only I'd had cover from the fire,   46
I'd willingly have flung myself among them.
(I think my teacher would have suffered this.)

But since, down there, I'd soon have singed and baked,   49
fear got the better of the good intent
that stirred my appetite for their embrace.

So I began: 'Great grief, not scornfulness,   52
to see your state was planted in my heart
(and only slowly will it shed its leaves)

the instant that my lord, in words to me,   55
led all my inner thoughts to understand
that persons such as you might soon come by.

I am of your place, too. So, I have heard –   58
and always with affection have proclaimed –
the deeds you've done and honour of your name.

I now take leave of galling fruits, to seek   61
sweet apples, promised by my lord in truth,
but first must reach the centre of the circle.'

64   'Se lungamente l'anima conduca
        le membra tue,' rispuose quelli ancora,
        'e se la fama tua dopo te luca,

67   cortesia e valor dì se dimora
        ne la nostra città sì come suole,
        o se del tutto se n'è gita fora:

70   chè Guiglielmo Borsiere, il qual si duole
        con noi per poco e va là coi compagni,
        assai ne cruccia con le sue parole.'

73   'La gente nuova e i sùbiti guadagni
        orgoglio e dismisura han generata,
        Fiorenza, in te, sì che tu già ten piagni.'

76   Così gridai con la faccia levata;
        e i tre, che ciò inteser per risposta,
        guardar l'un l'altro com' al ver si guata.

79   'Se l'altre volte sì poco ti costa,'
        rispuoser tutti, 'il satisfare altrui,
        felice te se sì parli a tua posta!

82   Però, se campi d'esti luoghi bui
        e torni a riveder le belle stelle,
        quando ti gioverà dicere "I' fui,"

85   fa che di noi a la gente favelle.'
        Indi rupper la rota, e a fuggirsi
        ali sembiar le gambe loro isnelle.

88   Un amen non saria possuto dirsi
        tosto così com' e' fuoro spariti;
        per ch'al maestro parve di partirsi.

91   Io lo seguiva, e poco eravam iti,
        che 'l suon de l'acqua n'era sì vicino,
        che per parlar saremmo a pena uditi.

94   Come quel fiume c'ha proprio cammino
        prima dal Monte Viso 'nver' levante
        da la sinistra costa d'Apennino,

97   che si chiama Acquacheta suso, avante
        che si divalli giù nel basso letto,
        e a Forlì di quel nome è vacante,

'Long may your soul lead forth your living limbs!'   64
So, in reply, said one of them. 'And – grant
your fame may long shine after you! – then say:

do courtesy and valour dwell, as once   67
they did, within the circuit of our city walls?
Or have they utterly departed thence?

Report of this, from courtly Borsiere   70*
(who only joined us here of late, and goes
with our companions there), has caused us pain.'

'That race of newly rich, and rapid gains,   73
these seeds, Fiorenza, bring to flower in you
excess and pride. And you already weep for that.'

With head thrown back, I cried this, all aloud,   76
and they, the three (accepting this response),
glanced each to each like those who've heard plain truth.

'If at so little cost,' they said, 'you speak   79
so well and satisfy what others seek,
then you may happily pronounce at will.

And so, should you escape from these dark haunts,   82
and go once more to see the lovely stars,
when you, with pleasure, say that "I was there",

then do, we beg you, speak of us to others.'   85
With this they broke their wheel and, as they fled,
their agile limbs in flight were quick as wings.

No 'amen' ever was so swiftly said   88
as these three disappeared before our eyes.
And now my teacher thought that we could leave.

I came behind. But now, not travelling far,   91
the sound of the water was so near at hand
that we could scarcely hear each other speak.

Compare: a river, near its native source,   94*
runs through the eastern Apennines due east,
and first descends the slopes of Monte Viso.

Its tranquil name up there is Acqua Cheta.   97
But then, on flowing to its lower bed,
at Forlì it assumes a different mode,

100   rimbomba là sovra San Benedetto
       de l'Alpe, per cadere ad una scesa
       ove dovria per mille esser recetto:

103   così, giù d'una ripa discoscesa,
       trovammo risonar quell'acqua tinta
       sì che 'n poc' ora avria l'orecchia offesa.

106   Io avea una corda intorno cinta,
       e con essa pensai alcuna volta
       prender la lonza a la pelle dipinta.

109   Poscia ch'io l'ebbi tutta da me sciolta,
       sì come 'l duca m'avea comandato,
       porsila a lui aggroppata e ravvolta.

112   Ond' ei si volse inver' lo destro lato,
       e alquanto di lunge da la sponda
       la gittò giuso in quell' alto burrato.

115   'E' pur convien che novità risponda,'
       dicea fra me medesmo, 'al novo cenno
       che 'l maestro con l'occhio sì seconda.'

118   Ahi quanto cauti li uomini esser dienno
       presso a color che non veggion pur l'ovra,
       ma per entro i pensier miran col senno!

121   El disse a me: 'Tosto verrà di sovra
       ciò ch'io attendo e che il tuo pensier sogna;
       tosto convien ch'al tuo viso si scovra.'

124   Sempre a quel ver c'ha faccia di menzogna
       de' l'uom chiuder le labbra fin ch'el puote,
       però che sanza colpa fa vergogna;

127   ma qui tacer nol posso, e per le note
       di questa comedìa, lettor, ti giuro,
       s'elle non sien di lunga grazia vòte,

130   ch'i' vidi per quell' aere grosso e scuro
       venir notando una figura in suso,
       maravigliosa ad ogne cor sicuro:

133   sì come torna colui che va giuso
       talora a solver l'àncora ch'aggrappa
       o scoglio o altro che nel mare è chiuso,

136   che 'n sù si stende e da piè si rattrappa.

and thunders here, in one great bound, above   100
the Alp Saint Benedict, where – were it eased
from ledge to ledge – the height would need a thousand.

So, likewise, down through one great shattered force,   103
we found, resounding there, a blackened stream –
the din of which would soon have stunned our ears.

Around my waist I wore a braided cord,   106*
and had on past occasion thought, by this,
to snare the leopard with its painted hide.

My leader told me I should slip this off.   109
And when I'd got it wound from round my waist,
I handed it across in twisted knots.

And then he turned towards his right-hand side,   112
and flung it, bunched, some distance from the bank.
It fell, to find the depths of that great sink.

'Astounding things,' I told myself, 'are bound   115
to come at this astounding sign, which now
my master follows with his waiting eye.'

How cautious we must always be when faced   118
with those who, far beyond observing deeds,
can gaze in wisdom on our very thoughts.

So now he said: 'There soon shall rise what I   121
expect (what you in thought now dream) will come.
All shall be, soon, uncovered to your eyes.'

Always, to every truth that looks, in face,   124
like lies, one ought (quite firmly) bar the lip
lest, guiltless, what one says should still bring shame.

I cannot, though, be silent here. Reader,   127
I swear by every rhyme this comedy
has caused to chime (may it not lack long favour)

that now, through dark and fatty air, I saw –   130
to strike sheer wonder in the steadiest heart –
approaching us a figure swimming up,

as any diver might who'd gone below   133
to loose an anchor snagged on rocks (or something
other, hidden in the sea) and now comes back,

arms stretching high, legs drawn to make the stroke.   136

CANTO 17

1   'Ecco la fiera con la coda aguzza,
     che passa i monti e rompe i muri e l'armi!
     Ecco colei che tutto 'l mondo appuzza!'

4   Sì cominciò lo mio duca a parlarmi;
     e accennolle che venisse a proda
     vicino al fin d'i passeggiati marmi.

7   E quella sozza imagine di froda
     sen venne, e arrivò la testa e 'l busto,
     ma 'n su la riva non trasse la coda.

10   La faccia sua era faccia d'uom giusto,
     tanto benigna avea di fuor la pelle,
     e d'un serpente tutto l'altro fusto;

13   due branche avea pilose insin l'ascelle;
     lo dosso e 'l petto e ambedue le coste
     dipinti avea di nodi e di rotelle:

16   con più color, sommesse e sovraposte,
     non fer mai drappi Tartari né Turchi,
     né fuor tai tele per Aragne imposte.

19   Come talvolta stanno a riva i burchi,
     che parte sono in acqua e parte in terra,
     e come là tra li Tedeschi lurchi

22   lo bivero s'assetta a far sua guerra:
     così la fiera pessima si stava
     su l'orlo ch'è di pietra e 'l sabbion serra.

25   Nel vano tutta sua coda guizzava,
     torcendo in sù la venenosa forca
     ch'a guisa di scorpion la punta armava.

CANTO 17

'Behold! The beast who soars with needle tail   1
through mountains, shattering shields and city walls!
Behold! The beast that stinks out all the world!'

   To me, my lord spoke thus, then beckoned up   4*
the monster to approach the jutting prow
that marked the end of all our marble paths.

   It came, that filthy image of deceit.   7
Its head and trunk it grounded on the shore.
It did not draw its tailpiece to the bank.

   The face was that of any honest man,   10
the outer skin all generosity.
Its timber, though, was serpent through and through:

   two clawing grabs, and hairy to the armpits,   13
its back and breast and ribcage all tattooed
with knot designs and spinning little whorls.

   No Turk or Tartar has woven finer drapes,   16*
more many-coloured in their pile or tuft.
Nor did Arachne thread such tapestries.

   Compare: on foreshores, sometimes, dinghies stand   19
in water partly, partly on the shingle –
as likewise, in the land of drunken Germans,

   beavers will do, advancing their attack.   22
So did this beast – the worst that there can be –
there on the rocky rim that locks the sand.

   Out into emptiness it swung its tail,   25
and twisted upwards its venomous fork.
The tip was armed like any scorpion's.

28   Lo duca disse: 'Or convien che si torca
la nostra via un poco insino a quella
bestia malvagia che colà si corca.'

31   Però scendemmo a la destra mammella
e diece passi femmo in su lo stremo,
per ben cessar la rena e la fiammella.

34   E quando noi a lei venuti semo,
poco più oltre veggio in su la rena
gente seder propinqua al loco scemo.

37   Quivi 'l maestro: 'Acciò che tutta piena
esperienza d'esto giron porti,'
mi disse, 'va, e vedi la lor mena.

40   Li tuoi ragionamenti sian là corti;
mentre che torni, parlerò con questa,
che ne conceda i suoi omeri forti.'

43   Così ancor su per la strema testa
di quel settimo cerchio tutto solo
andai, dove sedea la gente mesta.

46   Per li occhi fora scoppiava lor duolo;
di qua, di là soccorrien con le mani
quando a' vapori, e quando al caldo suolo:

49   non altrimenti fan di state i cani
or col ceffo or col piè, quando son morsi
o da pulci o da mosche o da tafani.

52   Poi che nel viso a certi li occhi porsi,
ne' quali 'l doloroso foco casca,
non ne conobbi alcun; ma io m'accorsi

55   che dal collo a ciascun pendea una tasca
ch'avea certo colore e certo segno,
e quindi par che 'l loro occhio si pasca.

58   E com' io riguardando tra lor vegno,
in una borsa gialla vidi azzurro
che d'un leone avea faccia e contegno.

61   Poi, procedendo di mio sguardo il curro,
vidine un'altra come sangue rossa,
mostrando un'oca bianca più che burro.

My leader said: 'We need to bend our path   28
a little further down, towards that vile
monstrosity that's lolling underneath.'

So down we went, towards the right-hand pap.   31
Ten paces, and we'd reached the very edge,
stepping well clear of flames and burning shoals.

And then, on getting to that spot, I saw,   34
a little further on along the sandbar,
a group just sitting near the gaping waste.

And here my teacher said: 'To carry back   37
experience of the ring that we're now in,
go over there and look at their behaviour.

But do not stay to talk at any length.   40
Till you return, I'll parley with this thing,
for him to grant us use of his great thews.'

So once again, along the outward brow   43
of Circle Seven I progressed alone
to where there sat these souls in misery.

The pain they felt erupted from their eyes.   46
All up and down and round about, their hands
sought remedies for burning air and ground.

Dogs in the heat of summer do the same,   49
stung by the bluebottle, gadfly and flea,
swatting at swarms with paw pads or with snout.

On some of these – these faces under showers   52
of grievous, never-ceasing rain – I set my eyes.
I recognized no single one, but noticed

round the neck of each a cash bag hung   55
(each with its own insignia and blaze),
on which their staring eyes appeared to graze.

So I, too, gazing, passed among them all,   58*
and saw, imprinted on a yellow purse,
a blue device, in face and pose a lion.

Then, as my view went trundling further on,   61
I saw another, with a blood-red field –
the goose it bore was whiter, far, than butter.

64   E un che d'una scrofa azzurra e grossa
segnato avea lo suo sacchetto bianco,
mi disse: 'Che fai tu in questa fossa?

67   Or te ne va; e perché se' vivo anco,
sappi che 'l mio vicin Vitaliano
sederà qui dal mio sinistro fianco.

70   Con questi Fiorentin son padoano:
spesse fiate mi 'ntronan li orecchi
gridando: "Vegna 'l cavalier sovrano,

73   che recherà la tasca con tre becchi!"'
Qui distorse la bocca e di fuor trasse
la lingua, come bue che 'l naso lecchi.

76   E io, temendo no 'l più star crucciasse
lui che di poco star m'avea 'mmonito,
torna'mi in dietro da l'anime lasse.

79   Trova' il duca mio ch'era salito
già su la groppa del fiero animale,
e disse a me: 'Or sie forte e ardito:

82   omai si scende per sì fatte scale.
Monta dinanzi, ch'i' voglio esser mezzo,
sì che la coda non possa far male.'

85   Qual è colui che sì presso ha 'l riprezzo
de la quartana c'ha già l'unghie smorte
e triema tutto pur guardando 'l rezzo:

88   tal divenn' io a le parole porte;
ma vergogna mi fé le sue minacce,
che innanzi a buon segnor fa servo forte.

91   I' m'assettai in su quelle spallacce;
'Sì,' volli dir, ma la voce non venne
com' io credetti: 'Fa che tu m'abbracce.'

94   Ma esso, ch'altra volta mi sovvenne
ad altro forse, tosto ch'i' montai
con le braccia m'avvinse e mi sostenne;

97   e disse: 'Gerion, moviti omai;
le rote larghe, e lo scender sia poco:
pensa la nova soma che tu hai.'

And then I heard (from one whose neat, white sack   64
was marked in azure with a pregnant sow):
'What are you after in this awful hole?

Do go away! Yet you – as Vitaliano is –   67
are still alive. Then understand me, please:
he'll sit on my left flank, my one-time neighbour.

I'm Paduan, among these Florentines,   70
and often they all thunder in my ears:
"Oh, let him come," they'll scream, "that sovereign knight,

    who'll bring the bag that bears three rampant goats."'   73
At which, in throes, he wrenched his mouth awry
and curled his tongue, like any ox, to lick his nose.

And I, who feared that, if I lingered long,   76
I'd irritate the one who'd said 'Be brief',
now turned my back upon these worn-out souls.

My leader, I discovered there, had jumped   79
already on that fearsome creature's rump.
'Come on,' he urged, 'be stalwart and courageous.

From now on we'll descend by stairs like these.   82
Mount at the front so I can come between,
to see the tail won't bring you any harm.'

Like someone shivering as the grip of 'flu   85
spreads over him, pale to the fingernails,
who trembles merely at the sight of shade . . .

well, that was me, as these words carried over.   88
The threat of shame, however, when one's lord
is near, emboldens one to serve him well.

I settled down between those gruesome shoulders.   91
I wished to say (my voice, though, would not come):
'Yes. Please! Be sure you hold me very firm.'

He, who in many an earlier 'perhaps'   94
had aided me, as soon as I got on,
flinging his arms around me, hugged me tight,

    and said: 'Go on, then, Geryon. Cast out!   97
Wheel wide about to make a smooth descent.
Think of the strange new burden on your back.'

100   Come la navicella esce di loco
         in dietro in dietro, sì quindi si tolse;
         e poi ch'al tutto si sentì a gioco,

103   là 'v' era 'l petto, la coda rivolse,
         e quella tesa, come anguilla, mosse,
         e con le branche l'aere a sé raccolse.

106   Maggior paura non credo che fosse
         quando Fetonte abbandonò li freni,
         per che 'l ciel, come pare ancor, si cosse,

109   né quando Icaro misero le reni
         sentì spennar per la scaldata cera,
         gridando il padre a lui, 'Mala via tieni!'

112   che fu la mia, quando vidi ch'i' era
         ne l'aere d'ogne parte, e vidi spenta
         ogne veduta fuor che de la fera.

115   Ella sen va notando lenta lenta;
         rota e discende, ma non me n'accorgo
         se non che al viso e di sotto mi venta.

118   Io sentia già da la man destra il gorgo
         far sotto noi un orribile scroscio,
         per che con li occhi 'n giù la testa sporgo.

121   Allor fu' io più timido a lo stoscio,
         però ch'i' vidi fuochi e senti' pianti;
         ond' io tremando tutto mi raccoscio.

124   E vidi poi, ché nol vedea davanti,
         lo scendere e 'l girar per li gran mali
         che s'appressavan da diversi canti.

127   Come 'l falcon ch'è stato assai su l'ali,
         che sanza veder logoro o uccello
         fa dire al falconiere: 'Omè, tu cali!'

130   discende lasso onde si move isnello,
         per cento rote, e da lunge si pone
         dal suo maestro, disdegnoso e fello:

133   così ne puose al fondo Gerione,
         al piè al piè de la stagliata rocca,
         e, discarcate le nostre persone,

136   si dileguò come da corda cocca.

Slowly astern, astern, as ferries leave   100
the quay where they had docked, so he moved out.
Then, only when he felt himself ride free,

he turned the tail where breast had been before,   103
and – stretching long, as eels might do – set sail,
paddling the air towards him with his paws.

No greater fear (so, truly, I believe)   106*
was felt as Phaeton let the reins go loose,
and scorched the sky as still it is today,

nor yet by ill-starred Icarus – his loins   109
unfeathering as the wax grew warm – to whom
his father screamed aloud: 'You're going wrong!'

And then with fear I saw, on every side,   112
that I was now in air, and every sight
extinguished, save my view of that great beast.

So swimming slowly, it goes on its way.   115
It wheels. It descends. This I don't notice –
except an upward breeze now fans my face.

By then I heard, beneath us to the right,   118
the roar of some appalling cataract.
And so I leant my head out, looking down.

More timorous of falling still, I saw   121
that there were fires down there and heard shrill screams.
Trembling, I huddled back and locked my thighs.

And then I saw, as I had not before,   124
the going-down – the spirals of great harm –
on every side now coming ever nearer.

A falcon, having long been on the wing,   127
and seeing neither lure nor bird to prey on,
compels the falconer to sigh: 'You're coming in,'

then sinks down wearily to where it left so fast.   130
A hundred turns – and then, far from its lord,
it lands, disdainful, spiteful in its scorn.

So, too, did Geryon, to place us on the floor,   133
the very foot of that sheer, towering cliff.
And then, unburdened of our persons now,

vanished at speed like barbed bolt from a bow.   136

CANTO 18

1   Luogo è in inferno detto Malebolge,
    tutto di pietra di color ferrigno,
    come la cerchia che dintorno il volge.

4   Nel dritto mezzo del campo maligno
    vaneggia un pozzo assai largo e profondo,
    di cui *suo loco* dicerò l'ordigno.

7   Quel cinghio che rimane adunque è tondo
    tra 'l pozzo e 'l piè de l'alta ripa dura,
    e ha distinto in dieci valli il fondo.

10 Quale, dove per guardia de le mura
    più e più fossi cingon i castelli,
    la parte dove son rende figura:

13 tale imagine quivi facean quelli;
    e come a tai fortezze da' lor sogli
    a la ripa di fuor son ponticelli:

16 così da imo de la roccia scogli
    movien che ricidien li argini e' fossi
    infino al pozzo che i tronca e raccogli.

19 In questo luogo, de la schiena scossi
    di Gerion, trovammoci; e 'l poeta
    tenne a sinistra, e io dietro mi mossi.

22 A la man destra vidi nova pieta,
    novo tormento e novi frustatori,
    di che la prima bolgia era repleta.

25 Nel fondo erano ignudi i peccatori;
    dal mezzo in qua ci venien verso 'l volto,
    di là con noi, ma con passi maggiori:

CANTO 18

There is in Hell a place called Rottenpockets,   1
rock, all rock, its colour rusted iron,
as is the wall that circles all around.

Dead in the centre of that poisoned plain   4
a well yawns open – empty, broad and deep.
Of that (when it's 'convenient') I'll have my say.

For now, between the well mouth and the clench   7
of cliff, a circling belt goes round, its floor
divided into ten deep trenches.

Compare: to guard the outer walls of castles,   10
moats in concentric multiples are dug,
and form the figure of a wheel around them.

That was the pattern that these trenches made.   13
And where, from fortresses, pontoons run out
to link each threshold to the other shore,

so, at the bottom of the precipice,   16
radials ride over every bank and ditch
till, at the pit, they're stopped and then sucked in.

This was the place where – shaken from the spine   19
of Geryon – we found ourselves. The poet
took the left-hand fork. I followed in his track.

Then, to my right, I saw fresh suffering: 22
new whips, new torments and new torturers,
and Pocket One, with these, was all a-flutter.

Down in those depths, stark naked, there were sinners   25
who came, on this side of a line, face on,
and faster, in our direction, on the other.

28   come i Roman per l'essercito molto,
        l'anno del giubileo, su per lo ponte
        hanno a passar la gente modo colto,

31   che da l'un lato tutti hanno la fronte
        verso 'l castello e vanno a Santo Pietro,
        da l'altra sponda vanno verso 'l monte.

34   Di qua, di là, su per lo sasso tetro
        vidi demon cornuti con gran ferze
        che li battien crudelmente di retro.

37   Ahi come facean lor levar le berze
        a le prime percosse! già nessuno
        le seconde aspettava né le terze.

40   Mentr' io andava, li occhi miei in uno
        furo scontrati, e io sì tosto dissi:
        'Già di veder costui non son digiuno.'

43   Per ch'io a figurarlo i piedi affissi;
        e 'l dolce duca meco si ristette
        e assentio ch'alquanto in dietro gissi.

46   E quel frustato celar si credette
        bassando 'l viso; ma poco li valse,
        ch'io dissi: 'O tu che l'occhio a terra gette,

49   se le fazion che porti non son false,
        Venedico se' tu Caccianemico.
        Ma che ti mena a sì pungenti salse?'

52   Ed elli a me: 'Mal volontier lo dico,
        ma sforzami la tua chiara favella,
        che mi fa sovvenir del mondo antico.

55   I' fui colui che la Ghisolabella
        condussi a far la voglia del marchese,
        come che suoni la sconcia novella.

58   E non pur io qui piango bolognese;
        anzi n'è questo loco tanto pieno
        che tante lingue non son ora apprese

61   a dicer sipa tra Sàvena e Reno;
        e se di ciò vuoi fede o testimonio,
        rècati a mente il nostro avaro seno.'

The Romans, in the Jubilee, devised   28*
a way for pilgrims and pedestrians,
in all their multitudes, to cross the Bridge

    so that, on one side (making for Saint Peter's),   31
they faced the Castle and took, conversely,
the other lane when heading for the Hill.

    This way, that way, over the dismal rock,   34
there were (I saw them!) horny demons lashing,
lashing the rear with their vicious scourges.

    Ouch! Even at the first stroke they lifted   37
their trotters; and none of them, for certain,
stayed for second helpings – fewer for thirds.

    But then, as I was moving on, looks clashed,   40
my own and one of theirs. I said straight off:
'There's one I've seen before. Once was enough.'

    To get him in my sights, I stopped my stride;   43
and, pausing quietly along with me,
my guide now let me turn a short way back.

    The body beaten abased its gaze, as if   46
it thought he really could hide. That didn't work.
'You there,' I said, 'Eyes-down! Bashful, are we?

    Assuming that your profile's not a lie,   49*
then you are Venedico Caccianemico.
So what brings you to this killing pickle?'

    And he to me: 'I grudge you my reply.   52
You and your bright words grind one out of me,
and make me call the world that was to mind.

    Foul tittletattle got this right. It's me;   55
I fixed it. My sister Ghisolabella
did let the marquis have his way with her.

    Don't think, though, I'm the only Bolognese   58
who's here in tears. The place is full of us.
Between the rivers Sàvena and Reno,

    far fewer tongues speak "yes" as "yeah" than here.   61*
And if you want to get this straight, recall
what money means to Bolognese hearts.'

64   Così parlando il percosse un demonio
        de la sua scuriada, e disse: 'Via,
        ruffian! qui non son femmine da conio.'

67   I' mi raggiunsi con la scorta mia;
        poscia con pochi passi divenimmo
        là 'v' uno scoglio de la ripa uscia.

70   Assai leggeramente quel salimmo;
        e vòlti a destra su per la sua scheggia
        da quelle cerchie etterne ci partimmo.

73   Quando noi fummo là dov' el vaneggia
        di sotto per dar passo a li sferzati,
        lo duca disse: 'Attienti, e fa che feggia

76   lo viso in te di quest' altri mal nati
        ai quali ancor non vedesti la faccia,
        però che son con noi insieme andati.'

79   Del vecchio ponte guardavam la traccia
        che venìa verso noi da l'altra banda,
        e che la ferza similmente scaccia.

82   E 'l buon maestro, sanza mia dimanda,
        mi disse: 'Guarda quel grande che vene,
        e per dolor non par lagrime spanda:

85   quanto aspetto reale ancor ritene!
        Quelli è Iasón, che per cuore e per senno
        li Colchi del monton privati féne.

88   Ello passò per l'isola di Lenno
        poi che l'ardite femmine spietate
        tutti li maschi loro a morte dienno.

91   Ivi con segni e con parole ornate
        Isifile ingannò, la giovinetta
        che prima avea tutte l'altre ingannate.

94   Lasciolla quivi gravida, soletta:
        tal colpa a tal martiro lui condanna,
        e anche di Medea si fa vendetta.

97   Con lui sen va chi di tal parte inganna;
        e questo basti de la prima valle
        sapere e di color che 'n sé assanna.'

And, as he spoke, a devil now struck out: 64
'Push off, you pimp,' he said, and swung his lash.
'There aren't tarts here for you to turn to cash.'

I turned to join my escort once again,   67
and walked with him a few steps further on,
then reached an outcrop jutting from the bank.

We made our way quite easily up that,   70
then, turning right along the splintered ridge,
we left that bunch to endless circulation.

So now we came to where the vault gapes wide   73
to let those beaten beings pass beneath.
'Pause here,' said Virgil, 'and ensure some glimpse

of all these woebegones now marks your eye.   76
They go in our direction. So, as yet,
you've had no chance to look them in the face.

We saw from that decrepit bridge the traces   79
of a second crew. These came towards us.
These, as well, were driven by whistling whips.

I did not prompt him, but my mentor said: 82
'Look at that hero there, advancing now!
He seems, for all his pain, to shed no tear.

How great an air of majesty he still retains!   85*
He is that Jason who, astute and strong,
made Colchos grieve to lose its gold-fleeced ram.

Journeying on, he passed the isle of Lemnos,   88
where cold and reckless women had, by then,
delivered death to every living male.

Yet he, with hints and eloquence of phrase,   91
beguiled the young Hypsipyle – a girl
who had herself proved guileful to the rest.

Alone he left her there, alone, with child.   94
That crime incurs for him this penalty
which also stands as vengeance for Medea.

Along with him go all who turned such tricks.   97
And that's enough to know about this vale,
or else of those who're caught within its fangs.'

100   Già eravam là 've lo stretto calle
con l'argine secondo s'incrocicchia
e fa di quello ad un altr' arco spalle.

103   Quindi sentimmo gente che si nicchia
ne l'altra bolgia e che col muso scuffa,
e sé medesma con le palme picchia.

106   Le ripe eran grommate d'una muffa,
per l'alito di giù che vi s'appasta,
che con li occhi e col naso facea zuffa.

109   Lo fondo è cupo sì che non ci basta
loco a veder sanza montare al dosso
de l'arco, ove lo scoglio più sovrasta.

112   Quivi venimmo; e quindi giù nel fosso
vidi gente attuffata in uno sterco
che da li umani privadi parea mosso.

115   E mentre ch'io là giù con l'occhio cerco,
vidi un col capo sì di merda lordo
che non parea s'era laico o cherco.

118   Quei mi sgridò: 'Perché se' tu sì gordo
di riguardar più me che li altri brutti?'
E io a lui: 'Perché, se ben ricordo,

121   già t'ho veduto coi capelli asciutti,
e se' Alessio Interminei da Lucca:
però t'adocchio più che li altri tutti.'

124   Ed elli allor, battendosi la zucca:
'Qua giù m'hanno sommerso le lusinghe
ond' io non ebbi mai la lingua stucca.'

127   Appresso ciò lo duca: 'Fa che pinghe,'
mi disse, 'il viso un poco più avante,
sì che la faccia ben con l'occhio attinghe

130   di quella sozza e scapigliata fante
che là si graffia con l'unghie merdose,
e or s'accoscia e ora è in piedi stante:

133   Taide è, la puttana che rispuose
al drudo suo quando disse, "Ho io grazie
grandi apo te?": "Anzi maravigliose!"

136   E quinci sian le nostre viste sazie.'

We'd come already to the point at which   100
the tight path crosses with the second bank
and makes a shoulder to another arch.

And now we heard, from Pocket Number Two,   103
the groans and griping of another lot,
the snuffling of their snouts, their slapping palms.

The banks were crusted with a slime and mould   106
that rose up in porridgy exhalations
and, scuffling, violated eye and nose.

The bottom of that pit goes down so deep   109
we saw it only when we climbed the ridge
and stood to see the rock rise straight above.

Reaching that point and looking down, we saw   112
that all of them were plunged in diarrhoea
flowing, it seemed, from human cubicles.

And while my eyes were searching deep within,   115
I noticed one whose head was foul with shit.
Had he the tonsure? It was hard to tell.

But he screamed out at me: 'Why gawp like that,   118
so hungry-eyed for me and not the other swill?'
'Because,' I said, 'if I remember well,

I've seen you once before, with drier coiffure.   121*
You are from Lucca. Alessio Interminei.
And that is why I've got my eye on you.'

He answered (battering his turnip top):   124
'I'm sunk this deep because of flatteries –
none were too sickly for my tongue to speak.'

When that was done, my leader now went on: 127
'Just poke your nose a little further out.
Your eyes may then be able to detect

a slut down there – filthy, with tangled hair,   130
scratting herself with cacky fingernails,
squatting at one time, upright at the next.

Thais! She's there, the whore, the one who cooed   133*
to her hot panting swain ("Yeees! Good for you?"),
"Angel, a miracle! My thanks indeed!"

Let that be all that here we need to view.'   136

CANTO 19

1   O Simon mago, o miseri seguaci,
che le cose di Dio, che di bontate
deon essere spose, e voi rapaci

4   per oro e per argento avolterate,
or convien che per voi suoni la tromba,
però che ne la terza bolgia state.

7   Già eravamo, a la seguente tomba,
montati de lo scoglio in quella parte
ch'a punto sovra mezzo 'l fosso piomba.

10   O somma sapienza, quanta è l'arte
che mostri in cielo, in terra e nel mal mondo,
e quanto giusto tua virtù comparte!

13   Io vidi per le coste e per lo fondo
piena la pietra livida di fóri,
d'un largo tutti e ciascun era tondo.

16   Non mi parean men ampi né maggiori
che que' che son nel mio bel San Giovanni,
fatti per loco d'i battezzatori;

19   l'un de li quali, ancor non è molt' anni,
rupp' io per un che dentro v'annegava:
e questo sia suggel ch'ogn' omo sganni.

22   Fuor de la bocca a ciascun soperchiava
d'un peccator li piedi e de le gambe
infino al grosso, e l'altro dentro stava.

25   Le piante erano a tutti accese intrambe,
per che sì forte guizzavan le giunte
che spezzate averien ritorte e strambe.

CANTO 19

You! Magic Simon, and your sorry school! 1*
Things that are God's own – things that, truly, are
the brides of goodness – lusting cruelly

    after gold and silver, you turn them all to whores. 4*
The trumpet now (and rightly!) sounds for you.
There you all are, well set in Pocket Three.

    Onwards towards this yawning tomb, mounting 7
the ridge, by now we'd reached its summit –
the point that plumbs the middle of the ditch.

    O wisdom in the height, how great the art 10
that you display in Heaven, on earth and even
in that evil world! How justly you deal power!

    I saw how all the livid rock was drilled 13
with holes – along its flanks, across its floor –
all circular, and all of equal measure.

    To me they seemed, in radius, no more nor less 16*
than fonts that, in my own beloved Saint John's,
allow the priest at baptisms a place to stand.

    (Not long ago, I shattered one of those. 19
Someone was drowning there. I got them out.
This, sealed and sworn, is nothing but the truth.)

    Out of the mouth of every single hole 22
there floated up a pair of sinner feet,
legs to the ham on show, the rest concealed.

    The soles of all these feet were set alight, 25
and each pair wriggled at the joint so hard
they'd easily have ripped a rope or lanyard.

28   Qual suole il fiammeggiar de le cose unte
     muoversi pur su per la strema buccia:
     tal era lì dai calcagni a le punte.

31   'Chi è colui, maestro, che si cruccia
     guizzando più che li altri suoi consorti,'
     diss' io, 'e cui più roggia fiamma succia?'

34   Ed elli a me: 'Se tu vuo' ch'i' ti porti
     là giù per quella ripa che più giace,
     da lui saprai di sé e de' suoi torti.'

37   E io: 'Tanto m'è bel, quanto a te piace:
     tu se' segnore, e sai ch'i' non mi parto
     dal tuo volere, e sai quel che si tace.'

40   Allor venimmo in su l'argine quarto;
     volgemmo e discendemmo a mano stanca
     là giù nel fondo foracchiato e arto.

43   Lo buon maestro ancor de la sua anca
     non mi dipuose, sì mi giunse al rotto
     di quel che sì piangeva con la zanca.

46   'O qual che se' che 'l di sù tien di sotto,
     anima trista come pal commessa,'
     comincia' io a dir, 'se puoi, fa motto.'

49   Io stava come 'l frate che confessa
     lo perfido assessin, che, poi ch'è fitto,
     richiama lui per che la morte cessa.

52   Ed el gridò: 'Se' tu già costì ritto,
     se' tu già costì ritto, Bonifazio?
     Di parecchi anni mi mentì lo scritto.

55   Se' tu sì tosto di quell' aver sazio
     per lo qual non temesti tòrre a 'nganno
     la bella donna, e poi di farne strazio?'

58   Tal mi fec' io quai son color che stanno,
     per non intender ciò ch'è lor risposto,
     quasi scornati, e risponder non sanno.

61   Allor Virgilio disse: 'Dilli tosto:
     "Non son colui, non son colui che credi!"'
     E io rispuosi come a me fu imposto.

As flames go flickering round some greasy thing   28
and hover just above its outer rind,
so these flames also, toe tip to heel end.

'Who, sir,' I said, 'is that one there? That one   31
who jerks in pain greater than his *confrères*,
sucked at by flames far more fiercely vermilion.'

'I'll lift you down,' he answered me, 'if you   34
insist. We'll take that bank the easier.
He'll talk to you himself about his twists.'

'Whatever pleases you,' I said, 'to me is good.   37
Lord, you remain: I'll not depart – you know –
from what you will. You read my silent thoughts.'

So on we went to the fourth embankment.   40
We turned around, descended on our left,
arriving at that pitted, straitened floor.

My teacher, kindly, did not set me down –   43
nor loose me from his hip hold – till we had reached
that fissure where (all tears) shanks shuddered.

'Whatever you might be there, upside down,   46*
staked, you unhappy spirit, like a pole,
if you,' I said, 'are able, then speak out.'

So there I stood like any friar who shrives   49
the hired assassin – head down in the earth –
who calls him back to put off stifling death.

And he yelled out: 'Is that you standing there?   52*
Are you there, on your feet still, Boniface?
The writings lied to me by quite some years.

Are you so sick of owning things already?   55
Till now, you've hardly been afraid to cheat
our lovely woman, tearing her to shreds.'

Well, I just stood there (you will know just how)   58
simply not getting what I'd heard come out,
feeling a fool, uncertain what to say.

Then Virgil entered: 'Say this – and make speed: 61
"No, that's not me. I am not who you think."'
And so I answered as he'd said I should.

64   Per che lo spirto tutti storse i piedi;
        poi, sospirando e con voce di pianto,
        mi disse: 'Dunque che a me richiedi?

67   Se di saper ch'i' sia ti cal cotanto
        che tu abbi però la ripa corsa,
        sappi ch'i' fui vestito del gran manto;

70   e veramente fui figliuol de l'orsa,
        cupido sì per avanzar li orsatti
        che sù l'avere e qui me misi in borsa.

73   Di sotto al capo mio son li altri tratti
        che precedetter me simoneggiando
        per le fessure de la pietra piatti.

76   Là giù cascherò io altresì quando
        verrà colui ch'i' credea che tu fossi,
        allor ch'i' feci 'l sùbito dimando.

79   Ma più è 'l tempo già che i piè mi cossi
        e ch'i' son stato così sottosopra,
        ch'el non starà piantato coi piè rossi;

82   ché dopo lui verrà di più laida opra,
        di ver' ponente, un pastor sanza legge,
        tal che convien che lui e me ricuopra.

85   Nuovo Iasón sarà, di cúi si legge
        ne' Maccabei; e come a quel fu molle
        suo re, così fia lui chi Francia regge.'

88   Io non so s'i' mi fui qui troppo folle,
        ch'i' pur rispuosi lui a questo metro:
        'Deh, or mi dì: quanto tesoro volle

91   nostro Segnore in prima da san Pietro
        ch'ei ponesse le chiavi in sua balìa?
        Certo non chiese se non: "Viemmi retro."

94   Né Pier né li altri tolsero a Matia
        oro od argento, quando fu sortito
        al loco che perdé l'anima ria.

97   Però ti sta, ché tu se' ben punito;
        e guarda ben la mal tolta moneta
        ch'esser ti fece contra Carlo ardito.

At which – all feet – the spirit thrashed about,   64
then, sighing loudly in a tearful voice:
'So what is it you want of me?' he said.

'If you're so keen to know who I might be,   67
and ran all down that slope to find me out,
you'd better know I wore the papal cope.

A true Orsini, son of Ursa Bear,   70
I showed such greed in favouring her brats
that – up there well in pocket – I'm in pocket here.

Below me, in great stacks beneath my head,   73
packed tight in every cranny of the rock,
are all my antecedents in the Simon line.

Down there I'll sink, in that same way, when he   76
arrives whom I supposed that you might be,
and uttered, therefore, my abrupt inquiry.

But I already – feet up on the grill, tossed   79
upside down – have passed more time
than Boniface will, stuck here with red hot toes.

For after him from westwards there'll appear   82*
that lawless shepherd, uglier in deed,
who then, for both of us, will form a lid.

He shall be known as a "Jason-Once-Again".   85
We read in Maccabees: "Priest Bribes a King."
This other will score well with one French prince.'

I may have been plain mad. I do not know.   88
But now, in measured verse, I sang these words:
'Tell me, I pray: what riches did Our Lord

demand, as first instalment, from Saint Peter   91
before He placed the keys in his command?
He asked (be sure) no more than: "Come behind me."

Nor did Saint Peter, or the rest of them,   94
receive from Matthias a gold or silver piece,
allotting him the place that Judas lost.

So you stay put. You merit punishment.   97*
But keep your eye on that ill-gotten coin
that made you bold with Charles the Angevin.

100 E se non fosse ch'ancor lo mi vieta
la reverenza de le somme chiavi
che tu tenesti ne la vita lieta,

103 io userei parole ancor più gravi;
ché la vostra avarizia il mondo attrista,
calcando i buoni e sollevando i pravi.

106 Di voi pastor s'accorse il Vangelista
quando colei che siede sopra l'acque
puttaneggiar coi regi a lui fu vista,

109 quella che con le sette teste nacque,
e da le diece corna ebbe argomento
fin che virtute al suo marito piacque.

112 Fatto v'avete dio d'oro e d'argento;
e che altro è da voi a l'idolatre,
se non ch'elli uno, e voi ne orate cento?

115 Ahi, Costantin, di quanto mal fu matre,
non la tua conversion, ma quella dote
che da te prese il primo ricco patre!'

118 E mentr' io li cantava cotai note,
o ira o coscïenza che 'l mordesse,
forte spingava con ambo le piote.

121 I' credo ben ch'al mio duca piacesse,
con sì contenta labbia sempre attese
lo suon de le parole vere espresse.

124 Però con ambo le braccia mi prese;
e poi che tutto sù mi s'ebbe al petto,
rimontò per la via onde discese.

127 Né si stancò d'avermi a sé distretto,
sì men portò sovra 'l colmo de l'arco.
che dal quarto al quinto argine è tragetto.

130 Quivi soavemente spuose il carco,
soave per lo scoglio sconcio ed erto
che sarebbe a le capre duro varco.

133 Indi un altro vallon mi fu scoperto.

And, were I not forbidden, as I am,   100
by reverence for those keys, supreme and holy,
that you hung on to in the happy life,

I now would bring still weightier words to bear.   103
You and your greed bring misery to the world,
trampling the good and raising up the wicked.

Saint John took heed of shepherds such as you.   106*
He saw revealed that She-above-the-Waves,
whoring it up with Rulers of the earth,

she who in truth was born with seven heads   109
and fed herself, in truth, from ten pure horns,
as long as she in virtue pleased her man.

Silver and gold you have made your god. And what's   112
the odds – you and some idol-worshipper?
He prays to one, you to a gilded hundred.

What harm you mothered, Emperor Constantine!   115*
Not your conversion but the dowry he –
that first rich Papa – thus obtained from you!'

And all the time I chanted out these notes,   118
he, in his wrath or bitten by remorse,
flapped, with great force, the flat of both his feet.

My leader, I believe, was very pleased.   121
In listening to these sounding words of truth,
he stood there satisfied, his lips compressed.

So, too, he took me up in his embrace.   124
Then, bodily, he clasped me to his breast
and climbed again the path where he'd come down.

Nor did he tire of holding me so tight.   127
He bore me to the summit of that arch
spanning the banks of Pockets Four and Five.

And there he gently put his burden down,   130
gently on rocks so craggy and so steep
they might have seemed to goats too hard to cross.

From there, another valley was disclosed.   133

CANTO 20

1   Di nova pena mi conven far versi
       e dar matera al ventesimo canto
       de la prima canzon, ch'è d'i sommersi.

4   Io era già disposto tutto quanto
       a riguardar ne lo scoperto fondo,
       che si bagnava d'angoscioso pianto;

7   e vidi gente per lo vallon tondo
       venir, tacendo e lagrimando, al passo
       che fanno le letane in questo mondo.

10   Come 'l viso mi scese in lor più basso
       mirabilmente apparve esser travolto
       ciascun tra 'l mento e 'l principio del casso,

13   ché da le reni era tornato 'l volto,
       e in dietro venir li convenia,
       perchè 'l veder dinanzi era lor tolto.

16   Forse per forza già di parlasia
       si travolse così alcun del tutto,
       ma io nol vidi, né credo che sia.

19   Se Dio ti lasci, lettor, prender frutto
       di tua lezione, or pensa per te stesso
       com' io potea tener lo viso asciutto,

22   quando la nostra imagine di presso
       vidi sì torta che 'l pianto de li occhi
       le natiche bagnava per lo fesso.

25   Certo io piangea, poggiato a un de' rocchi
       del duro scoglio, sì che la mia scorta
       mi disse: 'Ancor se' tu de li altri sciocchi?

CANTO 20

I now must turn a strange new pain to verse   1
and give some substance to this twentieth chant
that deals (*Cantica* 1) with sunken souls.

Already I had set myself to peer   4
intently on those now-discovered depths,
washed as they were with agonizing tears.

I saw there people circling round that trench.   7
And on they came in silence, weeping still –
as slow in pace as litanies on earth.

Then, as my gaze sank lower down these forms,   10
each was revealed (the wonder of it all!)
twisted around between the chin and thorax.

The face of each looked down towards its coccyx.   13
And each, deprived of vision to the front,
came, as it must, reversed along its way.

Seized by some paralytic fit, others   16
perhaps have been so turned awry. But I –
not having seen, myself – don't credit it.

That God may grant you, as you read, the fruit   19
that you deserve in reading, think, yourselves:
could I have kept my own face dry, to see,

close by, that image of our human self   22*
so wrenched from true that teardrops from the eyes
ran down to rinse them where the buttocks cleave?

Of this, be sure: that, leaning on a spur   25
of that unyielding cliff, I wept. 'Are you,'
my escort said, 'like them, an idiot still?

28   Qui vive la pietà quand' è ben morta:
chi è più scellerato che colui
che al giudicio divin passion comporta?

31   Drizza la testa, drizza, e vedi a cui
s'aperse a li occhi d'i Teban la terra,
per ch'ei gridavan tutti: "Dove rui,

34   Anfïarao? perché lasci la guerra?"
E non restò di ruinare a valle
fino a Minòs, che ciascheduno afferra.

37   Mira c'ha fatto petto de le spalle;
perché volse veder troppo davante,
di retro guarda e fa retroso calle.

40   Vedi Tiresia, che mutò sembiante
quando di maschio femmina divenne,
cangiandosi le membra tutte quante;

43   e prima, poi, ribatter li convenne
li duo serpenti avvolti, con la verga,
che riavesse le maschili penne.

46   Aronta è quel ch'al ventre li s'atterga,
che ne' monti di Luni, dove ronca
lo Carrarese che di soto alberga,

49   ebbe tra' bianchi marmi la spelonca
per sua dimora, onde a guardar le stelle
e 'l mar non li era la veduta tronca.

52   E quella che ricuopre le mammelle,
che tu non vedi, con le trecce sciolte,
e ha di là ogne pilosa pelle,

55   Manto fu, che cercò per terre molte;
poscia si puose là dove nacqu' io;
onde un poco mi piace che m'ascolte.

58   Poscia che 'l padre suo di vita uscìo
e venne serva la città di Baco,
questa gran tempo per lo mondo gio.

61   Suso in Italia bella giace un laco,
a piè de l'Alpe che serra Lamagna
sovra Tiralli, c'ha nome Benaco.

Here pity lives where pity's truth is dead.   28
Who is more impious, more scarred with sin
than one who pleads compassion at God's throne?

    Lift up your head! Stand straight. See, that one there?   31*
Under his chariot wheels, the earth yawned wide;
and Thebes – all eyes – yelled: "Where, Amphiaraus,

    headlong away? Why leave us in this strife?"   34
Into the ceaseless void he fell, until
he came where Minos stands, who seizes all.

    He's formed his chest – amazingly – from shoulder.   37
As once he wished to see too far ahead,
his tread is backward, and he stares to rear.

    See there Tiresias! Male-to-female switch.   40*
His looks, mutating, were entirely changed,
his members altering till each was each.

    And then, to win once more his virile plumes,   43
he needs must strike a second time, and shake
again at coupling snakes his witch's wand.

    Then, spine to gut, the prophet Arruns comes.   46
High in the Lunigiana hills – over
Carrara homesteads, so hard-hoed by serfs –

    he found a grotto in the marble cliffs   49
and took this for his dwelling place. Nothing,
from there, cuts off the view of sea or star.

    And then there's one whose breasts you cannot see   52*
(since these are mantled by her flowing strands)
who shows on that side all her shaggy fleece.

    She, once, was Manto, scouring many lands,   55
until she reached and settled at my birthplace.
And so – to please me – listen for a while.

    Her father, having left this life – and Thebes,   58
the place of Bacchus, being now in thrall –
for years she travelled, searching through this world.

    Above, in lovely Italy, there lies a lake   61*
(in Latin: Benacus) beneath those Alps
that lock out Germany beyond the high Tyrol.

64   Per mille fonti, credo, e più si bagna
        tra Garda e Val Camonica e Pennino
        de l'acqua che nel detto laco stagna.

67   Loco è nel mezzo là dove 'l trentino
        pastore e quel di Brescia e 'l veronese
        segnar poria, s' e' fesse quel cammino.

70   Siede Peschiera, bello e forte arnese
        da fronteggiar Bresciani e Bergamaschi,
        ove la riva 'ntorno più discese.

73   Ivi convien che tutto quanto caschi
        ciò che 'n grembo a Benaco star non può,
        e fassi fiume giù per verdi paschi.

76   Tosto che l'acqua a correr mette co,
        non più Benaco ma Mencio si chiama
        fino a Governol, dove cade in Po.

79   Non molto ha corso ch'el trova una lama,
        ne la qual si distende e la 'mpaluda;
        e suol di state talor esser grama.

82   Quindi passando la vergine cruda
        vide terra nel mezzo del pantano
        sanza coltura e d'abitanti nuda.

85   Lì, per fuggire ogne consorzio umano,
        ristette con suoi servi a far sue arti,
        e visse, e vi lasciò suo corpo vano.

88   Li uomini poi che 'ntorno erano sparti
        s'accolsero a quel loco, ch'era forte
        per lo pantan ch'avea da tutte parti.

91   Fer la città sovra quell' ossa morte;
        e per colei che 'l loco prima elesse,
        Mantua l'appellar sanz' altra sorte.

94   Già fuor le genti sue dentro più spesse,
        prima che la mattia da Casalodi
        da Pinamonte inganno ricevesse.

97   Però t'assenno che, se tu mai odi
        originar la mia terra altrimenti,
        la verità nulla menzogna frodi.'

From waters gathered in that standing pool   64
a thousand springs, I think, or more, refresh
the lands between those peaks, Camonica and Garda.

There is a place, the central point of these,   67
where pastors – if they choose to sail from Brescia,
from Verona and from Trent – have power to bless.

Here that brave citadel Peschiera sits,   70
built where the shoreline sinks to reach a low,
boldly outfacing Bergamese and Brescians.

Cascading from the lap of Benacus,   73
waters, unstayably, must run down here.
Through lush green meadows these all form a stream.

And this, when it begins to run, is known   76
by name as Mincio, not Benacus.
(It meets the river Po around Govérnolo.)

Moving, the Mincio at once dips down,   79
then, broadening in the plain, it forms a marsh –
and this in summer can be foul and brackish.

Manto, that bitter virgin, passing by,   82
saw, in the centre of that great morass,
a place unploughed and bare of population.

There, fleeing still from human fellowship,   85
she settled with her vassals, plied her arts,
in this place lived, here left her empty corpse.

Then other peoples came who had, so long,   88
been scattered all about. Because the marsh
surrounded it, the site was safe and strong.

They raised their city over those dead bones.   91
They called it Mantua (no magic charm!),
since Manto first had made the place her own.

Those living there were once more numerous,   94
before the idiotic Casalodi was
so taken in by Pinamonte's trick.

So, if in other stories you should hear   97
some tale of how my city came to be,
don't let the truth, I urge, be mocked by lies.'

100   E io: 'Maestro, i tuoi ragionamenti
mi son sì certi e prendon sì mia fede,
che li altri mi sarien carboni spenti.

103   Ma dimmi de la gente che procede,
se tu ne vedi alcun degno di nota;
ché solo a ciò la mia mente rifiede.'

106   Allor mi disse: 'Quel che da la gota
porge la barba in su le spalle brune,
fu – quando Grecia fu di maschi vòta

109   sì ch'a pena rimaser per le cune –
augure, e diede 'l punto con Calcanta
in Aulide a tagliar la prima fune.

112   Euripilo ebbe nome, e così 'l canta
l'alta mia tragedìa in alcun loco:
ben lo sai tu che la sai tutta quanta.

115   Quell'altro che ne' fianchi è così poco,
Michele Scotto fu, che veramente
de le magiche frode seppe 'l gioco.

118   Vedi Guido Bonatti; vedi Asdente,
ch'avere inteso al cuoio e a lo spago
ora vorrebbe, ma tardi si pente.

121   Vedi le triste che lasciaron l'ago,
la spuola e 'l fuso, e fecersi 'ndivine;
fecer malie con erbe e con imago.

124   Ma vienne omai, ché già tiene 'l confine
d'amendue li emisperi e tocca l'onda
sotto Sobilia Caino e le spine;

127   e già iernotte fu la luna tonda:
ben ten de' ricordar, ché non ti nocque
alcuna volta per la selva fonda.'

130   Sì mi parlava, e andavamo introcque.

'Sir,' I replied, 'to me your words are sure,   100
and capture so entirely what I think,
that differing versions are as burned-out coal.

But let me know some more of this parade,   103
that is, if any here still merit note.
My mind is waiting only for that word.'

And so he said: 'The one who there fans wide   106*
his beard from cheek to shadowed shoulderblade,
was – in those years when Greece was void of men,

when, even in the cradle, boys were few –   109
an augur. He, with Calchas, cast the hour
at which to cut the anchor rope in Aulis.

By name Eurypylus, there is some verse   112
in my great tragedy that sings of him.
But you'll know where. You know the whole thing through.

And then we meet, so withered in his flanks,   115*
a certain Scotsman, Michael. In the spheres
of fraud and magic, he was full of pranks.

There's Guido Bonatti. Look! Asdente, too!   118*
The cobbler must be wishing now he'd stuck
to thread and leathers. Too late to repent.

Then see those hags? They, one and all, forsook   121
for witchcraft distaff, needle, pin and spool.
They cast their spells with weeds and ju-ju dolls.

But come, now come. The zone where hemispheres   124*
both meet by now is gripped (and, under
Seville, waves are touched) by Cain, his bush and thorns.

And yestere'en the rounding moon was full.   127
You must remember this. It shone while you,
unharmed, were deep within that first dark wood.'

And so he chatted on and we fared forwards.   130

CANTO 21

1   Così di ponte in ponte, altro parlando
che la mia comedìa cantar non cura,
venimmo, e tenavamo 'l colmo quando

4   restammo per veder l'altra fessura
di Malebolge e li altri pianti vani;
e vidila mirabilmente oscura.

7   Quale ne l'arzanà de' Viniziani
bolle l'inverno la tenace pece
a rimpalmare i legni lor non sani,

10   ché navicar non ponno; in quella vece
chi fa suo legno novo e chi ristoppa
le coste a quel che più viaggi fece,

13   chi ribatte da proda e chi da poppa,
altri fa remi e altri volge sarte,
chi terzeruolo e artimon rintoppa:

16   tal, non per foco ma per divin' arte,
bollia là giuso una pegola spessa
che 'nviscava la ripa d'ogne parte.

19   I' vedea lei, ma non vedea in essa
mai che le bolle che 'l bollor levava,
e gonfiar tutta, e riseder compressa.

22   Mentr' io là giù fisamente mirava,
lo duca mio, dicendo: 'Guarda, guarda!'
mi trasse a sé del loco dov' io stava.

25   Allor mi volsi come l'uom cui tarda
di veder quel che li convien fuggire
e cui paura sùbita sgagliarda,

CANTO 21

So on we went from bridge to bridge, speaking   1
of things that I shan't, in this comedy,
commit to song. We gained the brow. Once there,
we paused and, down in Rottenpockets, saw   4
another fissure still, more empty tears.
I saw it all – a marvel of mere dark.
Compare: Venetians in their Arsenal,   7*
in winter when their ships cannot set sail,
brew up a viscous pitch which they then smear
on ailing boards, or else lay down new hulls.   10
Others will plug the ribs of hulks that have,
by now, made many a long-haul trip.
Some hammer at the prow, some at the poop,   13
some whittle oars, where others plait the rig.
Some mend the mainsail, others patch the jib.
So here – though more by art of God than fire –   16
a dense black gunge was brought to boiling point,
and splashed on all the banks in sticky smears.
I saw this stuff but nothing else within   19
but bubbles as the boiling bubbled on,
swelling to roundness, glue-ily sinking in.
In mesmerized amazement I just gazed.   22
But then, 'Look out! Look out!' my leader cried,
then dragged me, where I'd stood, towards his side.
And there I turned as one who may well pause –   25
all swagger, in his sudden panic, gone –
to peep at what he really ought to flee,

28   che, per veder, non indugia 'l partire:
     e vidi dietro a noi un diavol nero
     correndo su per lo scoglio venire.

31   Ahi quant' elli era ne l'aspetto fero!
     e quanto mi parea ne l'atto acerbo
     con l'ali aperte e sovra i piè leggero!

34   L'omero suo, ch'era aguto e superbo,
     carcava un peccator con ambo l'anche,
     e quei tenea de' piè ghermito 'l nerbo.

37   Del nostro ponte disse: 'O Malebranche,
     ecco un de li anzian di Santa Zita!
     Mettetel sotto, ch'i' torno per anche

40   a quella terra, che n'è ben fornita:
     ogn' uom v'è barattier, fuor che Bonturo;
     del *no*, per li denar, vi si fa *ita*.'

43   Là giù 'l buttò, e per lo scoglio duro
     si volse; e mai non fu mastino sciolto
     con tanta fretta a seguitar lo furo.

46   Quel s'attuffò, e tornò sù convolto;
     ma i demon che del ponte avean coperchio,
     gridar: 'Qui non ha loco il Santo Volto!

49   Qui si nuota altrimenti che nel Serchio!
     Però, se tu non vuo' di nostri graffi,
     non far sopra la pegola soverchio.'

52   Poi l'addentar con più di cento raffi,
     disser: 'Coverto convien che qui balli,
     sì che, se puoi, nascosamente accaffi.'

55   Non altrimenti i cuoci a' lor vassalli
     fanno attuffare in mezzo la caldaia
     la carne con li uncin, perchè non galli.

58   Lo buon maestro: 'Acciò che non si paia
     che tu ci sia,' mi disse, 'giù t'acquatta
     dopo uno scheggio, ch'alcun schermo t'aia;

61   e per nulla offension che mi sia fatta,
     non temer tu, ch'i' ho le cose conte,
     per ch'altra volta fui a tal baratta.'

yet, glimpsing this, does not delay his parting.   28
I saw there, right behind us, this black demon
running the ridge around in our direction.

Eek! How ferocious all his features looked.   31
How viciously his every move seemed etched,
wings wide apart, so lithe and light of foot.

The hunch blades of his shoulders, keen and proud,   34
bore up the haunches of some criminal,
his hook fixed firm in tendons at each heel.

Mounting our bridge, demonically he barked: 37*
'Get this, Rotklors! A boss man from Lucca!
You lot can dunk him. I'll get back for more.

I've got it stuffed, Saint Zita's place, with this sort.   40
They're at it there, the lot. (Oh! Not Bonturo!)
Cash on the nail, and "no" becomes "for sure".'

Dumping his load, he then dashed down   43
and crossed the flinty slope. No mad bullmastiff
ever was loosed so fast to catch a thief.

The sinner dived, but then turned, writhing up.   46
At which the demons, dossing by that bridge,
yelled: 'No place, black face, here for black-faced gods.

You can't swim here like bathers in the Serchio.   49
If you don't want to know what hooks can do,
then just don't poke your nose above that tar.'

They sank in him a hundred barbs or more.   52
'Down here,' they sang, 'you'll tango in the dark!
Get under cover! Pull what scams you can!

Chefs do the same. They get their kitchen boys   55
to fork the centre of a simmering pot,
so chunks of meat do not float up too high.

Here, too. 'Seem not to be here,' Sir now said.   58
'Just hunker down behind a spur of rock.
It may still offer you some place to hide.

Yet have no fear. Oppose me as they may,   61
my strategy – I know what's what – is clear.
I've been involved in rucks like this before.'

64   Poscia passò di là dal co del ponte;
        e com' el giunse in su la ripa sesta,
        mestier li fu d'aver sicura fronte.

67   Con quel furore e con quella tempesta
        ch'escono i cani a dosso al poverello,
        che di sùbito chiede ove s'arresta,

70   usciron quei di sotto al ponticello,
        e volser contra lui tutt' i runcigli;
        ma el gridò: 'Nessun di voi sia fello!

73   Innanzi che l'uncin vostro mi pigli,
        traggasi avante l'un di voi che m'oda,
        e poi d'arruncigliarmi si consigli.'

76   Tutti gridaron: 'Vada Malacoda!'
        per ch'un si mosse – e li altri stetter fermi –
        e venne a lui, dicendo: 'Che li approda?'

79   'Credi tu, Malacoda, qui vedermi
        esser venuto,' disse 'l mio maestro,
        'sicuro già da tutti vostri schermi,

82   sanza voler divino e fato destro?
        Lascian' andar, ché nel cielo è voluto
        ch'i' mostri altrui questo cammin silvestro.'

85   Allor li fu l'orgoglio sì caduto
        ch'e' si lasciò cascar l'uncino a' piedi,
        e disse a li altri, 'Omai non sia feruto.'

88   E 'l duca mio a me: 'O tu che siedi
        tra li scheggion del ponte quatto quatto,
        sicuramente omai a me tu riedi.'

91   Per ch'io mi mossi e a lui venni ratto;
        e i diavoli si fecer tutti avanti,
        sì ch'io temetti ch'ei tenesser patto:

94   così vid' io già temer li fanti
        ch'uscivan patteggiati di Caprona,
        veggendo sé tra nemici cotanti.

97   I' m'accostai con tutta la persona
        lungo 'l mio duca, e non torceva li occhi
        da la sembianza lor, ch'era non buona.

So now, beyond the bridge head, on he went,   64
and needed, when he neared Embankment Six,
the steadiest front that he could summon up.

With all the fury and tempestuous rage   67
of dog packs rushing on some poor old tramp –
who freezes there and pleads from where he'd reached –

so now those demons underneath the arch   70
stormed out at him and brandished all their hooks.
But he cried out: 'Don't even think of it.

Before you set on me with curving prongs,   73
let one of you who'll hear me out draw near,
and then discuss if hooking me is right or wrong.'

So, 'Go on, Rottentail,' they shrieked. 'That's you!'   76
And he advanced (the others kept their ground
and muttered: 'What will he get out of it?')

'Do you imagine, Rottentail,' my teacher said,   79
'who've seen me come already once, immune
to all your tricks, that I am here without

the favouring aid of fate or will divine?   82
Let us pass on. For Heaven wills that I
should guide another on the savage way.'

His arrogance at this took such a fall   85
he let his hook slip, dangling, to his heels.
'OK,' he told the others, 'let's not cut him.'

And now my leader turned and said: 'O thou   88
who sittest there, squatting by that splintered bridge,
return to me with confidence renewed.'

So shift I did, and reached him speedily.   91
At which the demons all came pressing forwards –
so I could not be sure they'd keep their word.

In this way, at Caprona once I saw   94*
the infantry come edging out, despite
safe conduct, chary of the hordes around.

Huddled against my leader's side, pressed hard   97
along him, head to toe, I could not wrench
my eyes from them. Their looks did not look good.

100   Ei chinavan li raffi, e: 'Vuo' che 'l tocchi,'
       diceva l'un con l'altro, 'in sul groppone?'
       E rispondien: 'Sì, fa che gliel'accocchi.'

103   Ma quel demonio che tenea sermone
       col duca mio, si volse tutto presto
       e disse: 'Posa, posa, Scarmiglione!'

106   Poi disse a noi: 'Più oltre andar per questo
       iscoglio non si può, però che giace
       tutto spezzato al fondo l'arco sesto.

109   E se l'andare avante pur vi piace,
       andatevene su per questa grotta:
       presso è un altro scoglio che via face.

112   Ier, più oltre cinqu' ore che quest' otta,
       mille dugento con sessanta sei
       anni compiè che qui la via fu rotta.

115   Io mando verso là di questi miei
       a riguardar s'alcun se ne sciorina:
       gite con lor, che non saranno rei.'

118   'Tra'ti avante, Alichino, e Calcabrina,'
       cominciò elli a dire, 'e tu, Cagnazzo;
       e Barbariccia guidi la decina.

121   Libicocco vegn' oltre e Draghignazzo,
       Ciriatto sannuto e Graffiacane
       e Farfarello e Rubicante pazzo.

124   Cercate 'ntorno le boglienti pane:
       costor sian salvi infin a l'altro scheggio
       che tutto intero va sovra le tane.'

127   'Omè, maestro, che è quel ch'i' veggio?'
       diss' io, 'deh, sanza scorta andianci soli,
       se tu sa' ir; ch'i' per me non la cheggio.

130   Se tu se' sì accorto come suoli,
       non vedi tu ch'e' digrignan li denti
       e con le ciglia ne minaccian duoli?'

133   Ed elli a me: 'Non vo' che tu paventi;
       lasciali digrignar pur a lor senno,
       ch'e' fanno ciò per li lessi dolenti.'

They cocked their barbs. Then one spoke out: 100
'Want me to touch him on his fat backside?'
And they replied: 'Yeah, get him in the notch.'

But then that devil who was still in speech   103
with my great leader swung around at speed,
and said: 'Just cool it, cool it, Tangletop!'

'Further along this crag,' he now declared,   106
'you just can't go. Bridge Six is broken down.
It lies in ruins on the valley floor.

But if you'd care to schlepp still further on,   109
then do so round this arching cliff. Nearby,
another outcrop makes a path for you.

Just yesterday (five hours ahead of now),   112
a thousand years, two centuries and sixty-six
from when the path was cut had then elapsed.

I'll send in that direction some of mine,   115
to watch for any sinner scenting air.
You go with them. They won't dare pull a stunt.'

'So, forward, Crackice! Forward, Flash Ali!'   118*
so he began: 'And Baddog! You as well.
And you, old Twirlitufts, can lead the squad.

Loveslot as well. And you, too, Dragonrunt,   121
Bigpig with tusks, and also Skratcherker,
Flutterby! For'ard! And you there, mad Glogob!

Search all around this pan of boiling lime: 124
until you reach the spur that arcs, unbroken,
over these dens, these two will go unharmed.'

'Sir, sir,' I said, 'what's this I see! Please, sir,   127
if you know how and where, let's go alone.
Myself, I didn't ask for this at all.

Your eyes are usually so very keen.   130
Can you not see? Just look! They grind their teeth.
Their frowns are warnings of what harm they mean.'

His answer was: 'I wouldn't have you frightened.   133
Let them scowl so, and grind as they may choose.
They mean it for the souls in this sad stew.'

136   Per l'argine sinistro volta dienno;
ma prima avea ciascun la lingua stretta
coi denti verso lor duca, per cenno,

139   ed elli avea del cul fatto trombetta.

About-face, leftwards on the rocky pass,   136
each poked a tongue, teeth clenched, towards their lord,
and he – to give the order now, 'Quick march!' –
in answer made a trumpet of his arse.   139

CANTO 22

1   Io vidi già cavalier muover campo
e cominciare stormo e far lor mostra,
e talvolta partir per loro scampo;

4   corridor vidi per la terra vostra,
o Aretini, e vidi gir gualdane,
fedir torneamenti e correr giostra,

7   quando con trombe, e quando con campane,
con tamburi e con cenni di castella,
e con cose nostrali e con istrane:

10   né già con sì diversa cennamella
cavalier vidi muover né pedoni,
né nave a segno di terra o di stella.

13   Noi andavam con i diece demoni.
Ahi fiera compagnia! ma ne la chiesa
coi santi, e in taverna coi ghiottoni.

16   Pur a la pegola era la mia 'ntesa,
per veder de la bolgia ogne contegno
e de la gente ch'entro v'era incesa.

19   Come i dalfini, quando fanno segno
a' marinar con l'arco de la schiena
che s'argomentin di campar lor legno:

22   talor così, ad alleggiar la pena,
mostrav' alcun de' peccatori 'l dosso
e nascondea in men che non balena.

25   E come a l'orlo de l'acqua d'un fosso
stanno i ranocchi pur col muso fuori,
sì che celano i piedi e l'altro grosso:

CANTO 22

I, in my time, have seen brave knights strike camp,   1
parade their power, launch an attack, and then,
at times, to save their skins, desert the field.

Yes, you, Aretines, I have seen our cavalry   4*
charge through your heartland. Skirmishes I've seen,
cut-and-thrust tournaments and running duels,

all to the sound of horns (at times) or bells,   7*
to beating drums or signals flashed from ramparts,
devices of our own and more exotic signs.

Yet never to so weird a pipe or whistle   10
have I, till now, seen foot or horse fall in,
nor ship set sail to signs like that, from land or star.

So, on we went, five friends on either side.   13
What fearsome company! Well, that's the way it is:
hobnob in church with saints, in pubs with sots.

The tar pit called for all my concentration   16
to note each facet of this rotten hole,
and also of the persons burning there.

As schools of dolphin when they arch their spines   19
provide a signal to the mariner,
to say the ship should soon be steered back home,

so too from time to time, to ease their pain,   22
a sinner gave his back some air, then quick
as any lightning flash would hide again.

Likewise, in ditches at the water's edge,   25
bullfrogs will stand, their snouts alone on show,
their feet concealed, with all their bulk below.

28 sì stavan d'ogne parte i peccatori;
ma come s'appressava Barbariccia,
così si ritraén sotto i bollori.

31 I' vidi, e anco il cor me n'accapriccia,
uno aspettar così, com' elli 'ncontra
ch'una rana rimane e l'altra spiccia;

34 e Graffiacan, che li era più di contra,
li arrunciglò le 'mpegolate chiome
e trassel sù, che mi parve una lontra.

37 I' sapea già di tutti quanti 'l nome,
sì li notai quando fuorono eletti,
e poi ch'e' si chiamaro, attesi come.

40 'O Rubicante, fa che tu li metti
li unghioni a dosso sì che tu lo scuoi!'
gridavan tutti insieme i maladetti.

43 E io: 'Maestro mio, fa, se tu puoi,
che tu sappi chi è lo sciagurato
venuto a man de li avversari suoi.'

46 Lo duca mio li s'accostò allato;
domandollo ond' ei fosse, e quei rispuose:
'I' fui del regno di Navarra nato.

49 Mia madre a servo d'un segnor mi puose,
che m'avea generato d'un ribaldo,
distruggitor di sé e di sue cose.

52 Poi fui famiglia del buon re Tebaldo;
quivi mi misi a far baratteria,
di ch'io rendo ragione in questo caldo.'

55 E Ciriatto, a cui di bocca uscia
d'ogne parte una sanna come a porco,
li fé sentir come l'una sdruscia.

58 Tra male gatte era venuto 'l sorco;
ma Barbariccia il chiuse con le braccia
e disse: 'State in là, mentr' io lo 'nforco.'

61 E al maestro mio volse la faccia:
'Domanda,' disse, 'ancor, se più disii
saper da lui prima ch'altri 'l disfaccia.'

In this same way, these sinners lolled around.   28
But then, whenever Twirlitufts came past,
they swiftly dived beneath the bubbling crust.

I saw – at this, my heart still skips a beat –   31
that one (as happens when a frog school springs,
but one stays dallying) was left behind.

And Skratcherker – as being nearest to him –   34
enmeshed his hook among those tar-caked locks
and yanked him out like any floppy otter.

I knew them all by name, the lot of them.   37
I'd noted each when they were first enrolled,
and then, between them, heard them call out names.

'Get in there, Glogob! Get him with your hook!'   40
(So, in damned unison, the chorus shrieked.)
'And tear the leather off his ugly rump!'

I turned, and to my master said: 'Find out,   43*
if you can manage it: who is that so-and-so
who's fallen foul of these antagonists?'

My leader went, and stood beside him there,   46
wanting to know the place where he was born.
He answered: 'I'm a native of Navarre.

My mother, having borne me to a lout,   49
who brought himself and all he had to ruin,
engaged me to the service of a nobleman.

And then I joined King Thibaut's retinue,   52
to practise arts of chartered bribery.
For which I pay my dues in this great heat.'

Then Bigpig, with his boar-like jowls – a tusk   55
stuck out from both his cheeks – supplied a sip
of how well one of these could rake and rip.

The mouse had got among the bad cats now.   58
But Twirlitufts enclosed him in his arms.
'Stay over there!' he said. 'I'll keep him pinned.'

He tilted up his face towards my guide: 61
'Go on, then. Ask him, if you want still more.
But quick,' he said, 'before they do him in.'

64   Lo duca dunque: 'Or dì: de li altri rii
conosci tu alcun che sia latino
sotto la pece?' E quelli: 'I' mi partii,

67   poco è, da un che fu di là vicino.
Così foss' io ancor con lui coperto,
ch'i' non temerei unghia né uncino!'

70   E Libicocco: 'Troppo avem sofferto,'
disse, e preseli 'l braccio col runciglio
sì che, stracciando, ne portò un lacerto.

73   Draghignazzo anco i volle dar di piglio
giuso a le gambe; onde 'l decurio loro
si volse intorno intorno con mal piglio.

76   Quand' elli un poco rappaciati fuoro,
a lui, ch'ancor mirava sua ferita,
domandò 'l duca mio sanza dimoro:

79   'Chi fu colui da cui mala partita
di' che facesti per venire a proda?'
Ed ei rispuose: 'Fu frate Gomita,

82   quel di Gallura, vasel d'ogne froda,
ch'ebbe i nemici di suo donno in mano,
e fé sì lor che ciascun se ne loda:

85   danar si tolse e lasciolli di piano,
sì com' e' dice; e ne li altri offici anche
barattier fu non picciol, ma sovrano.

88   Usa con esso donno Michel Zanche
di Logodoro; e a dir di Sardigna
le lingue lor non si sentono stanche.

91   Omè, vedete l'altro che digrigna;
i' direi anche, ma i' temo ch'ello
non s'apparecchi a grattarmi la tigna.'

94   E 'l gran proposto, vòlto a Farfarello,
che stralunava li occhi per fedire,
disse: 'Fatti 'n costà, malvagio uccello!'

97   'Se voi volete vedere o udire,'
ricominciò lo spaürato appresso,
'Toschi o Lombardi, io ne farò venire;

'So tell me, then,' my master now went on,   64
'among the criminals beneath the tar,
are any – can you tell? – Italian?' 'Just now,'
    he answered me, 'I left a man from there.   67
If only I were with him still beneath the lid,
I wouldn't need to dread these hooks and claws.'

    'We've taken quite enough of this!' So said   70
the Loveslot. Skewering an arm, he sliced
a muscle out in one long hookful.

    Then Dragonrunt must also have a go.   73
He ogled the ham. But their decurion
swung round and gave them all a filthy frown.

    Then, just a little, they all settled down.   76
The sinner lay there, wondering at his wound.
My lord without delay now turned and asked:
    'Who was the one from whom, you say, you took,   79
ill-fatedly, your leave to reach this shore?'
'Brother – as was – Gomita!' he replied.

    'Sard from Gallura, vessel of deceit!   82*
Palming (well-greased) his sire's worst enemies,
he treated all so well, each sang his praise.

    He took their cash, then let them off the hook.   85
In this – as he'll admit – and everything
a total crook. Not small time, though. The King!

    Don Michael Zanche, from the Logudor,   88
still hangs around with him. Their tongues don't tire
of banging on about "Sardin-i-ah".

    Ow! Look at how that demon grinds his teeth.   91
I could tell more but (oh! I'm terrified!)
he means to come and give my scabs a scrub!'

    The high commander swung on Flutterby,   94
whose moon eyes popped in eagerness to pounce.
'Butt out!' he hissed. 'You vulture! Over there!'

    Witless with fear, he started once again: 97
'If you would witness or hold audience
with Lombards or Tuscans, I can make them come.

100   ma stieno i Malebranche un poco in cesso,
       sì ch'ei non teman de le lor vendette;
       e io, seggendo in questo loco stesso,

103   per un ch'io son, ne farò venir sette
       quand' io suffolerò, com' è nostro uso
       di fare allor che fori alcun si mette.'

106   Cagnazzo a cotal motto levò 'l muso,
       crollando 'l capo, e disse: 'Odi malizia
       ch'elli ha pensata per gittarsi giuso!'

109   Ond' ei, ch'avea lacciuoli a gran divizia,
       rispuose: 'Malizioso son io troppo,
       quand' io procuro a' mia maggior trestizia.'

112   Alichin non si tenne e, di rintoppo
       a li altri, disse a lui: 'Se tu ti cali,
       io non ti verrò dietro di gualoppo,

115   ma batterò sovra la pece l'ali.
       Lascisi 'l collo, e sia la ripa scudo,
       a veder se tu sol più di noi vali.'

118   O tu che leggi, udirai nuovo ludo:
       ciascun da l'altra costa li occhi volse,
       quel prima ch'a ciò fare era più crudo.

121   Lo Navarrese ben suo tempo colse;
       fermò le piante a terra, e in un punto
       saltò e dal proposto lor si sciolse.

124   Di che ciascun di colpa fu compunto,
       ma quei più che cagion fu del difetto;
       però si mosse e gridò: 'Tu se' giunto!'

127   Ma poco i valse, ché l'ali al sospetto
       non potero avanzar; quelli andò sotto,
       e quei drizzò volando suso il petto:

130   non altrimenti l'anitra di botto,
       quando 'l falcon s'appressa, giù s'attuffa,
       ed ei ritorna sù crucciato e rotto.

133   Irato Calcabrina de la buffa,
       volando dietro li tenne, invaghito
       che quei campasse per aver la zuffa;

But let these Rotklors all stand well aside –   100
and no one need be frightened they'll attack –
while I, just sitting on this self-same spot,
    will whistle. Now I'm here alone. Presto!   103
And now we're seven! That's our usual trick
when any from below gets out of it.'

    Hearing this blag, old Baddog twitched his snout,   106
then shook his head and snarled: 'The little demon!
He means to take a dive and get back in.'

    That sinner up his sleeve had snares galore.   109
'O yeah! That's me,' he said. 'A demon! Sure!
Really? You think I'd bring my gang more grief?'

    Flash Ali, at these words, could not hold back.   112
Despite what his companions thought, 'Go on,'
he said. 'Slope off. I'll not come galloping.

    I will, though, stretch my wings across the pitch.   115
Let's leave the ridge. Let's make the slope our screen.
And then we'll see if you can get off clean.'

    O you there, as you read! Get this! Olympics!   118*
They all then turned to face the other bank,
even the one who first was most reluctant.

    The Navarrese chose his moment well.   121
Feet firmly planted, in a single flash,
he'd leapt and gone, scot-free of their intent.

    At this, the lot of them were pierced by guilt.   124
Yet, undeterred, the devil most at fault
drove onwards. 'Now you're for it!' he yelled out.

    To no avail. No wing could overhaul   127
the speed of fear. The sinner plunged. Square on,
the demon baulked and then shot up again.

    So, too, a rapid duck dives down, glimpsing   130
a falcon closing in. The duck's foe then
returns aloft, bitter in thwarted pique.

    Crackice, still seething at the doublecross,   133
zoomed ever onwards in his yen to see
the sinner free – then mix it with Flash Ali.

136   e come 'l barattier fu disparito
        così volse li artigli al suo compagno,
        e fu con lui sopra 'l fosso ghermito.

139   Ma l'altro fu bene sparvier grifagno
        ad artigliar ben lui, e amendue
        cadder nel mezzo del bogliente stagno.

142   Lo caldo sghermitor sùbito fue;
        ma però di levarsi era neente,
        sì avieno inviscate l'ali sue.

145   Barbariccia, con li altri suoi dolente,
        quattro ne fé volar da l'altra costa
        con tutt' i raffi, e assai prestamente

148   di qua, di là discesero a la posta;
        porser li uncini verso li 'mpaniati,
        ch'eran già cotti dentro da la crosta.

151   E noi lasciammo lor così 'mpacciati.

So, since the barrator had long since gone,   136
he turned his talons on his own best mate.
Above the ditch he locked him in his prongs.

   The other, though, a right old sparrowhawk,   139
returned the hook. And so the two of them,
as one, went tumbling to the boiling pond.

   The heat that instant made them come unhitched.   142
But, even so, they couldn't raise a thing,
so tightly glued together were their wings.

   Then Twirlitufts, condoling with his kin,   145
sent four of them towards the inner rim,
with all their grappling tackle, at top speed.

   This side and that they went to take their posts,   148
and bent their hooks towards those two, stuck fast.
By now they both were crisped within the batter.

   With that entanglement, we left the matter.   151

CANTO 23

Taciti, soli, sanza compagnia
n'andavam l'un dinanzi e l'altro dopo,
come frati minor vanno per via.

Vòlt' era in su la favola d'Isopo
lo mio pensier per la presente rissa,
dov' el parlò de la rana e del topo,

ché più non si pareggia *mo* e *issa*
che l'un con l'altro fa, se ben s'accoppia
principio e fine con la mente fissa.

E come l'un pensier de l'altro scoppia,
così nacque di quello un altro poi,
che la prima paura mi fé doppia.

Io pensava così: 'Questi per noi
sono scherniti con danno, e con beffa
sì fatta ch'assai credo che lor nòi.

Se l'ira sovra 'l mal voler s'aggueffa,
ei ne verranno dietro più crudeli
che 'l cane a quella lievre ch'elli acceffa.'

Già mi sentia tutti arricciar li peli
de la paura e stava in dietro intento,
quand' io dissi: 'Maestro, se non celi

te e me tostamente, i' ho pavento
d'i Malebranche. Noi li avem già dietro;
io li 'magino sì che già li sento.'

E quei: 'S'i' fossi di piombato vetro,
l'imagine di fuor tua non trarrei
più tosto a me che quella dentro 'mpetro.

CANTO 23

Silent, alone with no one now beside us,   1
we went our way – the one behind, the other
leading on – walking as meek Franciscans do.

My mind turned (thinking of that scuffle still)   4*
to Aesop and his fables, most of all
the one about the frog and rat and hawk.

For 'now' and 'noo' are hardly more alike   7*
than this fine mess to that – if parallels
are rightly drawn between the start and finish.

But thoughts pop up and then lead on to others.   10
So from this first a further set was born,
which now redoubled all my earlier fears.

'Because of us,' the sequence ran, 'that lot   13
have been so injured, put on, tricked and scorned,
they cannot fail, I think, to be upset.

Suppose their bile gets tangled now with anger,   16
then surely they'll come after us and snarl
more viciously than dogs that snout a hare.'

I felt already that my every curl   19
was bristling, on its end. So, gazing back,
stock still, I said: 'If you, sir, do not hide

yourself this second, me as well . . . I dread   22
the Rotklors gang. They're not now far behind.
I hear them now, imagine it, quite clear.'

'If I,' he said, 'were leaded mirror glass,   25
I could not make your outer image mine
more swiftly than I grasp your inward stress.

28   Pur mo venieno i tuo' pensier tra' miei,
        con simile atto e con simile faccia,
        sì che d'intrambi un sol consiglio fei.

31   S'elli è che sì la destra costa giaccia
        che noi possiam ne l'altra bolgia scendere,
        noi fuggirem l'imaginata caccia.'

34   Già non compié di tal consiglio rendere,
        ch'io li vidi venir con l'ali tese
        non molto lungi, per volerne prendere.

37   Lo duca mio di sùbito mi prese,
        come la madre ch'al romore è desta
        e vede presso a sé le fiamme accese,

40   che prende il figlio e fugge e non s'arresta,
        avendo più di lui che di sé cura,
        tanto che solo una camiscia vesta:

43   e giù dal collo de la ripa dura
        supin si diede a la pendente roccia
        che l'un de' lati a l'altra bolgia tura.

46   Non corse mai sì tosto acqua per doccia
        a volger ruota di molin terragno,
        quand' ella più verso le pale approccia,

49   come 'l maestro mio per quel vivagno,
        portandosene me sovra 'l suo petto
        come suo figlio, non come compagno.

52   A pena fuoro i piè suoi giunti al letto
        del fondo giù, ch' e' furon in sul colle
        sovresso noi; ma non lì era sospetto,

55   ché l'alta provedenza che lor volle
        porre ministri de la fossa quinta,
        poder di partirs' indi a tutti tolle.

58   Là giù trovammo una gente dipinta
        che giva intorno assai con lenti passi,
        piangendo e nel sembiante stanca e vinta.

61   Elli avean cappe con cappucci bassi
        dinanzi a li occhi, fatti de la taglia
        che in Clugnì per li monaci fassi.

Your thoughts just now came in upon my own,   28
in bearing similar, and look as well.
These, all together, formed a single plan.

Suppose that, on the right, the incline's such   31
that we can reach the pocket there beyond,
we shall elude the hunt we now imagine.'

No sooner had he offered up this thought   34
than, coming after us, I saw them, wings
stretched wide, now closer, meaning to get us.

My leader in an instant caught me up.   37
A mother, likewise, wakened by some noise,
who sees the flames – and sees them burning closer –

will snatch her son and flee and will not pause,   40
caring less keenly for herself than him,
to pull her shift or undershirt around her.

Down from the collar of that circling rock,   43
backwards he launched himself, and met the slope
that forms a bung against the other trench.

No mill race ever ran through any sluice   46
at such velocity, or streamed to meet
the scoops that drive, on land, the grinding stone,

as now my master slithered down that verge,   49
bearing me with him, bound upon his breast,
as though I were his son and no mere friend.

And hardly had his feet touched down to meet   52
the pocket floor than those were at the summit,
over us. We need have had no worries.

For that exalted providence that chose   55
such ministers to guard Ditch Five also
deprived them of the power to ever leave.

We found, down there, a people painted bright.   58
Their tread, as round they went, was very slow,
weeping, worn down and seemingly defeated.

They all wore robes with hoods hung low, that hid   61*
their eyes, tailored – in cut – to match those worn
by monks who thrive in Benedictine Cluny.

64   Di fuor dorate son sì ch'elli abbaglia,
        ma dentro tutte piombo, e gravi tanto
        che Federigo le mettea di paglia.

67   Oh in etterno faticoso manto!
        Noi ci volgemmo ancor pur a man manca
        con loro insieme, intenti al tristo pianto,

70   ma per lo peso quella gente stanca
        venìa sì pian che noi eravam nuovi
        di compagnia ad ogne mover d'anca.

73   Per ch'io al duca mio: 'Fa che tu trovi
        alcun ch'al fatto o al nome si conosca,
        e li occhi, sì andando, intorno movi.'

76   E un che 'ntese la parola tosca
        di retro a noi gridò: 'Tenete i piedi,
        voi che correte sì per l'aura fosca!

79   Forse ch'avrai da me quel che tu chiedi.'
        Onde 'l duca si volse, e disse: 'Aspetta,
        e poi secondo il suo passo procedi.'

82   Ristetti, e vidi due mostrar gran fretta
        de l'animo, col viso, d'esser meco,
        ma tardavali 'l carco e la via stretta.

85   Quando fuor giunti, assai con l'occhio bieco
        mi rimiraron sanza far parola;
        poi si volsero in sé, e dicean seco:

88   'Costui par vivo a l'atto de la gola;
        e s' e' son morti, per qual privilegio
        vanno scoperti de la grave stola?'

91   Poi disser me: 'O Tosco ch'al collegio
        de l'ipocriti tristi se' venuto,
        dir chi tu se' non avere in dispregio.'

94   E io a loro: 'I' fui nato e cresciuto
        sovra 'l bel fiume d'Arno a la gran villa,
        e son col corpo ch'i' ho sempre avuto.

97   Ma voi chi siete, a cui tanto distilla
        quanti' i' veggio dolor giù per le guance?
        e che pena è in voi che sì sfavilla?'

So gilded outwardly, they dazed the eye.   64*
Within, these robes were all of lead – so heavy
those capes that melt in torture would seem mere straw.

What labour to eternity to wear such dress!   67
We took once more the leftward path along
with them, intent on their distress and tears.

Because, though, of the labouring weight they bore,   70
these weary folk came on so slow that we,
at every hip swing, joined new company.

'Do all you can' – I put this to my guide –   73
'to find here someone known by name or deed.
As we move onward, scan around to see.'

Then one who'd recognized my Tuscan words   76
from close behind yelled out: 'You! Racing there
through all this murky air, just ease your stride.

You'll get, perhaps, from me what you desire.'   79
At this my leader turned. And, 'Wait,' he said,
'then follow forwards at the pace he sets.'

I stopped and saw there two who, from their look,   82
(though hampered by their load and narrow footings)
in mind were speeding on to reach my side.

At last, they caught me up. With eyes a-squint,   85
they gazed at me in wonder, spoke no word,
till muttering they turned and, each to each:

'This one, it seems – Just see his throat! It flicks! –   88
is still alive. If dead, why favoured so,
to go uncovered by a weighty cloak?'

And then to me direct they said: 'Tuscan,   91
you've reached the college of the hypocrites.
Do not disdain to say who you might be.'

'Born,' I replied, 'by the lovely Arno,   94
grown in the city that adorns its banks,
I still am in the limbs I've always worn.

But who are you, in whom, as I can see,   97
great pain distils such tears upon your cheeks?
What punishment strikes out these sparks from you?'

100   E l'un rispuose a me: 'Le cappe rance
son di piombo sì grosse che li pesi
fan così cigolar le lor bilance.

103   Frati godenti fummo e bolognesi,
io Catalano e questi Loderingo
nomati, e da tua terra insieme presi

106   come suole esser tolto un uom solingo,
per conservar sua pace; e fummo tali
ch'ancor si pare intorno dal Gardingo.'

109   Io cominciai: 'O frati, i vostri mali . . .'
ma più non dissi, ch'a l'occhio mi corse
un crucifisso in terra con tre pali.

112   Quando mi vide, tutto si distorse,
soffiando ne la barba con sospiri;
e'l frate Catalan, ch'a ciò s'accorse,

115   mi disse: 'Quel confitto che tu miri
consigliò i Farisei che convenia
porre un uom per lo popolo a' martìri.

118   Attraversato è nudo ne la via
come tu vedi, ed è mestier ch'el senta,
qualunque passa, come pesa pria.

121   E a tal modo il socero si stenta
in questa fossa, e li altri dal concilio
che fu per li Giudei mala sementa.'

124   Allor vid' io maravigliar Virgilio
sovra colui ch'era disteso in croce
tanto vilmente ne l'etterno essilio.

127   Poscia drizzò al frate cotal voce:
'Non vi dispiaccia, se vi lece, dirci
s'a la man destra giace alcuna foce

130   onde noi amendue possiamo uscirci,
sanza costrigner de li angeli neri
che vegnan d'esto fondo a dipartirci.'

133   Rispuose adunque: 'Più che tu non speri
s'appressa un sasso che da la gran cerchia
si move e varca tutt' i vallon feri,

And one replied to me: 'These orange robes   100
are thick with such a quantity of lead,
the weight of them would make a balance creak.

    We're good-time friars, Bolognese both.   103*
Our names? I'm Catalano. Loderingo's there,
captured together in that town of yours –

    although, by custom, there is one alone   106
whose mandate is to keep the peace. Our doings
still appear around the Watch, for such we were.'

    I then began: 'O brothers! All the harm that you . . .'   109
but said no more. Straight to my sight, there sped
one crucified. Three staves fixed him to earth.

    And he, on seeing me, writhed all around   112
and fluffed his beard up with the sighs he heaved.
Then brother Catalan, who saw all this,

    revealed to me: 'This figure, staked, whom you   115*
so wonder at, advised the Pharisees
that one man suffer for the sake of all.

    Across the road, stretched naked, as you see,   118
he first must feel, whoever passes by,
the toiling weight of those who come this way.

    Here too lies Annas – father of his wife –   121
racked in this ditch with others of that house
that proved an evil seed bed for the Jews.'

    Virgil, I saw, just stood there marvelling,   124
bending above that figure on the cross,
eternally in ignominious exile.

    But then, towards the friar he voiced: 'Please say   127
(though not to trouble you), if you're allowed,
is there some outlet lying to the right

    through which the two of us can make our way   130
without the need to call black angels here,
who might come down to further our departure?'

    'Far sooner than you hope,' the answer was,   133
'we'll near a rock that, jutting from the Ring,
vaults over all these savage valley floors –

136   salvo che 'n questo è rotto e nol coperchia;
       montar potrete su per la ruina,
       che giace in costa e nel fondo soperchia.'

139   Lo duca stette un poco a testa china;
       poi disse: 'Mal contava la bisogna
       colui che i peccator di qua uncina.'

142   E 'l frate: 'Io udi' già dire a Bologna
       del diavol vizi assai, tra 'quali udi'
       ch'elli è bugiardo e padre di menzogna.'

145   Appresso il duca a gran passi sen gì,
       turbato un poco d'ira nel sembiante;
       ond' io da li 'ncarcati mi parti'

148   dietro a le poste de le care piante.

except it's broken here and forms no covering.   136
You can, though, clamber up the ruined side.
The slope is gentle and the base piled high.'

My leader stood a moment, head hung down.   139
And then he said: 'He gave a false account,
that hooker-up of sinners over there.'

'I, in Bologna,' so the friar said, 'have heard   142
a good few stories told of devil vice,
not least "Old Nick's a liar – falsehood's dad".'

At this, with lengthened pace, my lord strode off,   145
clear signs of anger flitting on his face.
And so I left these beings with their loads
     to follow in the prints of his dear feet.   148

CANTO 24

In quella parte del giovanetto anno
che 'l sole i crin sotto l'Aquario tempra
e già le notti al mezzo dì sen vanno,

quando la brina in su la terra assempra
l'imagine di sua sorella bianca,
ma poco dura a la sua penna tempra,

lo villanello a cui la roba manca
si leva e guarda, e vede la campagna
biancheggiar tutta; ond' ei si batte l'anca,

ritorna in casa, e qua e là si lagna,
come 'l tapin che non sa che si faccia;
poi riede, e la speranza ringavagna,

veggendo 'l mondo aver cangiata faccia
in poco d'ora; e prende suo vincastro
e fuor le pecorelle a pascer caccia:

così mi fece sbigottir lo mastro
quand' io li vidi sì turbar la fronte,
e così tosto al mal giunse lo 'mpiastro;

ché, come noi venimmo al guasto ponte,
lo duca a me si volse con quel piglio
dolce ch'io vidi prima a piè del monte.

Le braccia aperse, dopo alcun consiglio
eletto seco riguardando prima
ben la ruina, e diedemi di piglio.

E come quei ch'adopera ed estima,
che sempre par che 'nnanzi si proveggia,
così, levando me sù ver' la cima

CANTO 24

In that still baby-boyish time of year,   1*
when sunlight chills its curls beneath Aquarius,
when nights grow shorter equalling the day,

  and hoar frost writes fair copies on the ground   4
to mimic in design its snowy sister
(its pen, though, not chill-tempered to endure),

  the peasant in this season, when supplies   7
run short, rolls from his bed, looks out and sees
the fields are glistening white, so slaps his thigh,

  goes in, then grumbles up and down, as though   10
(poor sod) he couldn't find a thing to do,
till, out once more, he fills his wicker trug,

  with hope, at least. No time at all! The features   13
of the world transform. He grabs his goad.
Outdoors, he prods his lambs to open pasture.

  In some such way, I too was first dismayed   16
to see distress so written on my leader's brow.
But he, as quickly, plastered up the hurt.

  And so, arriving at the ruined bridge,   19
my leader turned that sour-sweet look on me
that first he'd shown me at the mountain foot.

  He spread his arms, then, having in his thought   22
surveyed the landslip, and (a man of sense)
assessed it well, he took me in his grip.

  Then, always with adjustments in his moves   25
(so that, it seemed, he foresaw everything),
in hauling me towards the pinnacle

28   d'un ronchione, avvisava un'altra scheggia
dicendo: 'Sovra quella poi t'aggrappa;
ma tenta pria s'è tal ch'ella ti reggia.'

31   Non era via da vestito di cappa,
ché noi a pena, ei lieve e io sospinto,
potavam sù montar di chiappa in chiappa.

34   E se non fosse che da quel precinto
più che da l'altro era la costa corta,
non so di lui, ma io sarei ben vinto;

37   ma, perché Malebolge inver' la porta
del bassissimo pozzo tutta pende,
lo sito di ciascuna valle porta

40   che l'una costa surge e l'altra scende.
Noi pur venimmo al fine in su la punta
onde l'ultima pietra si scoscende.

43   La lena m'era del polmon sì munta
quand' io fui sù, ch'i' non potea più oltre,
anzi m'assisi ne la prima giunta.

46   'Omai convien che tu così ti spoltre,'
disse 'l maestro, 'ché seggendo in piuma
in fama non si vien, né sotto coltre;

49   sanza la qual chi sua vita consuma,
cotal vestigio in terra di sé lascia
qual fummo in aere e in acqua la schiuma.

52   E però leva sù; vinci l'ambascia
con l'animo che vince ogne battaglia,
se col suo grave corpo non s'accascia.

55   Più lunga scala convien che si saglia;
non basta da costoro esser partito.
Se tu mi 'ntendi, or fa sì che ti vaglia.'

58   Leva'mi allor, mostrandomi fornito
meglio di lena ch'i' non mi sentia,
e dissi: 'Va, ch'i' son forte e ardito.'

61   Su per lo scoglio prendemmo la via,
ch'era ronchioso, stretto e malagevole,
ed erto più assai che quel di pria.

of one moraine, he'd see a spur beyond   28
and say: 'Next, take your hold on that niche there.
But test it first to see how well it bears.'

This was no route for someone warmly dressed.   31
Even for us – he, weightless, shoving me –
we hardly could progress from ledge to ledge.

Had not the gradient been less severe   34
than that which faced it on the other side,
I'd have been beat. I cannot speak for him.

But Rottenpockets slopes towards the flap   37
that opens on the lowest sump of all,
and so, in contour, every ditch is shaped

with one rim proud, the other dipping down.   40
So, in the end, we came upon the point
where one last building block had sheared away.

My lungs by now had so been milked of breath   43
that, come so far, I couldn't make it further.
I flopped, in fact, when we arrived, just there.

'Now you must needs,' my teacher said, 'shake off   46
your wonted indolence. No fame is won
beneath the quilt or sunk in feather cushions.

Whoever, fameless, wastes his life away,   49
leaves of himself no greater mark on earth
than smoke in air or froth upon the wave.

So upwards! On! And vanquish laboured breath!   52
In any battle mind power will prevail,
unless the weight of body loads it down.

There's yet a longer ladder you must scale.   55*
You can't just turn and leave all these behind.
You understand? Well, make my words avail.'

So up I got, pretending to more puff   58
than, really, I could feel I'd got within.
'Let's go,' I answered, 'I'm all strength and dash.'

Upwards we made our way, along the cliff –   61
poor, narrow-going where the rocks jut out,
far steeper than the slope had been before.

64   Parlando andava per non parer fievole;
        onde una voce uscì de l'altro fosso,
        a parole formar disconvenevole.

67   Non so che disse, ancor che sovra 'l dosso
        fossi de l'arco già che varca quivi,
        ma chi parlava ad ire parea mosso.

70   Io era vòlto in giù, ma li occhi vivi
        non poteano ire al fondo per lo scuro;
        per ch'io: 'Maestro, fa che tu arrivi

73   da l'altro cinghio, e dismontiam lo muro;
        ché, com'i' odo quinci e non intendo,
        così giù veggio e neente affiguro.'

76   'Altra risposta,' disse, 'non ti rendo
        se non lo far; ché la dimanda onesta
        si de' seguir con l'opera tacendo.'

79   Noi discendemmo il ponte da la testa
        dove s'aggiugne con l'ottava ripa,
        e poi mi fu la bolgia manifesta;

82   e vidivi entro terribile stipa
        di serpenti, e di sì diversa mena
        che la memoria il sangue ancor mi scipa.

85   Più non si vanti Libia con sua rena;
        ché se chelidri, iaculi e faree
        produce, e cencri con anfisibena,

88   né tante pestilenzie né sì ree
        mostrò già mai con tutta l'Etiopia
        né con ciò che di sopra al Mar Rosso èe.

91   Tra questa cruda e tristissima copia
        correan genti nude e spaventate,
        sanza sperar pertugio o elitropia:

94   con serpi le man dietro avean legate;
        quelle ficcavan per le ren la coda
        e 'l capo, ed eran dinanzi aggroppate.

97   Ed ecco a un ch'era da nostra proda
        s'avventò un serpente che 'l trafisse
        là dove 'l collo a le spalle s'annoda.

Talking (to seem less feeble) on I went,   64
when, issuing from the ditch beyond, there came
a voice – though one unfit for human words.

I made no sense of it. But now I neared   67
the arch that forms a span across that pocket.
The speaker seemed much moved by raging ire.

Downwards I bent. But in such dark as that,   70
no eye alive could penetrate the depths.
But, 'Sir,' I said, 'make for the other edge,

and let us then descend the pocket wall.   73
From here I hear but do not understand.
So, too, I see, yet focus not at all.'

'I offer you,' he said to me, 'no answer   76
save "just do it". Noble demands, by right,
deserve the consequence of silent deeds.'

So where the bridgehead meets Embankment Eight   79
we then went down, pursuing our descent,
so all that pocket was displayed to me.

And there I came to see a dreadful brood   82
of writhing reptiles of such diverse kinds
the memory drains the very blood from me.

Let Libya boast – for all her sand – no more!   85
Engender as she may chelydri, pharae,
chenchres and amphisbaenae, jaculi,

never – and, yes, add Ethiopia, too,   88
with all, beyond the Red Sea, dry and waste –
has she displayed so many vicious pests.

And through all this abundance, bitter and grim,   91*
in panic naked humans ran – no holes
to hide in here or heliotropic charms.

Behind their backs, the sinners' hands were bound   94
by snakes. These sent both tail and neck between
the buttocks, then formed the ends in knots up front.

And near our point, at one of them (just look!)   97
a serpent headlong hurled itself and pierced
exactly at the knit of spine and nape.

100   Né O sì tosto mai né I si scrisse
       com' el s'accese e arse, e cener tutto
       convenne che cascando divenisse;

103   e poi che fu a terra sì distrutto,
       la polver si raccolse per sé stessa
       e 'n quel medesmo ritornò di butto.

106   Così per li gran savi si confessa
       che la fenice more e poi rinasce,
       quando al cinquecentesimo anno appressa;

109   erba né biado in sua vita non pasce,
       ma sol d'incenso lagrime e d'amomo,
       e nardo e mirra son l'ultime fasce.

112   E qual è quel che cade, e non sa como,
       per forza di demon ch'a terra il tira,
       o d'altra oppilazion che lega l'omo,

115   quando si leva, che 'ntorno si mira
       tutto smarrito de la grande angoscia
       ch'elli ha sofferta, e guardando sospira:

118   tal era 'l peccator levato poscia.
       Oh potenza di Dio, quant' è severa,
       che cotai colpi per vendetta croscia!

121   Lo duca il domandò poi chi ello era;
       per ch'ei rispuose: 'Io piovvi di Toscana,
       poco tempo è, in questa gola fiera.

124   Vita bestial mi piacque e non umana,
       sì come a mul ch'i' fui; son Vanni Fucci
       bestia, e Pistoia mi fu degna tana.'

127   E io al duca: 'Dilli che non mucci,
       e domanda che colpa qua giù 'l pinse;
       ch'io 'l vidi omo di sangue e di crucci.'

130   E 'l peccator, che 'ntese, non s'infinse,
       ma drizzò verso me l'animo e 'l volto,
       e di trista vergogna si dipinse;

133   poi disse: 'Più mi duol che tu m'hai colto
       ne la miseria dove tu mi vedi
       che quando fui de l'altra vita tolto.

Then, faster than you scribble 'i' or 'o',   100
that shape caught fire, flash-flared and then (needs must)
descended in cascading showers of ash.

There, lying in destruction on the ground,   103
the dead dust gathered of its own accord,
becoming instantly the self it was.

Compare: the phoenix (as the sages say)   106
will come to its five-hundredth year, then die,
but then, on its own pyre, be born anew.

Its lifelong food is neither grass nor grain,   109
but nurture drawn from weeping balm and incense.
Its shroud, at last, is fume of nard and myrrh.

The sinner, first, drops down as someone might   112
when grappled down, not knowing how, by demons
(or else some other epileptic turn),

who then, on rising, gazes all around,   115
bewildered by the overwhelming ill
that came just now upon him, sighing, staring.

So, too, this sinner, getting to his feet.   118
What power and might in God! How harsh it is!
How great the torrent of its vengeful blows!

My leader then demanded who he was.   121*
'I pelted down' – the sinner, in reply –
'to this wild gorge, right now, from Tuscany.

Beast living suited me, not human life,   124
the mule that once I was. I'm Johnny Fucci,
animal. Pistoia is my proper hole.'

I to my leader: 'Tell him, "Don't rush off!"   127
and make him say what guilt has thrust him down.
I've seen him. He's a man of blood and wrath.'

The sinner, hearing this, made no pretence.   130
He fixed on me a concentrated eye,
and coloured up in brash embarrassment.

'It pisses me right off,' he then declared,   133
'far more than being ripped away from life,
that you have got to see me in this misery.

136   Io non posso negar quel che tu chiedi:
in giù son messo tanto perch' io fui
ladro a la sagrestia d'i belli arredi,

139   e falsamente già fu apposto altrui.
Ma perché di tal vista tu non godi,
se mai sarai di fuor da' luoghi bui,

142   apri li orecchi al mio annunzio, e odi.
Pistoia in pria d'i Neri si dimagra;
poi Fiorenza rinova gente e modi.

145   Tragge Marte vapor di Val di Magra
ch'ì di torbidi nuvoli involuto,
e con tempesta impetuosa e agra

148   sovra Campo Picen fia combattuto;
ond' ei repente spezzerà la nebbia
sì ch'ogne Bianco ne sarà feruto.

151   E detto l'ho perché doler ti debbia!'

I can't say "no" to what you ask of me.   136
I'm stuck down here so deep 'cos it was me,
the thief who nicked the silver from the sanctuary.

   Then I just lied – to grass up someone else.   139
You won't, however, laugh at seeing this.
If ever you return from these dark dives,

   prick up your ears and hear my prophecy: 142*
Pistoia first will slim and lose its Blacks.
Then Florence, too, renews its laws and ranks.

   Mars draws up fireballs from the Val di Magra,   145
wrapped all around in clouds and turbulence.
And these, in acrid, ever-driven storms,

   will battle high above the Picene acre.   148
A rapid bolt will rend the clouds apart,
and every single White be seared by wounds.

   I tell you this. I want it all to hurt.'   151

CANTO 25

1
 Al fine de le sue parole il ladro
le mani alzò con amendue le fiche,
gridando: 'Togli Dio, ch'a te le squadro!'

4
 Da indi in qua mi fuor le serpi amiche,
perch' una li s'avvolse allora il collo,
come dicesse 'Non vo' che più diche,'

7
 e un'altra a le braccia, e rilegollo,
ribadendo sé stessa sì dinanzi
che non potea con esse dare un crollo.

10
 Ahi, Pistoia, Pistoia, ché non stanzi
d'incenerarti sì che più non duri,
poi che 'n mal fare il seme tuo avanzi?

13
 Per tutt' i cerchi de lo 'nferno scuri
non vidi spirto in Dio tanto superbo,
non quel che cadde a Tebe giù da' muri.

16
 El si fuggì che non parlò più verbo;
e io vidi un centauro pien di rabbia
venir chiamando: 'Ov' è, ov' è l'acerbo?'

19
 Maremma non cred' io che tante n'abbia
quante bisce elli avea su per la groppa
infin ove comincia nostra labbia.

22
 Sovra le spalle, dietro da la coppa,
con l'ali aperte li giacea un draco,
e quello affuoca qualunque s'intoppa.

25
 Lo mio maestro disse: 'Questi è Caco,
che sotto 'l sasso di monte Aventino
di sangue fece spesse volte laco.

CANTO 25

His words now reached their end. And then the robber   1*
hoisted hands on high – a fig-fuck formed in each –
and screamed: 'Take that! I'm aiming, God, at you!'

From that point on, the serpents were my friends.   4
For one entwined its length around his neck
as if to say: 'I'd have him speak no more.'

And then another bound his arms down tight,   7
and clinched itself so firmly round the front
he could not shake or shiver in either limb.

Pistoia! Ah! Pistoia! Why not take a stand?   10*
Just burn yourself to blackened ash, and be
no more. Your seed succeeds in doing only ill.

In all of Hell, through every murky ring,   13*
I saw no spirit facing God so proud,
even that king flung down from Theban walls.

Away he fled. He spake no further word.   16
And then there came, I saw, a wrathful centaur.
'Where? Where is he,' he called, 'so sour and crude?'

Maremma, I should think – with all its swamps –   19
has fewer snakes than he. They writhed from rump
to where, on human features, lips begin.

Above its shoulders, stretched behind the nape,   22
there lay a dragon, wings extended wide.
And all it hits against, it sets on fire.

'This centaur,' so my teacher said, 'is Cacus.   25
He is the one – so many times – who caused
a lake of gore to flood the Aventine.

28   Non va co' suoi fratei per un cammino,
      per lo furto che frodolente fece
      del grande armento ch'elli ebbe a vicino;

31   onde cessar le sue opere biece
      sotto la mazza d'Ercule, che forse
      gliene diè cento, e non sentì le diece.'

34   Mentre che sì parlava, ed el trascorse
      e tre spiriti venner sotto noi,
      de' quai né io né 'l duca mio s'accorse,

37   se non quando gridar: 'Chi siete voi?'
      Per che nostra novella si ristette,
      e intendemmo pur ad essi poi.

40   Io non li conoscea; ma ei seguette,
      come suol seguitar per alcun caso,
      che l'un nomar un altro convenette,

43   dicendo: 'Cianfa dove fia rimaso?'
      Per ch'io, acciò che 'l duca stesse attento,
      mi puosi 'l dito su dal mento al naso.

46   Se tu se' or, lettore, a creder lento
      ciò ch'io dirò, non sarà maraviglia,
      ché io, che 'l vidi, a pena il mi consento.

49   Com' io tenea levate in lor le ciglia,
      e un serpente con sei piè si lancia
      dinanzi a l'uno, e tutto a lui s'appiglia.

52   Co' piè di mezzo li avvinse la pancia
      e con li anterior le braccia prese;
      poi li addentò e l'una e l'altra guancia;

55   li diretani a le cosce distese,
      e miseli la coda tra 'mbedue
      e dietro per le ren sù la ritese:

58   ellera abbarbicata mai non fue
      ad alber sì, come l'orribil fiera
      per l'altrui membra avviticchiò le sue.

61   Poi s'appiccar, come di calda cera
      fossero stati, e mischiar lor colore,
      né l'un né l'altro già parea quel ch'era:

He does not tread the path his brethren take.   28
For spying, once, a mighty herd at hand,
he made it all his own by furtive fraud.

Beneath the mace of Hercules (that god   31
rained down a hundred blows, and he, perhaps,
felt ten, no more) his devious doings ceased.'

So Virgil spoke. The centaur sped away.   34
But now three spirits had approached beneath,
though neither of us noticed they were there

until they shouted out: 'So who are you?'   37
Our story-telling pausing at this point,
we fixed attention wholly on that trio.

Among the three was none I recognized.   40
And yet it chanced – as happens many times –
that one was forced to speak another's name,

inquiring: 'Where has Cianfa got to now?'   43*
At which (to shut my leader up) I placed
a finger slantwise from my chin to nose.

If you are slow, my reader, to receive,   46
in faith, what I'll say now – no miracle.
I saw it all, and yet can scarce believe.

While, eyebrows raised, I stared at these three men,   49
a reptile hurled itself with all six feet
at one, front on, and took a total hold.

It clenched the belly with its middle claws.   52
With each anterior it seized an arm.
It sank a forked fang deep in either cheek.

Along each loin it slithered out a leg,   55
then struck its tail between the two, to take,
now upwardly, a grip around the buttocks.

Ivy in tangles never barbed to tree   58
so tight as this ferocious awfulness,
linking its limbs in tendrils round that trunk.

As though the two were formed of warming wax,   61
each clung to each and, mingling in their hues,
neither now, seemingly, was what it was.

64 come procede innanzi da l'ardore,
per lo papiro suso, un color bruno
che non è nero ancora e 'l bianco more.

67 Li altri due 'l riguardavano, e ciascuno
gridava: 'Omè, Agnel, come ti muti!
Vedi che già non se' né due né uno.'

70 Già eran li due capi un divenuti,
quando n'apparver due figure miste
in una faccia, ov' eran due perduti.

73 Fersi le braccia due di quattro liste;
le cosce con le gambe e 'l ventre e 'l casso
divenner membra che non fuor mai viste.

76 Ogne primaio aspetto ivi era casso;
due e nessun l'imagine perversa
parea, e tal sen gio con lento passo.

79 Come 'l ramarro sotto la gran fersa
dei dì canicular, cangiando sepe,
folgore par se la via attraversa:

82 sì pareva, venendo verso l'epe
de li altri due, un serpentello acceso,
livido e nero come gran di pepe;

85 e quella parte onde prima è preso
nostro alimento a l'un di lor trafisse;
poi cadde giuso innanzi lui disteso.

88 Lo trafitto 'l mirò, ma nulla disse;
anzi, co' piè fermati, sbadigliava
pur come sonno o febbre l'assalisse.

91 Elli 'l serpente e quei lui riguardava;
l'un per la piaga e l'altro per la bocca
fummavan forte, e 'l fummo si scontrava.

94 Taccia Lucano omai, là dov' e' tocca
del misero Sabello e di Nasidio,
e attenda a udir quel ch'or si scocca.

97 Taccia di Cadmo e d'Aretusa Ovidio,
ché se quello in serpente e quella in fonte
converte poetando, io non lo 'nvidio,

Like that, a flame runs flaring up a page   64
and, just ahead, goes ever-darkening tints,
not black as yet, and yet the white still dies.

The other two, at this, stared on. And each   67
moaned out: 'Ohimé, Agnello, how you change!
Already, look, you're neither two nor one.'

And yes, those two by now were both as one.   70
That is: the outlines of the two appeared
in one face only, two-ness lost and gone.

Two arms were fashioned out of four long strips.   73
Thorax and stomach, loins and thighs and hips
became such organs as you've never seen.

In each, the primal signs were all struck out.   76
Two yet not either, as it seemed, this sick
apparition. So, treading slow, it went its way.

The great green lizard, at the summer's height,   79
lashed by a dog star rage from hedge to hedge,
crosses the path as though a lightning flash.

So, paunch high (darting at the two, of three,   82
who still remained), inflamed and fierce, there came
a snakelet, livid as a peppercorn.

This serpent pierced in one that spot where first   85
we draw our nourishment, transfixing him.
It then fell back, stretched out before his face.

The one transfixed gazed down but spoke no word.   88
Rather, he yawned, his feet just planted there.
Sick sleep, it seemed, had struck him hard, or fever.

He eyed the snake. The reptile eyed him back.   91
Each gave out smoke in streams – the wound of one,
the serpent's jaws. The smoke streams slowly met.

Lucan! Be silent now, and tell no more   94*
your snaky tales of poor Sabellus and Nasidius.
Give ear to what the bow will now unleash.

Ovid, be silent! Less 'Cadmus' and 'Arethusa'!   97
In turning verse, these two he may convert
to snake or stream. I do not envy him.

100   ché due nature mai a fronte a fronte
       non trasmutò sì ch'amendue le forme
       a cambiar lor matera fosser pronte.

103   Insieme si rispuosero a tai norme
       che 'l serpente la coda in forca fesse,
       e 'l feruto ristrinse insieme l'orme.

106   Le gambe con le cosce seco stesse
       s'appiccar sì che 'n poco la giuntura
       non facea segno alcun che si paresse.

109   Togliea la coda fessa la figura
       che si perdeva là, e la sua pelle
       si facea molle, e quella di là dura.

112   Io vidi intrar le braccia per l'ascelle,
       e i due piè de la fiera, ch'eran corti,
       tanto allungar quanto accorciavan quelle.

115   Poscia li piè di rietro, insieme attorti,
       diventaron lo membro che l'uom cela,
       e 'l misero del suo n'avea due porti.

118   Mentre che 'l fummo l'uno e l'altro vela
       di color novo e genera 'l pel suso
       per l'una parte, e da l'altra il dipela,

121   l'un si levò e l'altro cadde giuso,
       non torcendo però le lucerne empie,
       sotto le quai ciascun cambiava muso.

124   Quel ch'era dritto il trasse ver' le tempie,
       e di troppa matera ch'in là venne
       uscir li orecchi de le gote scempie;

127   ciò che non corse in dietro e si ritenne
       di quel soverchio, fé naso a la faccia
       e la labbra ingrossò quanto convenne.

130   Quel che giacea il muso innanzi caccia,
       e li orecchi ritira per la testa
       come face le corna la lumaccia;

133   e la lingua, ch'avea unita e presta
       prima a parlar, si fende, e la forcuta
       ne l'altro si richiude; e 'l fummo resta.

For he, through metamorphosis, did not   100
compose two species, glance on glance, whose forms
disposed themselves exchanging actual substance.

Each answered each in working through this rule: 103
the serpent fashioned (from his tail) a fork;
the wounded human dragged his footprints to.

The legs, now fastening at their inner thighs,   106
adhered so well that soon the join between
gave no clear sign of ever having been.

The cloven tail assumed the figure now   109
of that which, over there, was lost to view.
Hide softened here, but hardened over there.

I saw each arm retract and reach its pit.   112
The paws, conversely, of that stubby newt
lengthened as much as human feet grew short.

The hindmost toes then curled around and clinched;   115
these formed the member that a man conceals.
The other wretch wrenched his own part in two.

As now, around this pair, the fumes still hang,   118
a gauze of stranger colours – causing hair
to sprout fresh here, while there it plucks it sleek –

the one rose up, the other fell down flat,   121
yet, peering out, as this snout changed for that,
neither could wrest from either evil eye beams.

Upright, the one dragged jowl across to temple.   124
And then, from leakages of surplus pulp,
a pair of ears appeared, on thinned-out jowls.

Whatever residue did not run back   127
now gelled, and gave that face its human nose.
The lips, plumped up to meet the need, gained bulk.

The other, lying flat, extends his muzzle.   130
Then, just like snails when pulling in their horns,
he draws his ears back, flush along his skull.

And now the tongue – once whole, and quick to speak –   133
divides in two. The other finds his fork
has closed right up. The furls of smoke now cease.

136   L'anima ch'era fiera divenuta,
       suffolando si fugge per la valle,
       e l'altro dietro a lui parlando sputa.

139   Poscia li volse le novelle spalle,
       e disse a l'altro: 'I' vo' che Buoso corra,
       com' ho fatt' io, carpon per questo calle.'

142   Così vid' io la settima zavorra
       mutare e trasmutare; e qui mi scusi
       la novità se fior la penna abborra.

145   E avvegna che li occhi miei confusi
       fossero alquanto e l'animo smagato,
       non poter quei fuggirsi tanto chiusi

148   ch'i' non scorgessi ben Puccio Sciancato;
       ed era quel che sol, di tre compagni
       che venner prima, non era mutato;

151   l'altr' era quel che tu, Gaville, piagni.

The soul, transmogrified to fearful beast,   136*
flees – hissing, snuffling – off across the pit.
Spot on his track, the speaking presence spits.

And then he turns on him his novel back   139
to tell the third: 'I'll see slick Buoso go
as I did, bellyflop, around this track.'

Zymotic in the seventh bilge, I saw, then,   142
change and counterchange. My only plea, if here
my pen turns vain, must be sheer novelty.

And though my vision was a bit confused   145
(spirit quite drained of all its energies),
these souls could not so covertly pass by

that I should fail to see the cripple Puccio.   148*
Of three companions who had first come there,
he, all alone, escaped from alteration.

The last was him that you, Gaville, weep for.   151

CANTO 26

1   Godi, Fiorenza, poi che se' sì grande
che per mare e per terra batti l'ali,
e per lo 'nferno tuo nome si spande!

4   Tra li ladron trovai cinque cotali
tuoi cittadini onde mi ven vergogna,
e tu in grande orranza non ne sali.

7   Ma se presso al mattin del ver si sogna,
tu sentirai, di qua da picciol tempo,
di quel che Prato, non ch'altri, t'agogna;

10   e se già fosse, non saria per tempo.
Così foss' ei, da che pur esser dee!
ché più mi graverà, com' più m'attempo.

13   Noi ci partimmo, e su per le scalee
che n'avean fatto i borni a scender pria,
rimontò 'l duca mio e trasse mee;

16   e proseguendo la solinga via
tra le schegge e tra 'rocchi de lo scoglio,
lo piè sanza la man non si spedia.

19   Allor mi dolsi, e ora mi ridoglio
quando drizzo la mente a ciò ch'io vidi,
e più lo 'ngegno affreno ch'i' non soglio,

22   perché non corra che virtù nol guidi,
sì che, se stella bona o miglior cosa
m'ha dato 'l ben, ch'io stessi nol m'invidi.

25   Quante 'l villan ch'al poggio si riposa,
nel tempo che colui che 'l mondo schiara
la faccia sua a noi tien meno ascosa,

CANTO 26

Rejoice, Florentia! You've grown so grand 1
that over land and sea you spread your beating wings,
and through the whole of Hell your name resounds.

Among those thieves and robbers there, I found, 4*
were five of your own citizens. I am ashamed.
And you do not acquire, by this, great honour.

Yet if we dream, near dawn, of what is true, 7*
then you, not long from now, will surely feel
what Prato aches to see for you – others, as well.

And were it now it would not be too soon. 10
Would it were so, as rightly it should be.
It weighs me down the more that time drags on.

We now moved off. And climbing by those stairs 13
that, going down, had bleached us ivory,
my leader, mounting up, pulled me along.

And so, proceeding on this lonely way 16
through splintered rocks and outcrops from the ridge,
feet without hands would not have gained advantage.

It grieved me then, it grieves me now once more, 19
to fix my thoughts on what I witnessed there.
Now, more than usual, I must hold mind back,

lest brain should speed where virtue does not guide. 22
Thus if, by some propitious star (or more),
I've come to good, I'd best not make it void.

A farmer, leaning on his hillside, rests. 25
(It's summer time, when he who lights the earth
least hides his face from us.) This countryman,

28   come la mosca cede a la zanzara
        vede lucciole giù per la vallea,
        forse colà dov' e' vendemmia e ara:

31   di tante fiamme tutta risplendea
        l'ottava bolgia, sì com' io m'accorsi
        tosto che fui là 've 'l fondo parea.

34   E qual colui che si vengiò con li orsi
        vide 'l carro d'Elia al dipartire,
        quando i cavalli al cielo erti levorsi,

37   che nol potea sì con li occhi seguire
        ch'el vedesse altro che la fiamma sola,
        sì come nuvoletta, in sù salire:

40   tal si move ciascuna per la gola
        del fosso, ché nessuna mostra 'l furto,
        e ogne fiamma un peccatore invola.

43   Io stava sovra 'l ponte a veder surto,
        sì che s'io non avessi un ronchion preso,
        caduto sarei giù sanz' esser urto.

46   E 'l duca, che mi vide tanto atteso,
        disse: 'Dentro dai fuochi son li spirti;
        catun si fascia di quel ch'elli è inceso.'

49   'Maestro mio,' rispuos' io, 'per udirti
        son io più certo; ma già m'era avviso
        che così fosse, e già voleva dirti:

52   chi è 'n quel foco che vien sì diviso
        di sopra, che par surger de la pira
        dov' Eteòcle col fratel fu miso?'

55   Rispuose a me: 'Là dentro si martira
        Ulisse e Diomede, e così insieme
        a la vendetta vanno come a l'ira.

58   E dentro da la lor fiamma si geme
        l'agguato del caval che fé la porta
        onde uscì de' Romani il gentil seme;

61   piangevisi entro l'arte per che, morta,
        Deidamìa ancor si duol d'Achille;
        e del Palladio pena vi si porta.'

as now the fly makes way for the mosquito,   28
sees there, below him on the valley floor,
(where he perhaps will plough and gather grapes)
    glow-worms in numbers such as now I saw,   31
glittering around the dip of Pocket Eight,
when I arrived there, looking to its depths.
    Compare, as also in the Book of Kings: 34*
Elisha (once avenged by furious bears)
beheld Elijah's chariot drawn away
    by horses rising to the Heavens, straight.   37
His eye, unable to pursue, could see
only the flame, like cloud whisp, rising high.
    So, too, within the gullet of that ditch,   40
these fires move round. None shows its thievery.
Yet each fire stole some sinning soul away.
    I stood there on the bridge and craned to look.   43
Indeed, had I not clutched a nearby rock,
I surely would (unpushed) have fallen in.
    My leader, who had seen how hard I gazed,   46
informed me now: 'In all these fires are souls.
Each one is swaddled in its inward blaze.'
    'Well, sir,' I answered, 'to be told by you,   49
I am, of course, the surer. Myself, though,
I'd already thought of that. I meant to ask:
    "Who comes within that cloven-crested flame   52*
that seems to rise as from that pyre where, once,
Eteocles was laid beside a brother slain?"'
    'Within this flame,' so he now said, 'suffering,   55
are Ulysses and Diomed. As one, they face
their nemesis, as they in rage were one.
    Within their flame, the crime is now bewailed   58
of those whose cunning wrought the Trojan horse –
the door that freed the noble seed of Rome.
    They mourn as well the ruse by which – though dead –   61
young Deidamia must weep Achilles' loss.
They're punished, too, for theft, of sacred statues.'

64   'S'ei posson dentro da quelle faville
       parlar,' diss' io, 'maestro, assai ten priego,
       e ripriego che 'l priego vaglia mille,

67   che non mi facci de l'attender niego
       fin che la fiamma cornuta qua vegna:
       vedi che del disio ver' lei mi piego!'

70   Ed elli a me: 'La tua preghiera è degna
       di molta loda, e io però l'accetto;
       ma fa che la tua lingua si sostegna.

73   Lascia parlare a me, ch'i' ho concetto
       ciò che tu vuoi; ch'ei sarebbero schivi,
       perch' e' fuor greci, forse del tuo detto.'

76   Poi che la fiamma fu venuta quivi
       dove parve al mio duca tempo e loco,
       in questa forma lui parlar audivi:

79   'O voi che siete due dentro ad un foco,
       s'io meritai di voi mentre ch'io vissi,
       s'io meritai di voi assai o poco,

82   quando nel mondo li alti versi scrissi,
       non vi movete; ma l'un di voi dica
       dove per lui perduto a morir gissi.'

85   Lo maggior corno de la fiamma antica
       cominciò a crollarsi mormorando,
       pur come quella cui vento affatica;

88   indi la cima qua e là menando,
       come fosse la lingua che parlasse,
       gittò voce di fuori e disse: 'Quando

91   mi diparti' da Circe, che sottrasse
       me più d'un anno là presso a Gaeta,
       prima che sì Enea la nomasse,

94   né dolcezza di figlio, nè la pieta
       del vecchio padre, né 'l debito amore
       lo qual dovea Penelopè far lieta,

97   vincer potero dentro a me l'ardore
       ch'i' ebbi a divenir del mondo esperto
       e de li vizi umani e del valore;

'If they, within those tongues of fire, can speak,   64
I beg you, sir,' I said, 'and beg again –
so may each prayer be worth a thousand more –

    that you do not forbid my waiting here   67
until that flame with horns has come this way.
You see I bend to it with great desire.'

    'Your prayer,' he said, 'is worthy of great praise,   70
and I, most willingly, accede to it.
But you must keep your tongue in tight control.

    Leave me to speak. For I know very well   73*
what you desire. Nor would these two be quick,
perhaps, to hear your words. They both are Greek.'

    And when the flame had reached, in time and place,   76
a point at which my leader thought it fit,
I heard him form his utterances thus:

    'O you there, two within a single flame,   79
if I, when living, won, in your eyes, merit,
if merit, whether great or small, I won –

    in penning my exalted lines of verse –   82
do not move on. Let one of you declare,
where, lost, he went, to come upon his death.'

    The greater of those horns of ancient flame   85
began to tear and waver, murmuring
as fires will do when struggling in a wind.

    Drawing its pinnacle this way and that,   88
as though this truly were a tongue that spoke,
it flung out utterance, declaring: 'Once

    I'd set my course from Circe (she had kept   91*
me near Gaeta for a year or more,
before Aeneas, passing, named it that)

    no tenderness for son, no duty owed   94
to ageing fatherhood, no love that should
have brought my wife Penelope delight,

    could overcome in me my long desire,   97*
burning to understand how this world works,
and know of human vices, worth and valour.

100   ma misi me per l'alto mare aperto
     sol con un legno e con quella compagna
     picciola da la qual non fui diserto.

103   L'un lito e l'altro vidi infin la Spagna,
     fin nel Morrocco, e l'isola d'i Sardi
     e l'altre che quel mare intorno bagna.

106   Io e' compagni eravam vecchi e tardi
     quando venimmo a quella foce stretta
     dov' Ercule segnò li suoi riguardi

109   acciò che l'uom più oltre non si metta;
     da la man destra mi lasciai Sibilia,
     da l'altra già m'avea lasciata Setta.

112   "O frati," dissi, "che per cento milia
     perigli siete giunti a l'occidente,
     a questa tanto picciola vigilia

115   d'i nostri sensi ch'è del rimanente
     non vogliate negar l'esperienza,
     di retro al sol, del mondo sanza gente.

118   Considerate la vostra semenza:
     fatti non foste a viver come bruti,
     ma per seguir virtute e canoscenza."

121   Li miei compagni fec' io sì aguti
     con questa orazion picciola al cammino,
     che a pena poscia li avrei ritenuti;

124   e volta nostra poppa nel mattino,
     de' remi facemmo ali al folle volo,
     sempre acquistando dal lato mancino.

127   Tutte le stelle già de l'altro polo
     vedea la notte, e 'l nostro tanto basso
     che non surgea fuor del marin suolo.

130   Cinque volte racceso e tante casso
     lo lume era di sotto da la luna,
     poi che 'ntrati eravam ne l'alto passo,

133   quando n'apparve una montagna bruna
     per la distanza, e parvemi alta tanto
     quanto veduta non avea alcuna.

Out, then, across the open depths, I put to sea,   100
a single prow, and with me all my friends –
the little crew that had not yet abandoned me.

I saw both shorelines (one ran on to Spain,   103
the other to Morocco), Sardinia
and all those islands that our ocean bathes.

I and my company were old and slow.   106
And yet, arriving at that narrow sound
where Hercules had once set up his mark –

to warn that men should never pass beyond –   109
I left Seville behind me on the right.
To port already I had left Ceuta.

"Brothers," I said, "a hundred thousand   112
perils you have passed and reached the Occident.
For us, so little time remains to keep

the vigil of our living sense. Do not   115
deny your will to win experience,
behind the sun, of worlds where no man dwells.

Hold clear in thought your seed and origin.   118
You were not made to live as mindless brutes,
but go in search of virtue and true knowledge."

My men – attending to this little speech –   121
I made so keen to take the onward way
that even I could hardly have restrained them.

Wheeling our stern against the morning sun,   124*
we made our oars our wings in crazy flight,
then on, and always leftward making gain.

Now every star around the alien pole   127
I saw by night. Our own star sank so low
it never rose above the ocean floor.

Five times the light that shines beneath the moon   130
had flared anew – and five times, too, grown dim –
since we had set our course on that high venture.

Ahead of us, a mountain now appeared,   133
darkened through distance, soaring (to my eyes)
higher by far than any ever seen.

136 Noi ci allegrammo, e tosto tornò in pianto,
ché de la nova terra un turbo nacque
e percosse del legno il primo canto.

139 Tre volte il fé girar con tutte l'acque,
a la quarta levar la poppa in suso
e la prora ire in giù, com' altrui piacque,

142 infin che 'l mar fu sovra noi richiuso.'

We cheered for joy. This quickly turned to tears.   136
For now a wind was born from that new land.
Twisting, it struck at our forward timbers.

The waves and keel three times it swirled around.   139
And then a fourth. The afterdeck rose up,
the prow went down, as pleased Another's will,

until once more the sea closed over us.'   142

CANTO 27

1   Già era dritta in sù la fiamma e queta
per non dir più, e già da noi sen gia
con la licenza del dolce poeta,

4   quand' un'altra, che dietro a lei venìa,
ne fece volger li occhi a la sua cima
per un confuso suon che fuor n'uscia.

7   Come 'l bue cicilian, che mugghiò prima
col pianto di colui – e ciò fu dritto –
che l'avea temperato con sua lima,

10   mugghiava con la voce de l'afflitto,
sì che, con tutto che fosse di rame,
pur el pareva del dolor trafitto:

13   così, per con aver via né forame
dal principio nel foco, in suo linguaggio
si convertian le parole grame.

16   Ma poscia ch'ebber colto lor viaggio
su per la punta, dandole quel guizzo
che dato avea la lingua in lor passaggio,

19   udimmo dire: 'O tu a cu' io drizzo
la voce e che parlavi mo lombardo,
dicendo: "Istra ten va, più non t'adizzo,"

22   perch' io sia giunto forse alquanto tardo,
non t'incresca restare a parlar meco;
vedi che non incresce a me, e ardo!

25   Se tu pur mo in questo mondo cieco
caduto se' di quella dolce terra
latina ond' io mia colpa tutta reco,

CANTO 27

The flame was upright now, and still. It meant   1
to say no more. And so (the poet gently
gave his leave) it went its way, away from us.

But close behind, another blaze came up,   4
and made us turn (a sound, confusedly,
had issued out) and glance towards its top.

Compare the Torture bull of Sicily.   7
This bellowed its inaugural – and justly so –
with wailings from the smith who'd filed it smooth –

these bellows echoing its victim's moans –   10
so that, although, in form mere hollow bronze,
it was, it seemed, transfixed with living pains.

So now those words which, dreadfully, could find   13
no vent or outlet from their burning source,
were spoken in an accent of their own.

But when these sounds had made their way along,   16
and reached the tip which gave that flick and twist
that tongues will give to any stream of air,

we heard: 'You there! I square my words at you.   19*
I heard you say – Lombard tones – just now:
"Be out of it! I'll rile on you no more."

I'm here, perhaps belatedly. But you,   22
I hope, will not be loath to stay and speak.
You see how far from loath I am. And I burn!

If you have fallen even now to this   25
blind world, leaving the land of lovely Italy
(from which I carried any guilt I share),

28   dimmi se Romagnuoli han pace o guerra;
      ch'io fui d'i monti là intra Orbino
      e 'l giogo di che Tever si diserra.'

31   Io era in giuso ancora attento e chino,
      quando il mio duca mi tentò di costa,
      dicendo: 'Parla tu: questi è latino.'

34   E io, ch'avea già pronta la risposta,
      sanza indugio a parlare incominciai:
      'O anima che se' là giù nascosta,

37   Romagna tua non è, e non fu mai,
      sanza guerra ne' cuor de' suoi tiranni;
      ma 'n palese nessuna or vi lasciai.

40   Ravenna sta come stata è molt'anni:
      l'aguglia da Polenta la si cova,
      sì che Cervia ricuopre co' suoi vanni.

43   La terra che fé già la lunga prova
      e di Franceschi sanguinoso mucchio,
      sotto le branche verdi si ritrova.

46   E'l mastin vecchio e 'l nuovo da Verrucchio,
      che fecer di Montagna il mal governo,
      là dove soglion fan d'i denti succhio.

49   Le città di Lamone e di Santerno
      conduce il lioncel dal nido bianco,
      che muta parte da la state al verno.

52   E quella cu' il Savio bagna il fianco,
      così com' ella sie' tra 'l piano e 'l monte,
      tra tirannia si vive e stato franco.

55   Ora chi se', ti priego che ne conte:
      non esser duro più ch'altri sia stato,
      se 'l nome tuo nel mondo tegna fronte.'

58   Poscia che 'l foco alquanto ebbe rugghiato
      al modo suo, l'aguta punta mosse
      di qua, di là, e poi diè cotal fiato:

61   'S'i' credesse che mia risposta fosse
      a persona che mai tornasse al mondo,
      questa fiamma staria sanza più scosse;

tell me: Romagna – is it peace or war?   28*
I was myself from those Urbino hills,
the mountain yoke that first unlocks the Tiber.'

I held my head bowed low attentively,   31
until my leader lightly touched my side,
saying: 'You speak. This one's from Italy.'

And I, who had indeed got words prepared,   34
began without delay to speak to him:
'You, then, below! The soul that's hidden there!

Your dear Romagna (despots all the lot)   37*
is not without, nor ever was, some war-at-heart.
On leaving, though, I saw no open conflict.

Ravenna stands as she has stood for years.   40
The Eagle, blazon of the Clan Polenta,
broods in her skies; its vanes hide even Cervia.

Forlì (her towers withstood that lengthy siege   43
that left a blood-stained pile of French invaders)
goes ever on beneath the green-clawed Lion.

The Mastiffs, old and young, of Fort Verucchio,   46
vicious in lordship over Lord Montagna,
still, as is usual, gnash and suck their bone.

And where Lamone and Santerno flow,   49
the towns are schooled by Lion's-Whelp-sur-Argent.
Summer to winter, north to south, he cants.

And then that place whose rim the Savio bathes –   52
between the mountain and the plain it lies;
it lives between high tyranny and freedom.

So, who are you? I beg you now to say.   55
If you still wish your name to brave the world,
be no more stiff than others are with you.'

The flame, as was its wont, first roared a while.   58
Then, to and fro it writhed its pointed peak
and finally pronounced this speaking breath:

'Should I suppose, in answering, I spoke   61
to any person who should ever see
the world again, this flame would shake no more.

64   ma però che già mai di questo fondo
        non tornò vivo alcun, s'i' odo il vero,
        sanza tema d'infamia ti rispondo.

67   Io fui uom d'arme, e poi fui cordigliero,
        credendomi, sì cinto, fare ammenda;
        e certo il creder mio venìa intero,

70   se non fosse il gran prete, a cui mal prenda!
        che mi rimise ne le prime colpe;
        e come e *qua re*, voglio che m'intenda.

73   Mentre ch'io forma fui d'ossa e di polpe
        che la madre mi diè, l'opere mie
        non furon leonine, ma di volpe.

76   Li accorgimenti e le coperte vie
        io seppi tutte, e sì menai lor arte
        ch'al fine de la terra il suono uscie.

79   Quando mi vidi giunto in quella parte
        di mia etade ove ciascun dovrebbe
        calar le vele e raccoglier le sarte,

82   ciò che pria mi piacea allor m'increbbe,
        e pentuto e confesso mi rendei;
        ahi miser lasso! e giovato sarebbe.

85   Lo principe d'i novi Farisei,
        avendo guerra presso a Laterano,
        e non con Saracin né con Giudei –

88   ché ciascun suo nimico era cristiano,
        e nessun era stato a vincer Acri
        né mercatante in terra di Soldano –

91   né sommo officio né ordini sacri
        guardò in sé, né in me quel capestro
        che solea fare i suoi cinti più macri.

94   Ma, come Costantin chiese Silvestro
        d'entro Siratti a guerir de la lebbre,
        così mi chiese questi per maestro

97   a guerir de la sua superba febbre;
        domandommi consiglio, e io tacetti,
        perché le sue parole parver ebbre.

But since, if all I hear is true, there's none   64
who ever yet, alive, escaped these deeps,
I may reply without the fear of infamy.

I, once great warlord, was a friar next,   67
believing, bound by cord, I'd make amends.
And my beliefs would all have been assured,

had not there been (he'll rot!) that sovereign priest   70
who won me, firmly, back to former sins.
Qua re and "how" I mean that you should hear.

While I was still, in form, such pulp and bone   73
as, first, my mother gave to me, actions
of mine all favoured rather fox than lion.

Stratagems, wiles and covert operations –   76
I knew them all. These arts I so pursued
that word of me rang out throughout the world.

But when I recognized that now I'd come   79
to where we all in life ought, properly,
to furl our sail and take our rigging in,

whatever once had pleased me now annoyed.   82
I vowed – repentant, shriven – all obedience.
It might (what misery!) have worked out well.

The foremost lord of our new Pharisees,   85*
who waged in Rome a war around the Lateran
(never, of course, with Jew or Saracen;

his foes were faithful Christians everyone;   88
none had been present at the fall of Acre,
none worked as trader in the Sultan's souks),

did not, considering his own account,   91
consult his office or his holy rule,
nor mine – that cord which makes its wearer thin.

As once, on Mount Soracte, Constantine   94
required that Pope Silvester cure his leprosy,
so he, mi-lording it, commanded me

to cure him of his fevered arrogance.   97
He asked advice, and I maintained my silence.
He seemed plain drunk in what he had to say.

100   E' poi ridisse: "Tuo cuor non sospetti:
       finor t'assolvo, e tu m'insegna fare
       sì come Penestrino in terra getti.

103   Lo ciel poss' io serrare e diserrare,
       come tu sai; però son due le chiavi
       che 'l mio antecessor non ebbe care."

106   Allor mi pinser li argomenti gravi
       là 've 'l tacer mi fu avviso 'l peggio,
       e dissi: "Padre, da che tu mi lavi

109   di quel peccato ov' io mo cader deggio,
       lunga promessa con l'attender corto
       ti farà triunfar ne l'alto seggio."

112   Francesco venne poi, com' io fu' morto,
       per me; ma un d'i neri cherubini
       li disse: "Non portar, non mi far torto.

115   Venir se ne dee giù tra' miei meschini,
       perché diede 'l consiglio frodolente,
       dal quale in qua stato li sono a' crini;

118   ch'assolver non si può chi non si pente,
       né pentere e volere insieme puossi,
       per la contradizion, che nol consente."

121   Oh me dolente! come mi riscossi
       quando mi prese, dicendomi: "Forse
       tu non pensavi ch'io loico fossi!"

124   A Minòs mi portò; e quelli attorse
       otto volte la coda al dosso duro,
       e poi che per gran rabbia la si morse,

127   disse: "Questi è d'i rei del foco furo."
       Per ch'io là dove vedi son perduto,
       e sì vestito, andando, mi rancuro.'

130   Quand' elli ebbe 'l suo dir così compiuto,
       la fiamma dolorando si partio,
       torcendo e dibattendo 'l corno aguto.

133   Noi passamm' oltre, e io e 'l duca mio,
       su per lo scoglio infino in su l'altr' arco,
       che cuopre 'l fosso in che si paga il fio

136   a quei che scommettendo acquistan carco.

But still he urged: "Don't let your heart be doubtful.   100
I grant you henceforth total absolution.
Teach me how Penestrina may be razed.

The power is mine (you know it well) to unlock   103*
Heaven's door. Or lock it fast. Hence these two keys.
My predecessor held them far from dear."

Such points – all weighty – drove me to the view   106
that silence now was worse than quick assent.
"Father," I answered, "since you wash away

the sin that I must now be guilty of,   109
some promise – generous though of mean extent –
assures you triumph from your lofty throne."

Now dead, Saint Francis came for me. But then   112
a black alumnus of the Cherubim
cried out: "Don't cheat! *You* can't dispose of him.

Down must he come, to join my squalid thralls.   115
His sound advice was, after all, deceitful.
And since that hour, I've hovered round his hair.

Repentance fails? There can't be absolution,   118
nor penitence when willing ill goes on.
That is, by contradiction, *impossibile*."

The pain I felt! I shook myself awake.   121
To me he said (he took a grip): "Perhaps
you never knew: I practise logic, too."

To Minos he transported me, who then –   124
eight times! – coiled tail around relentless spine.
In utter ire, he bit this thing, and then

declared: "Condemned is he to thievish fire."   127
So that is why, as you see here, I'm lost,
and thus go dressed in inward bitterness.'

And once it reached the end of these few words,   130
grieving, the flame went off along its way,
thrashing its horn and wrenching it awry.

We now – my lord and I – went further on,   133
rounding the ridge to find another arch
to span Ditch Nine – wherein, a fee is paid,

incurred by those who force fair deals apart.   136

CANTO 28

1   Chi poria mai pur con parole sciolte
dicer del sangue e de le piaghe a pieno
ch'i' ora vidi, per narrar più volte?

4   Ogne lingua per certo verria meno
per lo nostro sermone e per la mente,
c'hanno a tanto comprender poco seno.

7   S'el s'aunasse ancor tutta la gente
che già, in su la fortunata terra
di Puglia, fu del suo sangue dolente

10   per li Troiani e per la lunga guerra
che de l'anella fé sì alte spoglie,
come Livio scrive, che non erra,

13   con quella che sentio di colpi doglie
per contastare a Ruberto Guiscardo,
e l'altra il cui ossame ancor s'accoglie

16   a Ceperan, là dove fu bugiardo
ciascun Pugliese, e là da Tagliacozzo,
dove sanz' arme vinse il vecchio Alardo,

19   e qual forato suo membro e qual mozzo
mostrasse, d'aequar sarebbe nulla
il modo de la nona bolgia sozzo.

22   Già veggia, per mezzul perdere o lulla,
com' io vidi un, così non si pertugia,
rotto dal mento infin dove si trulla.

25   Tra le gambe pendevan le minugia;
la corata pareva e 'l tristo sacco
che merda fa di quel che si trangugia.

CANTO 28

Who could relate – even in words set loose   1*
from rhyme, even by telling it over and over –
all that I witnessed now, the blood, the wounds.
   There is no doubt: all human speech would fail.   4
Our powers, whether of mind or tongue, cannot
embrace that measure of understanding.
   Suppose that, gathered in one single whole,   7
were all those people of the fated South
whose blood was shed in pain on the Apulian fields –
   be it as victims of the sons of Troy,   10
or else, as Livy writes unerringly,
in that long war where rings were heaped as spoils.
   Then add all those who suffered grievous wounds   13
in wars against the Norman king, Guiscardo,
and also add that band whose bones are gleaned
   at Ceperano still (where southerners, each one,   16
proved traitorous). To Tagliacozzo, then, move on.
There, ageing Elard won – by guile, not arms.
   Were every lopped-off limb or part pierced through   19
seen once again, that, even so, would far
from equal all the foul display in Pocket Nine.
   One I saw riven from his chin to fart hole.   22
No barrel – midslat or moon rib missing –
ever, I am certain, gaped as wide as that.
   Between his legs his guts all dangled down,   25
innards and heart on show, and that grim bag
that turns to shit whatever gullets swallow.

28   Mentre che tutto in lui veder m'attacco,
        guardommi e con le man s'aperse il petto,
        dicendo: 'Or vedi com' io mi dilacco!

31   Vedi come storpiato è Maometto!
        Dinanzi a me sen va piangendo Alì,
        fesso nel volto dal mento al ciuffetto.

34   E tutti li altri che tu vedi qui,
        seminator di scandalo e di scisma
        fuor vivi, e però son fessi così.

37   Un diavolo è qua dietro che n'accisma
        sì crudelmente, al taglio de la spada
        rimettendo ciascun di questa risma

40   quand' avem volta la dolente strada,
        però che le ferite son richiuse
        prima ch'altri dinanzi li rivada.

43   Ma tu chi se' che 'n su lo scoglio muse,
        forse per indugiar d'ire a la pena
        ch'è giudicata in su le tue accuse?'

46   'Né morte 'l giunse ancor, né colpa 'l mena,'
        rispuose 'l mio maestro, 'a tormentarlo;
        ma per dar lui esperienza piena,

49   a me, che morto son, convien menarlo
        per lo 'nferno qua giù di giro in giro;
        e quest' è ver così com' io ti parlo.'

52   Più fuor di cento che, quando l'udiro,
        s'arrestaron nel fosso a riguardarmi
        per maraviglia, obliando il martiro.

55   'Or dì a fra Dolcin dunque che s'armi,
        tu che forse vedra' il sole in breve,
        s'ello non vuol qui tosto seguitarmi,

58   sì di vivanda che stretta di neve
        non rechi la vittoria al Noarese,
        ch'altrimenti acquistar non saria leve.'

61   Poi che l'un piè per girsene sospese,
        Maometto mi disse esta parola;
        indi a partirsi in terra lo distese.

My eyes were fixed and gazed on him alone.   28
And he gazed back. Then, opening up his thorax,
hands at work: 'Look now,' he said, 'how wide I spread!

You see how mangled is the great Mohammed.   31*
Ali, ahead, wends weeping on his way,
cloven in countenance from quiff to chin.

So, too, the others that you here observe,   34
all in their lives sowed schism, scandal, discord.
And that is why they all are here so splintered.

Back there a devil deftly decks us out   37
in these cruel ornaments, and crops each page
in every quire that comes upon his sword edge.

For, as we pass around this road of pain,   40
each wound and gash is made entire and whole
before we come to face him once again.

But who are you, who there sniff down at us   43
and so perhaps are slow to meet the harm
that you've been sentenced to for your own crime?'

'Death has not reached him yet,' my teacher said,   46
'nor is he drawn by guilt to any pain.
I, being dead, to give him full experience,

am bound to lead him all through Hell, from gyre   49
to gyre from ring to ring through every round.
And this, I tell you, is the simple truth.'

To hear this said, a hundred (or yet more)   52
stopped short. They looked in wonder from the ditch
at me, in awe, forgetting their own agony.

'Since you, perhaps, will shortly hail the sun,   55*
then say: If Fra Dolcino is not keen
to join me soon, he'd better stockpile well,

lest winter snow in drifts makes barriers   58
bestowing triumph on the Novarese,
which they'd not lightly come by otherwise.'

That was Mohammed who – as now to leave –   61
had raised his foot while uttering these words.
He placed it flat to ground and went his way.

64   Un altro, che forato avea la gola
        e tronco 'l naso infin sotto le ciglia,
        e non avea mai ch'una orecchia sola,

67   ristato a riguardar per maraviglia
        con li altri, innanzi a l'altri aprì la canna,
        ch'era di fuor d'ogne parte vermiglia,

70   e disse: 'O tu cui colpa non condanna
        e cu' io vidi in su terra latina,
        se troppa simiglianza non m'inganna,

73   rimembriti di Pier da Medicina,
        se mai torni a veder lo dolce piano
        che da Vercelli a Marcabò dichina.

76   E fa sapere a' due miglior da Fano,
        a messer Guido e anco ad Angiolello,
        che, se l'antiveder qui non è vano,

79   gittati saran fuor di lor vasello
        e mazzerati presso a la Cattolica
        per tradimento d'un tiranno fello.

82   Tra l'isola di Cipri e di Maiolica
        non vide mai sì gran fallo Nettuno,
        non da pirate, non da gente argolica.

85   Quel traditor che vede pur con l'uno,
        e tien la terra che tale qui meco
        vorrebbe di vedere esser digiuno,

88   farà venirli a parlamento seco;
        poi farà sì ch'al vento di Focara
        non sarà lor mestier voto né preco.'

91   E io a lui: 'Dimostrami e dichiara,
        se vuo' ch'i' porti sù di te novella,
        chi è colui de la veduta amara.'

94   Allor puose la mano a la mascella
        d'un suo compagno e la bocca li aperse,
        gridando: 'Questi è desso, e non favella.

97   Questi, scacciato, il dubitar sommerse
        in Cesare, affermando che 'l fornito
        sempre con danno l'attender sofferse.'

Another then – his throat pierced through, his nose   64
shorn off and level with his hanging brows,
one ear alone, and only that to hear –

now paused with all the rest to stare at me,   67
but opened up, before the others might,
his windpipe, crimson in its outward parts.

'You there,' he said, 'whom guilt does not condemn,   70
I've met you once on our Italian soil,
unless I'm much beguiled by close resemblance.

If you should see once more the lovely plain   73*
that slopes between Vercelli and Marcabo,
then call to mind again Da Medicina.

And let the two best men of Fano know   76*
(Guido and Angiolello, his peer),
supposing that our foresight is not vain,

they'll both be slung, their necks bedecked with stones,   79
from boats that coast around Cattolica,
betrayed in this by a villainous baron.

From Cyprus on to the Majorcan isles,   82
Neptune has never seen a crime so great
pulled off by pirates or Argolian Greeks.

That traitor with his single seeing eye   85
(who rules a city that another with me here
might wish his sight had still to hunger for)

will work it so that they will come to parley,   88
then work it so they'll need no prayer or vow
to save them from the gales around Focara.'

And I in answer: 'Show me. Make it clear –   91
if you so wish I'll take back news of you –
who is that despot with the bitter view?'

At which, he put his hand around the jaw   94*
of one beside him, prising wide his mouth,
and yelled out: 'Here he is. And he can't utter.

Exiled, he drowned all Caesar's hesitations.   97
For, "Anyone," he said, "who's well prepared
will always suffer harm from titubation."'

100   Oh quanto mi pareva sbigottito
        con la lingua tagliata ne la strozza
        Curio, ch'a dir fu così ardito!

103   E un ch'avea l'una e l'altra man mozza,
        levando i moncherin per l'aura fosca,
        sì che 'l sangue facea la faccia sozza,

106   gridò: 'Ricordera'ti anche del Mosca,
        che disse, lasso! "Capo ha cosa fatta,"
        che fu mal seme per la gente tosca.'

109   E io li aggiunsi: 'E morte di tua schiatta.'
        Per ch'elli, accumulando duol con duolo,
        sen gio come persona trista e matta.

112   Ma io rimasi a riguardar lo stuolo,
        e vidi cosa ch'io avrei paura,
        sanza più prova, di contarla solo,

115   se non che coscienza m'assicura,
        la buona compagnia che l'uom francheggia
        sotto l'asbergo del sentirsi pura.

118   Io vidi certo, e ancor par ch'io 'l veggia,
        un busto sanza capo andar sì come
        andavan li altri de la trista greggia;

121   e'l capo tronco tenea per le chiome,
        pesol con mano a guisa di lanterna;
        e quel mirava noi, e dicea: 'Oh me!'

124   Di sé facea a sé stesso lucerna,
        ed eran due in uno e uno in due;
        com' esser può, quei sa che sì governa.

127   Quando diritto al piè del ponte fue,
        levò 'l braccio alto con tutta la testa
        per appressarne le parole sue,

130   che fuoro: 'Or vedi la pena molesta,
        tu che, spirando, vai veggendo i morti:
        vedi s'alcuna è grande come questa.

133   E perché tu di me novella porti,
        sappi ch'i' son Bertram dal Bornio, quelli
        che diedi al re giovane i ma' conforti.

How dismal and confused he seemed to be,   100
his tongue hacked out and hollow in his gullet,
so headstrong once, this Curio, in parley.

Then one came round with both his hands cut off.   103
He raised his flesh stumps through the blackened air;
he made his face drip filthy red with blood,

and yelled: 'Me too! I'm Mosca, you'll recall,   106*
who said, alas: "What's done, well, that is done."
And this sowed evil seed for every Tuscan.'

To which I added: 'Death to all your clan!'   109
So, piling always grief on top of grief,
he went his way, a melancholic madman.

But I stayed there and, staring at the throng,   112
I now saw something which, without more proof,
I fear that I could never hope to speak of.

Conscience, though, lends me confidence to try.   115
That good companion renders all men free
under its breastplate, knowing we are pure.

I saw – I'm sure – and still I seem to now,   118
in company with others in that herd,
a torso striding by without a head,

who held that head, though severed, by the hair.   121
It swung as might a lantern from his hand.
'Alas!' it said, and stared at us in wonder.

Himself he made a lamp for his own light.   124
So here were two in one and one in two.
How that can be He knows who orders so.

He stood directly by the bridge foot now.   127
He raised an arm (so, therefore, head and all)
to throw his words the closer to us there.

And these words came: 'See this, the harm, the hurt.   130
Breathing you go still, watching on the dead.
See now: is any punishment as great?

And so you may return with news of me,   133*
then know that I'm that Bertran de Born
who gave false comfort to the youthful king.

136   Io feci il padre e 'l figlio in sé ribelli:
       Achitofel non fé più d'Absalone
       e di Davìd coi malvagi punzelli.

139   Perch' io parti' così giunte persone,
       partito porto il mio cerebro, lasso!
       dal suo principio ch'è in questo troncone.

142   Così s'osserva in me lo contrapasso.'

Father and son, I set at mortal odds.   136
No worse, with Absalom, Ahithophel,
whose evil promptings prodded David on.

    Since persons so close-linked I put apart,   139
so I, alas, apart now bear my brain,
thus severed from its root in this great trunk.

    In me, then, counter-suffering can be seen.'   142

CANTO 29

1   La molta gente e le diverse piaghe
avean le luci mie sì inebriate
che de lo stare a piangere eran vaghe.

4   Ma Virgilio mi disse: 'Che pur guate?
perché la vista tua pur si soffolge
là giù tra l'ombre triste smozzicate?

7   Tu non hai fatto sì a l'altre bolge;
pensa, se tu annoverar le credi,
che miglia ventidue la valle volge.

10   E già la luna è sotto i nostri piedi;
lo tempo è poco omai che n'è concesso,
e altro è da veder che tu non vedi.'

13   'Se tu avessi,' rispuos' io appresso,
'atteso a la cagion per ch'io guardava,
forse m'avresti ancor lo star dimesso.'

16   Parte sen giva, e io retro li andava,
lo duca, già faccendo la risposta,
e soggiugnendo: 'Dentro a quella cava

19   dov' io tenea or li occhi sì a posta,
credo ch'un spirto del mio sangue pianga
la colpa che là giù cotanto costa.'

22   Allor disse 'l maestro: 'Non si franga
lo tuo pensier da qui innanzi sovr'ello.
Attendi ad altro, ed ei là si rimanga;

25   ch'io vidi lui a piè del ponticello
mostrarti e minacciar forte col dito,
e udi' 'l nominar Geri del Bello.

CANTO 29

This multitude, their wounds so various,   1
had made my eyes (the lights I look by) drunk.
So now they wished to stand there, and just gaze.

But Virgil said: 'Are you still staring on?   4
Why is your seeing plunged so deep among
such miserable, mutilated shades?

You've not done this in any other pocket.   7
Do you imagine you can count them all?
Well, think! This trench goes twenty miles around.

The moon already is below our feet.   10*
The time that we're allowed to stay is short.
And much is yet to see that still you've not.'

'If you had only cared,' I answered him,   13
'to know the reasons for that lingering look,
you would perhaps have let me stay still longer.'

But he (my leader), and myself behind,   16
was pressing on. I answered thus,
and added, as I went: 'Within that den

where I just now, with reason, fixed my eye,   19
there is a spirit of my blood who weeps,
grieving the guilt that, down there, sets its price.'

My teacher then: 'Allow no wave of thought   22
henceforth to break around his memory.
Attend to other things. And let him be.

I saw him standing by the bridge foot there,   25
still gesturing – a threatening finger raised –
and heard his name called out: Geri del Bello.

28   Tu eri allor sì del tutto impedito
      sovra colui che già tenne Altaforte,
      che non guardasti in là, sì fu partito.'

31   'O duca mio, la violenta morte
      che non li è vendicata ancor,' diss' io,
      'per alcun che de l'onta sia consorte,

34   fece lui disdegnoso; ond' el sen gio
      sanza parlarmi, sì com' io estimo,
      e in ciò m'ha el fatto a sé più pio.'

37   Così parlammo infino al loco primo
      che de lo scoglio l'altra valle mostra,
      se più lume vi fosse, tutto ad imo.

40   Quando noi fummo sor l'ultima chiostra
      di Malebolge, sì che i suoi conversi
      potean parere a la veduta nostra,

43   lamenti saettaron me diversi
      che di pietà ferrati avean li strali;
      ond' io li orecchi con le man copersi.

46   Qual dolor fora, se de li spedali
      di Valdichiana tra 'l luglio e 'l settembre,
      e di Maremma e di Sardigna, i mali

49   fossero in una fossa tutti 'nsembre:
      tal era quivi, e tal puzzo n'usciva
      qual suol venir de le marcite membre.

52   Noi discendemmo in su l'ultima riva
      del lungo scoglio, pur da man sinistra;
      e allor fu la mia vista più viva

55   giù ver' lo fondo, là 've la ministra
      de l'alto Sire infallibil giustizia
      punisce i falsador che qui registra.

58   Non credo ch'a veder maggior tristizia
      fosse in Egina il popol tutto infermo,
      quando fu l'aere sì pien di malizia

61   che li animali, infino al picciol vermo,
      cascaron tutti – e poi le genti antiche,
      secondo che i poeti hanno per fermo,

You were so caught, intent upon the sight   28
of that one there, once sire of Altafort,
you did not care to look around. So off he went.'

'His violent death,' I now addressed my lord,   31
'which goes yet unavenged by any kin,
whose fate must be to share this lasting shame,

inspires disdain in him. I judge that this   34
is why he left speaking no word to me.
This all the more makes clear to me my duty.'

Our talk went on in such-like terms until   37
we found the jutting spur that showed (or would have,
were there light to see) the floor beyond.

I stood there high above the final cloister   40
of Rottenpockets. All its postulants
were present and revealed for us to see.

A host of lamentations shot around me,   43
their iron barbs sharp-tipped with pain and pity.
I covered up my ears with both my hands.

Such sicknesses as here there'd be if all   46*
contagions born of summer heat – from wards
throughout Sardinia, the Chiana Vale, Maremma –

were brought together in one single hole.   49
That's what it was, the stench that came from it,
a fetor rising as from rotting limbs.

Veering still leftwards as we always did,   52
we searched that ridge and reached its final crag.
And there more vividly I came to view

the depths in which, unerringly, the power   55
of justice – minister of One on High –
will castigate those known on earth as frauds.

No greater woe, as I imagine it,   58*
was ever, even in Aegina, known – where plague
infected every citizen and air

so dripped malignancy, its creatures all –   61
down to the smallest worm – fell, sickening fast.
This ancient race was then restored (so say

64   si ristorar di seme di formiche –
         ch'era a veder per quella oscura valle
         languir li spirti per diverse biche.

67   Qual sovra 'l ventre e qual sovra le spalle
         l'un de l'altro giacea, e qual carpone
         si trasmutava per lo tristo calle.

70   Passo passo andavam sanza sermone,
         guardando e ascoltando li ammalati,
         che non potean levar le lor persone.

73   Io vidi due sedere a sé poggiati,
         com' a scaldar si poggia tegghia a tegghia,
         dal capo al piè di schianze macolati;

76   e non vidi già mai menare stregghia
         a ragazzo aspettato dal segnorso,
         né a colui che mal volontier vegghia,

79   come ciascun menava spesso il morso
         de l'unghie sopra sé per la gran rabbia
         del pizzicor, che non ha più soccorso;

82   e sì traevan giù l'unghie la scabbia,
         come coltel di scardova le scaglie
         o d'altro pesce che più larghe l'abbia.

85   'O tu che con le dita ti dismaglie,'
         cominciò 'l duca mio a l'un di loro,
         'e che fai d'esse talvolta tanaglie,

88   dinne s'alcun Latino à tra costoro
         che son quinc' entro, se l'unghia ti basti
         etternalmente a cotesto lavoro.'

91   'Latin siam noi, che tu vedi sì guasti
         qui ambedue,' rispuose l'un piangendo;
         'ma tu chi se' che di noi dimandasti?'

94   E 'l duca disse: 'I' son un che discendo
         con questo vivo giù di balzo in balzo,
         e di mostrar lo 'nferno a lui intendo.'

97   Allor si ruppe lo comun rincalzo,
         e tremando ciascuno a me si volse,
         con altri che l'udiron di rimbalzo.

those poets who believe it true) by seed   64
of ants. Such woe appeared across the dark pit floor.
See, in their different stooks, the spirits languishing.

Some sprawled across the stomach of the next,   67
some over shoulders. Others, on all fours,
dragged on (to make a change) along the road.

Without a word, we went on, step by step,   70
still gazing at and listening to the sick.
They could not lift their bodies from the ground.

I saw there leaning, one against the next –   73*
propped up as pairs of saucepans are to lose
their heat – two, scabby-spotted head to toe.

And never have I seen a currycomb   76
whisked (by a groom whose boss is waiting by,
or else disgruntled to be woken up)

so brisk as these attacked that raging itch –   79
for which no salve can ever now be found –
with biting fingernails to scrape at each.

With fingernails, each tore off showers of scabs,   82
as might a fish knife when it's skinning bream,
or else, perhaps, some type with larger scales.

'You there, whose fingers tear your chainmail off' –   85
to one of them my leader spoke these words –
'employing them as pincers sometimes, too,

now tell us (may your manicure endure,   88
your nails work well to all eternity!),
are there Italians sunk with you down there?'

'We, wrecked and ruined, are Italians both.'   91
So, weeping, one of them made this reply.
'But who are you that put to us this question?'

'I'm one,' my leader answered, 'who descends   94
with this still-living man from ledge to ledge.
My purpose is to show him all of Hell.'

At this, the coupling that had held them sheared,   97
and, trembling, each one turned himself to me,
as others did who heard these words in echoes.

100   Lo buon maestro a me tutto s'accolse,
       dicendo: 'Dì a lor ciò che tu vuoli';
       e io incominciai, poscia ch'ei volse:

103   'Se la vostra memoria non s'imboli
       nel primo mondo da l'umane menti,
       ma s'ella viva sotto molti soli,

106   ditemi chi voi siete e di che genti;
       la vostra sconcia e fastidiosa pena
       di palesarvi a me non vi spaventi.'

109   'Io fui d'Arezzo, e Albero da Siena,'
       rispuose l'un, 'mi fé mettere al foco;
       ma quel per ch'io mori' qui non mi mena.

112   Vero è ch'i' dissi lui, parlando a gioco:
       "I' mi saprei levar per l'aere a volo";
       e quei, ch'avea vaghezza e senno poco,

115   volle ch'i' li mostrassi l'arte; e solo
       perch' io nol feci Dedalo, mi fece
       ardere a tal che l'avea per figliuolo.

118   Ma ne l'ultima bolgia de le diece
       me per l'alchimia che nel mondo usai
       dannò Minòs, a cui fallar non lece.'

121   E io dissi al poeta: 'Or fu già mai
       gente sì vana come la sanese?
       Certo non la francesca sì d'assai!'

124   Onde l'altro lebbroso, che m'intese,
       rispuose al detto mio: 'Tra'mene Stricca,
       che seppe far le temperate spese,

127   e Niccolò, che la costuma ricca
       del garofano prima discoverse
       ne l'orto dove tal seme s'appicca,

130   e tra'ne la brigata in che disperse
       Caccia d'Ascian la vigna e la gran fonda,
       e l'Abbagliato suo senno proferse.

133   Ma perché sappi chi sì ti seconda
       contra i Sanesi, aguzza ver' me l'occhio,
       sì che la faccia mia ben ti risponda:

My good, kind teacher came up close to me,   100
saying: 'Just tell him what it is you want.'
And so, as he now wanted, I began:

'So may the thought of you be never robbed   103
from human memories in the first of lives,
but live on brightly under many suns,

tell me who you might be, and of what kin.   106
Dread not – for all your foul and loathsome pain –
but openly make known yourselves to me.'

'I was,' one answered, 'an Aretine once.   109
Albero of Siena had me burned alive.
But I'm not brought for what I died for here.

O yes! It's true, in jest I said to him: 112
"I've got the knowhow. I can fly through air."
Then he – all eyes, excited, but no genius –

was eager that I put my art on show.   115
I did not do a Daedalus. For that alone,
he got the one who called him son to burn me.

But Minos – not allowed to judge amiss –   118
condemned me to this final slot because,
in life, I practised as an alchemist.'

'On land or sea,' I turned towards the poet,   121
'was anyone as gormless as these Sienese?
The French themselves aren't that idiotic.'

At which, the other leper, overhearing,   124*
quipped in return: 'Except, of course, for Stricca,
who really knew what temperate spending is!

And Nick as well, the twit. He, in that garden   127
where the clove seed grows, discovered first
how rich the virtues of carnation are.

Omit, as well, those merry men with whom   130
Kid d'Ascian consumed both farms and vines.
Dazzledeye, too – who taught the boy such wisdom.

To see, however, who (like you) speaks here   133
so anti-Sienese, just sharpen up your eye.
My face – look hard – may give you your reply.

136   sì vedrai ch'io son l'ombra di Capocchio,
che falsai li metalli con l'alchìmia;
e te dee ricordar, se ben t'adocchio,
139   com' io fui di natura buona scimia.'

I am, you'll see, the shadow of Capocchio.   136
Alchemically, I falsified base metals
and, if I eye you well, then you'll recall
   how marvellous an ape of nature *I* was.'   139

CANTO 30

1   Nel tempo che Iunone era crucciata
per Semelè contra 'l sangue tebano,
come mostrò una e altra fiata,

4   Atamante divenne tanto insano
che, veggendo la moglie con due figli
andar carcata da ciascuna mano,

7   gridò: 'Tendiam le reti, sì ch'io pigli
la leonessa e 'leoncini al varco!'
E poi distese i dispietati artigli,

10   prendendo l'un ch'avea nome Learco,
e rotollo e percosselo ad un sasso;
e quella s'annegò con l'altro carco.

13   E quando la Fortuna volse in basso
l'altezza de' Troian che tutto ardiva,
sì che 'nsieme col regno il re fu casso,

16   Ecuba trista, misera e cattiva,
poscia che vide Polissena morta,
e del suo Polidoro in su la riva

19   del mar si fu la dolorosa accorta,
forsennata latrò sì come cane,
tanto il dolor le fé la mente torta.

22   Ma né di Tebe furie né troiane
si vider mai in alcun tanto crude,
non punger bestie, nonché membra umane,

25   quant' io vidi in due ombre smorte e nude,
che mordendo correvan di quel modo
che 'l porco quando del porcil si schiude.

CANTO 30

Think of that age when Juno – wracked with wrath,   1*
so envious of Semele – expressed her spite,
over and over, against the blood of Thebes.

That was the time when Athamas ran mad.   4
He saw his wife who carried, as she went,
in either arm the load of their two sons,

and yelled: 'Come on! Let's spread those nets! I mean   7
to stalk them all, both whelps and lioness.'
He then stretched out his unrelenting claws.

He grasped one child (Learchus was his name).   10
He whirled him round. He dashed him on a stone.
His wife drowned, loaded with their second son.

When, likewise, ever-turning Fate brought down,   13
in flames, the Trojans from all-daring height –
and so, together, king and kingdom broke –

Hecuba, grieving, wretched, now enslaved,   16
first saw Polyxena, her daughter, dead,
and then – to find there, lying on the margin

of the ocean, her youngest, Polydorus –   19
barked in her lunacy like any cur,
the pain of it so wrenched her mind askew.

And yet no fury known in Troy or Thebes   22
was ever seen, in anyone, to strike
so viciously at beast or human limb

as now I saw in two blank, naked shades –   25
who, racing round that circle, gnashed and gored
as swine do when their pigsty is unbarred.

28   L'un giunse a Capocchio, e in sul nodo
        del collo l'assannò, sì che, tirando,
        grattar li fece il ventre al fondo sodo.

31   E l'Aretin, che rimase, tremando
        mi disse: 'Quel folletto è Gianni Schicchi,
        e va rabbioso altrui così conciando.'

34   'Oh,' diss' io lui, 'se l'altro non ti ficchi
        li denti a dosso, non ti sia fatica
        a dir chi è, pria che di qui si spicchi.'

37   Ed elli a me: 'Quell' è l'anima antica
        di Mirra scellerata, che divenne
        al padre, fuor del dritto amore, amica.

40   Questa a peccar con esso così venne,
        falsificando sé in altrui forma,
        come l'altro che là sen va, sostenne,

43   per guadagnar la donna de la torma,
        falsificare in sé Buoso Donati,
        testando e dando al testamento norma.'

46   E poi che i due rabbiosi fuor passati
        sovra cu' io avea l'occhio tenuto,
        rivolsilo a guardar li altri mal nati.

49   Io vidi un, fatto a guisa di leuto,
        pur ch'elli avesse avuta l'anguinaia
        tronca da l'altro che l'uomo ha forcuto.

52   La grave idropesì, che sì dispaia
        le membra con l'omor che mal converte
        che 'l viso non risponde a la ventraia,

55   faceva lui tener le labbra aperte
        come l'etico fa, che per la sete
        l'un verso 'l mento e l'altro in sù rinverte.

58   'O voi che sanz' alcuna pena siete,
        e non so io perché, nel mondo gramo,'
        diss' elli a noi, 'guardate e attendete

61   a la miseria del maestro Adamo;
        io ebbi, vivo, assai di quel ch'i' volli,
        e ora, lasso! un gocciol d'acqua bramo.

One got Capocchio. At the very knot   28
of neck and spine, his tusks sank in. Then round
the hard pit floor he hauled him, belly scraping.

The Aretine (still there) spoke all atremble: 31*
'That banshee idiot is Gianni Schicchi.
He rages on, and treats us all like that.'

'Really?' I answered. 'Well, let's hope his fangs   34
don't pierce your rear. But (not to trouble you),
please say who's that, before it springs away.'

'That soul is known in legend,' he declared.   37
'It's Myrrha the Depraved, beyond the bounds
of love (as love should be) her father's friend.

She made her way to meet him in that sin,   40
shaping herself in counterfeit disguise.
So, too, the other, shooting off. To win

a mare (the queen of all the herd) he shaped   43
in counterfeit the guise of dying Buoso,
whose testament, attested thus, was sound.'

And now, when these two raging shades, on whom   46
till now I'd fixed my eye, had gone their way,
I turned and looked at other ill-created souls.

And one I saw was fashioned like a lute,   49
or would have been if severed at the groin,
to amputate those parts where humans fork.

Dropsy (osmosis of a morbid flux):   52
that discomposes, as the swellings rise,
all natural fit – so face and paunch mismatch –

constrained him, so his mouth hung open wide.   55
So, too, in fever victims, wracked with thirst,
one lip curls back, the lower meets the chin.

'O you who pass and know no pain (though why   58
I cannot understand) through this mean world,'
so he began, 'behold and hold in mind

the miseries of mastercraftsman Adam.   61
I had, alive, my share of all I sought;
and now I crave, alas, the merest water drop.

64   Li ruscelletti che d'i verdi colli
        del Casentin discendon giuso in Arno,
        faccendo i lor canali freddi e molli,

67   sempre mi stanno innanzi, e non indarno,
        ché l'imagine lor vie più m'asciuga
        che 'l male ond' io nel volto mi discarno.

70   La rigida giustizia che mi fruga
        tragge cagion del loco ov' io peccai
        a metter più li miei sospiri in fuga.

73   Ivi è Romena, là dov' io falsai
        la lega suggellata del Batista,
        per ch'io il corpo sù arso lasciai.

76   Ma s'io vedessi qui l'anima trista
        di Guido o d'Alessandro o di lor frate,
        per Fonte Branda non darei la vista.

79   Dentro c'è l'una già, se l'arrabbiate
        ombre che vanno intorno dicon vero;
        ma che mi val, c'ho le membra legate?

82   S'io fossi pur di tanto ancor leggero
        ch'i' potessi in cent' anni andar un'oncia,
        io sarei messo già per lo sentiero,

85   cercando lui tra questa gente sconcia,
        con tutto ch'ella volge undici miglia
        e men d'un mezzo di traverso non ci ha.

88   Io son per lor tra sì fatta famiglia:
        e' m'indussero a batter li fiorini
        ch'avean tre carati di mondiglia.'

91   E io a lui: 'Chi son li due tapini
        che fumman come man bagnate 'l verno,
        giacendo stretti a' tuoi destri confini?'

94   'Qui li trovai – e poi volta non dierno –'
        rispuose, 'quando piovvi in questo greppo,
        e non credo che dieno in sempiterno.

97   L'una è la falsa ch'accusò Gioseppo;
        l'altr' è 'l falso Sinon greco di Troia:
        per febbre aguta gittan tanto leppo.'

Those brooks that trickle down the high green hills   64
to reach the Arno from the Casentine
and, as they run, make channels, chill and moist,
    stand always in my sight. And not in vain: 67
the image of them parches me far more
than this disease that strips my face of meat.
    Unbending justice probes me to the core.   70
It takes its hint from regions where I sinned,
meaning the more to put my sighs to flight.
    Here Fort Romena stands, and here I forged   73*
fake specie, printed with the Baptist marque.
On that account, I left, up there, my body burned.
    Yet could I only glimpse those woeful souls –   76
Guido or Sandro or their brother – here,
I'd not exchange the Branda Spring for that.
    Already in, there's one of them, if those   79
crazed shadows as they whirl around speak truth.
What use is that to me? My limbs are bound.
    If only I were still so light and lithe   82
to travel in a hundred years one inch,
already I'd have started on that path,
    seeking him out from all this filthy clan.   85
And this ditch turns eleven miles around.
Nor is it less than half a mile across!
    I'm only in this mess because of them.   88
They led me on. I counterfeited florins
so each contained three carats-worth of dross.'
    'And who,' I said, 'are those two so-and-sos,   91
steaming as wet hands do on winter days,
those lying tight against your left frontier?'
    'I found them here,' he said, '(they've not turned since)   94
as soon as I showered down upon this midden.
I do not think they'll budge in all eternity.
    Joseph was falsely charged by that 'she' there.   97*
The other, just as false, is Sinon (Trojan-Greek!).
Their biting fever brews that curdled reek.'

100   E l'un di lor, che si recò a noia
forse d'esser nomato sì oscuro,
col pugno li percosse l'epa croia.

103   Quella sonò come fosse un tamburo;
e mastro Adamo li percosse il volto
col braccio suo, che non parve men duro,

106   dicendo a lui: 'Ancor che mi sia tolto
lo muover per le membra che son gravi,
ho il braccio a tal mestiere sciolto.'

109   Ond' ei rispuose: 'Quando tu andavi
al fuoco, non l'avei tu così presto;
ma sì e più l'avei quando coniavi.'

112   E l'idropico: 'Tu di' ver di questo,
ma tu non fosti sì ver testimonio
là 've del ver fosti a Troia richesto.'

115   'S'io dissi falso, e tu falsasti il conio,'
disse Sinon; 'e son qui per un fallo,
e tu per più ch'alcun altro demonio!'

118   'Ricorditi, spergiuro, del cavallo,'
rispuose quel ch'avea infiata l'epa;
'e sieti reo che tutto il mondo sallo!'

121   'E te sia rea la sete onde ti crepa,'
disse 'l Greco, 'la lingua, e l'acqua marcia
che 'l ventre innanzi a li occhi sì t'assiepa!'

124   Allora il monetier: 'Così si squarcia
la bocca tua per tuo mal come suole;
ché, s'i' ho sete e omor mi rinfarcia,

127   tu hai l'arsura e 'l capo che ti duole,
e per leccar lo specchio di Narcisso
non vorresti a 'nvitar molte parole.'

130   Ad ascoltarli er' io del tutto fisso,
quando 'l maestro mi disse: 'Or pur mira,
che per poco che teco non mi risso!'

133   Quand' io 'l senti' a me parlar con ira,
volsimi verso lui con tal vergogna
ch'ancor per la memoria mi si gira.

Then one of them, who took it much amiss –   100
or so I'd guess, to hear his name so sullied –
now thumped that tight-stretched belly with his fist.

It rumbled forth as though it were a drum.   103
Adam (the master) countered with his arm
to strike him no less hard across the face,

and said: 'It may well be I cannot move,   106
seeing how heavy I've become in limb.
But still my arms are free to do the job.'

The answer came: 'You weren't as free as that   109
when, arms trussed up, you went to mount the pyre.
Your arms were free, though, in their forging days.'

'There,' the hydroptic said, 'you speak mere truth.   112
Yet, as a witness, you were not so true
at Troy, when true words were required of you.'

'Well, I spoke false, and you struck dodgy coin.   115
But I'm here,' Sinon said, 'for one plain fault.
You were accused of more than any demon.'

'The horse! Remember that, you lying cheat!'   118
(This came in answer out of Swollenguts.)
'Tough luck on you that all the world knows that.'

'And tough on you,' the Greek replied, 'the thirst   121
that cracks your bloated tongue, the bilge that swells
that belly to a hedgerow round your eyes.'

At which: 'Yeah, yeah' (the coiner). 'Sickness   124
has stretched your mouth (what's new?) to tearing point.
I may be dry. I'm swollen, ripe with pus.

But you're burnt-out. Your sick head throbs and aches.   127*
It wouldn't take too much – a word or so –
to make you lick the mirror of Narcissus.'

All ears, I strained to listen in – until   130
I heard my teacher speak: 'Go on! Just gaze!
It won't take much for me to fight with you.'

And when I heard his words, so near to wrath,   133
I turned towards him with a shame that still,
on calling it to mind, brews vertigo.

136 Qual è colui che suo dannaggio sogna,
che sognando desidera sognare,
sì che quel ch'è, come non fosse, agogna,

139 tal mi fec' io, non possendo parlare,
che disiava scusarmi, e scusava
me tuttavia, e nol mi credea fare.

142 'Maggior difetto men vergogna lava,'
disse 'l maestro, 'che 'l tuo non è stato;
però d'ogne trestizia ti disgrava.

145 E fa ragion ch'io ti sia sempre allato,
se più avvien che Fortuna t'accoglia
dove sien genti in simigliante piato:

148 ché voler ciò udire è bassa voglia.'

Like someone dreaming of a harm to come,   136
who, dreaming, yearns for this to be some dream,
and hence desires what is as though it weren't,

so was I now. For wishing I could speak,   139
and so excuse myself, I so excused myself,
and did not think that all along I did.

'Less shame,' my master said to me, 'makes clean   142
far greater fault than yours has been. And so
cast off the weight of all your misery.

Consider well. I'm always by your side.   145
Remember this, if Fortune leads you on
to where such spats as this are played out loud.

To wish to hear such stuff is pretty low.'   148

CANTO 31

1   Una medesma lingua pria mi morse
sì che mi tinse l'una e l'altra guancia,
e poi la medicina mi riporse:

4   così od' io che solea far la lancia
d'Achille e del suo padre esser cagione
prima di trista e poi di buona mancia.

7   Noi demmo il dosso al misero vallone
su per la ripa che 'l cinge dintorno,
attraversando sanza alcun sermone.

10   Quiv' era men che notte e men che giorno,
sì che 'l viso m'andava innanzi poco;
ma io senti' sonare un alto corno

13   tanto ch'avrebbe ogne tuon fatto fioco,
che, contra sé la sua via seguitando,
dirizzò li occhi miei tutti ad un loco.

16   Dopo la dolorosa rotta, quando
Carlo Magno perdé la santa gesta,
non sonò sì terribilmente Orlando.

19   Poco portai in là volta la testa,
che me parve veder molte alte torri;
ond' io: 'Maestro, dì, che terra è questa?'

22   Ed elli a me: 'Però che tu trascorri
per le tenebre troppo da la lungi,
avvien che poi nel maginare abborri.

25   Tu vedrai ben, se tu là ti congiungi,
quanto 'l senso s'inganna di lontano;
però alquanto più te stesso pungi.'

CANTO 31

The self-same tongue that bit me first so hard   1
that both my cheeks had coloured up, bright red,
now offered once again its remedy.

So, too (as I have heard the story told),   4
the spear that both Achilles and his father bore
would cause a wound that spear alone could cure.

We turned our back upon the dismal deep,   7
riding the bank that circles it around,
and made our way across without more speech.

Here it was less than night and less than day,   10
so that our seeing went no way ahead.
But then I heard a horn ring out so loud

that thunder in comparison is vapid,   13
and, turning back to see the echoing source,
I fixed my eyes upon one single place.

After the great and grievous rout at which   16
was lost the sacred band of Charlemagne,
great Roland sounded notes of no such terror.

I had not held my head turned there for long   19
when (so it seemed) I now saw many towers.
And therefore, 'Sir,' I said, 'what town is this?'

'Because,' he said, 'through all these wreaths of shade   22
you rush ahead too far from what's at hand,
you form of it a blurred and empty image.

You'll see quite clearly when you soon arrive   25
how greatly distance may deceive the sense.
So drive yourself a little further on.'

28   Poi caramente mi prese per mano,
        e disse: 'Pria che noi siam più avanti,
        acciò che 'l fatto men ti paia strano,

31   sappi che non son torri, ma giganti,

        e son nel pozzo intorno da la ripa
        da l'umbilico in giuso tutti quanti.'

34   Come, quando la nebbia si dissipa,
        lo sguardo a poco a poco raffigura
        ciò che cela 'l vapor che l'aere stipa:

37   così, forando l'aura grossa e scura,
        più e più appressando ver' la sponda,
        fuggiemi errore e crësciemi paura,

40   però che, come su la cerchia tonda
        Montereggion di torri si corona,
        così la proda che 'l pozzo circonda

43   torreggiavan di mezza la persona
        li orribili giganti, cui minaccia
        Giove del cielo ancora quando tuona.

46   E io scorgeva già d'alcun la faccia,
        le spalle e 'l petto e del ventre gran parte,
        e per le coste giù ambo le braccia.

49   Natura certo, quando lasciò l'arte
        di sì fatti animali, assai fé bene
        per tòrre tali essecutori a Marte.

52   E s'ella d'elefanti e di balene
        non si pente, chi guarda sottilmente
        più giusta e più discreta la ne tene;

55   ché dove l'argomento de la mente
        s'aggiugne al mal volere e a la possa,
        nessun riparo vi può far la gente.

58   La faccia sua mi parea lunga e grossa
        come la pina di San Pietro a Roma,
        e a sua proporzione eran l'altre ossa;

61   sì che la ripa, ch'era perizoma
        dal mezzo in giù, ne mostrava ben tanto
        di sovra, che di giungere a la chioma

Then, with great tenderness, he took my hand.   28
He then went on: 'And yet before we step
ahead – so all these facts may seem less odd –
   you ought to know that these aren't towers. They're
      giants.   31
These stand within the well around its rim,
navel height downwards, all the lot of them.'

   As when a mist is thinning out, the gaze   34
will, point by point, begin to recompose
the figure hidden by the steam-thick air,
   so, boring through that dense, dark atmosphere,   37
approaching ever closer to the edge,
false knowledge fled and fear grew yet more great.

   For, as above its circling curtain wall,   40*
Montereggione boasts a crown of towers,
so too above the bank that rings the well
   stood, towering here to half their body height,   43
the dreadful giants, who are under threat
from highest Jove whenever he wields thunder.

   By now I saw, in each of these, the face,   46
the chest and shoulders, areas of paunch,
and, down the ribcage, all their dangling arms.

   Nature did well, desisting from the art   49
of forming animals like that. She thus
deprived great Mars of his executors.

   If she, on that account, did not repent   52
of whales and elephants, to subtle minds
this will seem right, and most intelligent.

   For when the powers of working intellect   55
are wed to strength and absolute illwill,
then humans cannot find a place to hide.

   In bulk and length, his face could be compared   58
to that bronze pine cone in Saint Peter's, Rome.
His other bones were all in due proportion.

   And so that bank (his fig leaf, 'zone' or apron,   61*
hanging around his loins below) displayed,
above, up to his mane, as much of him

64   tre Frison s'averien dato mal vanto,
        però ch'i' ne vedea trenta gran palmi
        dal loco in giù dov' omo affibbia 'l manto.

67   'Raphèl maì amècche zabì almì,'
        cominciò a gridar la fiera bocca,
        cui non si convenia più dolci salmi.

70   E 'l duca mio ver' lui: 'Anima sciocca,
        tienti col corno, e con quel ti disfoga
        quand' ira o altra passion ti tocca!

73   Cércati al collo, e troverai la soga
        che 'l tien legato, o anima confusa,
        e vedi lui che 'l gran petto ti doga.'

76   Poi disse a me: 'Elli stessi s'accusa:
        questi è Nembrotto per lo cui mal coto
        pur un linguaggio nel mondo non s'usa.

79   Lasciànlo stare e non parliamo a vòto;
        ché così è a lui ciascun linguaggio
        come 'l suo ad altrui, ch'a nullo è noto.'

82   Facemmo adunque più lungo viaggio,
        vòlti a sinistra; e al trar d'un balestro
        trovammo l'altro assai più fero e maggio.

85   A cigner lui qual che fosse 'l maestro
        non so io dir, ma el tenea soccinto
        dinanzi l'altro e dietro il braccio destro,

88   d'una catena che 'l tenea avvinto
        dal collo in giù, sì che 'n su lo scoperto
        si ravvolgea infino al giro quinto.

91   'Questo superbo volle esser esperto
        di sua potenza contra 'l sommo Giove,'
        disse 'l mio duca, 'ond' elli ha cotal merto.

94   Fialte ha nome, e fece le gran prove
        quando i giganti fer paura a' dèi;
        le braccia ch'el menò, già mai non move.'

97   E io a lui: 'S'esser puote, io vorrei
        che de lo smisurato Briareo
        esperienza avesser li occhi mei.'

as three tall Frisians would boast in vain.   64
I saw their thirty-eight-inch finger spans
down from the point where cloaks are buckled on.

'*Raphèl maì amècche zabì almì*,'   67
so screaming it began, that fearsome mouth,
unfit to utter any sweeter psalm.

My leader aimed: 'You idiotic soul!   70*
Stick to your horn. With that, give vent to wrath,
or any passion that you chance to feel.

Just fumble round your neck, you great dumb thing.   73
You'll find the cord it's tied to. There it rests.
A chevron – see? – across your mighty breast.'

And then to me: 'He stands his own accuser.   76
It's Nimrod there. Through his sick whim
no single tongue is spoken anywhere.

So, let him be. We'll not speak in that vein.   79
For every tongue, to him, remains the same
as his tongue is to others: quite unknown.'

Now, turning left, we made a longer march;   82
and there (the distance of a crossbow shot)
we found a bigger ogre, fiercer still.

Who that lord was I cannot tell, who locked   85
these shackles round him and about. He held
his right arm bound in front, his left behind,

by one tight chain that – tangling down – was hitched   88
a full five turns around the bits we saw,
netherwards stretching from his neck to waist.

'This one, in pride, was quick to prove his power   91
against the majesty of Jupiter.'
Thus spoke my leader. 'His reward is this.

By name Ephialtes, his deeds were done   94*
when giants caused the deities such dread.
He can't now budge the arm he wielded then.'

And I to him: 'If it were possible   97
to gain with my own eyes experience
of measureless Briareus, *that* I'd like.'

100   Ond' ei rispuose: 'Tu vedrai Anteo
       presso di qui, che parla ed è disciolto,
       che ne porrà nel fondo d'ogne reo.

103   Quel che tu vuo' veder più in là è molto,
       ed è legato e fatto come questo,
       salvo che più feroce par nel volto.'

106   Non fu tremoto già tanto rubesto
       che scotesse una torre così forte
       come Fialte a scuotersi fu presto.

109   Allor temett' io più che mai la morte,
       e non v'era mestier più che la dotta,
       s'io non avessi viste le ritorte.

112   Noi procedemmo più avante allotta,
       e venimmo ad Anteo, che ben cinque alle,
       sanza la testa, uscia fuor de la grotta.

115   'O tu che ne la fortunata valle –
       che fece Scipion di gloria reda
       quand' Anibàl co' suoi diede le spalle –

118   recasti già mille leon per preda,
       e che, se fossi stato a l'alta guerra
       de' tuoi fratelli, ancor par che si creda

121   ch'avrebber vinto i figli de la terra:
       mettine giù, e non ten vegna schifo,
       dove Cocito la freddura serra.

124   Non ci far ire a Tizio né a Tifo;
       questi può dar di quel che qui si brama;
       però ti china e non torcer lo grifo.

127   Ancor ti può nel mondo render fama,
       ch'el vive, e lunga vita ancor aspetta,
       se 'nnanzi tempo grazia a sé nol chiama.'

130   Così disse 'l maestro; e quelli in fretta
       le man distese, e prese 'l duca mio,
       ond' Ercule sentì già grande stretta.

133   Virgilio, quando prender si sentio,
       disse a me: 'Fatti qua, sì ch'io ti prenda.'
       Poi fece sì ch'un fascio era elli e io.

'Antaeus,' he in answer said, 'you'll see   100
not very far from here. And he – unchained
and speaking, too – will lower us to sin's last floor.

The one whom you so keenly wish to see   103
is over there, a good way further on,
constrained like these but fiercer still in mien.'

No earthquake, rude in vigour, ever struck   106
a tower with such great force as Ephialtes,
writhing round suddenly, now shook himself.

And, more than ever now in mortal fear,   109
sheer terror would have done the trick, had I
not seen the fetters that restrained him there.

And now, as we proceeded on our way,   112
we came upon Antaeus, rising high
(omitting head) five yards above the pit.

'You there! Yes, you! In that propitious vale   115*
where Hannibal turned tail with all his men –
and so made Scipio the heir of fame –

you brought as spoils a thousand lions back.   118
And if, like all your brothers, you had joined
in battle with the gods above, then (some

believe) those earthborn sons might well have won.   121
Then set us down – and please, no dark disdain –
deep in Cocytus, locked by freezing keys.

Don't make us trudge to Tityos or Typhon.   124
This man can give you what you yearn to have.
Therefore bend down. And do not twist your snout.

To earth he can still carry back your name.   127
He's living still – and so expects to, long,
unless grace summons him before his time.'

My teacher spoke. The giant in great haste   130
stretched out his hands – whose powerful clutch had once
been felt by Hercules – to take him in his fist.

And Virgil, when he felt himself well held,   133
now said to me: 'Come here. Let me take you!'
He packed us in – one bundle, him and me.

136   Qual pare a riguardar la Carisenda
       sotto 'l chinato, quando un nuvol vada
       sovr'essa sì ched ella incontro penda:
139   tal parve Anteo a me che stava a bada
       di vederlo chinare, e fu tal ora
       ch'i' avrei voluto ir per altra strada.
142   Ma lievemente al fondo che divora
       Lucifero con Giuda ci sposò;
       né, sì chinato, lì fece dimora,
145   e come albero in nave si levò.

    Just as the Garisenda tower, when viewed   136
beneath its leaning side, appears to fall
if any floating cloud should pass behind,
    so, too, Antaeus seemed to me, as there   139
I stood expecting him to bend. And now
I'd willingly have gone some other way.
    Yet lightly he set us, lightly, in those depths   142
that eat at Lucifer and Judas, too.
He did not, bowing so, make long delay,
    but swayed again up straight as ship masts do.   145

CANTO 32

1   S'io avessi le rime aspre e chiocce
come si converrebbe al tristo buco
sovra 'l qual pontan tutte l'altre rocce,

4   io premerei di mio concetto il suco
più pienamente; ma perch' io non l'abbo,
non sanza tema a dicer mi conduco:

7   ché non è impresa da pigliare a gabbo
discriver fondo a tutto l'universo,
né da lingua che chiami mamma o babbo.

10   Ma quelle donne aiutino il mio verso
ch'aiutaro Anfïone a chiuder Tebe,
sì che dal fatto il dir non sia diverso.

13   Oh sovra tutte mal creata plebe
che stai nel loco onde parlare è duro,
mei foste state qui pecore o zebe!

16   Come noi fummo giù nel pozzo scuro
sotto i piè del gigante assai più bassi,
e io mirava ancora a l'alto muro,

19   dicere udi'mi: 'Guarda come passi!
Va sì che tu non calchi con le piante
le teste de' fratei miseri lassi.'

22   Per ch'io mi volsi, e vidimi davante
e sotto i piedi un lago che per gelo
avea di vetro e non d'acqua sembiante.

25   Non fece al corso suo sì grosso velo
di verno la Danoia in Osterlicchi,
né Tanai là sotto 'l freddo cielo,

CANTO 32

If I had rhymes that rawly rasped and cackled   1*
(and chimed in keeping with that cacky hole
at which, point down, all other rock rings peak),
    I might then squeeze the juices of my thought   4
more fully out of me. But since I don't,
not without dread, I bring myself to speak.
    It's not (no kidding) any sort of joke   7
to form in words the universal bum,
no task for tongues still whimpering 'Mum!' and 'Dad!'
    The Muses, though, may raise my verse – women   10*
who once helped Amphion lock Thebes in walls –
so fact and word may not too far diverge.
    You ill-begotten zombies, worst of all,   13*
who stand there where to utter is so hard,
better had you been born as sheep or bezoars!
    Now deep within the darkness of that well   16
and further even than those giant feet,
I stood and gazed sheer upwards at that wall
    when, out of nowhere, I heard: 'Watch your step!   19
Don't plant those feet of yours on some poor head;
we're here all brothers in this sorry crowd.'
    I turned at this, and now could see – around,   22
and all beneath, my feet – a lake of ice
that seemed far less like water than clear glass.
    The Danube, even in winter Österreich,   25
never congealed its currents to so thick
a veil (the Don, neither, under freezing skies)

28   com' era quivi; che se Tambernicchi
        vi fosse sù caduto, o Pietrapana,
        non avria pur da l'orlo fatto cricchi.

31   E come a gracidar si sta la rana
        col muso fuor de l'acqua, quando sogna
        di spigolar sovente la villana,

34   livide insin là dove appar vergogna
        eran l'ombre dolenti ne la ghiaccia,
        mettendo i denti in nota di cicogna.

37   Ognuna in giù tenea volta la faccia;
        da bocca il freddo, e da li occhi il cor tristo
        tra lor testimonianza si procaccia.

40   Quand' io m'ebbi dintorno alquanto visto,
        volsimi a' piedi, e vidi due sì stretti
        che 'l pel del capo avieno insieme misto.

43   'Ditemi, voi che sì strignete i petti,'
        diss' io, 'chi siete?' E quei piegaro i colli;
        e poi ch'ebber li visi a me eretti,

46   li occhi lor, ch'eran pria pur dentro molli,
        gocciar su per le labbra, e 'l gelo strinse
        le lagrime tra essi, e riserrolli.

49   Con legno legno spranga mai non cinse
        forte così, ond' ei come due becchi
        cozzaro insieme, tanta ira li vinse.

52   E un ch'avea perduti ambo li orecchi
        per la freddura, pur col viso in giùe,
        disse: 'Perché cotanto in noi ti specchi?

55   Se vuoi saper chi son cotesti due,
        la valle onde Bisenzo si dichina
        del padre loro Alberto e di lor fue.

58   D'un corpo usciro; e tutta la Caina
        potrai cercare, e non troverai ombra
        degna più d'esser fitta in gelatina:

61   non quelli a cui fu rotto il petto e l'ombra
        con esso un colpo per la man d'Artù,
        non Focaccia, non questi che m'ingombra

  as this. And if the crags of Tambernic   28*
had crashed down here – or Pike Pietrapana –
its very fringe would not have cracked or creaked.

  As frogs sit croaking in the harvest month   31
(when country girls will dream of gleaning corn),
their snouts just poking from the water line,

  so too these shadows, fixed in ice lead-blue,   34
to where, in shame, we start to blush, their teeth
as rhythmic, beakily, as chattering storks.

  And each one kept his face bent down. From mouths   37
the cold, from hearts their miseries force
a public testament of suffering.

  I stood a while just gazing all around,   40*
then, glancing to my feet, I saw here two
embraced so closely that their head hair mixed.

  'Go on,' I said, 'so tell me who you are,   43
straining so tightly, tit to tit.' Coupled,
the two eased back their necks. Their faces now

  were straight to mine. Once moist within, their eyes   46
welled up. The teardrops flowed toward their lips.
But chill gripped these, to lock them in their holes.

  To wood wood never has been clamped so hard   49
as these two were; and, overwhelmed with ire,
each butted each like any pair of goats.

  Another in the frost had lost both ears.   52
Still gazing downwards, he was first to speak:
'Why eye us so, as though we were your mirror?

  If you're so keen to know who these two are,   55
that valley where Bisenzio streams down
belonged to them, as to their father, earlier.

  They issued from a single womb. And you   58*
may go, if you so please, through all of Cain
finding no shadow freeze in aspic fitter,

  not Mordred, even – breast and shadow pierced   61*
by thrusts his "uncle", great King Arthur, gave –
neither Focaccia (source of strife), nor this one here,

64   col capo sì ch'i' non veggio oltre più,
        e fu nomato Sassol Mascheroni:
        se tosco se', ben sai omai chi fu.

67   E perché non mi metti in più sermoni,
        sappi ch'i' fu' il Camiscion de' Pazzi,
        e aspetto Carlin che mi scagioni.'

70   Poscia vid' io mille visi cagnazzi
        fatti per freddo, onde mi vien riprezzo,
        e verrà sempre, de' gelati guazzi.

73   E mentre ch'andavamo inver' lo mezzo
        al quale ogne gravezza si rauna,
        e io tremava ne l'etterno rezzo,

76   se voler fu o destino o fortuna,
        non so, ma, passeggiando tra le teste,
        forte percossi 'l piè nel viso ad una.

79   Piangendo mi sgridò: 'Perché mi peste?
        se tu non vieni a crescer la vendetta
        di Montaperti, perché mi moleste?'

82   E io: 'Maestro mio, or qui m'aspetta,
        sì ch'io esca d'un dubbio per costui;
        poi mi farai, quantunque vorrai, fretta.'

85   Lo duca stette, e io dissi a colui,
        che bestemmiava duramente ancora:
        'Qual se' tu che così rampogni altrui?'

88   'Or tu chi se' che vai per l'Antenora
        percotendo,' rispuose, 'altrui le gote,
        sì che, se fossi vivo, troppo fora?'

91   'Vivo son io, e caro esser ti puote,'
        fu mia risposta, 'se dimandi fama,
        ch'io metta il nome tuo tra l'altre note.'

94   Ed elli a me: 'Del contrario ho io brama.
        Lèvati quinci e non mi dar più lagna,
        ché mal sai lusingar per questa lama!'

97   Allor lo presi per la cuticagna
        e dissi: 'El converrà che tu ti nomi
        o che capel qui sù non ti rimagna.'

whose head, so annoyingly, cramps my view.   64
His name was Sassolo Mascheroni,
and you, if you are Tuscan, know him well.

However, not to drag out speeches further,   67
be told that I'm Camiscion de' Pazzi.
I wait for Carlin. He'll acquit me here.'

And then I saw a thousand mongrel faces   70*
bitten by frost. (I shiver, remembering –
and always will – to see a frozen puddle.)

Trembling, as ever, in the endless nip,   73
onwards we went to reach the cone's last core,
where all the weight of everything weighs down.

And whether by intention, chance or fate   76
(well, I don't know!) pacing among these heads,
hard in the face of one, I struck my foot.

It screeched out, whingingly: 'Why stamp on me?   79
Unless, of course, you're here to take revenge
for Montaperti. If not, why do me harm?'

I to my teacher: 'Wait a little here.   82
I'll go and free myself of doubts with him.
Then push me on as much as you desire.'

My leader paused. And, turning to the one   85
still spitting curses out, I now inquired:
'So who are you, to go on scolding others?'

'And who are you? You trek through Antenora,   88
bashing,' he said, 'at other people's cheeks.
Were you alive, I wouldn't stand for it.'

'I am alive,' I answered him. 'How dear to you   91
I might become, if fame is what you thirst for!
I could well note your name among the rest.'

'I yearn,' he answered, 'for the opposite.   94
Just go away and give me no more grief.
You don't know how to flatter in a bog like this.'

And so I grasped him tight against the scalp.   97
'You'll name yourself,' I said to him. 'If not,
you'll find no single bristle on your topknot.'

100   Ond' elli a me: 'Perché tu mi dischiomi,
       né ti dirò ch'io sia né mosterrolti,
       se mille fiate in sul capo mi tomi.'

103   Io avea già i capelli in mano avvolti,
       e tratti glien' avea più d'una ciocca,
       latrando lui con li occhi in giù raccolti,

106   quando un altro gridò: 'Che hai tu, Bocca?
       non ti basta sonar con le mascelle,
       se tu non latri? qual diavol ti tocca?'

109   'Omai,' diss' io, 'non vo' che più favelle,
       malvagio traditor, ch'a la tua onta
       io porterò di te vere novelle.'

112   'Va via,' rispuose, 'e ciò che tu vuoi conta;
       ma non tacer, se tu di qua entro eschi,
       di quel ch'ebbe or così la lingua pronta.

115   El piange qui l'argento de' Franceschi:
       "Io vidi," potrai dir, "quel da Duera
       là dove i peccatori stanno freschi."

118   Se fossi domandato: "Altri chi v'era?"
       tu hai dallato quel di Beccheria
       di cui segò Fiorenza la gorgiera.

121   Gianni de' Soldanier credo che sia
       più là con Ganellone e Tebaldello,
       ch'aprì Faenza quando si dormia.'

124   Noi eravam partiti già da ello,
       ch'io vidi due ghiacciati in una buca,
       sì che l'un capo a l'altro era cappello;

127   e come 'l pan per fame si manduca,
       così 'l sovran li denti a l'altro pose
       là 've 'l cervel s'aggiugne con la nuca:

130   non altrimenti Tideo si rose
       le tempie a Menalippo per disdegno,
       che quei faceva il teschio e l'altre cose.

133   'O tu che mostri per sì bestial segno
       odio sovra colui che tu ti mangi,
       dimmi 'l perché,' diss' io, 'per tal convegno,

'Don't think,' he said, 'because you pluck my curls,   100
I mean to say or show you bugger all,
bomb as you may my skull ten thousand times.'

I'd got him twisted in my fingers now,   103
and had, already, yanked out several tufts.
He barked, but kept his eyes held firmly down.

Another yelling now: 'What's with you, Big Mouth?   106
Not satisfied to castanet cold jaws?
You bark as well. What devil's got to you?'

And then I said: 'I'd have you speak no more.   109
You're vile, you traitor. I'll augment your shame,
I'll carry in your name a true report.'

'Go on,' he answered, 'gossip all you like.   112
But don't, if you get out of here, be silent
when it comes to him, his tongue so slick.

He weeps for having fingered French-y silver.   115
Now you can say: "I saw that man from Duera.
He dwells where all the sinners keep quite cool."

And should you ask me: "Are there others here?"   118
Beside you, there is Abbot Beccheria,
the one whose gizzard Florence sawed right through.

Then Ghibelline Jack, I guess, is further on,   121
with Ganelon and Tebaldello, too.
He slid the doors of sleeping Faience back.'

By now we had already gone our way.   124*
But then I saw two frozen in one single hole,
one head a headpiece to the one below.

As bread is mangled by some famished mouth,   127
so too the higher gnawed the lower head,
precisely where the nape and brainstem meet.

The dying Tydeus in this same way,   130
in loathing, chewed the brows of dead Menalippus,
gnawing the skull and everything besides.

'O you who by so bestial a show   133
make known your hatred for the one you eat,
now tell me – why? I give my word,' I said,

136   che se tu a ragion di lui ti piangi,
        sappiendo chi voi siete e la sua pecca,
        nel mondo suso ancora io te ne cangi,
139   se quella con ch'io parlo non si secca.'

'if you complain of him with proper cause,   136
then once I know his name and how he sinned,
I'll make you in the world a fair return,
  provided means of speech do not fall dry.'   139

CANTO 33

1   La bocca sollevò dal fiero pasto
    quel peccator, forbendola a' capelli
    del capo ch'elli avea di retro guasto.

4   Poi cominciò: 'Tu vuo' ch'io rinovelli
    disperato dolor che 'l cor mi preme
    già pur pensando, pria ch'io ne favelli.

7   Ma se le mie parole esser dien seme
    che frutti infamia al traditor ch'i' rodo,
    parlare e lagrimar vedrai insieme.

10 Io non so chi tu se' né per che modo
    venuto se' qua giù; ma fiorentino
    mi sembri veramente quand'io t'odo.

13 Tu dei saper chi'i' fui conte Ugolino,
    e questi è l'arcivescovo Ruggieri:
    or ti dirò perché i son tal vicino.

16 Che per l'effetto de' suo' mai pensieri,
    fidandomi di lui, io fossi preso
    e poscia morto, dir non è mestieri;

19 però quel che non puoi aver inteso,
    cioè come la morte mia fu cruda,
    udirai, e saprai s'e' m'ha offeso.

22 Breve pertugio dentro da la Muda
    la qual per me ha 'l titol de la fame,
    e che conviene ancor ch'altrui si chiuda,

25 m'avea mostrato per lo suo forame
    più lune già, quand' io feci 'l mal sonno
    che del futuro mi squarciò 'l velame.

CANTO 33

Jaws lifted now from that horrible dish,   1
the sinner – wiping clean each lip on hair that fringed
the mess he'd left the head in, at its rear –
    began: 'You ask that I should tell anew   4
the pain that hopelessly, in thought alone,
before I voice it, presses at my heart.
    Yet if I may, by speaking, sow the fruit   7
of hate to slur this traitor, caught between my teeth,
then words and tears, you'll see, will flow as one.
    Who you might be, I do not know, nor how   10
you've come to be down here. But when you speak,
you seem (there's little doubt) a Florentine.
    You need to see: I was Count Ugolino.   13*
This is Ruggieri, the archbishop, there.
I'll tell you now why we two are so close.
    That I, in consequence of his vile thoughts,   16
was captured – though I trusted in this man –
and after died, I do not need to say.
    But this cannot have carried to your ears: 19
that is, how savagely I met my death.
You'll hear it now, and know if he has injured me.
    One scant slit in the walls of Eaglehouse   22*
(because of me, they call it now the Hunger Tower.
Be sure, though: others will be locked up there)
    had shown me, in the shaft that pierces it,   25
many new moons by now, when this bad dream
tore wide the veil of what my future was.

28   Questi pareva a me maestro e donno,
      cacciando il lupo e' lupicini al monte
      per che i Pisan veder Lucca non ponno.

31   Con cagne magre, studiose e conte
      Gualandi con Sismondi e con Lanfranchi
      s'avea messi dinanzi de la fronte.

34   In picciol corso mi parieno stanchi
      lo padre e' figli, e con l'agute scane
      mi parea lor veder fender li fianchi.

37   Quando fui desto innanzi la dimane,
      pianger senti' fra 'l sonno i miei figliuoli,
      ch'eran con meco, e dimandar del pane.

40   Ben se' crudel, se tu già non ti duoli
      pensando ciò che 'l mio cor s'annunziava;
      e se non piangi, di che pianger suoli?

43   Già eran desti, e l'ora s'appressava
      che 'l cibo ne solea essere addotto,
      e per suo sogno ciascun dubitava;

46   e io senti' chiavar l'uscio di sotto
      a l'orribile torre, ond' io guardai
      nel viso a' mie' figliuoi sanza far motto.

49   Io non piangea, sì dentro impetrai:
      piangevan elli; e Anselmuccio mio
      disse: 'Tu guardi sì, padre! che hai?'

52   Perciò non lagrimai, né rispuos' io
      tutto quel giorno né la notte appresso,
      infin che l'altro sol nel mondo uscìo.

55   Come un poco di raggio si fu messo
      nel doloroso carcere, e io scorsi
      per quattro visi il mio aspetto stesso,

58   ambo le man per lo dolor mi morsi;
      ed ei, pensando ch'io 'l fessi per voglia
      di manicar, di sùbito levorsi,

61   e disser: 'Padre, assai ci fia men doglia
      se tu mangi di noi: tu ne vestisti
      queste misere carni, e tu le spoglia.'

This thing here then appeared to me as Master   28*
of the Hounds, who tracked the wolf – his cubs as well –
out on the hill where Lucca hides from Pisa.

In front, as leaders of the pack, he placed   31
the clans Gualandi, Sismond and Lanfranchi,
their bitches hunting eager, lean and smart.

The chase was brief. Father and sons, it seemed,   34
were wearying; and soon – or so it seemed –
I saw those sharp fangs raking down their flanks.

I woke before the day ahead had come,   37
and heard my sons (my little ones were there)
cry in their sleep and call out for some food.

How hard you are if, thinking what my heart   40
foretold, you do not feel the pain of it.
Whatever will you weep for, if not that?

By now they all had woken up. The time   43
was due when, as routine, our food was brought.
Yet each was doubtful, thinking of their dream.

Listening, I heard the door below locked shut,   46
then nailed in place against that dreadful tower.
I looked in their dear faces, spoke no word.

I did not weep. Inward, I turned to stone.   49
They wept. And then my boy Anselmo spoke:
'What are you staring at? Father, what's wrong?'

And so I held my tears in check and gave   52
no answer all that day, nor all the night
that followed on, until another sun came up.

A little light had forced a ray into   55
our prison, so full of pain. I now could see
on all four faces my own expression.

Out of sheer grief, I gnawed on both my hands.   58
And they – who thought I did so from an urge
to eat – all, on the instant, rose and said:

'Father, for us the pain would be far less   61
if you would chose to eat us. You, having dressed us
in this wretched flesh, ought now to strip it off.'

64   Queta'mi allor per non farli più tristi;
      lo dì e l'altro stemmo tutti muti:
      ahi dura terra, perché non t'apristi?

67   Poscia che fummo al quarto dì venuti,
      Gaddo mi si gittò disteso a' piedi,
      dicendo: "Padre mio, ché non m'aiuti?"

70   Quivi morì; e come tu mi vedi,
      vid' io cascar li tre ad uno ad uno
      tra 'l quinto dì e 'l sesto; ond' io mi diedi,

73   già cieco, a brancolar sovra ciascuno,
      e due dì li chiamai, poi che fur morti.
      Poscia, più che 'l dolor, poté 'l digiuno.'

76   Quand' ebbe detto ciò, con li occhi torti
      riprese 'l teschio misero co' denti,
      che furo a l'osso, come d'un can, forti.

79   Ahi Pisa, vituperio de le genti
      del bel paese là dove 'l sì suona,
      poi che i vicini a te punir son lenti,

82   muovasi la Capraia e la Gorgona
      e faccian siepe ad Arno in su la foce,
      sì ch'elli annieghi in te ogne persona!

85   Che se 'l conte Ugolino aveva voce
      d'aver tradita te de le castella,
      non dovei tu i figliuoi porre a tal croce.

88   Innocenti facea l'età novella,
      novella Tebe, Uguiccione e 'l Brigata
      e li altri due che 'l canto suso appella.

91   Noi passammo oltre, là 've la gelata
      ruvidamente un'altra gente fascia,
      non volta in giù, ma tutta riversata.

94   Lo pianto stesso lì pianger non lascia,
      e 'l duol che truova in su li occhi rintoppo
      si volge in entro a far crescer l'ambascia;

97   ché le lagrime prime fanno groppo
      e, sì come visiere di cristallo,
      riempion sotto 'l ciglio tutto il coppo.

So I kept still, to not increase their miseries.   64
And that day and the day beyond, we all were mute.
Hard, cruel earth, why did you not gape wide?

As then we reached the fourth of all those days,   67
Gaddo pitched forward, stretching at my feet.
"Help me," he said. "Why don't you help me, Dad!"

And there he died. You see me here. So I saw them,   70
the three remaining, falling one by one
between the next days – five and six – then let

myself, now blind, feel over them, calling   73
on each, now all were dead, for two days more.
Then hunger proved a greater power than grief.'

His words were done. Now, eyes askew, he grabbed   76
once more that miserable skull – his teeth,
like any dog's teeth, strong against the bone.

Pisa, you scandal of the lovely land   79*
where 'yes' is uttered in the form of *sì*,
your neighbours may be slow to punish you,

but let those reefs, Capraia and Gorgogna,   82
drift, as a barrage, to the Arno's mouth,
so that your people – every one – are drowned.

So what if – as the rumour goes – the great Count   85
Ugolino did cheat fortresses from you.
You had no right to crucify his children.

Pisa, you are a newborn Thebes! Those boys   88
were young. That made them innocent. I've named
just two. I now name Uguiccione and Brigata.

We now moved on, and came to where the ice   91
so roughly swaddled yet another brood.
And these – not hunched – bend back for all to view.

They weep. Yet weeping does not let them weep.   94
Their anguish meets a blockage at the eye.
Turned in, this only makes to their heartache more.

Their tears first cluster into frozen buds,   97
and then – as though a crystal visor – fill
the socket of the eye beneath each brow.

100   E avvegna che, sì come d'un callo,
       per la freddura ciascun sentimento
       cessato avesse del mio viso stallo,

103   già mi parea sentire alquanto vento;
       per ch'io: 'Maestro mio, questo chi move?
       non è qua giù ogne vapore spento?'

106   Ond' elli a me: 'Avaccio sarai dove
       di ciò ti farà l'occhio la risposta,
       veggendo la cagion che 'l fiato piove.'

109   E un de' tristi de la fredda crosta
       gridò a noi: 'O anime crudeli
       tanto che data v'è l'ultima posta,

112   levatemi dal viso i duri veli,
       sì ch'io sfoghi 'l duol che 'l cor m'impregna
       un poco, pria che 'l pianto si raggeli.'

115   Per ch'io a lui: 'Se vuo' ch'i' ti sovvegna,
       dimmi chi se', e s'io non ti disbrigo,
       al fondo de la ghiaccia ir mi convegna.'

118   Rispuose adunque: 'I' son frate Alberigo,
       i' son quel da le frutta del mal orto,
       che qui riprendo dattero per figo.'

121   'Oh,' diss' io lui, 'or se' tu ancor morto?'
       Ed elli a me: 'Come 'l mio corpo stea
       nel mondo sù, nulla scienza porto.

124   Cotal vantaggio ha questa Tolomea,
       che spesse volte l'anima ci cade
       innanzi ch'Atropòs mossa le dea.

127   E perché tu più volontier mi rade
       le 'nvetriate lagrime dal volto,
       sappie che, tosto che l'anima trade

130   come fec' io, il corpo suo l'è tolto
       da un demonio, che poscia il governa
       mentre che 'l tempo suo tutto sia vòlto;

133   ella ruina in sì fatta cisterna.
       E forse pare ancor lo corpo suso
       de l'ombra che di qua dietro mi verna;

My own face now – a callus in the chill –   100
had ceased to be a throne to any kind
of sentiment. And yet, in spite of all,
   it seemed I felt a wind still stirring here.   103
'Who moves these currents, sir?' I now inquired.
'At depths like these, aren't vapours wholly spent?'

   He in reply: 'Come on, come on! You soon   106
will stand where your own probing eye shall see
what brings this drizzling exhalation on.'

   A case of icy-eye-scab now yelled out: 109
'You must be souls of such malignancy
you merit placement in the lowest hole.

   Prise off this rigid veil, to clear my eyes.   112
Let me awhile express the grief that swells
in my heart's womb before my tears next freeze.'

   I answered: 'Are you asking help from me?   115
Tell me who you are. Then I'll free your gaze,
or travel – promise! – to the deepest ice.'

   'I,' he replied, 'am Brother Alberigo,   118*
I of the Evil Orchard, Fruiterer.
Here I receive exquisite dates for figs.'

   'Oh,' I now said, 'so you're already dead?'   121
'Well, how my body fares above,' he said,
'still in the world, my knowledge is not sure.

   There is, in Ptolomea, this advantage,   124*
that souls will frequently come falling down
before Fate Atropos has granted them discharge.

   I very willingly will tell you more,   127
but only scrape this tear glaze from my face.
The instant any soul commits, like me,

   some act of treachery, a demon takes   130
possession of that body form and rules
its deeds until its time is done. Swirling,

   the soul runs downwards to this sink. And so   133*
the body of that shade behind – a-twitter
all this winter through – still seems up there, perhaps.

136   tu 'l dei saper, se tu vien pur mo giuso:
    elli è ser Branca Doria, e son più anni
    poscia passati ch'el fu sì racchiuso.'

139   'Io credo,' diss' io lui, 'che tu m'inganni,
    ché Branca Doria non morì unquanche,
    e mangia e bee e dorme e veste panni.'

142   'Nel fosso sù,' diss' el, 'de' Malebranche,
    là dove bolle la tenace pece,
    non era ancora giunto Michel Zanche,

145   che questi lasciò il diavolo in sua vece
    nel corpo suo, ed un suo prossimano
    che 'l tradimento insieme con lui fece.

148   Ma distendi oggimai in qua la mano,
    aprimi li occhi.' E io non gliel' apersi;
    e cortesia fu lui esser villano.

151   Ahi Genovesi, uomini diversi
    d'ogne costume e pien d'ogne magagna,
    perché non siete voi del mondo spersi?

154   Ché col peggiore spirto di Romagna
    trovai di voi un tal, che per sua opra
    in anima in Cocito già si bagna,

157   e in corpo par vivo ancor di sopra.

You're bound to know, arriving only now,   136
that this is Signor Branca ("Hookhand") d'Oria.
Years have gone by since he was ice-packed here.'
    'I think,' I said, 'that this must be a con.   139
For how can Branca d'Oria be dead?
He eats and drinks and sleeps and puts his clothes on.'
    'Recall that ditch,' he said, 'named Rotklorsville,   142
where, higher up, they brew adhesive pitch?
Well, long before Mike Zanche got to that,
    Hookhand was history. He, as proxy, left   145
a devil in his skin (his kinsman's here as well,
the one who planned with him the double-cross).
    But please, now reach your hand to me down here.   148
Open my eyes for me.' I did not open them.
To be a swine in this case was pure courtesy.
    You Genovese, deviant, deranged   151
and stuffed with every sort of vicious canker!
Why have you not been wiped yet from the earth?
    Among the worst of all the Romagnuoli   154
I found there one of yours, whose works were such
his soul already bathes in Cocytus.
    His body, seemingly, lives on above.   157

CANTO 34

1   '*Vexilla regis prodeunt inferni*
verso di noi; però dinanzi mira,'
disse 'l maestro mio, 'se tu 'l discerni.'

4   Come, quando una grossa nebbia spira
o quando l'emisperio nostro annotta,
par di lungi un molin che 'l vento gira:

7   veder mi parve un tal dificio allotta;
poi per lo vento mi ristrinsi retro
al duca mio, ché non lì era grotta.

10   Già era, e con paura il metto in metro,
là dove l'ombre tutte eran coperte,
e trasparien come festuca in vetro.

13   Altre sono a giacere; altre stanno erte,
quella col capo e quella con le piante;
altra, com' arco, il volto a' pié rinverte

16   Quando noi fummo fatti tanto avante
ch'al mio maestro piacque di mostrarmi
la creatura ch'ebbe il bel sembiante,

19   d'innanzi mi si tolse e fé restarmi,
'Ecco Dite,' dicendo, 'ed ecco il loco
ove convien che di fortezza t'armi.'

22   Corn' io divenni allor gelato e fioco,
nol dimandar, lettor, ch'i' non lo scrivo,
però ch'ogne parlar sarebbe poco.

25   Io non mori' e non rimasi vivo:
pensa oggimai per te, s'hai fior d'ingegno,
qual io divenni, d'uno e d'altro privo.

CANTO 34

'*Vexilla regis prodeunt inferni*,   1*
marching towards us. Fix your eyes ahead,'
my teacher said, 'and see if you can see it.'

As though a windmill when a thick fog breathes –   4
or else when dark night grips our hemisphere –
seen from a distance, turning in the wind,

so there a great contraption had appeared.   7
And I now shrank, against the wind, behind
my guide. There were no glades to shelter in.

I was by now (I write this verse in fear)   10
where all the shades in ice were covered up,
transparent as are straws preserved in glass.

Some lay there flat, and some were vertical,   13
one with head raised, another soles aloft,
another like a bow, bent face to feet.

And then when we had got still further on,   16
where now my master chose to show to me
that creature who had once appeared so fair,

he drew away from me and made me stop,   19
saying: 'Now see! Great Dis! Now see the place
where you will need to put on all your strength.'

How weak I now became, how faded, dry –   22
reader, don't ask, I shall not write it down –
for anything I said would fall far short.

I neither died nor wholly stayed alive.   25
Just think yourselves, if your minds are in flower,
what I became, bereft of life and death.

28   Lo 'mperador del doloroso regno
        da mezzo 'l petto uscia fuor de la ghiaccia;
        e più con un gigante io mi convegno

31   che i giganti non fan con le sue braccia:
        vedi oggimai quant' esser dee quel tutto
        ch'a così fatta parte si confaccia.

34   S'el fu sì bel com' elli è ora brutto,
        e contra 'l suo fattore alzò le ciglia,
        ben dee da lui procedere ogne lutto.

37   Oh quanto parve a me gran maraviglia
        quand' io vidi tre facce a la sua testa!
        L'una dinanzi, e quella era vermiglia;

40   l'altr' eran due, che s'aggiugnieno a questa
        sovresso 'l mezzo di ciascuna spalla
        e sé giugnieno al loco de la cresta:

43   e la destra parea tra bianca e gialla;
        la sinistra a vedere era tal, quali
        vegnon di là onde 'l Nilo s'avvalla.

46   Sotto ciascuna uscivan due grand' ali,
        quanto si convenia a tanto uccello:
        vele di mar non vid' io mai cotali.

49   Non avean penne, ma di vispistrello
        era lor modo; e quelle svolazzava,
        sì che tre venti si movean da ello;

52   quindi Cocito tutto s'aggelava.
        Con sei occhi piangea, e per tre menti
        gocciava 'l pianto e sanguinosa bava.

55   Da ogne bocca dirompea co' denti
        un peccatore, a guisa di maciulla,
        sì che tre ne facea così dolenti.

58   A quel dinanzi il mordere era nulla
        verso 'l graffiar, che talvolta la schiena
        rimanea de la pelle tutta brulla.

61   'Quell' anima là sù c'ha maggior pena,'
        disse 'l maestro, 'è Giuda Scariotto,
        che 'l capo ha dentro e fuor le gambe mena.

The emperor of all these realms of gloom   28
stuck from the ice at mid-point on his breast.
And I am more a giant (to compare)
     than any giant measured to his arm.   31
So now you'll see how huge the whole must be,
when viewed in fit proportion to that limb.

     If, once, he was as lovely as now vile,   34
when first he raised his brow against his maker,
then truly grief must all proceed from him.

     How great a wonder it now seemed to me   37
to see three faces on a single head!
The forward face was brilliant vermilion.

     The other two attached themselves to that   40
along each shoulder on the central point,
and joined together at the crest of hair.

     The rightward face was whitish, dirty yellow.   43
The left in colour had the tint of those
beyond the source from which the Nile first swells.

     Behind each face there issued two great vanes,   46
all six proportioned to a fowl like this.
I never saw such size in ocean sails.

     Not feathered as a bird's wings are, bat-like   49
and leathery, each fanned away the air,
so three unchanging winds moved out from him,

     Cocytus being frozen hard by these.   52
He wept from all six eyes. And down each chin
both tears and bloody slobber slowly ran.

     In every mouth he mangled with his teeth   55
(as flax combs do) a single sinning soul,
but brought this agony to three at once.

     Such biting, though, affects the soul in front   58
as nothing to the scratching he received.
His spine at times showed starkly, bare of skin.

     'That one up there, condemned to greater pain,   61
is Judas Iscariot,' my teacher said,
'his head inside, his feet out, wriggling hard.

64   De li altri due c'hanno il capo di sotto,
        quel che pende dal nero ceffo è Bruto –
        vedi come si storce, e non fa motto –

67   e l'altro è Cassio, che par sì membruto.
        Ma la notte risurge, e oramai
        è da partir, ché tutto avem veduto.'

70   Com' a lui piacque, il collo li avvinghiai;
        ed el prese di tempo e loco poste,
        e quando l'ali fuoro aperte assai,

73   appigliò sé a le vellute coste;
        di vello in vello giù discese poscia
        tra 'l folto pelo e le gelate croste.

76   Quando noi fummo là dove la coscia
        si volge, a punto in sul grosso de l'anche,
        lo duca, con fatica e con angoscia,

79   volse la testa ov' elli avea le zanche,
        e aggrappossi al pel com' om che sale,
        sì che 'n inferno i' credea tornar anche.

82   'Attienti ben, ché per cotali scale,'
        disse 'l maestro, ansando com' uom lasso,
        'conviensi dipartir da tanto male.'

85   Poi uscì fuor per lo fóro d'un sasso,
        e puose me in su l'orlo a sedere;
        appresso porse a me l'accorto passo.

88   Io levai li occhi e credetti vedere
        Lucifero com' io l'avea lasciato,
        e vidili le gambe in sù tenere;

91   e s'io divenni allora travagliato,
        la gente grossa il pensi che non vede
        qual è quel punto ch'ío avea passato.

94   'Lèvati sù,' disse 'l maestro, 'in piede:
        la via è lunga e 'l cammino è malvagio,
        e già il sole a mezza terza riede.'

97   Non era camminata di palagio
        là 'v' eravam, ma natural burella
        ch'avea mal suolo e di lume disagio.

The other two, their heads hung down below,   64*
are Brutus, dangling from the jet black snout
(look how he writhes there, uttering not a word!),

    the other Cassius with his burly look.   67
But night ascends once more. And now it's time
for us to quit this hole. We've seen it all.'

    As he desired, I clung around his neck.   70
With purpose, he selected time and place
and, when the wings had opened to the full,

    he took a handhold on the furry sides,   73
and then, from tuft to tuft, he travelled down
between the shaggy pelt and frozen crust.

    But then, arriving where the thigh bone turns   76
(the hips extended to their widest there),
my leader, with the utmost stress and strain,

    swivelled his head to where his shanks had been   79
and clutched the pelt like someone on a climb,
so now I thought: 'We're heading back to Hell.'

    'Take care,' my teacher said. 'By steps like these,'   82
breathless and panting, seemingly all-in,
'we need to take our leave of so much ill.'

    Then through a fissure in that rock he passed   85
and set me down to perch there on its rim.
After, he stretched his careful stride towards me.

    Raising my eyes, I thought that I should see   88
Lucifer where I, just now, had left him,
but saw instead his legs held upwards there.

    If I was struggling then to understand,   91
let other dimwits think how they'd have failed
to see what point it was that I now passed.

    'Up on your feet!' my teacher ordered me.   94
'The way is long, the road is cruelly hard.
The sun is at the morning bell already.'

    This was no stroll, where now we had arrived,   97
through any palace but a natural cave.
The ground beneath was rough, the light was weak.

100   'Prima che de l'abisso mi divella,
       maestro mio,' diss' io quando fui dritto,
       'a trarmi d'erro un poco mi favella:

103   ov' è la ghiaccia? e questi com' è fitto
       sì sottosopra? e come, in sì poc' ora,
       da sera a mane ha fatto il sol tragitto?'

106   Ed elli a me: 'Tu imagini ancora
       d'esser di là dal centro, ov' io mi presi
       al pel del vermo reo che 'l mondo fóra.

109   Di là fosti cotanto quant' io scesi;
       quand' io mi volsi, tu passasti 'l punto
       al qual si traggon d'ogne parte i pesi.

112   E se' or sotto l'emisperio giunto
       ch'è contraposto a quel che la gran secca
       coverchia, e sotto 'l cui colmo consunto

115   fu l'uom che nacque e visse sanza pecca;
       tu hai i piedi in su picciola spera
       che l'altra faccia fa de la Giudecca.

118   Qui è da man, quando di là è sera;
       e questi, che ne fé scala col pelo,
       fitto è ancora sì come prim' era.

121   Da questa parte cadde giù dal cielo;
       e la terra, che pria di qua si sporse,
       per paura di lui fé del mar velo,

124   e venne a l'emisperio nostro; e forse
       per fuggir lui lasciò qui loco vòto
       quella ch'appar di qua, e sù ricorse.'

127   Luogo è là giù da Belzebù remoto
       tanto quanto la tomba si distende,
       che non per vista, ma per suono è noto

130   d'un ruscelletto che quivi discende
       per la buca d'un sasso ch'elli ha roso
       col corso ch'elli avvolge, e poco pende.

133   Lo duca e io per quel cammino ascoso
       intrammo a ritornar nel chiaro mondo;
       e sanza cura aver d'alcun riposo

'Before my roots are torn from this abyss,   100
sir,' I said, upright, 'to untangle me
from error, say a little more of this.

Where is the ice? And why is that one there   103*
fixed upside down? How is it that the sun
progressed so rapidly from evening on to day?'

And he in answer: 'You suppose you're still   106
on that side of the centre where I gripped
that wormrot's coat that pierces all the world.

While I was still descending, you were there.   109
But once I turned, you crossed, with me, the point
to which from every part all weight drags down.

So you stand here beneath the hemisphere   112
that now is covered wholly with dry land,
under the highest point at which there died

the one man sinless in his birth and life.   115
Your feet are set upon a little sphere
that forms the other aspect of Giudecca.

It's morning here. It's evening over there.   118
The thing that made a ladder of his hair
is still as fixed as he has always been.

Falling from Heaven, when he reached this side,   121
the lands that then spread out to southern parts
in fear of him took on a veil of sea.

These reached our hemisphere. Whatever now   124
is visible to us – in flight perhaps from him –
took refuge here and left an empty space.'

There is a place (as distant from Beelzebub   127
as his own tomb extends in breadth)
known not by sight but rather by the sound

of waters falling in a rivulet   130
eroding, by the winding course it takes (which is
not very steep), an opening in that rock.

So now we entered on that hidden path,   133
my lord and I, to move once more towards
a shining world. We did not care to rest.

136   salimmo sù, el primo e io secondo,
        tanto ch'i' vidi de le cose belle
        che porta 'l ciel, per un pertugio tondo.
139   E quindi uscimmo a riveder le stelle.

We climbed, he going first and I behind,   136
until through some small aperture I saw
the lovely things the skies above us bear.
Now we came out, and once more saw the stars.   139

Commentaries and Notes

For each canto, under Notes the reader will find broadly factual references and cross-references to texts cited by Dante that are worth reading alongside Dante's own. The asterisks in the text show the beginning of the *terzina* in which such a reference occurs. Sometimes this points to a sequence of *terzine* in which, by consolidating these references, readers may discern some pattern of concerns – with, say, the minutiae of thirteenth-century politics – that will better emerge than in a strictly line-by-line treatment. This edition attempts to disturb as little as possible the reader's enjoyment of the narrative flow of Dante's poem. Where a pattern or point of critical interest has been pointed up, the explanatory note is subsumed into the interpretative Commentary which precedes the notes and is marked by bold type. Traditional annotations in sequential form are to be found in the excellent editions by Robert Durling and Ronald Martinez (Oxford, 1996) and the well-conceived apparatus by David Higgins in his commentary on C. H. Sissons's translation (London, 1980). To both of these editions the present editor is glad to acknowledge a warm debt of gratitude. Quotes from the Bible are from the Authorized Version.

CANTO 1

The dark wood and the sunlit hill. The appearance of Virgil. The beginning of the path down through Hell.

Commentary

The *Commedia* begins on a quiet and questioning note. Only in canto 3 does Dante describe his dramatic entry into a subterranean Hell. Until that point, his narrative is set at some deliberately unspecified point on the surface of the earth and explores the doubts and difficulties that beset the mind of Dante himself as he first confronts the conditions of loss, sin and exile, and sets himself – as poet no less than as protagonist – to discover a comprehensive remedy.

From the first, the text acknowledges that, beyond the experience of confusion, there must be design and order. The way forwards may be confused (lines 1–3) but a path, with its geometry of beginnings, middles and ends, exists. The first *terzina*, with its own steady rhythmic balance, reflects that understanding. So, too, the purpose of the poet (8) – registered in coolly scholastic phrases – is to demonstrate the extent of the *good* that he finds, even in Hell or in the confusions that assail him in his earthly existence. In the concluding phase of canto 1 (112) he is already able to give in outline the plan of a work that will lead him through the three realms of eternity, as if he could not even begin without knowing what his end would be.

For all that, the whole of Dante's narrative is impelled by a spirit of exploration and experiment. Even in the *Paradiso* (at canto 4, lines 130–33), Dante celebrates doubt as an intellectual impulse that leads always onwards to a greater discovery of truth. The drama of *Inferno* 1 anticipates in its own way the connections that Dante always makes between journeying, narrative and the life of the awakening mind. This canto is far less sharply focused in its visual effects than most of the subsequent cantos. It hovers in an area of dream and dazed waking (10) between archetypal images of light and dark, matter and immateriality, movement and stasis. But little by little – through a sequence of setbacks – a careful and unexaggerated advance is achieved.

The first phase of the canto (1–66) describes a condition of isolation and lonely effort. Notoriously, Dante never hesitates in the *Inferno* to pass cruel judgements on his fellow human beings. But the opening cantos represent a judgement on his own vacillations and frailty – to the extent that some of his phrases anticipate the psychology of Shakespeare's Hamlet (e.g. 55–7; see also *Inferno* 2: 37–9). This is not, however, to say that Dante wholly consents to the introspectiveness that has characterized European ethics since the Renaissance. The dark wood represents his own involvement in sin. But if the way forwards is lost, it is because others as well as he have deserted and obscured the road ahead. The experience of exile is already registered in the apprehension of a barbaric and dangerous world beyond the confines of a city wall. Nor will Dante find a remedy by his own efforts alone. By line 66 – having made his single-handed but unsuccessful attempt to escape from the wood – the forward narrative has become an anti-narrative as Dante heads downhill to a place where there are no words or light to guide him. As soon as he sets out on the climb, his mind begins to generate hallucinatory terrors and confusions – as, for instance, when the leopard of line 32 terrifies but also fascinates him and gives him false reasons for hope. The three beasts of this sequence are all introduced by the word for 'seeming' (*parea*) or with the evocation of unrealized or unreal conditions that are expressed by the Italian subjunctive: these are not actual beasts, but rather beasts of the mind. Rhythm and tempo are correspondingly agitated, flickering constantly between forward movement and sudden decline.

Left to itself, the mind of the individual erodes all its best motivations. The remedy is to be found in the rediscovery of resources that lie beyond its own limits. The text reflects this understanding in its constant reference to a biblical tradition in which ethical 'paths' are lost and the 'hill of hope' stands in significant juxtaposition with the 'valleys' of despair. However, it is, above all, the figure of Virgil who expresses Dante's understanding of a solution.

Virgil dominates the second phase of the canto, introducing (particularly in lines 67–75) a range of narrative and rhetorical considerations. He alludes to the history of Rome – which began when the Greeks destroyed Troy and the Trojan Aeneas set out on his predestined journey to discover a new home for his refugee compatriots. From this example Dante – as a Florentine descended from Roman seed – may take the strength to turn his own disasters into unexpected successes. Thus, with the appearance of Virgil, the diction of the canto moves from interior monologue into a conversation marked by the adoption of a distinctly public style of rhetorical address – by elevated circumlocutions (73–5), eloquent claims to attention (85–7) and explicitly Latinate elements (70). Dante has been drawn out of himself into a world where the traditions of civilization deriving from Rome can be enlisted against the confusions of the dark wood.

The final line of the canto registers a minimal but none the less real advance. This line, balanced around a central caesura, depicts the firm footing that Dante has now achieved in his relationship with Virgil. But in canto 2 Dante will come to renewed doubts when he realizes that his journey, which should lead him to the light of the hill, is after all a journey into the depths of Hell, under the guidance of a figure who is self-confessedly one of the damned (124–6). The concluding phase of canto 1 has already prepared for some of this paradox. Virgil may in most respects be taken to represent the resources of rational discourse. Yet from the outset there are ambiguities surrounding him. He himself confesses that he remains a rebel against the divine law (125), and movingly he is one who 'did not know' the name of the true God (131). Indeed, his first appearance is marked by enigmas and riddles, as of some old man encountered in a fairytale landscape. So, too, in offering his picture of Roman history, Virgil is given a sequence of cryptically oracular lines, as he looks prophetically to the future, and to the salvation that will come either on the unknown Day of Judgement or else with the advent of a saviour in the form of the mysterious *veltro* or 'hound' of lines 103–5. Beyond the clear schemes that the civilized world provides, there are, for Dante, forces which reason alone cannot clearly define. It thus becomes significant that, at his first appearance, Virgil's very dignified and clear words should also be characterized – as many of his utterances are – by negative constructions: '*Non omo, omo già fui*' (67).

Notes

1–6   Biblical references to the span of human life as three score years and ten are to be found in Psalms 90: 10, which Dante quotes in *Convivio* book 4, where he discourses at length on the ages of man and their proper function. The notion of a road of righteousness is contained in Psalm 23 along with that of the 'valley' of death. Isaiah 38: 10 reads: 'in the cutting off of my days I shall go to the gates of the grave'. The wood recalls the Romance wood that in, say, Arthurian legend the hero may encounter in his search for the Holy Grail.

13–18   The hill is a figure for hope in Psalms 24: 3; 43: 3; 121: 1.

28–30   Dante's obscure reference to his 'firm foot' has provoked much discussion. The best explanation is that Dante has in mind here Aristotle's observation that our stride is led by the *right* foot, leaving the *left* foot to impel our movement forwards. The line may also be taken as an example of the extreme precision of mind which leads Dante to note exactly where, in any narrative scene, his own body is placed and what lies to left and right of him.

31–60   The three beasts seem to be drawn from The Lamentations of Jeremiah 5: 6, an old Testament book to which Dante showed particular devotion. Allegorically, the leopard has been taken to represent false (and possibly sexual) pleasure, which fascinates but also irritates the mind. The lion may stand for pride, haughty but in reality a dangerous void. The wolf may be taken as avarice and is of particular importance, being the only beast of the three to which Dante refers in his appeal to Virgil. (See also *Purgatorio* 20: 10–12). Avarice, for Dante, characterizes the corrupt culture of capitalist Florence, and is above all a pointless and never-ending pursuit of false and unsatisfying goods. In this sense it is a '*bestia sanza pace*' – a 'brute which knows no peace' (line 58), a restlessness of mind that erodes the harmony of civic life.

64–6 Though Dante, without yet realizing it, is speaking to a pagan figure, he invokes here the great penitential psalm 'Miserere Domine' (Psalm 51):

> Have mercy upon me, O God, according to thy loving kindness; according unto the multitude of thy tender mercies blot out my transgressions.

67–75 Virgil (70 BC–19 BC) here links his own success as a poet with the major themes of his narrative in the *Aeneid*, which tells of the fall of Troy (Ilion being its great citadel), the travels of Aeneas and the foundation of Rome as a new homeland (106–8) which achieves imperial glory under Augustus. Virgil will act as Dante's guide and companion until his disappearance in *Purgatorio* 30. In the *Inferno*, Dante is especially influenced by – and competes with – book 6 of the *Aeneid*, which describes the descent of the epic hero Aeneas into the underworld in pursuit of prophetic vision (see especially *Inferno* 3). The *Purgatorio* pays particular attention to Virgil's pastoral poems, the *Eclogues* (see *Purgatorio* 21–2).

94–105 The 'hound' ('*veltro*') has been variously identified as Can Grande della Scala (1291–1329) (one of Dante's patrons in exile), the Emperor Henry VII (*c.* 1275–1313), whom Dante hoped, vainly, would restore imperial rule to Italy (see Introduction p. xvii) and even as Dante himself. The phrase 'between the felt and felt' may refer to geographical location (between the towns of Feltre and Montefeltro in northern Italy). We are sometimes reminded that in the star sign Gemini the 'twins' are thought to wear felt caps, so that anyone born under that sign – as Dante was – would have been born 'between the felt and felt'. Scholarly ingenuity (of a kind which henceforth these notes will not indulge) can, however, all too easily diminish the imaginative impact of enigma itself. Dante is rarely enigmatic. But when he is, it is with poetic purpose.

CANTO 2

Virgil explains how Beatrice chose him as Dante's guide.

Commentary

In canto 2, the word 'why' (*'perché'*) becomes a leitmotif, occurring with particular urgency at lines 31 and 122–3. The advance towards Hell in the company of Virgil is now seen to raise as many questions as it answers. The canto opens with the realization that Dante is, after all, alone on his journey: he is a living being but Virgil, his guide, is no more than a shadow. The emotions aroused by this realization are suggested by the exceptionally emphatic ending of line 3 – *'io/sol/ uno'* (*'I/alone/ . . . the only one'*) – where pride and apprehension at confronting this mad journey (34–5) are present in equal measure. From this point, too, the pronoun I (*io*) – which Italian does not normally need to be employed in verbal constructions – is also a repeated focus of attention. Dante least of all believes himself worthy for the enterprise ahead (32). May it not simply be crazy to undertake it? In canto 1, the primal impulsions of the human being – perception, physical motion, question and answer – were dramatically explored. Now Dante's attention falls upon the *conscious* apprehension of selfhood. Canto 2 opens in an attempt at self-knowledge, but reveals that sophistication of mind can be no less a source of difficulty than the disorientated confusions of the opening canto.

In addressing these questions, Dante summons up modes of thought and speech which initially reflect his new devotion to Virgil and in some measure confirm that Virgil represents for him the range of resources available in rational culture. The introductory phase of the canto (1–9) includes the invocation to the Muses which might have been expected at the opening of canto 1. The penetratingly beautiful lines with which the canto begins, evoking evening and heroic endeavour, are drawn on Virgilian models. Dante then attributes to himself one of the longest speeches that he as a character delivers in the *Commedia*, syntactically sustained in long periodic sentences. But these are also punctuated by moments of colloquial utterances as Dante – asking, essentially, 'Why me?' – acknowledges the incalculable distance between himself and the saints and heroes of the past (10–33). (Geoffrey Chaucer recognized the bathos and comic potential of these verses in *The House of Fame* (*c.* 1378–81).)

Reason and eloquence lead here not to a resolution but to an aggravation of Dante's self-doubt. A familiar interpretation would insist that, if Virgil represents reason, then already the limitations of reason are displayed here, as they are also in *Inferno* 1 and 9 and *Purgatorio* 30. Reason may teach us how to act but delivers no explanation as to our ultimate purpose, or *raison d'être*. That is a task for revelation. Thus the central phase of the canto (43–126) is dominated by a scene in Heaven where Beatrice is enlisted as the agent of providence to strengthen Dante's resolve, revealing that he is sustained by the divine love that created him in the first place.

This simple paraphrase should not distract from the extraordinarily inventive choreography that characterizes Dante's language and narrative in canto 2. Virgil, now speaking of Beatrice, abandons the epic elevation of his earliest utterances in favour of a lyric style that traces the interplay of many voices in the court of Heaven. Where Virgil had previously insisted (as he does throughout the *Inferno*) upon a manly forward march, he here records a sequence of feminine voices all interlaced, calling, one to the other, in long melodic lines of praise and concern. The loneliness of heroic endeavour and the apparent self-sufficiency of the human ego are shown to be dependent upon, and supported by, a chorus of other human beings, whose minds comprehend not merely reason and effort, but also love.

The concluding phase of the canto (127–42) – a renewed conversation between Dante and Virgil – modulates to reflect the implications of its central episode. Virgil's voice is now uncharacteristically flurried, enthusiastic and even irritated that Dante should waste the advantages that come to him (though not to Virgil himself) through the intercession of the Christian saints. So, too, the Virgilianism of the epic simile (127–32) is modified so as to emphasize regeneration and light rather than untimely destruction. (See Introduction p. c). Notably, the ethical terms that punctuate this phase of the canto point not simply to the sphere of military (or epic) prowess, but to a medieval romance tradition in which deeds are done in love service to a lady or *donna*. Momentarily, even Virgil speaks here (123–8) of courtesy, pity, '*franchezza*' (as in the moral liberty of the Carolingian Franks) and boldness of address ('*ardire*'). (Such notions drawn from the culture of courtly love are also at issue in *Inferno* 5.) Dante concludes the canto able once more to march ahead, but he does so in a way that contrasts with the subdued conclusion of canto 1. Now (142) Dante advances with the daring of a romance hero eager for adventure in a mysterious forest.

Notes

1–9   These lines, like others in the canto, make liberal reference to
       Virgil's *Aeneid* (see lines 127–9). Here, in delicately responsive
       pastiche, Dante recalls the many passages where Virgil's Aeneas
       is left alone at night wondering how best to serve his needy
       companions:

> *Nox erat et terra animalia fessa per omnia*
> *alitum pecudumque genus sopor altus habebat*
>   *cum pater . . .*

       (Night it was and night through every land held the weary
       creatures, the creatures of flight and the flocks while the
       father . . .)   *Aeneid* 8: 26–7

       For Virgilian invocations to the Muses, see *Aeneid* 1: 1–11.

13–27 Like Virgil in canto 1, Dante adopts here an elevated circum-
       locutory style: the 'sire of Silvius' is Aeneas himself. Aeneas's
       vision in the underworld of the future glories of Rome – revealed
       to him by his own father, Anchises – is here combined, syn-
       cretically, with a Christian vision of Rome's future. Compare, as
       a parallel to the meeting of Aeneas and Anchises, Dante's own
       meeting with his forefather Cacciaguida in *Paradiso* 15–17.

28–30 Like Aeneas, Saint Paul – while still in his human body – was
       granted a vision of divine glory:

> I knew a man in Christ above fourteen years ago, (whether in the
> body, I cannot tell; or whether out of the body, I cannot tell: God
> knoweth;) such an one caught up to the third heaven.
>   And I knew such a man, (whether in the body, or out of the
> body, I cannot tell: God knoweth;)
>   How that he was caught up into paradise, and heard unspeakable
> words, which it is not lawful for a man to utter.
>   2 Corinthians 12: 2–4

       For Dante's treatment of his own bodily vision, see *Paradiso* 2:
       37–9.

52–81 The figure of Beatrice who here speaks to Virgil is (in Dante's
       account) the central figure in the *Commedia*, and also of his
       Christian understanding. (See Introduction.) The *Vita nuova* is
       Dante's early account of his love for her, of the poetry he wrote

in her name and of the way in which he responded to her death. An example of the style of this early poetry, which exerts a strong influence over the present passage, is the last sonnet in the *Vita nuova*, which anticipates Dante's attention here to both universal spaces and intimate effects of emotion, to tears, sighs and the light of eyes:

> *Oltre la spera che più larga gira,*
> *passa 'l sospir che esce del mio cuore:*
> *intelligenza nova, che l'Amore*
> *piangendo mette in lui, pur su lo tira ...*

(Beyond the sphere that circles most widely,/ there passes the sigh that leaves my heart/ a new understanding which Love,/ weeping, imparts to him, draws him ever higher.)

Vita nuova 41

94–126 The first lady to speak in Heaven is the Virgin Mary. Dante talks of his devotion to her at *Paradiso* 23: 88, and a sustained prayer to the Blessed Virgin prepares for Dante's vision of God in *Paradiso* 33: 1–39. Saint Lucy is the patron saint of sight. According to an anecdote in the commentary written by Dante's son Jacopo, Dante was especially devoted to this saint, and Dante himself in *Convivio* 3: 9 records how he prayed to her when his eyesight had been endangered by too much study. Saint Lucy has an important role in *Purgatorio* 9 and appears in *Paradiso* 32: 13–18. Rachel is the second wife of Jacob (Genesis 29). She was frequently regarded as a figure for contemplation, and fulfils this role in *Purgatorio* 27: 104–8. (See also *Paradiso* 32: 8–9.)

CANTO 3

The entry into Hell. Charon and the apathetic sinners.

Commentary

In contrast to the oblique but measured eloquence of canto 1, and the polyphonic conversations of canto 2, canto 3 opens abruptly with a single voice and a chain of sentences – authoritarian, menacing, alien, yet brutally clear – that conclude with the seemingly doomladen imperative: '*Lasciate ogne speranza, voi ch'intrate*': 'Surrender as you enter every hope you have' (9). No narrative scene-setting prepares the reader for these words. Nor is it apparent until lines 10–11 that these lines, far from being uttered by some human prison guard, or even the voice of God, are phrases scratched on the lintel of a decrepit gateway (*'una porta'*, meaning here merely some door or other).

As always, the shock, and even the confusion (12) that Dante generates in his narrative are themselves significant. In the present case, Dante dramatizes a shift away from the introspective consideration of his own doubts and almost-extinguished potentialities to an encounter with unchangeable and eternal reality. Hell is not for Dante merely a state of mind; it is a condition of being which predates even the creation of human nature and will last eternally. Hell, brought into existence to receive the fallen angels, will never end, and at the Last Judgement (see *Inferno* 6: 94–111) will become even more agonizing. Hell is thus the first expression that Dante encounters of the divine will; and the words of Hell Gate do not shrink from the profound paradox which recognizes that, where divine justice searches the moral character of all created beings and divine wisdom orders and disposes according to unbending principles, so, too, divine love contributes to the damnation of those who have rejected the demands of love.

In conjunction with this terrible but unwavering vision, canto 3 in its second phase (22–69) offers a first view of the damned themselves and the nature of their failings. Neither here not at any other point in the *Inferno* does Dante suggest that sin is an offence against some encoded table of divine rules. The sinners of canto 3 are the 'apathetic', '[t]hese wretched souls [who] were never truly live' (64). Sin, on this view, is a rejection of the energies that feed our lives, and the sufferings of damnation arise essentially from the revelation that life, which proceeds from the ardour and urgency of divine love, cannot be avoided. To those who have been too pusillanimous to impel their own existence, committing themselves (rightly or wrongly) to some cause, 'life' continues, but only in the form of external stimuli, the bites of hornets and flies (65–9).

For all that, canto 3 is only the first step in a process (not completed until *Paradiso* 33) in which Dante progressively unfolds the implications of the divine nature and of human participation in divine life. In the *Paradiso*, Dante comes to reveal that order is a form of liberation rather than constraint. Correspondingly, in the subtext of *Inferno* 3, the reader is encouraged to recognize that, while the reality of Hell cannot be questioned, it is also fundamental that the Hell Gate should not be allowed the final word. By lines 14–15 Virgil has begun to utter gentler and more humane imperatives, which lead one to recognize that, after all, the paralysing pronouncements of the gate cannot be allowed to stand in Dante's way. It is written that Dante should pass through Hell. It is also true that he will pass beyond Hell in a way that these words themselves do not anticipate. Courage – the opposite of the sin for which the sinners in this canto are condemned – resides precisely in an ability to see beyond the opening sentences on the gate.

In parallel with the subtlety of Dante's moral vision, the third canto represents an extremely daring piece of imaginative invention. Notably, the condition of the damned is first registered in the Babelic confusion and lack of clarity in speech, which isolates them from human relationship and from participation in divine understanding. Conversely, Dante summons up a power of literary virtuosity that draws on Virgil but never hesitates to modify the original text. The most sustained of a series of Virgilian allusions is the central encounter (82–99 and 109–20) with Charon, the boatman of Hell. Here is a figure drawn directly from Virgil's own account of the underworld, in book 6 of the *Aeneid*. But the melancholic sublimity of Virgil's description is here transformed into a highly visual depiction of demented power (compare with the representation of Minos in *Inferno* 5: 4–15). Imperatives in Charon's mouth become the self-important fussings of some minor functionary, and are countered by the extreme energy that Virgil displays in his famous injunction at **lines 95–6** (repeated at *Inferno* 5: 23–4): '*vuolsi così colà dove si puote/ ciò che si vuole, e più non dimandare*': 'For this is willed where all is possible that is willed there. Question no further.' Here Dante attributes to Virgil a syntactically complex and rhythmically energetic expression of divine power. Virgil does not know God and cannot name Him. But his words – in their emphatic use of the verbs 'to will' and 'to be able' – summon up an understanding of the essential activity that God initiates and human beings can share in, which immediately (and comically) deflates the pretensions of Charon's false authority.

In a canto that ends with a thunderous earthquake, paralleling the abruptness and violence of its opening, power has been explored in both its divine and literary aspects. Michelangelo recognized this and drew on the pose and torsion of Dante's Charon when painting his version of the Last Judgement in the Sistine Chapel (1535–41). T. S. Eliot also recognized the sapping awfulness of apathy when, in *The Waste Land* (1922), he refers to this canto in his own vision of spiritual dereliction.

Notes

1–9 The originality of Dante's treatment of Hell may be gauged by comparing these lines (and the plan of Hell offered in canto 11) with visual representations such as Giotto's in the Scrovegni chapel at Padua or in the mosaics of the Baptistery (reproduced on the cover of this volume). Where, traditionally, Hell is pictured as chaos, violence and ugliness, Dante sees a vision of terrifying order expressing the underlying structure of a world that God has created but sinners have refused to contemplate. Hell Gate is not simply an awe-inspiring threat, but a demand that intelligence and understanding should be engaged anew in the analysis and exploration of divine purpose. (See also the plan of Hell on p. cxii, and Dante's own discussion of the moral categories of Hell in *Inferno* 11.)

16–18 'The good that intellect desires to win' is a phrase much influenced – as is so much of Dante's thinking – by Aristotle's *Ethics*. Aristotle writes in the *Nicomachean Ethics* 6: 2: 1139a:

> What affirmation and negation are in thinking, pursuit and avoidance are in desire; so that since moral virtue is a state of character concerned with choice, and choice is deliberate desire, therefore must the reasoning be true and the desire right, if the choice is to be good, and the latter must pursue just what the former asserts. Now this kind of intellect and of truth is practical. But of the intellect which is contemplative, not practical nor productive, the good and bad state are truth and falsity respectively . . . The origin of action . . . is choice, and that of choice is desire and reasoning with a view to an end.
>
> D. Ross (trans.), *The Nicomachean Ethics of Aristotle*
> (Oxford, 1954)

Compare with Dante, *Convivio* 4: 7, 12.

34 For the apathetic, see Revelation 3: 15–16:

> I know thy works, that thou art neither cold nor hot: I would thou wert cold or hot.
> So then because thou art lukewarm, and neither cold nor hot, I will spue thee out of my mouth.

55 T. S. Eliot alludes to these lines when he writes:

> *Unreal City,*
> *Under the brown fog of a winter dawn,*
> *A crowd flowed over London Bridge, so many,*
> *I had not thought death had undone so many.*
>   *The Waste Land*, lines 60–63

For Eliot's continuing engagement with Dante's poetry, see especially *Inferno* 27, *Purgatorio* 26 and the introduction to *Purgatorio*. Eliot's phrase in *Four Quartets* (1935–42) 'human kind/ Cannot bear very much reality' accurately interprets Dante's thinking about the apathetic.

58–60 The apathetic are unlike almost all other sinners in Hell in being unnamed. It is a mark of particular contempt for their wasted lives that names should be denied them. It is, however, generally accepted that the figure referred to here is more likely to be Pietro da Morrone (1215–96), who became Pope Celestine V in 1294, than other candidates such as Pontius Pilate or Judas Iscariot. History (though not Dante) speaks well of Celestine. A saintly figure, known to be a spiritual reformer who founded the Order of Celestines, Celestine was canonized shortly after his death. But the 'great denial', which in Dante's eyes seems to have damned him, was his abdication after only five months, under pressure from the Curia and his successor, Boniface VIII (1235–1303). This act of *viltà* (or cowardice) put an end to the possibility of reform, and opened the way to the election of the pope whom Dante hated and despised above all others. (For Boniface, see especially *Inferno* 19.)

82–111 Dante here offers an animated variation on Virgil's treatment of Charon:

> A terrifying ferryman is guardian of these waters. His filth is fearsome; his chin is covered with a thick straggle of grey whiskers; his eyes are flames.   *Aeneid* 6: 298–300

112 Here again, as at 2: 127–9, Dante deliberately alludes to the *Aeneid* 6: 309–12 and suggests the measure of both his stylistic and moral differences from Virgil. Milton makes comparable use of the autumn leaf simile in *Paradise Lost* 1.

CANTO 4

The First Circle of Hell. Limbo. Unbaptized children.
Virtuous pagans.

Commentary

Canto 4 depicts Limbo, the region of Hell in which all those who have died without benefit of baptism are held 'suspended' (45) in a state that reflects the moral condition of the unbaptized. These souls have committed no sin and consequently do not suffer any particular pain. None the less (34–42), they remain overshadowed by the original sin which, for the Christian, is removed at baptism, and they will never be able to enjoy to the full the revelation and joy of the divine, which (as the *Purgatorio* and *Paradiso* demonstrate) Dante firmly believes lies at the centre of Christian experience. As **line 42** declares, the unbaptized live in desire of the vision of God – who alone can bring human beings to happiness – without any possibility of ever reaching it.

The souls in Limbo include not only unbaptized children but also many pagans. It is to the latter group that Dante pays especial and characteristic attention, imagining a place of special dignity in Limbo where the great figures of pagan antiquity are confined. This is the great hemisphere of light – and within it a 'noble fort' – which dominates canto 4 from **line 67** onwards. Here in a great catalogue of resonant names, Dante celebrates a group who (in total contrast to the apathetic) have lived lives of heroism, intellectual ambition and perfect moral virtue and thus provided an illumination even for the Christian mind. The word 'honour', and its cognates, is repeated at **lines 73, 74, 76 and 80.**

Supreme among these honoured individuals is Virgil, celebrated by a great chorus of ancient poets at **lines 80–81.** Dante, the Christian poet, imagines himself to be received as a sixth member of the great school or 'college' which includes Virgil, Homer, Horace, Lucan and Ovid – which points to the extreme confidence that Dante has in his own genius. This confidence leads him in later cantos to challenge, and even claim to outdo, almost all the members of this school. (See *Inferno* 25–6.) Canto 4 brings into sharp relief some of the most fundamental tensions in his work, in particular those that arose in canto 1 with the choice of Virgil as his guide. What place does poetry and personal talent have in the search for Christian salvation? Above all, what contribution can the great traditions of classical learning and literature make to such a search?

These questions, which run through the whole *Commedia*, emerging particularly in *Purgatorio* 21 and 22, and even in the *Paradiso* (at cantos 19 and 20), remain largely unresolved.

On the one hand, Dante is profoundly committed to the notion that human nature, as created by God, was potentially good and that, even without the benefit of revelation, the resources of human communities and human traditions can provide a beacon of security (or a hemisphere of light) in the dark wood created by human violence. Language, too, is a human resource which the classical world can illustrate, often more effectively than the Christian world.

On the other hand, the Limbo sequence does point to limitations and shortcomings in the pagan mentality. Even in the hemisphere of light, these souls are neither happy nor sad (84). They are characterized by a stoic preservation of dignity. But they are also unresponsive to the great redemptive event, which ensures that some at least who lived before Christ – the patriarchs and prophets of Israel – will be saved. Here as elsewhere, Virgil speaks only obliquely and with muted awe of the 'power' (53) of divine action – as if the extreme mysteries of Christian faith were as anti-pathetical to him as the extremes of human emotion. By contrast, Dante's poem progressively recognizes that rationality and human discourse can themselves become restrictive, limiting the full spectrum of human possibilities – a 'noble fort', a defence of the self which is also a prison.

Linguistically, the canto moves across a gamut of effects, ranging from elegiac melancholia to the resonant catalogue of pagan names that dominates its second half. Lines such as 25–7 delicately register the emotions of sadness and loss which Dante would have found expressed in the 'tears of things' that Virgil invokes in *Aeneid* 6. So, too, in glorifying the names of those figures (including Aristotle; see Introduction p. xl) who have illuminated Dante's own intellectual life, there is an evident exuberance, even pride, in the capacity of the vernacular to stretch its rhythms under Dante's hand and harmonize in Italian such exotic names as (137) 'Diogenès, Anassagora e Tale'. Virgil's speeches (especially 31–42), though sober and restrained, are also characterized by a certain bareness, even repression, as Dante wishes to show Virgil talking about Christian history at the very limit of his understanding and tolerance. Later cantos (especially *Purgatorio* 3) return to this idiom, even enriching its pathos and raising more acutely the question of why Virgil should be a dweller in Limbo.

The canto ends with a verse that draws directly upon the elegiac tonality and plainness of Virgilian diction. But these lines also 'tremble' (see 150). The verb *tremare* is, from the *Vita nuova* onwards, consistently associated with moments of revelation when the individual is challenged, by revelation, to abandon settled habits and beliefs. (See also *Purgatorio* 21: 55–60.) Here, it resonates with apprehension and adventure. Leaving the dignified unity of the hemisphere of light, Dante (against all reason) goes out once more into the darkness of Hell, where he and the reader will experience anew the unknown extremes of human viciousness and divine power.

Notes

46–63 The Harrowing of Hell – when Christ entered Hell and broke open its gates on Easter Saturday – brought salvation to those among the Hebrew patriarchs who had anticipated or prophesied Christ's coming, but not to the noble pagan. This event is also much in Dante's mind in *Inferno* 12 and 21–2.

88–90 Of the four classical poets who here welcome Dante and Virgil, Homer alone was unavailable to Dante, who knew no Greek. But Dante did know of his reputation through his reading of Cicero, Virgil and other Latin poets; and in canto 26 of the *Inferno* he offers his own, highly revisionary account of the Odysseus legend. The other three are Quintus Horatius Flaccus (65–8 BC), Publius Ovidius Naso (43 BC–*c*. AD 17) and Marcus Annaeus Lucanus (AD 39–65). The influence of all these poets upon Dante's *Commedia* is evident at later points, notably in *Inferno* 25, where Dante claims he can outdo anything which Ovid and Lucan can achieve.

121–9 The Electra referred to here is not the daughter of Agamemnon but of Atlas. As the mother of Dardanus, one of the legendary founders of Troy, she occupies a legitimate position – alongside Hector, Aeneas and Julius Caesar – among the heroes of the Trojan line which eventually became the lineage of Rome. Camilla and Penthesilea, queen of the Amazons, are both virgin warriors mentioned by Virgil (see *Aeneid* 1: 490–93, 7: 803–17, 11: 648–835). The former was supposed to be an ally of Latins, the latter an ally of the Trojans. Brutus and Cornelia, as figures in Roman history, were known to Dante from Livy, Lucan and others. Brutus was first consul of the Roman republic after the expulsion of the kings; Cornelia was the wife of its first emperor, Julius Caesar. Saladin (Salah ad-Din, 1137–93) was sultan of

Egypt. He drove the Crusaders out of the Holy Land. But many legends concerning his heroism and generosity proliferated in the west.

130–44 The 'master of those who know' is Aristotle (384–322 BC). Dante knew about Plato (427–347 BC) and his treatment of Socrates through Latin texts. Diogenes the Cynic (fourth century BC) rejected the claims of supposedly civilized existence. Anaxogoras (fifth century BC) was both philosopher and mentor of Pericles. Thales (seventh century BC) was considered the founder of Greek philosophy. Empedocles of Sicily (fifth century BC) was both a rhetorician and the inventor of the notion of the four elements. Heraclitus of Ephesus (fifth century BC) held that fire was the fundamental element. Zeno of Cyprus (third century BC) is praised by Dante in *Convivio* 4, and is considered the founder of the Stoic school. Dioscorides of Anazarba (first century AD) founded pharmacology. Orpheus and Linus are mythical poets. Tullius is Marcus Tullius Cicero (106–43 BC), Roman statesman and philosopher, whose *De Amicitia* and *De Officiis* were acknowledged influences on Dante's thought. Seneca (d. AD 65) influenced Dante through his Stoic philosophy. Euclid (fourth century BC) is the Greek geometrician. Ptolemy of Alexandria (second century BC) devised the astronomical system, posited on a geocentric universe that Dante adopts in imagining the universe of the *Commedia* (see P. Boyde, *Dante, Philomythes and Philosopher* (Cambridge, 1981)). Hippocrates (fourth century BC) founded medical studies. Avicenna (d. 1036) was an Arabic physician and philosopher. Galen of Pergamum (second century AD) wrote medical text books. Averroes (d. 1198) was one of the most important philosophers of the Middle Ages. Born in Arabic Spain – his name in Arabic is Ibn-Raschd – his great commentary on Aristotle won him the name of 'the commentator' (see also *Purgatorio* 25: 63–5). Scholasticism – and Dante – owed much to his influence, even if inclined to resist its implications.

CANTO 5

Minos, judge of the underworld. The lustful. Francesca da
Rimini.

Commentary

The second half of canto 5 contains, probably, the most celebrated episode in the *Commedia*. The canto as a whole is concerned with the sins of lust and sexual licence. But, beginning at **line 73**, Dante focuses his attention on two figures from thirteenth-century Italian history – Francesca da Rimini, wife of Gianciotto Malatesta (marriage *c.* 1275) and Paolo, Gianciotto's brother. Francesca was married by political arrangement to Gianciotto, a member of the ruling family of Rimini, but began an affair (as described here) with Paolo. When he discovered this, Gianciotto murdered both his wife and his brother. This was a great scandal in its day. Remarkably, Dante, having consigned Francesca to Hell, was supported between 1317 and 1320 by the patronage of her nephew, Guido Novello da Polenta.

Though Dante alludes only indirectly to the historical event, debate continues as to the stance he adopts in representing the fate that Paolo and Francesca suffer in Hell. On the one hand, the second half of canto 5 – from the moment at which Dante compares Paolo and Francesca to a pair of homing doves (**82**) – is coloured by effects of sentiment and pathos. There is also, in the two speeches that Dante attributes to Francesca, a degree of lyrical subtlety and syntactical sophistication (as in the sustained six-line sentence of the Italian text, **lines 88–93**), of elegant and persuasive rhetoric (as in the repeated '*Amor*' of **lines 100–106**) and an erotic tension, particularly in the rhythms of the passage from **line 127** to **line 138** where Francesca alludes to the first moments of her love-making. These features combine to give a greater psychological depth to the episode than any previous canto of the *Inferno* has generated. Such qualities have evoked a sensitive response from artists such as Pyotr Tchaikovsky in his symphonic poem *Francesca da Rimini* (1877) or Auguste Rodin in his many sculptures; and a familiar reading of the episode (particularly in the nineteenth century) stresses the extent to which love and death are here movingly at one, and suggests that Dante felt a sympathy for these lovers that over-rode his condemnation of their adultery. These lovers, after all, are eternally intertwined (**74** and **135**) and seem to enjoy in Hell the closeness that they sought in their earthly love.

More recent readings argue that Dante means not only to condemn these sinners but also to create a subtext in Francesca's voice which, read carefully, betrays a mind dominated as much by self-delusion and moral passivity as by lust. For instance, Francesca may declare at line 91 that if the Sovereign of the Universe were her friend, she would pray for Dante's peace of mind. But God, who condemns her to Hell, is not her friend; and so the prayer must fail. Likewise, the sweetness of Francesca's rhetorical repetition of 'Amor' is matched by an emphasis on violent actions hidden in the second line of each of these terzine. A phonetic modulation from a voice of love to a voice of hatred occurs at line 107, as the dominant 'm' alliterations of the preceding lines suddenly give way to a biting 'c' and 's' pattern, which enunciates Francesca's detestation of her murderous husband. Correspondingly, Francesca displays a continuing evasiveness, seeking to shift the blame for her fate away from her own person. It is 'Love' which takes possession of her. It is the book (133–4 and 137) rather than her own passion which leads her into adultery. Thus the particularly mellifluous line 103: 'Amor, ch'a nullo amato amar perdona': 'Love, who no loved one pardons love's requite' reveals itself on examination to be a morally dubious justification of love as an obsessive submission to fate, in which no one who is the object of love has the right to deny love in return to the person that projects that love. On this view, Dante does not condemn Francesca for lust alone. (Among those redeemed in the Purgatorio and Paradiso are figures who submitted to lust, including the sodomites and bestialists of Purgatorio 26 and the court-esans and whores who appear in Paradiso 8 and 9.) Her sin is rather a sin of moral apathy and failed intelligence. Noting how inclined Francesca is to think within the imprisoning conventions of romantic love literature (127–38), some would now compare her to Flaubert's Madame Bovary, destroyed by a fevered but banal imagination, who fails to take seriously the intellectual and emotional drives that are central to her personality.

Neither of these views does full justice to canto 5. Read as a whole, the canto does not merely offer a realistic portrayal of Francesca's seductive personality, but introduces a range of issues concerning the nature of human individuality and the relations between judgement and sensibility, sex and literature, love and death, which were increas-ingly central to Dante's own culture, and have subsequently resonated throughout the culture of western Europe. The first half of the canto emphasizes the importance of judgement. In unambiguously diagnos-tic terms, Dante speaks of those who have submitted reason to instinct and produces a list of figures who are standard examples of the vice, often drawn from the classical past. Notable among these is the empress of Assyria, Semiramis (58–60), who changed the law of her realm to legitimize her own incestuous relationship with her son, who eventually assassinated her. Here, as throughout, it is clear that for Dante there is no such thing as private sin. The consequences of sin are always likely to reverberate throughout the public body. In Dante's understanding, the core of human personality lies in an intellectual appetite or intelligent desire to attain the good. It is this appetite that ultimately leads Dante – through his contemplation of Beatrice – to the recognition, in the last line of the *Commedia*, that '*amor*' is the power 'that moves the sun and other stars' and sustains all created beings in harmonious relationship one with the other. By contrast, '*amor*', as understood by Francesca, leads only to death, to her actual death and to the swoon into which Dante descends, falling 'as bodies fall, for dead' in the final line of canto 5.

For all that, Dante does not represent judgement and reason as merely regulatory and neutral standards of action. From the first, the delicacy of Dante's portrayal of Francesca stands in marked contrast to the harsh and even comic depiction of the judge Minos who, at lines 4–6, not only barks like a dog but consigns the damned to their circle of Hell with the twirl of a tail. Judgement in the hard-line sense may be necessary, but it is also absurd in its crude assessments of human particularity. But judgement can also proceed in the form of self-judgement, and in the direction and development of intelligence and sensibility. Francesca, as Dante represents her, may not possess such powers. Nor does any other figure in the *Inferno*. But the canto at large may be seen as Dante's own attempt to judge himself and to develop the understanding of love which is central to his view of human personality, from the *Vita nuova* to the last lines of the *Paradiso*. Francesca's words '*Amor, ch'al cor gentil ratto s'apprende*' (100) are calculated to mirror a line from the sonnet in chapter 20 of the *Vita nuova* which begins '*Amore e 'l cor gentil sono una cosa*': 'Love and the noble heart are one thing.' But in fact, where Francesca's line speaks of the violence that love does to the noble soul, Dante's insists that love and moral integrity are absolutely identical, literally 'one thing'.

This crucial understanding of the dignity of love is one that Dante in part derives from the tradition of Italian love poetry that had preceded him. But that tradition had also been aware of the close proximity of love to death – of '*amore*' to '*morte*'. (See below Dante's treatment of earlier poets, especially Cavalcanti and Pier della Vigna, in *Inferno* 10 and 13.) In his representation of himself in canto 5,

Dante dramatizes his awareness of the fine line that distinguishes salvific from lethal '*amor*'. The very word '*amor*' can have an hallucinating effect. This is registered at the point in the canto (**68–9**) where the repetition of the consonant 'm' – which in the *Vita nuova* itself generates a lyrical sequence of '*amore*': '*morte*': '*memoria*' – produces an hypnotic cadence that already dissolves inelligent attention into sympathetic resonance. Sinners here become romantic knights and ladies of old, drawing character (and many readers of the canto) into rose-tinted reverie. But such sympathy is also under scrutiny in the course of the canto. The constantly repeated word *pietà* or its cognates (**72, 93, 117, 140**) certainly acknowledges the sort of empathy which readers of modern novels tend to invoke when they speak of their feelings for 'three-dimensional characters'. But for Dante the word has other and richer meanings. His Italian word is etymologically akin to the Latin *pietas*, which Virgil sees as the heroic virtue of Aeneas devoted to the well-being and ultimate good of his band of Trojan refugees. It is that same quality of concern for the salvation of a particular individual which Beatrice displays in her love for Dante in *Inferno* 2. (compare with *Purgatorio* 30.) As for Dante – carrying forward the native love tradition in his devotion to Beatrice and his new attention to Virgilian ethics – *Inferno* 5 may be seen as the profound and ambiguous first move in a long redefinition of love and pity which only concludes with the final line of the *Paradiso*.

Notes

4   In classical legend, Minos, king of Crete, is the son of Zeus and Europa. He appears as the terrifyingly sombre judge of the underworld in Virgil's *Aeneid* 6: 566–9.

40–48 Among the stylistic developments that occur between Dante's writing of the *Vita nuova* and the *Commedia* is a sequence of poems, the *Rime Petrose*, or *Stony Verses* (1296–7), which speak of frustrated love, winter, petrifaction and obsession in a peculiarly harsh diction entirely unlike the 'sweetness' of the *Vita nuova* and its *dolce stil nuovo* manner. One feature of these poems, especially '*Io son venuto al punto della ruota . . .*', is an attention to bird flight across a winter sky. These lines reflect such developments, revealing, pre-emptively, the dark subtext of Francesca's delicate sentiment. (Compare with the 'harsh' diction of *Inferno* 6 and 32.)

52–67 Semiramis, widow of King Ninus, the legendary founder of the Babylonian empire, was, according to Saint Augustine of

Hippo, Paulus Orosius and Brunetto Latini (see below, *Inferno* 15), guilty of incest with her son and used her political position to make this crime legitimate. Dido, queen of Carthage, deserted the memory of her first (dead) husband Sichaeus out of love for Aeneas, but committed suicide when Aeneas left Carthage to continue his journey to Italy and found Rome. The marriage of Cleopatra, queen of Egypt, to Mark Antony precipitated a civil war between Antony and Octavius, who was to become Roman emperor. Helen of Troy was the wife of Menelaus, king of Sparta, whose abduction by Paris, son of the Trojan king Priam, led to the Trojan War. Achilles the Greek warrior was ready to betray his countrymen when he fell in love with Polysena, daughter of Priam, but was ambushed and killed by Paris before he could complete his act of betrayal. Tristan – in love with Iseult, wife of his uncle King Mark of Cornwall – was killed as a traitor by the king's poisoned spear.

106–7 Caina in the geography of Hell is the region in the lowest circles (32) assigned to those who, like Cain, murdered members of their kin.

121–38 Francesca and Paolo are here reading a version of *The Book of Launcelot of the Lake* (an early thirteenth-century prose account of the Arthurian legend). The 'single point' which overcame them is Lancelot confessing his love to Guinevere, under persuasion from Galehault (Galeotto in Italian). 'Galeotto' thus came to mean the type of a go-between or pander. Note that, whereas Francesca claims to have been kissed by Paolo, Guinevere is always presented as giving the first kiss to Lancelot.

CANTO 6

The circle of the gluttons, guarded by Cerberus. Ciacco.
The politics of Florence in 1300.

Commentary

Canto 5 concerned the conflicting and distracting emotions aroused in the inner self by sexual impulse and love. In canto 6 Dante, for the first time in the *Inferno*, explicitly addresses issues specific to the world of contemporary Florentine politics and begins here a sequence of political cantos – continuing, for instance, in *Inferno* 10 and 16 and extending as far as *Paradiso* 16 – where (as here at lines 79–80) he directly names and judges some of the most important public figures of his day. The shift in emphasis between canto 5 and canto 6 mirrors the shift that occurred in Dante's personal career when, at the death of Beatrice, he turned his attentions, at least temporarily, away from the refined diction and rarefied sentiment of his love poetry in the *Vita nuova* to engage directly in the public arena and the world of philosophical debate.

The shock of re-entry into the contentious world of politics is registered by the rude awakening depicted in the opening lines of canto 6, centred upon an ironic repetition of the word '*novi*' (4). In the *Vita nuova* (*The New Life*) 'newness' is associated with the capacity for seeing miraculous evidence of the value of human life represented – as it is again in the *Paradiso* in Dante's constantly 'new' perception of Beatrice. That capacity is wholly contradicted in Hell. The savage repetitiveness of political strife also reduces the history of the world to a dismal and unrelieved sequence, where the same causes of strife are endlessly re-iterated (compare with *Inferno* 27). In particular, greed – which is the sin punished in this circle and which, along with pride and avarice, Dante regularly identifies as the source of civic strife – is here identified as a central factor in the political malaise.

In the political theory which Dante begins to develop in the first years of his exile, greed is seen as the antithesis of justice: where there is the slightest evidence of acquisitiveness, there can be no justice at all (*Monarchia* 1: 1), since justice is concerned with a proportionate distribution of goods, while greed seeks for personal satisfaction which will disturb that proportion. But greed also distorts the intellectual and ethical ambitions which, for Dante, are specific to any truly human life, and must inspire the social and political conduct of citizens. This is a theme throughout the *Convivio* – a title that signifies the 'banquet' of true knowledge and the harmonious living-together that Dante imagines to be possible in a just social order. Thus in *Convivio* 4: 13, Dante writes:

> The good traveller constantly journeys towards a certain and reliable end, and there comes to rest. The mistaken traveller never reaches that. But at the expense of great labour to his soul, always gazes with gluttonous eyes ahead of him.

The philosophical life is here seen as a constant but orderly moving forwards to new goods, which are constantly satisfying and refreshing, whereas the appetite for material goods condemns humanity to unrelieved dissatisfaction and fret.

The issues raised by these considerations are focused in the central encounter of the canto between Dante and his fellow Florentine, the glutton Ciacco. It is significant that the gluttons, suffering in Hell the consequences of the dismal world that their own gluttony has created, are represented in a surrealistic image as 'voided nothings only seeming men' (36). The mere bulk which corporeal appetite may nourish is an ironic parody of what a human being truly is. Momentarily Ciacco emerges from the slime; and a conversation begins which has the initial appearance of sympathy, but is shot through with dissensions and crossed wires: Ciacco – though a historical figure who is the subject of a lively anecdote by Giovanni Boccaccio in the *Decameron* 9: 8 – is allowed no name save a nickname which means 'porker' or 'hog'. He has no standing or stable position within the order of society; and indeed, when he speaks of his fellow citizens, he divisively relishes the fate they will suffer. Such *schadenfreude* extends even to his attitude to Dante. Through Ciacco's mouth Dante alludes for the first time to his own political exile (64–84). But this is seen as a vicious slur (as it will be also in *Inferno* 24), a nervous attempt to distract Dante from his mission – and discompose the breadth of vision that true philosophy would generate, and which Dante, in writing the *Commedia*, is attempting to cultivate. Above all, there can be no recognition between Dante and Ciacco. The emotional core of the canto is focused upon the three words at line 41: '*riconoscimi, se sai*': '[T]ell me you know me'. Ciacco here voices an agonizing desire (which the exiled Dante may himself have shared) for recognition in the eyes of his fellow citizens. But such reciprocity is a reflection of a fundamental commitment to the life of justice in which human beings truly are human. Ciacco's attitudes are the opposite of that. This is not to deny the value of recognizable human form. Indeed, it is significant that the final section of the canto (94–115) makes reference to the Day of Judgement and the Resurrection of the Body – a constant and central theme in Dante's thinking. (See *Inferno* 10 and *Paradiso* 14.) The '*carne*' and '*figura*' ('flesh' and 'figure') are part of human identity and will be given eternal significance in the final eternal state. But that identity once again depends upon justice, not upon the indulgence of acquisitive appetites.

The language of the sixth canto, in contrast to the heady *dolcezza* that characterized canto 5, is here harsh in both sound and implication: the classical and mythic figure of Cerberus becomes a howling mongrel. Note especially the harsh sequence of rhymes at lines 14–18 – *latra/atra/isquatra* – in which barking, darkness and tearing to bits are linked. There is something here of the violent, dissonant language that

Dante practises in the deliberately harsh *Rime Petrose* of his lyric poetry. In later cantos (particularly canto 32) there is a bleak and hard-headed virtuosity about such usages. Here the aim is to produce a vivid play on physical and material spiritual forms (shadows being torn to pieces) which produces a cartoon-like perception of the human being. Dogs howl; sinners struggle. Only the voice of Virgil in the concluding parts harmonizes this, producing the great sonorities in which he evokes the sound of the eternal trumpet, or else a clear, almost clinical resort to practical science in **lines 106–8**.

Notes

13–32 Cerberus (here, like Charon in canto 3, a modification and intensification of Virgil's original) is to be found as the watchdog of Hades in *Aeneid* 6: 417–22.

58–73 The exchange here between the two Florentines and Dante provides a (sometimes allusive) account of the factional strife between White and Black Guelfs (see Introduction p. xx) which came to a head around 1300–1302 and brought about Dante's exile. The Blacks had rioted in 1301 and Dante, in his role as one of the priors of Florence, had been obliged to exile members of both Black and White factions. The Whites were the 'country' – hence (here) 'Wildwood' party; their leaders, the Cerchi, came from the rural environs of Florence – and in 1300 the Whites had won a temporary superiority. But the Blacks regrouped, and within the span of three years ('three ... suns') they returned to power. Their cause was supported by the one who 'now just coasts between' – that is, Pope Boniface VIII – keeping open the option of alliance with both Blacks and Whites.

79–84 All the great Florentines that Dante here disingenuously inquires about are found in the lower circles of Hell. Notes on Farinata can be found in canto 10, on Rusticucci and Tegghiaio in canto 16 and on Mosca in canto 28. Arrigo is not mentioned elsewhere.

106–8 This principle is enunciated by Aristotle in the *Nicomachean Ethics* 10:4.

115 Plutus, the god of riches, dominates the first phase of canto 7.

CANTO 7

The avaricious and the spendthrift. The doctrine of
fortune. The wrathful and the melancholic.

Commentary

Canto 7 shifts attention from the pursuit of physical appetite in glut-
tony to the perversion of intelligence that, for Dante, is displayed in
the avaricious pursuit of money wealth. Two other distortions of
intellectual appetite are also considered in this canto. These are, firstly,
anger (a violent frustration in the face of the obstacles that are pre-
sented by the material presence of other persons and other things)
and, secondly, melancholia (a refusal to admit the rightful claims that
material and earthly objects exert on us by virtue of their beauty).

Where canto 6 pursues a taste for satirical violence in its style and
diction, canto 7 opens with pure gibberish (1). Here as elsewhere (for
example, in *Inferno* 26: 67) Dante combines an irrepressible linguistic
inventiveness with a profound sense that corruptions of mind and
sensibility are directly reflected in corrupted applications of language,
or in the lessening of a capacity for coherent thought and word. Where
Ciacco is denied the dignity of a personal name, the sinners of canto
7 are not identified by any sort of address. Nor do they enter into any
conversation with Dante. The canto concludes with a richly evocative
– and comic – indication of Dante's linguistic preoccupations: the
unseen souls of the melancholic, plunged in the slime of the Styx, create
speech bubbles in the viscous element, which Virgil – the exemplar of
articulate and rational utterance – then translates on their behalf as a
dark but lyrical expression of sullenness in the face of earthly beauty.

The failures of language that begin and end the canto throw into
relief the brilliantly lucid poetry that Dante attributes to Virgil in its
central section (73–96). Here Virgil discourses on the theme of fortune.
This is a theme to which Dante might be thought especially sensitive,
considering the evidence that he faced of a cruel and changing world
in the history of his own exile from Florence. So at significant moments
in the *Commedia* Dante returns to this theme, until in *Paradiso* 15–17
he eventually offers his most extended and sophisticated account of
the relation of providence to fortune and human suffering. Already in
canto 7 he writes a passage that in style and imagery anticipates the
scintillating philosophical poetry of the *Paradiso*. To Virgil (who is
shown initially as reluctant to speak in any detail about fortune) Dante

here attributes a sensitivity to the imagery of light; and here, as always, there lies at the core of Dante's own style a syntactical articulation (for example, in the result clause of line 75 and the gerunds of lines 76 and 83 ('*distribuendo*' and '*seguendo*'), which serves to ensure both a clarity of logical outline and a lyrical fluency, as thought combines in sequence with thought. It is notable that Virgil at line 72 invites Dante, literally rendered, 'to take into his mouth' or, in the terms of the *Convivio*, 'feast' on this doctrinal disquisition. The style of the passage helps to focus the sort of pleasure its savour might bring to the intellectual appetite. But in substance, too, Dante here introduces certain original emphases, involving a vigorous rewriting of a standard medieval representation of fortune drawn from Anicius Boethius's *Consolation of Philosophy* (524–5). In its popular form, the Boethian conception of fortune pictures the world as subject to a constant shift of fortune's wheel:

> So with imperious hand she turns the wheel of change
> This way and that like the ebb and flow of the tide.
> And pitiless she tramples down those once dread kings,
> Raising the lowly face of the conquered –
> Only to mock him in his turn.
> Careless she neither hears nor heeds the cries
> Of miserable men.   *Consolation of Philosophy* 1: 1

Our consolation must be to lift our gaze beyond this world to eternal and unchanging truths. However, Dante at no point adopts the grim tonalities conventionally associated with this conception, nor even recommends that we should abandon, in a certain fashion, our love of earthly things. From the first, he demands that fortune should be seen as an eternal principle, ensuring a proper distribution of goods in the world. Goods are scarce and therefore it is a condition of our enjoyment of them that we should accept intellectually that they will move from hand to hand. Like Boethius, Dante fixes his mind on an eternal verity. But, unlike Boethius, he refuses to dismiss the 'splendours of the world', the '*splendor mondani*' of line 77. The created world is, for Dante, inherently good. That is why fortune should be praised. If we understand the nature of the goods of this world, we have a right to enjoy them, and should praise fortune rather than blame her for effecting an appropriate distribution of these goods.

A key to this passage is the repeated references to '*permutasse/ permutazion*', 'permutations'. In contrast to the mechanical model offered in popular versions of Boethius's work, this pictures intelligent variation and is consistent with the final version of the doctrine (offered in *Paradiso* 15–17) that pictures providence as the intelligent working-through of the divine plan. Dante sees participation in this plan as possible. At the same time, in canto 7, he throws into relief the activities of the money men who create a materially minded geometry which is reflected in the blank regularity of their punishment. Intelligence here is reduced to the rolling of boulders, a subjection of mind and energy to mere materiality.

Notes

8   The wolf referred to here recalls the she-wolf of *Inferno* 1: 49–60 and anticipates a further reference in *Purgatorio* 20: 10.

10–12 The archangel Michael leads the attack that drives Satan from Heaven.

22–7   Compare with Virgil, *Aeneid* 3: 420–23. Charybdis is the mythological name for the whirlpools in the Straits of Messina. The reference to the sea in this canto recalls that, in Boethius's *Consolation of Philosophy*, it was merchants who originally disturbed the harmony of the Golden Age by their maritime enterprise. The punishment of the rocks recalls the labours of Sisyphus in *Aeneid* 6: 616.

43–5   Avarice is here punished alongside its opposite, prodigality. Aristotle suggests this coupling in *Nicomachean Ethics* 4: 1: 1121a. Following Aristotle here as elsewhere, Dante would identify virtue as a mean between two vicious extremes. In this case, liberality would constitute the virtuous mean.

73–96 In the course of this passage Dante attributes to fortune angelic powers. Angels (on the understanding that Dante offers in *Paradiso* 28) are the purest forms of created intelligence, and are set as governors over the movements of the physical cosmos.

97–9   The reference to the stars here establishes the hour as just past midnight on Good Friday.

115–29 The swamp formed by the river Styx contains within it two groups of sinners, the wrathful and the sluggardly. (One etymology for 'Styx' suggests the word means 'sorrow', which can be taken as the source of both anger and hatred.) Again, Dante is using conceptions of the Aristotelian mean to identify anger and wrath as vicious extremes.

CANTOS 8 AND 9

*The swamp of the Styx. Encounter with Filippo Argenti.
Arrival at the city of Dis. Entry secured by the messenger
from Heaven.*

Commentary

Cantos 8 and 9 form a sustained and connected narrative unit unusual
for the *Inferno*. (Compare, however, *Inferno* 21–3.) In terms of sub-
ject, this sequence spans the transition from the first major division of
Hell – where the trivial, though still damnable, sins of appetite and
intemperance are punished – to the city of Dis, which runs down to
the very bottom of the pit and comprises the punishment of all those
sins that involve some active and conscious application of rational
will. Explanations are offered for such divisions in canto 11; and these
explanations (in common with the philosophical lyric of canto 7)
demonstrate the extent of Dante's philosophical ambitions, even in
the *Inferno*. Yet in cantos 8–9 there is no explicitly philosophical
discussion. The issues that concern Dante here are, rather, approached
obliquely through the suggestions of scene, imagery and dramatic
action. Indeed, the ambition that Dante seems to be pursuing involves a
strikingly new development in cultivating the potentialities of narrative
and even epic poetry. From the first, the poet here displays an acute
awareness of his own artistic purposes. Thus the opening lines of canto
8 have been supposed (originally by Boccaccio) to mark the point at
which Dante abandoned an early attempt to write his poem in Latin
and turned to the vernacular, as if he were determined now – '*Io dico,
seguitando*', 'And so I say (continuing)' (8:1) – to prove that the
vernacular was capable of anything that a classical language could
achieve. Whether or not Boccaccio's contention is true, Dante himself
(9: 61–3) draws the attention of the reader to the high meaning of the
sequence, assuming an authority over his audience which he has never
previously displayed. Correspondingly, the great twentieth-century
critic Erich Auerbach discerns in the episode that immediately follows
these lines an example of epic sublimity unmatched since the works
of Virgil and Homer. (See his 'Camilla and the Rebirth of the Sublime'
in *Literary Latin and Its Public in Late Latin Antiquity* (New York,
1965).)

At the core of canto 8 is the defeat that Virgil suffers when he
attempts to negotiate a safe conduct for Dante across the threshold of

Dis. Canto 9 revolves around the effortless entry into Dis which is secured on Dante's behalf by an unnamed figure sent from Heaven, who (at 9: 64–99) comes with heroic power (but also walking like Christ across the waters) over the filthy swamp that surrounds the city. Why is it that Virgil, as Dante's chosen leader and the river of discourse of canto 7, line 80, should be prevented so early in the journey from performing his function as a guide? What significance does Dante expect his reader to find in the appearance of the messenger?

In terms of moral allegory, the defeat of Virgil may be seen as an expression of the limitation of rational thought when confronted with sins such as those within the city of Dis that are themselves, perversely, the product of rational thought and endeavour. From the first, the city of Dis – whose inhabitants spit out their opposition to Dante's advance '*stizzosamente*': '[s]pitting in wrath' at **canto 8, lines 83–4** – is a place in which the powers of rational calculation that Virgil devotes to Dante's salvation are themselves seen to be capable of producing such deviations as heresy, suicide, flattery, false propaganda and manifold forms of treachery. At the same time, the appearance of the messenger from Heaven, the '*Messo da Ciel*', as the unnamed figure is usually referred to, suggests that for Dante there is a power – whom even Virgil longs to see (**9: 9**) – that can intervene to save humanity from its own self-imposed confusions and make possible its advance towards salvation. In canto 2 Virgil was obliged to invoke the aid of Beatrice to further Dante's advance. Already in that canto, Beatrice, who embodies and demonstrates the truth of God's creative power, was invoked by Virgil himself to solve the first questions and delays that Dante suffers. There is a direct correspondence between the power of Beatrice and that of the *Messo da Ciel*, though Dante is not prone to emphasize the effects of grace. (See Introduction p. li). There is some sense here, however, that the beauty and vigour and purposefulness of human action can only be assured by association with powers that reflect the actions of the divine.

The moment of transition that Dante's narrative here represents is in some measure a moment of conversion – recognition of the dependence of human beings upon their maker, an assertion of a spiritual freedom that can only be claimed by moving ever forwards, as faith demands, into surprising and unexpected situations. But here, as at other great moments of transition (as, for example, *Purgatorio* 9, 20 and 30), Dante magnifies the personal drama of conversion by relating it to the points of intersection between providence and history. In its imagery and drama, canto 9 recreates the moment when Christ entered the world – when a threshold was crossed between the world before and after redemption. If Virgil is shown here to wait so longingly for the coming of the *Messo*, this must reflect the tragic paralysis of the pagan mind (represented also in the Limbo sequence of canto 4), needing to be delivered from its own self-imprisonment, yet incapable of seeing where that deliverance will come from. So, too, a dominant image in canto 8 is the stagnant swamp that surrounds the city of Dis. Archetypally, the waters of life, of regeneration and fertility, have been transformed, as if by the malignant chemistry of original sin, into the '*schiuma antica*'. The 'age-old scum' of **canto 9, line 74** that surrounds the city of Dis could be taken as an image of the corruption that has grown under the influence of original sin and poisoned the springs of life and rebirth. A further indication of this are the Furies and the Medusa, drawn from classical legend (9: 37–51), who threaten to paralyse Dante with a vision of how humanity in its unredeemed condition inexorably preys upon itself.

These two cantos, taken together, express a growing confidence and experimental vigour on Dante's part as he extends the stretch of his own narrative stride and produces a sequence of extraordinary variety in its dynamics and tonal colour. So, too – in a sequence where Virgil as a character is shown at times to be tongue-tied and capable of only rather pallid forays into narrative – Dante begins to challenge the achievements of classical poetry (as he will quite explicitly in *Inferno* 25). Not only is he capable of matching the classics in his depiction of the Furies (as described by Virgil in *Aeneid* 6: 570–75), he is also able to offer his own highly redefined version of epic heroism – in the form exemplified by the *Messo da Ciel*. Here, too, there are classical precedents for the great similes that introduce the advent of the *Messo*: in the *Aeneid* 2: 416–19 and in Ovid's account of the transformation of the Lycians (*Metamorphoses* 6: 370–81), while there are features drawn from Mercury as described in Statius's *Thebaid* 2: 1–3. Yet there is no brute force here, but rather an effortless, almost nonchalant display of energy, which is captured in the characteristically graphic detail of the figure moving his hand (his left hand) to dispel the smoke and the tiny disdainful gesture he makes with his diminutive wand, the '*verghetta*' (9: 89).

In canto 4 Dante showed Virgil speaking of the '*possente*' – the powerful one who breaks open the depths of Hell. This figure, though (again) not named as Christ, displays that same concentrated power. It is characteristic of Dante to see Christ's actions in terms more of power than of gentleness or suffering. (Compare with the earthquakes created by the Harrowing of Hell referred to in *Inferno* 12 and 22.) In the present sequence, however, Dante places a strong emphasis upon effects of anger. The sinners confined within the marsh that surrounds the city of Dis are themselves condemned for their instinctual anger. But it is also impossible to enter this city 'without anger'. The Messenger's self-possessed vigour is the supreme example of righteous wrath. But Virgil himself grows (repressedly) angry at **canto 8, line 121.** And Dante too, at **lines 31–63,** portrays himself in peculiarly vicious contest with one of the damned and (most remarkable of all) draws a daring, even scandalous connection between his own violent demeanour and the actions of Christ. In this highly problematical episode, Dante encounters a fellow Florentine, the notoriously arrogant Filippo, a member of the Black Guelf Adimari clan, which is condemned by Dante in *Paradiso* 16: 115–20. Though now so caked in mud – '*pieno*', so 'full' of it that it seems to flow out of him, Filippo was in life nicknamed Argenti, the Silver One, apparently because he had his horses shod in silver. Concentrated in this figure is the spirit of pride and divisiveness that Dante constantly identifies among the sources of Florentine corruption. Dante's violence towards Argenti – who, like Francesca in canto 5, seeks to evoke pity but receives none – may be an understandable expression of political and moral fervour. Yet at this same point, Virgil is shown – in a way that challenges any such rationalization – to defer to Dante and explicitly address to him in all his wrath words that were originally in Luke 11: 27: 'Blessed is the womb that bare thee.' As the rational Virgil dimly anticipates, beyond the limitations of his own reason, the coming of a messenger from Heaven, so here he momentarily seems to recognize in Dante's wrath an anticipation of that coming. A capacity for energy and surprising power are, for Dante, hallmarks of the Christian mind. Correspondingly, the Christian poet may be expected to reflect this in the vitality or even disruptiveness of his own style. So in the Argenti episode, the quarrel between the two Florentines is characterized by the exceptional violence of phrase and colloquial roughness of **canto 8, lines 39** and **52–4.** Such qualities as these – which Dante develops to yet greater extremes as the *Commedia* proceeds – are in marked contrast to the measured words that Dante regularly attributes to Virgil as his guide.

For all that, the initially frustrated and ultimately exultant energies that the sequence generates are paralleled throughout by passages in which doubt, self-questioning and even humiliation are the dominant features. Dante allows himself no triumphalism in his encounter with Filippo Argenti. **Canto 8, lines 64–6** record an uncomfortable attempt to exclude the agonizing cries of Filippo from his story: '*più nonne narro*' ('Of him, my story tells no more'), and leads to a section in which he contemplates the possibility that his own story might itself have no future. The repeated word '*rimanere*' – 'to remain' – becomes a motif, along with the verb '*forse*' – perhaps (8: 34, 38, 110 and 116). In canto 9 Dante is threatened with the Medusa who, by turning him to stone, would deprive him of all power to continue his journey. Already in the final phase of **canto 8**, beginning at **lines 109–11**, the rhythms of the canto have begun to evoke paralysis of mind and body as Virgil leaves Dante to parley with the devils. Suddenly, far from producing an epic advance, Dante seems to have returned to the state in which Virgil first found him in the dark wood; and Dante does indeed refer, at **canto 8, line 102**, to the possibility of abandoning the whole enterprise.

Beneath these vacillations are the experiences of the Florentine exile, faced with the acute drama that the crossing of any gate or threshold is likely to inspire in him, as he resuscitates the emotions of being driven out and ever-after seeking some place to which he might return. (Compare with the entry into Purgatory at *Purgatorio* 9.) Thresholds familiarly evoke both panic and exhilaration. But the ambiguity of emotion that underlies this sequence is entirely consistent with that of a thinker such as Dante who believed the city to be the true arena for human action, loved Florence and yet was driven out by its citizens. Dis and Florence are analogous. But the journey towards a new home and a new city needs to be continued. Heroic endurance (and the writing of a poem aimed at salvation) may be one mode in which this can be accomplished. At the same time, patience and humility are portrayed as being a part of this endurance. Thus, one of the most moving features of the episode is the picture of Virgil and Dante – both suffering defeat and perplexity – that emerges in **canto 9, lines 16–30 and 58–60**. To pass the time and give Dante some confidence, Virgil speaks in necessarily obscure terms of the help that might be offered, and in pathetically feeble tones – especially when compared with the high drama that the sequence elsewhere generates – musters stories that might encourage a renewal of Dante's trust. Then, at the point when the *Messo* might be expected, the Furies appear, and to save Dante from the sight of the Medusa, Virgil spins Dante round and, to be doubly sure of protecting him, places his own hands over the hands with which Dante has covered his eyes. The very fragility of these two human figures summoning what resources they can (including the physical support for one another) produces a solidarity in such circumstances of waiting which itself establishes its own form of restrained and modest heroism. (Compare with the importance of 'waiting' in *Purgatorio* 4–8.)

It is a feature of the sequence that Dante's literary and moral focus should move constantly between effects of confusion and command, of violence and energy, of stasis and kinesis, of humanity and inhumanity both divine and monstrous, of pride in literary skill and an awareness of how feeble the resources of reason and language may be.

Thus, in the first phase of the sequence, in the opening lines of canto 8, suspense is created by the signal lights flashing at the top of the towering vertical that impedes Dante's progress. What do they signify? On one level, they mark the secret opposition that is now mustering against Dante's advance. The apprehension they arouse also points remotely to the coming of the power that will overthrow that opposition. Signs themselves are ambiguous here and that ambiguity may itself contain, beyond reason, a providential subtext. But initially the signs trigger a sudden change of tempo as Dante is opposed by the guardian of this circle, Phlegyas, impelled by rage across the stagnant swamp (8: 19). This arrival is depicted in a dynamic syntactical movement, sustained over six lines, in an exceptionally sharp focus – 'una nave piccioletta', 'un sol galeoto' – and a violent climax in the raucous voice of the pilot. This is immediately countered in the worldweary tones of Virgil, who already sees in Dante's journey a manifestation of providential design, which is emphasized by the dipping of the boat as the miraculously physical presence of Dante enters it (8: 27). In the second phase of the canto (8: 31–63), Florence itself, in the person of Filippo Argenti, puts an immediate obstacle in Dante's way. Here, as throughout the sequence, the narrative constantly draws attention to the axis of vision, whether horizontal or vertical. This filmic control also carries with it its own symbolism, the horizontal signifying the axis of human endeavour, the vertical being the axis of mysterious intervention, be that intervention demonic or divine, from below or from above. The steady progress which Dante is attempting to make – though shortly to be interrupted by the tower of the malignant city – is initially interrupted by the figure of Filippo Argenti from these depths. Virgil defends the gunwales of the ship, himself adopting momentarily an uncharacteristically violent mode of speech.

In the third phase of the canto (8: 64–81) there is a stolid interlude as Dante and Virgil steadily advance. But this horizontal advance is increasingly threatened by premonitions of what the city holds in store. Its vividly burning minarets (71–2) fixate the eyes of the traveller and visually anticipate the strenuous syntax and onomatopoeic truculence that record the appearance of a thousand devils on the threshold at lines 82–4. With this begins the long evocation of defeat and delay that concludes the eighth canto. Even the reader is invited, at lines

94–6, to enter into the stasis of this phase. Eventually, in **canto 9, lines 61–6,** the 'sane' intellect of the reader is encouraged to discover a meaning beneath the surface of the 'alien' fiction that Dante has here created. For the moment, attention is concentrated on discomfiting emotions and accursed utterances. Virgil's words, addressed now to the devils on the threshold (**8: 87** and **112**), are unavailable to Dante – as secret in significance as the signs that at the opening of the canto had threatened Dante's advance. Dante is left, already paralysed with doubt – between the 'yes' and the 'no' – mulling over his own story so far, attempting to draw comfort from it (**8: 97–102**), but also imagining how it might all unravel.

The poet who has contrived this meditation on his own invented journey now employs the canto break not – as he normally does – to create an effect of surprise, but rather to challenge the reader with the prospect of an unchanging and unchangeable scene. In the opening phase of canto 9 (**9: 1–33**) Virgil is as nonplussed as Phlegyas was at the opening of canto 8. His words break down into inarticulate silence at **line 8,** and broken utterance (**line 14**), which by its ambiguity serves only to terrify Dante further. He is capable of speaking only in indefinites of the help that might be offered ('*Tal*' – 'such a one', 'someone' (**line 8**)). Nor when he attempts to tell the story of his own earlier journey through Hell (**9: 22–30**) does he succeed in capturing Dante's attention. On the contrary, at this point the tension of the canto begins to build with the vividly colouristic and intricate vision of the Furies, blood-stained, girt around with brilliant green snakes, their hair formed out of snakelets. This picture of violent motion builds to a crescendo at the point at which the Medusa might be expected to appear. It is against that monstrous possibility that Virgil closes his hands so humanely over Dante's eyes.

Yet it is not the Medusa who arrives but – from behind Dante and Virgil, coming across the waters – the providential and wholly surprising figure of the *Messo da Ciel*. The narrative of suspense continues. But its character now changes to anticipation of meaning and resolution. In contrast to all previous effects of sluggishness, the elemental forces of wind and natural power are evoked rhythmically and onomatopoetically (**9: 64–75**). These effects are first expressed through sound. But to sharpen the effect Dante, instead of allowing a simple increment of sounds, crosscuts at **canto 9, line 73** to the timorous figure of his *alter ego* – eyes still tight shut – who now is allowed to release his eyes, in sinewy concentration, to witness the arrival of the *Messo*. The orchestration of the scene again is exact: first a 'thousand' figures fanning out in chaotic flight from the power of the *Messo* and then a refocused concentration on 'one' who walks effortlessly across the air towards them. The verse itself effects its own effortless modulation at lines 80–81 with an alliterative repetition across the enjambment of '*passo*' – 'pace' and '*passava*' – 'passed'. In almost languorous tones, the *Messo* speaks of irreconcilable conflicts: evil in the form of the devils constantly repeats its history of opposition, refusing to hear the story that has, time and again, brought providential power triumphantly into Hell (9: 91–9).

Though the *Messo* undoubtedly must – to the 'sane' intellect' (see 9: 61) – be seen as a figure for the hidden power of Christ, this is the last occasion in Hell when Dante will portray any such intervention. At later moments of transition (*Inferno* 17 and 30) his descent into Hell is facilitated by figures who are themselves representative of sin, in the form of deceit and brutish pride. To that degree, sin again proves to be self-defeating. Yet it needs to be emphasized that the Messenger, far from appearing in the form of an angelic being (the agents of grace in the *Purgatorio*), is a distinctly anthropomorphic figure. He does not descend from the vertical – so often the symbol of the divine – but moves along the human horizontal. This implies that grace, in Dante's view, does not eliminate or replace human action, but rather enables the fulfilment of recognizably human effort. This, too, is the implication of the final phase of the sequence (9: 100–33). As Dante now enters the city of Dis there is an immediate anticlimax. All resistance has gone. What is left is a city of the dead, of tombs eerily illuminated by fires burning within them. For Dante and Virgil there remains the humdrum heroism of picking their painstaking way through a landscape in which it becomes ever more apparent how easily human beings, even the most heroic, can reduce themselves to nothing.

Notes to Canto 8

19–24 Phlegyas is drawn (much altered) from *Aeneid* 6: 618–20, where he appears as king of Thessaly. His anger there is a response to his daughter's rape by Apollo.

31–42 This episode is illustrated in all its violence by Eugène Delacroix in his *Dante and Virgil in Hell* (1822), now in the Louvre.

43–5 It should be noted that in the passage in Luke 11: 28 to which this alludes, Christ replies by rejecting the praises offered to him.

124–6 This is the gate of Hell (*Inferno* 3) which since the Harrowing of Hell has always stood open.

Notes to Canto 9

7–9 Because the verb *'s'offerse'* and its subject *'Tal'* have no gender, this broken utterance may be taken to refer to Beatrice or the *messo da ciel*.

22–30 Dante – drawing on Lucan's *Pharsalia* 6: 507 and so on – seems to have invented the story of Virgil's earlier journey through Hell to the depths where Judas is punished, conjured to do so by the witch Erichtho. Throughout the Middle Ages Virgil had a reputation for witchcraft – which Dante repudiates implicitly in *Inferno* 20.

37–51 Compare with Virgil, *Aeneid* 6: 570–75. The Three Furies, or Eumenides, or Erinyes, specifically pursue those who are guilty of crimes of blood. Hecate is the queen of Hell spoken of here.

52–4 The story of the Medusa and of her power to turn men to stone is told in Ovid's *Metamorphoses* 6: 606: 249. The Furies at line 54 show regret that they did not kill Theseus (see also notes to *Inferno* 12), when they had him in their power, and thus dissuaded other travellers from passing through Hell.

97–9 Hercules is said to have defeated and chained Cerberus, who appears in canto 3.

112–15 These lines refer to Roman cemeteries at Arles, near the mouth of the river Rhône, and at Pola (now Pulj) on the Istrian peninsula.

CANTO 10

The heretics. Farinata and Cavalcante.

Commentary

The first sinners that Dante encounters in the city of Dis are those condemned for heresy. Strictly speaking, heresy is the result of obstinacy or confusion in the minds of Christian thinkers which leads them into contention with orthodox understanding. Dante includes an example in the coda to this episode which appears in canto 11, lines 7–9, where Anastasius is led to believe only in the human nature of Christ. Yet little is explicitly said about heresy in this canto. The canto is above all characterized by Dante's encounter with two Florentine figures from the generation preceding his own, the Ghibelline warlord Farinata degli Uberti (d. 1264), and the Guelf aristocrat and one-time chief magistrate of Gubbio, Cavalcante de' Cavalcanti (d. *c.* 1280), who was the father of Guido, Dante's closest friend in his early years as a poet. These men are likely to have held heterodox views, and are associated here with those who believe that as the body dies, 'so too the soul' (15). But the conversation that unrolls here concerns Farinata's patriotic, if flawed, devotion to the Florentine cause. He speaks (at **lines 89–93**) of an occasion when his party were in a position to destroy the city of Florence yet were restrained by his rhetoric. Correspondingly, Cavalcante's mind is obsessed with paternal pride and envy: if Dante should be so favoured as to travel through the other world, then why should not his highly intelligent son (59) be similarly favoured? In his response to both, Dante attributes to himself a lively independence of mind, amounting to truculence (49–51), which contributes to his developing picture of Florence as a place of division and misapprehension.

It says something for the intellectual temper of thirteenth-century Florence that it could foster adherence to doctrines (here associated with pre-Christian philosophers such as Empedocles and Lucretius) which were wholly at odds with Christian teaching. Dante himself – a decidedly independent thinker – is frequently thought to have brushed up against heretical thinking in *De Monarchia*. Certainly, the work was eventually condemned by the Catholic Church. But beneath the political cut-and-thrust of canto 10 there runs a desire to see heresy as itself a cause of political division and a determination to re-affirm, however obliquely, Dante's devotion to the figure of Beatrice, who throughout the *Commedia* demands of him an absolute devotion to Christian truth. In choosing to focus on the philosophical propositions of those who deny that human life is eternal (among the many possible heresies he might have attacked), Dante resuscitates in the drama of the canto a view that he vigorously expresses in the *Convivio*, that it is an inhuman and irrational stupidity to deny a life after death to human beings:

> Of all brutish opinions none is more stupid, more base or more pernicious than the belief that there is no other life after this; every poet who writes in the faith of the gentiles seems to say as much and every code of moral law asserts the same, be it of the Jews, the Saracens, the Tartars or any other that lives according to rational principle. And to suppose that all these were mistaken would be an absurdity.   *Convivio* 2: 8

Human life, then, is too dignified to be erased by death. The solidarity of human agreement to this proposition demands that we should accept it as a rational tenet of our existence. This also is one of the beliefs that Dante was driven to explore in his desolation at the death of Beatrice – to whom he alludes at lines 63–4. But without this profound assertion of human worth, all the particular manifestations of human love and value – such as Farinata's patriotism or Cavalcante's devotion to his son – are likely to come to nothing. Love of cities and love of sons may be good. Indeed, they are so good that they point to an unassailable belief in the endurance of these dispositions, which ironically enough Farinata and Cavalcante have denied in their heretical beliefs but demonstrate to the full in the speeches that Dante now gives to them. Nor is a city likely to live in harmony with itself unless it is inspired by an unwavering belief in the ultimate value of the human person.

The landscape and dialogues of canto 10 depict a city which has become an eerie graveyard, and where talk itself is as likely to be as divisive as it is concordant. After the violent scenes at the gate of Dis, Dante now enters a place which is empty of all signs of life, until suddenly a voice arrests Dante's progress and demands that he should speak as one Tuscan to another. Farinata's words are sonorous and rhythmically sustained (lines 22–5). Yet they inspire only terror in his fellow citizen, as does the monumental and graphic image of a figure expanding its massive chest and raising a disdainful eyebrow at line 45. Dante's own words only add to the dissension as he reaches back in history to recall the antipathy of his Guelf ancestors to Farinata's Ghibelline cause.

Wires cross even further with the appearance of Cavalcante. Notably, Farinata says nothing at all to Cavalcante – despite the fact that his daughter had been married (in the interests of civic harmony) to Guido Cavalcanti. Indeed, a faintly comic contrast now emerges, as the rigid Farinata (moving neither his neck nor his waist (75)) looks over the head of a Cavalcante, whose rhythms of speech and syntax desert the archaic gravitas that Farinata had displayed and fall into broken and distracted confusion. Dante adds to that confusion by a grammatical mistake, which he refers to at lines 110–11, an incorrect use of the past remote *ebbe*, which Cavalcante takes to imply that his son's life has ended.

Beyond this picture of civic and personal misapprehension there lies the story of Dante's complex relationship with Guido Cavalcanti (see Introduction p. xxvii). The phrase that Dante at line 59 puts in the mouth of Cavalcanti's father identifies intellectual acumen as a quality displayed by Guido and Dante alike. Yet that Guido should not be travelling alongside Dante through the other world implies a distinction in the application of intelligence. (This distinction emerges even more clearly in *Inferno 26*.) Guido may not have held Virgil in the same regard that led Dante to make him his guide on a journey inspired by the desire to rebuild a shattered civilization. He was to remain a poet simply of lyrical brilliance. Nor did his poems recognize, as Dante increasingly does in the *Commedia*, that love is a harmonious and sustaining power. Guido's persistent vision of the destructive influence of love on the self-possession of intelligent men rejects the claims of a community that gathers (as do the Christian philosophers of *Paradiso* 14) to celebrate the resurrection of the body.

This canto offers a strangely musical trio – with the largely silent voices of Guido Cavalcanti and Virgil adding their vestigial presence – in which the resonances of Farinata, the whimper of Cavalcante and the impertinence of Dante all play their parts. Visually, too, the marked contrasts in physical form and gesture between Farinata, Cavalcante and Dante create a monumental (but also at times comic) choreography in which, imaginatively as well theologically, Dante's invariable concentration on the significance of the human body is immediately perceptible.

Notes

10–12   Jehoshaphat, according to Joel 3: 2, is where the Last Judgement will be announced and conducted.

13–15   Dante speaks of the Greek philosopher Epicurus with admiration in *Convivio* 47: 6 but here as elsewhere (see *Inferno* 12: 40–43) resists the implications of materialist metaphysics.

31–54 and 76–93   The references underlying Farinata's first and, explicitly, his concluding speech are to the events surrounding the battle of Montaperti, near Siena – where the battlefield is traversed by the river Arbia. Here in 1260 the Florentine Guelfs were defeated by a coalition of Tuscan Ghibellines. It was Farinata who at the subsequent war council in Empoli persuaded his allies to refrain from destroying Florence. When the Guelfs recovered their supremacy, Farinata and his descendants were excluded from the amnesties of 1280. The Uberti palace, occupying the present Piazza della Signoria in Florence, was pulled down and left in Dante's lifetime as rubble, *pour encourager les autres*.

67–9   Dante has here used the past remote *ebbe*, which in Italian signifies an action in the past that has no continuing connection with the present, hence implying Guido Cavalcanti's death. Here, too, Dante gives Cavalcante's speech a Bolognese inflection: *lume* (light) here becomes '*lome*'.

97–108 Dante imagines a form of myopia by which the sinners are condemned to have no knowledge of present things and to see more clearly into the distant future than into the past.

119–20 For Frederick II of Hohenstaufen (1194–1250), Holy Roman Emperor, see Introduction p. xvii. The cardinal is the Ghibelline Ottaviano degli Ubaldini (d. 1273), who is said to have declared: 'If I have a soul at all, I have lost it a hundred times in the interests of the Ghibellines.'

131–32 The reference here, as above at line 63, is to Beatrice in Heaven.

CANTO 11

The plan of Hell.

Commentary

Adopting, for the most part, a very plain and often compressed style of writing, in canto 11 Dante enunciates, through the mouth of Virgil, some of the major principles on which the moral plan or geography of Hell has been constructed. Particular attention is given to the sins of '*ingiuria*' (23), a scholastic term designating the injustices which are committed with the conscious and intentionally malicious aim (22) of causing harm to other people or to their legitimate possessions. Sins of this sort are punished within the walls of the city of Dis, which Dante and Virgil have now entered and which extend to the lowest regions of Hell. From point to point, Dante analyses and grades the severity of these sins, with a subtlety that sometimes eludes the general scheme offered in the eleventh canto (see the plan of Hell p. cxii). But the canto does offer a key to certain general preoccupations and specific emphases in Dante's ethical thinking. The upper circles (visited in cantos 12–17) contain various forms of violent behaviour, all of which in some way – as in gang warfare, suicide, or blasphemy – set the mind against the sustaining relationship it should enjoy with others, with its own being, with nature or with God. But fraud – or, better, deceit – which underlies sins such as flattery, fallacious leadership and, ultimately, treachery – is judged by Dante to be worse than violence, in that it turns the best faculties and capacities that God has given to human beings (reason and rational speech) to destructive ends. Sin, in all its forms, is seen as an erosion of divinely created possibilities. Where the capacities that would allow human beings to cultivate the good are employed to evil ends, then this – a form of sin, which is specific to mankind – 'incurs the hatred of Heaven' (23).

In constructing this speech for Virgil, Dante draws far more directly on classical than on specifically Christian authorities, creating an eclectic ethical mixture of Aristotle and Cicero, along with allusions to the principles of Roman law. (See Introduction p. lxxvii.) This might be seen as a way of characterizing the intellectual principles embodied in Virgil's pre-Christian mentality. However, Virgil does not attempt to explain his own presence among the damned, as a dweller in Limbo – though this highly problematical issue does come to the surface in the *Purgatorio* 3 and *Paradiso* 19. At the same time, the dependence here upon classical authorities confirms the interest which Dante takes in the way that human resources might themselves, when properly used, be employed, independent of revelation, to identify and categorize human failings. Indeed, following the representation, in canto 10, of those whose minds had been too confused or inflexible to perceive the truth, Virgil's masterclass in analytical philosophy might suggest that rational clarity was a distinct part of the remedies for sin.

On the other hand, it would be a mistake to suppose that Virgil's schematic account of sin represents the only moral impulse in the canto. At line 94, following a paean of praise to Virgil's therapeutic rationality, Dante urges clarification of a specific point, the simultaneous condemnation of sodomy and usury as sins which violate the bond in nature between human beings and God. Usury, in particular, is a sin which scarcely merits attention from classical philosophers. But it is one of the main targets in Dante's attack on the ethical and social decline of Florence. Thus, beneath the disingenuous question of the Dante character, there is the beginnings of a highly polemical assault upon the sins of contemporary Florence. (Compare with *Inferno* 15 and 16.) And anger (as in *Inferno* 8) proves time and again to be as important as rational deliberation in Dante's ethical armoury. In this section of the canto, also, there is a more direct reference to sin as an offence against the creative power of God than anywhere else in the canto. Where in Genesis 9: 1 God demands that human beings should be fruitful and multiply, the usurers – like the sodomites – seek to evade this demand. Instead of working directly with the given nature of the world, they employ their 'arts' – or their capacities for productive work – on the manmade resource of money, and thus break the link of love which, through our engagement with the natural world as a creation of God, joins us to the creative processes of divine love. Sin is an offence against love – an understanding that is developed in the more explicit discussion of sin offered by Virgil in *Purgatorio* 17–18.

One reason given for Virgil's discourse is that it will make it possible for his pupil simply to 'see' (or merely glance at) the subsequent manifestations of sin in the following phases of his journey. The reader of the *Commedia* may likewise be thought to receive a comparably clear orientation. Yet the technique that Dante adopts in the following cantos, far from allowing detached analysis, often involves the reader in a close dramatic engagement with the confusions and nuances of a particular sin. The exact character of the sin and the degree of its offensiveness, as Dante saw it, is established in and through the imaginative picture the poet develops here. Indeed, canto 11 itself – though principally interesting because of its intellectual rigour and economy – does contain its own elements of drama and narrative invention. There are moments of slight intellectual friction between master and pupil, as for instance when Dante reminds Virgil (at **lines 94–6**) that he has omitted to give an account of the earlier groups of sins and is reminded rather curtly by Virgil that Aristotelian principles explain why intemperance is less blameworthy than sins where the will and reason are active participants. More significant still is the ruling conception of this episode, which imagines Virgil's discourse as a compensation for the time lost in accompanying the senses to the stench of lower Hell. Allegorically, an opposition arises between the rotting odour of corrupt rationality and the clear illumination offered by reason well employed. One also notes that Virgil's discourses – as in *Purgatorio* 4 or *Purgatorio* 17–18 – often serve as moments of pause in the otherwise vivid and imaginative thrust of Dante's narrative. The implication must be that, while truths will eventually be seen directly as visions of Paradise, our rational conversations about the truth are a necessary, if only provisional, means to approach that truth. Canto 10, so far from expounding everything needful for understanding, prepares for an ever more precise encounter in seeing, in imagination and in emotional engagement, which is to be pursued in the cantos that follow.

Notes

7–9   The references to Anastasius and Photinus are not entirely clear, historically or syntactically. Pope Anastasius II (d. 498) was believed by medieval historians (though not by modern scholars) to have been led into an heretical denial of the divinity of Christ by his friend Photinus, deacon of Thessalonica.

25-7   Human beings share with beasts a capacity for violence. But only human beings are capable of fraud – which therefore more severely offends a higher principle. Compare with *Convivio* 3: 2: 14–19.

49-51 The destruction of Sodom as an archetypal city of corruption is described in Genesis 13: 10. Cahors (a city in southern France) was notorious as a centre of money-lending and usury.

52-66 Fraud can only be practised against our fellow human beings, since God is omniscient. In its worst form, as treachery, fraud violates the special bonds of love and trust that have been established between particular persons. Simple fraud is somewhat less heinous but still violates the relationships that exist between humans by virtue of their common humanity.

97-100 The term '*arte*' (100) that Dante uses here may be taken to mean 'intelligent and purposeful work'. In this sense, divine art creates nature. Human art, operating in the natural sphere, may and – properly – must affiliate itself harmoniously with the divine original.

112-14 The references here to the constellations of the Fish and the Great Wain and also to the north-west wind ('Coro' in Dante's text) establishes – in an 'artful' reading of the natural order – that the time on the April morning of Dante's journey is about 4 a.m.

CANTO 12

The Minotaur, centaurs and those who are guilty of violence against the person or possessions of others.

Commentary

After the discursive interlude of canto 11, the twelfth canto returns to the realm of the imagination, and begins to establish a narrative setting which, progressively over the next five cantos, will transform the ethical principles enunciated in canto 11 into precise and dramatic imagery. Violence here is seen to have produced an infernal wasteland threaded by rivers of blood, beaten by snowstorms of fire, and peopled not only by sinners but also by hybrid beings in whom human form is yoked to animal form, producing monstrous displays of bestial impulse, as in the Minotaur of canto 12 or the Harpies of canto 13. This is a world turned upside down by sin. The motif is frequent enough in medieval literature. (See, for a survey, Ernst Curtius, *European Literature and the Latin Middle Ages*, trans. Willard R. Trask (New York, 1953).) But Dante – concerned, as always, to demonstrate the ways in which sin destroys the possibility of human flourishing – embarks on a very exact search for remedies, focused often upon the analysis of specific historical cases. Cantos 13 and 15, in common with canto 10, show a continuing interest in the history of thirteenth-century Italy, evoking a tragic picture of a sterile moral wasteland in which great possibilities are squandered and set at nothing. But these historical considerations are enriched by the mythic and archetypal references that the poet develops in canto 12, and carries still further in canto 14. In these cantos, too, Dante draws liberally on classical antecedents, reviving and redirecting the myths and legends that he had received from Ovid and Virgil.

Canto 12 opens with an evocation of a savage but natural mountain landscape, apparently drawing on observations that Dante could well have made during his long stay in the Veneto. But at **line 10** this swivels, camera-like, into fictional focus, and produces ancient perceptions of extreme perversion, as Dante and Virgil descend towards the Minotaur – offspring of the union between a bull and the Cretan queen Pasiphae – which guards the base of the cliff in Hell. Dante shows himself to be thoroughly aware of every aspect of the Minotaur legend. But he does not indulge the lubricious and spectacular horrors of the tale. On the contrary, Virgil, acting almost as arbiter to the moral sensibility of the classical world, treats him with a disdain that consigns the monster to the comic impotence of its own frustrated violence. At **lines 22–4** the Minotaur is reduced to its taurine essence, comically (or pathetically perhaps, if this truly were a bull) behaving with the dazed fury of a pole-axed steer.

Dante's own narrative, here and throughout the canto, interests itself above all in contrasted effects of motion. Thus, as Dante moves further down the cliff face, an arena opens to view at **line 52** in which two modes of movement are dominant: the first is the rapid and decisive actions of the centaurs (**55–60**) who guard this circle with purposeful showers of arrows; the second (**100–102**) the steadily deepening current of the river of boiling blood in which the sinners are plunged at differing heights, according to the severity of their crimes, as a punishment for robbery, brigandry and tyranny. (An early illustration of this canto, to be found in C. S. Singleton's *Illuminated Manuscripts of the Commedia* (London, 1970), emphasizes the textural and colouristic contrast between vermilion blood and the silvery hide of the haunches of the centaurs.)

This stream is to become one of the main topological features in the following sequence. Its source is traced in canto 14, and in canto 16 it cascades, along with all the other rivers of Hell, into the empty depths. The symbolism is plain: violence begets violence in a constantly degenerating stream that mimics the effects of natural fertility. But motion is not merely a symbol, but the physical agent of violent acts of will. Here, as in cantos 8 and 9, Dante contemplates the possibility that violence can be countered by the apparently violent but essentially regenerative action of the divine. The shrewd, even beautiful, adroitness of the centaurs as appointed guardians of the circle is one indication of this, rendered in the light and rapid rhythms of **lines 56** and **73–4**. But an interlude in the action, from **line 31** to **line 43**, alerts one to a Christian myth which lies beyond the world envisaged in classical legend. Here Virgil focuses (as does Dante's narrative elsewhere – for instance, cantos 4 and cantos 21–2) on the effect of divine power which – with Christ's entry into Hell on Easter Saturday – sent a great earth tremor through Hell, leading to landslides and ruin in this, as in every other, circle of Hell. The tremor, however, is a redemptive power which shatters the hold exerted by human violence on humanity itself, in the restoration of universal harmony. A compressed but startling reference to this occurs at **lines 40–45**, where Virgil speaks of how, according to certain philosophers, any touch of love would paradoxically reduce the world to chaos. The philosophy that Virgil alludes to here is the atomistic school (representatives of which are found in Limbo at canto 4, lines 136–8) which maintained that the existence of created forms depended upon the constant collision of streams of atomic particles. On this view, violence is essential for the creation of all that we know. But Dante will eventually end his poem with a vision of how the harmony of the created order depends upon 'the love that moves the sun and other stars'. Virgil's words (which are, of course, the words of a pagan) dimly anticipate this realization, which throughout his career Dante associates with the effects of physical 'trembling' that love inspires as the first indication that a revelation or lifechanging conversion is occurring. (Compare with *Vita nuova* and *Purgatorio* 21: 55–60 and 30: 36).

The narrative of canto 12 offers a subtle articulation of this underlying notion. For the Minotaur and the centaurs are not the only hybrid beings in this episode. Dante himself is another, who in his doubleness of spirit and body points beyond Hell, and serves as a sign of the providential plan that, through the Resurrection, makes him immune to violence or death. Dante's bodily presence in the spiritual realm of Hell is registered by attention to the way in which his 'new' (or miraculous) burden at **lines 28–30** sends scutters of stones from beneath his descending feet. (Compare with the fastidious detail that draws attention to the human dignity of Chiron at **lines 77–8**.) This violation of common sense – that a redeemed soul should also be a redeemed body – is a premonition of the great theme of resurrection that is central to Dante's conception of Purgatory and Paradise: the creative love which human violence denies but aims to sustain human form in its physical as well as its spiritual identity.

Notes

4–9   These lines probably refer to the Slavini di Marco, twenty miles south of the city of Trento in northern Italy.

10–27   The Minotaur was the offspring of the union between Pasiphae, wife of King Minos of Crete, and a white bull with which she became infatuated (compare with *Purgatorio* 26: 40–42). Minos ordered Daedalus to construct the labyrinth in which the Minotaur would be confined. With the aid of the Minotaur's sister, Arianna, the duke of Athens, Theseus, entered the labyrinth and slew the monster. (See Ovid, *Metamorphoses* 8: 152–82 and *The Art of Love* 2. Also Virgil, *Aeneid*, 6: 14–33.)

55–72   The centaurs are treated at length in Ovid's *Metamorphoses* book 12. Nessus is slain by Hercules when the hero finds the centaur stealing from him his wife Deianira. As he dies, Nessus plans his revenge, offering a shirt dipped in his own blood to Hercules' wife, declaring it to be a fitting love token for Hercules. When later she offers him the shirt, the poisoned blood begins to consume Hercules' flesh. To maintain command over his own destiny, he builds a funeral pyre and immolates himself, thus becoming a god. In this canto of two-fold beings, there are clearly parallels to be drawn between Dante, himself painfully in search of divinity, and the demi-god Hercules.

Chiron is reputedly the wisest of the centaurs, said (in Statius's *Achilleid* 1) to be the teacher of both Hercules and Achilles. Pholus (Virgil, *Georgics* 2: 256 and Ovid, *Metamorphoses* 12: 306) is renowned for his violence. Another centaur, guilty of violent theft and also slain by Hercules, appears in *Inferno* 25: 17–33.

88   It is Beatrice – the inspiration for Dante's heroic journey and for his poem – who sings this alleluia.

106–38   The list of tyrants here surveys history from the time of Dionysius of Syracuse (d. 397 BC) to Alexander the Great (356–

323 BC) and Pyrrhus (319–272 BC) on to Sextus Pompeius (75–35 BC), son of Pompey the Great (106–47 BC), and Attila (d. AD 453), who was thought (incorrectly) to have destroyed the city of Florence. These remote figures are interspersed with figures from the history of Europe in Dante's time. Opizzo d' Este, lord of Ferrara, who was famous for his cruelty, died in 1293 at the hand of his (probably) illegitimate son and heir, Azzo. The assassin of **line 119** is Guy de Montfort (d. *c.* 1288), who murdered a cousin of the English King Edward I in 1271 in a church at Viterbo where the cardinals had gathered to elect a pope. Renier the Mad and Renier da Corneto were notorious brigands.

CANTO 13

Suicides and squanderers. Pier della Vigna – transformed into a thorn tree – tells his story as later the anonymous Florentine suicide tells his.

Commentary

The subject of canto 13 is the damage that human beings can do to their own Godgiven persons and possessions. Suicide is the prime instance of such self-destruction. Thus the central episode of the canto (25–108) and its coda (130–51) present two contrasted instances of suicide. The first is that of the historical Pier della Vigna, now transformed by way of punishment into a 'great hawthorn' (32). The second is that of an unidentified Florentine who hanged himself in his own house, and who now appears as a torn and bleeding shrub (131–2). (It appears that in Dante's day an epidemic wave of suicide had run through the city of Florence.) But alongside suicide, profligacy – in the irresponsible waste of one's own possessions – is here condemned with comparable rigour (109–29). It is an indication of Dante's unfailing commitment to the potential goodness of the material world that offences against property should be judged in the same measure as offences against the physical body: both life and the ownership of goods are the gift of a loving God (compare with *Inferno* 11 and, especially, 25). More noticeable in canto 13 is a marked contrast in narrative tempo and linguistic level between the principal phases of the canto. The suicides are viewed tragically, in a stasis of pity and terror. Then the profligates interrupt that attention in a grimly farcical intervention, where the frantic sins of the spendthrift are reflected in a sudden frenzy of rapid movements and raucously trivial language.

The suicide Pier della Vigna was one of the most important figures in the political and cultural life of the early thirteenth century. Born in Capua around 1200 in modest circumstances, Piero became the spokesman and chief minister of the Emperor Frederick II (1194–1250), while also contributing, in verse and political rhetoric, to the development of Italian as a literary language. But in 1249 Piero fell victim to scandal; and though (as Dante seems to allow at lines 73–5) innocent of any treachery to his overlord, he was still disgraced. He seems to have committed suicide by beating his brains out against his prison walls.

In meditating on these events, Dante produces a canto which is probably the most complex and multi-levelled of the whole *Commedia*. There can be no doubt (arguing from the moral scheme of canto 11) why suicide is a sin: we come into existence not by our own volition but by the action of God and are sustained in existence by our relationship with the human and physical universe. Dante does not, however, stress this theological reasoning in the canto itself. On the contrary, his emphasis falls, in a characteristically secular fashion, on the political and social origins of Piero's suicide – above all, on a fatal distortion to which Piero fell victim in the pursuit of loyalty. Though court gossip turned against him, Piero was loyal to Frederick. Indeed, the culture of Frederick's court in its neo-feudal aspects depended upon the maintenance of hierarchical fealties. Yet on the view offered here, such loyalty was built upon fragile foundations. The emperor himself – though sometimes spoken of by Dante with admiration – is consigned to the circle of the heretics at *Inferno* 10: 119; and the court he ruled is one which is riven by the scandal and gossip which destroy Piero's reputation. (An irony that English translation can hardly reproduce occurs at line 59: the root of Frederick's name in Italian, Federigo, contains '*fede*', the Italian word for 'faith'.) The tragedy is that Piero should have devoted his energies to a government that could not fully reward his best intentions or ultimately provide any grounds for self-belief. His words in Hell reflect the continuing myopia of an official who was 'only following orders', who wore himself out by his devotion to duty and, not unsurprisingly, alienated his fellow courtiers by locking them all out from the 'secrets' of his imperial master (58–72).

The moral issues deepen when one considers the grotesque punishment that Dante has devised for the suicides. The logic of this punishment may be that the suicides have attempted to give up life, but life is not theirs to dispense with, so that, while they have abdicated human existence, they cannot shrug off the minimal existence that they now must suffer in vegetative form. Throughout, in the symbolism and imagery of the canto, there are remote references to the central stories of the Christian faith. The tree (especially a thorn tree) points to the Crucifixion and the Crown of Thorns, and thus to Christ's atonement, which could have made sense of sufferings such as Piero's. Equally, Piero's name reminds one of the disciple Peter, who did betray or at least deny his master (Piero did *not* betray Frederick) and yet still formed the rock of the Church.

More immediately, the wood, along with Dante's selection of Piero as an illustration, draws to mind the situation of the poet Dante himself. He, too, once found himself in a dark wood; and the wood of the suicides represents an intensified version of that '*selva oscura*' of canto 1. Like Piero, Dante suffered political disgrace, yet could not follow Piero's desperate example. Nor, it seems, could the poet in Dante allow himself to be content with Piero's *poetic* example. It is typical of Piero's poetry that it should cultivate a theme of desperation and death as attributes of the experience of love, as, for instance, in the opening verses of '*Amando con fin core e con speranza*':

> Loving with loyal heart and with hope,
> I was promised by Love a greater joy
> than I deserved,
> for Love exalted me in my very heart
> And I would never be able to separate from it,
> however much I longed to do so,
> so deeply is her image imprinted in my heart,
> even though Death has parted me
> in body from her –
> Death, bitter, cruel and violent.

Here the theme of feudal loyalty is translated, as it regularly is in the courtly love tradition, into a metaphor for faithful service in love. But in Piero's poem death haunts both forms of fidelity. This poem stands at a great distance in thought from Dante's *Vita nuova*, where service to Beatrice illuminates the moral life of the 'noble heart' and endures beyond death in the Christian hope of redemption and resurrection. Piero's poem painfully anticipates his suicide – hollowing out the inner self as an echo chamber for death.

This difference between Piero's position and Dante's (on poetic as well as political grounds) is enforced by a peculiarly tense concentration on effects of rhetoric and linguistic complication in all parts of the canto. For instance, at line 25 there is the famously entangled verse: '*Cred'io ch'ei credette ch'io credesse* . . .' – 'Truly I think he truly thought that, truly, I might just have believed . . .' Here, a gap opens up in the understanding that Dante portrays between himself and Virgil – the final subjunctive, '*credesse*', suggesting that Virgil had after all misapprehended the true state of Dante's thinking. This could be viewed as being in parallel with the disastrous misunderstanding between Piero and his own imperial leader, Frederick. At the same time, the linguistic irony here is that repetition should reduce the '*credere*' – which in Italian indicates the certainties of rational discourse, trust and belief – to a repetitive jingle. Likewise in Piero's speeches, rhetorical repetitions and metaphoric flourishes produce a disturbing incongruity, when one observes that these elegant utterances proceed from the trunk of a bleeding tree. Dante emphasizes this when, on introducing the highly sophisticated and mannered words of the suicide at line 55, he denies to the sinner the verb for human speech (the predictable 'he said') to suggest the gap in being, between human and vegetative form, across which these words are spoken. From the first, Piero's language may be taken as a pastiche of his own historical writings. But there is also a propensity to self-entanglement, or even self-destruction, in the obsessive crescendo of lines 67–9, which picture the incendiary riot of gossip and scandal that led to his disgrace. Even the pathos of his proud affirmation of innocence is undermined at line 72 ('*ingiusto*'/'*giusto*' – 'unjust'/ 'just') by a suspiciously artificial balance between the first word and the last. Finally, at line 73, when Piero attempts to swear an oath of loyalty and self-vindication, he does not swear 'on the Bible' or 'on his own honour', but rather – in a moment of eerie comedy – by the weird new roots of the vegetable substance into which he has been transformed.

By contrast, Dante's authorial voice begins the canto with a series of repetitions and firmly marked divisions in the metrical structure ('*Non . . . ma*': 'No . . . but'), which drive the reader to an unwavering contemplation of the negative and of inconceivable violence. Suicide, the implication must be, would sink in despair before such a vision. But the thirteenth canto engages vividly throughout (in comic as well as tragic mode) with a linguistic and intellectual disorientation that sees even Virgil reduced to inciting an act of cruelty from his pupil (28–30) and also engaging absurdly (in science-fiction fashion) with the talking tree about the mechanics of germination in the underworld (94–105).

Notes

7–9 The reference here is to the Cécina (a stream) and Corneto (a village), in the swampy area on the borders of Tuscany and Lazio.

28–30 The Italian metaphor here ('*monchi*') refers to the 'chopping-off' of human limbs. Dante's doubts will end, chopped off like a hand at the wrist, if he puts his hand forward to pluck a twig.

31 onwards The episode throughout runs parallel to that in Virgil's *Aeneid* 3: 3–65, where Aeneas encounters Polydorus, youngest son of the Trojan King Priam, transformed into a tree.

55–7 Piero here is given metaphors drawn from fishing (*adescare*: to bait) and bird hunting (*invescare*: to catch with bird lime). But the violence of these phrases is hidden away beneath the sophisticated surface of the rhetoric.

106–9 Early commentators objected that Dante is guilty of heresy here, in suggesting that a soul can be hung from a tree and therefore can be divided from its body. A more subtle interpretation is that Dante deliberately entertains this theological absurdity – which contradicts his own fundamental sense of body in its relation to soul – to add to the grotesqueness of the scene.

115–23 The spendthrifts here are: Arcolano da Squarcia di Riccolfo Maconi (murdered 1288 near Pieve al Toppo), who, according to Boccaccio, was a member of the Sienese 'spendthrifts' society; and Iacopo da Santo Andrea (also the victim of murder) who was, like Pier della Vigna, a member of Frederick II's court and is said in an early commentary on the *Commedia* to have set fire to his own property out of a desire to witness a good blaze.

142–50 This speech obliquely recalls legends of the violent history of Florence in the early Middle Ages. As a Roman city, Florence had been founded under the influence of Mars (its first patron). But the pagan god was displaced by the Christian Saint John, to whom the Florentine Baptistery is dedicated. Yet enough of Mars' temple remained in the city for his influence to continue. The city was destroyed, in the account given by the anonymous suicide, by Attila (in fact it was besieged by Totila in AD 410) and, traditionally, refounded by the Emperor Charlemagne in 801. The suicide thus suggests that without the warlike strain in its inheritance – represented by a fragment of statuary near the river Arno – the city would not have survived.

CANTO 14

*The blasphemers. Capaneus. The Old Man of Crete. The
source of the rivers of Hell.*

Commentary

The sinners represented in the first half of canto 14 are blasphemers.
To Dante, a clear connection exists between moral disposition and the
ways in which words are shaped and employed. Indeed, the very first
impression that Dante has of Hell is the confusion of tongues that
issues out of it, denying all possibility of clear communication or
thought. Conversely, the conditions of prayer and praise emerge in
the *Purgatorio* and *Paradiso* as the fundamental modes of language.
Even in the opening lines of canto 14, Dante pictures a bizarre yet
moving attempt to restore a bond of understanding and harmony
between himself and the shrub of the Florentine suicide, as he is driven
by charity to restore to the shrub (its voice now fading) the leaves that
have been stripped from its trunk. But blasphemy is a deliberate assault
upon any such bond.

The first half of this canto is dominated by the portrayal of the
Greek king Capaneus (46–72). This (apparently) heroic figure is drawn
from Statius's *Thebaid* where, at book 3, line 605, Capaneus – laying
siege to the city of Thebes – is described as the great contemner of the
gods, and is finally struck down at book 10, lines 935–9 by Jove's
thunderbolt. In Statius's account, Capaneus possesses undoubted
stature. In the *Inferno*, he appears as the empty shell of heroic postur-
ing. He is repeatedly said to 'seem' great (46, 69–70). Yet his words
have no foundation. On the contrary, Dante attributes to him a speech
which, while superficially brilliant in its rhetorical gestures, is confused
and disproportionate in syntax and logic. The stoic magniloquence of
line 51 – 'What I, once living, was, so dead I am' – proves on inspection
to be mere bombast, leaving the reader with the question of what,
after all, he was when he was alive. Lines 52–60 produce nine lines of
vigorous but confusing bluster, wholly disproportionate in length and
syntactic complexity to the single line that concludes his very single-
minded speech.

At lines 61–3 Virgil is said to speak louder here than at any other
point in Hell, as if to signify his rational opposition to Capaneus's
display of irrational blasphemy. From this point on, the canto is
dominated by the voice of Virgil, speaking, however, in a range of

subtly differentiated tones – from the elegiac to a precise topographical definition – as if he intends to re-establish, within the acknowledged limits of reason, the competence and variety of rational discourse.

Virgil's function here is to explicate, for the benefit of Dante as protagonist, the plan of the poem that Dante as poet is here developing. The plan is not now seen merely in terms of the philosophical scheme that Virgil expounded in canto 11. Rather, Virgil draws on myth and legend (assembled in inventive new conjunctions by Dante) to expose some of the imaginative principles that govern the central cantos of the *Inferno*. His ostensible concern is to explain the geography of the rivers that run their course through Hell. To do this, however, he reaches back to the origins of time. In a cave in ancient Crete there stood a statue with a head of gold, a body of various costly metals and a foot of clay. But the statue was cracked, and the tears that issued from it descended to form the infernal rivers. The allegory here (though obscure in detail) points to the realization that the great possibilities inherent in human nature have – in a way mysterious to Virgil – all come to nothing. Crete is seen as a world where human beings once were happy, and where the god Zeus, as a child, could live in safety. But all such happiness is in the distant past. This melancholic understanding is re-enforced in the speech by the rhythmic repetition of the words *fu* and *già* (96, 97 and 100) where *già* expresses 'once upon a time' and *fu* – 'was' – which is an Italian past remote, speaks as English cannot of a time now gone, wholly separate from the present.

In the second phase of this speech (115–29), myth gives way to something akin to science-fiction as Virgil traces the course of the rivers of tears down through the circles of Hell. By question and answer, he leads his pupil to an understanding of a plan (which his pupil has himself constructed), pointing eventually beyond the plan of Hell to the final river, Lethe, which in the earthly Paradise (*Purgatorio* 30–33) will cancel the effects of the rivers of sin and provide redemption (though not for Virgil) through penitential oblivion.

Behind the contrasting voices of Capaneus and Virgil, and then through all the modulations of voice that Virgil himself produces, there is, of course, the art of Dante, producing here a peculiarly witty and moving play of narrative voices. The consciousness that Dante displays of his own narrative plan demonstrates an awareness of how far his own art has distinguished itself from its immediate predecessors in the Italian vernacular. This much is suggested by a single but very poignant allusion at lines 28–30 to a line of verse by Guido Cavalcanti. (See notes to canto 10.) In praise of the incomparable beauty of his lady, Cavalcanti had written in '*Biltà di donna e di saccente core ...*'

that she exceeds the 'white snow descending in the windless air': '*e bianca neve scender senza venti*'. Dante takes the exquisite rhythm of this line and (almost) matches it with his own. But Cavalcanti's line is evocative rather than descriptive, whereas Dante shows – with '*dilatate falde*': 'broad-winged fire flakes' – an interest in the observation of actual phenomena. There is also a vicious irony here. For Dante is not after all describing snowflakes, nor immediately writing a love poem, but rather imagining the flakes of fire that descend in judgement on the blasphemers. He cruelly wrenches Cavalcanti's line to the service of his own fiction and a retributive moral vision.

The novelist and critic Italo Calvino, in his *Lezioni Americane* (Milan, 1989), speaks admiringly of the lightness of touch, the wit and charm, of Cavalcanti's poetry and less admiringly of Dante's gravity and moral weight. Dante might well have accepted this judgement but would still have insisted that Cavalcanti (to whom his attitude was always so ambiguous) had only begun a poetic tradition that Dante himself was now in the process of developing. Indeed, the allegory of the Old Man of Crete may itself be seen as a further allusion to Cavalcanti's verse, carrying with it a tragic sense of the fractured relationship with his erstwhile poetic mentor. In a characteristically melancholic consideration of the destructive effects of love, Cavalcanti, in '*Tu m'hai sì piena di dolor la mente . . .*', speaks of himself as being 'outside life', appearing to be a hollow, walking statue 'made out of bronze or stone or wood': '*fatto di rame o di pietra o di legno*'. This line, like his 'snow' line, displays the indefiniteness of reference that Calvino describes as 'lightness' in the sequence of repeated 'or's – as if there were no way of deciding what substance he was now made of. Again Dante (through the mouth of Virgil) replaces such indefiniteness with extreme visual clarity and a vigorous pursuit of allegorical meaning. Cavalcanti's introspective melancholia is here translated into a universal vision of the tragic state of mankind.

That seriousness, that ambition for new meaning, is part of the remedy that Dante seeks in the *Commedia* for the tainted inheritance – the sadness and disaffection – that Cavalcanti has bequeathed. In literary terms, too, the canto is a measure of the distance that Dante has travelled from the delicately lonely world of Cavalcanti's vernacular lyrics. Canto 14 echoes with the competing voices of Virgil and Capaneus, ransacks the classical past and the scientific present for apposite allusions (as at lines 31–4) and offers, above all, a bravura display of invention and lexical variety. None of this would have been possible if Dante had remained content with Cavalcanti's lyricism. Nor, in the end (despite Calvino's comments), is the canto lacking in lightness. Throughout, there runs the witty (but wry and sometimes tragic) play upon authorial voices as Dante ventriloquizes his Christian vision through the mouth of the pagan Virgil. Blasphemy – a single-minded violence of utterance of which Cavalcanti certainly seems to have been capable – would disallow any such flexibility and cultivation of nuance.

Notes

13–15 Cato the Younger (95 BC–AD 46) (as described in Lucan's *Pharsalia* 9: 382 and so on) crossed the northern Sahara in Libya during his campaign in support of Pompey the Great against Julius Caesar. Further references to Lucan's account occur in canto 25.

31–6 This reference to an incident in Alexander the Great's campaign in India draws on Albertus Magnus's *De meteoris* 1: 4: 8, which in turn cites a description of this event that Alexander is said to have written to his tutor, Aristotle.

55–7 'Mongibello' or Mount Jabal (a compound of the Latin *mons* and the Arabic *jabal*, both signifying 'mountain') is the popular name for Mount Etna. This is here imagined as the smithy in which Jupiter prepares his thunderbolts.

79–81 The Bulicame (literally, 'the boiling thing') is the name of a stream near Viterbo that runs red with sulphur. Early commentators spoke of how this stream was reserved for the prostitutes of the town to bathe in.

94–120 Though the detail of the allegory here has never been fully explained, Dante, in constructing the image of the Old Man of Crete, draws on a wide variety of sources. The primary source is the dream of Nebuchadnezzar recorded in the Book of Daniel 2: 31–5. Daniel interprets the dream to represent the successive rise and fall of world empires, beginning with Nebuchadnezzar's own. Christian interpreters such as Richard of Saint Victor took the dream as a representation of the corruption of humanity – the head of gold being symbolic of the freedom of the will – and the coming of Christ. Other sources include Ovid's *Metamorphoses* 1: 89–150, which offers an account of the ages of gold, silver and brass. Saint Augustine in *The City of God* book 15 draws on the account of the excavation of a statue in Crete offered in Pliny's *Natural History* 7: 16. Dante's own references to Crete see it as the birthplace of Zeus (lines 100–102), where his mother Rhea had fled to save her son from the murderous rage of his father Saturn. It is she who caused dances and music to be performed to conceal the cries of her baby boy. In canto 12, the troubled history of Crete as the realm of King Minos is recorded. Minos himself, as judge of the underworld, appears in canto 5.

CANTO 15

The sodomites. Brunetto Latini.

Commentary

In canto 15 the myths and legend which characterize cantos 12 and 14 disappear as Dante imagines a conversation – extending throughout the canto from **line 22** – between himself and the historical figure of Brunetto Latini (*c.* 1220–*c.* 1294: see Introduction p. xxv). In the Guelf republic of Florence, Brunetto occupied a political and cultural position comparable to that which Pier della Vigna held in the imperial court of Frederick II. He was not – as is sometimes thought – Dante's 'old school master', but an administrator, intellectual and one-time exile of the first importance; and Dante seems to have had some association with the circle that gathered around Brunetto, gaining from him an interest in classical rhetoric and, perhaps, French literature.

The elder Florentine and Dante here concern themselves – as did Dante and the Ghibelline Farinata in canto 10 – with the divided state of their native city and the consequences of these divisions for Dante's own future. (It is notable that Virgil, who is now Dante's chosen model of political and rhetorical practice, remains silent throughout the canto, save for a tight-lipped, sardonic intervention at **line 99**.) The central conversation is edgy – even embarrassing – but also puts on display two deeply tragic perceptions, one concerning the divided state of Florence, the other concerning the differences between the inexplicably damned Brunetto and the inexplicably redeemed Dante.

Doubts persist as to the sin for which Brunetto has been condemned to Hell. According to the plan provided by Virgil in canto 11, the fifteenth canto (set in the third subcircle of the circles of wilful violence) represents those who have violated nature and thus offended the manifestation of God's creative power. Sodomy, along with usury, is for Dante an example of such violence. This may well be reflected in the imagery of the canto, where fire falls from the sky as it did on the city of Sodom, and the ground beneath the feet of the sinners is an infertile plain where procreation seems to have no place. Equally, there is enough, in the portrayal of Dante's conversation with the naked Brunetto – who touches Dante's hem at line 24 – to suggest the reverberations of some obscure sexual shock. On the other hand, Brunetto is known to have spoken out against sodomy and no direct charge is laid against him in this canto. Dante's silence here has led critics to look for other ways in which Brunetto may be thought to have committed a sin against divinely created nature. Some speak of a political antipathy on Dante's part to a politician who might have denied the claims of the imperial cause (represented by Virgil) to advance and regulate the interests of the human race. Others discern heretical tendencies in Brunetto's thinking. The great French critic André Pezard argues that Brunetto's decision to write his major work, the *Livres dou Trésor* (1262–6), in French might itself have seemed an unnatural act given Dante's own passionate devotion to the vernacular. (See Introduction p. xxxviii). Certainly, the conclusion of the canto envisages a link between the literary life and unnatural acts, with the naming of Priscian, the great Latin grammarian (109). Such charges were commonly levelled against intellectuals and academics, as they were in the important medieval text *De planctu naturae* (1160–70) by Alain de Lille.

The very ambiguity generated by these competing suggestions contributes directly to the drama of a canto which investigates how finely poised the human mind must always be between achievement and self-destruction. Brunetto is a historic equivalent of the Old Man of Crete in the preceding canto (lines 94–114), endowed with great qualities yet in some mysterious way fissured and self-destroyed. He is also the very image of a 'dear, good father' (83). But, in common with Farinata in canto 10, Pier della Vigna in canto 13 and the Guelf nobles whom Dante meets in canto 16, Brunetto is also a failed father, the representative of a generation preceding Dante's own which erected many great monuments in the political and cultural arena but also bequeathed a wasteland riven by violence to heirs such as the exiled Dante.

Dante would have undoubtedly agreed with some of the principal tenets of Brunetto's thinking. Thus, in his commentary on Cicero's rhetoric writings, Brunetto writes:

> What is a city? A city is a coming-together of persons as one to live according to reason: citizens are not those who live simply in the same community surrounded by the same city walls but those rather who are brought to live according to rational principle.

A city, on this understanding, is not merely a market place or defensive stronghold but the expression of common interest in rational values. Dante's own devotion to the life of a small city, understood in such terms, persists into *Paradiso* 8 and (especially) 15–17. Likewise, his portrayal of the intellectual companionship between himself and Virgil is entirely consistent with Brunetto's dictum: 'A companion is one who joins himself to another through contract and agreement for the sake of pursuing some particular purpose.' It is even possible that Brunetto's writing suggested to Dante the ways in which he might begin his quest in the dark wood. For Brunetto – himself suffering exile – had written in his vernacular verse allegory *Tesoretto* (lines 190–94) of how in 'a dark wood, coming back to conscious mind', he turned his thoughts to the ascent of a great mountain. (Compare with *Inferno* 1: 1–18.) But Brunetto would not be in Hell if, in some way, he had not failed to live up to the principles that he expresses here. He has been displaced as teacher, in respect of civic understanding, companionship and intellectual exploration, by the figure of the Roman Virgil.

The tensions at work in this critique penetrate the language, conversational interchanges and narrative rhythm of the canto. The opening similes already picture a world where human beings are at odds with nature, and need to defend themselves against its impact. The same lines (4–6) reflect this tension linguistically in a knotty, tense syntax and a sequence of puns, which associate *Fiamminghi* (Flemings) with *fiamme* (flames), *Bruggia* (Bruges) with *brucia* (burning) and *Guizzante* (Wissant) with *guizzare* (wriggling). The North Sea coast displays, it seems, some of the properties of burning Hell.

These pressures come to a crucial point in Dante's meeting with Brunetto, which is staged throughout in an extremely uncomfortable posture. Brunetto, walking on the floor of the infernal trench, touches the hem of his pupil, who walks in safety on the bank above him, drawing attention to the awkward inversion of status between master and pupil. Brunetto is seared with fire while his pupil is protected from the fire flakes by convection currents rising to deflect them. Dante dare not leave this vapour capsule. He depicts himself in a painfully distorted position as one who 'seems' to show reverence. But this is the visual correlative to a distortion of words which begins as soon as Brunetto's cry of '*Qual maraviglia!*': 'How marvellous!' (24) is met by Dante's '*Siete voi qui, ser Brunetto?*': 'Brunetto, sir, are you here?' (30). There is no sense at all here that Brunetto understands the 'marvel' or miracle that has brought his erstwhile companion safely through Hell. Indeed, his phrase has something of the modern cocktail-party rhetoric: 'How marvellous to see you.' Conversely, Dante attributes to himself the painful task of registering the brute facts of the case in the stark indicatives of his own question. (T. S Eliot, in his famous rewriting of this episode in 'Little Gidding' (1942), experienced considerable difficulties of his own, revealed in his drafts for this section of his poem: after very lengthy deliberation, Eliot chose to repress all personal names and designate his own 'dead master' as some 'familiar compound ghost'.)

Misregistration (in posture and language) continues throughout the canto. At lines 49–54, Dante attempts to press upon Brunetto a fuller version of his experiences in the dark wood and his salvation at Virgil's hands than he offers to any other sinner. But Brunetto's reply deflects the urgency of Dante's account, resorting, first, to a series of rhetorically vapid flatteries (55–7) and then descending to an obsessive political diatribe against the sources of corruption in Florentine life. There are sentiments here with which Dante himself would undoubtedly agree (see *Paradiso* 15–17). But the language he attributes to Brunetto is an uncomfortable and unstable oratorical mix of insults drawn from the farmyard, earthy sayings (65–6, 72–5) and biblical allusions to the fruits by which 'ye shall know them' and to the sterile trees of Matthew 7: 16–20. In contrast, Dante's reply, as protagonist, displays an extraordinary balance of emotion and discriminating intelligence, admitting much of the affection he may have felt for his former exemplar while still maintaining distance and reserve. The feeling response to the dear and good image of the father produces an emotional surge reflected in the enjambment of lines 83–4. Yet this is only the 'image' of fatherhood. So, too, at line 85 a distinction is implied between the glory that Brunetto may have sought in his teaching of politics and rhetoric (see *Trésor* 2: 120) and the glory that comes to Dante eternally in the *maraviglia* (wonder) of his journey. Dante's speech parallels Brunetto's in its use of the conditional clause introduced by 'If . . .' (Compare line 55 and so on with line 79 and so on.) But it is Dante, not the rhetorician Brunetto, who in the dextrous rhythms of his sentence – with all its qualifying subclauses – displays a mentality that is free from paranoia, obsession and violence.

A similar spirit of careful and reserved discrimination is required of the reader in interpreting the concluding lines of the canto. To some (including T. S. Eliot) it has seemed that Dante repents his condemnation of Brunetto to Hell when he pictures him running off like one who wins a race rather than loses it. Yet 'loses' is the last word of the canto. Brunetto's 'race' is one that endlessly encircles Hell. Dante's own painful progress has to encompass experiments in intellect, word and spirit of which the Brunetto represented in this canto would not have been capable.

Notes

61–3 The legend (recorded in Brunetto's *Livres dou Trésor* 1: 37: 1–2 and also in Giovanni Villani's *Cronica* 1: 37–8 (*c.* 1322)) is that the hilltown of Fiesole was a hotbed of revolt against Rome during the Catiline conspiracy of 62 BC and was razed to the ground by Julius Caesar. Florence was then founded in the valley as a loyal imperial colony, while the remnants of the original Fiesoleans gathered themselves over the centuries in continuing opposition to the 'true seed of Rome'. (Compare with *Inferno* 16 and *Paradiso* 15–17.)

109–14 Priscian (491–518) was the author of the most influential Latin grammar of the Middle Ages. Francesco d'Accorso (1225–93), doctor of civil law, acted as counsellor to the English King Edward I. Andrea de' Mozzi (d. 1296), member of an important banking family in Florence, was appointed bishop of that city in 1287. When accused of various abuses, he was transferred by Pope Boniface VIII (see cantos 19 and 27) from Florence (the Arno) to Vicenza (identified in the Italian text by the river Bacchiglione which runs through it). Boniface is here ironically given the traditional appellation of the popes: *servus servorum*: '*servo de' servi*': 'Slave of Slaves'.

119 In the *Tesoretto* Brunetto writes: '*Poi vi presento e mando/questo ricco Tesoro/che vale argento ed oro*': 'I send and present to you this rich Treasure worth its weight in silver and gold.'

121–3 The race referred to here is a palio for naked athletes, run in the environs of Verona on the first Sunday in Lent.

CANTO 16

The sodomites continued. The Guelf nobles. The call to Geryon.

Commentary

The scene in canto 16 is dominated by the sounds of a waterfall. These sounds are compared in the opening lines to the hollow rumbling, as head from a distance, of bees in a hive. Later, at lines 94–102, the cataract is compared, with geographical precision, to the exhilarating leap of waters in the Apennines at San Benedetto dell Alpe where (on one reading of these disputed lines) a stream that might have descended by a thousand intermediate steps hurtles down in a single cascade. There is, however, no such sublimity or exhilarating vigour to the scene in Hell. This, after all, is no waterfall, but rather a blood fall: it is at this point that the rivers of Hell, seeping in tears from fissures in the body of the Old Man of Crete (see canto 14) and contaminated with blood, pitch down into the pit near the bottom of Hell, which is the setting for cantos 18–30. There is nothing here of the natural energy of the mountain stream or beehive, but rather the violence and confusion wrought by the accumulated perversities of human action. Dante and Virgil are scarcely able to make themselves heard above the roar (93): the very bond of rational and ethical understanding that exists between them seems to be under threat. A further instability is given to the episode by its unresolved conclusion. In suspense, Dante and Virgil await the arrival from the pit of the unknown being that will transport them into its depths.

The sinners whom Dante meets in this agitated scene are – like Brunetto Latini in canto 15 – Florentines of great political and social standing who have been guilty of unnatural vice – identified as sodomy more clearly in this case than in Brunetto's. In canto 17 a further group of once-noble Florentines are to appear, condemned for the sin of usury. So in these two cantos Dante completes the polemical connection he drew in canto 11 between sodomy and usury, incriminating Florence itself as a prime source of both forms of 'unnaturalness'. However, where, in canto 17, the position that Dante adopts is one of scathing satire, in canto 16 there remains something of the ambiguity and tragic tension that characterized the meeting with Brunetto. Where Brunetto ran off like a naked participant in the palio at Verona, so the four sinners appear like naked wrestlers. Their whole conversation with Dante is conducted to the contorted rhythms of a struggling dance, impelled by falling fire flakes, in which their heads swivel continually to align themselves with Dante (26–7). There is a strange and strained courtesy in this, the more so because the Florentine nobles maintain a stately and rather old-fashioned mode of address, especially in their proclamations of personal names (28–45).

Dante responds in kind, particularly in the uncomfortably elaborate syntax of lines 52–63. His situation here is somewhat similar to that which he adopted in his encounter with the first great Florentine of this sequence, Farinata degli Uberti, in canto 10. But a development has taken place since that earlier canto. For now, in the dynamic confusions of the present scene, it is to Dante that the struggling aristocrats appeal for news of their native city. And his response is to raise his voice against the roar of the cascade to speak out with unprecedented directness against the degeneracy of the race that had sent him into exile (73–5). The implication is clear: standing against the degeneracy of Florence, Dante, as here he portrays himself, has become the representative and source of redemption, the spokesman for all that Florence should truly be. The short speech – spoken against the confusion wrought by the waterfall – re-asserts polemically what Virgil cannot rise to. Here too a theme is introduced (compare *Inferno* 28) that will become especially emphatic in the course of the *Purgatorio*, in which Dante's physical form is recognized. Remotely (and consistent with the emphases of canto 10) Dante sees that politics must ultimately be illuminated by the doctrine of the Resurrected Body.

It is particularly difficult in this canto (and probably not very profitable) to distinguish between Dante as poet and Dante as protagonist. The *Commedia* has here become a medium for political polemic comparable to the poet's *Epistles*, and a record of spiritual, intellectual and artistic ambition. But the final phase of canto 16 draws attention to the figure of Dante himself in two ways which, together, profoundly complicate our sense of what Dante's person might actually be.

The first of these complications proceeds from the enigmatic moment at **lines 106–14**, where Dante casts the cord of his tunic into the depths of the pit, declaring that he had once sought to lasso the *lonza*, or leopard, of canto 1 with this cord. (There is no mention of a cord in that earlier episode, though in *Purgatorio* 1 Dante girds himself again with a reed.) Few moments in the *Commedia* are more obscure; and critics have offered a variety interpretations, ranging from the suggestion that Dante had once considered becoming a Franciscan – to save himself from the false pleasures of the flesh – to the notion that, as he now begins to contemplate the sin of fraud, he flings off the temptation to fraudulence that he recognizes in his own political dealings. (Compare the qualms of conscience that Dante admits in his post-exile *canzone* 'Tre Donne . . .' (*c.* 1296).) In either case, the allusion must be to some aspect of Dante biography beyond the confines of the actual text. (Compare with *Inferno* 19: 16–21.)

Equally disconcerting is Dante's affirmation of his own authority as poet that occurs at **lines 127–9**. At **lines 124–6** Dante introduced the rather prim moral maxim that one must be cautious about speaking truths which have the appearance of lies. (Compare with the guarded tone of **lines 118–20**.) But this is immediately followed by an address to the reader, which draws the reader into a receding and teasing perspective of truth, trust, illusion and the fictive suspension of disbelief. To assert the truthfulness of the account that will follow, Dante takes an oath. But instead of swearing on the Bible or some obvious source of sacred authority, he swears, tautologically enough, by the very text whose veracity he purports to assert. (Contrast with the address to the reader in *Inferno* 9: 61–3; but compare with *Inferno* 22: 118–20.) The extreme poetic self-consciousness of this passage prepares for the virtuosity of *Inferno* 17. It also includes the first of only two references that Dante makes to his poem as a 'comedy' (see also *Inferno* 21: 1–3). And with this a series of questions, concerning the literary as well as the moral principles on which the poem is built, immediately begins to emerge. How authoritative, after all, is a 'comedy'? What trust should we place in a text where logic is so evidently unstable? Is there any sense in which Dante might seriously think his text is a source of magical – or scriptural – powers? Just as the narrative leads the reader in the final moments of this canto to a dramatic point of suspense, so the metatext generates a swirl of enticing illusions and sleights of hand.

Notes

37–44 Guido Guerra (1220–72) came from the noble family of the Conti Guidi and was leader of the Tuscan Guelfs. He was the grandson of Gualdrada di Bellincione Berti de' Ravagnani, who is mentioned, along with her husband, in the great account of Florence in her golden age that Dante offers in *Paradiso* 15, at lines 97–9. His companions in sodomy are the Guelf aristocrat Tegghiaio Aldobrandi (d. before 1266) and the minor nobleman Iacopo Rusticucci (fl. 1235–66). The words that 'ought to have more pleased the world' are a speech he made to dissuade the Florentines from engaging in the battle of Montaperti. (Compare with Farinata in *Inferno* 10: 88–93.) The presence of all these figures in Hell was first announced by Ciacco in canto 6.

70 Nothing is known of Guglielmo Borsiere, save for the picture of his courtesy and generosity that Boccaccio offers in *Decameron* 1: 8.

CANTO 17

The usurers. The descent on the back of Geryon to lower Hell.

Commentary

In common with cantos 8 and 9 of the *Inferno*, canto 17 depicts a moment of dramatic transition in the journey of the traveller, and also demonstrates Dante's skill in the portrayal of such moments and the profound importance of motion itself to his moral understanding of human existence. In the moral plan of the *Commedia* the episode has a place of considerable importance. Dante refers back later to the dangers and distractions that are depicted here (at *Purgatorio* 27: 23). The episode marks a transition in the *Inferno* from a consideration of the sins of wilful violence to a consideration of the sins of deceit. Dante is now transported downwards to the lower reaches of Hell on the back of the monstrous Geryon, who possesses the face of a benign and honest man but the body of a reptile and the tail of a scorpion (10–12 and 25–7). The Old Man of Crete had a head of gold and a fractured body. Brunetto Latini was 'a dear, good father' ('*cara e buona imagine paterna*'). The logical point of arrival in this sequence, expressing an appalling disappointment over human possibilities, is Geryon as the 'filthy image of deceit' (the '*sozza imagine di froda*') (7) that destroys the integrity of all civilization.

From canto 18 until canto 30 Dante's theme in the *Inferno* is the manifold ways in which deliberate deceit can destroy the productive relationships that exist between human beings. The descent into the pit offers a vision of utter helplessness: the very faculties of reason and language, which hitherto have sustained the possibility of co-operation, are themselves now seen to be capable of manipulative untruth. Such sentiments are in some ways deeply uncharacteristic of Dante. In the *Purgatorio* and the *Paradiso* he subtly and sustainedly re-asserts that confidence in the rational activity he first displayed in choosing Virgil as his guide in the other world. His conception of God is one that insists upon the possibility of a meeting between divine and human wisdom. Yet now Dante develops subtextually an apocalyptic vision, in which the helplessness of human beings can only be remedied by the intervention of divine justice. In the Apocalypse (as treated in the Book of Revelation) the disasters that human beings visit on themselves are taken to be the very signs that a second coming and the Day of Judgement are at hand. The imagery and punishments of the following sequence often reflect the images of disaster that will appear in the days preceding the Last Judgement: fire (cantos 26–7); war (canto 28); disease (cantos 29–30). But the conception of Geryon in canto 17 anticipates this sequence. Where Geryon, scorpion-like, horse-like, rises out of the abyss, so at Revelation 9: 2–7 we read:

> And [the fifth angel] opened the bottomless pit; and there arose a smoke out of the pit, as the smoke of a great furnace . . . And there came out of the smoke locusts upon the earth: and unto them was given power, as the scorpions of the earth have power . . . And the shapes of the locusts were like unto horses prepared unto battle; and on their heads were as it were crowns like gold, and their faces were as the faces of men.

Dante draws on the full resources of his narrative invention – especially in effects of surprise and suspense – of linguistic versatility and precision in observation. Geryon is presented over the cliff-hanging break between cantos 16 and 17. The descent on his back is deferred; and in the parenthesis that occurs in the second phase of the canto between lines 37 and 78, Dante offers his account of the usurers, significantly perched on the edge of the abyss, all of them tainted by the malignant aura of Geryon's deceitfulness. In contrast to the tortured and ambiguous depiction of the sodomites in canto 16, the picture of the usurers is scathingly satirical, focusing on the acid colours of the money bags that hang around their necks. These bear the arms of once-noble families, reduced now to the banking logos of figures who, like the avaricious of canto 7, are otherwise anonymous, worthy of neither speech nor name. The one usurer who does speak in truculent and divisive tones (64–75) is the Paduan Reginaldo Scrovegni (d. 1290), whose heirs, in expiation for his banking activities, commissioned Giotto to paint the Arena Chapel in Padua. Dante pays no such respect.

The third phase of the canto is an extended account of Dante's descent on Geryon (85–136), orchestrated in contrasting rhythms of slowness and speed, caution and terror. Classical references to Phaeton and Icarus elevate the linguistic register. But this is interspersed with farce in Dante's depiction of his own panic, trembling between the 'gruesome shoulders' ('*spallacce*') of the monster (91). Virgil's position is hardly less absurd. As always in Dante's poetry, highly detailed reference is made to observable phenomena (to the movement of ships and eels at lines 100 and 104, as earlier to dinghies and beavers at lines 19 and 22). But the slow, almost imperceptible descent into deceit also produces a disorientation and decomposition of any natural reference. The four elements are here systematically confused: a flight through the air is seen in terms of the motions performed in water-borne travel; earth dissolves into mere emptiness; fire threatens from the floor of the pit. A final simile (127–32) offers an animated analogy between Geryon's flight and that of a falcon. Yet the effect is again of dislocation, as the hallucinatory gyrations of the monster are converted to the sudden speed of his disappearance in the concluding line.

Some critics have read the Geryon episode as a metaphor for Dante's own illusionistic art – an art in which textures are as varied as they are on Geryon's hide, where deceit is as beguiling as truth, where Scripture – even the Book of Revelation – can be challenged and outperformed. However, the episode is equally a fantasia on the themes which are essential to Dante's own poem: perception, hallucination, motion, journeying, arrival and rest. In both respects, the canto is a comedy, preparing for a sequence of cantos that will reveal a whole gamut of possibilities in that genre.

Notes

4 onwards This figure is Geryon, only named at line 97, who originally was one of the monsters overcome by Hercules (see *Aeneid* 6: 288).

16–18 In Ovid's *Metamorphoses* 6: 1–145, a Lydian girl, Arachne, challenges the goddess Athena to a weaving contest and, losing, is transformed into a spider. (Compare with *Purgatorio* 12: 43–5.)

58–73 Identified by their armorial bearings these figures are, respectively, members of the following families: the Yellow Purse – the Gianfigliazzi, of Florence Guelfs, becoming Black Guelfs after 1300; the White Goose – the aristocratic Florentine Ghibelline Obriachi; the Blue Sow ('*scrofa*') – the Scrovegni of Padua; the Three Goats – the Florentine Buiamonte, of whom Giovanni di Buiamonte de' Becchi became Gonfaloniere (chief of police) in 1293.

106–11 Phaeton, driving the chariot of the sun, loses the reins in terror at the sight of the constellation of Scorpio (Ovid, *Metamorphoses* 2: 200) while (*Metamorphoses* 8: 226) Icarus, climbing towards the sun, finds that his wax wings melt.

CANTO 18

*The plan of Malebolge where deceit is punished. Pimps,
seducers and flatterers.*

Commentary

Cantos 18–30, describing the ten '*bolge*', or pockets, that contain the
various sinners of deceit, have usefully been described as comic in their
prevailing character. Dante himself, at canto 16, line 128 and at canto
20, line 2, refers to the poem here as his comedy. This designation is
highly significant in the perspective of Dante's own theory. It may
also, however, be taken to indicate the wide range of developments in
narrative and linguistic procedure that the reader is to encounter in
the second half of the *Inferno*.

   Hitherto, Dante has tended to build his cantos around highly dra-
matic encounters with figures such as Francesca, Pier della Vigna or
Brunetto Latini. In many of these the reader has been confronted with
contradictions and ambiguities of position comparable to those that
characterize the greatest works of tragic literature. In the pockets of
the Malebolge – with the notable exception of canto 26 – the emphasis
distinctly changes. Here we are concerned, as comedy often is, with
the behaviour of groups rather than individuals. The sins of deceit –
from flattery and seduction to false science and misleading propaganda
– are sins which involve a perversion of relationships; and the sinners
here are regularly seen in a perverse or parodic version of the commu-
nal order which they themselves exploited in their lives.

   The very circumstances in which the pockets are set point more to
the city than to the country. The ten concentric circles in which the
sinners are confined are cut in rock and variously recall the architec-
tural features of a corrupt urban environment: the castle fortifications
or sewers to which Dante alludes in canto 18; the dangerous alleyways
of cantos 21 and 22; the parade ground of canto 28; the hospitals of
canto 30. Nor is Dante as protagonist often allowed to display in this
sequence anything of that sympathy for the damned that was a central
feature of cantos 5, 13 and 15. The architecture of the Malebolge
provides him at every point with a solid vantage point from which to
view at a distance the contemptible and often farcical doings of the
sinners beneath him.

   It is consistent with this aspect of these cantos that, for the first time
in the *Inferno*, the scene should be dominated by the familiar devils

of medieval iconography, with horns, whips and pitchforks. This feature continues the emphasis that began in canto 17 with the appearance of Geryon. There is, in short, a perceptible (if temporary) shift from the rationalism that characterized the early cantos towards a darkly religious perception of the helplessness of human beings when left to their own deceitful devices. At the same time, evil will progressively be revealed as a mere nothing (see notes to canto 33). Here, as for instance in the drama of the mystery plays, the empty violence of the devils is itself revealed in a comedic form which comes to its climax in cantos 21 and 22.

If a great variety of emotion and imaginative effect is largely replaced by the grim repetitiveness and squalor of the Malebolge, then compensation is to be found in an extreme virtuosity of language and constantly varying shifts of authorial perspective. Canto 18 represents a notable example. Comparing, for instance, the opening of canto 18 with the opening of canto 1, it initially appears that Dante has abandoned the oblique, exploratory approach that characterized the opening phases of the poem. Now he apparently offers us an authorial overview of the Malebolge, designating the number, colour and disposition of the region in a detailed plan. Yet, as the narrative proceeds, such authorial omniscience proves less than reliable as we learn that an earthquake has destroyed the structure of the bridges that Dante led us to suppose would ensure him safe passage. (See notes to cantos 21–32.)

Linguistically, too, the eighteenth canto is far less stable than its confident exordium suggests, producing a peculiarly varied range of textual shifts. The subject of the canto – concerning in the first pocket (25–63) seducers and in the second (79–136) flatterers – points to the ways in which language may be manipulatively employed in sinful deceit. But Dante, in response to this theme, allows his own language (and even the language he attributes to Virgil) to become in places complicit with the sinners, mirroring their corrupted practices. The sequence adopts a deliberately low, even scatological register, which reaches a climax when, in the first description of the flatterers (103–8) plunged deep among the filthy exhalations of excrement, the diction and rhyme carry this emphasis to exceptional lengths: 'scuffa', 'muffa', 'zuffa' – 'snuffling', 'porridgy exhalations', 'scuffling'. The first encounter with a sinner (40–63) is likewise an aggressive exchange into which Dante as character willingly enters. The story told here is a dirty story of sexual depravity, more suitable, one might suppose, to a Boccaccian novella than a spiritual epic such as the Commedia.

In the second encounter (82–99), Virgil momentarily elevates the stylistic level in a miniature epic describing the exploits of the heroic Jason. Yet the subtext to Virgil's fine words involves stories of sexual violence and double-dealing. Jason is said at **line 91** to have employed '*parole ornate*' ('eloquence of phrase') in his betrayal of Hypsipyle. Yet the same phrase was used in *Inferno* 2: 67 to refer to the persuasive rhetoric on account of which Beatrice had originally chosen Virgil as Dante's guide. The possibility arises that, even at its best, language may prove devious. Are Virgil's elevated words themselves anything more than seductive flattery?

Progressing further into excremental extremes, the final phase of the canto (103–36) confirms these disconcerting suggestions. Here Dante finally encounters the prostitute Thais. She does not speak on her own account. It is Virgil who adapts his tongue to record her words in a scene where Thais fakes sexual satisfaction in order to flatter the prowess of her customer. In this scene, Dante allows two of the central terms of his own ethical vocabulary to be drawn into the scatological vortex. For the words that Virgil here employs on Thais' behalf are words that elsewhere Dante associates with his understanding of Beatrice. The words for 'grace' and 'marvel' or 'miracle' (*grazie* and *maravigliose*) are here reduced to pornographic sweet talk.

Notes

28–33 In 1300 Pope Boniface VIII (see especially *Inferno* 19) proclaimed a jubilee year which brought an influx of some 200,000 pilgrims to Rome. Dante here refers to the methods of crowd control devised at the time. Central barriers were erected on the Ponte degli Angeli to divide those pedestrians approaching Saint Peter's from those who were leaving it – that is, those who were heading towards the papal fortress of Castel Sant' Angelo from those who were going in the direction of Monte Giordano, a small hill opposite the fortress.

49–63 Venedico Caccianemico (d. *c.* 1302) was a Bolognese noble of the Guelf party and military governor of various cities. No record remains as to how or to whom he prostituted his sister Ghisolabella. At line 51 the word translated here as 'pickle' is *salse*, which may also refer to an area of Bologna in which the bodies of excommunicants and suicides were buried.

61 *Sipa* – translated here as 'yeah' – is Bolognese dialect for 'yes'.

83–95 The story of Jason and Hypsipyle appears in Ovid's *Metamorphoses* 7: 1–424, his *Heroides* 6 and also in Statius's *Thebaid* 5: 29–485. Jason, the first sea traveller voyaging in pursuit of the

Golden Fleece, becomes an important point of reference for Dante in *Paradiso* 2: 16–18 and 33: 94–6. His appearance here is accounted for by his acts of infidelity and seduction. When Jason and his Argonauts arrive at the island of Lemnos, they find that the women of the island have resolved to kill all men – but that Hypsipyle has enabled her father, the king, to escape. The Argonauts are accepted as husbands by the women of Lemnos. And Hypsipyle (to whom Dante also refers at *Purgatorio* 22: 112 and 26: 95) marries Jason, only to be deserted and left pregnant when he sails from Lemnos. Medea, at **line 96**, after bearing two children to Jason, is outraged when Jason abandons her for Glauce, daughter of the king of Corinth and, in revenge, murders both Glauce and her own children in the sight of Jason.

121–2 Alessio Interminei (alive 1295) was a white Guelf of Lucca. For further satirical references to Lucca, see *Inferno* 21: 37–51.

133 Thais the prostitute appears in Terence's comedy *The Eunuch* (161 BC), but Dante would have found references to her in Cicero's *De Amicitia* (45–44 BC) and John of Salisbury's *Policraticus* (1159), where flattery is treated as a form of fraud.

CANTO 19

Simony exemplified by papal corruption. Dante reproves
Pope Nicholas III.

Commentary

Canto 19 represents the most sustained attack on the corruptions of the medieval Church that Dante offers in the *Inferno*. In *Purgatorio* 32–3 and *Paradiso* 27 and 29, the assault will be yet more confident and explicit, to the point at which (*Paradiso* 27: 22–4) Saint Peter cries out, in agonized indignation, against those of his successors who have turned the holy ground of Rome – 'my place, my place, my place' – into a 'sewer'. *Inferno* canto 19 pictures a history of corruption which runs parallel to the true history of the apostolic succession which came to a head in Dante's time, under the papacies of Nicholas III, Boniface VIII and Clement V. The sin that is punished in this pocket is simony, which is to say, the abuse of sacramental authority for the purposes of gain. This sin is traced to the apostolic era: in the Acts of the Apostles 8: 9 onwards, Simon of Samaria (the 'Magus') is condemned by Saint Peter when he seeks to buy from the Apostles the sacramental powers of their priesthood (1–4). The apocryphal Acts of Saint Peter represents Simon as chief magician to the Emperor Nero, defeated in miracle-working contests by Saint Peter. The punishment that Dante devises for the followers of Simon – plunged absurdly one above the other in a well, with the soles of their projecting feet set alight – involves a continuous line of corrupt pontiffs which parodies the apostolic succession. Likewise, the fundamental sacraments of baptism are parodied in allusions to the Florentine Baptistery at lines 16–18 – and to confession at lines 49–51. So, too, as in Acts, tongues of fire descend on the heads of the Apostles, fire here licks at the feet of corrupt priests, while the chrismatic oil that is used in the consecration of priests is here the burning grease that adds to their torment (28–30).

In the perspective of the first *cantica*, which is prevailingly political and secular in its concerns, the religious themes of canto 19 make this canto something of an exception. The language of the canto is marked by explicit references to scriptural texts, notably the Book of Revelation (106–8). At the same time, the canto is tightly connected in theme to the developing context of the circles of deceit, the Malebolge. In the previous canto Dante depicted the perversions of human relationships that occur in flattery and seduction. Now his concern is with the perversion of those fundamental bonds between the Divine Creator and the human individual which the Church, in its sacramental function, is called upon to nourish. Without the nourishment of the sacraments, human identity is pitched into absurdity. This absurdity is reflected in the poetic practice of the canto – above all, in the black comedy that Dante here conceives in his attack on the scandalous corruption of the Church. Thus the sequence from line 52 to line 63 represents a stunning moment in which he is mistaken for his own worst enemy, Pope Boniface VIII. Here, in a perversion of the fundamental sacrament of baptism, Dante receives from the papal priest a wholly false name and identity. His only recourse is to the rational Virgil (who, for most of the canto, stands aloof from this drama of Christian nonsense). At an earlier point (19–21), Dante makes elliptical reference to an episode in his own life when he seems to have damaged one of the fonts in the Florentine Baptistery in order to save a child from drowning. There exists no independent corroboration for this episode. But its implications are consistent with Dante's concerns in canto 19: Dante has attempted to act as the true priest in saving life; and for doing so, his own name and reputation have been attacked by materially minded Church authorities.

In re-asserting his own identity, Dante here draws together the poetic persona and the authorial voice more obviously than at any other point in the *Inferno*. Where canto 18 began with a seemingly omniscient author laying out the plan of lower Hell, the unprecedented opening lines of canto 19 are dominated by a vehement voice breaking in on the narrative flow with stark scriptural references and agitated, driving rhythms which closely resemble those Dante adopts in some of his own political letters. But very similar characteristics are to be found in the long speech that Dante gives to himself from **line 90** to **line 117**, where references to the fundamental truths of the Gospels are combined with visionary anger and political polemic. Where the institutional Church has failed, Dante must draw upon all the resources of his own voice – 'plain mad' (88) as this may seem – to maintain some sanity in an absurd world.

Notes

4–6 The trumpet call – a feature of the military epic – is here translated into the prophetic instrument that will sound, once and for all, on Judgement Day. See Hosea 8 and Matthew 24: 31.

16–21 The Baptistery in Florence contained octagonal fonts into which four pits were built, where the priest would stand to administer the sacrament of baptism.

46–51 The upturned sinner is Pope Nicholas III (*c.* 1225–80), a member of the noble Orsini clan, whose family emblem was the Bear (see **line 70**). Under Florentine law, hired assassins were condemned to be executed by being buried head down in the earth.

52–7 Boniface VIII was born into the noble clan of the Caetani in 1235, became cardinal in 1281 and pope on the resignation of Celestine V (see note to *Inferno* 3: 58–60) in 1295. In his attempts to advance the temporal ambitions of the Church he came into conflict with Philip IV of France over the right of the king to tax the clergy. He excommunicated Philip and issued the bull *Unam sanctam* (1302) asserting (contrary to Dante's philosophy, as discussed in the Introduction p. xxxiv) the supremacy of the Church over secular rulers. Philip replied by declaring his election invalid and arresting Boniface at his birthplace, Anagni, in 1303. (See especially *Inferno* 26 and *Purgatorio* 20.)

82–97 The 'lawless shepherd' is the third pope to be mentioned here. This was Bernard Le Got (*c.* 1260–1314) (a Frenchman from Gascony), who became Pope Clement V. His election seems to have depended upon the influence of Philip the Fair of France.

Clement immediately appointed a considerable number of French cardinals and then established the Papal Curia in Avignon, preparing for the long period in which, under French dominion, the papacy was 'exiled' from Rome. Dante is referring here not to Jason the Argonaut, who appears in canto 18, but Jason Maccabaeus, who attempted to bribe the Seleucid King Antiochus IV Epiphanes (2 Maccabees 4: 7 onwards). Clement V is the 'new' Jason in that he may have bribed Philip IV of France into supporting his election as pope.

97–9   There is a (now discredited) story which suggests that Nicholas accepted a bribe to join the conspiracy that led to the expulsion of the Angevins from Sicily in 1282.

106–11   Saint John the Evangelist (*Vangelista*), who in the Book of Revelation speaks of the utter corruption which will immediately precede the Second Coming (see notes to *Inferno* 16). The Whore of Babylon is a great sign of this corruption, as at Revelation 17: 3–6:

> I saw a woman sit upon a scarlet coloured beast, full of names of blasphemy, having seven heads and seven horns. And the woman was arrayed in purple and scarlet colour, and decked with gold and precious stones and pearls, having a golden cup in her hand full of abomination and filthiness of her fornication . . . And I saw the woman drunken with the blood of the saints, and with the blood of the martyrs of Jesus.

The seven heads may be taken to represent the seven sacraments, the ten horns the Ten Commandments that were once a source of virtue and have now been polluted. Dante shares with the 'spiritual Franciscans' of his time a willingness to identify this monstrosity with the corruption of the Church.

115–17   The Emperor Constantine (*c.* 274–337), having been converted to Christianity (see also *Inferno* 27: 94–5 and *Paradiso* 20: 55) was thought to have donated the temporal power of the western part of the empire to the Church. The document of donation was proved during the sixteenth century to be an eighth-century forgery. Dante had already argued that the donation was legally invalid and an offence against the spirit of Christian poverty. (See *De Monarchia* 3: 10: 1.)

CANTO 20

The soothsayers. Virgil's account of the founding of Mantua.

Commentary

Canto 20 is sometimes taken to be a 'prosaic' canto – though not by Samuel Beckett, who makes very powerful use of it in *The Unnameable* (1953). It is true, of course, that there are certain passages in the *Commedia* which do not at first sight display the dramatic intensity that readers have rightly come to expect of Dante's poem. Yet in a work as concentrated and as precise in its organization, there is little room for insignificant digression or imaginative relaxation; and passages that might at first defeat our initial expectations usually reveal, if we are willing to abandon our preconceptions, some tightly drawn connection with cantos in its immediate context, or else some experimental departure in thought and language. In the case of canto 20, lines 1–2 display (almost wearily) the author's own consciousness of the organizational task he has undertaken. Then, at lines 19–21, he addresses the reader, alerting us to the conditions under which we will derive benefit from reading Dante's text. This is paralleled at the conclusion of the canto by references that allude to Dante himself as an attentive reader of Virgil's *Aeneid* (112–14). In addition, Dante here consciously (and by no means wearily) undertakes to compress episodes from classical authors such as Statius, Lucan and Ovid, which in the original can extend to something like 250 lines, into four lines of his own (31–4). In the major phase of the canto (55–99) attention falls on Virgil in a way that invites one to re-assess his contribution to Dante's poetic enterprise: where Virgil has hitherto provided Dante with a model for epic procedure, here – for reasons that the reader is bound to investigate – Dante ascribes to the Virgilian voice an extremely vivid piece of landscape poetry.

Literary considerations of this sort give depth and resonance to the subject of the canto. The sinners in this circle are all soothsayers or false prophets (most of them pagans), who are grouped among the fraudulent because they have deceived themselves and others into believing that the human mind can exercise its power over the unknowable future. Yet one of the things that Dante learns from Virgil himself is that poets can also claim the power of prophecy. What difference is there between the false examples of prophecy and the true? What difference is there between pagan acts of prophecy and such acts as have been recorded in canto 19 in the references to the Book of Revelation, as visions of Christian providence? Is there any distinction to be drawn between Dante and Virgil as prophetic poets? (Compare with *Purgatorio* 21–2 and *Purgatorio* 28: 139–44.)

Canto 19 concerns itself with relationships that are essential to human existence but which can be violently disrupted by sin. Now, in a canto which is more concerned with the pagan than with the Christian world, Dante meditates on the ways in which the human mind, by its prophetic pretensions to know the unknowable, can distort our natural relationship to a particular time and place. Our bodies define us in our connections with the world around us, and suffer when the mind seeks to transcend those limits. (See Introduction pp. liv.) The canto also continues to interest itself in the theme of identity. In canto 19, Dante defends his own baptismal identity from the corruptions of the Church. Virgil (who was considered a soothsayer in the Middle Ages) now distinguishes himself from all foolish prophets of the era, and even from Ovid (to whom the canto makes significant allusion), who delighted in the perverse metamorphoses to which the human body is subject. The landscape poetry of Virgil's speech here reminds one that Virgil is not only the poet of the epic underworld, but also the poet who in his *Eclogues* (42–37 BC) and *Georgics* (37–30 BC) celebrated the harmony between the natural world and the human world of shepherds and farmers.

The opening phase of the canto (1–18) pictures a procession of apparently dignified figures, comparable to those who chant the prayers of a litany. But prayer is the antithesis of soothsaying and, as the camera eye of Dante's narrative closes on the procession, he sees that each figure is unnaturally distorted. The sight produces a three-fold response from Dante (19–30). Virgil reprimands Dante for the shock and pity he feels. Yet surely Virgil is mistaken here (contrast the treatment of pity in cantos 2 and 5). Dante is not empathizing with the sinners. He is, rather, horrified at how seriously the sins of the mind can damage the integrity and goodness of human identity, in physical as well as spiritual form. Indeed, the reader is asked to realize that he will only benefit from reading the poem if he is capable of acknowledging the claims of compassion (19–20).

The third phase of the canto (31–60) is almost a mock-epic procession of great names reminding one that the classical world is as capable of stupidity as of the wisdom celebrated in canto 4. But this catalogue of follies is also enlivened by a piquant sensitivity, aroused by this strange perception of our normal lineaments which, especially in lines 40–45 – with its reference to Tiresias's '*verga*' ('wand') and the restoration of masculine '*penne*' ('plumes') – approaches the realm of sexual innuendo.

Virgil's great speech on the foundation of Mantua abandons the intense concentration on the human form that characterizes the opening phases of the canto to reveal a sweeping panorama that follows the course of the river Mincio down from the Alps and Lake Garda to the swamps that serve as a defence for his native city. The speech is conducted in an elevated version of the plain style, in which prophetic suggestion is wholly cancelled in favour of a sequence of place names and geographical phenomena.

In the penultimate phase of the canto (106–23), Dante introduces a further emphasis, displaying how easily the normal, everyday activities of shoemaking and housewifery can be turned into nightmare by the superstitious ambitions of soothsayers and witches. In the coda of the canto (124–30), Dante's own language briefly turns enigmatic in its references to the moon. There is a touch of the uncanny (and some archaism of language) in the reference to the folk tale of Cain as the Man in the Moon. But the purpose of this reference is not necromantic. Rather, it is an attempt, by reference to natural phenomena, to establish a timetable for Dante's onward journey. Notable, too, is the air of casual and easy conversation in the exchange between Dante and Virgil here: at line 114, Virgil has already addressed Dante as a familiar reader of his own books. The canto concludes, as the next will begin, with a suggestion of the comfortable literary discussions that Dante and Virgil enjoy.

Notes

22–30 Samuel Beckett meditates on the painful meaning of line 28 in his early story 'Dante and the Lobster' (1934) and clearly has this passage in mind when in *The Unnameable*, p. 279, he writes:

> If I am, I am but lightly. For I feel my tears coursing over my chest and all down my back. Ah yes I am truly bathed in tears. They gather in my beard and from there, when it can hold no more – no, no beard, no hair either, it is a great smooth ball I carry on my shoulders, featureless, but for the eyes, of which only the sockets remain.

This passage also conflates allusions to *Purgatorio* 10 and 20. (For Beckett's deep interest in the *Commedia*, especially the

Purgatorio, see the Introduction to *Purgatorio*.) The wordplay at line 28 which attracted Beckett depends upon the double meaning of '*pietà*' (see notes to canto 5) deriving from a tension between the Virgilian notion of *pietas* as the public duty of a Roman to the gods and to the state and the Romance understanding which indicates compassion and sentiment. (See also commentary on canto 26.)

31–9 In Statius's *Thebaid*, the Amphiaraus episode runs to over 250 lines, from book 7, line 688 to book 8, line 126. Amphiaraus, one of the Seven Against Thebes, is an augur who has foreseen his own death in battle and yet, against his better judgement, is driven to participate in the war by his wife. His death and arrival in the underworld is described by Statius in characteristically spectacular and ornate style:

> Behold in a gaping chasm the ground yawns sheer and deep, and stars and shade feel mutual terror. The huge abyss engulfs him and swallows the horses as they try to leap across it . . . When on the sudden the prophet fell among the pallid shades and burst into the homes of the dead and the mysteries of the deep-sunken realm and affrighted ghosts with his armed corpse, all were horror-struck . . .   *Thebaid* 7: 816–19; 8: 1–4

Statius (a poet whom Dante read with especial attention) appears as an important character in the *Commedia* at *Purgatorio* 21–5. (Compare also Dante's references to Thebes in *Inferno* 32–3.)

40–46 Tiresias and Arruns appear respectively in Ovid's *Metamorphoses* 3: 324–31 and Lucan's *Pharsalia* 1: 585–638. The Theban seer Tiresias is asked by Jove and Juno whether men or women take greater pleasure from lovemaking – Tiresias would know, since he has been both a man and a woman. Ovid then recounts how 'once with a blow of his staff Tiresias had outraged two huge serpents while mating; and immediately was changed from man to woman. Eight years later he saw the same serpents again, struck them once more and was changed back into a man.'

Lucan describes Arruns as 'one who dwelt in the deserted city of Lucca: the course of thunderbolts, the marks on entrails yet warm and the warning of each wing that strays through the sky had no secrets from him'. Arruns foresees the disasters of civil war between Caesar and Pompey but conceals the whole truth.

Ovid is arguably as important an influence on Dante's narrative style as Virgil. The references here anticipate the great description of metamorphosis in canto 25, where Dante claims to outdo both Ovid and Lucan.

52–60 Manto is the daughter of Tiresias and herself a sorceress, who at the fall of Thebes – the city sacred to the god Bacchus – searched over many lands for a new home (as Aeneas did at the fall of Troy), eventually settling in the marshes around Mantua. The (modified) account that Dante here offers draws on the *Aeneid* 10: 198–201.

61–99 This lengthy account of the foundation of Mantua follows the downward course of the river Mincius, or Mincio, and attempts to dissociate the city from any taint of sorcery. The city is founded for good military and defensive reasons. The words that Dante attributes to Virgil contain topographical references to an Italian landscape that Dante himself may have travelled through, and define the place in terms of modern and Christian history. Garda is a city on the shores of Lake Benacus (the Latin name for Lake Garda). The 'central point' is, presumably, the island of Lechi, at which the dioceses of Trent, Brescia and Verona meet. Peschiera in Dante's time was controlled by the Scaligeri, lords of Verona; Govérnolo is a mile north of the point at which the Mincio meets the Po; in 1291 Pinamonte dei Bonacolsi (d. 1293) tricked the then-ruler of Mantua, Alberto de Casalodi, into withdrawing his nobles from the city. Pinamonte then stirred up the populace of the city in rebellion and massacred most of the noble families.

106–12 Eurypylus is mentioned along with Calchas in *Aeneid* 2: 114. Dante seems to have misread this passage, assuming that Eurypylus was an augur associated with Calchas in deciding when the Greek fleet should cast off for Troy from Aulis (where the oracles of Apollo were heard). In the period of the Trojan War, Greece was 'void of men', in that all its males had gone off to battle.

115–17 Michael Scott (d. *c.* 1235) was employed by the Emperor Frederick II (see 9: 119) as a futurologist. He also translated from Arabic and from Aristotle's Greek texts.

118 Guido Bonatti (b. *c.* 1220) was, like Michael Scott, an astrologer at Frederick II's court and influential in Ghibelline circles. Asdente (meaning 'the Toothless') was a soothsaying shoemaker, whom Dante refers to in *Convivio* 4: 16: 6 as the most famous man in Parma.

124–30 As seen from Jerusalem, the moon is now setting south of Seville. The time is 6 a.m. The moon had been full when Dante entered the dark wood, and had cast an imperfect light that hindered rather than guided him. The Man in the Moon, as legend has it, is Cain carrying a bramble branch on his back. The last line of the canto includes the Florentine dialect word *introcque* (meaning 'meanwhile') which Dante in *De Vulgari Eloquentia* 1: 13: 1 declares unsuitable for poetry in the high, tragic style. This usage is the more striking in view of the mention of Virgilian 'tragedy' at **line 113** and of Dantean 'comedy' in the opening verse of the following canto. (On tragedy and comedy, see Introduction p. xcvii.)

CANTOS 21 AND 22

The sinners here have been guilty of corruption in public office (barratry). The mock epic of the demon guardians of the circle.

Commentary

The sin under punishment in the fifth pocket is corruption in the exercise of public office – an offence which was once known as barratry, and has more recently been designated 'sleaze'. It is an indication of how closely Dante connects ethical and political considerations that this form of deceit should occupy so low a place in the infernal hierarchy. The barrators are those who, in their willingness to take bribes for their consent to policies and contracts, effectively buy and sell the 'yes' and 'no' (**21: 42**). The sin thus represents a fundamental distortion of the mechanisms by which the human mind arrives at truth in argument and attestation. The consequences of this radical distortion are traced in an episode which runs in a continuous narrative over two cantos and is only fully concluded in the closing section of canto 23.

In cantos 21 and 22 Dante offers a sustained vision of a violently disordered society, detached from truth, caught in a spiral of deception and mutual contempt. The focus falls less upon the sinners than upon the devils who act as guardians of this society. Of the human sinners plunged in pitch, only one emerges (in canto 22) to enter into a dialogue with Dante and Virgil, which is characterized by badinage and trickery. The devils are parodically presented as a viciously disordered squad of authoritarian thugs – recognizably akin, in retrospect, to a gang of mafiosi or fascist bullies – who in their actions represent the disintegration that Dante seems to envisage when good government is eaten away by the fraudulent pursuit of self-interest. The bonds of civilized or productive discourse dissolve and the result is a proliferating violence which erodes human identity and threatens – as in 21: 52–7 and 22: 72 – even the physical safety of those who are subject to corrupt jurisdiction. (Parallels could be drawn between this appalling vision and that of Ambrogio Lorenzetti's fresco *Bad Government*, painted during the 1330s in the Palazzo Pubblico of Siena, where civic order has fallen into the clutches of a horned and scowling demon.)

A notable feature of Dante's picture is that, while sinners in human form are largely absent from the scene, the poet represents himself and Virgil as a principal focus of narrative attention, threatened and drawn into very risky reliance on the devils who guard this pocket. It is the devils, ironically enough, who act as a very uncomfortable bodyguard to Dante in the transition from canto 21 to canto 22. This focus is all the more remarkable in that Dante himself was accused, while in exile, of corruption during the period of his priorate. We might therefore have expected at this point some vigorous expression of self-justification, or at least as much self-approbation as Dante displays in the diatribes of canto 19. Instead, cantos 21 and 22 carry to an extreme conclusion the elements of self-ridicule which began to appear in that earlier canto, and consistently represent Dante and Virgil in postures of ludicrous and demeaning fear or dangerous involvement with the devils themselves – as when one of their number threatens to hook the cowering traveller 'on his fat backside' (21: 101). Either Dante wished to evoke the utter absurdity of a world in which the charge of barratry could be laid against him. Or, in a world where 'yes' and 'no' are bought and sold, Dante's evident self-confidence has been eroded to the point of half-admitting his own involvement in a corrupt and corrupting political process.

The prevailing tone of these two cantos – where violence and farcical comedy are vertiginously intermingled – has been brilliantly caught in an illustration for his own version of the *Inferno* by the painter Tom Phillips in which Dante and Virgil are represented, on a torn strip of cinema film, as Laurel and Hardy. Much here is knockabout, and Dante's command of narrative tempo uncannily anticipates the stutter and dash of early film comedies. But Phillips also identifies the moral core of this sequence when, in the same film frame, he introduces two trademarks, still familiar in Italian supermarkets, in one of which Dante's profile advertises Dante Olive Oil, while in the other Virgil's features are the stamp of Virgil Butter. In a venal society, dignity and moral identity are not merely undermined, but themselves become marketing devices.

Dante's own narrative generates a terrible but also hallucinatory cartoon, in which many of the principles on which his art and moral vision depend are called mockingly into question. For instance, whereas Dante frequently focuses his attention on the historical personages and the implications of their historical lives, here, at the conclusion of canto 21, he indulges an anarchically inventive taste for fictional names in the titles he gives to members of the devil gang. This is a mock-heroic catalogue (in direct contrast to the honour roll of philosophers in canto 4), and the mock-epic character of the episode is sealed by the famous fart which ends canto 21 and provides a lingering *segue* into the opening of canto 22.

Here, too, the narrative of the *Commedia* comes to a standstill. Where so much in Dante's journey reflects moral purpose and courage, here the forward march of the pilgrimage or epic adventure is paralysed in the stasis produced by the unusual linkage of two cantos (otherwise only to be found at cantos 8–9 – where significant parallels are to be observed in the comparable inability of Virgil to ensure Dante's onward progress). Forward movement is for two cantos replaced by a frenzy of pointless activity introduced by the devil who comes nightmarishly running, profiled in blackness and carrying a sinner on his sharp black shoulders. Throughout, the sequence is punctuated by more varied reference to types of hook than the English lexicon allows. And it ends with the self-defeating collision of devils who, hooked together, themselves tumble into the pitch (22: 133–51).

In a similar way, question and answer, so far from producing (as they will pre-eminently in the *Purgatorio*) the cogs of productive conversation, here descend into the exchange of insults, equivocation and lies, as in the prolonged game of lethal cat and mouse that takes place at 22: 97–132, in which a human sinner seeks to outwit the devils and return to the relative safety of the pitch – while the devils themselves, barely restrained by their supposed leader, jockey divisively to satisfy their appetite for violence.

In lexical character, the canto is a virtuoso display of Dante's low style, where rhymes themselves underline and exaggerate an entangled violence of diction (as, for instance, at 22: 130–41) at the wholly opposite pole from the delicate evocations of Virgilian style in canto 4. The descent into the Christian iconography of devils and pitchforks is very markedly in contrast to the often classical register of punishment seen before. The absurdity and banality of evil here appears in a way which reflects the treatment of devils as comic figures in the cycles of English mystery plays, but is also consistent with Dante's own representation of Satan as a brute manifestation of nothingness.

Virgil, as a character in the narrative, is drawn into this empty spiral. Thus a signal that a style change is consciously anticipated occurs in the opening lines of canto 21. Here for a moment Dante alludes to the sort of conversation that will be wholly absent from the next two cantos. But he also alludes to a 'comedy' (21: 2) which will displace the gravitas of the opening lines. And Virgil is not immune to contamination in the negotiations that follow. Having secured a safe conduct for Dante, he calls his pupil forwards with a high rhetorical flourish – 'O thou . . .' (21: 88), but is forced to address these words to the decidedly unheroic figure of Dante squatting behind a rock – and, in doing so, he sullies his tongue with the quacking phonemes of '*quatto quatto*' (21: 89).

It is not only Virgil but the reader of the *Commedia* who is offered here an exhilaratingly dangerous ride through a literary fairground. In the plan provided by an apparently omniscient author in canto 18 there was no mention of broken bridges (and Virgil is much disturbed at the conclusion of canto 23 to discover that the devils have been lying to him). But the reader too has to negotiate a series of lies in approaching this sequence. It is Dante, in his authorial voice, who, at the height of the farce in canto 22, invites the reader to enter not into a process of judgement such as the *Inferno* regularly promotes but rather into a 'new game', where the word for game is '*ludo*' (22: 118), a mockingly high-level Latinism. So, too, our first introduction to the scene is one in which the mechanics of Dante's simile, far from offering the orientation that his similes almost always will in the *Commedia*, contrive to deny us any such security. From line 7 to line 18, we are offered a picture of work in the Arsenal at Venice, specifying the many kinds of productive and co-operative labour needed to prepare a ship to sail. Yet the purpose of this evocation is to focus on one single feature of the factory scene – the pitch that in blackness and viscosity is the negation of all the variety and agility described in the foregoing scene. Here as also in 22: 1–12, the functions of human activity and the phenomena of the natural world are shown to be at the mercy of human contrivance and deceitful manipulation. As in the Geryon episode (canto 16), we are brought to ask where Dante's own poem stands. Does it belong to the realm of true endeavour or else of sophisticated fiction?

Notes to canto 21

7–18 The Arsenal, or shipyard, of the Venetian empire had been in existence about 200 years when Dante visited it. It developed very early a form of production-line manufacture, accurately depicted by Dante in contrast to the unproductive activity of Hell.

37–49 Rotklors ('*Malebranche*') is an invented collective noun referring to the devils of this pocket. Much of this sequence is punctuated by reference to the Black Guelf city of Lucca, in north-western Tuscany, which had a reputation for rampant civic corruption. Santa Zita (d. *c.* 1272) is the patron saint of Lucca. The Holy Face of Lucca is a crucifix – still on show in the city – carved in ebony (hence reference to 'black-faced gods'), supposedly by the Apostle Nicodemus. Its face is said to have been completed by a miracle while the Apostle slept. The Serchio is a river popular with bathers a few miles from Lucca.

　　The speaker (newly arrived in Hell) has been identified as Martino Bottaio, a political boss in Lucca, who died on the night of Good Friday 1300 – and hence at the same time as Dante's journey through Hell supposedly began. Exception from judgement is here made, ironically, on behalf of one of the most infamous of the Lucchese politicians, Bonturo Dati (d. after 1324). Bonturo, while ostensibly leader of the people's party, was driven out of the city by a popular uprising in 1313.

94–6 Caprona, a Pisan fortress, surrendered to Florence in August 1289. Dante was probably present at the siege, as a member of the Florentine cavalry.

112–14 Since the Passion of Christ and the Harrowing of Hell, which on Easter Saturday broke down the bridges of the Malebolge through the aftershock of the earthquake, 1266 years have passed to noon of Good Friday 1300, which is now 'yesterday' in the timetable of Dante's journey. If noon is five hours later than the present time, the hour is now Saturday, 7 a.m.

118–23 Some of the names given to the Malebranche may be deformations of family names from Lucca. Most are purely fantastical. A roughly literal translation of each would be as follows: *Alichino* – Harlequin; *Barbariccia* – Curly Beard; *Cagnazzo* – Nasty Dog; *Calcabrina* – Trample Frost; *Ciriatto* – Big Pig; *Draghignazzo* – Big Little Dragon; *Farfarello* – Flutterby; *Graffiacane* – Scratching Dog; *Libicocco* – (following suggestions by Robert Durling) Love Notch; *Malacoda* (**lines 76** and **79**) – Evil Tail; *Rubicante* – Red Face; *Scarmiglione* (**line 104**) – Tangled Hair.

Notes to canto 22

4–6 In a letter now lost, but recorded by the leading fifteenth-century historian Leonardo Bruni, Dante speaks of his own participation in the battle of Campaldino (11 June 1289) between the Florentine and Aretine Guelfs (see also *Purgatorio* 5: 88). 'Tournaments' involved group fights with hand weapons, as contrasted with jousts, which were mounted 'duels' with lances in the lists.

7–9 Medieval armies would go into battle with bells born on great war wagons. The 'signs' referred to here are drawn from the constellations, from which appropriate auguries might be read.

43–54 Though commentators traditionally give this figure the name of Ciampolo (Jean-Paul) he is, perhaps significantly, not named in the text but simply identified by the king under which he was born, Thibaut II of Navarre (1255–70).

82–90 Between 1275 and 1296, Brother Gomita (a member of the *frati godenti* – see notes to *Inferno* 23) acted as deputy to Nino Visconti (see *Purgatorio* 7) as governor of Gallura, which was one of the four administrative districts of Sardinia. Logodoro was another of these districts, governed, it seems, by Lord Michel Zanche as deputy of King Enzo (1239?–72). At *Inferno* 33: 134, Michel Zanche is said to have been murdered by his son-in-law, Branca Doria.

118–20 To designate the 'sport' which Dante now describes to his readers, the poet ironically uses the elevated Latinism '*ludo*' (*ludus*). Compare with his address to the reader at *Inferno* 16:127–8.

CANTO 23

The conclusion of Dante's encounter with the devils. The hypocrites. Caiaphas.

Commentary

Though canto 23 continues and concludes the encounter with the devils that began in canto 21, its tempo and tone are markedly different. An adagio movement is announced by the rhythmic gravitas of the opening line (which pictures Dante and Virgil as 'little' Franciscans walking in line) and continues until eventually a new acceleration of pace occurs at **line 37**. Diction changes, too. In place of mock-epic burlesque, there now appears an allusion to the popular wisdom of Aesop's *Fables* (4–6), carrying with it a solid simplicity of reference and a wry, ruminative humour. Correspondingly, the knockabout action of the previous two cantos is now replaced by an extended piece of interior monologue (13–24). This is a device that Dante very rarely uses in the *Commedia*. His concern throughout is with public rather than private utterance, with persons in their relationship with others rather than their inner selves. But hypocrisy plainly concerns the relationship of the inner life to the outer. In this canto, too, the inward fluctuations of Dante's mind, fearful that the devils will pursue him, produce a spontaneous, psychosomatic response – Dante's hair stands on end at the thought (19–20) – and a renewed conversation with Virgil who, in measured and leisurely tones (25–33), speaks of how the leaded mirror glass of mind reflects Dante's own thinking, and assesses the ways in which the landscape might afford them safety. The ease, frankness and sincerity of this exchange sets a measure against which to gauge the mentality of the hypocrites.

At least momentarily, the canto re-establishes the relationship between Dante and Virgil, which had been endangered in the previous episode. But in the second, allegro phase of the narrative (37–57), the renewed vigour of their advance through Hell is expressed in the rapidity and spontaneity of their physical actions: seeing the devils draw near, Virgil speeds their escape by seizing Dante, placing him on his own stomach and sledging down the cliff that divides the fifth pocket from the sixth (43–56). The similes describing this action are epic in form, but comic in effect (37–51). Here the perception of Virgil as a mother saving her son from a burning house (too hurried to put on a stitch of clothing), or as water rushing through a mill race, suggests a renewed relationship between Virgil and Dante and institutes a play of elemental sentiments and phenomena – of unthinking love, of action, of light, fire and speed – which all prove significant in the subtext of the canto.

The filmic rush of this sequence leads to a new focus and a further change of rhythm to an all-but-elephantine lento (58–69), which also introduces the hypocrites – the sinners who inhabit the fifth of the pockets – whose punishment is to wear cloaks made of lead, so heavy as to reduce the pace of the sinners to an imperceptible crawl. At every point in the canto, there are subtle variations on the rhythmic, imagistic and stylistic motifs that Dante has introduced in its opening phases. For instance, comedy returns at **lines 76–8**, when Dante, who is travelling at a natural walking pace, is observed by two of the hypocrites (who at **lines 82–4** are said to show haste in their minds, if not in their tread) and perceived in comparison with them to be 'racing there through all this murky air'. So, too, the canto ends with Virgil, who, after discomfitures which continue in the second half of the canto (124 and 139), is able at last to restore a dignified, if emphatic pace (145). In a similar way, suggestive correspondences arise between 'the leaded mirror glass' of Virgil's understanding and the lead of the hypocrites' cloaks, between the references to the mill race and the reference to the lovely river Arno of Dante's birthplace (94–5) and, above all, between the clothed form of the sinners (save that at line 118 one of them appears dramatically exposed) and recurrent allusions to nakedness or visible movements of the body (19, 72, 88, 113 and 148). Speech moves between a sane simplicity of style in the opening sequence to bursts of formal, and sometimes bombastic rhetoric (67, 91–3, 109).

All of these features contribute to the imaginative definition of hypocrisy that Dante is here developing. Behind his conception lie references to the Gospels in which hypocrisy is denounced (as, for example, at Luke 20: 46–7 and Matthew 6: 1–6). It is clear that Dante also has in mind the false etymology which (according to Uguccione da Pisa's dictionary, *Magnae derivationes* (*c.* 1200)) suggests that 'hypocrite' signifies 'gilded over' by compounding the Greek words *hyper* (above) and *chrysis* (gold). But, knowingly or not, the canto as a whole is closer in its implications to the true definition, which derives from the Greek verb 'to judge' but also came to be associated with 'interpretation', 'acting' and 'simulation'. This canto specifically concerns acts of judgement (especially at lines 109–11), challenges our powers of discerning truth from falsehood and exposes the psychological dissimulations that even the protagonist can be guilty of. In the context of the Malebolge, the canto is concerned with deceit as a self-deceit that denies the practitioner all access to the springs of generous or truthful behaviour. Thus, the moral measure of the canto is the naked mother whose wholly true, wholly sincere concern – pursued instinctively at speed – is the well-being of her child. Hypocrisy, in contrast, is self-enclosure in dress, mind and word, a defensiveness in relation to the claims that need and truth may make on us. It is an inner world that refuses to allow itself to be the subject of interpretation by other eyes.

These implications are dramatically carried through in the two most striking moments of action in the canto: Dante's interrupted address to the hypocrites at line 109; and Virgil's astonishment at the sight of the crucified Caiaphas (124).

The first of these shows Dante adopting a magniloquent posture of secure judgement. Yet such judgement would itself, if delivered, carry with it the danger of hypocritical, or pharisaic rigidity of mind. And the stumbling block (the scandal) which prevents this moment in the canto is the astonishing, even blasphemous vision of Caiaphas, whose actions in defence of the Old Law led him to urge Christ's crucifixion. But now he, too, is crucified. His nakedness is emphasized texturally by the vivid reference to the beard, his only covering. He puffs ludicrously into his facial hair as the weighty ranks of the hypocrites pass over him. If Christ as sacrificial victim bore the sins of the world, so in this parodic version the weight of self-deception now falls on Caiaphas.

It is sometimes said that the only possible responses to the often-outrageous truths contained in Christ's teaching and example are either scandal or discipleship. Caiaphas, though offered direct acquaintance with Christ, turns aside from it, tearing his garments (as in Duccio di Buoninsegna's presentation of the scene in the Passion panel of his Maestà (1308–11), now displayed in the Museo del Duomo at Siena). Dante – and any reader of this episode – is likely to be shocked out of all complacency. Certainly Virgil is. The sight of Caiaphas is one that he did not encounter on his earlier journey through Hell, just as he knew nothing of the earthquake that Christ had caused in the Harrowing of Hell. The whole effect of Christ's providential action falls beyond his competence. Thus painfully Dante speaks of the 'wonder' that Virgil experiences at this sight, using the word '*maravigliar*', which always signifies a response to the miracles which save the mind from its own rational self-imprisonment (compare with *Purgatorio* 21: 55–7). But Virgil, tragically, has no way of benefiting from such illuminating scandals. Rather, the last phase of the canto shows him extricating himself from the effects of another mystery, the enduring deceitfulness that led the devils to mislead him as to the existence of bridges over the Malebolge. Troubled and angry as he is, his stride at the conclusion of the canto marks out a visible and steady track for Dante to follow.

Notes

4–6 A great many versions of Aesop's *Fables* circulated in the late Middle Ages. In the fable to which Dante refers here, a frog offers to transport a mouse across the water and ties its leg to his, meaning to dive and drown it. As frog and mouse struggle together, a hawk descends and carries off both of them.

7–9 The Italian words *mo* and *issa* both mean 'now' or 'soon' – *issa* being a form used in the dialect of Lucca. (See notes to canto 21.)

61–3 Cluny was the Benedictine monastery in Burgundy, founded in 910, which by the twelfth century possessed the largest church in Christendom – but also a growing reputation for easy living.

64–6 The Emperor Frederick II (see canto 9) punished traitors by encasing them in leaden cloaks, then melting these encasements around them, over a slow fire.

103–8 'Frati godenti' was the disparaging nickname given to the religious order of the Knights of Saint Mary, founded in Bologna in 1261, which allegedly devoted itself to civic peace but was notorious for corruption. One of its founding members was Catalano dei Malavolti (1210–85), another was Loderingo degli Andalo (1210–93). These men – the first a Guelf, the second a Ghibelline – were appointed to the governorship of Florence in 1266 by Pope Clement IV (d. 1268), ostensibly to maintain a troubled peace. Dante clearly suspected their motive. It was they who ordered the demolition of many Ghibelline houses in the Gardingo ('Watchtower') district of Florence, close to the present Palazzo della Signoria, including the dwelling of Farinata degli Uberti. (See canto 10 and Villani's *Cronica* 7: 13.)

115–23 Caiaphas, the High Priest of Jerusalem (son-in-law of Annas, who is mentioned at **line 121**), judges Christ and declares that it is expedient that one man should die for the people (John 11: 45–52), thus ignoring the redemptive significance of Christ in favour of a partial, pragmatic judgement.

CANTO 24

Climbing from the pocket of the hypocrites, Dante and Virgil arrive at a point where they can look down into the pocket of the thieves.

Commentary

At various points in the last fifteen cantos of the *Inferno* Dante draws the reader's attention to the difficulty of his authorial task and the virtuosity with which he addresses it. Instances are to be found in the opening lines of cantos 28 and 32. But the most notable case occurs in 25: 94–102, where Dante claims to outdo two of the classical poets, Lucan and Ovid, who were members of the great school of poets with whom Dante claimed to be associated in the Limbo episode of canto 4. Canto 24, linked in theme and narrative orchestration with its successor, prepares for this great poetic crescendo with a sequence of elaborate flourishes in style and lexical effect.

The most notable of these is the extraordinary simile – extending for no less than fifteen lines – which opens the canto. Here, Dante chronicles the changes of expression that flit over Virgil's face: first of all, frosty disapproval of the lies the devils of the previous episode have told him; then (20) a more encouraging expression which he first showed to Dante at the foot of the mountain in canto 1. But here – with that marked ability to move in imagination from the small to the great, from the cosmic to the microcosmic, which appears in all parts of the *Commedia* – Dante invokes the meteorological changes that occur on a winter's day when frost at first prevents a peasant from getting down to the work on which his survival depends and then, as the suns comes out, allows him to get outdoors with his flock of lambs. The simile is epic in its length, and its rhetorical level is often extremely elevated – with references to Aquarius, personifications of frost as the 'sister' of snow, and phrases alluding directly to classical originals. The '*giovanetto anno*' of **line 1** reflects the '*iuvenes annos*' of Ovid's *Metamorphoses* 7: 295. The '*'l sole i crin . . . tempra*' (2) echoes Statius's '*crinem temperat*' in *Silvae* 2: 14–15, and also Virgil's '*crinitus Apollo*' in *Aeneid* 9: 638. At the same time, the simile is unmistakably pastoral, not only focusing on the day-to-day doings of a '*tapin*' ('poor sod') (11) complete with wicker baskets and cattle prods, but also referring to the inner fluctuations and psychosomatic shifts of doubt and apprehension that run (unheroically) between Dante and Virgil. This is no mere imitation of classical forms, but a peculiarly Dantean compound of styles in which the 'low' has as much prestige as the 'high'.

In his recent volume of poetry *The Orchards of Syon* (London, 2002), Geoffrey Hill writes of 'Dantean eclogues. Relentless, a toothed/mill-wheel baptizes the mill-race' (compare with 23: 46–8), and continues:

> The spirit materializes; once for all
> we know its oratory . . .
> . . . I fancy this light
> fantastic carries itself as completion
> somewhere that I am not.

He is right in suggesting that the eclogue is a form that matters a good deal to Dante. Virgil, the great writer of the prophetic eclogues, is recognized as such in *Purgatorio* 21, as if the humble level style (however elevated its linguistic texture) could touch upon truths unavailable to higher forms of verse.

It seems that, in canto 24, Purgatory is already in Dante's mind. The 'longer ladder' that at **line 55** Virgil says Dante must climb probably refers to the Mountain of Purgatory. But the climb into the depths of Hell represents a descent into a world that denies all the material beauty of the potentially golden world that divine creation offers. As early as canto 7 Dante spoke of the '*splendor mondani*'. The wasteland of cantos 12–16 confirms the extent to which he believes that sin is a clouding of that view. Now, in cantos 24 and 25, there develops a massive vision of 'Paradise lost'.

The dominant images of the sequence involve a desert landscape peopled by naked figures who (as in the Garden of Eden) are at the mercy of serpents, represented here in the utmost variety of reptilian forms that have descended from that original (**82–96**). These are archetypal evocations of ever-burgeoning original sin. But Dante, as always, focuses his attention on human culpability. The sin punished in this pocket is theft and, far from celebrating theft as an illustration of human cunning or astuteness, Dante envisages this sin as a radical assault upon the order and harmony of mind and matter that human beings were meant to enjoy in the physical world. In the final phase of the canto, Dante moves from myth to history and pictures a political antagonist, Vanni Fucci (d. 1300) (**97–151**), whose particular crime against sanctified order was to steal silver images from the sacristy of Pistoia – and then lay the blame on someone else. Psychologically and linguistically, the concluding phase of canto 24 presents a complete contrast to the opening section. Where the frustrated peasant both submits to and profits from the changes of weather, Vanni Fucci sets himself in violent opposition to that order. In place of the delicate reciprocations of expression and word that pass between Dante and Virgil here and elsewhere in the canto, there is a malicious determination to 'steal' from Dante any pleasure he may take at the sight of sin so justly encountering the due order of its punishment. Here is a figure who rejoices in being bestial – as his brutal, rhythmically disrupted words suggest (**124–6**). His mulish determination not to enter into any intelligent interplay with others, and the punishment he suffers – which is constantly to have his possession of form reduced to ashes – parodies the productive change that Virgil, Dante and the peasant are all part of. Finally, where the Dantean 'eclogue' may prove a prophetic form, anticipating a return to the golden world, Vanni Fucci's deliberately obscure and disturbing words, foreshadowing

Dante's exile, evoke a Tuscan landscape destroyed and desecrated by meteorological conflict (145–51).

Between the stylistic extremes represented by the opening simile and Vanni Fucci's words, canto 24 displays a particularly wide gamut of lexical and tonal effects. There is, for instance, the account of the climb to a vantage point which – suggesting an acquaintance with mountaineering techniques on Dante's part – also represents the Dante character in a state of comic exhaustion, his lungs 'milked of breath' (43). Virgil, on the other hand, can adopt a high-minded tone of heroic exhortation (46–51), quoting biblical and classical sources, the Book of Wisdom 2: 1–5 and *Aeneid* 5: 740. But even he can be reduced to low-level references, as in the quilt and cushions of line 48. Then, too, there is the exoticism of lines 85–90. Here, anticipating references to Lucan in canto 25, Dante produces, with rhythmic relish, a list of the technical terms for snakes drawn from the whole of the unknown eastern territories. This picture of desolation in the natural deserts of the world also contrasts with the mystic terms in which the phoenix is referred to at lines 106–11. Dante's description of the phoenix draws directly on Ovid's *Metamorphoses* 15: 392–407. But the phoenix is also a familiar medieval figure for the Resurrection – in which, according to Christian belief, human beings are finally assured of the eternal possession of their own physical identities. It is an irony underlying all the transformations of form that are suffered in this canto and the next by the thieves themselves, that their punishment should be a mirror image of that ultimate transformation – which is also a restoration of identity. The Ovidian reference points beyond its own sensational and mythic forms to a truth which Christianity will bring to fulfilment. Here, too, beyond the shifts of natural weather and even the depredations of sickness, there is the assurance of an order which will eventually be restored. In the tears and ever-repeated death and resurrection of the phoenix – reflected in a magical sequence of alliterations on 'm', rhymes on '-omo' and negative constructions – canto 24 opens up a promise to be fulfilled in the region of religious eclogue.

Notes

1–3 Aquarius (the zodiacal sign of the Waterbearer) is in the ascendant between 21 January and 21 February. Thus here the winter solstice has passed and night has begun to come closer in length to day – or else, in some interpretations, 'runs southwards'.

55–7 For the geography of Purgatory (conceived as a mountain in the southern hemisphere), see commentary on canto 34, below, and the Introduction to *Purgatorio*.

91–3 The heliotrope is a stone that was believed, in medieval studies of the properties of minerals, to render its possessor invisible.

121–6 Vanni Fucci was a member of the White Guelf faction in Pistoia. He was responsible for the murder of a fellow White Guelf in 1293 or 1294. In 1293 (as recorded here), he stole two silver tablets bearing images of the Blessed Virgin and the Apostles from the sacristy of the church of San Zeno at Pistoia. A certain Rampino di Francesco Foresi was arrested for the crime and only released in 1295, when Vanni Fucci informed on one of his accomplices, who was subsequently executed in Rampino's place.

142–51 This violent and perhaps deliberately enigmatic prophecy pictures the factional conflicts of the Tuscan Blacks and Whites in terms of the geography of the region. Mars, the god of war, stirs up the leader of the Blacks of Lucca, Moroello Malaspina, from his native place in the Val di Magra. (For Dante's eulogy of the Malaspina family, see *Purgatorio* 8.) The 'clouds' (**146**) are probably the Tuscan White Guelfs. Conflicts flared in 1302 and in 1306, when, in alliance with the Blacks of Florence, Moroello defeated the Whites of Pistoia.

CANTO 25

The thieves continued, their punishment to be constantly metamorphosed from human form to reptile and back again.

Commentary

Using the canto break to spectacular effect, Dante brings the final moments of Vanni Fucci's appearance in the narrative to an abrupt act of disruptive violence – involving the ferocious blasphemy of his words and a graphic obscenity in his gesture, as he directs towards God the sign of the figs in both hands, thrusting thumb between forefingers in imitation of the female pudendum. To critics of a Romantic persuasion, Vanni Fucci's gesture might be viewed as a titanic rebellion against divine repression, betraying a division in Dante's own mind between a sympathy for human self-affirmation and a deference to the demands of divine judgement. Remembering,

however, that Dante has himself written the scabrous words that he
attributes to Vanni Fucci, and remembering, too, that the climax of
the canto is marked by a challenge to the great poets of antiquity,
Ovid and Lucan, it may be more appropriate to view the canto in
terms of a continuing textual conflict, in which the extremes of Dante's
literary and linguistic inventiveness are constantly in tension with his
desire to reconcile his own art with the workings of divine order.
Thus, at the conclusion of the canto, Dante asks forgiveness of his
reader (144) – disingenuously, many might say – for the 'sheer novelty'
of the phantasmagoric account of transmutation which he has just
offered. Indeed, at lines 64–6 there is a momentary apprehension that
paper (the material on which words are written) might be destroyed
by the burning spread of so ferocious a description. (Compare the
association of transformation with the writing of 'I' and 'O' at 24:
100.) Nor is it possible in a canto where the theme is theft to ignore
the question of whether Dante here, in his allusion to Ovid and Lucan,
is effecting some sort of literary theft or malignant metamorphosis.

The climax of the canto is marked by Dante's overt challenge to
Ovid and Lucan. But, from the first, the poet has conducted a more
muted contest between himself and his principal literary model, Virgil.
The Pistoian thug Vanni Fucci is chased from the scene by a figure
from classical legend, the centaur Cacus. And Virgil proceeds (25–33)
to offer a brief account of the doings of that Cacus, himself a thief,
and of his death at the hands of Hercules (as he did in Aeneid 8: 193
and so on). Yet there is a certain flatness in the narrative that Virgil
offers which is utterly at odds with the dramatic picture that Dante
provides of a half-man half-horse wreathed around with snakes, all
surmounted by a fire-breathing dragon. For the Virgil of the Aeneid,
Cacus was no centaur at all, but merely a 'semi-homo', a dismal
half-man. Dante the poet has already produced an account of the
centaurs in canto 12. Now he exceeds his original in mythic imagina-
tion, and Dante, as a character in his own poem, almost truculently
silences his master's prosaic ramblings with a finger raised from chin
to nose.

The comic detail of this gesture – contrasting with and yet also
paralleling Vanni Fucci's obscenity – is the last moment in the canto
when the simple lineaments of the human body will be allowed any
interest or integrity. Where the emphasis in canto 24 fell upon the
sinful desecration of the natural world, the emphasis in canto 25 is on
sin as a desecration of the human body. In the numerically parallel
canto, Purgatorio 25, Dante offers a luminous vision of human pro-
creation in which the dignity of the human person depends upon a

union of body and soul as indissoluble as the union of grape juice and the sun's heat in a draught of wine (see *Purgatorio* 25: 76–8; see also Introduction p. iii). But, beginning with Vanni's mockery of the female organ, continuing at **lines 85–6** with a reference to the umbilicus 'where first we draw our nourishment' and the reference to 'the member that a man conceals' at **line 116**, the parody of divine order offered here is seen in large part as a frustrated parody of sexual activity, not least in that the only creatures involved are male.

This is particularly evident in the first of the two sets of metamorphoses that Dante depicts. An apparently normal street scene in which one person inquires as to the whereabouts of another (43) is suddenly galvanized, rhythmically as well as imaginatively, by the leaping up of a six-legged lizard which attaches itself, in a parody of copulation, to the front of the other. Yet as the figures begin to fuse like melting wax, no third figure is brought to life as in natural birth. Rather, the slow process produces only the lurching monstrosity – whose movements are replicated in the rhythm and enjambment of the verse at **lines 76–8**). In this figure, too, the fundamental principles of numerical identity are equally dissolved. The whole passage is scanned by references to the numbers two and one and none. But there is no reference to three. In *Paradiso* 14: 28–30, Dante produces a peculiarly lyrical account of the Trinity which, through its three-in-one-ness, creates the life that the Resurrection will ensure to eternity: 'the one and two and three eternally in life that reigns for ever in three and two and one'.

The passage from the first transformation scene to the second is marked by a momentary reference back to the natural world (81), where lizards simply *as* lizards can produce the brilliant flash of movement across a country road. To the poet Eugenio Montale, in his lyric collection *Mottetti* (1973), this passage deserved to be put alongside Shakespeare's phrase from *The Tempest* (1611) in which something 'rich and strange' can be created epiphanically in the momentary brilliance of the created world. For Dante, the insight contrasts with a dire vision of black magical action wholly at odds with the workings of the natural world.

Where proximity and miscegenation were the key to the first transformations, the key here is distance. A man is bitten by a tiny snake that drops down before him and gazes at him, until, beneath a pall of magical smoke, the one form fuses and the other splits apart to take on the characteristics of the other. Here, finally, the degradation of language is also seen, as the newly created man uses his mouth to spit out and utter words of *Schadenfreude* and vengeance. It is this vision that, in Dante's view, marks his superiority to Ovid. What justifies this superiority? In Lucan's original, there is a sensational concern with deliquescence and death: a tiny snake bites his victim, who dissolves into a pool of slime (*Pharsalia* 9: 767). In Ovid, there is an equally sensational concern with sex and sensuality: when his characters are transformed into snakes, they are a husband and wife who go away interweaving their coils. Dante is no less sensational than his originals and, like them, differs from Virgil in being so. But behind his lines there is a world view which cannot accept the Ovidian concept of atomic flux or the Stoicism of Lucan (with its interest in natural process), nor allow that literature is there only for the frisson of the fictional. An even greater horror than either of these two classical authors could muster comes from the recognition that the metamorphosis of the human body offends the profound principles of creation and resurrection that are central to a Christian understanding. The recuperation of that understanding, which emerges in the course of the *Purgatorio* and the *Paradiso*, is a fundamental part of his purpose in writing the poem. The twenty-fifth canto of the *Inferno* stands as a pre-emptive parody of much that Dante will see in a positive light in the final cantos of the *Paradiso*.

Meanwhile Dante remains dangerously and energetically involved in a battle with his own frenzied imagination and total commitment to moral truth. Thus, in a coda (142–51), he cannot rest until he has accounted for (and incriminated) all the sinners who appear in the canto. One alone remains unchanged. But with the total lack of compassion that has characterized his account of the central transformations, Dante's eye viciously focuses on this named individual. In a restless desire for linguistic novelty he produces the word '*zavorra*' (142) – the bilges of contaminated water (or sand) swirling in a ship. (The oddity of that word is reflected in the translation here that speaks of the 'zymotic'.) And with similar venom, in line 148 Dante identifies a historical figure whose nickname, '*Sciancato*' ('The Lame'), speaks of the crippled state of a sinner whose physical malformation seems to be itself metamorphosis enough.

Notes

1–3 The obscene sign of the figs is made by thrusting the thumb between the two forefingers. The Florentine chronicler Villani reports (*Cronica* 6: 5) that in 1228 Pistoia set up a marble representation of the figs aimed at Florence. The name Pistoia is derived, says Villani at *Cronica* 1: 32, from the Latin *pestis*: pestilence.

10–12 These lines represent the first of a series of polemical outbursts against the cities of Tuscany, including Florence itself (compare with cantos 26 and 33), and also the satire against Siena that concludes canto 29. In his authorial voice, Dante enters vigorously into the political animosities of the period.

13–18 Dante here employs the elevated and latinate locution '*verbo*' – which he also uses in referring to the Word of God or *Logos*. The rhyme '*verbo*' ('word') and '*acerbo*' (here, 'sour') also occurs in the account of Satan's fall in *Paradiso* 18. It is a further sign of the literary self-consciousness that characterizes this canto that Dante should introduce two cross-references to earlier passages in his own fiction: Capaneus (who was 'flung down from Theban walls' (15)) appears at canto 14: 49–75; the centaurs from whom Cacus is separated are guardians of the circle of Hell described in canto 12.

43 onwards Though little is known about the historical lives of the five figures who participate in these metamorphoses, all were Florentines. The first two to appear may have been Agnello, of the prominent Brunelleschi family, and Buoso Donati, who is referred to again in canto 30. Cianfa (who is, presumably, the lizard that responds to the question posed by Agnello and Buoso) was another member of the important Donati clan.

94–9 For Lucan's *Pharsalia* – an account of the Roman civil wars fought in the deserts of Libya – see notes to canto 20. In *Metamorphoses* 6: 571–603, Cadmus, founder of Thebes, is transformed into a serpent as a punishment for impiety, along with his wife Harmonia. Arethusa, in *Metamorphoses* 5: 572–641, is transformed into a stream while escaping the advances of Alpheus – who is himself transformed into a stream and so mingles with her.

136–8 Human spittle was thought in Dante's day to be venomous to snakes.

148–51 The last two Florentines are probably Puccio Galigai, who was nicknamed '*Sciancato*' – 'the Lame' – and Francesco de' Cavalcanti – originally the 'snakelet' of line 84 – whose nickname was '*Guercio*', or 'Cross-eyed'. Francesco was murdered by the inhabitants of the village of Gaville, on whom the Cavalcantis took extreme vengeance. In that sense Gaville weeps on his account.

CANTO 26

*The first of two cantos describing the eighth pocket,
where the sinners, transformed into flames, are those
who have made deceitful or destructive use of their
intellectual gifts.*

Commentary

The episode that runs in the twenty-sixth canto from line 85 to its conclusion has come to be seen as a definitive examination of features central to the intellectual identity of European culture. (See Piero Boitani, *The Shadow of Ulysses* (Oxford, 1994).) Here, continuing the challenge to classical literature that he issued in canto 25, Dante undertakes to represent the figure of the famously intelligent Ulysses, the Greek hero who devised the stratagem of the Trojan horse. Dante did not know Homer's Greek original, and so relied for his knowledge of the Ulysses legend on references in Latin sources such as Cicero, Seneca and, above all, Horace's *Art of Poetry* and Ovid's *Metamorphoses* 14: 157 and so on. But these sources all tend to represent Ulysses in terms of low cunning rather than intelligence – as does Virgil in lines 55–63 of Dante's canto. Nor has any precedent been found that anticipates the account which Dante puts in Ulysses' own mouth of a last journey beyond the limits imposed by the gods upon human endeavour (108–9), a journey which ends in death but is impelled by a desire for knowledge of the world and of the vices and virtues of human beings (98–9 and 116–20).

Taken out of context, Dante's account of Ulysses can readily be seen as a restatement of the myth of Prometheus, or a precursor of the story of Faust, in which the desire for knowledge and the affirmation of intellectual freedom bring the human mind into heroic conflict with all the restraints imposed by the gods or by human frailty. Thus Alfred Lord Tennyson puts in Ulysses' mouth the noble sentiments of an explorer: 'To strive, to seek, to find, and not to yield' ('Ulysses' (1842)) Likewise Primo Levi, in *If This is a Man* (1947), meditates on lines 118–20 of the canto – 'Hold clear in thought your seed and origin./ You were not made to live as mindless brutes,/ but go in search of virtue and true knowledge' – and finds there a truth, born of the best of European culture, that can sustain him against the worst, as displayed in Auschwitz. Nor can there be any doubt that Dante himself saw in the Ulysses of his own conception a possible model for intellec-

tual heroism. In canto 26 a certain friction arises between the protag-
onist and Virgil, as Dante, driven by vertiginous curiosity (22 and
43–5) seeks to speak directly to Ulysses and yet is restrained (64–75)
by a cautious Virgil. Virgil may be Dante's master and guide in matters
of reason, but here he speaks in far less inspiring terms than those that
Dante ascribes to the Ulyssean flame. There is no episode in the
Commedia to which Dante makes more frequent cross-reference. At
salient moments in his subsequent narrative, he regularly and often
explicitly compares his own progress to the voyage he has invented
for Ulysses, as for instance in *Inferno* 28: 48, when Virgil sees Dante's
journey through Hell as one which is intended to provide full '*esperi-
enza piena*': 'full experience' of the other world. (See also, and especi-
ally, *Purgatorio* 1: 131 and 19: 22–4; *Paradiso* 2: 1–6 and 28: 82–4.)

For all that, in the wider context of both canto 26 and of the
Commedia at large, it becomes clear that Ulysses is a problematical
figure, to be seen as an intellectual exemplar only with extreme quali-
fication. In canto 15 Dante focused attention on the historical figure
of Brunetto Latini and established an indissoluble link between the
intellectual life and the ethical life. In inventing the figure of Ulysses
as an imaginative *alter ego*, Dante now holds up a critical mirror to
many of the principles which underlie not only his fictional journey
through the other world, but also the intellectual, narrative and lin-
guistic procedures on which his poem is founded.

After all, Ulysses is in Hell. Nor is he in that part of Hell – Limbo
– that is occupied by other intellectual heroes from the pagan past,
such as the Greek Aristotle or the Roman Virgil himself. Moreover,
as in the case of Francesca or Farinata or Pier della Vigna, the initial
brilliance and emotional charge of his words reveal, on closer reading,
flaws and deficiencies in the claims he makes. The power and glamour
of this speech is beyond question. Virgil – almost as if he were speaking
to some ancient oracular flame – conjures words from the fire that
Ulysses has now become (twinned with his now-silent partner in strat-
egy, Diomed). These words begin with the magnetic energy and drive
of '*Quando*' (a grandiose version of 'once upon a time') isolated at
the end of line 90. For the duration of a single verse, utterance struggles
through a series of subordinate clauses, but then generates an un-
stoppable forward motion producing the vibrant rhythms of line 97,
and onwards into the high rhetoric of Ulysses' address to his old and
weary shipmates (112–20). This may be a 'little' speech – as Ulysses
puts it at line 121, with rhetorical understatement (see the use of
'*picciola*' at lines 102 and 114). Yet it elicits an immediate spurt of
revitalized energy from the crew, who row wordlessly into the

uncharted territory of a world illuminated – in Ulysses' narrative atmospherics – by moonlight and stars unknown in the northern hemisphere, until he arrives at the only land mass which (in Dante's atlas) existed in the southern hemisphere, the Mountain of Purgatory, and is sunk by a mysterious whirlwind before reaching its shores.

Yet if the issue here is knowledge and the use of the intellect, why do the crew men not enter into the debate? What part have they in the journey that Ulysses impels them to undertake? What knowledge is achieved when the last sight they enjoy is of an unattainable mountain, 'darkened through distance'? Seen from their angle, Ulysses' posture is as much that of demagogue – unthinking as to purpose or effect – as heroic adventurer. This view is the more likely when one notes, beneath the wake of Ulysses' words, a reference to Aeneas (93) and a gleeful delight in an intellectual curiosity lead him to ignore the bonds of family life, the calls of wife and son and the '*pieta*' (sacred 'duty') that he owed to his father. The defining virtue of Aeneas, in Virgil's account of him, was *pietas* – a high sense of public responsibility. Whereas Ulysses leaves Troy as victor, and enters on a sequence of piquant adventures, the defeated Aeneas begins his journey in a spirit of concern for those who depend upon him, with the desire, above all, to found a new homeland in Rome for his refugee companions. Nor, on this point, are the sympathies of Dante the exile likely to be in doubt. His journey under the tutelage of Virgil is, like Aeneas's journey, one that seeks (as does Dante's own poem) to establish a home, a place of ethical security, of relationship and discourse, to replace the ruined Florence. On that understanding, Ulysses' journey – which is, confessedly, a mad flight (125) – is an absurdity, a blind desire to enter an empty world 'where no man dwells' (117), where the bonds, and equally the possibilities, of human intercourse do not pertain.

Denying the claims of *pietas* may appear to assert a Promethean freedom. It is, however, an illusory freedom, not simply because it offends divine restraints, but because it denies the claims of relationship that define and foster our human existence. It is significant that the wind that sinks Ulysses and his crew is stirred up by '*altrui*', 'Another's will'. This is the absolute otherness of God, unknown to the pagan Ulysses. But this divine otherness avenges all those manifestations of human otherness – father, child, wife, crew men and even the figure of Diomed who goes unacknowledged in the same flame as Ulysses – whom Ulysses has consigned to oblivion. Of course, in recent centuries the notion of rationality as a form of neutral inquiry that locates truth, as it were, in some laboratory beyond the taint of human value or relationship, has come to dominate our conception of what reason properly is. And Dante undoubtedly recognized the importance of such modes of inquiry: his own encyclopaedic work the *Convivio* begins with the Ulyssean and Aristotelian dictum: 'All human beings by nature desire to know . . .' At the same time, in canto 26 and subsequently throughout the *Commedia*, he provides a critique of any exercise of intellect which denies the demands of other persons, and progressively defines and develops an alternative view, whereby rationality resides in the propagation of and participation in the common endeavours of human discourse. The *Purgatorio* and the *Paradiso* will reveal how rich in significance such rationality may be, and will eventually rename it as love. But it is an indication of the continuing distinction that Dante draws between Ulyssean rationality and his own that, in the opening cantos of the other two *cantiche* he should introduce a perceptible allusion to *Inferno* 26. In *Purgatorio* 1, Dante arrives at the shores where Ulysses had been wrecked. What, for Ulysses, was a mountain looming darkly in the distance is, for Dante, a little island surrounded by seas that catch the rays of dawning light. Ulysses' grand ambitions saw, finally, only a darkness; Dante's restrained and steady application of mind accepts natural limits but – as in some mental microscope – sees more clearly and in greater detail by virtue of seeing small. Then again, at the opening of *Paradiso* 2: 1–15 Dante turns to his own readers as Ulysses turned to his crew men, addressing those who follow his poetic 'ship' in little boats of their own. But far from attempting to sweep these readers into an excited literary frenzy, his advice is that, in an act of free self-knowledge – such as Ulysses' 'little speech' disallows – they should assess their own competence, and turn back without disgrace to their home shores if they decide that they are not yet ready for the rigours of Dante's narrative. In both cases, the true functioning of the intellect demands a closeness of attention, whether to persons or to things. Ulysses is a false counsellor in forbidding any such attention. His ancient flame, noble as that image may be, is a flame that destroys a homeland such as Troy.

Such conclusions are anticipated within canto 26 by a number of features that constitute the context of the Ulysses episode. The first half of the canto depicts a journey which, far from exciting the emotions of a mad flight, draws attention – in terms, as always, verging on the comic – to the awkward and laborious progress that Dante and Virgil make, scrambling over cliff faces and splintered rock (17–18). Knowledge – of the gradients and textures of the physical world – is carried as much in the abraded knee as in the fine flights of mind. There are two linked similes at **lines 25–39**, which serve as a frame and chorus

to the Ulyssean venture. The second of these refers to the punitive
flames of the pocket in terms that recall Elijah's ascent to Heaven
in a chariot of fire. Here, as ultimately in the *Paradiso*, knowledge is
seen as a prophetic re-establishment of the relationship between the
human mind and the divine mind, and by the *Paradiso* Dante will
indeed see revelation as a form of rationality. But this is not to deny
that knowledge of this world – the world of space and time in which
human lives are lived – may also be revelatory. So, the first of these
two similes (in common with the pastoral simile of canto 24) pictures
a wholly productive engagement with the natural order. A peasant
rests on a hillside, contained within and supported by its slopes.
Ulysses seeks the 'open depths' (100) and is wrecked by a sudden
vertical movement. For the peasant, however, containment is the con-
dition of at-homeness, and knowledge is the detailed perception of
what is already to hand, an awareness of the productive schemes of
winter and summer, of ploughing and harvest, a sensitivity to the
nuances through which time shifts 'as now the fly makes way for
the mosquito'.

Finally there is the evidence offered by the violent authorial voice
that opens the canto (1–12). In contrast to the dynamic attraction of
Ulysses' narrative, Dante's voice speaks out in prophetic fury and
vicious irony against his native city, Florence. Ulysses may have willed
the destruction of Troy. Dante here likewise longs for the fall of a city
that seeks ever-greater dominion over the world, and even over Hell
itself. Yet, simultaneously, this is the voice of an Aeneas who, by
his own journey through the other world, endeavours to restore the
homeland that ambition and acquisitiveness have destroyed. This voice
is as abrasive and gnarled as the rocks over which Dante clambers.
But if it lacks the brilliance and charm of Ulysses' eloquence, it is also
free of the illusions that the pretension to knowledge can itself tragic-
ally generate.

Notes

4–6   Behind this sarcastic encomium one may discern the words
       inscribed in 1255 on the walls of the Bargello Palace in Florence
       (see Introduction p. xx) claiming for the republic (ironically
       enough) imperial dominion over the world and the right to make
       its Tuscan subjects 'happy': '*Que mare, que terram, que totum
       possidet orbem*' – 'Who possesses land, sea and all the earthly
       globe' (a phrase from Lucan's *Pharsalia* 1: 109, describing the
       self-destructiveness of Rome, also quoted in Dante's *De Mon-*

archia 2:8). A connection is clearly drawn between intellectual appetitiveness and commercial greed. (See *Convivio* 4: 12: 11.)

7–9 As with the reference to Pistoia in canto 25, this allusion points to the strife, particularly between Black and White Guelf factions, that had arisen in the last decade of the thirteenth century between Florence and the Tuscans cities that were its immediate neighbours.

34–9 These lines refer, in highly compressed form, to the two Old Testament prophets Elijah and Elisha, contained in 2 Kings 2. Elijah is, like Ulysses, hidden in flame, but ascends to Heaven (as, of course, Ulysses does not):

> And it came to pass, as they still went on, and talked, that, behold, there appeared a chariot of fire, and horses of fire, and parted them both asunder; and Elijah went up by a whirlwind into heaven. And Elisha saw it, and he cried, My father, my father, the chariots of Israel, and the horsemen thereof.   2 Kings 2: 11–12

Elisha is 'avenged by furious bears' for being mocked by the urchins of Bethel:

> . . . there came forth little children out of the city, and mocked him, and said unto him, Go up, thou bald head; go up thou bald head . . . And there came forth two she bears out of the wood, and tare forty and two children of them.   2 Kings 2: 23–4

46–8 The destructive fire within is now displayed in the outward fire that consumes them.

52–63 Statius describes how the two sons of Oedipus, Eteocles and Polynices, kill each other in mutual hatred and are laid on the same funeral pyre, their hatred dividing its fire (*Thebaid* 12: 429–32). Drawing on a number of classical sources including *Aeneid* 2 and *Metamorphoses* 13: 123–380, Dante here puts into Virgil's mouth references to three events in Ulysses' life, all of which might be taken as evidence of a destructive or impious intellect worthy of damnation. First, Ulysses devises the strat-agem of the Trojan horse, which allows the Greeks to enter Troy and destroy it – thus opening the way to the ultimate foundation of Rome. (Both Ulysses and Diomed entered Troy in the wooden belly of the horse.) Secondly, Ulysses persuades Achilles (in Stat-ius's *Achilleid* 1) to abandon his love for his wife Deidamia, daughter of the king of Scyros, and go off to the Trojan War, in which he meets his death. Thirdly, in both the *Aeneid* and the *Metamorphoses*, Ulysses is held to have been guilty of profanity, when he stealthily enters Troy and steals from its inner sanctum the sacred image of Pallas Athene (the Palladium) on which the security of the city depends.

73–84 The rhetorical devices that Dante here attributes to Virgil reflect features of Virgil's own usage in, for instance, *Aeneid* 4: 317–18.

91–3 The sorceress Circe, daughter of the sun, demanded that Ulysses – on his adventurous return from the Trojan War – should remain with her on the island of Aeaea, near Cumae, for a full year after she has transformed his men from swine back to human form (see Ovid, *Metamorphoses* 14). Aeneas on his more purposeful and 'pious' journey renames a promontory in the vicinity Gaeta, in honour of his nurse who died there.

97–9 In attributing to Ulysses this burning intellectual curiosity, Dante draws directly on phrasing in Horace's *Ars Poetica* 141–42, which in turn refers to the opening lines of Homer's *Odyssey*.

124–42 The geography of this invented journey represents Ulysses as travelling through the Mediterranean – seeing both its northern and southern shores and the island of Sardinia – and then passing through the Straits of Gibraltar (the rocks of which were supposed, since Pindar's *Fourth Nemean Ode*, to have been set up by Hercules as a limit on human travel), leaving Seville on the right and Ceuta in Morocco on the left. Turning south – and therefore left – Ulysses journeys for five months, telling time by the phases of the moon; and as he enters the southern hemisphere he sees the stars around the northern pole disappear as those stars of the southern hemisphere (never before seen by human eyes since the fall of Adam – see *Purgatorio* 1: 22–4) gradually appear to view. The mountain that Ulysses encounters is the Mountain of Purgatory. This is, in Dante's view, the only land mass in the southern hemisphere. It stands at the antipodes of Jerusalem and its formation is described in the final canto of the *Inferno*. (See notes to *Inferno* 34 and the Introduction to *Purgatorio*.)

CANTO 27

Abuse of intellect continued; the case of Guido da Montefeltro.

Commentary

Dante's critique of pure intellect – his own no less than that of the damned – continues and evolves in canto 27, though its stylistic and dramatic terms are very different from those of canto 26. The damned soul encountered here is not a legendary pagan but a historical figure from the Christian era – who enjoyed a close working relationship with the Pope – the Ghibelline warlord and politician Guido da Montefeltro (1223–98).

There had been a time when Dante admired Guido. In the *Convivio* 4: 28: 8, he spoke of him as 'the most noble Guido of Montefeltro', and praised him for the wisdom with which he brought his life to an end. Guido, after a history of excommunications, finally reconciled himself with the Church, and, having associated himself with the Franciscans, died in Assisi. In this early work, then, Guido is taken to exemplify an important piece of Dantean ethics. According to the view offered in the *Convivio*, human life goes through four phases and each phase has its characteristic virtues, which the intellect should seek to cultivate to the full. For instance, in what we should now call middle age and Dante calls youth – or '*gioventute*' – we should usefully be involved in practical and public affairs (since etymologically the word *gioventute* can be derived from *giovare*: 'to be useful'). Both Ulysses and Guido continue to behave as though they were, in this sense, youthful and useful. Yet both were old men at the time of their deaths, and by that time should have begun to develop the virtues of contemplation, considering the life-to-come. Considerations such as these are, for Dante, built into the natural (or, as we might now say, genetic) pattern of human life and thus provide a reliable pattern which the sane mind should consult and rely upon in seeking ethical happiness. It is on this pattern that Dante, at the age of thirty-five (and thus at the pinnacle of his usefulness), should seek, in writing the *Commedia*, to perform a work of public benefit. By the same token it is absurd that, at a point in life when Guido (like Ulysses) should have furled the sail and settled to the contemplation of the divine, he perversely chose to cultivate the behaviour of a younger man and plunge back into the political arena. It seems that, belatedly, Dante came to realize that Guido had been guilty of some such reversion to political type. For, as depicted in the central conversation (61–111), there came a point when he was inveigled out of his religious retirement by the pope of the day, Dante's *bête noire*, Boniface VIII (see notes to canto 19), and persuaded by a meretricious promise of salvation to advise in matters of worldly strategy: How should the city of Palestrina be brought under papal rule? Guido's brutally simple answer is: Promise the city a truce, then break that promise.

The abuse of intellect here lies in the near-treachery of Guido's strategy. But it also involves a perverse refusal to recognize those truths that are available in the spheres of both natural existence (the arc of human life) and revealed religion. And in complete contrast to canto 26, with all its drive and unselfconscious energy, Dante here depicts a mind so confident of its own sophistications that it entangles itself in self-conscious calculation. Ulysses has (to borrow a phrase from Friedrich Nietzsche) 'the profound surface' of an archaic Greek statue, brilliant in its pure spontaneity. Guido, by contrast, is a study in tortured, self-conscious pinstripe, unable to distinguish truth from the bureaucratic stamps of approval and safe conducts that were increasingly available in the corridors of ecclesiastical power. So, too, where Ulysses speaks his monologue with hubristic flourish, Guido – who engages in conversation with Dante throughout the canto – is involved in a chain of winks, nudges and (ultimately) total misapprehensions. The result is a canto which, in its contorted syntax and banal political chicanery, is peculiarly difficult to read (and to translate). The canto also offers a scathing criticism of any culture that thrives on the self-delusions of placemen and insider dealing. It is no accident that Guido's description of himself, as being more inclined to adopt the cunning of the fox than the courage of the lion, should provide titles for volumes on the *realpolitik* of Machiavelli.

The bitterly contorted irony that characterizes much of this canto displays itself first in the opening simile where, in contrast to the elemental flame of Ulysses, the flame into which Guido has been transformed is associated with art, craft and industry – all devoted to destructive and perverse ends. Early lines of the canto (7–12) recall how the despotic Perillus of Sicily demanded that his workman should make an instrument of torture in the fashion of a bronze bull, and include in the structure a subtly contrived mechanical larynx which would be able to translate the roars of any victim roasted within its hollow body into the bellowing of a bull. The first victim was the artificer himself. The passage is syntactically disturbed and marked by unusual repetitions. But the essential message is almost blatantly clear:

'the biter bit', a villain hoist with his own petard. Correspondingly, at the end of the canto, a surreal farce takes place when Guido, despite safe conduct from the Pope – for the sin he is about to commit (see line 109) – is snatched in all his official dignity from the hands of Saint Francis by a devil who demands: 'Perhaps you never knew: I practise logic, too' (122–3). If rationality is to be identified with logic, then the devil is as competent as any other in arriving at destructive conclusions.

The two central phases of the canto pursue these psychological and linguistic negotiations very closely. Guido, impelled by the urgent demands of a mind that cannot do without news of the day and bulletins on the hour, demands to know of Dante what the state of Romagna (Guido's dukedom) currently is. Dante's reply is marked by a weary sense that there is no *new* news at all, save the taunting reminder that Guido's party has been replaced by vicious representatives of his opponents, the Guelfs.

There is a heraldic (but ironic) blazon of violence about the whole of Dante's speech (36–57). Colour words identify the familiar factions that cause such strife in Romagna and point up the violence that wrecks the natural landscape. But there is no colour in Guido's words. Instead, there is the total misapprehension expressed in the highly sophisticated syntax of lines, which leads him again to self-delusion: he would not speak if he supposed Dante would return to the world. Just as Guido has ignored the implications of revealed truth, so now he has no eyes for the fact that, miraculously, Dante is going to return in bodily form to the world above. Equally, the lines show a complete misunderstanding of that inward nature which Dante once believed Guido understood so well. In the phrase (73) 'While I was still, in form, such pulp and bone . . .', Guido displays his repugnance at any manifestation of physical nature, and expresses a desire to make mind as superior to matter. So, comparably, Ulysses preferred the glamour of far intellectual horizons to the physical bonds represented by home and family. Guido, thus, ignores that insistence on the value of body which has been voiced repeatedly in the *Inferno* since canto 25. He also falls victim once again to self-imposed vengeance. Elegantly sophisticated as Guido's words may be, they also betray the onomatopoeic hissings and snortings of a physical flame. Regardless of Guido's intentions, physical form makes its claims upon him.

It is significant that T. S. Eliot chooses these lines as an epigraph for 'The Love Song of J. Alfred Prufrock' (1917). Eliot is picturing a worn-out world, a husk in which the mind has become nothing but a self-engrossing engine of doubt. 'I am not Prince Hamlet,' says Prufrock. But Guido is the forebear of Hamlet, and Prufrock the degenerate heir of both. Ulysses may stand in canto 26 as an exemplar of the hubris of which the western culture of information may be guilty. Guido correspondingly exemplifies that aspect of supposedly civilized order which translates self-conscious devotion to office and workmanlike craft into an instrument of torture. But here – as in all his subsequent allusions to Ulysses – Dante works to devise a remedy for such possible corruptions of mind. In canto 5 of the *Purgatorio* a scene occurs that exactly parallels the farcical tussle over Guido's soul at the gate of Paradise. But in this case, Guido's son, Buonconte da Montefeltro (d. 1289), receives unexpectedly the salvation which his father, for all *his* expectations, is firmly denied. Buonconte was no contemplative. He was a warrior who died in battle, fighting on the opposite side from Dante himself. Yet Buonconte's final act on earth is pictured as an infinitesimally small moment of repentance in which he weeps a penitent tear and locks his arms over his chest in the form of a cross. The question is, how do we use the time that is given us? Is it to be frittered away in the erosive self-regarding prolixities and chicanery of a Guido (or a Hamlet or Eliot's Prufrock)? Or else, should our minds be concentrated on those myriad split seconds in the natural world which provide an insight into the redemption of each being in its physical and mental entirety?

Notes

19–21   It may be taken as a sign of Guido's political divisiveness that, far from recognizing in Virgil a representative of true imperial authority, he focuses, perhaps disparagingly, on Virgil's Lombard accent and turn of phrase: '*Istra*' ('now') being used for the more regular '*issa*'. Note that Virgil at line 33 may respond by allowing Dante to speak to this mere Italian in the vernacular.

28–54   Where most of the cities of Italy in the last decades of the thirteenth century had come under Guelf control, the Romagna, in the north-west of the peninsula, had remained Ghibelline in sympathy, largely through the military and strategic efforts of Guido, who locates his birthplace at lines 29–30 between Urbino (where he became duke in 1293) and the source of the Tiber. But Ghibelline control had begun to slip, leaving in its wake Guelf despotisms. In response to Guido's question, Dante ascribes to himself a survey of the political state of the seven major cities of the Romagna. Notably, these cities are described as despotisms at line 37, suggesting – against the claims of true empire – the assumption of violent and unlawful rule. Despots, as Aristotle (quoted in *De Monarchia* 3: 4) declares, 'do not follow laws for the common good but attempt to wrench them to their own benefit'. Dante then proceeds to describe these cities in terms, usually, of the heraldic emblems and coats-of-arms of their leading families. Since 1275 Ravenna had been ruled by the Guelf Guido Vecchio da Polenta (father of Francesca, who appears in canto 5) and in 1283 Guido da Montefeltro lost control of the town of Cervia to the Polenta, whose family emblem was a red eagle on a golden field. Forlì had been defended successfully by Guido against troops dispatched by Pope Martin IV. These troops included French mercenaries whom Guido massacred, leaving a 'blood-stained pile' (44) of the dead. In 1296, however, the city came under the control of the Guelf Ordelaffi. Their shield bore a green lion with prominent claws in its upper half. Rimini was ruled by the Malatesta, whose ancient stronghold was Verucchio and whose emblem was the bullmastiff – its teeth sucking the life blood out of its opponents. Ferocious adversaries of Guido, the Malatesta had driven the Ghibellines from Rimini in 1295 and imprisoned and murdered their leader, Montagna de' Parcitati, in 1296. Faenza and Imola are identified by the rivers that flow through them, the Lamone and the Santerno. These cities were ruled by the Pagani family, under the emblem of a blue lion on a white field. Maghinardo Pagani (d. 1302) fought as a Ghibelline in Romagna, north of the Apennines, and as a Guelf to the south, in Tuscany. The last of these seven cities is Cesena on the river Savio, which was governed nominally by Guido's nephew Galasso, but in 1300 was a Guelf commune, living politically – as it did topographically – between the high mountains of tyranny and the plains of republican democracy.

85–97 The 'lord of our new Pharisees' is Pope Boniface VIII (see notes to canto 19). He had called on Guido for advice in prosecuting his quarrel with the Colonna clan of Rome, who refused to admit the legitimacy of his election in 1294. The Colonna had retreated to their fortress at Penestrina (or Palestrina, now Praeneste), twenty miles south of Rome. Boniface's campaign against this citadel is contrasted with what Dante might have considered more legitimate objects of military action, particularly the recovery of Acre in the Holy Land, which had been seized by Muslim forces in 1291. Further ironies in the corrupting complicity of Church and state are identified by the parallel drawn between the Emperor Constantine (see notes to canto 19) and Pope Sylvester I (314–35) and himself and Guido. The legend is that Constantine was stricken by leprosy for his persecution of the Christians, was cured on Mount Soracte, north of Rome, by Sylvester and subsequently converted to Christianity. Boniface's disease is not leprosy but a frenzied political ambition. The 'cure' is not a conversion but the involvement in an intrigue and abuse of absolution that leads Guido to Hell.

103–23 The devil identifies the false logic that runs through the previous lines: that absolution cannot be given in advance of the crime that it is intended to pardon. Willing a sin and not willing it cannot, logically, be simultaneous.

CANTO 28

The ninth pocket, where those whose words have deliberately fomented discord between others are punished by the suffering of wounds.

Commentary

In this canto Dante imagines, apocalyptically, a connection between language and violence. Just as human intellect can prove destructive of itself and others, so words – as the primary agent of human intellect – can be used in inflammatory speeches to foment divisions in the social and domestic order. The punishment envisaged for this sin is submission to physical mutilation in an endless circling around the point (37–9) where a devil continually re-opens the same wounds that have just healed during the march the sinners make around the pocket.

The significance of such a sin to Dante – a poet, and therefore wholly committed to language – can be gauged by his treatment in lines 118–42 of the final figure in the canto, the troubadour poet Bertran de Born (c. 1140–c. 1215), lord of the castle of Altaforte in Périgord. Famously, the poetry of Bertran displays a positive relish in the destructive energies released by warfare and battle, as for instance in his 'Be.m plai lo gais temps de pascor' with its great, ironic crescendo of blood lust:

How pleased I am with the season of Easter, which makes leaves and flowers flourish. And I am pleased when I hear birds in all happiness send their song ringing through the woodland. And I am pleased when across the fields I see tents and pavilions pitched and am greatly cheered when I see lined up on the plain the ranks of horsemen and horses. And

I am pleased when the skirmishers put crowd and all their possessions to flight, and cheered when after them I see a great host of men in arms come in pursuit.

In the *De Vulgari Eloquentia* 2: 2: 8 Dante speaks highly of Bertran. Lamenting that the Italian vernacular has yet to provide an example of military poetry, he points to Bertran's poetry as an exemplar of what the Occitan vernacular has already achieved. Now, however, this surreal picture of the brilliant Bertran carrying his own severed head like a lantern markedly modifies the earlier celebration. If Bertran is in Hell, it is because – in a spirit of political realism – his interference in the affairs of the English court has led to acrimony between father and son. An exact correspondence of crime and punishment is observed.

Dante puts in Bertran's mouth, in the final line of the canto, the one use of the word *contrapasso* ('counter-suffering'), which is sometimes taken to characterize the whole vengeance system of the *Inferno*. One way in which Dante may be thought to have moved on is to realize that only God's apparent vengeance is a guarantee of wholeness. The only violence appropriate to a poet is in recording this. Yet this conclusion does not do full justice to the imaginative force of the canto, or to the problem it raises. From the opening section (as, with a different emphasis, in canto 25) the canto itself is written, almost, with the same relish that it ostensibly condemns. Even the notion of the *contrapasso* might be thought to be part of that, as Dante, with all the eloquence at this command, employs graphic figures and rhetorical tropes to equal the violence of the scene. The opening section (1–21), confessing to linguistic inadequacy, manages none the less to depict an historical panorama of the violence that has beset Italy from the arrival of the Trojans up to the thirteenth century. Then, descending from this epic account to a lower, more comic level, Dante focuses the eye upon guts spilling from wounded bellies, as though from a shattered barrel. At each subsequent point in the canto, there is a peculiar concentration on the effects of colour, especially blood spilling out over the face through the dark air (104–5).

The rhetoric of canto 28 is marked at times by bravura flourishes in both the low style and the high style (the former, for instance, at lines 25–30, the latter in the ellipses of the great opening passage, as for instance at lines 10–12). A particularly dense example occurs at lines 34–9. Here there occurs a sequence of elegantly difficult rhymes: *scisma/accisma/risma*. '*Accisma*' in archaic Italian means 'to fit' or 'to adorn', ironically enough when the adornment here is the wound inflicted by the devil's sword. But suggestion and significance deepen with '*risma*'. This – as an archaism – can signify 'rhyme', but it also means a 'ream of paper'. The result is the suggestion of a connection between the material of literary authorship and acts of violence. These grow the stronger when one notes that the density of metaphorical implication is akin to some of the more extreme usages of Occitan poetry. Bertran de Born celebrates the 'cut' or slicing of swords in 'Un sirventes fatz dels malvatz barons'. But, skilful as Dante may be in his emulation of Occitan verse, canto 28 also indicates two of the most important respects in which Dante has advanced beyond the Occitan lyric: in his strong sense of narrative sequence, and in the extreme intensity of his descriptive imagery. Thus the organizing principle of this canto is the repeated motif '*Un diavolo . . .*', '*Un altro . . .*', '*E un ch'avea . . .*' at the opening of lines 37, 64 and 103. Each figure in the violent procession is isolated in turn under the beam of imaginative attention. Language, misused, can lead to a recrudescence of violence. Here Dante constructs a mode of attention in which we are led almost silently to contemplate the tragedy of what the sowing of discord may produce.

Notes

1–21 'Set loose' – Italian: *sciolte* – in line 1 points to a distinction between tightly disciplined verse and the laxer form of prose, as used by historians such as Livy. Apulia in Dante's day was the whole of southern Italy, forming the kingdom of Naples. The following lines make rapid but detailed reference to the wars that were fought in this territory from ancient times up to the present. These include the wars fought by the Trojans (that is to say, the original Romans) in their battles with native Latin tribes. The 'long war where rings were heaped' (line 12) refers to the Punic Wars of 264–146 BC, fought between Rome and Carthage for dominion over the Mediterranean, as recounted by Livy; it is reported by Saint Augustine of Hippo and Paulus Orosius that, following the battle of Cannae (216 BC), the Carthaginians gathered three bushels of rings as spoils from the Roman dead. Robert Guiscard (*c.* 1015–85) was the first of a line of Norman rulers of Sicily and southern Italy invited to stake a claim to these territories by Pope Nicholas II (d. 1061) in 1059. Southern domination of Italy was extinguished with the death of Emperor Frederick II's natural son, Manfred, at the battle of Benevento in 1266 (see *Purgatorio* 3.) On Dante's understanding, the battle was lost when Apulian barons deserted their positions near the Ceperano pass. At Tagliacozzo, in the Abruzzi hills north-east of Naples, the last remaining hopes of the imperial cause were extinguished in 1268 with the defeat of Coradino, Frederick's grandson, by Charles d'Anjou (1227–85), following tactical advice from 'Alardo' (Érard de Valéry, Constable of Champagne (c. 1220–77).

31–3 The Prophet Mohammed (c. 570–632) was thought to have been a Nestorian Christian before arriving at his own religious vision. He may thus be judged a schismatic. Ali (c. 600–661) was Mohammed's cousin and son-in-law.

55–60 These lines refer to the agitated religious scene – evoked powerfully by Umberto Eco in *The Name of the Rose* (1980) – which developed in Italy around the year 1300. Dolcino de' Tornielli (in some measure similar to Dante in his radical view of social order) was leader of the band of Apostolic Brothers and preached that possessions should be held in common. Pope Clement V moved against him 1305, with soldiers drawn from Dolcino's native Novara. Dolcino was captured and burned at the stake in 1307.

73–5 Though little is known about Pier da Medicina, early commentators suggest that he was responsible for sowing strife among the members of the Polenta and Malatesta families in the 1280s. (See notes to canto 27.)

76–90 Guido del Cassero and Angiolello da Carignano, leading figures in the city of Fano, were drowned sometime between 1312 and 1317 (with stones slung round their necks) off the coast of Cattolica, near Rimini, on the orders of Malatestino, the despotic lord of Rimini. The currents and winds were particularly dangerous on this coast line. But since these two men were doomed to be murdered, there was no point in their praying for safe passage.

94–102 It was Gaius Scribonius Curio (d. 49 BC) who first advised Caesar to cross the river Rubicon near Rimini, thus precipitating the Roman civil wars.

106–8 Mosca de' Lamberti (fl. 1200), a Florentine, first mentioned by Ciacco in canto 6, is thought to have stirred up the strife that ran through the families of Florence throughout the thirteenth century. When Buondelmonte de' Buondelmonti (fl. 1200) rejected the wife from the Amidei clan to whom he was betrothed, Mosca – whose Lamberti family were allied to the Amidei – incited his allies to revenge with the words, 'What's done, well, that is done.' On Easter Sunday 1215, Buondelmonte was dragged from his horse and stabbed to death.

133–42 For Bertran, see commentary above. In 2 Samuel 15–19, Ahithophel, the friend and adviser to King David, incites David's son Absalom to rebel against his father.

CANTO 29

Conclusion to the ninth pocket. Entry into the tenth and last pocket, where deceit in the form of false science, counterfeiting and impersonation is punished.

Commentary

The extreme concentration on human vulnerability that marks canto 28 is dissipated as Dante moves into the last ditch of the Malebolge, where the sinners, instead of marching in well-defined circles, lie at random around the trench, suffering various forms of spectacular disease from dropsy to leprosy, which bloat their human features and render them unrecognizable. Over the whole scene, as described in this canto and the next, there hangs a miasmic stench (46–51). The tragic tones of the previous canto descend into a ghastly comedy and the text returns to the low levels of diction that were exemplified most notably in cantos 21 and 22. Sinners lie against each other like draining saucepans (73–5) and scratch their itches like sleepy grooms wielding currycombs (76–81). A classical allusion – recorded in a singularly disjointed trio of *terzine* (58–65) – recalls how the whole population of Aegina died and was nightmarishly reborn from the seed of ants.

The transition to the final pocket is marked by a moment of distraction on the part of the Dante character. The rapt attention that Dante gave to the sinners in the previous canto has already led to confusion and distraction: while Dante is gazing at the fantastic vision of Bertran de Born, he is approached by one of his own kin who, though unnoticed, reminds Dante with a stabbing motion of his finger that the Alighieri family has still to avenge his death. This is Geri del Bello (25–7), the first cousin of Dante's father, who was murdered by the Sacchetti clan around 1280 and (according to the commentary on the *Commedia* written by Dante's son Pietro) eventually requited in 1310. But such apparently heroic acts of violence which, in canto 28, were seen to lead to an unending circle of strife, are replaced in cantos 29 and 30 by the squalid quarrels that involve the sinners of the final pocket and even, to an extent, Dante and Virgil themselves. There is a hint in the tetchy exchange between Dante and Virgil at **lines 22–36** of the dissension between them that will come to a head at the conclusion of canto 30.

The vision offered in cantos 29 and 30 is of humanity in the grip, not merely of its own malign intentions, but also of an uncontrollable corruption that distorts the dignity of its form and expresses itself in pointless banter and fruitless violence. The sinners here, as examples of deceit, have consciously wedded themselves to illusion in the pursuit of false science, alchemy, counterfeiting and even acts of impersonation. In 30: 31–45 Dante introduces the crazed figure of Gianni Schicchi (d. before 1280). The story runs that Gianni Schicchi, a Florentine noble famous for his arts of mimicry, was persuaded to imitate a dying man, climbing into his deathbed to dictate a last will and testament in favour of Simone Donati (father of Forese: see *Purgatorio* 23 and Piccarda in *Paradiso* 3). In fact, Gianni employed the occasion to utter a will in his own favour, 'bequeathing' to himself the best mare in the dead man's stable. The dead man, Buoso Donati, appears as a serpent in canto 25. (See notes to 25: 140–41.) There is material for comedy here; indeed, Giacomo Puccini turned the episode into a well-known comic opera, *Gianni Schicchi* (1918). Dante maintains throughout his own comedy a firmly judgemental grip on the degeneracy implied in such acts of deceit.

The rationale in the equation of sin and punishment here seems to be that mimicry, false coining and misguided science interfere with the trustworthy relationship between humans and the world around them, substituting illusion and deceit for the truthbearing realities of natural phenomena. In such a world no one can be sure of their own identity, or even be granted the solemnity of a final moment on their deathbed.

The last phase of canto 29 (**109–39**) pictures the working of such a world as revealed in the scams and idiotic projects of a decadent Sienese society: even the French are not as idiotic as the Sienese (**121–3**). (See notes below.) One example is the alchemist Griffolino of Arezzo, executed in 1272, whose claim to be able to fly was taken seriously by a Sienese nobleman, Albero of Siena, who was greatly favoured by, and possibly the son of, the bishop inquisitor of Siena. When Griffolino failed to perform the promised miracle, Albero persuaded the bishop to have him burned at the stake. The second example is the Sienese (or possibly Florentine) Capocchio (**136**). Anecdotes recorded by Dante's early commentators tell of how, one Good Friday, Capocchio the impersonator succeeded in painting the whole story of Christ's Passion on his fingernails. Dante caught him in the act and, when Capocchio hurriedly erased these images, berated him for having destroyed such a wonderful work of art. This anecdote suggests an early sympathy between Dante and Capocchio. They may have been friends and fellow students in Florence. But in cantos 10–12 of the *Purgatorio*, Dante shows a certain reserve in regard to the value of mimetic or 'realistic' representation. And while in canto 29 Dante does not himself allude to his own dealings with Capocchio, his characterization of him as a 'marvellous . . . ape of nature' (139) points to the trivialization that the human mind can foist upon the world it inherits.

Notes

10–12   This reference establishes the time on the journey as about 1 p.m. on Holy Saturday. Dante must hurry on if he is to arrive at Purgatory by Easter Sunday morning.

46–51   The Valdichiana and Maremma areas in Tuscany were, along with Sardinia, notorious for malaria in Dante's day.

58–66   Ovid tells in *Metamorphoses* 7: 523–660 how the people of Aegina (an island off the coast of Athens) were struck by a plague visited on them by Juno. Aeacus, king of Aegina, prayed for help to Jupiter and in a dream saw ants becoming men. The new inhabitants of the island, the Myrmidons, were transformed into human form from the ants that lived in an oak sacred to Jupiter. (See also *Convivio* 4: 37: 17.)

124–39   Continuing his satirical attack on Sienese folly, Dante – through the mouth of Capocchio, who is said in one early commentary to have been a student friend of Dante's in Florence – names a group of prominent figures who formed the '*Brigata Spendereccia*' (the 'Spendthrifts Club'). Of these it has been possible to identify Caccia d'Asciano (d. after 1293) and Bartolommeo dei Folcacchieri (d. 1300), also known as *L'Abbagliato* ('Dazzledeye'), who held important posts in the Guelf administration of Tuscany, and Caccianemico degli Scialenghi d'Asciano. The unidentified Nick (127) seems to have dabbled in the expensive trade of spice cloves.

CANTO 30

*Falsifiers continued: Master Adam, the counterfeiter;
quarrels between Adam and Sinon, Virgil and Dante.*

Commentary

The last phase of canto 30 (130–48) is dominated, like the end of
canto 29, by a quarrel that threatens to escalate into disagreements
between Dante and Virgil over whether Dante should debase himself
by contemplating such scenes as he has witnessed here. And certainly
canto 30 deepens and extends the hallucinatory vision offered in canto
29. Far from entering a world of reciprocities and relationship, such
as begins to be recovered in the *Purgatorio* and ultimately enjoyed by
the souls in the *Paradiso*, the sins depicted here leave figures isolated
in the cartoon versions of their beings that disease has wrought, where
repeatedly effects of twinning and mirroring are seen to lead not to
the confirmation of identity but only to further fragmentation. One
sinner, swollen to unrecognizable dimensions by dropsy, is thus ready
to lick 'the mirror of Narcissus' (129) and, in his raging thirst, derive
from the mere appearance of water further pain rather than refresh-
ment. In describing the same figure, Dante invents the neologism
'*dispaia*' (52) to indicate the total lack of correspondence between the
bodily parts of the sinner.

This theme begins in the highly unusual references to madness that
open the canto. Dante – more concerned with badness than madness
– rarely interests himself in states of pathological distraction. Even
here the potentially tragic stories of Athamas, who attacked his own
wife and baby sons (4–12), and Hecuba, who witnessed the death of
her children at the fall of Troy (13–21), are reduced to a brutally
unsympathetic narrative (in which the crazed Hecuba barks 'like any
cur' (20)). Rather than providing the reader with any clear understand-
ing of the scene, these highly condensed accounts of classical episodes
create a receding perspective of narrative-within-narrative, where
derangement seems to lie at the heart of human history. This impres-
sion is confirmed when the classical comparisons attach themselves to
a scene in Hell which descends to the comic level, with the image of
swine unloosed from their pen (25–7).

The swine in this case – again an incongruous yoking of classical
and contemporary reference – are the souls of the trickster Gianni
Schicchi (see commentary to canto 29) and Myrrha (mother of Adonis)

who, in Ovid's *Metamorphoses* 10: 298–513, adopts a disguise in order to seduce her own father, King Cinyras of Cyprus. If Gianni Schicchi plays fast and loose with the solemnities of death, Myrrha does likewise with those of birth and parental kinship.

The central episode of the canto (49–129) focuses upon the counterfeiter Master Adam, now so swollen with dropsy as to resemble a lute, ironically enough, considering how far from harmonious he is in his moral character. Little is known of him. The historical Adam was employed by the ancient feudal clan of the Conti Guidi (see notes to canto 16) at their stronghold of Romena in the Casentino hills above Florence, to which he refers at lines 73–8. Adam was burned at the stake in 1281. It is hard, however, to ignore the resemblance between his name and that of Adam of the Garden of Eden, particularly when the quarrel into which he enters at line 100 is conducted with another archetypal figure, the Trojan Sinon, who impersonated a Greek in order to bring disaster on Troy. To Adam, Dante attributes a peculiar sensitivity of intellect and diction. Yet these very qualities of mind – employed to deceitful purposes in counterfeiting the coinage – are a greater source of pain than the punitive disease he suffers. So it is Adam who speaks – in phrases that, out of context, would ring with exquisite sensuality – of the refreshing streams that run through 'channels, chill and moist' (66) from the hills of the Casentino where he worked. Yet in Hell, as Adam himself says, this mental perception is a greater torment than the physical consequences of his disease (68–9). Moreover, the rhetoric and narrative that Dante attributes to Adam also constitute – as in the case of Ulysses – a moment of reflection on the author's own poetic practices. The opening lines of Adam's speech (58–60) mirror phrases from Dante's own *Vita nuova* 7: 'O voi che per le vie d'amor passate . . . guardate e attendete' ('O you who pass along the paths of love, look and attend'). These phrases in turn echo the prophetic utterances of Jeremiah in Lamentations 1: 12: 'behold, and see if there be any sorrow like unto my sorrow'. But if Adam is a counterfeiter of coins, he is also a counterfeiter of the verbal motifs that might, in other mouths, underlie a living tradition. His words are an invitation to dissension and contamination. Similarly, when Adam speaks (82–7) of how he would travel an inch at a time around the eleven miles of the pocket to revenge himself on a soul that has insulted him (though his disease deprives him of all movement), his malicious purposes parallel and invert those of Dante himself as he travels through Hell. Mind and motion – the defining characteristics of a free human being – are in Adam perversely and pointlessly devoted to purely destructive ends.

The end of canto 30 sees a fatuous quarrel developing between figures whose archetypal names point back to the origins that the deceptions of sin have destroyed. But the quarrel between Dante and Virgil which threatens at line 131 also produces a vertiginous piece of wordplay at lines 136–41: someone dreaming of danger longs to believe that he is dreaming, so that danger should be merely a dream, and thus desires what already is the case – even though it seems not to be the case. In the insistence here upon on the word 'dream', as also in the play between indicative and subjunctive moods in line 138 ('*sì che quel* ch'e, *come non* fosse, *agogna*'), there is something of a parallel to the play of lunatic illusions with which the canto begins, save that the canto ends with an attempt to orient itself by returning to a Virgilian stability of utterance. Virgil's words offer some apparent alternative to the hall of mirrors that Dante's own fiction has here induced one to enter.

Notes

1–21 In Ovid's *Metamorphoses* 4: 465–542, Juno is stirred to jealousy by Jove's adultery with Semele, daughter of Cadmus, founder of Thebes. She takes revenge by driving Athamas (husband of Ino, another daughter of Cadmus) to bring about the deaths of both his wife and sons in a fit of madness. (For Semele, see *Paradiso* 21: 6.) Hecuba, queen of Troy at the fall of the city, sees her daughter Polyxena sacrificed on the tomb of Achilles and then finds the mutilated body of her son Polydorus, murdered by King Polymnestor, thrown up on the seashore. Driven mad, she barks like a dog and kills Polymnestor by thrusting her fingers into his eyes. (Ovid, *Metamorphoses* 13: 408–575.)

31–3 For Gianni Schicchi, see commentary to canto 29.

73–90 The gold florin of Florence carried on one side the lily, emblem of the city, and on the other the mark of Saint John the Baptist, its patron saint. By adding three carats of dross, Adam reduces the florin from its official twenty-four carats to twenty-one. The Branda Spring has not been securely identified. It may refer to the well of that name in Siena, or else another in the Casentino.

97–9 Sinon and Potiphar's wife are both guilt of false testimony. Sinon persuaded the Trojans to accept the gift of the Trojan horse. Potiphar's wife, in Genesis 39: 7–21, accused Joseph of rape when he rejected her advances.

127–9 The 'mirror' into which Narcissus looked (Ovid, *Metamorphoses* 3: 370–503) is the water in which he drowned. (See also *Paradiso* 3: 17–18.)

CANTO 31

The giants Nimrod, Ephialtes and Antaeus. Antaeus
lowers Dante into the last region of Hell.

Commentary

The opening phase of this canto promises a dramatic climax as, leaving the squalor of the Malebolge, Dante and Virgil approach the final region of Hell, where traitors are confined in ice – and where, in canto 34, the gigantic Satan will be revealed to view. An epic reference dominates the second *terzina* at lines 4–6, comparing Virgil's words in the moment of friction that ended canto 30 to the spear that Achilles inherited from his father which alone could heal the wounds it caused (see Ovid, *Art of Love* 4: 43–8). Then, at lines 10–15, a trumpet blast is heard through the half-light. Given the apocalyptic imagery that has formed the background to the Malebolge – war, fire, disease and pestilence – the reader might remember that the Last Judgement is supposed to be announced by a trumpet blast. (See cantos 6 and 19.) But this trumpet is no sign of divine power, nor an announcement of redemption. Instead, in the allusion at lines 16–18, Dante recalls the disaster, described in the French epic poem *Chanson de Roland* (*c.* 1100), that overcame the troops of Charlemagne in 778 at the battle of Roncesvalles in the Pyrenees, supposedly against the forces of Muslim invaders. Betrayed into an ambush by Ganelon, Roland, leader of Charlemagne's rearguard, blew his horn until his brains spilt out, but to no avail. The flower of Charlemagne's 'sacred band' (17) received no help. (See especially *La Chanson de Roland*, line 1765 and so on.)

But this blast is blown by the giant Nimrod, whom Virgil derides at lines 70–75 for being so stupid as not to be able to recover his bugle, on its rope around his neck, once it has dropped from his lips. From this point on, the canto enters a realm of comedy, which contrasts (like the final canto of the *Inferno*) the childlike naivety – but animation – of human actions with the bluster of massive, yet blockish piles of insentient matter.

In classical literature the giants are usually represented as the sons of Gaia, the earth goddess, who rise against the heavenly gods and wrestle with the demigods. Dante makes reference to these myths at lines 91–129. But he has interpretations and emphases of his own to offer, corresponding partly to biblical considerations (in which the giants of Numbers 13: 32–3 are seen as the inhabitants of a self-devouring wasteland) and partly to the demands of his own thought and fiction. As he declares with an ironic turn at lines 49–51, Nature did well when she left off making these figures. Whales and elephants have their place in the natural order, presumably because they have minds adapted to their size and habitat. But giants – in whom minimal intelligence is wedded to corporeal mass – are moral dinosaurs that can only serve as engines of martial violence. So, too, in Dante's perception, the giants are represented in terms of cities and their towers (40–41 and 136–8), emblems of crude materialism and perverse ambition that Dante discerns in the corrupt city state. Immobile and shackled, the function of the giants in the *Commedia* is to emphasize an attention to the lifeless fixity that will prevail in the punishments of the final cantos of the *Inferno* – and also, farcically enough, to provide a means of transport for Dante and Virgil as human travellers through this realm of disproportion. In both respects, the giants anticipate the metaphysical comedy that characterizes Dante's portrayal of Satan in canto 34.

Particularly significant among the giants is Nimrod (58–81). He was the builder of the tower of Babel and, as such, has been in Dante's mind since *De Vulgari Eloquentia* 1: 7, in which false pride, in merely material domination, is associated with the confusion of tongues and the creation of vernacular languages. The canto confirms this emphasis, attributing to Nimrod the nonsense that he speaks at line 67. Running throughout the *Commedia* there is a linguistic drama in which confusions in language – the primary resource of intelligent life in human beings – are seen to reflect confusion of moral purpose. (See *Inferno* 2 and 7; *Purgatorio* 26; and *Paradiso* 26.) Against this, the relationship between Dante and Virgil frequently demonstrates the ways in which human discourse may be restored to effective life. In canto 31 this may account for a certain childlike tone in the authorial voice itself that marks the canto off from its neighbours. Though the dissemination of vernacular languages was a consequence of Babel, Dante never abandons his love for, and desire to refine, his own native tongue. The very value of the vernacular, for him, lies in its association with the child who learns to speak that tongue innocently 'at the breast of its nurse' (*De Vulgari Eloquentia* 1: 1). So, in the present canto, high rhetorical levels are assumed only in Virgil's ironically flattering speech to Antaeus which, at lines 115–29, contortedly recalls the supposedly epic exploits of the giants against the gods. Elsewhere, the text adopts very simple syntactical constructions, as at lines 10, 31 and 82–4. The giants are measured by a distinctly human module

(64–90), or else are presented with a picture-book clarity, which delights in the twisting of chains five times around an overweening and musclebound torso. (William Blake registers this in his representation of the episode in his 102 illustrations of the *Commedia*, commissioned by John Linnell (*c.* 1824–5).) At times, indeed, the eye assumes the wonder that typifies the first-time tourist at a spectacular sight – as when, at lines 58–60, Nimrod's face is compared to the great bronze pine cone which is still to be seen in the Vatican in Rome. Or else there is a *frisson* of illusion in the encounter with these pantomime giants, as in lines 136–41 when, bending, Antaeus is compared to the Garisenda tower in Bologna, which looks like it is about to fall when a cloud passes behind it. In all these respects, canto 31 contrasts significantly with the violent sophistications of tongue that the authorial voice adopts in future cantos of the *Commedia*, especially in the opening of canto 32.

Notes

40–43 Montereggione is a fortress with fourteen towers rising above its circular curtain wall, eight miles north-west of Siena, built as a defence by the Sienese after their victory over Florence at Montaperti in 1260.

61–6 Here (at a point when he is shortly to register the nonsense language of Nimrod) Dante employs the word '*perizoma*', which in the sacred tongue of Hebrew is used to refer to the apron or fig leaf with which the first humans modestly covered themselves. From folklore and encyclopaedias, Dante gained the impression that the northern Frisians were especially tall.

94–124 The giants named in this sequence are as follows: Ephialtes, son of Neptune, who was sent by his father to pile up the mountains of Ossa and Pelion (in Macedonia) so as to reach Mount Olympus and challenge the gods. He is noted for his ferocity (*Aeneid* 6: 583–4); Briareus, who is spoken of here as being nothing special – similar to Ephialtes – contrary to Virgil's account of him in *Aeneid* 10: 564 (see also Statius, *Thebaid* 2: 596); Antaeus, who does not speak, though he is able to do so, did not attack the gods, and so is not bound. He did, however, ruin crops and attack men and cattle in the vale of Zama in northern Africa, until Hercules arrived to conquer him by lifting him clear of contact with his mother – the earth – from whom he drew his strength. (See Lucan, *Pharsalia*: 4: 593–660.) It was in the vale of Zama that the Roman general Scipio defeated

Hannibal and ended the Carthaginian attempt to dominate the Mediterranean; Tityos, who attempted to rape Latona, the mother of Apollo and Diana (see Servius on *Aeneid* 6: 595). In punishment he was stretched out over the earth, his body covering nine acres, as a vulture fed on his liver (*Aeneid* 6: 595–7); Typhon, who was struck by a thunderbolt sent from Jupiter and buried under Mount Etna (Ovid, *Metamorphoses* 4: 303 and 5: 354 and so on. Compare with *Paradiso* 8: 70).

CANTO 32

The first two subdivisions of treachery, Caina (treachery against kin) and Antenora (treachery against party or state). The Ninth Circle of Hell.

Commentary

A brilliant characterization of the linguistic texture of this canto is offered by the poet Osip Mandelstam, who writes:

> I should like to speak about the auditory coloration of Canto XXXI of the *Inferno*. A peculiar labial music: 'abbo' – 'gabbo' – babbo' – Tebe' – 'plebe' – 'zebe' – 'converrebbe'. It's as if a nurse had participated in the creation of phonetics. Now the lips protrude in a childish manner, now they extend into a proboscis. The labials form some kind of 'numbered bass' – *basso continuo* ... They are joined by smacking, sucking and whistling sounds and also by the dental 'zz' and 'dz' sounds. I pull out a single thread at random: *cagnazzi–ripresso–guazzi–mezzo–gravezza*. The tweaking, smacking and labial explosives do not cease for a single second.   *Conversation about Dante* (1933), p. 430

In terms of Dante's own poetic development, a precedent for the deliberate cultivation of a 'harsh style' is to be found especially in the four lyric poems that make up his *Rime Petrose*, or *Stony Verses* (see Introduction p. xci). Where Dante's poems to Beatrice are cast in a *dolce stile* that cultivates fluency of phonetic effect and simplicity of diction, the *Rime Petrose* – dedicated to a 'stony', or resistant lady and set in a winter scene – explore experiences of sexual frustration, stasis and spiritual aridity and experiment in modes of technical virtuosity in a way which suggests that Dante had been impressed by some of the more extreme instances of Occitan poetry that are to be found, for example, in the writings of Arnaut Daniel (fl. 1180–1210) (who appears in *Purgatorio* 26). Thus, in 'Così *nel mio parlar* . . .', Dante declares his wish to be as harsh in his poetic words as the lady is in her treatment of him and, in the '*Al poco giorno* . . .', Dante describes the dead season in the year in the extremely complex form of a *sestina* – where the poem is constructed of six stanzas of six lines each, in which the end words of each line, though unrhymed within in the first stanza, appear in every subsequent stanza in constantly permutated position. The act of writing itself in such a poem comes to reflect the author's own imprisonment in the form he has developed.

As soon as Dante begins the *Purgatorio*, he starts to recover, in developed form, the 'sweet style' – or *dolce stil novo* – that characterized his early lyric poetry, as the '*dolce*' – or 'sweet' – colour of sapphire spreads across the dawning sky. But the harsh style is never wholly absent from Dante's stylistic palette, and can even re-emerge – in the constant process of experimentation that characterizes Dante's writing – in altered form in the *Paradiso* (as, for example, in cantos 7, 21 and 29). As for canto 32, a direct connection with the *Rime Petrose* occurs at lines 103–5. In 'Così *nel mio parlar* . . .' Dante spoke of how, in his frustration, he wished he could get his hands into the hair of the unresponsive lady and haul her up and down from morning to night 'like a bear at play'. Now he tears the hair from the frozen scalp of the traitor Bocca degli Alberti.

But the present sequence also introduces variations of its own upon the earlier lyric poems. Some of these are moral in character. Where the winter scenes of the *Rime Petrose* were the reverse pole of the springtime scenes of sexual love, winter in Hell identifies the ethical character of the worst of all sins. All sin, for Dante, is the extinction of human possibility. Treachery deliberately assumes the mask of love and loyalty in order to pervert and undermine all those relationships that express the participation of human beings in the flow of divine creation. In the *Paradiso*, that participation is expressed in part through the image of the great river of light that flows towards Dante in the thirtieth canto. But in the lowest circles of Hell it is part of the punishment that the sinners suffer that they should have no access even to the emotions that they traduced in their earthly existences: the very tears they weep freeze in their eye sockets (46–8; see also 33: 94–9).

In stylistic terms, too, in this canto Dante far extends the range of harsh or surprising rhymes, to include the exotic conclusion of a rhyme sequence (10–15) with the startling '*zebe*' – 'bezoars' – and to create an outlandish phonetic knot around the rhymes '*Osterlicchi* . . . *Tam-*

bernicchi . . . cricchi' (26–30), which in some editions is rendered even more striking by the unprecedented adoption of masculine rhymes on '-*ic*'. Similarly, there are few more peculiar locutions in the *Commedia* than the clamping repetition of '*Con legno legno . . .*' (meaning wood clamped to wood) in line 49. At the same time, the sheer materiality of such phrases is yoked together, across the barriers of lexical decorum, with a high style, so that Dante can move in the space of a line from the use of 'Mum' and 'Dad' to an invocation to the Muses who assisted Amphion in the building of the ill-fated city of Thebes (9–11). Finally the linguistic pressures of this canto can produce an extraordinary variant upon the precise visual style that typifies Dante's writing in all parts of the *Commedia*. At lines 31–6, Dante finds the traitors sitting like frogs, half in and half out of the water, their teeth chattering like the beaks of storks. The *Rime Petrose* showed birds in precise formation clattering across a winter sky (compare 5: 40–48). But only here do we find the play of sound, colour and sensation which imagines shadows which are purple through the cold fringing of a pond which is white with ice, while contributing the dry percussion of their teeth to the staccato symphony of the canto. The complication of the passage grows only the greater when Dante compares the winter scene in Hell to a summer scene on earth – which is itself signified by the dreams of a peasant girl haunted by thoughts of harvesting.

The canto is no less inventive in its narrative structure. Hitherto, Dante's journey has been purposefully downward-moving. But now he stands on a plain of ice, and the forward dynamic which has hitherto impelled his journey is now arrested. Virgil plays little part in this phase of the poem; it is as if Dante were deliberately eclipsing any awareness of how the final exit from Hell is to be accomplished. The protagonist wanders among the frozen heads that protrude from the ice and, far from expressing the pity or curiosity that he showed in earlier sections of the poem, he represents himself either as a random, robotic agent of pain for the sinners (76–8) or else as a torturer who could be mistaken for a demon (108).

It may even be argued that the author here, as in the *Rime Petrose*, is implicated in the frustrated and fruitless violence of his own text. In lines 1–12, Dante summons the most extreme sophistication to aid him in his last descriptions of Hell, declaring in tones of disparagement that the task is not one for an infant voice. Yet the preceding canto displayed much of the inherent virtue of the innocent speech (as, in its own way, does 33: 61–9). Canto 32 is as much a demonstration of the self-imprisoning violence of highly wrought language as canto 28, a brilliant cage of linguistic icicles.

Notes

1–6 The opening lines of this canto develop a thought from Cicero's *Somnium Scipionis* 4: 9, which speaks of the distribution of the planetary spheres: 'The earth is the lowest sphere and does not move. So it bears the weight of all the other heavens.' Following this logic, Dante sees the centre of the earth as the point at which all weight is concentrated.

10–12 The city of Thebes (for Dante, the image of violence and corruption; see 33: 88–90) was built by the poet Amphion, whose verses, aided by the Muses, caused the rocks to move and become the city walls (Statius, *Achilleid* 1: 13).

13–15 The exotic reference to '*zebe*' – 'goats' or, more exotically, 'bezoars' – recalls the scriptural separation of sheep and goats at Judgement Day. See Matthew 25: 32.

28–30 Tambernic and Pietrapana (now called Tambura and Pania della Croce) are mountain peaks in the Apuan Alps, near Lucca.

40–57 The two figures referred to here are the brothers Alessandro and Napoleone degli Alberti, who killed each other around 1282 in a quarrel over inheritance. The Conti Alberti, including their father Alberto, owned lands and castles – Vernia and Cerbaia – in the valley of the Bisenzio, which flows into the Arno at Signa, some ten miles downriver from Florence.

58 Caina, the setting of the present episode, is the region of the lowest circle of Hell reserved for those who treacherously murder their kin.

61–9 In the French prose work *Mort le roi Artu* (*c.* 1237), King Arthur kills Mordred (officially his nephew; actually his illegitimate son by Morgan le Fay). The other figures here recorded are historical, all belonging to the last decades of the thirteenth century. Focaccia is Vanni de' Cancellieri of Pistoia, who is said variously to have murdered his cousin (in a tailor's shop), his uncle or his cousin, and to have been responsible for the division of the Guelfs into the Black and White factions (see 25: 142). Sassolo Mascheroni, probably of the Florentine Toschi clan, murdered his cousin for an inheritance and was beheaded after being rolled through Florence in a barrel of nails. Alberto (or Uberto) Camiscione de' Pazzi, from the Val d'Arno, killed his kinsman Ubertino for his castles. But his crime is outweighed (hence 'He'll acquit me here' (**69**)) by another of the Pazzi (the name means 'the Mad') who more grievously betrayed a fortress of the White Guelf faction for money during the campaign of the White exiles in 1302.

70–123 At this point Dante passes from Caina into Antenora, where those who betray their country are punished. The concluding sinner at line 122 is the archetypal traitor Ganelon who in *La Chanson de Roland* (see commentary on 31: 16–18) betrayed his stepson Roland into the hands of the Saracen King Marsilio at the massacre of Roncesvalles. Among the contemporary traitors mentioned here is the major protagonist of this phase of the canto, Bocca degli Alberti ('Big Mouth', 106), who, as a Ghibelline treacherously assuming the role of a Guelf, showed his true colours at the battle of Montaperti in 1260 (see canto 10), when he conspired in the defeat of the Guelfs by cutting the Florentine standard from the hand of its bearer. Hence the reference to 'revenge for Montaperti' at lines 80–81. Buoso da Dovero (Duera) was a Ghibelline leader of Cremona who was bribed (115) to allow the armies of Charles d'Anjou to pass through his territory in a campaign against the imperial representative, Manfred (see *Purgatorio* 3). Tesauro dei Beccheria, abbot of Vallombrosa and papal legate in Tuscany (119–20), was beheaded in 1258 for treachery towards the Guelfs. Gianni de' Soldanier (here 'Ghibelline Jack' at line 121) became a Guelf after the defeat of Manfred in 1266 in his attempt to secure power. Tebaldello, a member of the Ghibelline Zambrasi clan of Faenza (122), opened the gates of Faenza on the morning of 13 November 1280 to allow in the enemies of a certain family – the Bolognese Lambertazzi, who had taken refuge there – against whom he bore a grudge.

124–39 Here begins the episode that will dominate the first phase of canto 33. The reference to Tydeus and Menalippus at lines 130–32 draws on Statius's *Thebaid* 7: 745–64, where the hero Tydeus, who is dying by a wound from Menalippus's spear, asks that the severed head of Menalippus, whom he himself has slain, should be brought to him. Spurred on by the Furies, he sets his teeth into the skull, just at the moment when the goddess Minerva is about to honour his victory with a laurel crown.

CANTO 33

Antenora continued. Ugolino. The passage to Giudecca.
Treachery against guests.

Commentary

Dante and Virgil, at the beginning of this canto, remain in the circle of Antenora – where traitors against their own countries are confined in the ice of a frozen lake – and only move on across the surface of the ice at **line 91** to another region, Ptolomea, where those who have betrayed their guests are similarly imprisoned. Ugolino (who was first seen in the previous canto gnawing at the skull of a fellow sinner, Archbishop Ruggieri) pauses in his 'horrible dish' to describes how, on the orders of the archbishop, he and his four sons were starved to death in the Hunger Tower at Pisa (**13–18**). Dante as pilgrim says nothing to Ugolino in this canto. But at the end of Ugolino's speech, the authorial voice bursts out in indignation against the corruption of Pisan society (**79–90**). The narrative then focuses, from **line 118** onwards, upon Friar Alberigo in Ptolomea, who confesses that, while his soul is dead and eternally damned, his body continues to live in the temporal world, as does the body of another traitor, the Genovese Branca d'Oria (**137**). Dante has gained this information by offering to free Alberigo's eyes of their frozen tears, but then refuses to honour that promise (**149**). The canto ends with a further authorial diatribe, this time directed at the city of Genoa (**151–7**).

The emphatic image in **line 1** of the canto is that of the mouth; and references to mouths – and also to prisons and ice – dominate Dante's vision of evil in the final cantos of the *Inferno*. Evil is imagined to be the extinction of life, which, on Dante's understanding, is the capacity for growth and for free and independent motion. Sin is a condition of willing self-imprisonment. So Satan – deprived of all movement in the final circle of Hell – exercises the jaws of his three faces in a debased version of all that a human mouth can do in discoursing with or smiling at others, gnawing endlessly at the bodies of his victims. But Ugolino anticipates this ultimate distortion of human possibilities. Even when he abandons the act of eating, his words continue to express only hatred and a desire to destroy the reputation as well as the physical form of Archbishop Ruggieri. His language is initially marked by eloquent appeals for pity. Yet eloquence and pity are themselves intended here to sow the seeds of hatred.

Language – as, in Dante's view, the most characteristic of human attributes – is a matter of great importance in this canto. Far from displaying any obvious violence or brutality, Ugolino's opening words (4–6) are pitched in a high register (marked by allusions to Virgil's *Aeneid*) and are syntactically complex, suggestive of a mind that is struggling to sustain a firm grip on its own defamatory intentions while also recalling the tragedy that befell his family. As Ugolino proceeds to the climax of the tragedy, his words become increasingly bare and unadorned, emphasizing – as if drained of all emotion – the number of children who died and the number of days they took to die (70–75). Perceptible, though, beneath this stark surface, are parodic analogies between the situation in the tower and some of the fundamental features of Christian belief: the prayer for 'daily bread', the eucharistic eating of the divine body; the Crucifixion where Christ's words 'My God, my God, why has thou forsaken me?' (Matthew 27: 46) are paralleled in the words of Ugolino's son: 'Help me . . . Why don't you help me, Dad?' (69). In these passages, Dante (unusually) allows the rhythms of his verse to lose their normally emphatic pattern and come close to prose.

In the second part of the canto, questions may be asked as to whether Dante's authorial voice is itself a voice of love or hate, of loyal principle or of treachery. The narrative, in contrast to the realism of view that dominates Ugolino's speech, is here characterized by effects of verbal conceit (the 'crystal visor' (98) that is formed by the frozen tears of the damned), or by desperate flights of fantasy, as for instance in the wholly unorthodox suggestion that a body under the influence of demonic possession 'eats and drinks and sleeps and puts his clothes on' (141) when the soul has already entered Hell. Black comedy here replaces the tragic tonalities that dominated the central part of the canto.

Notes

13–18 Count Ugolino (?1230–89) was descended from an ancient Longobard Ghibelline family with possessions in the region of Pisa. He had been the imperial representative in Sardinia but, with the fall of the Hohenstaufen dynasty, he returned to Pisa and, changing his allegiances, joined the Guelf party, in the hope of gaining control of the city. While military governor of the city he gave up certain Pisan fortresses (see **lines 85–6**) to the Guelf cities of Lucca and Florence, meaning to weaken the antagonism to Pisa which these cities displayed in alliance with Genova.

When the Ghibelline party, under Archbishop Ruggieri degli Ubaldini, came once again to dominate Pisan politics, it was this action that led them to accuse Ugolino of treachery and to imprison him along with his children.

22–4 The prison in which Ugolino was confined was the Muda (or 'Mew') where, it is thought, the hunting birds and civic eagles of Pisa were kept during the moulting season.

28–36 Ruggieri is the 'master' of the hunt. The Gualandi, Sismondi and Lanfranchi were powerful families belonging to the Ghibelline faction in Pisa.

79–90 Thebes, the city of Oedipus and subject of Statius's epic *Thebaid*, is regularly regarded by Dante as the archetypal city of corruption. (See *Inferno* 32 and *Purgatorio* 22.) Pisa was also thought to have been founded by Theban travellers. Capraia and Gorgogna are two islands off the coast of Pisa at the mouth of the Arno. If they were to drift together, Pisa would be flooded with river water.

118–20 Frate Alberigo was a leading member of the Guelf families of Faenza and also a member of the lay order of *Frati godenti* (see notes to canto 23). In 1285, he invited several members of his family with whom he was in dispute over land rights to dinner – and had them murdered. The sign he gave for the assassination was, 'Let the fruits be brought in.' Hence his reference to figs and dates. Figs are a poor fruit, dates are exotic and expensive: for his act of treachery Alberigo now receives more than abundant recompense in Hell.

124–6 Atropos is one of the three Fates: Clotho spins the thread of life; Lachesis measures it; Atropos severs it.

133–8 Branca d'Oria, member of a noble Genovese family, invited his father-in-law Michel Zanche to dinner (see 22: 89–90) and had him murdered. Branca (a personal name, but also the Italian word for 'hook' and 'branch') was still alive in 1325, some four years after Dante's own death.

CANTO 34

*Giudecca, where treachery against sovereigns and
benefactors is punished. Satan. The climb out of Hell
through the centre of the earth.*

Commentary

Evil, for Dante, is pure negation (see Introduction p. lxxiv). Part of
the function of the journey that Dante makes through Hell is to realize
that false goods pursued – confusedly or deliberately – in acts of sin
deliver only a reduction of human possibilities. In the course of the
Commedia Dante does not say much about Satan. But when he does,
for instance in a final brief reference in *Paradiso* 19, he stresses not
rebellion but stupidity, impatience and passivity. Satan was once
Lucifer, the highest being in creation, who would progressively have
been given as much light as any finite creature could possibly receive.
Instead of 'waiting' for light he falls '*acerbo*': 'unripe'. It is for this
reason that, in canto 34, Satan is represented in a peculiarly mechanical
and negative form.

As canto 33 has suggested, even in the final moments of their lives
human beings are likely to be capable of sins of the most devastating
sort, betraying others by their silences and by their distortions of
emotional relationships. But Satan remains a principle of inertia. Com-
paring Dante's vision of Satan, for instance, with the monstrous figure
that the poet would have seen depicted from his childhood onwards
in the Baptistery at Florence, the first half of canto 34 (1–67) abandons
the anarchic vigour of the mosaic. His Satan is a mere refrigerator
whose flapping wings cool the ice of lower Hell, and a grinding mill
whose teeth bear down on the three great traitors, Judas, Brutus and
Cassius. In common with Brutus and Cassius, who betrayed their
emperor, Julius Caeser (at least in Dante's view), Satan has betrayed
the just purposes of God. But above all, like Judas, he has betrayed
the creative love that is enacted in the divine relationship of the Trinity.
Thus Dante's Satan is a parasitical figure, existing only as a negative
image of the ultimate truth. His three faces are parodic reflections of
the Trinity. His movements are wholly different from the harmonious
and productive movements of the universe that finally gather Dante
up in the concluding moments of the *Paradiso*. Even as an emperor of
evil, he is a mere shadow of what an emperor might truly be. So the

opening lines (1–3) of the canto appropriately offer a burlesque version
of the hymn '*Vexilla regis*', sung in Holy Week before Easter:

> The battle standards of the King advance,
> the mystery of the Cross shines out,
> by which the very creator of flesh
> was hung in flesh upon the gallows.
>
> Venantius Fortunatus (AD 535–600)

In the plan of the *Commedia*, canto 34 of the *Inferno* serves as both
a conclusion and a transition, and draws to the attention of the reader
some of the most significant techniques and interests that underlie
the architecture of Dante's poem. Two closely connected features –
reflecting Dante's narrative procedure and his moral vision – are dis-
played here, the first being a concern with the minute detail of the
fiction, the second, the poet's constant awareness of the plan which
governs the work as a whole.

Dante's narrative inventiveness is displayed in the two contrasted
halves of the canto, each with its own *tempi*, dynamics and tonal
colorations. Satan is located in an unreal space. He does not touch the
sides of the pit. Nor is he physically supported there, but rather
suspended by the forces that play around the absolute density of his
material form. His proportions can be calculated, to indicate that his
torso rises some 800 feet above the ice (31–3). The textures and the
details of Satan's pelt are invoked in close-up at lines 73–5, with their
alliterative emphasis on a climb that moves '*di vello in vello*', from
'tuft to tuft' of shaggy hair, and an exact visualization of these tufts is
offered, as being frozen on a rigid skin. In complete contrast to the
picture of perverse and gigantic materiality which dominates the first
half, the second half of the canto evokes the emptiness of an awe-
inspiring but natural cavern (97–9). This space is slowly filled by the
quiet but intelligent voice of Virgil as he orients Dante within his new
setting. Then, increasingly, as the travellers proceed from the little
ledge on which they have deposited themselves (85–7), the cavern is
filled by the sound of a natural stream making its way through rock
from the surface of the earth beyond (127–35).

Such detailed attention to topography and the process of climbing
is at all points accompanied by an ever-clearer perspective in which
the workings of the cosmos and of divine providence are both brought
to light. The canto divides with unusual precision exactly around its
middle point, and Dante is plainly aware of the parallels between this
final episode and two earlier episodes, involving the giants of canto

30 and, at lines 88–90, especially the corrupt popes in canto 19, who are seen, as Satan finally is, with their legs wafting absurdly in the air. But this awareness is also related to a fundamental sense in which the search for and enjoyment of order is, in Dante's view, the essential aim of intellectual and ethical existence. In the opening lines of canto 1 he spoke of his poem attempting to derive 'good' even from the confusions of Hell. In his portrayal of Satan at the end he depicts the reverse of any such intention – the ultimate death of mind that results from offending the life-sustaining vitality of divine order. Yet in two ways the second half of canto 34 evokes anew the order that Satan offended and reveals it to be a satisfaction to the seeking human mind.

In the first place, through Virgil's quiet discourses, one sees that, beneath the science-fiction of this canto and so many others, there is a serious attempt to provide a precise understanding of the structure of the universe. To the end of his days, in one of his last extant works – the *Quaestio de Acqua et Terra*, delivered as a lecture in Verona in 1320 – Dante interested himself in geographical questions concerning the distribution of land and sea around the terrestrial globe. Describing the fall of Satan (121–6) he provides a similar account of the distribution of land and water. Satan, descending from Heaven, penetrates the surface of the earth at the point where Jerusalem would eventually stand and, impelled through the globe to its core, displaces the mass of earth which will form Purgatory, the only land mass in the southern hemisphere, which is also the site of the Garden of Eden (see introduction to *Purgatorio*). Satan's fall, then, positively contributes to the development of providential purpose, establishing the realm in which human beings first enjoy their relationship with God and then, after the Fall and atonement, eventually come to be purged of their sins.

Yet science in Dante does not stand at odds with religion. As he makes clear in *Paradiso* 10, human wisdom – in science and philosophy – is stimulated above all by a recognition that the order we explore in our rational investigations is also the order created by divine reason. There is, however, the dawning realization in canto 34 that the created order can be seen not simply as a place in which the human mind and the divine mind meet, but also as symbol and representation of the ultimate relationship in love that exists between human beings and their creator. The liturgies of the Church translate our everyday understanding of the yearly calendar, which articulates our progression through time and space, into a dramatic re-enactment of the providential design that leads us to God. The *Purgatorio*, in particular, is punctuated by moments in which the always-valuable observation of daily detail – the dawn, the evening – is translated and converted by the religious imagination into a recognition that the time and space of our earthly existences may also serve as a scheme recalling us to the celebration of the divine action as displayed, for instance, in the events of the Incarnation, of Good Friday and Easter Sunday.

Satan isolates himself from any such animating understanding in merely parodic relationship with the Easter hymn and the three persons of the Trinity. But the canto itself constantly measures the earth from the redemptive places of Jerusalem and Purgatory, and with a time scheme that acknowledges how easily darkness can be turned into light (118): 'It's morning here. It's evening over there.' This is an entirely logical phenomenon if we look, macrocosmically, at the circlings of the sun around the terrestrial globe. (In Dante's science the sun *does* circle round the earth but the earth is emphatically *not* flat.) The same observation prepares one, liturgically, to recognize that, in the providential scheme, sin is ultimately as insignificant as Satan here appears, and that correspondingly the enjoyment of light is the essential duty of any created being.

In common with the *Purgatorio* and *Paradiso*, the first *cantica* of the *Commedia* ends with the word '*stelle*': 'stars'. Yet reference naturally opens a new vertical and evokes sentiments of liberty and delight, long repressed in the *Inferno* itself. At the same time, this sequence of repetitions – presumably planned by the author – points very precisely to the kind of universe in which Dante wishes to locate himself. Stars are fixed points in the sky inviting mathematical calculation and allowing a traveller to take his bearings. They are an indication that the world responds to intelligent inquiry. Stars are also symbols of an infinity of possibilities beyond our immediate horizons, drawing the mind constantly into further questioning. In the *Paradiso* Dante gives his fullest account of how these human questions and possibilities may be realized among those who have taken the stars as their guide. Indeed, when the *Paradiso* ends with the word *stelle* – where it might have ended with the word God or an 'Amen' – the effect, like that of the conclusion of the *Inferno*, is one of significant and surprising anticlimax, revealing that – this side of eternity, at any rate – the proper function of human beings is to continue in our exploration of the created order and to seek intelligently to move, as at the end of the *Paradiso*, in harmony with the 'sun and the other stars'. It is, however, the *Purgatorio* – displaying a peculiarly subtle interest in natural landscapes and human community – that most delicately reveals, as the *Inferno* could not, what a life lived in pursuit of perfection *beneath* the stars might, in Dante's view, be like.

Notes

1   Translation: 'The battle standards of Hell advance . . .'

64–7   It is said of Judas Iscariot, the apostle who betrayed Christ, that 'Satan entered into him' (John 13:27). Marcus Junius Brutus (85–42 BC) and Gaius Cassius Longinus (d. 42 BC) led the conspiracy to assassinate Julius Caesar in 44 BC, when Caesar sought to become emperor. The view Dante takes of this conspiracy is significantly different from Shakespeare's. It is consistent with Dante's increasingly imperial sympathies that he should condemn the conspiracy against Caesar as treachery. However, it is remarkable that in the next canto of the *Commedia*, *Purgatorio* 1, a fellow opponent of Caesar, Cato, who like Brutus and Cassius committed suicide in defeat, should appear as the first soul in Purgatory and the 'guardian' of the purgatorial mountain. In the *Purgatorio* Dante's standards of judgement are by no means identical to those in the *Inferno*.

103–33   Space and time in this canto are measured from Jerusalem, which in medieval cartography was thought of as the central point of the northern hemisphere. It was at Jerusalem, through Christ's crucifixion in the city (see lines 112–15), that humanity was redeemed from sin. In the southern hemisphere, at the antipodes of Jerusalem, there is, on Dante's view, the mountain of Purgatory, where human beings as described in the second *cantica* of the *Commedia* purify themselves for their earthly sins. The formation of Purgatory is described in canto 34 at lines 121–6. On this understanding, when it is midnight in Jerusalem, it is night in the northern hemisphere from the Ganges to Gibraltar. Dante's journey down through Hell, which lies directly beneath Jerusalem, began on the evening of Good Friday. It is now at the end of its first full day, about 6 p.m. on the evening of Holy Saturday in Jerusalem (line 68). The journey up through the empty subterranean sphere, described in the second half of this canto, continues until just before dawn on Easter Sunday. (See also the commentary above.) The 'highest point' (114) is the zenith or point in the sky directly above any terrestrial point, in this case Jerusalem. Thus Satan, falling from Heaven, penetrates the earth at Jerusalem and is fixed at its central point. The mass of land which his fall displaces rises into the southern hemisphere to form the only land there, Mount Purgatory.

THE STORY OF PENGUIN CLASSICS

Before 1946 ...'Classics' are mainly the domain of academics and students, without readable editions for everyone else. This all changes when a little-known classicist, E. V. Rieu, presents Penguin founder Allen Lane with the translation of Homer's *Odyssey* that he has been working on and reading to his wife Nelly in his spare time.

1946 *The Odyssey* becomes the first Penguin Classic published, and promptly sells three million copies. Suddenly, classic books are no longer for the privileged few.

1950s Rieu, now series editor, turns to professional writers for the best modern, readable translations, including Dorothy L. Sayers's *Inferno* and Robert Graves's *The Twelve Caesars*, which revives the salacious original.

1960s The Classics are given the distinctive black jackets that have remained a constant throughout the series's various looks. Rieu retires in 1964, hailing the Penguin Classics list as 'the greatest educative force of the 20th century'.

1970s A new generation of translators arrives to swell the Penguin Classics ranks, and the list grows to encompass more philosophy, religion, science, history and politics.

1980s The Penguin American Library joins the Classics stable, with titles such as *The Last of the Mohicans* safeguarded. Penguin Classics now offers the most comprehensive library of world literature available.

1990s The launch of Penguin Audiobooks brings the classics to a listening audience for the first time, and in 1999 the launch of the Penguin Classics website takes them online to a larger global readership than ever before.

The 21st Century Penguin Classics are rejacketed for the first time in nearly twenty years. This world famous series now consists of more than 1300 titles, making the widest range of the best books ever written available to millions – and constantly redefining the meaning of what makes a 'classic'.

The Odyssey continues ...

The best books ever written

PENGUIN 🐧 CLASSICS

SINCE 1946

Find out more at www.penguinclassics.com

PENGUIN CLASSICS

TROILUS AND CRISEYDE
GEOFFREY CHAUCER

The tragedy of *Troilus and Criseyde* is one of the greatest narrative poems in English literature. Set during the siege of Troy, it tells how the young knight Troilus, son of King Priam, falls in love with Criseyde, a beautiful widow. Brought together by Criseyde's uncle, Pandarus, the lovers are then forced apart by the events of war, which test their oaths of fidelity and trust to the limits. The first work in English to depict human passion with such sympathy and understanding, *Troilus and Criseyde* is Chaucer's supreme evocation of the joy and grief inherent in love.

In his critical introduction to this original-spelling edition, Barry Windeatt discusses the traditions, sources and interpretations of *Troilus and Criseyde*. The poem is provided with on-page glosses, explanatory notes and full glossary, and appendices explore topics such as metre and versification.

Edited with an introduction and notes by Barry Windeatt

PENGUIN CLASSICS

FAIRY TALES
HANS CHRISTIAN ANDERSEN

Blending Danish folklore with magical storytelling, Hans Christian Andersen's unique fairy tales describe a world of beautiful princesses and sinister queens, rewarded virtue and unresolved desire. Rich with popular tales such as *The Ugly Duckling*, *The Emperor's New Clothes* and the darkly enchanting *The Snow Queen*, this revelatory new collection also contains many lesser-known but intriguing stories, such as the sinister *The Shadow*, in which a shadow slyly takes over the life of the man to whom it is bound.

'Truly scrumptious, a proper treasury ... Read on with eyes as big as teacups'
Guardian

'With J. K. Rowling and Lemony Snicket bringing black magic to the top of today's children's literature, the moment seems ripe for a return to the original'
Newsweek

'Tiina Nunnally's wonderful new translations of Andersen are an invitation to open-ended, mind-engaging reading' Rachel Cusk

Translated by Tiina Nunnally

Edited by Jackie Wullschlager

CLASSICAL LITERARY CRITICISM

'Sublimity is the echo of a noble mind'

The works collected in this volume have profoundly shaped the history of criticism in the Western world: they created much of the terminology still in use today and formulated enduring questions about the nature and function of literature. In *Ion*, Plato examines the god-like power of poets to evoke feelings such as pleasure or fear, yet he went on to attack this manipulation of emotions and banished poets from his ideal Republic. Aristotle defends the value of art in his *Poetics*, and his analysis of tragedy has influenced generations of critics from the Renaissance onwards. In *The Art of Poetry*, Horace promotes a style of poetic craftsmanship rooted in wisdom, ethical insight and decorum, while Longinus's *On the Sublime* explores the nature of inspiration in poetry and prose.

This edition of these landmark texts includes an introduction by Penelope Murray, which discusses the literary background since Homer and sets the work of each critic in context. It also includes suggestions for further reading, a chronology and explanatory notes.

Translated by Penelope Murray and T. S. Dorsch with an introduction and notes by Penelope Murray

PENGUIN CLASSICS

DON QUIXOTE   MIGUEL DE CERVANTES

'Didn't I tell you they were only windmills? And only someone with windmills on the brain could have failed to see that!'

Don Quixote has become so entranced by reading romances of chivalry that he determines to become a knight errant and pursue bold adventures, accompanied by his squire, the cunning Sancho Panza. As they roam the world together, the ageing Quixote's fancy leads them wildly astray. At the same time the relationship between the two men grows in fascinating subtlety. Often considered to be the first modern novel, *Don Quixote* is a wonderful burlesque of the popular literature its disordered protagonist is obsessed with.

John Rutherford's landmark translation does full justice to the energy and wit of Cervantes's prose. His introduction discusses the traditional works parodied in *Don Quixote*, as well as issues surrounding literary translation.

'John Rutherford ... makes *Don Quixote* funny and readable ... His Quixote can be pompous, imposingly learned, secretly fearful, mad and touching' Colin Burrow, *The Times Literary Supplement*

Voted greatest book of all time by the Nobel Institute

Translated with an introduction and notes by John Rutherford

PENGUIN CLASSICS

THE DEATH OF KING ARTHUR

'Lancelot has brought me such great shame as to dishonour me through my wife, I shall never rest till they are caught together'

Recounting the final days of Arthur, this thirteenth-century French version of the Camelot legend, written by an unknown author, is set in a world of fading chivalric glory. It depicts the Round Table diminished in strength after the Quest for the Holy Grail, and with its integrity threatened by the weakness of Arthur's own knights. Whispers of Queen Guinevere's infidelity with his beloved comrade-at-arms Sir Lancelot profoundly distress the trusting King, leaving him no match for the machinations of the treacherous Sir Mordred. The human tragedy of *The Death of King Arthur* so impressed Malory that he built his own Arthurian legend on this view of the court – a view that profoundly influenced the English conception of the 'great' King.

James Cable's translation brilliantly captures all the narrative urgency and spare immediacy of style. In his introduction, he examines characterization, narrative style, authorship and the work's place among the different versions of the Arthur myth.

Translated by James Cable

PENGUIN CLASSICS

REVELATIONS OF DIVINE LOVE
JULIAN OF NORWICH

'Just because I am a woman, must I therefore believe that I must not tell you about the goodness of God?'

After fervently praying for a greater understanding of Christ's passion, Julian of Norwich, a fourteenth-century anchorite and mystic, experienced a series of divine revelations. Through these 'showings', Christ's sufferings were revealed to her with extraordinary intensity, but she also received assurance of God's unwavering love for man and his infinite capacity for forgiveness. Written in a vigorous English vernacular, the *Revelations* are one of the most original works of medieval mysticism and have had a lasting influence on Christian thought.

This edition of the *Revelations* contains both the short text, which is mainly an account of the 'showings' themselves and Julian's initial interpretation of their meaning, and the long text, completed some twenty years later, which moves from vision to a daringly speculative theology. Elizabeth Spearing's translation preserves Julian's directness of expression and the rich complexity of her thought. An introduction, notes and appendices help to place the works in context for modern readers.

Translated by Elizabeth Spearing with an introduction and notes by A. C. Spearing

---

PENGUIN CLASSICS

LA VITA NUOVA (POEMS OF YOUTH)   DANTE

'When she a little smiles, her aspect then
No tongue can tell, no memory can hold'

Dante's sequence of poems tells the story of his passion for Beatrice, the beautiful sister of one of his closest friends, transformed through his writing into the symbol of a love that was both spiritual and romantic. *La Vita Nuova* begins with the moment Dante first glimpses Beatrice in her childhood, follows him through unrequited passion and ends with his profound grief over the loss of his love. Interspersing exquisite verse with Dante's own commentary analysing the structure and origins of each poem, *La Vita Nuova* offers a unique insight into the poet's art and skill. And, by introducing personal experience into the strict formalism of Medieval love poetry, it marked a turning point in European literature.

Barbara Reynolds's translation is remarkable for its lucidity and faithfulness to the original. In her new introduction she examines the ways in which Dante broke with poetic conventions of his day and analyses his early poetry within the context of his life. This edition also contains notes, a chronology and an index.

Translated with a new introduction by Barbara Reynolds

PENGUIN CLASSICS

THE DECAMERON   GIOVANNI BOCCACCIO

'Ever since the world began, men have been subject to various tricks of Fortune'

In the summer of 1348, as the Black Death ravages their city, ten young Florentines take refuge in the countryside. They amuse themselves by each telling a story a day for the ten days they are destined to remain there – a hundred stories of love, adventure and surprising twists of fate. Less preoccupied with abstract concepts of morality or religion than earthly values, the tales range from the bawdy Peronella hiding her lover in a tub to Ser Cepperallo, who, despite his unholy effrontery, becomes a Saint. The result is a towering monument of European literature and a masterpiece of imaginative narrative.

This is the second edition of G. H. McWilliam's acclaimed translation of *The Decameron*. In his introduction Professor McWilliam illuminates the worlds of Boccaccio and of his storytellers, showing Boccaccio as a master of vivid and exciting prose fiction.

Translated with a new introduction and notes by G. H. McWilliam

---

THE BOOK OF THE COURTIER
BALDESAR CASTIGLIONE

'The courtier has to imbue with grace his movements, his gestures, his way of doing things and in short, his every action'

In *The Book of the Courtier* (1528), Baldesar Castiglione, a diplomat and Papal Nuncio to Rome, sets out to define the essential virtues for those at Court. In a lively series of imaginary conversations between the real-life courtiers to the Duke of Urbino, his speakers discuss qualities of noble behaviour – chiefly discretion, decorum, nonchalance and gracefulness – as well as wider questions such as the duties of a good government and the true nature of love. Castiglione's narrative power and psychological perception make this guide both an entertaining comedy of manners and a revealing window onto the ideals and preoccupations of the Italian Renaissance at the moment of its greatest splendour.

George Bull's elegant translation captures the variety of tone in Castiglione's speakers, from comic interjections to elevated rhetoric. This edition includes an introduction examining Castiglione's career in the courts of Urbino and Mantua, a list of the historical characters he portrays and further reading.

Translated and with an introduction by George Bull